Post-Communist Politics

AN INTRODUCTION

Karen Henderson
University of Leicester

and

Neil Robinson
University of Essex

Prentice Hall

London   New York   Toronto   Sydney   Tokyo   Singapore
Madrid   Mexico City   Munich   Paris

First published 1997 by
Prentice Hall Europe
Campus 400, Maylands Avenue
Hemel Hempstead
Hertfordshire, HP2 7EZ
A division of
Simon & Schuster International Group

Typeset in 10/12½pt Times East European by
Hands Fotoset, Ratby, Leicester

Printed and bound in Great Britain by
Hartnolls Limited, Bodmin, Cornwall

Library of Congress Cataloging-in-Publication Data

Available from the publisher

British Library Cataloguing in Publication Data

A catalogue record for this book is available from
the British Library

ISBN: 0-13-442039-X

1 2 3 4 5   01 00 99 98 97

Post-Communist Politics

AN INTRODUCTION

Post-communist Europe, 1996

Contents

List of figures, tables and textboxes

Figures

Tables

Textboxes

Glossary and abbreviations

AFD	Alliance of Free Democrats (Hungary)
apparat	The bureaucracy of former ruling communist parties
APU	Agrarian Party of Ukraine
BANU	Bulgarian Agrarian National Union
BCP	Bulgarian Communist Party
BSP	Bulgarian Socialist Party
CDC	Croatian Democratic Community
CDP	Civic Democratic Party (Czech Republic)
CDPP	Christian Democratic People's Party (Hungary)
CDU	Christian Democratic Union (Germany)
CF	Civic Forum (Czechoslovakia)
CIS	Commonwealth of Independent States
CMEA	Council of Mutual Economic Assistance (Comecon)
Council of the Federation	Upper chamber of the Russian parliament
CP RSFSR	Russian Communist Party
CPB	Communist Party of Belarus
CPD	Congress of People's Deputies
CPM	Communist Party of Moldova
CPRF	Communist Party of the Russian Federation
CPSU	Communist Party of the Soviet Union
CPU	Communist Party of Ukraine
CSCE	Conference on Security and Cooperation in Europe
CSFR	Czechoslovak Federal Republic
CSR	Czechoslovak Republic
CSSR	Czechoslovak Socialist Republic
DAPM	Democratic Agrarian Party of Moldova
DCR	Democratic Convention of Romania

Democratic Platform	Democratic group in the CPSU
DEMOS	Democratic Opposition of Slovenia
DEPOS	Democratic Movement for Serbia
DLA	Democratic Left Alliance (Poland)
DNSF	Democratic National Salvation Front (Romania)
DP	Democratic Party (Albania)
DU	Democratic Union (Slovakia)
Duma	See State Duma
EBRD	European Bank for Reconstruction and Development
EC	European Community
ENIP	Estonian National Independence Party
EU	European Union
FDP	Free Democratic Party (Germany)
FIDESZ	Alliance of Young Democrats (Hungary)
FSB	Federal Security Service (one of the successor organisations to the KGB)
G-7	Group of Seven
GDP	Gross Domestic Product
GDR	German Democratic Republic
glasnost	'Openness' (policy of allowing wider discussion of social, historical and political issues initiated by Mikhail Gorbachev)
GRP	Greater Romania Party
HDF	Hungarian Democratic Forum
HDFR	Hungarian Democratic Federation of Romania
HSP	Hungarian Socialist Party
HU(CL)	Homeland Union (Conservatives of Lithuania)
I-RBR	Inter-Regional Bloc of Reforms (Ukraine)
I-RDG	Inter-Regional Deputies' Group
IFIs	International financial institutions (like the IMF)
IMF	International Monetary Fund
Interfront	International Front (Ethnic Russian organisations in pre-independence Baltic republics)
Isamaa	Fatherland (Estonian electoral alliance)
ISP	Independent Smallholders Party (Hungary)
KGB	Committee for State Security (Soviet secret police)
KRO	Congress of Russian Communities
LCY	League of Communists of Yugoslavia
LDLP	Lithuanian Democratic Labour Party
LDPR	Liberal Democratic Party of Russia
LNIM	Latvian National Independence Movement
MFDS	Movement for a Democratic Slovakia

MRF	Movement for Rights and Freedoms (Bulgaria)
Narodna Rada	People's Council (Rukh faction in the Ukrainian Supreme Council/Rada elected in March 1990)
NATO	North Atlantic Treaty Organisation
NDR	Our Home is Russia (Russian political party establised by Prime Minister Chernomyrdin in 1995)
neformaly	Informal (independent) political groups established during *perestroika*
NIS	Newly independent states (all of the former states of the USSR)
NLP	National Liberal Party (Romania)
nomenklatura	The appointments system under communism. Used colloquially to mean the ruling elite under communism and communist elite members who have kept their power since communism's demise.
NSF	National Salvation Front (Romania)
oblast'	Region (territorial unit in the USSR and Russia)
OECD	Organisation for Economic Cooperation and Development
OMON	Special police units
OMONIA	Democratic Union of the Greek Minority (Albania)
OSCE	Organisation for Security and Cooperation in Europe
Parlamentul	Parliament (Moldova)
PAV	Public Against Violence (Czechoslovakia)
PDL	Party of the Democratic Left (Slovakia)
PDS	Party of Democratic Socialism (Germany)
perestroika	'Restructuring' (generic name for the reform policies of Mikhail Gorbachev)
PFB	Popular Front of Belarus
PFE	Popular Front of Estonia
PFL	Popular Front of Latvia
PFM	Popular Front of Moldova
PLA	Party of Labour of Albania
PPOs	Primary party organisations
PPP	Polish Peasant Party
PR	Proportional representation
PRES	Party of Russian Unity and Accord
PRNU	Party of Romanian National Unity
PSDR	Party of Social Democracy of Romania
PU	People's Union (Bulgaria)
Rada	See Verkhovna Rada
RCP	Romanian Communist Party

Riigikogu	Parliament (Estonia)
RSFSR	Russian Soviet Federal Socialist Republic (communist period name of Russia)
Rukh	Popular Movement of Ukraine
Saeima	Parliament (Latvia)
Sajudis	Movement (Lithuanian independence movement)
Samnieks	In Charge (Latvian political party)
SCSE	State Committee for the State of the Emergency
SDU	Social Democratic Union (Romania)
SED	*Sozialistische Einheitspartei Deutschlands* (Socialist Unity Party of Germany – GDR)
Seimas	Parliament (Lithuania)
Sejm	Polish parliament
SLP	Socialist Labour Party (Romania)
SNP	Slovak National Party
Soyuz	Union (Conservative faction in the USSR CPD)
SPA	Socialist Party of Albania
SPD	*Sozialdemokratatische Partei Deutschlands* (Social Democratic Party of Germany)
SPU	Socialist Party of Ukraine
START	Strategic Arms Reduction Treaty
State Duma	Lower chamber of the Russian parliament
UDF	Union of Democratic Forces (Bulgaria)
UHU	Ukrainian Helsinki Union
UIE	Union of Industrialists and Entrepreneurs (Russia)
USSR	Union of Soviet Socialist Republics
Verkhovna Rada	Supreme Council, the Ukrainian parliament
Yabloko	Lit. 'apple'. Acronym of the Yavlinsky-Lukin-Boldyrev bloc (Russia)
Yedinstvo	Unity (Russian organisations in Lithuania and Moldova)

N.B. The initials of the English name for political parties and organisations have been used to assist reader recognition unless it is customary to use the foreign language initials in English-language texts.

Preface

In the 1990s, the study of post-communist states has become a central focus of interest in many disciplines. Whereas communist societies were frequently viewed as a world apart – a special case of peripheral concern – the (sometimes chaotic) developments in the newly emerging democracies provide fascinating test cases for some long-established wisdom.

This book is about the politics of post-communist states. It is aimed at three main groups of readers: first, students of politics who want an introduction to what is happening in the other part of Europe; secondly, area studies specialists seeking a background to the government structures and political contro-versies which are crucial to so much else that happens in the region; and thirdly, the more general reader who is interested in the post-communist world and wants more information about, and a deeper understanding of, countries about which previously so little was known.

The scope of the book is broad. We have chosen to write about all the European states – old and new – which were previously subject to communism in all its many forms. This includes what were once the East European members of the Warsaw Pact (Bulgaria, the Czech Republic, eastern Germany, Hungary, Poland, Romania and Slovakia); Albania and the states of the former Yugoslavia; the Baltic Republics of Estonia, Latvia and Lithuania; Belarus, Moldova and Ukraine, and, last but not least, the largest and most pivotal part of the communist world, Russia. We look at the political developments of them all individually, giving comprehensive election results and a background to the political dilemmas which determined the choices made by their leaders and their voters. But we also draw attention to the underlying themes which united, and sometimes divided, them.

Our aim is to provide clarity in the explanation of events which so often appear complex and confusing. We start with an Introduction containing basic details about how European states became communist, and the ways in which this system made them so very different from Western Europe. This is not intended to be a substitute for the many excellent texts on the communist period which have recently appeared, and references to these are given to advise on further reading. But it does provide the essentials for a reader approaching the rest of the book with no prior knowledge of the region. Developments are then examined chronologically in four sections. Post-communist politics is *not* unstructured chaos. All the new political systems have passed through definable stages, and while there are marked differences in the progress which individual states achieved in each, and reasons for such divergence, these can be defined.

In Part I, we look at the year 1989, and the ways in which different parts of the communist world exited from communism. In Part II, we examine the electoral processes which confirmed the end of communism. In Eastern Europe, we deal solely with 1990, but in the Soviet republics we follow events up until the demise of the Soviet Union a year later. In Part III, we examine the crucial period up to the end of 1993, when the new or emergent state structures confronted – with greater or lesser success – the challenges of post-communist transition. Finally, in Part IV, we analyse events from 1994 until late 1996. These illustrate the divergence in the outcomes of 'negotiated revolution' in countries which were once largely viewed, from the outside, as an undifferentiated mass following a uniform Soviet model (unless identified, as in the case of Yugoslavia and Albania, as curious 'escapees').

All parts of the book are similarly structured. An opening chapter alerts the reader to general themes and points of analysis which will emerge in discussion of individual states. It also points out the relevance of experiences in Eastern Europe and the former Soviet Union for general political science theories which have been developed in regard to more established democratic states. The second chapter deals with the states of the former Soviet Union, and the third chapter with what was once called 'Eastern Europe', but which is now increasingly referred to as 'East-Central Europe'.[1] We attempt to give equal weight to all states, with two major exceptions. First, Russia is not just another post-communist country. In terms of both geographic and population size, it is nearly four times larger than its nearest rival, and this is reflected in both its international importance and in its significance for students of the post-communist world. We therefore deal with developments in Russia in enough detail to make the book useful for readers whose primary interest is Russia. Secondly, we pay less attention to internal political developments in the successor states of Yugoslavia. This is because we have written a book which is primarily about the domestic politics of post-communist states, and in much of former Yugoslavia, this is heavily interlinked with the course of the war and internationally brokered agreements. Whereas international relations and the desire for integration into European structures are an important factor in the internal politics of all the states we discuss, in the former Yugoslavia the intervention of NATO, the EU and the UN exists on a fundamentally different level, and this can be dealt with more effectively in works dedicated to the subject. Nevertheless, former Yugoslavia cannot be ignored in a book of this kind, since – its own traumas notwithstanding – it does provide an interesting illustration of some of the general themes in post-communist politics.

Since this book is primarily intended as an introduction to a very broad area of study, much detailed information and analysis of events has necessarily had to be omitted. We have tried, however, to remedy this deficiency by providing notes guiding the reader to a comprehensive bibliography of English-language material about the region's politics.

Finally, we would like to express our thanks to everyone who has helped during the course of our work on this book. The large number of countries that we have covered has made us especially dependent on the resources and staff of the Open Media Research Institute (OMRI) in Prague, who have done so much in making up-to-date information and analysis on the post-communist world accessible to English-speaking scholars. We would particularly like to thank those members of the OMRI staff who gave their time and expertise in reading and commenting on draft chapters. Colleagues in the United Kingdom also provided much needed assistance and information. Maura (this one's for you SP – TB) Adshead, Sarah Birch and Peter Frank read draft chapters and provided much needed corrections. Rachel Walker provided encouragement and advice. The usual disclaimer applies.

Note

1. For the sake of standardisation, we retain the label 'Eastern Europe' throughout the book for all the states which were not formerly Soviet republics. It should be noted, however, that current usage tends to extend the term to cover all the European states which were once in the Soviet Union with the exception of Russia, while it increasingly excludes the formerly communist states in Central Europe.

Introduction

The breakdown of the communist systems in Eastern Europe and the Union of Soviet Socialist Republics in 1989–91 was hailed as the triumph of capitalism and democracy. The peoples of the old communist bloc wanted the freedoms that democracy provides and the economic development and material prosperity created by capitalist economic efficiency, innovation and profit-seeking. Triumphalism was moderated somewhat by the realisation that some of the newly liberated peoples of Eastern Europe would not enjoy the wealth of the market or democracy immediately or easily. But on the whole the future of the new post-communist states seemed assured. For a great many analysts – from both the East and the West – there was no economic alternative to capitalism and no political option other than democracy. History had disposed of communism, the main competitor to liberal democracy, and it had done so for the most part in the name of freedom of choice, economic diversity and efficiency, political pluralism and tolerance.[1]

Just over half a decade later triumphalism had vanished almost completely. The former communist states have developed unevenly and fitfully towards democracy and the market, and any progress made looks delicate and ethereal. Significant economic progress is limited to those states that border the European Union (EU) and these were the most economically developed of the communist states anyway. Most of the more backward countries, such as Bulgaria or the majority of the newly independent states (NIS) in the former Soviet Union, have yet to emerge from economic crisis. Political progress towards democracy has been equally patchy. Some states have hardly broken with the past. Old political elites rule under new banners. Successor parties to the Communist Parties have not been swept away by popular revulsion at past abuses of power. They have been successful in elections in several countries and play a significant role in the political life of many of the other 'post'-communist states. Nationalism, a force for liberation from communism in much of the former USSR, has frequently degenerated into xenophobic hatred of other ethnic groups, and has led to racial discrimination and, most tragically in the former Yugoslavia, to violence and war.

What explains the different fates of post-communist states, the differences

1

that they display both to one another and to advanced capitalism and developed liberal democracy? Unfortunately, there is no single factor which by its presence or absence can explain the magnitude and variance of post-communist experiences. The communist states of Eastern Europe and the USSR were, despite some important common features, very different from one another in many important respects. These differences were sufficient to ensure that the countries of Eastern Europe and the former Soviet Union entered the period of post-communism with distinctive capabilities and by different means. The different routes out of communism and the different resources that post-communist leaders had available to them – together with such things as the timing of elections, the ethnic mix in a country and many other factors – affected the way that institution-building was approached, the choices that were made about economic reform and the outcomes of political and economic processes. The result is the variation that we can see – and shall explore in this book – among post-communist states.

The differences between the communist states of Eastern Europe and the Soviet Union were a product of history, culture, leadership and fortune. In the rest of this chapter we shall explore these differences and also look at what the countries of Eastern Europe and the former Soviet Union had in common. We shall examine three particular features of communism in the USSR and Eastern Europe: the origins of communism, the Communist Parties and political life, and the economic development of communism. These three features of communism show us the stresses and strains that existed both within the communist bloc and inside individual countries, the destruction of independent political activity and civil society under communism, and the different socio-economic foundations upon which post-communist economy has to be built. Understanding something about these three features of communism will enable us to appreciate the roots of contemporary change and its different forms. We shall also be able to judge the profundity of change that has taken place over the last few years and the scope of the problems that have yet to be mastered.

The origins of communism in Eastern Europe and the USSR

There were two main ways in which communism came to Eastern Europe and the Soviet Union. In the majority of states it was *imposed* by the Soviet Red Army after World War II. In other states it was founded largely by *indigenous* forces (see Textbox I.1).[2] However, neither of these two methods of attaining power is a clear-cut type: where the system was imposed, power ultimately came from, and rested on, the military might of the Red Army, yet it was channelled through local communist leaderships. Where Communist Parties

Textbox I.1 Key dates in communist history, 1917–85

1917	Russian Revolution.
1918–21	Civil war in Russia.
1924	Death of Lenin. Stalin begins his rise to power.
1928–32	Forced industrialisation and collectivisation in USSR. Millions die in famine.
1934–38	Purges in Soviet Union.
1939–40	Forced incorporation into USSR of Moldova, western Ukraine and the Baltic states.
1941	German invasion of USSR.
1945	Reincorporation into USSR of Baltic states, Moldova and western Ukraine. Communist Parties take power in Albania and Yugoslavia.
1946–49	Russian-backed communist takeovers in Bulgaria, Czechoslovakia, GDR, Hungary, Poland and Romania.
1948	Yugoslavia breaks with USSR.
1949	CMEA established.
1949–53	Stalinisation of Eastern Europe, including show trials.
1953	Death of Stalin. Khrushchev begins rise to power. Worker demonstrations put down by Soviet troops in Berlin.
1955	Formation of Warsaw Treaty Organisation.
1956	Khrushchev's denunciation of Stalin followed by crises in Poland and Hungary. Soviet invasion of Hungary to restore Soviet hegemony.
1961	Berlin Wall built. Soviet–Albanian split.
1963	Self-management introduced throughout the Yugoslav economy.
1964	Khrushchev removed from power. Brezhnev becomes new Soviet leader.
1968	Czechoslovak reform attempts crushed by USSR. 'Brezhnev Doctrine' formulated. New Economic Mechanism introduced in Hungary.
1970	Worker riots in Poland.
1971	Attempts at reform by party in Croatia suppressed by Tito.
1976	Worker riots in Poland and the formation of KOR (Committee for Workers' Defence), the intellectual progenitor of Solidarity.
1977	Charter 77 (human rights group) founded in Czechoslovakia.
1979	Pope John Paul II visits Poland. USSR invades Afghanistan.
1980	Death of Tito. Formation of Solidarity in Poland.
1981	Introduction of martial law in Poland and repression of Solidarity. Movement goes underground.
1982	Death of Brezhnev. Andropov becomes Soviet leader.
1983	Death of Andropov. Chernenko becomes Soviet leader.
1985	Death of Chernenko. Gorbachev becomes leader. Reform process begins in USSR.

came to power by their own efforts, they did so in situations of great social, economic and political instability. And in all cases, the communist rise to power owed as much to the weakness of the opposition in the struggle for power as to the strength of communism. Once the reins of power were grasped, however, the remaining opposition had to be destroyed through coercion, so that even takeovers by indigenous Communist Parties also imposed communism to a large degree.

The USSR was the first socialist state in the world.[3] The October 1917 revolution was prompted by the failure of the Tsarist empire in World War I, but it was led by a domestic Russian revolutionary movement, the Bolshevik Party (as the Communist Party of the Soviet Union was then known). The Bolsheviks fought off both native counter-revolutionary forces and foreign armies of intervention in the civil war that followed the revolution. The combination of domestic revolutionary war and rallying to the cause of national defence gave the Bolsheviks a measure of security and legitimacy as an indigenous revolutionary movement. But the civil war that followed the October 1917 revolution was also the first stage of imposing communism in the USSR. The Bolsheviks forcibly coerced much of the old Tsarist empire – most of Ukraine, the Caucasian states of Georgia, Armenia and Azerbaijan, and the peoples of Central Asia – into the new Union of Soviet Socialist Republics. The new communist state claimed this was not a re-creation of the Russian empire, but a coming together of the peoples collectively oppressed by Tsarism and capitalism. The Bolsheviks thus represented the construction of communism as an endogenous process for the whole USSR. Events inside and outside the Soviet Union helped promote this self-image. The USSR's international isolation in the 1920s and rapid development in the 1930s contributed to the image of the Soviet state and the CPSU as bulwarks against foreign, capitalist aggression.

More people came to support the Soviet communist regime in World War II (known to Russians as the 'Great Patriotic War'). Victory over Germany confirmed the greatness and legitimacy of the communist state since it led to the USSR achieving superpower status. However, it also completed the second stage of imposing communism in the USSR. The USSR seized much of what is now western Ukraine from Poland in 1939. In 1940 it annexed the Baltic states of Estonia, Latvia and Lithuania and took Moldova from Romania.[4] It lost these areas to the Germans very quickly once war broke out in 1941, but in 1944 it forcibly reincorporated them into the USSR. These lands had all been a part of the Tsarist empire, but had achieved independence or escaped Soviet control as that empire had collapsed. Their seizure by the USSR was followed by the arrest of national elites, mass deportations, the forced collectivisation of agriculture and the general imposition of Soviet political, social and economic practices.

In Albania and Yugoslavia, communism was introduced by native guerrilla armies which liberated their countries from German occupation at the end of World War II. Since they had seized power through their own efforts and as part of a national liberation struggle, the communist regimes of Albania (under Enver Hoxha) and Yugoslavia (under Josip Broz Tito) had a greater claim to legitimacy than the other communist states of Eastern Europe. It was easier for them to ignore Moscow's orders and instructions because they did not depend on the USSR for their existence or day-to-day survival, and the same geographical distance from the Soviet border which had prevented the Red Army from reaching most of the area in 1945 also made it more difficult for Moscow to impose its will by force later in the communist period. Eventually, both countries rejected Soviet commands and broke off relations with Moscow. Tito split with Stalin in 1948 because Stalin could not tolerate Tito's independent foreign policy and his refusal to allow Soviet interference in Yugoslav political affairs. The Soviet Union was not strong enough to attempt the invasion of an Eastern European state which was both more populous and more skilled in guerrilla warfare than many others. Although initially one of the most Stalinist states of Eastern Europe, Yugoslavia later used its freedom to become the most open communist state and to experiment with economic organisation. Albania exploited the Tito–Stalin split to break free from the danger of Yugoslav domination, and eventually went in the opposite direction to Yugoslavia. It broke with the USSR in 1961 after several years of acrimony caused by Khrushchev's denunciation of Stalin and Soviet attempts at rapprochement with Yugoslavia, and proceeded to become the most closed and repressive of European communist states.

The seizure of power by Tito was, like the formation of the USSR, a partial imposition of communism. Yugoslavia had not existed as a state until after World War I, and the interwar years had been marked by great instability and tension between its constituent ethnic groups (Serb, Slovene, Bosnian, Croat, Macedonian, Albanian, Montenegrin). This was then exacerbated by the multiple division of the country during World War II, during which nationalist and communist guerrilla armies fought against the common enemy as well as each other. During this struggle, the communists, who were the only multinational force, became dominant in Yugoslav politics. Yet although they were the most popular political force, the re-creation of Yugoslavia as a communist state by Tito and the partisans papered over real ethnic divisions and amounted to some extent to the imposition of communism.

The partial imposition of communism in Yugoslavia and the USSR created problems for both states. The dividing line between areas where communism had been imposed and areas where there had been an indigenous movement for communism was largely ethnic. This created tensions between the core nations – Russians and Serbs – which had most strongly supported the revolution or war of liberation, and the peripheral areas which had been forcibly incorporated and had communism imposed upon them. This tension was preserved and institutionalised in Yugoslavia and the USSR because of their federal structure. Although communist federalism provided little scope for political autonomy of any sort, federalism in both countries perpetuated the identification of ethnic groups with specific territories, and provided a geographic and political space inside which ethnic identity and culture could be preserved and indigenous national elites developed. The basic building blocks of nationalist movements (identity and leadership) and a cause (getting rid of imposed communism) were thus created by the state structures of both Yugoslavia and the USSR. Czechoslovakia was also a federal state after 1968, and this played a considerable role in the development of the Slovak national elite. Here, however, nationalism did not become an overwhelming political issue or destroy the Czechoslovak state until after the defeat of communism, an alien ideology that had been imposed on both Czechs and Slovaks.

The inadvertent promotion of nationalism in the Soviet Union and Yugoslavia was ironic because communism was supposed to promote international solidarity amongst peoples and lead to the creation of a community that would be above nation-states. This irony extended to the countries that had communism imposed upon them by the Soviet Red Army (Bulgaria, Czechoslovakia,[5] GDR, Hungary, Poland and Romania). The fate of these countries was different from that of Albania and Yugoslavia. They remained under Soviet domination until 1989 and formed the Soviet bloc with the USSR. They were a part of the Soviet military alliance system (the Warsaw Treaty Organisation or Warsaw Pact) and the Soviet-dominated economic bloc, the Council for Mutual Economic Assistance (CMEA).

Their membership of the Soviet bloc did not mean that the countries where communism was completely imposed were totally alike. Even the 'reimposition' of Soviet hegemony after local challenges (GDR in 1953, Hungary in 1956 and Czechoslovakia in 1968) did not create homogeneity. The Soviet invasion of Hungary in 1956 was followed by several years of harsh repression, but this eased in the early 1960s. The country went on to introduce economic reform and the most market-based economic system in the Soviet bloc. Czechoslovakia, on the other hand, suffered under one of the most orthodox leaderships after the 1968 Warsaw Pact invasion ended the attempts at democratisation labelled by the Czechoslovak leader Dubček as 'socialism with a human face'.[6] Poland, unlike Czechoslovakia, was placed under martial law in 1981, but never 'normalised' by direct Soviet interference. As a result, party control of society was never fully re-established.

Soviet hegemony, whether imposed or reimposed, did not produce uniformity. Rather, Soviet hegemony provided a general blueprint and constrained development to follow certain broad lines. This meant that the Communist Parties within the Warsaw Pact were only partly sovereign, i.e.

only partly able to rule free of outside interference. Soviet hegemony was both ideological and military in nature. The USSR claimed to be more advanced as a socialist state (in other words, closer to communism) than its allies. The Soviet bloc states of Eastern Europe were initially referred to as 'people's democracies'. This term partly revealed the postwar origins of the imposed communist regimes. The USSR introduced Communist Party rule by stealth, setting up anti-fascist coalition governments before allowing full Communist Party rule to emerge. Power was thus 'shared' for a time in a version of democracy. Gradually, the Communist Party became dominant, but in some countries other political parties were allowed to survive as 'puppets' under close Communist Party and police supervision and to 'represent' the people in a mock multi-party system. More generally, the concept of people's democracy indicated that relations between social groups in Eastern Europe were – in the language of Marxism-Leninism – more 'antagonistic' than in the USSR. This meant that the 'people's democracies' could not be full socialist democracies like the USSR where broad social unity and support for the Communist Party had been achieved (or so it was claimed).[7] By the early 1960s, however, as the first generation of the intelligentsia to have been educated under socialism emerged, and agriculture had been collectivised (except in Poland), this ideological distinction between the USSR and the 'people's democracies' was eroded.

From the 1960s onwards, the patterns of Communist Party control varied throughout the Warsaw Pact, and local leaderships were free to shore up their own position at home as they saw fit, provided that their tactics did not appear dangerous to the Soviet leadership. Countries like Romania and Albania, which were not strategically sensitive and where internal Communist Party control was strong, were allowed to exploit nationalism and exercise independent foreign policy lines up to the point where, in 1968, the Romanians refused to participate in the Warsaw Pact invasion of Czechoslovakia, and Albania formally left the Warsaw Pact (with whom it had already ceased to cooperate in 1961). However, in Czechoslovakia, where the Communist Party led the move towards democracy in 1968, the precedent for its Warsaw Pact neighbours was considered too dangerous and invasion followed. This was indicative of how Soviet military hegemony limited local Communist Parties' sovereignty over national affairs, a notion which was summed up by the 'Brezhnev Doctrine'. Although the 'Brezhnev Doctrine' was first articulated after the invasion of Czechoslovakia, it had existed in practice for much longer. It claimed that the USSR and other socialist states had a 'fraternal' duty to intervene in a fellow socialist state that was departing from a correct, socialist path of development and threatening the socialist interests of its people (and the strategic interests of the USSR).[8] It was only with the advent of the Gorbachev period that this was replaced by what was colloquially known as the 'Sinatra Doctrine' (because, as in the popular song, the East

European leaderships could do it 'their way'). Sovereignty was restored as communist governments ceased to worry about whether their actions might destabilise their neighbours' regimes. And in what might be regarded as the ultimate proof of the Brezhnev Doctrine's rationality, they all fell together.

The political system of communism

No matter what their origins, the communist states of Eastern Europe and the USSR shared one, essential, common political feature: they were all ruled by Leninist political parties. Such Communist Party rule was notorious for restricting the freedom of the citizen and creating a closed society. There was strict censorship of all newspapers, books, radio and television, and freedom to travel abroad was severely limited. Only Yugoslavs were able to travel where they wished and to seek temporary or permanent employment in the West; most Soviet and Albanian citizens never left their own country, while the bulk of East Europeans holidayed with increasing frequency in other Warsaw Pact countries, but had access to the West blocked by obstacles which ranged – from country to country and from decade to decade – from the inconvenient to the insuperable. However, the power of the party did not merely circumscribe society on the level of individual freedom; it also over-shadowed any of the structural differences that existed in electoral systems, federal arrangements and party systems in Eastern Europe. The party's power dominated and corrupted all these variations in political structure in some way or other so that all the post-communist states shared a common legacy and problem: overcoming the destruction of independent social, economic and political life wrought by their ruling communist power.

Such independent activity is the basis of what is commonly called 'civil society'. Civil societies take many different forms throughout the world. Their form, extent and the way in which they support democracy or not are conditioned by such things as religion, social structure and economic organisation. The wide number of variables that influence the formation and function of civil society makes it difficult to define precisely.[9] However, it is generally recognised that civil society is the sum of non-state and extra-familial activity in a nation. In other words, it is things like trade union activities, participation in protest groups (like environmental groups), church and religious activities, membership of neighbourhood and community associations and campaigns, charity work, participation in political parties, etc. A civil society need not support democracy, but democracy needs civil society because without the activities listed above and the groups, parties and organisations they create there are insufficient checks on state power and few institutions to channel interests into the policy-making process.

Historically, civil society had been relatively weak in most of the eastern part of Europe, and the advent of communism destroyed it almost completely. Commentators have for years argued about whether or not the communist systems of Eastern Europe and the Soviet Union were totalitarian and exercised total control of society.[10] It is now largely accepted that there were ways in which the power of Communist Parties was subverted and incomplete. The totalitarian label applies best to the period when Stalin was in power in the Soviet Union, and random terror was used to cow the population into compliance. Since Stalin died in 1953, the Stalinist period only lasted for about four years in Eastern Europe, compared to nearly two decades in the Soviet Union. Thereafter, society was 'post-totalitarian': while the changes enforced under Stalinism, such as state control of the economy and the political control of one party, continued to dominate the structure of everyday life, there were also some activities that escaped the oversight of party and state. There was even some negotiation and bargaining within political systems as competing interest groups within the state and party bureaucracies contended for resources.

But despite, indeed perhaps because of, these flaws in control, the ruling parties of the old communist states were driven by a totalitarian impulse. They desired and sought to control everything from work to leisure activities. This led them to break down the distinction between public and private life, and to dominate all activities in the public sphere. Civil society was destroyed as an independent entity. Trade unions, youth groups, charities, sports clubs, arts societies, neighbourhood associations, hobby groups, any form of activity that involved people coming together on the basis of mutual interest were subject to party control. Communist societies are often described as having been monolithic because there was one of everything: there was one approved organisation for each form of activity, and the one party determined whether or not they were permitted to exist. Any group that endeavoured to organise independently of the party faced sanctions. The partial exceptions to this were churches and religious organisations, which were the only hierarchically organised bodies to exist outside the framework of state and party. However, although they were nominally independent, they were closely watched, distrusted, persecuted and infiltrated by the secret police. A problem post-communist countries faced was that while the individual freedom of citizens can be re-established fairly quickly, re-creating complex, autonomous organisational mechanisms within society takes much longer.

The totalitarian impulse to control was the product of Marxism-Leninism, the body of ideas culled from the writings of Karl Marx and Vladimir Lenin that made up official ideology in the communist states. The ruling Communist Parties claimed that Marxism-Leninism was scientific and provided the means to understand all human development, and that their leaderships comprised the people most able to interpret and apply Marxism-Leninism. They knew the true interests of the people, and could represent them and guide them to communism, the highest possible stage of human development. The Communist Parties were therefore entitled to have a 'leading role' in society.[11] This leading role was enshrined in the constitutions of their states, and was the legal basis for Communist Party power. What it meant was that the party usurped the authority of all representative, executive and judicial institutions, occupied a central place in all decision-making and intervened in all executive actions. Legislatures were turned into rubber-stamping bodies, which ratified the party's instructions to the populace. The alleged infallibility of Marxism-Leninism also meant that the Communist Party could not legitimately be challenged by the populace: since party ideology was held to be objectively correct, those who disagreed with it had to be wrong; and since the Communist Party did everything for the good of the people, those who opposed it were acting against the interests of the people.

The monolithic role of the party in the communist system was very inefficient. There was a huge duplication of structures. At every level, representative bodies (the councils and parliaments which were voted for in sham elections) and the state's administrative organs were matched by party organisations which guided and controlled them. However, although the party interfered everywhere, there were limits to the actual knowledge that any party worker or leader could possess, and to the work that party organisations could carry out. The result was bad policy and an inefficient use of resources. Since the party was all-powerful and usurped the functions of state, legislatures and judiciary, there were no checks on bad policy. The party stood above the law and exhibited little sympathy for society's concerns even as its workers interfered in all aspects of life. The party's enormous power encouraged arrogance and corruption.[12] Individual initiative was frowned on and often repressed since it came from outside of the omniscient party.

The fundamental flaw of the communist system was thus simple: Marxism-Leninism was not objectively right, and the goal of building communism was unattainable. Since communist regimes could never concede either point without undermining their right to rule, they were innately incapable of solving their problems. Elaborate party structures disguised the failure of their ideology, and conformism, paper-pushing and pointless bureaucracy became the party's main activities. The reporting of activity became a substitute for activity itself, as each level of the party hierarchy desperately attempted to prove that it had reached its targets so that it would not be subject to unwelcome scrutiny.

A look at the organisational structures of Communist Parties illustrates the full extent of the massive bureaucracies which were established from the desire to dominate all activity.[13]

Political parties in advanced democracies are generally organised on a territorial basis, with territorial divisions (district, city, county, province and nation) corresponding to electoral constituencies. The ruling Communist

Parties of the USSR and Eastern Europe were organised on a territorial basis too (see Figure I.1). But their lowest level of organisation, the Primary Party Organisations (PPOs), were predominately extra-territorial because they were based at the workplace, in schools, factories, shops, farms, theatres, universities and military barracks, etc. Each party had thousands of PPOs so that it infiltrated, and had a means of checking, work – the main social activity of everyday life. Above the PPO stood the territorial organisation of the party. Conferences and congresses were elected at district, city, county, republic (for the federal states) and national level. The congresses and conferences met sporadically and elected committees and bureaux to oversee party work on a day-to-day basis. Both committees and bureaux, and the party administrative departments that worked under them, were headed by the local party First Secretary. At national level the party congress would elect the Central Committee, which would in turn elect the Central Committee Secretariat and the Politburo. These were supervised by the General Secretary of the Central Committee of the party, who was the leader of both the party and the country – men (never women) like Gorbachev in the USSR or Honecker in the GDR. At all levels party committees served to integrate people in positions of power into the party and bind them to it. Committee elections were not free and fair. The majority of committee members were the most important people in the area, with a few token workers and peasants included to show that this was a 'party of all the people'.

The organisation of the party secretariats and departments reproduced the party's supervision of all activity through the workplace PPOs. Party departments at every level covered such things as industry, agriculture, education, commerce, construction, energy, media and propaganda, and party affairs. At the apex of the party the Central Committee Secretariat would also have departments for foreign and security affairs. The departments were the party's civil service and employed thousands of people; they supervised their sector and the work of party committees and departments below them. There was thus a chain of command and oversight that stretched from every factory floor, classroom and office through the local party departments to the Central Committee Secretariat. Almost no decisions were taken anywhere without advice from the party leader at the workplace and the local party department.

Party control was further assured by its personnel policy. Party organisations controlled all major appointments in their area. The Central Committee Secretariat and the General Secretary, for example, controlled appointments to ministerial posts, key jobs in the military, security and foreign services, the appointment of directors of major economic concerns and regional party and government leaders. At lower levels (town or district, for example), the party committee and First Secretary would control the appointment of school headteachers, PPO chairs, local council chairs, shop and small factory managers, etc. This system was known as the *nomenklatura*

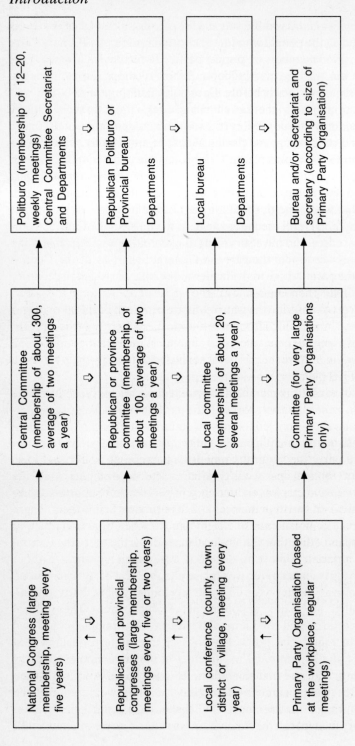

Figure I.1 Typical Communist Party organisational structure

system. The *nomenklatura* was literally the list of jobs controlled by the party. At the lowest level, the people who filled them did not necessarily have to be communists, or even members of 'puppet parties', where these existed. What was important was that the post-holder and their secret personnel file were vetted by the Communist Party before the appointment was made. A person's chances of promotion could therefore be blocked throughout their career by a secret (and possibly untrue) report of a youthful indiscretion entered by an informer in their peer group; and having a close relation living in the West – which was common, for example, in Czechoslovakia and the GDR – could place a 'glass ceiling' on the aspirations of even a conformist party member.

Symbolically, the *nomenklatura* was much more than an administrative device. *Nomenklatura* came to stand for the ruling elite of communism. (As we shall see, the term is still used today to describe those members of the new post-communist elites who have survived from the old system and kept their power.) The pressure to join the party and conform to its wishes was strong among the educated and those in – or who wanted to occupy – any position of responsibility. This phenomenon was known as party saturation (a term coined in the West to describe the way in which certain jobs were reserved for party members).[14] As a result, although the party comprised 10 per cent of the adult population on average, the ratio among middle-aged, professional males was often 1 in 2. Since the party was supposed to reflect the composition of the country in its membership and, most particularly, the working class, the demands placed on aspiring members in professional jobs were often stricter than those for a female factory worker.

The *nomenklatura* system led to the vast majority of people of importance being subject to party discipline and control. Every workplace or social organisation contained a party group which was supposed to enforce the party line. Uniformity within the party was created and enforced by the principle of *democratic centralism*. This was an idea specific to Communist Parties. It was supposed to ensure unity within their ranks and around the correct ideological line defined by Marxism-Leninism. Democratic centralism was variously defined in the rules of different Communist Parties. But the concept generally had four main aspects:

- all leading party bodies are elected;
- party bodies report periodically to their organisations and to higher bodies;
- there is strict party discipline and subordination of the minority to the majority;
- the decisions of higher bodies are obligatory for lower bodies.[15]

As Holmes points out, the first thing to note about the idea of democratic centralism 'is that the noun is centralism, the *adjective* democratic . . . [so] the basic tenet is centralism, not democracy'.[16] The lines of election and authority that such rules created can be seen in Figure I.1. Party secretaries and departments approved who was elected to attend and serve on committees so that electoral choice was heavily curtailed in the party. This meant that the 'democratic' element of the concept did not work. There was no means to organise for an alternative political line to that of the central authorities. Factional activity inside the party was banned and discussion of policy was virtually non-existent because decisions from the centre could not be questioned. Lower bodies and individual members had to accept as binding orders from above.

The organisation, ideology and personnel policies of ruling Communist Parties created close control over political life. Regular elections to councils and parliaments did not interfere in this. Elections had two main purposes. One was to provide the party's actions with a veneer of respectability. The other was to assure the party that most citizens were prepared to consent to its rule. Electoral choice was as constrained as it was inside the party. Elections to local and national legislatures usually involved no choice at all: voters either accepted or rejected the single name or list of names on the ballot paper. Most voters accepted the candidates put forward (who had always been approved by the party, even if they were not actually a member) because it was easy for the authorities to see who entered the polling booth to amend the ballot paper by crossing out names rather than placing it directly in the ballot box. The existence of other political parties in some countries made no difference to this. Their candidates appeared on the same approved lists as party candidates. While initially, in the late 1940s, the purpose of these parties had been to give a veneer of democracy to a *de facto* communist monopoly of power, they later served to harness as many citizens as possible to the goals of communism. For example, a practising Christian in the GDR, who would be unable openly to embrace Marxism-Leninism in the way required by Communist Party membership, could none the less demonstrate support of the state's other goals and participate in the administration of their workplace or the state by joining the puppet Christian Democratic Union. It could be argued that the existence of such parties kept some notion of party political representation alive, and in some cases they did gain in importance as communism collapsed (see Chapters 6 and 9).

The power of the party, the corruption of elections and subversion of minor parties destroyed the mass of independent activity that is found in western democracies and elsewhere. Independent political activity was not stamped out totally, however, because of the struggles of dissident groups. These very often saw and described themselves as being civil society, an alternative, morally superior and uncorrupted, political environment to the party. The level of dissident activity varied from country to country and over time, and it is hard to assess the extent of political activity since the line between actual political protest and mere deviance in culture or lifestyle was blurred by the ruling party's desire to control everything.

The USSR, Bulgaria and Yugoslavia had small dissident movements from the 1960s onwards.[17] The dissidents suffered imprisonment, internal exile and banishment. In the USSR, support for dissent was highest in western Ukraine and the Baltic republics, areas that had been forcibly annexed. In Albania and Romania, open dissent was rarer and was rapidly and harshly repressed when it did occur. In Central Europe, however – Poland, the GDR, Czechoslovakia and Hungary – discontent with the communist regime manifested itself not only by the existence of dissident movements, which usually comprised urban intellectuals, but also at times through mass popular protest. The Communist Parties here suffered from a double disadvantage: they not only ruled countries where communism had been imposed, they also had populations that were more open to Western influences, both through geographical proximity, culture and history and the presence of large émigré communities abroad. The consequence was that these regimes were much more obviously dependent on Soviet military support for their continued existence.

The influence of dissidents and their legacy was mixed, and as we shall see later, their role in the defeat of communism varied. When communism finally collapsed, a very large role was played by economic failure, the inability or unwillingness of communist leaders to reform or adapt and the USSR's disengagement from the Soviet bloc. In part, communism decayed from within, as the ruling parties increasingly comprised members who had joined for purely instrumental reasons (they wished to gain practical advantages in everyday life) rather than ideological conviction. It was also doomed, however, because far too high a percentage of the population were passive through coercion rather than consent. Although post-totalitarian communism rarely used physical force to control citizens, this was largely because it did not need to. The party exercised sufficient control over society for citizens to be compliant for fear of more minor sanctions than imprisonment: for example, anxiety that one's children would not be allowed to go to university was enough to make many people avoid any open sign of protest. However, once Communist Parties began to relinquish rigid control in the hope that they might, somehow, be able to rule by consent, the lack of popular allegiance to communism among the masses became very clear.

Communism and economic development

Party control covered the economy as well as politics. Most of the economies of the communist bloc were centrally planned. Almost everything was owned and run by the state: not just waterworks and railways, or even car factories and steelworks, but also restaurants, small shops and housing. Except in Poland and Yugoslavia, farming was carried out on large collective or state farms, rather than land and animals belonging to individual farmers. Some legal private enterprise did exist, but mostly this took the form of peasants being allowed to grow produce for the market on small private plots. This made up for the shortfalls in production on collective farms. Most other forms of private enterprise were illegal and formed part of the huge black market in scarce goods and services that sprang up because of the official system's inefficiency in distribution and inability to produce what people desired.

State ownership of the economy was important because it helped the Communist Parties control people politically. Because most people worked for the state, the communists controlled how they earned their money; and because the communists controlled prices, and determined the distribution of goods such as housing and foreign holidays largely by non-market mechanisms, they were also able to influence how people spent their money. Salaries and salary differentials were not high, but state welfare provision, particularly free health care, nurseries and higher education, was relatively advanced compared to the generally rather low standard of living. Transport, rents and utilities (gas, electricity, water) were heavily subsidised, but for those with money left over, luxuries such as cars and fashionable clothing were both scarce and expensive. This meant that citizens' everyday lives were to a large extent homogenised in communist states – that is, there were more similarities in the way families lived than in the West. Professors and factory-workers lived side-by-side in small flats in high-rise blocks; their children would go to the same schools and holiday camps; and a person's financial position and social standing would not be immediately apparent from the clothes they wore or the car they drove.

State control of the economy also affected citizens' family lives. Most women worked in full-time employment unless on maternity leave, encouraged by both easy availability of crèche and nursery places, and by social pressures, including their husbands' low salaries. Couples also tended to have children earlier than in the West since state provision for families meant that they never had to establish their economic independence. Having children normally came before obtaining one's own home, since it was virtually impossible to buy a flat on the open market, and the state allocated homes only to families with children. It is often assumed that communist states encouraged women to work and to have children early for economic reasons: there was a labour shortage. However, there were also political reasons for both policies. First, communist regimes did not want the next generation to be brought up by (possibly religious) housewives over whom they had no control. By moving the small children to nurseries and their mothers to the workplace, Communist Party structures had daily access to both. Secondly, people were encouraged to have children as soon as possible because families with responsibility for children were far more vulnerable to the risks involved in open dissent (not being allowed to work, imprisonment, etc.) than single people, and were also likely to be too engrossed in the everyday logistics of both working and bringing up a family to be concerned about politics.

However, whatever advantages state ownership had for the Communist Parties in terms of social engineering, there was a major economic disadvantage: central planning could not work. Economic planning requires accurate information. Without accurate information planners cannot make decisions that meet needs and are efficient. It was impossible to gather such reliable information so as to plan whole economies in the communist bloc. There are simply too many products and too many operations to be performed in the course of production. Moreover, the planners had to accommodate the demands made upon them by party leaders. Also, central planning was very inflexible, and could not adapt quickly to unforeseen problems.[18]

The result of these logistical problems with information was not the economics of *planning* – if planning means the issuing of measured, considered, economic targets with a balance of inputs and outputs – but *command* economics. Planners issued orders based on previous targets. These were often arbitrary and politically defined. Increases in production were achieved by raising targets by a certain percentage year on year, no matter what production capacity or demand was. Targets could not be set for all products, only for gross production. For example, a glass factory would not be told to produce x amount of glass for shop windows, y amount of glass for houses and z amount of glass for car windscreens; it would simply be told to produce so many square metres of glass. The result was a shortage of certain types of glass and huge amounts of waste as thin glass broke when used inappropriately. Production was further hampered and made wasteful by bottlenecks. Deliveries of supplies could not be guaranteed between different stages in the production process. As a result factories and workers would stand idle while waiting for a vital component. When it arrived workers would have to insert it quickly to meet the monthly plan target. The result was goods of poor quality and limited life: fridges with their doors nailed on, television sets with the parts not wired up, etc. The constant need to meet the plan target also prevented innovation and modernisation. Factories were not given time to introduce new machinery or techniques into production because there was no let-up in the plan targets. As a result, they would carry on using old machines and techniques while expensive new machinery rusted unused. Making a profit, breaking even or using materials economically did not matter. Factory directors did not have to worry about the financial health of their enterprise because they worked under 'soft-budget constraints': loss-making enterprises could always squeeze more subsidies from the state. There were none of the 'hard-budget constraints' imposed in capitalist economies by markets, commercial banks, shareholders and the bottom line of profit and loss.

Table I.1 Selected statistics on socio-economic development in Eastern Europe and the USSR

	% of population employed in agriculture 1985	*No. of cars per 1000 inhabitants*
Albania	50	
Bulgaria	23	127
Czechoslovakia	12	174
GDR	10	209
Hungary	20	157
Poland	30	111
Romania	28	12
USSR	19	44
Yugoslavia	30	129

Source: Kornai (1992, pp. 6–7, 305).

Two caveats need to be made to this bleak economic picture.

First, waste, inefficiency and failure to meet consumer demands were not the whole story. The countries we are interested in did not become as powerful or as wealthy as the countries of the Organisation for Economic Cooperation and Development (OECD) countries (Western Europe, United States, Canada, Japan, New Zealand and Australia), or as strong in the world economy as the NICs (Newly Industrialised Countries such as South Korea). But in some ways, they were development successes. With a few exceptions (most notably the Czech part of Czechoslovakia), the countries of Eastern Europe and Russia were economically backward when the communists came to power and/or were devastated by war. By the end of the communist period they had developed industrial economies and welfare states. Social developments were particularly impressive. The communist states fostered high levels of literacy, narrowed the gap between rich and poor, brought electricity to rural areas, created towns and provided healthcare for all. True, services were often rudimentary, the towns that were built were ugly and there were costs attached to nearly every social gain. But the communists left populations that were skilled and educated and used to certain standards in the public provision of social services. This had both pluses and minuses for communism and post-communism. An educated, skilled citizenry is necessary for development, a plus for both political forms. But education led to dissatisfaction with the limits of communist politics and awareness of communism's failings as an economic system. This helped to bring about the collapse of communism. An educated, skilled, urban population is important for the development of democracy and market economy. Yet at the same time, many people in Eastern Europe and the former Soviet Union are now unhappy about the loss of welfare rights that they enjoyed under communism. Citizens of communist states were used to the notion that all people were supposed to be equal. Although it was well known that leading communists enjoyed great privileges, including access to closed shops and normally unobtainable goods, there was a general consensus that such advantage was illegitimate. This affected attitudes to the conspicuous wealth that was flaunted throughout the region after the fall of communism.

The second caveat to the general picture of communism as a disastrous economic system is that there were variations to the basic economic model and in the economic fortunes of the communist countries. The main variation to the planning model was found in Yugoslavia. Economic management in Yugoslavia took the form of 'worker self-management'.[19] The central planning organs and economic ministries were abolished and a semi-market system developed. This blended the setting of prices by markets with self-management of economic activity by collectives and managers and some planning by central and (particularly) republican authorities. Other economic experiments took place in Hungary (the New Economic Mechanism, which included some free prices and hard-budget constraints),[20] and there were frequent attempts at reforming economies based on reorganising economic institutions, correcting the way that plan targets were set, etc., throughout the area.

Economic experimentation combined with different levels of development at the onset of communism to produce uneven development. We can see one aspect of this in the figures for the number of people employed in agriculture in Table I.1. The more people engaged in agriculture, the less industrialised and developed the economy. Unevenness also occurred within states: the Baltic republics were more advanced economically than the rest of the USSR, the Czech Republic was more developed than Slovakia,[21] Croatia and Slovenia were wealthier than Serbia and Montenegro. These disparities caused problems within states and within the Soviet trading bloc, the CMEA. The regional and national variations in economic fortune under communism influenced its end and post-communist developments. Tensions between republics in the federal states of Czechoslovakia, the USSR and Yugoslavia fuelled centrifugal forces in all of the countries. The level of economic development achieved under communism has also influenced the speed at which the new states have been able to react to the market.

When we consider development as well as the fundamental flaws of the command-planning system the image of communist economics becomes more varied than if we look at just the basic design flaws of the system. But in the end, and despite its successes in socio-economic development and the variations that could be found within it, the system told. The communist economic experiment was all but finished by the mid-1980s. It was under pressure because of its technological backwardness, consumer pressure for higher living standards and international indebtedness. (East European leaders had borrowed heavily from the West in the 1970s and their economies did not produce goods that could earn foreign revenue to pay off this debt.) These problems could not be solved without technological modernisation, and productivity and efficiency gains. However, there was no way that the communist economic system could achieve these needed improvements. The planning system could not become more efficient and was unresponsive to reform. Productivity would not rise because there were no incentives for workers, and the lack of innovation in the economy made the communist bloc countries dependent on the West, the ideological enemy, for technology. In the end, communism could not compete with capitalism in technology and living standards. Table I.1 shows just one area in which the communist bloc was falling behind advanced capitalist states: the number of cars per 1000 people. The GDR led the communist bloc with 209 cars per 1000 people. At the same time there were 388 cars per 1000 people in West Germany. Similar disparities could be produced for telephones, televisions, larger ones for such things as personal computers and video recorders.

For communist states, this was not merely an economic problem, but also an ideological one. Marxism-Leninism was understood by many ordinary people to contain at least the promise of ever-increasing material well-being for the population. After all, the economic systems were based on an ideology that was supposed to be scientific and infallible, and the communist regimes committed themselves publicly to doing everything for the good of the people. If capitalism performed so very much better, then Marxism-Leninism could not be faultless, and the Communist Party's right to rule was non-existent.

Conclusion

Communism in Eastern Europe and the USSR was not uniform. This is particularly true of communism as it entered the 1980s. There were huge political differences between Stalinist Albania, the political turmoil in Poland caused by Solidarity, the fetid orthodoxy of Czechoslovakia and the GDR, and the struggling superpower politics of the USSR.

Such huge differences all played their part in the way that communism fell and what has followed it. The crises that beset communist leaders were broadly similar: they were politically illegitimate, the economic systems that they managed were inefficient and decaying, the political systems they headed were corrupt and unresponsive to pressures for change. But the way in which crisis visited each communist regime, the way that they tried to deal with it and the result, the manner in which post-communism began, was very different.

Notes

1. The most famous of these arguments was Francis Fukuyama's claim that history had 'ended'. The ideological struggle between communism and capitalist democracy was

over and a political system (democracy) that recognised human differences and sought to accommodate them had triumphed. There would thus be no more major conflicts such as the Cold War, no more struggles between grand ideas. See Fukuyama (1989 and 1992).

2. On the different routes to communism and communist takeovers in Eastern Europe, see Hammond (1975) and McCauley (1977). The best histories of communism in Eastern Europe are Rothschild (1993) and Schöpflin (1994).

3. The best general histories of the USSR are Hosking (1990) and McAuley (1992b). Introductions to specific periods include Fitzpatrick (1994) (for the 1917 revolution and its immediate aftermath), Ward (1993) (for the Stalin period) and Keep (1995) (for the 1945–91 period).

4. We shall use post-communist geographic terminology for Belarus and Moldova throughout this book: Belarus rather than 'Byelorussia', and Moldova rather than 'Moldavia'.

5. It is more accurate to talk of Soviet pressure than Red Army intervention in Czechoslovakia, since the armies of both the USSR and the United States left the country in December 1945.

6. On events in Hungary in 1956, see Lomax (1976) and for Czechoslovakia in 1968, Skilling (1976) and Mlynář (1980).

7. See Berglund and Dellenbrant (1994) for a useful summary of the concept of 'people's democracies'.

8. For a complete description of the 'Brezhnev Doctrine', see Jones (1989).

9. See Keane (1988) for definitions of civil society.

10. For the classic statement on totalitarianism, see Friedrich and Brzezinski (1956). The concept's history and development is traced in Tormey (1995). The main criticisms made of the idea can be found in Holmes (1986, pp. 383–90), and most other textbooks on communism.

11. Robinson (1995, pp. 20–7).

12. See Holmes (1993) for details of corruption in communist states.

13. The best description of a ruling Communist Party is Hill and Frank (1986) on the CPSU. The day-to-day work of party cadres is described in Horvárth and Szakolczai (1992) on the Hungarian Socialist Workers' Party in Budapest.

14. Hough (1977, pp. 125–39).

15. Taken from Hill and Frank (1986, p. 73).

16. Holmes (1986, p. 121).

17. For details on dissent in Eastern Europe, see Tökés (1979) and Skilling (1989). For a history of dissent in the USSR see Alexeyeva (1987).

18. For fuller descriptions of the operation of planned economies, see Kornai (1992), Nove (1986) and Rutland (1985).

19. Comisso (1979) and Lydall (1990).

20. For a fuller analysis of Hungarian reform, see Berend (1990).

21. Differences in living standards between Czechs and Slovaks were greatly reduced during their 40 years under communism, but Slovakia, which had attained modernisation under communism, was more vulnerable in the changes which took place after 1989. See Musil (1995).

PART I

1989 – DECLINE AND REVOLUTION

CHAPTER 1

Describing radical change and post-communist politics

The changes that have occurred in Eastern Europe and the USSR since 1989 are difficult to classify. Two standard social science classifications of radical political change have been invoked to describe the collapse of communism and post-communist attempts at democratisation: revolution and transition. However, what has happened in Eastern Europe and the USSR does not fit neatly with the classical definitions of either transition or revolution. The collapse of communism and post-communism seem to blend aspects of revolution and transitional politics. This, perhaps, should not be too surprising. If communism was unique as a social, economic and political system, its end and aftermath should also be distinctive. Moreover, just as communism was not uniform in its origins and its form throughout the Soviet Union and Eastern Europe, so too were there differences in the processes by which various states exited from communism.

To see how distinctive (or not) the processes of change from communism have been, we need to look first at what we mean by revolution and transition. We shall do this by looking first at the ideal-typical definitions of revolution and transition, the abstract examples against which messy reality can be compared, and how change in Eastern Europe and the USSR stand up against them. We shall then see how blending ideas about revolution and transition might better capture the complexity of communism's end and aftermath. Finally, we will look at the various classifications which have been suggested for differentiating the processes of regime change in the various countries.

Revolution and transition

Revolution is one of the most overused and overextended terms in the lexicons of history and social science. It is frequently and promiscuously associated with dramatic changes of vastly different types and various outcomes.

The term has also been widely and loosely used about the end of communism. The collapse of communism in Czechoslovakia was quickly christened the 'Velvet Revolution', and descriptions of Gorbachev's reforms as 'revolution from above' and the popular response to it as 'revolution from below' are common. The overuse of revolution threatens to make it meaningless because it has become a synonym for any large-scale change. However, some clear defi-nitions are available for us to use. The most appropriate is the concept of social revolution. When we talk of revolution in the rest of this book we are most frequently referring to this type of radical social, political and economic transformation.

The ideal-type of social revolution has been most clearly defined by Theda Skocpol in her comparison of the great social revolutions in France (1789), Russia (1917) and China (1911–49):

> Social revolutions are rapid, basic transformations of a society's state and class structures; and they are accompanied and in part carried through by class-based revolts from below. Social revolutions are set apart from other sorts of conflicts and transformative processes above all by the combination . . . of societal structural change with class upheaval . . . and of political with social transformation.[1]

There are two important things to note about this definition of social and political revolution. First, social 'revolutions are not made; they come'.[2] Secondly, a revolution's outcome is as important in defining it as a revolution as the type of actors involved in the overthrow of an old regime and the actions that they undertake to ensure a change in power. Class revolt (by workers or peasants and involving violence) helps to make a social revolution but the post-revolutionary transformation of society through changes in the economy are equally important.

The fact that revolutions 'come' unbidden and the importance of looking at outcomes when defining revolution are both explained by the causes of revolution. Social revolutions take place in states that are struggling to compete internationally because of economic backwardness. As they fall behind their international rivals crisis occurs, generally during or after a war. A revolutionary situation thus occurs owing to *systemic* factors (the effects of international competition and economic backwardness) and not because of the actions of revolutionary parties. The uncalled for development of a revolutionary situation enables the overthrow of the ruling class. State, society and economy are then reconstructed by a fresh ruling group. The state, society and economy created by this new ruling group are qualitatively different from those that preceded them since they are rebuilt in a way that makes them capable of sustained international competition; 'basic changes in social structure and in political structure occur together and in a mutually reinforcing fashion'.[3] The combination of political and socio-economic change to deal with the pressures of international competition also means that social revolution is nation-building. New ideas of nation and citizenship are developed in the course of social and political reconstruction.

The collapse of communism is comparable to a social revolution in terms of both causes and consequences. As we noted in the Introduction, communism as an economic system could not match its western ideological opponents in technological innovation or consumer goods production. The lag in technological development meant that the Soviet bloc in general, and the USSR in particular, were falling behind in the arms race. The United States' plans to develop the Strategic Defence Initiative (SDI or 'Star Wars') in the 1980s exposed the technology gap between the United States and the USSR, and threatened the Soviets with an expensive new round of arms development that they could ill afford because of the lamentable state of the Soviet economy. Further, the USSR was burdened by the costs of empire. These included direct costs, such as those incurred by the war in Afghanistan and the stationing of troops in Eastern Europe, and indirect costs, like the subsidised sale of energy to CMEA countries at prices lower than those that could be earned on the world market. All in all the USSR, and by extension the whole Soviet bloc, were competing internationally with the West at a level they could not afford. The Gorbachev reforms were – at least in part – an attempt to ease the burden of empire by encouraging reform in the Soviet bloc and reducing international tension and the pace of the arms race. Since these reforms stimulated the breakdown of Communist Party power in the USSR and Soviet hegemony in Eastern Europe the collapse of communism could be said to have 'come' from systemic factors – Soviet failure in international competition and relative economic backwardness. Additionally, within Eastern Europe, the protests of 1989 were also preceded by a gradual breakdown of what was often termed a 'social contract': an unspoken agreement that citizens remained politically passive in return for a low, but gradually increasing, standard of living. This delicate balance was disturbed when the ailing economies of the region could no longer afford to keep the communists' side of the 'bargain'.

The end of communism is even closer to social revolution in outcomes. There has been a complete coincidence between major and radical social and political transformation. Monolithic ruling Communist Parties have been swept away in favour of political pluralism and constitutional government (albeit imperfect and not fully developed). Privatisation and marketisation policies have been pursued (with various degrees of success and enthusiasm) so that planning has been largely destroyed and socio-economic stratification has begun to emerge. The aim of much of this change is not necessarily to create economies that can support strategic military competition with the West, but to create economies that can compete with advanced capitalist economies in the world market. The creation and re-creation of nations and the reconstruction of citizenship is also more marked in the collapse of communism because of the need to create new nation states in the former Soviet Union, Yugoslavia and Czechoslovakia.

However, in many other respects the collapse of communism does not fit the ideal-typical paradigm of social revolution. We could argue that communism's collapse was caused by *non*-systemic variables as much as by international competition. Particularly important here would be the decision to reform taken by Mikhail Gorbachev and the Soviet leadership. Moreover, communist leaderships were often not overthrown but gave up power through negotiation. Hungary and Poland would be the best examples of this in 1989; the communist elites of the Baltic republics in the USSR also compromised significantly with opposition forces. The part played by communist elites, as we shall discuss below, could be described as setting in train a classical process of transitional, rather than revolutionary, politics.

The events surrounding the collapse of communism are equally at odds with what we might expect to find taking place during a social revolution. Communism was not defeated by class-based revolt from below, and violence was not a major instrument of change in most countries. Violence was rare and generally perpetrated by the ailing communist regime (for example, the Soviet attempts at suppressing the Lithuanian independence movement in 1991). Romania suffered the worst bout of violence, for reasons discussed in Chapter 3. However, these cases notwithstanding, the most remarkable feature of communism's collapse was the *lack* of violence attendant on the Communist Parties' defeat. Most of the violence that occurred was incidental to the defeat of ruling parties and consisted of ethnic groups contesting the spoils of communism's demise, or reliving older hostilities. Ethnic conflict is, in fact, another of the differences between social revolution and the end of communism. Class conflict is the main form of social involvement in social revolution. Class cleavages as we know them in the West had been distorted in communist systems. As a result class did not, and could not, serve as the base for protest action. Protest stimulated by distinct socio-economic strata occurred only among tight-knit communities concentrated in specific regions and with 'trade', not 'class', consciousness. The Soviet miners who took action against the state from 1989 onwards would be a good example of this; they were concentrated geographically, had grievances specific to their industry and a sense of themselves as a distinct group of workers. More usually, protest against the communist system cut across class lines and transcended ethnicity in a fight against a common enemy. The mass movements that emerged in 1989 like Civic Forum/Public Against Violence in Czechoslovakia or Sajudis (Movement) in Lithuania were led by intellectuals but aspired to express the grievances of different occupations, and a wide array of socio-economic and cultural groups.

Finally, the outcome of social revolutions has been at odds historically with the declared aims of change in Eastern Europe and the former Soviet Union. None of the great social revolutions, whatever their proclaimed initial aims, led to democracy – at least not quickly or directly. The great social revolutions were legitimated in part by *ideology*, but revolutionary ideologies failed to achieve their aims when attempts were made at practical implementation. Post-revolutionary rulers created repressive, centralised, closed, authoritarian or totalitarian political systems. Authoritarianism or totalitarianism enabled them to rebuild their state, economy and society and compete internationally. Social revolution in France was followed by the military authoritarianism of Napoleon, in Russia and China by communism. These outcomes are very much at odds with the aim of most post-communist rulers in Eastern Europe and the former USSR – building democracy, a system based on legal and human rights, some decentralisation of power and openness.[4] Building democracy was the nearest thing to an ideology propelling the opponents of communism. It might even be argued that the changes in Eastern Europe and the former Soviet Union would be better described as 'counter-revolutions' – a return to the *status quo ante* and an attempt to reassert old links with the rest of Europe.

The different aims of post-communist rulers, the lack of violence, the compromise by elites and initiation of change by some of them, the absence of class-based revolt – all point analysis towards looking at the end of communism as transition rather than revolution. However, the idea that post-communism is a type of 'transitional politics' has been very hotly contested.[5] The main ideas about transitional politics describe the 'third wave' of democratisation – the establishment of democracy in southern Europe (Spain, Portugal and Greece) in the 1970s, and the collapse of military dictatorships in Latin America in the same period.[6] The literature on these regime changes can be divided into two broad approaches: functionalist and genetic.[7]

The functionalist approach focuses on long-term socio-economic changes and argues that the development of modern, capitalist economy and social structure is the main cause of collapse in authoritarian systems and ensures the growth of democracy. As capitalism develops, and especially as it becomes more advanced, it creates social classes and groups with defined interests and an ability to act autonomously. In short, development creates interests and the ability to organise institutions (parties, community and interest groups, etc.) to satisfy those interests. Development thus creates civil society. The bourgeoisie (sometimes also referred to as the middle class) is traditionally seen as playing the main role in pressing for and supporting democratic politics. The bourgeoisie was born as a class with capitalism and is supposed to have a clear idea of its interests and the means to organise for them before other modern classes (such as the working class). This leads it to demand democratic political rights and freedoms to match and safeguard its economic position. A variant on this long-term approach has been put forward by

Rueschemeyer *et al.* They argue that social structure helps to nourish democracy not because of the rise of the middle class, but because the development of capitalist economy creates an organised working class. The organised working class prevent the concentration of power in elite hands and force the development and spread of rights.[8] Whichever class is seen as the most important agent of democratisation the result and its ultimate cause are the same: democracy is created to bring the political system into line with socio-economic pressures created by the evolution of modern capitalist economy; political change is thus *functional*, it occurs to balance socio-economic change and ensure harmony within a nation-state.

The genetic approach qualifies the functionalist, long-term approach. It acknowledges that socio-economic development might promote change and that historically the development (or not) of democracy is linked to the presence or absence of classes, particularly a bourgeois class. But the genetic approach does not see socio-economic change as ultimately being a guarantee of democratic development. Instead, the genetic approach stresses 'contingency', the provisional, uncertain nature of transitions from authoritarianism: transitions can lead to democracy but they do not do so necessarily.

The focus of the genetic approach is the specific political processes of transitions, the details of which are unique to each country (hence its label). However, certain common problems can be identified and theorised. In particular, genetic approaches to transition look at relationships within political elites. These are examined to see what promotes peaceful movement from authoritarianism to democracy. Two factors are identified as being most important: the nature of the move from authoritarianism and the choices – the political and economic strategies – that leaders and elites make during and just after the move.

The nature of the move from authoritarianism is important because it determines which institutions are inherited from authoritarianism and who (which sectors of the old elite) is involved in the political game of transition. By selecting which institutions are inherited from authoritarianism and who is involved in the political game, the move from authoritarianism establishes the 'path' of a transition: it makes certain courses of action and outcomes more likely than others. This idea is sometimes called 'path dependency'.[9] Some 'paths', like revolution, cannot lead to democracy. Institutions of all kinds (social, economic and political) are destroyed during revolution; revolutionary leaders centralise power so that they can rebuild their state, economy and society.[10] The result, as we have discussed already, is the creation of a new authoritarian polity. The most secure 'path' to democracy is through the building of pacts, compromises between leaders and elites. Successful transitions by pact start with a stage of liberalisation. This stage sees reforms being introduced to an authoritarian polity by a ruling regime. These reforms (such as the *perestroika* – restructuring – reforms introduced by Gorbachev in the USSR) give citizens and groups limited political rights (some freedom of speech and association, for example). When reform starts, elites are divided on how far it should go. However, these divisions are neutralised because elite members join in a pact for reform: they see the need to change some aspect of the authoritarian system and consequently are willing to embark on at least limited reform. In successful transitions, pacts expand to incorporate both original elite members and any new elites that emerge with liberalisation (for example, leaders of new political parties or interest groups). Such expanded pacts help to ensure that the second stage of change, democratisation, follows liberalisation and is peaceful. This second stage of change sees the expansion of rights, their full institutionalisation and the construction of democratic citizenship.

Pacts are thus important for two reasons. First, they help to get reform – and the movement away from authoritarianism – moving. Secondly, once the authoritarian system has begun to crack they ensure that a sufficiently large number of elite members have a stake in the political game and do not see themselves as having lost too much from change. If a section of the elite thinks at any stage that it has lost too much, it will not abide by the rules of a fledgling democratic polity. In particular a 'losing' elite will reject the rule central to democratic politics: the notion that power should be transferred between elite members only via free elections. The losing elite will appeal to its supporters and, if powerful enough, will return the state to authoritarianism by a coup or some other clampdown.

The calculation of gain or loss by elite members is influenced by the second factor stressed by genetic approaches to transition: elite strategies. If the wrong strategy is chosen by dominant elite members, their rivals will think that they are losing from change and will not be bound by pacts. Indeed, because the transition process starts with reform of the authoritarian system, strategy (in the shape of a reform package around which elite members can cluster) comes before pacts. How elites appreciate strategies and calculate their losses and gains is a complex process and there are no firm rules to guide analysts. We can guess that some strategies are obviously dangerous and likely to provoke some elite members into counteraction (for example, arresting them for crimes against humanity committed under the authoritarian system). However, there is no sure way that anyone can fully know what strategies are most likely to result in democracy's consolidation and thus predict the future. Elites have different characters in different countries, sections of the elite (like the military) vary from state to state, and political leaders suffer the full range of human personality disorders.

The fact that there are many ways in which national elites can make calculations about their losses and gains during a period of change leads the genetic approach to transitions to conclude that transitions are very uncertain processes that need not lead to a fixed end, democracy. Rather, transitions are:

from certain authoritarian regimes toward an uncertain 'something else'. That 'something' can be . . . political democracy or the restoration of a new, and possibly more severe, form of authoritarian rule . . . [or] the rotation in power of successive governments which fail to provide any enduring or predictable solution to the problem of institutionalising political power.[11]

Waves of democratisation can, in short, go into reverse as the tide of democracy surges and ebbs.[12]

Some aspects of genetic transition theory seem to fit with the post-communist experience of many countries in Eastern Europe and the former USSR.[13] The collapse of communism did begin with an elite strategy/reform package – *perestroika* – in the USSR. This was a liberalisation policy and required an elite pact/compromise to initiate it and maintain it for its first few years. Some of the changes of rulers in the area took place through what appear to be negotiation and pacts: institutions were not destroyed. Instead, attempts were made to transform them legally. Parliaments were not shut down and constitutions were not suspended. The composition of parliaments was changed by a process of painstaking negotiation and elections, and constitutions were changed either by successive amendments passed through the parliament, or by a new constitution passed by post-communist parliaments.

The functionalist approach too seems to have some mileage. Development did create pressures for change during the communist period: better education created dissatisfaction with communist ideology and awareness of the outside world; technological advancement, although slower than in the West, gave skilled workers and experts a greater role in the economy and led some to believe that they could manage their own affairs without the party; material expectations rose as economies developed so that people began to hunger for the consumer goods of advanced capitalism.

However, as with the concept of revolution, the validity of both functionalist and genetic approaches to transition has been questioned for post-communism. First, both have been criticised – somewhat unfairly in the case of the genetic approach – for being determinist. The word transition suggests to many that the final destination of the society undergoing change is known: they are in transition to democracy. Making such an assumption can lead us to ignore political phenomena that are running counter to democratic development. As a result, we might misjudge the future quite badly.

Secondly, the idea that democracy is a result of socio-economic development does not explain the onset of post-communism or its democratic prospects. Development created pressure for change and these pressures contributed to the loss of legitimacy by communist regimes. But these pressures do not on their own explain why communism collapsed when it did and how it did. Factors such as Soviet non-interference in Eastern Europe in

1989, national history and state form also had an immense influence on the way that communism collapsed.

Thirdly, the tasks involved in post-communist democratisation are much greater than in Latin American and Southern European transitions so that elite choices are more complex, uncertainty much greater and the number of factors and forces that need to be considered is far larger. In Southern Europe and Latin America the most important strategic choices concerned political questions such as the nature of electoral system, presidentialism or parliamentarianism, etc. (see Chapter 7 for a fuller discussion of these questions). There were few fundamental economic issues involved in transition because capitalism was firmly installed and society was stratified by it. In Eastern Europe and the former USSR the creation of a democratic institutional framework coincides with the need to remove the economy from state control and with the need to build nations; the former communist countries are undergoing a 'triple transition'.[14] The need to build political nations means that we have to take into account ethnic minorities and culture in ways that were not a problem for analysts of earlier transitions. The need to build capitalism as well as democratic institutions means that 'path dependency' is more complex than before. Economic institutions and actors have survived as well as political ones and these have to be taken into account both by domestic elites and by outside observers.[15]

Classifying negotiated revolutions

The collapse of communism sits awkwardly between revolution and transition. This has led some analysts simply to fuse the terms and talk of 'revolutionary transitions'.[16] However, a preferable alternative is to talk of 'negotiated revolution'. This is a better expression than 'revolutionary transitions' or 'peaceful revolutions' because it asserts the depth and significance of the changes that have been underway in Eastern Europe and the former USSR since 1989. The con-cept of change at the forefront of analysis is revolution: total and fundamental social, political and economic transformation occurring at the same moment of time and originating in systemic crisis. The roots of the crisis that affected the communist regimes in the USSR and Eastern Europe in the 1980s were created by communism's unworkability as an economic system, its illegitimacy as either an economic system, an imposed or partly imposed order, the difficulty of reforming the communist system due to the bureaucratisation of Communist Parties, and the ruling Communist Party's arrogance and isolation from the population which fostered corruption and mismanagement. This communist system was swept away in 1989 in most of Eastern Europe and between 1989 and 1991 in Albania, the USSR and Yugoslavia. Although this was not achieved by class-based revolt, it was accomplished by mass social protest, the only form of protest that could occur given the levelling of social differentiation by communist rule. The changes that have followed are of world-historical importance and amount to a basic and simultaneous reconstruction of society, polity and economy. Change of this magnitude and world-historical importance can only be captured by the use of the term 'revolution'.

The second reason that we prefer 'negotiated revolution' is that it both modifies the description of how change takes place and contains an idea of what may make the outcome of total change different to the usual outcome of social revolution. Change is described both by the concept used (revolution) and the adjectival prefix (negotiated); revolution indicates that change is fundamental, negotiated indicates that there are limits to change, that change is permanently subject to rectification as revolution is continually being redefined in practice. The degree to which negotiation mediates revolution – particularly revolutionary strategies for rapid change – is decided by resources. Resources can be many things: money, culture, international aid, organisations and institutions. For example, in the GDR negotiation was conditioned by the GDR's existence as a state within a larger German nation. The larger nation was a resource in many different ways. In the first instance it created opportunities for flight to the West, which forced change on an unresponsive communist elite. Later it meant that there were political and economic resources (West German parties and finance) to balance the power of the old elite. In the USSR the limits to change were imposed at first by the need to deal with entrenched local party leaders. The attitudes of these leaders influenced the speed at which opposition, and hence change, could develop. Later, political development was influenced by the continued existence of the central Soviet state. This had to be dealt with before post-communism proper could begin. The means used were the struggle for legal precedence between central and republican laws and elite bargaining. In Romania, Bulgaria and Albania the balance between revolution and more gradual change was set by the limited resources available to the people for overthrowing the communist elite. Change was dependent on the support of a section of the communist elite, who consequently could control the form that post-communism took.

The use of the term 'negotiated revolution' should not be allowed to disguise the differences between the processes of change in individual communist countries. Such differences are particularly important, because it is becoming increasingly evident that the 'mode of transition' – the precise circumstances in which Communist Party rule was replaced – is one of the factors affecting the eventual outcomes. A number of attempts have been undertaken to classify differing ways in which countries exited from communism, and these should be borne in mind when considering the events analysed in the following chapters.

One of the most common classifications is the 'pairing' of the six Warsaw

Pact countries in Eastern Europe: Czechoslovakia and the GDR; Poland and Hungary; Bulgaria and Romania. These six form a natural group, since communism had been externally imposed upon all of them, and there was therefore an element of decolonisation in the regime changes of 1989–90. The fall of the communist rulers in Czechoslovakia and the GDR is commonly described as 'implosion' or 'capitulation of the old elites': the party leaderships had no strategy for coping with popular protest and collapsed rapidly. Changes in Hungary and Poland are labelled 'negotiated transitions', 'bargaining among the old and new elites' or 'party competition/election'. Here, Communist Parties contained some elements who were willing to compromise and carry out change, partly because they believed that the best way of stabilising their own power was by increasing their legitimacy. Bulgaria and Romania are described as 'preventive reform of communist elite groups' or 'compromise'. These were states with a weak tradition of dissent, where part of the ruling elite took the initiative to democratise in the wake of the first signs of public protests.

The most systematic attempt at pairing has been undertaken by Claus Offe, who isolated seventeen factors which distinguished each pair.[17] Apart from the mode of regime change, these included per capita industrial production (high for Czechoslovakia and the GDR, low for Bulgaria and Romania), the predominant mode of social integration (economic for Czechoslovakia and the GDR, national for Hungary and Poland, and repressive for Bulgaria and Romania), the level of repression under the old regime (low in Hungary and Poland, high in Bulgaria and Romania, and medium in Czechoslovakia and the GDR) and geostrategic position (the GDR and Czechoslovakia were 'front-line states' while Bulgaria and Romania were distant from Western Europe). The identification of so many factors clearly points to the fact that many elements that structured communist societies have since impacted on elite strategies and the mode of regime change, with the interconnection between factors being particularly important. One summary of the changes describes them as taking 'ten years in Poland, ten months in Hungary, ten weeks in the GDR and ten days in Czechoslovakia'. (Offe adds that the duration of the regime change was even shorter in Bulgaria and Romania.) Why were some changes quicker than others? In Poland and Hungary, the communists were prepared to compromise and negotiate with the opposition over a longer period of time so that they initially achieved smoother transitions. The intransigent, authoritarian communist regimes in Czechoslovakia and the GDR, on the other hand, collapsed almost totally in a relatively short time. Bulgaria and Romania are different cases, because – although the deposing of the elderly leaders Zhivkov and Ceaușescu was effected rapidly – there was a question mark over whether the rest of the ruling elites had at this point changed at all.

An extension of Offe's classification of the East European 'democratic transitions' is provided by Herbert Kitschelt.[18] He refines the pairing of the six Warsaw Pact states by dividing Czechoslovakia, and suggesting, controversially, that while the Czech Republic and the GDR were clearly similar cases, events in Slovakia to some extent bore more resemblance to those in Bulgaria and Romania. While the regime initially imploded, brought down together with the communists in Prague, the Slovak *nomenklatura* was later able to take pre-emptive action and re-emerge as new parties formed. Kitschelt also incorporates some of the other communist states into his analysis. Slovenia, Croatia and the Baltic states are aligned with Hungary and Poland as cases of bargaining between old and new elites, while Russia, the Ukraine, Belarus and most other former Soviet Republics, as well as Serbia and Albania, are classified together with Bulgaria and Romania as examples of preventive reform by communist elite groups. (Montenegro, and to a slightly lesser extent Macedonia, would also fit this category.)

Kitschelt's distinctions between the modes of transition is further underpinned by linking them to the structure of authoritarian rule, that is, by differentiating between types of communist regime.[19] *Patrimonial communism* was distinguished by a lower level of contestation over policy-making within the Communist Party elite, and little popular interest articulation, as well as 'low to intermediate rational-bureaucratic institutionalization'. The latter feature entails a low level of professionalism in the bureaucracy, and consequently extensive patronage networks and clientelism. Since there was little opposition to communism in such systems, changes were brought about through pre-emptive attempts at reform by parts of the communist elite. This type of communism was characteristic for South-East Europe and Russia, the Ukraine and Belarus. *Bureaucratic-authoritarian communism* is largely a description of the system in the Czech Republic and the GDR. It applies to a lesser extent to Slovakia, where there were also elements of patrimonial communism. Such systems contain little internal or external contestation of communist power, but the communist bureaucracy demonstrates a greater level of competence. Such regimes were marked by inflexibility, and therefore collapsed under pressure because of their inability to undertake preventive reform. Finally, Poland and Hungary are described as *national* or *national consensus communism*. Interest articulation was possible, both within and outside the party, and communist elites presented themselves as trying to maintain national autonomy from Soviet hegemony. This stance opened the way to negotiations with the opposition and 'negotiated transitions'. Slovenia and Croatia are included in this category, as are the Baltic Republics, as borderline cases.

A somewhat different classification to that of Offe and Kitschelt is provided by Samuel P. Huntington, who looks at the democratisation of communist regimes together with regime changes in Latin America and southern Europe.[20] Huntington's classification is particularly interesting for two reasons. First, his three basic categories of transition processes disrupt the familiar pairing of the six Warsaw Pact countries of Eastern Europe. Hungary and Bulgaria are designated 'transformations', the GDR and Romania 'replacements', and Czechoslovakia and Poland 'transplacements'. Secondly, distinctions are made between the factions within both the ruling elites and the opposition. Governing elites are divided into 'standpatters', who would countenance no change, 'liberalisers', who supported limited reform, and 'democratisers', who were prepared to share power with the opposition. The opposition is divided into moderates and extremists.

In *transformations*, 'those in power in the authoritarian regime take the lead and play the decisive role in ending that regime and changing it into a democratic system . . . Transformation requires the government to be stronger than the opposition'.[21] Apart from Hungary and Bulgaria, the Soviet Union is also tentatively placed in this category. Transformation is a gradual process: as a first step, the 'standpatter' leaders (Kádár in Hungary, Zhivkov in Bulgaria, Chernenko in the Soviet Union) are replaced by liberalisers (Grosz, Mladenov, Gorbachev). However, liberalisation fails to stabilise the systems, and so its representatives are merely transitional leaders; democratisers take over and a complete transfer of power becomes possible.

Replacements are substantially different. 'Reformers within the regime are weak or non-existent. The dominant elements in government are standpatters staunchly opposed to regime change. Democratisation consequently results from the opposition gaining strength and the government losing strength until the government collapses or is overthrown.'[22] This category is useful because it caters for some of the exceptional (by communist standards) features of Ceauşescu's rule and how it was ended. In most cases of replacement, military disaffection was essential to bringing down the regime,[23] and this clearly was an important factor in Romania (and it was also present in East Germany, where the use of force against mass demonstrations was favoured by the communist leader Honecker, but prevented by his fellow standpatters, who were more conscious of the likely consequences of bloodshed). The category also makes a distinction between Romania, where the regime is classified as a personal dictatorship, and the GDR, which is the only one-party state of six in Huntington's *replacement* group (the others are the personal dictatorships in Portugal and the Philippines, and the military dictatorships in Greece and Argentina).[24] The weakness of the category, however, is that it fails to distinguish between the total replacement of the previous elites which was to take place in the GDR and the very different situation in Romania, where it was only the personal dictatorship of Ceauşescu and his family which was replaced.

Transplacement is a category which sometimes blurs with transformation:[25]

Democratization is produced by the combined actions of govern-ment and opposition. Within the government the balance between standpatters and reformers is such that the government is willing to negotiate a change of regime – unlike the situation of standpatter dominance which leads to replacement – but it is unwilling to initiate a change of regime. It has to be pushed and/or pulled into formal or informal negotiations with the opposition . . . In transplacements, unlike transformations and replacements, government leaders often negotiated the basic terms of regime change with opposition leaders they had previously had under arrest . . .[26]

There are several advantages to using the idea of transplacements rather than concepts such as 'negotiated transition' and 'implosion'. It permits a distinction between Czechoslovakia, where there were some ineffectual attempts at reform in the late 1980s, marked by the ouster of Husák in late 1987, and the GDR, where there were no such events. It also distinguishes between, on the one hand, Czechoslovakia and Poland, where mass protest played a role in democratisation, and Hungary, where the opposition who negotiated with the communist democratisers were not supported by a broad popular movement. Finally, interesting results can be obtained by applying the notion of transplacement to Yugoslavia in 1990, where the Presidents Tudjman and Izetbegović in Croatia and Bosnia-Herzegovina, respectively, had both spent terms in prison under communism. In both cases, the former communist regimes had been more authoritarian than in Slovenia, where liberalisation and democratisation had taken place over a much long time period.

The significance of differing modes of transition becomes apparent when one examines the fate of federations, whose constituent republics used different exit paths from communism. All came apart. The fact that Czechoslovakia was the only federation to survive much more than a year of post-communism is not unrelated to the modes of transition in the two republics, which at first appeared very similar. While the Socialist Federal Republic of Yugoslavia, whose constituent republics were marked by different modes of transition from communism, disintegrated, the new Federal Republic of Yugoslavia was formed from Serbia and Montenegro, the two republics where reform was most limited. Likewise, cooperation between former Soviet republics is smoothest where new leaders were produced by similar processes of change. It is not necessarily being suggested that these federations disintegrated because their republics broke with communism in different fashions, but rather that the differing elite strategies chosen by the republican leaderships were symptoms of the divergent environments and structures of power which existed in individual republics. Modes of transition were a symptom as much as a cause of the problems which eventually destroyed the federations.

Notes

1. Skocpol (1979, p. 4).
2. Wendell Phillips, quoted in Skocpol (1979, p. 17).
3. Skocpol (1979, p. 5).
4. Only by the use of the term 'revolution' in the broader sense of the Industrial Revolution in Britain can a more direct link with democratisation be ascertained in the great 'revolutions' of history.
5. See, for example, the ongoing debate in *Slavic Review* between analysts keen to highlight the social, cultural and political specificities of Eastern Europe and the former USSR, and specialists in transitional politics who want to look at change in the region using concepts from comparative politics. The debate began with Terry (1993) and Schmitter with Karl (1994).
6. Huntington (1991). The first wave were the attempts at constitutional government that followed the American and French revolutions in the late eighteenth century. This gradually spread through Western Europe and to selected countries in the rest of the world. The second wave followed World War II and covered the defeated Axis Powers (Italy, Japan and West Germany) and some of the colonies that achieved independence in the 1950s.
7. We are borrowing these labels from Pridham (1994).
8. Rueschemeyer *et al.* (1991, especially pp. 269–81).
9. Path dependency is also sometimes used in social science to describe patterns of development that are fixed by socio-economic conditions. The idea that democracy is only possible with capitalist development (described above) is one example of this other way of using path dependency.
10. For details on other 'paths' see Karl and Schmitter (1991). Karl and Schmitter identify four ways of moving from authoritarianism: pact (described in the main text of this chapter); imposition (where elites use force to change political regime); revolution (again described in the main text of this chapter); and reform (where mass popular action forces elites to compromise). See also categorisation of modes of transition in the second section of this chapter.
11. O'Donnell and Schmitter (1986, p. 3).
12. Huntington (1991, especially p. 25).
13. For attempts at applying functionalist approaches to Eastern Europe and the USSR see Rau (1991); Vanhanen and Kimber (1994). For attempts at applying genetic approaches, see Bova (1992); Gill (1995); Löwenhardt (1995, Chapter 5); Przeworski (1991); Steenbergen (1992); Rutland (1996, pp. 261–5); and Welsh (1994).
14. Offe (1991). For further discussion of this term, see Chapter 7.
15. On 'path dependency' and economic change, see Stark (1992 and 1995).
16. See for example McFaul (1993a and 1993b).
17. Offe (1994, pp. 241–9).
18. Kitschelt (1995a, pp. 11–15 and 1995b).
19. The definitions below are taken from Kitschelt (1995b, pp. 453–5).
20. Huntington (1991, pp. 121–63).
21. *Ibid.*, pp. 124–5.
22. *Ibid.*, p. 142.
23. *Ibid.*, p. 145.
24. *Ibid.*, p. 113.
25. *Ibid.*, p. 124.
26. *Ibid.*, pp. 151, 159.

CHAPTER 2

The USSR: The difficult rebirth of politics

Introduction

The reform policies of Mikhail Gorbachev, known collectively as *perestroika* (restructuring), began to fail in 1989. Gorbachev was successful as a leader between 1985, when he became General Secretary of the Communist Party of the Soviet Union (CPSU), and 1989. In 1985–86 he secured his power and began to introduce the policy of *glasnost'* (openness) and the concept of *perestroika*. In 1987 he began to reform the CPSU and took the first steps towards economic reform. In 1988 he convened the 19th CPSU Conference, introduced proposals for radical reform of the representative system and parliament and secured his election to the Chairmanship of the USSR Supreme Soviet Presidium.[1] Gorbachev had endured many political battles to secure these reforms, and numerous obstacles and problems had emerged to prevent the smooth passage of his policies (see Textbox 2.1). But despite these problems he managed to retain control over the agenda of *perestroika* by manipulating the Soviet political system and trading on his foreign policy successes. All this was to change in 1989: by the end of the year, Gorbachev was struggling to control the fragmentation of his power-base in the CPSU and to forestall the rise of radical democrats and nationalists.

The chief cause of this turnaround in Gorbachev's political fortunes was the formation of the USSR Congress of People's Deputies (CPD). The CPD was a new legislature and replaced the old Supreme Soviet, which was a typical communist-style parliament that rubber-stamped decisions made by the party. The elections to the CPD were supposed to demonstrate the support of the Soviet people for the CPSU and *perestroika*, and confer a new legitimacy upon the Soviet system. Instead, the opposite was to occur. The elections to the CPD in March 1989 and its first sessions in June demonstrated the contradictions and limits of *perestroika* as Gorbachev conceived it. Opposition grew to the CPSU, and the true nature of the CPSU's bureaucratic power was shown.

Two things followed once the new parliament made the shortcomings of reform, and the Soviet political system as a whole, both visible and the focus of intense political discussion.

First, radical democrats and nationalists were motivated to organise and agitate more vigorously for political change and the dissolution of Soviet power. As a result, the formation of the CPD precipitated the election of nationalist governments in the March 1990 republican and local elections, and the struggle for power between the central Soviet government and the republics (see Chapters 4 and 5).

Secondly, the formation of the CPD brought confusion to the CPSU, the institution that lay at the heart of Soviet, and hence Gorbachev's, power. The failure of the CPSU to perform as Gorbachev expected in the elections to the CPD enabled the divisions within the party to emerge publicly. The result was that the party, which following Leninist fashion was supposed to be the symbol of political unity and decisive political action, began to destroy itself in acrimonious debate. It lost effectiveness both as an organisation and as a barrier to the development of independent political activity.

The contradictory nature of *perestroika*

The formation of the CPD resulted in the weakening of the party because it demonstrated the impossibility of both democratising the USSR and having the CPSU continue to be 'the leading and guiding force', as Article 6 of the 1977 Soviet Constitution put it, of the Soviet political system.[2]

Gorbachev believed reform was needed because the CPSU had degenerated into a bureaucratic machine under the leadership of Leonid Brezhnev (CPSU General Secretary from 1964 to 1982). Gorbachev called the Brezhnev era the period of *zastoi* (stagnation). For Gorbachev, the party had ceased to carry out its proper, political functions of disseminating socialist ideals, representing the socialist interests of the Soviet people, and drawing them into the daily life of the political system in order to make it effective and legitimate. The party, in short, was failing to live up to its own rhetoric about the moral, economic and political superiority of the 'socialist way of life': under Brezhnev, Gorbachev wrote, 'the world of day-to-day realities and the world of feigned prosperity were diverging more and more'.[3]

Gorbachev had few plans about how to correct this failure of the party when he came to power in 1985. His actions on becoming General Secretary were a mixture of traditional Soviet politics – such as making personnel changes in the party and state – and of innovation. The most important innovation was the introduction of *glasnost'*. Under *glasnost'* previously taboo socio-economic problems (such as prostitution and drug abuse) were talked of in the press for the first time and historical events (particularly those of the

---

Textbox 2.1 Main events in the USSR, 1982–88

1982

November   Leonid Brezhnev dies after 18 years as leader of the
                     USSR. Yuri Andropov succeeds as General Secretary of
                     the CPSU Central Committee. Soviet Union bogged down
                     in war in Afghanistan, troubles in Poland and engaged in
                     expensive second Cold War. Andropov launches anti-
                     corruption campaign, tries to increase labour discipline
                     and begins to assemble what will eventually be reform
                     team under Gorbachev.

1984

February   Andropov dies. Konstantin Chernenko succeeds him.
                     Chernenko temporarily stops reform.

1985

March   Chernenko dies. Gorbachev succeeds as General Secretary.

1986

February/March   27th CPSU Congress. Gorbachev begins to broaden and
                     deepen reform.
April   Disaster at Chernobyl increases financial crisis of Soviet
                     state but allows Gorbachev to extend *glasnost'*.
December   Andrei Sakharov released from internal exile. Riots in
                     the capital of Kazakhstan are the first sign of nationalist
                     unrest.

Stalin period) were discussed more honestly.[4] These discussions were supposed to demonstrate to the Soviet people that the system needed reforming
and build a consensus for change.

Gorbachev's initial policies led to removal of some old, incompetent and
corrupt officials from their posts and created a feeling that – as he is reported
to have remarked to close colleagues – 'we cannot go on living like this, we
must change'.[5] This was not sufficient to alter the part played by the CPSU in
the Soviet system. Consequently, Gorbachev began, from mid-1986 onwards,
to question more fully the work of the CPSU, and introduced reform of the
party by insisting on the election of party First Secretaries (chief party
administrators) up to *oblast'* (regional) and territorial level, and of the central
committees of republican Communist Parties (like the Communist Party of
Ukraine or the Communist Party of Latvia).[6]

1987

January/June	Two major CPSU Central Committee plenums. Gorbachev begins internal party reform.
June	Experiment with multi-candidate elections in 5 per cent of constituencies at local elections.
July	Major law on industrial organisation passed allowing limited autonomy for economic enterprises from central bureaucracy and planners.
August	Rallies in Baltic republics against their forced inclusion in the USSR.
October	Boris Yeltsin criticises slow pace of reform at Central Committee meeting. Is removed as head of Moscow City CPSU in November and begins drift into opposition.
November	70th anniversary of October 1917 revolution. Gorbachev talks of different paths to socialism in different countries – a sign of weakening control over Eastern Europe.

1988

June	19th CPSU Conference. Gorbachev launches reform of state structures. Promises new parliaments and multi-candidate elections.
August	Independent political activity grows throughout USSR in response to 19th CPSU Conference.
October	Gorbachev becomes Chair of USSR Supreme Soviet.
December	Constitutional amendments passed establishing Congress of People's Deputies and new electoral system.

Textbox 2.2 Main events in the USSR, 1989

March	Elections to CPD.
April	Army kills peaceful demonstrators in Tblisi, capital of Georgia.
May/June	First CPD sessions. Election of Supreme Soviet. Gorbachev elected Chair of the Supreme Soviet.
July	First outbreak of labour unrest in mining regions.
September	CPSU Central Committee plenum on nationalities policy.
Autumn/Winter	Outbreak of revolutions in Eastern Europe.
December	Lithuanian Communist Party declares itself independent of the CPSU. Sakharov dies.

However, this too was not enough. Democratisation of the CPSU was slow and modest. Even if it had been effective, the relationship between the CPSU and the Soviet people as a whole, Gorbachev's major concern, would not necessarily have altered at any speed. Internal party reform did not automatically change the work of the party or make it less bureaucratic. Gorbachev concluded that the only way to alter the CPSU's relationship with the people, change its methods of work and make it earn its power was to force it to work in a new political environment. Such a change would force the party to confront the people and the nature of its activities by setting it a new and different range of political tasks.

A small experiment with multi-candidate elections in local council elections in June 1987 seemed to demonstrate that elections were the best method of setting such tasks and creating a new political environment.[7] The experiment had been popular and made some party cadres face up to the electorate. Gorbachev therefore moved to extend it at the 19th CPSU Conference in 1988. He announced the creation of a new, two-tier parliamentary structure.[8] The Supreme Soviet, previously a large and ineffective body that rubber-stamped party directives, would in future be made into a smaller, full-time legislature with 542 deputies. Instead of being directly elected by the people, the Supreme Soviet would be elected by a new parliamentary body, the Congress of People's Deputies (which would have 2250 deputies). This new body – which would be popularly elected – would meet twice a year and set out the strategic goals of policy. The Supreme Soviet would transform these goals into legislation. Elections for the new Congress of People's Deputies were set for March 1989. The new Supreme Soviet would be elected when the Congress met in June 1989.

The work of the CPSU and its relationship to the Soviet people were supposed to change because of the demands that electing the CPD would impose upon the party. Gorbachev saw the CPD as representing two things: it would be a physical symbol of what he called the 'socialist pluralism of opinions', and it would be the pinnacle of a new 'socialist law-based state'.[9] The concept of 'socialist pluralism of opinions' described the Soviet people as holding differing views according to such things as their ethnic origin and their socio-economic position. These differences of belief were not recognised as fundamental. Gorbachev, like earlier Soviet leaders, believed that the Soviet people were united at the most basic level of interest: they were all committed to the 'socialist choice' made during the October 1917 revolution when the party had come to power. Gorbachev wanted this unity to be developed and made apparent to the people by the CPSU: the CPSU was to show that all were committed to socialism by demonstrating that its policies reflected the people's deepest, socialist aspirations. Gorbachev believed that the party would encounter the various forms that the people's socialist interest took during the elections to the CPD and would merge them together in a new, active whole. This would ensure the legitimacy of the party and the Soviet system, and would concentrate the support of the people behind reform.

Gorbachev intended that the party be aided in developing unity among the people by the creation of a 'socialist law-based state'. The party's degeneration into a bureaucratic machine, Gorbachev argued, was a result of its being too intimately involved in day-to-day administration of the economy and local affairs. This, Gorbachev maintained, associated the party too greatly with the concerns of bureaucrats, caused it to forget that it was supposed to lead and mobilise the people, and meant that it failed to develop a strategy that developed the country and fulfilled the people's socialist interests. The formation of a 'socialist law-based state' would create respect for the legal definition of the roles of state agencies. Creating respect for the law and definitions of administrative roles would narrow the number of tasks the party had and enable party workers to concentrate on developing their political relationship with the people. The party would be freed from doing work that was the responsibility of other bodies and from their concerns, so as to do its own, proper job. Other organisations would, in turn, be able legally to demand their right to take decisions that were in their sphere of competence. The CPD as the apex of this new 'socialist law-based state' would, by its creation and operation, help to achieve this liberation of the CPSU from the mundane management of daily life. The CPD was legally charged with the determination of state policy. Party workers would have to secure their control over politics by winning election to the CPD. This would automatically turn party workers away from administrative to political work (in the form of electioneering) and demonstrate to them how they would in future control politics via their domination over elected representative institutions at all levels of the Soviet system. The CPSU would not lose power but exercise it in a new way.

There was, however, a contradiction at the heart of these proposals. Gorbachev, while talking of the need for the CPSU to stimulate and represent the socialist interests of the people, continued to portray the party in terms that were quite traditional. He insisted that despite its failings, the CPSU knew what the best interests of the people were and was the only body capable of representing them faithfully. As a result, the party, and only the party, knew the contours of the unity that was to be brought out from within the diverse interests of the Soviet people. Being so aware the party could – indeed had – to decide which popular interests could be appropriately represented in the 'socialist pluralism of opinions'. Gorbachev thus sent out contradictory messages about the formation of the CPD. On the one hand, he was instructing party cadres to work with and through the people, to listen to and appreciate popular concerns and modify their behaviour and labour accordingly. On the other, he was telling them that they alone knew what was best for the people and that they should act to secure representation for the people that corresponded to this knowledge no matter what they found out about the people during the election campaign. 'Interests', Gorbachev argued, 'should be moulded and directed . . . [because] in the long run the purpose of *perestroika* is to take interests into account, to influence interests and to effect control over them and through them.'[10]

The pressure on party workers to change their methods of work was thus inconsistent. The pluralism that the party was supposed to create was not intended to be a free outpouring of political opinion. 'Socialist pluralism of opinions', as one Soviet commentator noted, was 'supposed to be a substitute for political pluralism', for multi-party democracy, interest group politics, etc.[11] In order for this substitute to work two things had to exist or occur: first, there had to be a latent unity among the diverse interests of Soviet society for the CPSU to uncover and work with; and secondly, the CPSU had to pay attention to Soviet society and incorporate the interests that it discovered within society in the political system. If a basic unity of interests did not exist among the Soviet people as Gorbachev imagined, and/or if the party failed to pay attention to and assimilate the interests of the people, then the people would seek representation by forces other than the CPSU in the elections. If this happened, the façade of unity that Gorbachev was seeking to promote would be shattered, and, more importantly, the CPSU would be challenged. Deputies who were elected to represent interests not fixed and absorbed into the 'socialist pluralism of opinions' by the party would have to seek means of articulating the views of their constituents. This would bring them into conflict with the party which was supposed to rule through the CPD and ensure the harmonisation of interests within it. Procedural rules and real debate about principles and policy, both of which were alien to the party, would be required to manage this conflict. Unfortunately for Gorbachev, such conflict with the CPSU and debate about rules, principles and policy were inevitable: the elections to the CPD proved that there was no unity among the Soviet people, and that the CPSU was incapable of changing its working practices to win its place at the head of the Soviet political system.

The election of the Congress of People's Deputies

The 2250 deputies of the CPD were elected in one of three ways.

One third of the CPD's deputies were elected on the basis of 'national-territorial' districts. These seats were distributed according to the federal-ethnic structure of the Soviet state. Each union-republic (like Latvia or Russia) had 32 constituencies; smaller ethnic groups with their own territories within union-republics were allocated between 1 and 11 seats according to the size of their territory.[12] Deputies were chosen directly by the population and had to secure over 50 per cent of the vote to be elected. Where no candidate received this level of support in the first round of voting (26 March 1989) a run-off election was held. A further 750 deputies were elected from ordinary 'territorial' constituencies created according to population distribution. The rules governing election to these 'territorial' seats were the same as those for the 'national-territorial' constituencies. Finally, 750 seats were reserved for representatives of all-Union 'public organisations'. Thirty-seven organisations were deemed to meet the legal criteria for representation and they were all official organisations of some form or other. The largest blocs of seats were allocated to the CPSU and trade unions (100 seats each). Other organisations represented included cultural unions (like the Union of Writers), officially sanctioned campaigning groups (like the 'All-Union Society for the Struggle for Sobriety') and official leisure associations (like the 'All-Union Society of Book Lovers').[13]

The reservation of 750 seats for delegates from 'public organisations' proved to be an immediate bone of contention. Gorbachev argued that electing deputies from 'public organisations' would help democratise them. This did not prove to be the case. Ordinary members and branches of 'public organisations' were able to nominate candidates for deputy. But the election of deputies was the preserve of the central plenary meeting of each 'public organisation', which voted on a list presented to it by the organisation's electoral commission (which was formed by the central plenary meeting). The results were less than encouraging. For example, 31,500 nominations were received from CPSU PPOs. However, by the time that a list was presented to the CPSU Central Committee and voted on, only 100 candidates (including Gorbachev and other party leaders) remained for the party's 100 guaranteed seats.[14] Most other 'public organisations' followed the CPSU's lead. In total there were just 871 candidates for the 750 'public organisation' seats, and in some 'public organisations', like the Academy of Sciences, members had to launch public protests to secure the (s)election of radical candidates like the dissident physicist Andrei Sakharov.

Matters were better handled for the election of deputies to the 'national-territorial' and 'territorial' constituencies, but only just. There was no legal requirement for the election of deputies from these constituencies to be by multi-candidate contests. Candidates could be nominated by 'public organisations', from workplaces or from public meetings of at least 500 voters. Nominations were then considered by district electoral commissions which produced the final ballot sheet. Bureaucratic interference occurred at both stages in the nomination process. Meetings were manipulated to produce the 'right' results; 'undesirable' candidates who secured nomination were pressured to withdraw from the race; and public meetings were cancelled on spurious grounds. Finally, electoral commissions, which were established by local Soviets and were thus under the control of the CPSU, whittled the number of prospective candidates down by over two-thirds.[15] The result of this manipulation of the nomination procedures was that although there was competition in the vast majority of seats, it was frequently only between two candidates, and in over a quarter of constituencies there was only one name on the ballot. Overall, the bureaucracy managed to limit the number of candidates standing in the 1500 'national-territorial' and 'territorial' constituencies to 2895. A little over 20 per cent of these candidates stood in the 10 per cent of seats fought by more than two deputies so that competition was contained as far as possible.

The results of the elections were mixed because of the manipulation of electoral procedures. In aggregate terms the CPSU was victorious: 87.5 per cent of the deputies to the CPD were party members. But this tremendous showing actually meant little for three reasons.

First, some party members elected were successful in spite of their CPSU membership. The success of future president Boris Yeltsin in the Moscow 'national-territorial' constituency is the best example of this. Yeltsin had been a candidate member of the CPSU Politburo and Moscow Party Secretary until 1987, when he was removed from his party posts for criticising the slow pace of reform. Although still a party member and government minister, Yeltsin was vilified by the official press during the campaign. However, his victory over the official candidate, Yevgeny Brakov, was resounding: Yeltsin received 5.1 million votes (89.6 per cent of the total electorate) to Brakov's 400,000.[16]

Secondly, there was a marked failure on the part of many CPSU leaders to face up to the challenge of the elections. Gorbachev, who avoided electoral contest by being one of the CPSU's 100 nominated deputies, is one example of this. Most regional Party Secretaries opted to stand for election unopposed and in rural constituencies where there was less opposition from the new, independent *neformaly* (informal) political groups.[17] Most were successful in the elections thanks to this strategy. But it meant that they evaded the task that Gorbachev had set them in the elections: they did not interact with and absorb popular interests, they avoided them. Moreover, there were still some spectacular failures by party leaders and officials who had manipulated the nomination process so as to stand unopposed, but who failed to secure 50 per cent of the vote because voters crossed their name from the ballot paper. Yuri Solovev, the head of the Leningrad regional party organisation and a candidate member of the Politburo, was the most prominent of these failures. These illustrious losers focused public awareness of the CPSU's failure to reform itself and live up to its claims of omniscience and omnipotence.

Thirdly, there was a widespread popular perception that the elections had not been democratic. One survey found that over one-third of those polled were dissatisfied with the nomination process. Further evidence of dissatisfaction are the complaints received by central political authorities. The Central Electoral Commission received over 14,500 complaints about the work of local election commissions.

Popular perceptions and complaints about the elections, and the fact that voters were able to distinguish between party members committed to reform and those who were ambivalent to it, meant that there was a difference between the 'real', statistical victory of the CPSU and the 'symbolic' results of the election, the open recognition of electoral malpractice and demonstration that the CPSU could be defeated. Gorbachev tried to put a positive gloss on the results and use them to further reform. The party, he argued, had generally been successful; losses had occurred because some cadres had not been diligent enough in changing their style of work and relations with the people. Gorbachev had some factual grounds for making this claim given that 87.5 per cent of the CPD deputies were CPSU members. But his argument was not accepted by either party conservatives or some of the new deputies. Conservatives began to lay the blame on Gorbachev personally for the damage that *perestroika* was doing to the CPSU. Their main criticism – which was to become the bulwark of their future arguments against reform – was that Gorbachev had failed to sufficiently prepare and arm the party for the electoral challenge. The idea of 'socialist pluralism of opinions' was, they claimed, too weak and amorphous to allow them properly to control and structure popular political participation.[18] The conservatives' desire once more to tighten the criteria for entry into the political system further demonstrated that a significant section of the CPSU membership, and most particularly its administrative apparatus, had not begun to work or think in a reformed manner. The CPSU was thus unprepared to meet the next assault on its power, which would come with the first convocation of the CPD.

The failure of Gorbachevian parliamentarianism: the first convocation of the CPD and the summer of 1989

The Soviet leadership's preparations for the first meeting of the CPD in June 1989 were paradoxically flawed in that they were both too extensive and yet not extensive enough.

The leadership had very definite ideas about what the CPD would do: it would elect the Chairman of the new Supreme Soviet (Gorbachev) and the new Supreme Soviet, and it would confirm the people's support for the main principles of *perestroika*. Having done this it would adjourn and allow the full-time Supreme Soviet to get on with the business of approving Gorbachev's choice of ministers and converting *perestroika* into legislation. The leadership was not prepared to deal with opposition to these plans. Gorbachev and those around him had not 'taken into account the difference between a party conference and a parliamentary session'.[19] They expected the CPD to be compliant and unanimous in its support for the official platform; there were no rules for the conduct of discussion or voting and no procedures to show that the administration of parliamentary life was *politically neutral*.

The result was that when radical deputies tried to oppose or modify the agenda of the CPD, to make Gorbachev account for his activities before his election as Chairman of the Supreme Soviet, or simply to express alternative political views, they were brusquely pushed to one side by Gorbachev or one of the other sessional chairmen. While this made for captivating political theatre on Soviet television, it also made proceedings appear *politically biased* against radical deputies, who were mandated by their constituents to present their ideas and had a right to express their constituents' views. (The political bias in the CPD was made to seem worse by the virulent opposition to radicals by what one of them was later to call the 'aggressive-obedient majority' of party hacks and state officials in the Congress.) Together, political bias and the activities of the radicals called the quality of representation in the new legislatures into question and showed that the CPD was not an example of 'socialist pluralism' and could not be so. Different interests were represented within the CPD and they did not want to be submerged in a collective will represented by the CPSU. Gorbachev's vision of a Soviet parliamentarianism was thus flawed from the very start. Moreover, it became apparent that the new legislatures would not be able to function as Western parliaments either. The absence of any notion of parliamentary procedure meant that the CPD was like the CPSU – unable to provide for the free and fair representation of popular interests.

The CPD thus began to fail very rapidly. It could not satisfy radicals (since it was not a parliament) nor could it deliver support for Gorbachev and *perestroika* by representing a fictitious popular unity. Instead the CPD appeared as yet another institution that only paid lip-service to popular interests. This, and the hostility that was demonstrated towards them during the CPD's sessions, forced radicals to break with Soviet political practice and organise themselves in opposition to the official platform. On the third day of the Congress sessions, a Moscow deputy, Gavriil Popov, announced the formation of a faction, the Inter-Regional Deputies' Group (I-RDG).[20] Although its leaders claimed otherwise, the I-RDG was an opposition group.[21] It was not the first opposition group of the *perestroika* era, since it was preceded by the rise of the *neformaly* and the Popular Fronts in the Baltic republics (see below). But it was the first organised opposition within the official political structure of the Soviet state since the 1920s. This gave the I-RDG an immense symbolic status and enabled it to have two practical effects.

First, although the group never had a large membership (it peaked at 269 members), it was successful in forcing the pace of political debate. Almost immediately after Popov announced the group's formation, and again at the second convocation of the CPD at the end of 1989, the I-RDG tried to have Article 6 (the Article of the 1977 Soviet Constitution that put the CPSU at the centre of the Soviet political system) discussed. Although the group was not successful, the constant allusion to Article 6 brought the unchecked power of the CPSU into sharper focus and finished what the elections had started: it became possible to question and oppose the party almost without check from the authorities. The televised debates in the CPD helped the development of opposition too: they showed that dissent need no longer lead to punishment.

Secondly, the formation of the I-RDG prompted further political organisation and fragmentation. The I-RDG's creation demonstrated to radicals the need to organise in order to avoid being marginalised in the future. This led to a linking up of reformist intellectuals with some of the *neformaly*, and to radicals organising within the CPSU. These developments weakened the CPSU further and made conflict between the centre and the republics more likely. The I-RDG's legitimation of parliamentary factions and effect on the political agenda prompted conservatives to organise too. The main conservative faction to emerge in the CPD was the Soyuz (Union) group. Soyuz was dedicated to preserving the integrity of the USSR and the Soviet state. It put pressure on Gorbachev to be harsher in his dealing with the republics, and its activities in 1990–91 were to sharpen the division between the centre and the republics.

The reaction in the republics

The election and formation of the CPD and the emergence of the I-RDG changed the political environment in the USSR by accelerating and formalising the development of many latent political conflicts. Some of these conflicts would have emerged anyway, and they often had no direct relationship to the events in the CPD. The most significant example of such a conflict were the miners' strikes in the summer of 1989.[22] The strikes, which spread rapidly from Siberia to Vorkuta in northern Russia, and the Donbass in Ukraine, were caused by the miners' economic grievances and frustration at the lack of reform within their industry. Political demands were not generally made by the strikers.[23] However, by coming so rapidly on the heels of the I-RDG's formation, the strikes gave the impression of a complete split between the official political system and Soviet society. Miners were potent symbols of the industrial working class, the social group the party claimed was its natural supporter. Their protests marked the beginnings of an alignment between radical political causes and the people. From this point onwards, calls for change could not plausibly be derided as the pipedreams of ambitious, self-serving politicians and intellectuals, or the anti-Soviet propaganda of nationalists. The strikes showed that a desire for change was a mass social phenomenon which could not be contained within the channels of the Soviet system as Gorbachev had planned with his idea of a 'socialist pluralism of opinions'.

The reaction against official reformism and its limits took different forms throughout the USSR. Broadly speaking there were three trends in 1989: there were the beginnings of mass organisation against the CPSU and the Soviet state in the Russian Soviet Federal Socialist Republic (RSFSR) and Ukraine; there was the deepening and acceleration of nationalist protest in the Baltics; and there was a struggle to escape from under the dead hand of republican communist parties in Belarus and Moldova. The differences between the republics were the result of a number of factors: levels of economic devel-opment, geographic size, demographic fears about the influx of Russians, concern over cultural rights, historical relations with Russia, ethnic splits in the republics and the amenability of local party leaders to nationalist movements. However, the different rates of development were to a degree evened out by a domino effect. Success for the opposition in one republic provided encouragement and example for the others, weakened the central state's ability to intervene in republican politics generally, and demoralised communist officials across the USSR.

The Russian Soviet Federal Socialist Republic and Ukraine

There were many *neformaly* political groups and small nationalist groups in the RSFSR and Ukraine prior to 1989.[24] In the RSFSR, groups like the Moscow and Leningrad Popular Fronts, Pamyat' ('Memory', an extreme Russian nationalist group), and the Democratic Union had become vocal political actors in 1987–88. In Ukraine, nationalist and human rights groups like the Ukrainian Helsinki Union (UHU), and cultural groups like the Ukrainian Association of Independent Creative Intelligentsia, had been stimulated by the release of political prisoners and the more liberal cultural climate of *glasnost'*. Some of these groups took part in the elections to the CPD in March 1989. In Russia, for example, *neformaly* supported Yeltsin's campaign in Moscow. In Ukraine, the UHU called for a boycott of the elections and supported only a few radical candidates.[25] However, the influence of the *neformaly* on the elections was uneven and limited. Access to resources and organisational sophistication were variable, and *neformaly* influence was geographically confined to urban areas. The results of the elections and the events at the CPD were, however, a great incentive to the *neformaly*. The I-RDG's activities at the CPD showed how legislative forums could be used to broaden the political agenda. The miners' strikes of the summer showed that there was a potential support base for them too in both Ukraine and Russia. However, this potential support had to be organised and captured. The struggle to organise was conditioned by very different circumstances in the two republics.

In the RSFSR, the existence of leaders like Yeltsin and Sakharov, and of new politicians with strong local support (like Anatoly Sobchak who would become mayor of Leningrad in 1990), gave the democratic movement a republic-wide focus. Moreover, the grouping of these prominent political actors in the I-RDG provided the movement with a common political platform. Various organisations were set up in late 1989 to link political leaders with grassroots groups. These organisations provided the basis for the foundation of 'Democratic Russia' in January 1990.[26] 'Democratic Russia' created a means of getting information about what candidates stood for to voters in a vast country where there were limits to national political communication. By approving certain candidates, 'Democratic Russia' gave voters a more distinct political choice in March 1990 than they had in March 1989: they could now vote – albeit indirectly – for anti-establishment politicians like Yeltsin (Sakharov died in December 1989) and causes. Moreover, being a part of 'Democratic Russia' empowered local voters' associations and democratic *neformaly*. This allowed them to overcome some of the residual resistance of local CPSU officials. The overall result, as we shall see in Chapter 5, was that the Russian CPD was a very different body from the all-Union CPD discussed above.

It was more difficult to overcome resistance to radical change in Ukraine for two reasons. Volodymyr Shcherbytsky, the Communist Party of Ukraine (CPU) First Secretary since 1972, was removed from power only in September 1989. Shcherbytsky had been appointed to counter nationalist influences in Ukraine and the CPU. His extended tenure in office meant that the CPU retained an organisational culture that was pro-Russian. This limited the political spaces (media, power vacuums, etc.) that nationalist organisations could exploit. Russian democrats were not faced with this problem since there was no RSFSR communist party until June 1990. They therefore only had to struggle against local party bodies. Matters improved slightly after the replacement of Shcherbytsky with the more pragmatic Volodymyr Ivashko in the autumn of 1989, but the CPU remained a powerful force against change.

The attitude of the CPU was compounded by the demography of the republic. Rukh (Popular Movement of Ukraine, which grew out of student and cultural organisations and groups like the UHU at the start of 1989) was able to build on mass popular support for independence in western Ukraine (where Ukrainian culture was less diluted by Russian speakers and shored up by the Uniate Church) and possessed some energetic leaders (released dissidents from western Ukraine and members of the Kiev cultural intelligentsia). Eastern and southern Ukraine are largely populated by Russians and russified Ukrainians.[27] While not necessarily pro-Moscow or pro-communist, these areas were difficult for ethnic nationalist movements to penetrate and mobilise within since the people there were wary of nationalist symbols and cultural demands. Only 15 per cent of delegates at the September 1989 founding congress of Rukh were from the south and east of the republic. The vast majority of delegates were from the west and the central districts around the capital, Kiev.[28] This gave Rukh, which was to be the main partner in the 'Democratic Bloc' (the electoral alliance that opposed the CPU in the 1990 elections), an uneven influence and ensured that there were tensions in the nationalist movement and potential sources of support for the CPU.

The Baltic republics: Estonia, Latvia and Lithuania

Traditions of hostility to Moscow were strong in the Baltic republics. They had enjoyed independence from Russia from the end of World War I to 1940 (when they were forcibly reincorporated into the USSR under the terms of the Molotov–Ribbentrop Pact) and had long-standing historic links to Western Europe and Scandinavia. In the immediate aftermath of World War II Baltic guerrilla forces fought the reimposition of Stalinist rule. Later, all three republics developed nationalist-dissident movements. National sentiment was further fuelled by resentment of Russian immigration. The Russian population grew in all three republics during the Soviet period (see Table 2.1), and was of particular concern in Estonia and Latvia where the native population were only just in a majority. Finally, the Soviet federal system produced regional political elites who were more willing to protect and promote the interests of the republics than the Ukrainian leadership under Shcherbytsky.[29]

Together, these factors made it possible for political activists in the Baltic republics to organise protests against the Soviet system more quickly and across a broader front than in other republics. Protest started in 1986 and 1987 with ecological and anti-Stalinist demonstrations, which were implicitly nationalist because of the forced incorporation of the republics into the USSR. In 1988 Estonian political elites began to push for autonomy by demanding greater control over the republican economy.[30] The real leap

Table 2.1 The ethnic composition of the Baltic republics in 1989 and in comparison to the interwar years

	Estonia		Latvia		Lithuania	
	%	1989 as a % of 1934 population	%	1989 as a % of 1935 population	%	1989 as a % of 1923 population
Natives	61.5	97	52.0	94	79.6	168
Russians	30.3	512	34.0	439	9.4	679
Poles	—		2.3		7.0	
Others	4.9		10.3		4.0	

Sources: Lieven (1994, pp. 432–4) and Raun (1994b, pp. 158–9).

forward came with the 1988 19th CPSU Conference. The Balts took advantage of the opportunities for political debate that the Conference afforded to establish popular fronts: the Popular Front of Estonia (PFE), the Popular Front of Latvia (PFL) and Sajudis (Movement) in Lithuania.[31] The creation of these new organisations and their ability to draw upon popular nationalist sentiment from both the population and the Baltic communist parties accelerated the development of politics in two ways.[32]

First, the popular movement for change began to have an effect on republican communist parties much earlier than anywhere else in the USSR, liberating the republics from pro-Moscow officials a year before the Ukrainians were freed of Shcherbytsky. The activities of the PFE helped secure the removal from office of the republican party First Secretary and the resignation of the Chairman of the republican Council of Ministers (the Prime Minister) in mid-1988. They were replaced by reformists who, together with the Chairman of the Estonian Supreme Soviet, Arnold Rüütel, were prepared to negotiate with the PFE.[33] In Lithuania, the First Secretary of the party, Algirdas Brazauskas (appointed in October 1988), had a rocky relationship with Sajudis, but furthered the drive towards independence by promoting the cause of Lithuanian sovereignty.[34] Events moved more slowly in Latvia, but even there the appointment of Anatolijs Gorbunovs as Chair-man of the Latvian Supreme Soviet in 1988 gave popular sentiment a voice in the party-state apparatus.[35]

Secondly, the establishment of the popular fronts in 1988 allowed them to demonstrate the strength of nationalist feeling and gain some electoral experience in the March 1989 elections. In Lithuania, Sajudis candidates won 36 out of 42 seats.[36] In Estonia, candidates (including Rüütel) supported by the PFE won 27 of the republic's 36 seats.[37] The PFL was equally successful in Latvia, but this was as much due to electoral gerrymandering as to its mobilising electoral support.[38]

The success of the popular fronts in March 1989 and the sympathetic attitude towards them in at least a part of the communist establishment in the Baltics created a tidal wave of protest and change in the rest of the year. Baltic deputies at the CPD forced the establishment of a commission to examine the Molotov–Ribbentrop Pact, which had brought the Baltic republics under Soviet control at the start of World War II. The popular fronts called for complete independence. The Lithuanian and the Latvian Supreme Soviets passed declarations of sovereignty which made republican law higher than federal legislation. The Estonian Supreme Soviet proclaimed the Soviet annexation of the republic illegal and declared sovereignty in November. (Declaring sovereignty was the first step towards declaring independence for the majority of republics. By declaring sovereignty republics asserted that their legislatures were the main policy- and law-making bodies in the republic, and that their legislation and decisions were superior to those of central government.) A human chain (the 'Baltic Way') of two million people joined the three capitals (Tallin in Estonia, Riga in Latvia and Vilnius in Lithuania) on the fiftieth anniversary of the Molotov–Ribbentrop Pact in a demonstration for independence.

The cumulative effect of these changes was to make the popular fronts 'governments in waiting' by the year end. Any remaining hopes that Gorbachev and the central political leadership might have had about the Baltic republics staying in the USSR were shattered by the Communist Party of Lithuania's break with the CPSU in December (the Estonian and Latvian parties followed early in 1990). The only real cloud on the horizon for the popular fronts and their supporters were the Russian minorities in the three republics. Many supported Baltic independence, but some joined the Interfronts (Internationalist Fronts). These were set up with help from Soviet conservatives as associations of Moscow-loyalists, retired Soviet military officers and Russian industrial workers worried about becoming second-class citizens after independence.[39] While these organisations were not able to hold back the tide of nationalism, they were to provide an excuse for intervention into Baltic affairs by Moscow and legitimated the call for discriminatory citizenship laws by the extreme nationalist wings of the popular fronts.

Belarus and Moldova

Belarus and Moldova lagged behind the other republics of the European USSR. Unlike the Baltic republics they had no real history of independence to draw on. Belarus had been part of the Livonian and Russian empires. Most of Moldova was annexed by the USSR from Romania after World War II and had never existed as a modern independent state.[40] Belarusians were assimilated to Russian culture and language to a greater extent than any of the other peoples of the USSR. The Communist Party of Belarus (CPB) displayed no signs of a national consciousness and was implacable in its opposition to any deviation from the centre's commands.[41] Moldovan culture and language were likewise suppressed and diminished by Soviet rule, and the Communist Party of Moldova (CPM) was dominated by Russians and Ukrainians because of Moscow's desire to reinforce the republic's isolation from Romania.[42] The republic was also ethnically divided, with the Russian, Ukrainian and Gagauz (an Orthodox Christian Turkic group) minorities clustered together in Transdnestr in the east of the republic (Russians and Ukrainians), and in the south (Gagauz).[43]

The development of oppositional politics was slow in both republics. The most significant demonstrations in Belarus prior to 1989 were anti-Stalinist demonstrations, which were given an added impetus after the discovery of the mass graves at Kuropaty in 1988. Various *neformaly* (mostly youth and cultural groups) had also been organised.[44] These groups came together at the

Table 2.2 The ethnic composition of Moldova, 1989 (per cent)

Moldovan	64.37
Russian	12.93
Ukrainian	13.83
Gagauz	3.52
Bulgarian	2.02
Jews	1.51
Others	1.80

Source: Fane (1993, p. 137).

end of 1988 and took the first steps towards the formation of the Popular Front of Belarus (PFB). However, Belarusian society was so depoliticised that it took another six months for the PFB to hold its founding conference in Vilnius (the capital of Lithuania). The PFB had little influence on the 1989 CPD elections. It supported only seven candidates, all of whom stood in the capital, Minsk. Five were elected but the CPB dominated the other contests and controlled the media tightly.[45]

In Moldova, protest revolved around the question of language. The Latin script of Moldovan Romanian had been replaced by the Soviet state with Russian-style Cyrillic. This, the poor provision of Moldovan language litera-ture, press and teaching, and the extensive use of Russian as the language of administration, were the main issues addressed by the first opposition groups in 1988. The recalcitrance of the CPM under Semyon Grossu radicalised this struggle and the Popular Front of Moldova (PFM) was created in 1989. The depth of feeling created by the PFM and other groups over the language issue forced the authorities to consider some of their demands. In March 1989 the Moldovan Supreme Soviet passed a draft law making Moldovan the state language and supporting the use of Latin script. This, however, produced a Russian backlash. Yedinstvo (Unity), an Interfront-style movement, was formed and there was an outburst of strikes and demonstrations by Russian workers when the draft law on language was considered by the Supreme Soviet in August. The opposition countered with mass demonstrations in the capital, Chișinău. Ill-feeling continued after the law was passed. Violent demonstrations prevented the annual parade commemorating the 1917 revo-lution on 7 November in Chișinău. Symbolically this was a serious loss of control and Grossu was removed nine days later. His replacement, Petr Lucinschi, adopted some of the PFM's proposals. The growing influence of the PFM and the prospect of reunification with Romania that arose with the overthrow of Ceaușescu in December made it unlikely that Moldovans, Russians and the Gagauz would be reconciled.

Conclusion

The growing strength of nationalist movements at the end of 1989, although uneven, left them poised to take power in the forthcoming republican elections. Gorbachev had little response to them. A Central Committee plenum in September considered the party's policy on the nationalities question, but failed to produce a concrete plan for changing federal relations. Moreover, and despite the failure of the CPD elections to force change on the party, Gorbachev did not articulate a vision of change radically different from the one he had held at the start of the year. He continued to insist that Article 6 of the Constitution did not need changing and rejected calls for the establishment of a presidency. The former, in particular, meant that he had no chance of affecting a compromise with the Russian democrats, which might have enabled him to keep a stronger hold over the centre ground of politics. When in early 1990 he changed his mind over both Article 6 and the presidency it was too late: radical forces were establishing other channels of political influence.

The only reform that Gorbachev did bring about at the end of 1989 was a change in the electoral law. Originally, republican legislatures were to have been elected in the same way as the CPD. The activities of popular fronts and protests from all over the USSR forced Gorbachev to reconsider. Republican Supreme Soviets were allowed to make changes to the nomination process and means of election. Most responded by abolishing the electoral commissions that had undermined the March 1989 vote and scrapped the system of reserved seats for 'public organisations' (Belarus kept the reserved seats system). While this ensured that elections would not be boycotted by popular fronts as undemocratic, it did nothing for the prospects of the CPSU in the elections. The changes to electoral laws guaranteed that nationalist and democratic forces would grow in influence and that the struggle for power between the centre and the republics would dominate the politics of 1990–91.

Notes

1. On the development of *perestroika*, see Remington (1989); Sakwa (1990); White (1991a and 1991b); Brown (1992 and 1996); Walker (1993); Robinson (1992 and 1995). Detailed descriptions of economic reform can be found in Åslund (1991) and Goldman (1991).
2. For alternative views on the contradictory nature of *perestroika*, see Braun and Day (1990); Sakwa (1990, pp. 357–93).
3. Gorbachev (1987c, p. 22).
4. For details of *glasnost'* see Sakwa (1990, pp. 10–11); Gill (1994, ch.2); Davies (1989); Nove (1989).
5. Cited in Roxburgh (1991, p. 8).

6. Gorbachev (1987a); Gill (1994, p. 37).

7. Hahn (1988); White (1989, pp. 7–13).

8. Hazan (1990, pp. 26–7, 130–1).

9. Evans (1993, ch. 11); Robinson (1995, ch. 5).

10. Gorbachev (1987b, p. 10).

11. Robinson (1993, p. 93).

12. These territories were classified according to their size as autonomous republics, oblasts or okrugs and were administrative districts within union-republics (like Ukraine) in which a large proportion of the population were of a different ethnic group from the titular nationality of the union-republic. The vast majority of these areas where within the Russian Soviet Federative Socialist Republic.

13. Lentini (1991, p. 74).

14. Urban (1990, p. 93).

15. *Ibid.*, p. 101. A firsthand account can be found in Sobchak (1992, pp. 5–19).

16. Morrison (1991, pp. 89–93); Yeltsin (1990, pp. 108–11, 187).

17. Berezkin *et al.* (1989, pp. 629–32).

18. Robinson (1995, pp. 159–61).

19. Kagarlitsky (1990, p. 147).

20. *Ibid.*, pp. 174–5; Tolz (1990, pp. 72–4).

21. If nothing else, the I-RDG was in opposition to the way in which deputies were officially organised within the CPD. All deputies, even those elected by 'public organisations', were grouped together according to their region of origin. These regional caucuses were to consider legislation and propose amendments, determine who should stand for election to the Supreme Soviet, etc. The problem with the regional group system for the radicals was that they were even more marginalised within them than they were in the CPD itself. (The exceptions were the Moscow group, from which many of I-RDG leaders and members would emerge, and the Baltic republic groups which had a substantial number of popular front representatives.) As its name suggested, the Inter-Regional Deputies Group wanted to overcome the regional system. For this reason it included among its five co-chairmen one Estonian, Viktor Palm (the other co-chairs were Sakharov, Popov, Yeltsin and Afanasyev).

22. Friedgut and Siegelbaum (1990); Rutland (1991); Clarke and Fairbrother (1993).

23. Dunlop (1993, p. 106).

24. Tolz (1990, pp. 10–25); Hosking *et al.* (1992); Fish (1995a).

25. Kuzio and Wilson (1994, pp. 92–3).

26. Hosking *et al.* (1992, pp. 78–80); Brudny (1993).

27. Krawchenko (1993, pp. 84–6).

28. Paniotto (1991, p. 177).

29. For extended discussion of the fate of the Baltics under Soviet power, see Misiunas and Taagepera (1993); Gerner and Hedlund (1993, ch. 3); Lieven (1994, pp. 82–108); Shtromas (1994). Descriptions of the Soviet period in the individual states can be found in Dreifelds (1996); Vardys (1978); Taagepera (1993, pp. 77–109).

30. Misiunas and Taagepera (1993, pp. 303–12); Gerner and Hedlund (1993, pp. 70–3, 77–93).

31. For details see Lieven (1994, pp. 219–30); Vardys (1989, pp. 56–8); Dreifelds (1989, pp. 84–6); Senn (1990a, pp. 55–73); Hosking *et al.* (1992, pp. 180–93); Karklins (1994, pp. 77–80).

32. For example, half the initiative group that founded Sajudis were members of the Lithuanian Communist Party. See Senn (1996, p. 125).

33. Taagepera (1989, p. 18).
34. Senn (1990b).
35. Dreifelds (1989, pp. 89–90).
36. Vardys (1990, p. 71).
37. Taagepera (1990a, pp. 336–9).
38. Latvia's large Russian minority (see Table 2.1) was based in the urban areas of the republic. These areas were under-represented in the elections because urban electoral districts were larger (150,000 voters per seat) than in the Latvian-dominated rural areas (28,000 voters per seat). See Tishkov (1990, p. 113).
39. Gerner and Hedlund (1993, pp. 107–9); Lieven (1994, pp. 188–91).
40. Zaprudnik (1993); Eyal (1990, pp. 109–12).
41. Clem (1990, p. 115); Urban (1989, p. 133).
42. Eyal (1990, pp. 128–9).
43. See Fane (1993, pp. 138–49) for a description of the ethnic minorities in Moldova.
44. Urban and Zaprudnik (1993, pp. 109–10); Zaprudnik (1993, pp. 125–41).
45. Zaprudnik (1989, p. 49).

CHAPTER 3

Eastern Europe: Negotiated revolution and popular revolution

Introduction

As *perestroika* began to fail in the Soviet Union in 1989, a train of events took place in Eastern Europe which, by the end of the year, had overshadowed even the remarkable changes that Gorbachev had brought about in his own country. For the first time in decades, the fate of the six smaller Warsaw Pact states was being decided at home and not in Moscow.

Gorbachev had undoubtedly been a catalyst in these events. Since 1985, East European communists had reacted to the confusing Soviet lead in different ways. In Poland and Hungary, *perestroika* gradually removed the externally imposed limits to reform, which had previously constrained communist rulers willing to countenance change. Yet these leaders were to discover that their own greater freedom of manoeuvre was insufficient to underpin their rule because the advantages *perestroika* brought them were more than matched by the impetus it gave to their opponents. In the more authoritarian states of the GDR and Czechoslovakia, it was clear to the communists from the outset that, for reasons peculiar to their own states which will be discussed below, *perestroika* fundamentally jeopardised their claims to govern. In Romania and Bulgaria, events in the Soviet Union did not initially appear as problematic, though for quite different reasons: Romania's Ceauşescu had rejected the Soviet lead two decades previously and established an idiosyncratic and increasingly obsessive dictatorship of his own design, whereas Bulgaria merely continued in the mode of apparent compliance to the Soviet model which had characterised it for much of the communist period.

Developments in the Soviet Union would not, however, have had the spectacular outcomes witnessed in Eastern Europe in 1989 if the states there

---

Textbox 3.1 Main events in Eastern Europe, 1989

January   *Czechoslovakia* A demonstration commemorating the 20th
anniversary of Palach's self-immolation is attacked by police;
Havel is arrested and sent to prison.
Hungary An official investigation concludes that the events
of 1956 were a 'popular uprising' and not a counter-
revolution.

February   *Hungary* The Hungarian Socialist Workers' Party agrees on a
multi-party system.

March   *Romania* Six former leading communists issue an open letter
criticising Ceaușescu's policies.

April   *Poland* Parliament accepts round table decisions on semi-free
elections.
Romania It is formally announced that the country has
finished paying off its foreign debt.

May   *Czechoslovakia* Havel is released from detention.
Hungary Shooting at persons illegally crossing the border
with Austria ceases, leading to wave of East Germans using
Hungary as an escape route to the West.

June   *Hungary* Nagy, the 1956 revolution leader, is reburied.
Poland Solidarity wins almost all the seats open to it in semi-
free Polish elections.

July   *Poland* Parliament elects Jaruzelski President.

August   *Poland* Mazowiecki becomes Prime Minister of a Solidarity
government including communists.

September   *Hungary* The communists and opposition agree on
constitutional changes to bring about a multi-party system,
with free elections in 1990.

October   *Bulgaria* The CSCE holds environment conference in Sofia,
which becomes a focus for dissident protest.
GDR Gorbachev attends celebrations for the GDR's 40th
anniversary on 7th; Monday demonstrations in Leipzig grow
in size throughout the month; Honecker is replaced by Krenz
as SED leader on 18th.
Hungary The Hungarian Socialist Workers Party becomes the
Hungarian Socialist Party (HSP); Hungary becomes a

---

had not been suffering from deep-rooted problems of their own. First, the
communist regimes all lacked legitimacy, and the economic failures of the
1980s reduced the will to passive compliance among largely depoliticised
populations. Secondly, generational change took its toll. The minority of
citizens who had, in their youth, been genuinely inspired by the early years of
communist construction were long past their prime. The subduing experiences of the worst years of communist repression were not a living memory

Republic, rather than a Socialist Republic; constitution is changed, removing the leading role of the party.

November

Bulgaria Mladenov replaces Zhivkov as state and party leader.

GDR Modrow replaces Stoph as Prime Minister on 8th; Berlin Wall opened on 9th.

Czechoslovakia A student demonstration in Prague on 17th leads to widespread protests, the formation of Civic Forum (CF) and Public Against Violence (PAV), and the replacement of Jakeš as Communist Party leader.

Hungary A referendum rejects direct election of President prior to free elections; these are fixed for March 1990.

Romania The 14th Congress of the Romanian Communist Party enthusiastically endorses Ceauşescu's leadership.

December

Albania Anti-government demonstrations in Shkodër are put down by force.

Bulgaria The Union of Democratic Forces (UDF), a coalition of opposition parties, is formed, with Zhelyu Zhelev as Chair; 'Bulgarisation' campaign is ended, ethnic Turks invited to return.

Czechoslovakia Čalfa, a moderate Slovak communist, becomes Prime Minister of a Government of National Understanding mainly comprising non-communists; Čič, also a communist, becomes Prime Minister of a similar Slovak government; Havel becomes President in place of Husák.

GDR Gysi replaces Krenz as Communist Party leader; round-table talks commence and agree free elections for May 1990, and the removal of the leading role of the party from the constitution; Leipzig demonstrators call for the first time for German unification.

Romania Protests in Timişoara are violently suppressed, leading to uprisings throughout the country; Ceauşescu flees Bucharest, is arrested and executed with his wife Elena on the 25th; the National Salvation Front (NSF) is formed with Iliescu Chair and Roman Prime Minister; leading role of the party abolished.

for the majority of the population either. The younger generation took even the modest material securities of their countries for granted, and, as access to Western information sources increased, were impressed only by the stark differences between the performance of their own states and those in the West. Thirdly, Communist Party membership had increasingly been based solely on instrumental considerations rather than on any ideological conviction. In the late 1980s, communists were disoriented as the certainties upon which they had built their careers evaporated. The leaderships could no longer rely on their support; nor, by 1989, could they rely on the ultimate sanction of Soviet military intervention if all else failed. In most cases, all else did fail. As the 'domino effect' of examples of communist weakness in neighbouring states gained momentum, the risks of non-compliance with orthodox modes of behaviour diminished for the average citizen.[1]

The above considerations apply to a lesser extent to two of the states under consideration in this chapter, which, purely for reasons of alphabetical ordering, come first and last. Albania and Yugoslavia were not in the Soviet bloc. Albania received virtually no attention at all in the Western press, for the changes taking place did not appear radical, and the extremely closed nature of the country meant that accounts of incipient public disturbances at the end of the year were hazy in the extreme. Yugoslavia – the most open of the communist states – received less attention than it merited. Fundamental processes of change were occurring, and they were radically different at opposite ends of the country. It was a complex story which could not easily be conveyed by a single photograph, unlike the single, starkest image of the year – a pickaxe being driven into the top of the Berlin Wall.

Albania

Albania was an exception to the other communist countries of Europe in almost all respects. It was the poorest, least known and most isolated European country. After having very close relations with Yugoslavia in the years immediately after World War II, it had escaped the danger of being absorbed into its larger communist neighbour by siding with the Soviet Union when Yugoslavia left the Soviet bloc in 1948. However, it also turned against the Soviet Union in 1961, at the time of the Sino-Soviet split, and adhered to China as its sole communist model until the 1980s, when its relations with China also cooled.[2]

In April 1985, the month after Gorbachev came to power, Albania underwent its first leadership change in forty years. Enver Hoxha, the last of the 'little Stalins' of Eastern Europe,[3] died and was replaced as First Secretary of the Party of Labour of Albania by Ramiz Alia. The country's relations with its Balkan neighbours improved, and the level of internal political repression eased somewhat, but these processes were less a form of *perestroika* and more belated first steps towards destalinisation – the capital, Tirana, still boasted a large statue of Stalin, and a Lenin and Stalin Museum. In 1989, Albania remained the only European state not to have joined the Conference for Security and Cooperation in Europe, it had no diplomatic relations with the United Kingdom, the United States or the USSR, and it was an 'atheist state', in which all religious practices were banned.

In view of such international isolation and domestic totalitarianism, it is not surprising that the revolutions of 1989 appeared to pass Albania by. However, the year was not completely uneventful. A limited amnesty of prisoners was declared in November, and in December there were the first reports of unrest in the northern city of Shkodër.

Bulgaria

While the Bulgarian regime felt no affinity with the reforms Gorbachev began to introduce in the Soviet Union, they did not pose quite such an uncomfortable dilemma for the communist leader, Todor Zhivkov, as for his counterparts in Czechoslovakia and the GDR. Bulgaria was known for being the Warsaw Pact country whose people felt the nearest to genuine historical friendship for the Russians (albeit weakened by forty-five years of communist rule): not only were there some similarities in their languages and Cyrillic alphabets, but the armies of the Russian Tsar had suffered enormous numbers of deaths during Bulgaria's liberation from the Ottoman domination in 1877–8. It might also be suggested that the closeness of the Russians and Bulgarians stemmed precisely from the fact that they were *not* neighbours. Russian support was valued in part because the Bulgarians had three non-Warsaw Pact neighbours, the Yugoslavs, Greeks and Turks, who were traditional enemies, even though relations with Greece had been relatively good in recent times. Additionally, there had been a border dispute with the Romanians to their north at the time of World War II. Bulgarian communism had a further advantage in that its non-communist neighbours were scarcely models of prosperous Western democracies, unlike Austria and Germany, whose mere existence served to undermine the claims of economic success trumpeted by their Eastern neighbours, Hungary and Czechoslovakia. The Bulgarian Communist Party (BCP) also had some indigenous strength, as it had enjoyed substantial support in the interwar period.[4]

When *perestroika* came, Zhivkov reacted with his normal compliance in following Soviet models.[5] However, Bulgaria was by now suffering from a number of problems which added to the destabilising effects of Gorbachev's policies. One was the fact that Zhivkov, born in 1911, was the oldest and longest-serving Warsaw Pact leader, having been in power since the mid-1950s. This impaired his ability to respond flexibly and realistically to the challenges of the late 1980s. The second problem was the state of the economy. The general economic decline experienced in Eastern Europe in the 1980s was exacerbated in Bulgaria by adverse weather conditions in the middle of the decade. This was particularly problematic because of the importance of agriculture to Bulgaria, but it also led to a permanent energy crisis – conspicuously manifested in regular power cuts. Additionally, Gorbachev was less inclined than his predecessors to reward Bulgaria's sycophancy with economic advantages, and since the majority of the country's foreign trade was with the Soviet Union, this hampered efforts to solve the country's difficulties. Finally, Bulgaria's image abroad had been tarnished in the late 1970s and early 1980s by the country's alleged complicity both in the sensational assassination by poisoned umbrella of Gyorgy Markov, a Bulgarian dissident in exile in London, and in the attempted assassination of the Pope. In the mid-1980s, Zhivkov again attracted adverse publicity when he tried to promote Bulgarian nationalist feeling through the forced assimilation of the country's Turkish minority. Most notable was the campaign to force them to adopt Bulgarian names.

Perestroika undermined Zhivkov precisely because links with the Soviet Union were so close, particularly among the communist-inclined intelligentsia. This meant that such people were greatly influenced by the changes and by the increased freedom of information enjoyed by the Russians, whose television programmes they were able not only to receive, but also easily to understand. Zhivkov's attempts to respond to Gorbachev by initiating economic reform – which was undoubtedly necessary – were unsuccessful. His 'July Concept' announced in 1987 was a reform plan that went further than Soviet intentions at the time, although there were no signs that Zhivkov had any idea how to implement it. Simultaneously, opposition to Zhivkov was growing on two fronts: within the party itself, where he was seen as a liability by an increasing number of colleagues, and outside.

Although Bulgaria had been notable for the lowest level of protest within the Warsaw Pact, between 1987 and 1989 an interesting range of opposition groups formed, which corresponded to the main dissident movements in their communist neighbours. Ecoglasnost was an ecological group which grew out of protests against the massive pollution of the northern border town of Ruse, which was being simultaneously poisoned by the Romanians and by the Bulgarians themselves; Podkrepa was an independent trade union; there was a Club for the Support of Perestroika and Glasnost (the latter word soon replaced by 'democratisation'); an Association for the Protection of Human Rights; a Committee for Religious Rights, Freedom of Conscience and Spiritual Values; and, eventually, a number of resuscitated political parties whose pre-communist forerunners were thought to have expired forty years previously. The fact that these opposition groups were small and disunited was a problem that had an effect beyond the fall of communism.

In the course of 1989, intra-party opposition to Zhivkov strengthened. He exacerbated problems with the Turkish minority, eventually opening the border with Turkey and encouraging them to leave. When, in the summer of 1989, in excess of 300,000 actually went, the fact that the Turks had mainly been engaged in agricultural production led to a further economic problem for the regime. By the autumn, the advantages for the Bulgarian Communist

Party of deposing Zhivkov were becoming overwhelming: the elderly Husák and Kádár had been removed by fellow communists in Czechoslovakia and Hungary in 1987 and 1988, and Honecker was ousted in East Germany in October 1989. Gorbachev had never liked Zhivkov, and it was by this stage completely clear that there would be no Soviet objections to Zhivkov's despatch. Bulgaria's image abroad was further dented when an ecological conference in Sofia, held under the auspices of the CSCE and intended by the regime to enhance the country's prestige, backfired on them: it became a focus for protests by Ecoglasnost, and demonstrators were subject to sometimes violent police reprisals in the glare of international press coverage. By 9 November, there was a Politburo majority against Zhivkov, and he resigned. His resignation was made public at a meeting of the Communist Party's Central Committee the following day.

Zhivkov was replaced as party leader and President by the Foreign Minister, Petar Mladenov, who had led the plot against him. Mladenov proceeded, almost immediately, to make all the concessions to which communist leaders elsewhere had been forced: the leading role of the party was abolished, freedom of speech and an end to internal activity by the secret service were proclaimed, and free elections were announced for 1990. Roundtable discussions with the opposition were agreed in order to make the necessary arrangements for the elections, largely under pressure from the Union of Democratic Forces, which had been founded on 7 December to bring together ten organisations and parties which opposed the communists. However, in spite of these momentous changes in Bulgarian politics, it is questionable whether they constituted a revolution. Bulgaria is an example of a country where the transfer of power was relatively smooth because the Communist Party was prepared to change. While popular protest clearly influenced the radical shift in direction of the Bulgarian Communist Party, it was discontent and an awareness of events in the rest of the communist world among leading communists themselves that were the main cause of Zhivkov's downfall. The party itself had yet to be defeated.

Czechoslovakia

Perestroika confronted the Czechoslovak regime, like its counterpart in the GDR, with insuperable problems. Local jokes in the late 1980s ran along the lines of 'What's the difference between Gorbachev's *perestroika* and the Prague Spring?' with varying answers such as 'Twenty years' or 'None, but they haven't realised it yet'. The Prague Spring reforms of 1968, presided over by Communist Party leader Alexander Dubček, had represented the most far-reaching attempt at democratisation – that is, the redistribution of power – ever attempted by a communist regime.[6] This was ended by the Warsaw Pact invasion of August 1968, and the 'normalisation' process which followed had entailed the removal of the most imaginative and dynamic forces in the Communist Party.[7] The communist leadership was replaced by orthodox apparatchiks in their forties, who were still in post when the Gorbachev effect hit Eastern Europe. While the Czechoslovak regime was not, by East European standards, particularly geriatric, the communist leadership had been marked by inordinate stability from the early 1970s onwards. Since these men owed their advancement to their predecessors' disgrace as 'counter-revolutionaries', they could not reassess the events of 1968 without conceding that their own installation in power had been illegitimate and unnecessary. The similarity between *perestroika* and the Prague Spring was therefore highly problematic for them.

However, it is not true to say that the late 1980s saw no change in Czechoslovakia until the 'Velvet Revolution' of November 1989.[8] Communist tactics in the 1970s and 1980s had been a typical example of rulers trying to ensure public passivity by maintaining a tolerable level of material security: the standard of living was arguably the highest of all communist countries (the main competitor being the GDR), and this had not been achieved by the accumulation of hard currency debts seen in Poland and Hungary. Yet by the late 1980s, the need to revitalise the economy was perceived, and in December 1987 Gustáv Husák, the communist leader since 1969, was replaced by Miloš Jakeš, although Husák retained the presidency he had held since 1975. Jakeš was scarcely a radical change, since he had been heavily identified with the normalisation process of the early 1970s. However, he did embark upon an attempt to reform the economy, albeit without tackling the more problematic question of political change.

At the same time, the mood in society at large subtly shifted. The Gorbachev example meant that younger professional rank-and-file Communist Party members – those who had joined since 1970 in order to pursue their careers unhindered – were able to promote innovations they considered desperately overdue by citing Soviet precedents. Other citizens acutely sensed an innate absurdity in the fact that Czechoslovak politics were now lagging behind even those of the Soviet Union, and claimed to watch the (easily accessible) Soviet television broadcasts because they were more interesting than those of Czechoslovak television. This may have been less the objective truth than an acerbic critique of the failings of Czechoslovak information policy. In the case of young people, however, another fact was of importance: while their parents remembered the extreme demoralisation and sense of hopelessness of the normalisation years in the early 1970s, their children did not, and to an extent, they were less fearful. Youth culture was also thoroughly Western in orientation, and as increasing opportunities to visit the West became available towards the end of the 1980s, these were enthusiastically taken up.

On the level of open dissent, the mainly Prague-centred dissident movement, Charter 77, encompassed a wide range of regime opponents, comprising disgraced 1968 reform communists and Catholic activists as well as non-communist intellectuals such as the playwright Václav Havel.[9] While its support did not increase markedly in the late 1980s, it was none the less noteworthy for its resilience and ability to survive in the face of persistent regime persecution, including the frequent imprisonment of its spokespeople. A feature of the late 1980s, however, was the emergence of new forms of dissent. In 1987 and 1988, a petition demanding religious freedom obtained over half a million signatures collected mainly in Slovakia and Moravia, which were areas not normally associated with dissident activity. In March 1988, a peaceful religious demonstration in Bratislava was brutally attacked by the police, despite the large number of elderly women taking part. In August 1988, on the twentieth anniversary of the invasion, the established dissident movement was surprised by a demonstration of largely young people, who could not even remember the events commemorated, in Prague's Wenceslas Square. In January 1989, the police attacked demonstrators commemorating the self-immolation of the student Jan Palach twenty years earlier, and Václav Havel was among those arrested. He was imprisoned and not released until May. The regime clearly did not know how to cope with such protests, and by the end of 1989 what was virtually a pattern could be observed, whereby demonstrations were alternately attacked by the police and allowed to pass off peacefully.[10] Neither approach achieved the intended aim of preventing further protest. At the same time, the gradual development of what might be termed a broader 'civil society' could be observed, particularly in Prague. Groups formed voicing protests about environmental issues, and in the summer of 1989, a petition entitled 'several sentences' containing demands for political freedom accumulated far more signatures that Charter 77 ever did.

In such an uneasy situation, the Czechoslovak authorities were less than pleased when, in August 1989, the GDR's emigration problems settled near to President Husák's residence in Prague Castle as disaffected East Germans turned the garden of the West German Embassy into a grossly overcrowded campsite, and local Czechs passed them supplies over the fence. The final débâcle came, however, on 17 November, when the students in the official Socialist Union of Youth were authorised to hold a commemoration of the day, fifty years earlier, when Czech students had demonstrated against Nazi occupation, leading to the execution of the leaders and the closing for the duration of the war of all Czech universities. This anniversary was part of the approved 'communist calendar'. However, in the atmosphere of Eastern Europe in late 1989, it became politicised, with banners demanding democracy and freedom. When the authorised commemoration was over, some of the thousands of students present attempted to march to Wenceslas Square, gathering in additional crowds en route. The way was blocked by police, and as the students attempted to escape a brutal baton charge, they discovered that all the side streets had been blocked off in advance.[11]

Hereafter, events developed with enormous speed. News of the full extent of police violence was spread by foreign radio stations the next day, and protest began to form based around the theatres, whose actors went on strike after reading proclamations from the students. The small but established dissident community, led by Havel, formed 'Civic Forum' over the course of the weekend, and as news of what had happened filtered down to Bratislava, Slovak regime opponents set up their own counterpart, 'Public Against Violence'. During the next few days, spontaneous crowds of up to several hundred thousand gathered intermittently in central Prague. These assemblies culminated on 23 November with the appearance of Prague Spring leader Dubček next to Havel on a balcony in Wenceslas Square. The day before, Dubček had emerged from twenty years of near-silence to speak to a crowd of about 80,000 in Bratislava.[12] Finally, a two-hour strike on Monday, 27 November proved that the protest was supported not just by students and intellectuals, but also by the workers – the first time in the postwar history of Czechoslovakia that such an alliance had effectively been formed.[13]

A week after the first demonstration, the communist leadership resigned, but the new party leader was not acceptable to the citizens' movements; nor was a new, but still communist-dominated government formed on 3 December. On 10 December, Husák resigned as President, and a Government of National Understanding was formed in which communists were a minority. Free elections and economic reforms were announced, and in late December, Dubček was elected Chair of the national parliament, the Federal Assembly, and some of the more clearly disgraced communist deputies were replaced. The day after, the Federal Assembly elected Václav Havel President. It was less than a year since he had last been arrested and imprisoned.

GDR

While the changes in the Soviet Union after 1985 were to some extent welcomed by the communist leaderships of Hungary and Poland, the German Democratic Republic is one of the two examples of regimes for whom *perestroika* posed insuperable problems. The legitimacy not only of the communist rulers in East Germany, but also of the state itself, was based on the fact that they were socialist: two separate German states had been founded in 1949 because the communist system being imposed in the East was incompatible with the democratic order developing in the West.[14] Therefore, if the GDR's socialism were in any way to be diluted by ideas of the 'socialist market' so that it became less distinct from the 'social market economy' of the larger Federal Republic of Germany, then the GDR's right to exist as a separate state would also be diminished.

Although the GDR's rulers had paid lip-service to the aim of German unification in the early decades after the war, from 1970 it had increasingly been officially maintained that an independent socialist German nation was being formed in the GDR, and the amended 1974 constitution deleted all references both to 'Germany' and to the mission of striving for German reunification. This led to the absurd situation whereby the text of the country's national anthem, which contained the phrase *Deutschland, einig Vaterland* – Germany united fatherland – could no longer be sung when the anthem was played. However, attempts to develop a GDR national consciousness in the 1970s and 1980s were not entirely in vain. The party leader Erich Honecker, who took over from Walter Ulbricht in 1971, presided over a steady increase in the standard of living, and many East Germans felt that their 'economic miracle' was equal to that of the West Germans, since it had been achieved in far more adverse circumstances. The phenomenal number of Olympic gold medals the country won in 1976 relative to its modest population size also made a contribution to national pride and identity. By the 1980s, the regime felt sufficiently secure to rehabilitate traditional historical figures from their part of Germany, such as Frederick the Great and Martin Luther.

However, the communist leadership proved unable to cope with the growing problems that emerged during the 1980s, having made the false assumption that the increase in its popular acceptance in the 1970s was destined to continue indefinitely.[15] The well-educated population felt increasingly oppressed by the restrictions on travel to the West, which were in stark contrast to the exceptionally high level of information which it received from West German television. Moreover, the younger generation took for granted what was, by communist standards, a relatively high level of material security, and no longer perceived this to be an achievement of socialism. And ironically, despite the efforts of the regime to cut its people off from the West, the rulers themselves became, in the course of the 1980s, more and more financially dependent on West Germany in order to maintain living standards at home.

Confronted by *perestroika*, the GDR maintained that it did not need to reform, since it had already carried out the economic reforms being attempted by Gorbachev in the Soviet Union – an idea immortalised in one Politburo member's statement in March 1987 that one did not have to change the wallpaper in one's flat just because the neighbours had done it. However, beneath the surface, the party was dividing, as many members were becoming demoralised by Soviet admissions that the party had not always been right.

The final insoluble dilemma for the communists was presented in May 1989, when the Hungarian authorities ceased to shoot people illegally crossing their border into Austria. A trickle of East Germans, which in the course of the summer became a flood, began to try to escape by this route. Those who were apprehended retreated to the West German embassy in Budapest, having had a stamp put in their passport which made return to the GDR an unwelcoming prospect. By August, almost everyone in the GDR knew someone who had gone on holiday to Hungary and failed to return, but in an atmosphere that was becoming increasingly surreal, the communist leadership refused even to address the fact that they had a problem, maintaining that those who had left were merely an undesirable minority.[16]

The problem intensified on 11 September, when Hungary opened its border to Austria for GDR citizens, against sharp protests from their government; East Germans unable to reach Hungary had also led to the closing of West German embassies in Poland and Czechoslovakia, and its mission in East Berlin, when they were flooded by people seeking to emigrate. Internally, September saw the start of mass protest by groups pressing for change at home in the GDR rather than emigration rights under the slogan 'We are staying here', and within the GDR of citizens' groups such as New Forum were formed. The core of such protests comprised long-standing peace movement dissidents under the protection of the Protestant Church; small marches after regular Monday evening 'peace prayers' in the Nikolai Church in Leipzig turned into spontaneous demonstrations of ever growing size.

On 7 October, as Gorbachev attended grandiose celebrations of the 40th anniversary of the GDR's foundation in East Berlin and warned that 'He who comes too late is punished by life', the East German leadership confronted two unwelcome choices. To stop the emigration wave, it would have to seal for its own citizens not only the GDR's borders to the west but also to its socialist partner countries. This would scarcely be meekly tolerated by the population. To stop the demonstrations, it would have to imitate the behaviour of the Chinese in Peking's Tiananmen Square in June 1989 by using brutal force against its own people. However, neither option would have produced a long-term solution, and the regime began to retreat. On 17 October, the Politburo removed Honecker, who was replaced by Egon Krenz. Krenz's more conciliatory attitude solved nothing: on 4 November, a million people demonstrated in East Berlin; on 7 November, the government resigned; on 8 November the Politburo resigned; and on 9 November – amid astonishing official confusion – the Berlin Wall was opened.[17] Hans Modrow, a more moderate communist, was made Prime Minister, and on 8 December, Gregor Gysi replaced Krenz as party leader. The day before, round-table talks had begun between opposition groups and official organisations, but negotiation came too late. A minority of demonstrators was already calling for German unification.

In the last analysis, it had been the GDR's status as part of a nation which brought the regime down. In the communist world, discontent could manifest itself as either 'voice' or 'exit': citizens could either voice their protest about the prevailing system of rule, the political costs of such action depending on the repressiveness of the individual states; or they could merely exit from the system through emigration, the ease with which they could leave likewise varying from country to country.[18] What distinguished the GDR from its neighbours was that, although the political costs of protest were high, and travel to the West very restricted (most notably for families travelling together), the personal costs of exit were very much lower for East Germans than for any other communist bloc citizens once a family had reached the West. They were automatically entitled to citizenship, including welfare benefits and permission to work, as soon as they reached the Federal Republic of Germany, and they faced no language barriers when integrating into their new surroundings. Emigration – if physically possible – was thus an option for ordinary people, whereas elsewhere, it was only attractive for the adventurous and those so persecuted they had little left to lose.

Hungary

Hungary is distinguished by being the clearest example within the Warsaw Pact of a negotiated transition. After the failed revolution and Soviet invasion of 1956, both the communist leadership and the people from the 1960s onwards tacitly accepted that everyone was making the best of a bad job, given the circumstances – i.e. the geopolitical reality that Hungary was part of the Soviet bloc and that exceeding certain limits would therefore trigger military invasion. This delicate arrangement was disturbed by Gorbachev's advent to power in the Soviet Union. While, in theory, *perestroika* gave the Hungarian leadership new possibilities for rationalising their system of rule, in practice the fact that the outer limits of change were no longer fixed allowed the emergence of new forces which questioned the communist monopoly of power.

The dominant figure in Hungarian politics from 1956 onwards, the party leader János Kádár, was in his seventies by the 1980s, and unable to cope when his established strategy of depoliticising the population in return for economic reform ceased to function.[19] His New Economic Mechanism, introduced in 1968 in an attempt to combine central planning with market forces, gave Hungary significant advantages over the other countries of Eastern Europe. However, by the mid-1980s it was inadequate to stave off economic stagnation, and from 1986 onwards, criticism was increasingly articulated both by the intelligentsia within the party, and by dissidents. Popular protest, however, was largely lacking: Hungarian shops were the best supplied in the Warsaw Pact, and most citizens responded to their inability to afford what was on offer by exhausting themselves through working in two or three jobs at the same time.

From within the system, economists led by Imre Pozsgay initiated debate in late 1986 with an unpublished report entitled 'Turning Point and Reform', which contained a sharp critique of central planning and advocated increased marketisation; this in turn prompted a dissident response in the form of an article entitled 'A New Social Contract' in the opposition *samizdat* journal Beszélő which promoted the idea of open negotiation of a new social contract based on political pluralism. At the same time that fundamental economic problems came under discussion, journalists were becoming more vocal, and also voiced nationalist grievances.[20] While the economists viewed the catastrophic situation in neighbouring Romania as a dire warning of the economic consequences of failure to reform, others were more concerned by the increasing repression of the substantial Hungarian minority there. By 1988, there were mass demonstrations in Budapest against the policies of the Romanian government, to which the Hungarian government belatedly responded in an attempt to mobilise nationalist sentiment in its support.

In the meantime, changes were taking place within the political leadership, and it can be argued that Hungary was a classic case of a divided party being unable to counter attacks on its legitimacy. In 1987, Károly Grósz became Prime Minister, and in March 1988, he replaced Kádár as First Secretary of the party. Miklós Németh became leader of a government which soon separated itself from the previously tight control of the party, and Grósz himself came under increasing pressure within the party leadership from reformers such as Rezső Nyers and Imre Pozsgay. It was, however, in retrospect often regarded as the most competent 'government of expertise' that Hungary had ever had.

The changes taking place among communists were matched by developments in political life outside, and an embryonic party system began to form. The 'urbanist intellectual' dissident movement formed the Alliance of Free Democrats; a radical Alliance of Young Democrats (AYD, usually known by its Hungarian acronym FIDESZ) also emerged, and the Hungarian Democratic Forum constituted a more populist party.[21] At the same time, the traditional political parties eradicated by the communists in the late 1940s were reborn, most notably the Smallholders Party and the Social Democrats. These developments distinguished Hungary from the other Warsaw Pact countries: the communists were not a strong and united universal enemy, so the opposition could afford the luxury of disunity. A later consequence of this was that when post-communist Hungary faced its first free elections in 1990, it already possessed a multi-party system that was not dominated by the communist/anti-communist divide.

By 1989, the reformers among the communist leadership had accepted that a solution to the country's economic problems could only follow genuine political change.[22] Politics changed both on a symbolic and a practical level. At the beginning of the year, Pozsgay announced the results of a party historical commission report on the events of 1956: it had been an uprising (rather than a counter-revolution, as had previously been officially asserted). In June, the executed 1956 leader, Imre Nagy, was moved from an unmarked grave and reinterred in a ceremony attended by some 200,000 people. Three weeks later, Kádár died. The transformation of Hungarian communism continued at a special party congress in October, at which the party changed its formal name from 'Hungarian Socialist Workers Party' to 'Hungarian Socialist Party', thereby becoming the first Communist Party to embark on the road to social democratisation. Grósz was replaced as Secretary-General of the party by Nyers, and the hardliners left the congress and reformed under the old party name.[23]

By this time, however, round-table talks between the communists and their satellite organisations on the one side, and a variety of opposition parties on the other, had already been completed. In October, the agreement they had reached was passed by the parliament (whose members, while technically mostly communists, had long felt unrestrained by any instructions from their party): there was to be a presidential election on 26 November, followed by parliamentary elections three months later. The contentious issue was the direct election of the President. This had been calculated by the communists to improve the chances of Imre Pozsgay winning this office, but while the proposal was also supported by the HDF, it led to refusal to sign the agreement by the AFD and FIDESZ. The latter forced a referendum, which narrowly came out against electing the president before the parliament.

The smoothness of the transition from communism can be attributed in part to the fact that the regime had been the most open to both political and economic reform: the party had retained dynamic elements within it which meant that – unlike its Polish counterpart – it was capable of leading change as well as reacting to irresistible pressure from society. Additionally, it was the only country where the dynamic elements within the party felt that they had a real chance of gaining electoral legitimation for their party. Had it not been for the example of the more radical changes which took place elsewhere in the Soviet bloc in late 1989, their calculation might have proved correct in the short term, and they might indeed have won a real election.

Poland

Poland differed from the rest of the Warsaw Pact in that it had been characterised throughout the communist period by instability, most notably popular protests in 1956, 1968, 1970, 1976, 1980–81 and 1988–89. To an extent, it suffered from the same problems as the rest of Eastern Europe – regime illegitimacy and economic decay – but in a more extreme form. However, it also had its own distinctive features, such as extreme russophobia, deriving both from its history and from more recent events, and a strong national consciousness reinforced by its post-war ethnic homogeneity and its strong Catholicism.

The weakness of Polish communism is demonstrated by the fact that response to popular protest was the *usual* reason for changing the leader of the Communist Party, the Polish United Workers Party (PUWP). This occurred on four occasions: in 1956, in 1970, in 1980 and in 1981. In recognition of the weakness of Polish communism, the Soviet Union permitted a laxness in party control over Poland that was not tolerated elsewhere. This was facilitated by the fact that Poland's weak and hence unattractive economy diminished the country's influence as a model for protest elsewhere in the bloc. After the Solidarity period of 1980–81, when the shipyard electrician Lech Wałęsa emerged to lead a ten million-strong trade union movement, the party never fully regained control. In December 1981, martial law was imposed under the party leader, General Jaruzelski.[24] This move was dubbed 'self-invasion': the Soviet Union eschewed Warsaw Pact invasion not only because of the bloodshed which would have ensued, but also because it would not have provided any realistic prospect of 'normalising' the country. The Polish army, however, had a relatively high standing at home and was felt to have a somewhat greater chance of controlling the situation.

Despite the initial imprisonment of Wałęsa and other Solidarity leaders, Communist Party control in the 1980s remained weak. It confronted the power not only of the remnants of Solidarity, but also of the Catholic Church, whose already high prestige had been enhanced by the appointment of a Polish Pope in 1978. Failure to resolve Poland's economic problems, which had been exacerbated by the huge legacy of debt resulting from the irresponsible use of excessive Western loans in the 1970s, undermined the regime's last hope of being accepted by the population at large. As in the Hungarian case, events in the late 1980s can be regarded as a negotiated transition, although in Poland negotiations with society were forced upon the party from without.

The advent to power of Gorbachev in the Soviet Union should have strengthened Jaruzelski's hand. He met with Gorbachev's favour as the youngest, and most recently appointed, party leader among the Warsaw Pact allies, and he should have been assisted by increased scope for Soviet-approved reform in the second half of the 1980s. However, his attempts at implementing economic reform were stymied not merely by the division of the party between hardliners and reformers, but also by the fact that even when the latter prevailed, there was an unwillingness to cooperate on the part of Polish society at large. A full amnesty for political prisoners declared in September 1986 led, in February 1987, to the lifting of the US economic sanctions imposed after martial law was decreed at the end of 1981. In November 1987, Jaruzelski held a referendum in which Poles were invited to decide upon a government programme for economic recovery and the democratising of political life. The result of the referendum was a victory for nobody. About two-thirds of the population voted despite Solidarity's calls for abstention, but the government did not win, since approval of the referendum's proposals required half of all *eligible* voters to say 'yes', and as about a third of the electorate abstained, and a third of those who did vote rejected the proposals, only 45 per cent of the electorate had registered positive approval. This set the scene for Poland's final showdown.

In early 1988, the regime proceeded to implement price rises despite their lack of endorsement in the referendum. Food price rises had been the traditional catalyst for public protest in Poland, and an initial strike wave hit the country in April/May of that year. This represented not merely opposition to the regime, however, but also a split within the underground Solidarity movement, since the strikes were led by younger militants among the workers, while the leadership under Wałęsa was ambivalent. Yet when a second strike-wave hit the country in August, the regime conceded the strikers' non-economic demands – the recognition of Solidarity – by offering talks with Solidarity. This represented a victory of the more reformist wing of the regime and was a great enhancement to Wałęsa's prestige.

Round-table talks between the regime and the opposition finally commenced early in 1989.[25] The agreement they reached in April led to the formal re-legalisation of Solidarity, a liberalisation of the media and the holding of semi-free parliamentary elections in June of that year. The distribution of seats was partly arranged in advance: 65 per cent of seats in the Sejm (the lower chamber) were reserved for the party and its smaller satellites, but all 100 seats in the newly created Senate (upper chamber) were open to all-comers. In subsequent elections all seats were to be freely contested.

The election results took almost everyone by surprise by demonstrating two facts: first, how strong opposition to the Polish communists was, and secondly, how clearly Solidarity was perceived as the embodiment of Polish opposition to communism.[26] Not only did Solidarity win almost every seat for which it was allowed to stand, as illustrated in Table 3.1, but the communists, due to a quirk of communist election rules, even managed to lose seats where they stood unopposed. This was because voters had the right to cross out the names of candidates they did not support – which the Poles did with relish – and any candidate who did not receive 50 per cent 'positive' votes in the ballot was disqualified. The communist coalition finally managed to fill its 65 per cent of seats because Solidarity decided to let its candidates through on a second ballot, but the communists' problems did not end there.

Jaruzelski was elected President by the Sejm, but with an embarrassingly small majority, and was left trying to find an acceptable Prime Minister and government. Solidarity did not wish to endanger its popularity by serving in a government under the communists, and, in view of its stunning election success, finally adopted the slogan Your President, our Prime Minister . Jaruzelski might have been in a position to ignore this demand had the communists actually held 65 per cent of Sejm seats. In fact, however, only

Table 3.1 Polish elections, 4/18 June 1989

Sejm (Lower House)	Seats
Polish United Workers' Party	173
United Peasant Party	76
Democratic Party	27
Catholic groups	23
[Communist coalition total	299]
Solidarity Citizens' Committee	161
Total	460
Senate (Upper House)	*Seats*
Solidarity Citizens' Committee	99
Independent	1
Total	100

Source: Lewis (1990, pp. 99–100).

38 per cent of deputies were communists, and a further 27 per cent belonged to the smaller satellite parties.[27] In a development later mirrored elsewhere in the communist bloc, these former communist puppets responded to the shift in power relations by starting to assert their independence from the communists and behaving like real political parties. When Wałęsa raised the possibility of Solidarity forming a coalition government with the communists' erstwhile allies, which was by now a political as well as an arithmetical possibility, Jaruzelski finally began to negotiate on the basis of a Solidarity-led 'grand coalition' government, containing communists in control of certain key ministries such as Defence and Internal Affairs. Since a non-communist Defence Minister representing Poland at Warsaw Pact meetings was still hard to imagine at this point, the option chosen appeared to represent the most radical likely to be acceptable to the Soviet Union.

On 18 August 1989, President Jaruzelski asked the Solidarity-backed Catholic intellectual, Tadeusz Mazowiecki, to form a government, and six days later he formally became the first non-communist Prime Minister in Eastern Europe for over forty years.

Romania

By the 1980s, Romania represented a rather divergent case among the Warsaw Pact countries. Under the leadership of Nicolae Ceauşescu, it enjoyed relatively good relations with the West, which valued the country's independent policy stance vis-à-vis the Soviet Union rather on the principle that 'my enemy's enemy is my friend', and chose to overlook Romania's increasingly blatant infringements of basic human rights. The Soviet Union, in turn, tolerated the country's maverick foreign policy because Ceauşescu's repressive internal regime maintained communist power and did not provide any kind of reformist model likely to contaminate the country's neighbours. Additionally, Romania did not provide any obvious security threat since it did not border any NATO country: it was geographically positioned firmly between the Soviet Union, the loyal Soviet ally Bulgaria and Romania's historical enemy Hungary, with only a very short border to socialist Yugoslavia.[28]

This rather unusual political balancing act was disturbed by the advent of *perestroika* in the Soviet Union. Outwardly, changes in Soviet policy presented no insuperable problem to the Ceauşescu regime, as the communists had, since the 1960s, attempted to legitimate their rule on nationalism rather than slavish adherence to the Soviet model. However, as the West gradually ceased to regard Gorbachev as a Soviet sworn enemy, it became more alive to the iniquities of Romania's treatment of its own citizens, and this led to the withdrawal of Most Favoured Nation trading status by the United States. Gorbachev also made no secret of his distaste for Ceauşescu, and as the Romanian economy worsened in the late 1980s, the country's dependence on the Soviet Union grew. At the same time, relations with its historic enemy Hungary deteriorated, and as Romanians started to escape across the border, Hungary became the first communist state to grant political asylum to citizens fleeing from a Warsaw Pact ally.

These events were but a backdrop to Romania's internal travails. The country's difficulties can be divided into three categories, all largely of the dictator's own making. First, there were economic problems. While economic decline was a feature of all communist regimes in the 1980s, in Romania the situation was exacerbated by Ceauşescu's declaration at the beginning of the decade that the country would pay off its entire foreign debt. Consequently, food was exported while people went hungry, and energy was saved through domestic power-cuts which became the norm rather than the exception. Secondly, the privations of ordinary citizens contrasted with the resources lavished on the ludicrous and monstrous construction projects which emanated from the crazed imagination of the country's megalomaniac leader. Large parts of historic central Bucharest were bulldozed to pave a broad and grandiose avenue leading to Ceauşescu's new palace, but more contentious for the outside world was what was known as 'systematisation'. This involved the razing of entire villages and the resettlement of their inhabitants in more controllable blocks of flats in larger centres of population. Although the plan remained to a large extent unimplemented, the fact that many of the villages targeted were Hungarian produced a lobby abroad anxious to publicise the issue.

Above all, however, the specifically Romanian factor in the 1989 revolution was that the everyday oppression of the regime reduced its citizens to a position where they had very little to lose; however harsh the penalties for dissent, in the end the marginal cost of protest was reduced by the intolerable nature of the status quo. While there was some increase in the previously minimal levels of dissent from late 1988, the flashpoint came in December 1989, when the authorities attempted to evict a dissident Hungarian pastor, László Tökés, from his house in Timişoara. A crowd of Hungarian parishioners, who surrounded his house to protect him, were gradually joined by the non-Hungarian citizens of Timişoara, and on 17 December, the army opened fire. Assuming this was the end of the affair, Ceauşescu left the following day for a short trip to Iran, but unrest in Timişoara continued. By the time the leader returned two days later, the protests were beginning to spread to other cities.

At this point, Ceauşescu began to lose control. The army, which he had alienated over the years by his preference for the Securitate secret police, were often unwilling to fire on Romanians. On 21 December, he attempted to stage a mass demonstration in his support in Bucharest, but television viewers across the country watched as the crowd turned hostile. Confusion reigned throughout the country, and on the evening of 22 December, Ceauşescu was forced to flee ignominiously by helicopter, as the mob closed in on him. Shortly after the helicopter landed, in the Romanian countryside, Ceauşescu and his wife were taken prisoner. After being subjected to a trial of sorts on Christmas Day, they were shot by a firing squad, and pictures of their corpses were broadcast around the world on television.

The Romanian revolution was by far the most bloody of all in Eastern Europe. The reasons for this were several. Not only were the Romanians the most desperate victims of communist rule, but Ceauşescu was also the only communist ruler sufficiently divorced from reality to bring himself to give the order to shoot regardless of the consequences. Yet even this decision contained elements of rationality, since – as Ceauşescu's eventual fate demonstrated – his own position was in a sense as desperate as that   of his people: his previous excesses made it unlikely that he could expect   any mercy when he lost his power. A further reason for the bloodshed was that the defection of the army left two bodies of men – the army and the Securitate secret police – confronting each other with weapons in their   hands.

Yet although the fall of Ceauşescu appeared in many ways to be more of a classic revolution than those elsewhere in Eastern Europe, questions remained about whether it was in fact far more of a 'palace coup', in which power stayed in the hands of a communist elite. The identity and motivation of the National Salvation Front, a group of anti-Ceauşescu plotters who ensconced themselves in the television building and confronted the Securitate in the last days of Ceauşescu's life, remained obscure. While few people mourned the dictator's death, his summary execution in many respects averted the fuller examination of his tenure of power and the role of others in it which would have been brought out by an open trial.[29]

Yugoslavia

```
                        Textbox 3.2  Main events in Yugoslavia, 1989

January          Marković becomes President of the Federal Executive
                 Council (Yugoslav Prime Minister).
February         The Serbian constitution is altered, changing the status of the
                 Autonomous Provinces of Kosovo and Vojvodina, and leading
                 to disturbances in Kosovo.
March            Further massive demonstrations in Kosovo and Belgrade.
April            Slovenia holds an election to choose their member of Federal
                 State President, and the non-communist Drnovšek wins.
May              The Marković government announces that there are to be
                 multi-party elections.
                 Milošević becomes Serbian President.
                 The Slovene Drnovšek becomes President of rotating
                 Federal State Presidency.
September        Slovenia reaffirms its sovereignty, and declares the right to
                 secede from the federation.
November         Relations between Slovenia and Serbia deteriorate, and
                 economic boycotts begin.
December         Slovenia passes a Law on Political Associations, following the
                 formation of associations within the Socialist Alliance of
                 Slovenia (a move to be followed by the other republics during
                 the course of 1990).
                 The Federal government introduces an economic reform
                 programme.
```

Yugoslavia differed substantially from the other communist states of Eastern Europe in two important respects. First, it removed itself from Soviet influence in 1948, and was never a member either of the Warsaw Pact or of the CMEA. It therefore gradually developed, after seemingly orthodox Stalinist beginnings in 1944–48, a different kind of socialism, in terms of its legitimating ideology, its economic and political structures and the freedoms allowed to citizens. Secondly, its ethnic and cultural diversity were great even by East European standards, as can be seen from Table 3.2. Other countries contained territories which had previously belonged to different empires: Czechoslovakia mainly comprised two Slav nations – the Czechs and Slovaks – who, prior to 1918, had been separated in, respectively, the Austrian and Hungarian parts of the Habsburg Empire; Romania's dominant nation had experienced both Hungarian and Turkish rule; and the Poles had for more than a century been divided between the German, Austrian and Russian empires. Yet Yugoslavia's diversity of historical experience was even greater.

Table 3.2 National composition of Yugoslavia, 1981

	Albanians	Croats	Hungarians	Macedonians	Montenegrins	Muslims	Serbs	Slovenes	Yugoslavs	Others
Yugoslavia	**8**	**20**	**2**	**6**	**3**	**9**	**36**	**8**	**5**	**4**
Bosnia/H.	0	18	0	0	0	40	32	0	8	2
Croatia	0	75	1	0	0	1	12	1	8	3
Macedonia	20	0	0	67	0	2	2	0	1	8
Montenegro	6	1	0	0	69	13	3	0	5	2
Serbia	14	2	4	1	2	2	66	0	5	5
Kosovo	*77*	*1*	*0*	*1*	*2*	*4*	*13*	*0*	*0*	*3*
Vojvodina	*0*	*5*	*19*	*1*	*2*	*0*	*54*	*0*	*8*	*9*
Serbia	*1*	*1*	*0*	*1*	*1*	*3*	*85*	*0*	*5*	*3*
Slovenia	0	3	1	0	0	1	2	91	1	1

N.B. All figures relate to the percentages of citizens in each republic (left-hand column) who identified themselves as belonging to the given nationality (in top row). Statistics derive from the last full census taken in Yugoslavia. For Serbia, figures are given for the entire republic, and also separately in italics for Serbia proper and its two autonomous republics.

Source: SFRJ Savezni zavod za statistiku (1989, p. 453); Vojnić (1995, pp. 88–9).

It was founded in 1918 from the Slovenes, who had been under Austrian rule, the Croats, who had been dominated by Hungary, and the Serbs, who had been under the rule of the Ottoman Empire until the nineteenth century. Communist Yugoslavia after 1945 was then divided into six republics, also including Bosnia and Herzegovina, Macedonia and Montenegro. While all the republics were predominantly Slav, Serbia also contained non-Slav minorities whose nations ruled the contiguous states of Hungary and Albania. When a new Yugoslav constitution was passed in 1974, Vojvodina with its Hungarian minority and Kosovo with its Albanian majority obtained the status of autonomous provinces within Serbia. Religious diversity matched the national diversity of Yugoslavia: while Poland and Czechoslovakia were predominantly Catholic and Romania predominantly Orthodox, Europe's great religious faultline dividing Catholics and Protestants from members of Orthodox communities ran through the middle of Yugoslavia. Slovenia and Croatia were Catholic, while Serbia, Montenegro and Macedonia were Orthodox. Bosnia-Herzegovina contained a multi-ethnic mix of Catholic Croats, Orthodox Serbs and Muslims, and the Albanians of Kosovo and the inhabitants of the Sandžak region (split between Serbia and Montenegro) were also largely Muslim.[30]

The historical origins of Yugoslavia are being emphasised because of the overwhelming extent to which, with the partial exception of Slovenia, it was the dividing of Yugoslavia along national lines which was to dominate domestic politics in the Yugoslav successor states of the post-communist period.

Communist Yugoslavia was distinguished both by the way in which communism had been established there and its national composition. The state was based on a number of 'legitimating myths':[31] first, there was the charismatic leadership of the wartime communist leader Tito, backed up by the prominent political role played by former partisans; secondly, there was adherence to the principles of socialism, in which devotion to the specifically Yugoslav doctrine of socialist self-management substituted for the loyalty to the Soviet Union and its Marxist–Leninist ideology which was demanded within the Warsaw Pact countries;[32] thirdly, there was a belief that federalism, together with the advantages of socialist self-management, would overcome all ethnic differences; and finally, there was the concept of non-alignment, under which Yugoslavia belonged to neither East nor West. Backing up the acceptance of the communist regime which stemmed from its indigenous and mythologised heroic origins were more pragmatic considerations, such as the fact that the country was clearly more Western in its economic development (particularly of tourism) and its citizens enjoyed far greater freedom to travel than in other communist countries. The latter characteristic not only removed a source of psychological tension, but also brought with it economic advantages, since the large number of Yugoslavs working in the West reduced unemployment at home, while it provided an influx of Western currency to their families.

By the 1980s, however, the foundations of Yugoslavia's always tenuous stability had begun to crumble. Wartime memories had faded as a potent legitimating force, and the death of Tito in 1980 removed the unifying symbol of Yugoslav communism. The practical failure of self-management as an effective economic strategy became ever more evident, and as federalism mutated into confederation, the chances of implementing vitally needed economic reforms receded.[33] The advantages of non-alignment diminished too as closer integration with the West became an increasingly desirable option (most particularly to Slovenia and Croatia) and, at the same time, the Soviet threat receded after Gorbachev's coming to power.

An important factor which contributed to the eventual demise of Yugoslavia was that the country's federalism – unlike that in the Soviet Union and Czechoslovakia – contained some genuine elements of decentralisation of power. It was a principle which underlay the organisation of the state, and not a mere empty shell, although Tito acted as a unifying force. Preparations were made prior to Tito's death for there to be a rotating presidency, and decision-making in the 1980s was based on a real need to obtain a consensus of opinion between the republics. Frequently, this led to immobilism and stagnation and a weakening of federal institutions. Whereas, in the other communist federations, the centralisation of power in the hands of the Communist Party overrode any nominal institutional independence of republican parliaments, in Yugoslavia the Communist Party power bases were also divided along republican lines (something that developed only in 1990–91 in the USSR). By the late 1980s, the last real federal force was not the party, but the Yugoslav People's Army, which had a special role in view of the history of communist Yugoslavia. The Army was also an institution in which Serbian predominance was particularly strong.[34]

By 1989, the dynamics of Yugoslav politics were driven by the potent mixture of national and economic interests. The more prosperous western republics, most notably Slovenia, advocated economic reform and closer links to the European Community, and resented the fact that their more profitable economies were subsidising the more backward, Balkan areas of the country. At the level of federal decision-making, however, they could be effectively outvoted by Serbia, which could rely on the support both of Montenegro and its own two autonomous provinces (which had equal voting rights on federal matters). At the same time that Slovenian discontent with the slow pace of economic reform and democratisation in Yugoslavia was growing, Serbian nationalism was also on the increase.[35] The mobilising cause for the Serbs was the situation in the autonomous province of Kosovo, where stories abounded of the Albanian majority violently forcing out the remaining Serbs from what the latter regarded as the historical heartland of their nation. It was the decision of the Serbian communist leader, Slobodan Milošević, in spring 1987 to deflect the Kosovo Serbs' criticism of the communist authorities in

Belgrade by himself adopting the nationalist mantle that fatally politicised the issue.[36] Over the next two years, Milošević consolidated his power over Serbia, and the volume of nationalist propaganda in the media there grew. Increasing Serb repression in Kosovo was followed in March 1989 with amendments to the Serbian constitution, which removed the autonomy of both Kosovo and Serbia's other autonomous province, Vojvodina.[37] The Albanians in Kosovo responded by demanding full republican status. Slovenia was generally sympathetic towards the Albanians' predicament, and in December 1989 Serbia retaliated with economic reprisals against the republic. The stage was thus set for the unravelling of Yugoslavia, which progressed in the course of 1990 and finally led to the country's disintegration in 1991.

Conclusion

The events in Eastern Europe in 1989 – with the exception of those in Yugoslavia and Albania – were soon labelled 'revolutions'. Emphasis was laid on what they had in common: popular protest and the demise of Communist Party power. However, in the years that followed, the diversity of the states of Eastern Europe, which had been evident since the 1960s, rapidly took on completely new dimensions. It also became increasingly apparent that the developments which had taken place in 1989 were not uniform. The communists had approached the threats to their power in differing social, political and economic environments, and their strategies had also been different – some less effective, as in the case of Czechoslovakia and the GDR, and some more effective, as in Romania (with the exception of Ceauşescu's personal fate) and Bulgaria. In federal Yugoslavia, the League of Communists was already in practice an association of independent republican communist leaderships, and all were preparing strategies of their own. The different preludes to the fall of Communist Party power were later reflected in the outcomes of the 'negotiated revolution'.

Nor had the removal of the old communist leaderships completed the process of change. As 1990 began, almost all the countries under discussion were faced with the enormous task of choosing what to put in their place. While there was a fairly broad consensus that Western-style democracy and a market economy were desirable goals, this did little to relieve the enormous decision-making burden with which they were confronted.

Notes

1. See Kuran (1991).
2. There are few good histories of Albania in the communist period. For background, see J. F. Brown (1988, pp. 371–83); Vickers (1995).

3. In the Stalinisation period from the late 1940s until Stalin's death in 1953, each East European state had a communist leader – a 'little Stalin' – who was deified in a 'cult of personality' similar to that surrounding Stalin in the Soviet Union; apart from Hoxha, only Ulbricht of the GDR (ousted in 1971) and Tito of Yugoslavia (died 1980) remained in power after the end of the 1950s.

4. For the history of Bulgaria, see Bell (1985) and Crampton (1987).

5. For more details of Bulgaria in the late 1980s, see J. F. Brown (1991, pp. 181–97); Stokes (1993. pp. 141–8); Todorova (1992).

6. For details of events in the Prague Spring, see Kusin (1972); Mlynář (1980); Skilling (1976).

7. The best account of the normalisation period is Simecka (1984).

8. See J. F. Brown (1991, pp. 149–79); Wolchik (1991, pp. 39–49, 245-8).

9. On Czech dissent, see Bugajski (1987); Skilling (1981).

10. Note that 'cycles of protest and repression' are considered by Huntington to be typical of the mode of regime change he defines as 'transplacement'. Huntington (1991, p. 153).

11. For details of events in November 1989, see Wheaton and Kavan (1992).

12. On Dubček's role in both the Prague Spring and 1989/90, see Shawcross (1990).

13. Nationalism united the population in the wake of the Warsaw Pact invasion in August 1968, but it can be argued that this had little effect in reversing the tide of events.

14. A good analysis of the communist period in the GDR is Fulbrook (1995); for a shorter history, see Fulbrook (1992).

15. For discussion of this point, see Henderson (1992).

16. Osmond (1992) contains systematic detail of the events in 1989 and the following reunification of Germany. Friedheim (1993) and Lohmann (1994) contain theoretical analysis of the train of events.

17. See Sarotte (1993).

18. For discussion of this concept, see Joppke (1993).

19. Good discussion of this period is contained in Batt (1991); for background also covering the preceding decades see Swain (1992).

20. Sword (1990, pp. 100–16).

21. On the nature of the parties, see Körösényi (1994); also Glenny (1993).

22. On reform circles within the party, see O'Neil (1996).

23. See Batt (1990).

24. For the rise of Solidarity, see Ascherson (1981); Ash (1983); Staniszkis (1984).

25. See Colomer and Pascual (1994); Kaminski (1991).

26. On Solidarity's campaign, see Zubek (1991).

27. Batt (1991, pp. 31–2); Lewis (1990).

28. For the communist period in Romania, see Deletant (1995); Gilberg (1990); Rady (1992); Ratesh (1991); Tismaneanu (1989).

29. For a theoretical view of the Romanian revolution, see Roper (1994); for further details of events, Calinescu and Tismaneanu (1991); Rady (1992).

30. For historical background on Yugoslavia, see Akhavan and Howse (1995); Bennett (1995); Carter and Norris (1996); Cohen (1995); Singleton (1985).

31. See Allcock (1994c, pp. 617–18); Brown (1991, pp. 221–2).

32. See Okey (1994, pp. 131–2).

33. For the problems of Yugoslav federalism, see Bebler (1993); Dubravčić (1993); Popovski (1995).

34. On the Yugoslav Army, see Gow (1992).

35. On Serbian nationalism, see Crnobrnja (1994, pp. 93–106); Pavković (1994).
36. For an account of this, see Almond (1994, pp. 9–10); Bennett (1995, pp. 90–6); Silber and Little (1995, pp. 36–48).
37. See Janjić (1993); Popovski (1995).

PART II

ELECTIONS AND THE FIRST FOUNDATIONS OF DEMOCRACY

CHAPTER 4

Creating democratic legitimacy

1990 was a year of elections. Regular elections had been held throughout the communist period, but these had been rituals. The public displayed the fact that they were not going to oppose ruling communist regimes openly by turning out and endorsing the candidates put forward by the authorities. As a result, the elections had not been about *choice*. Nor had they been about the *distribution* of power, since most parliaments were tame bodies that met infrequently to rubber-stamp decisions taken by the Communist Party.

The elections of 1990 were very different. As democratic (if often less than perfect) elections, they were about *choice* and the *distribution* of power: governments were elected from a range of options in most of the countries we are looking at in this book. But they were also much more than the means by which power was transferred from one set of rulers to another. The 1990 elections were also 'referendums on democracy', in which the main task was to deliver a verdict on forty years of communist rule and affirm the people's desire to live under a different, non-communist system, and/or 'referendums on stateness' in which the legitimacy of the territorial state in which people were living was put to the vote.

Depending on whether they were 'referendums on democracy' or 'referendums on stateness' elections played a very different role in the development of 'negotiated revolution' (see Chapter 1). 'Referendums on democracy' rectified the revolutionary drive that was a part of the 1989 overthrow of communism in Eastern Europe by establishing forums in which the negotiation of the revolution could take place, created forces (political parties and electoral alliances) that could take part in this negotiation, and put in place some basic democratic norms (such as the idea that power should be transferred by electoral choice) to govern political interaction.

'Referendums on stateness', although not wholly separate from 'referendums on democracy', in that voters also often cast their lot for democratic politics and politicians, played a different role in 'negotiated revolution'. The

91

'referendums on stateness' took place in Yugoslavia and the USSR. Yugoslavia and the USSR were both federations. Communist federations were a contradiction in terms. Federalism is about the dispersal of power and the mediation of conflicts between lower units and central authorities within a clear, legal and authoritative framework of rights and prerogatives. Communism, however, centralised power in the hands of Communist Parties, and denied that there might be legitimate conflicts of interest between nations or regions. Communist federations, therefore, had the constitutional form of federations, but not the content.

The 1990 elections changed this in both the Soviet Union and Yugoslavia and show that the sequence of elections is important in multinational federations trying to reach democracy. Juan Linz and Alfred Stepan have contrasted the electoral experience in Spain after Franco and the USSR and Yugoslavia in 1990.[1] In all three cases there were pressures for greater regional autonomy or independence before elections were held (from Catalonia and the Basque country in Spain, from the republics – particularly the Baltic republics and western Ukraine, Croatia and Slovenia – in the Soviet Union and Yugoslavia). Electoral politics came to Spain in a way that cemented regions together. The first Spanish election in 1977 was country-wide. This marginalised parties organised on regional lines in favour of parties that cut across regional and ethnic lines and represented national socio-economic groups and ideological positions. As a result, the ballot was not a test of the Spanish 'stateness', but a 'referendum on democracy', in which the vote was 'about democratisation; it was a nationwide general election to select deputies who would create a government and draft a new constitution' for the whole country.[2] In contrast, Linz and Stepan argue that in the USSR and Yugoslavia the 'policies followed . . . were virtually the *optimal* sequence to be followed *if* one wanted to disintegrate the state and heighten ethnic conflict'.[3] The 1990 elections in Yugoslavia and the USSR filled federalism with a content that it lacked under communism. (This was particularly true of the USSR.) The elections took place within the territorial boundaries imposed by communism, and in federal states that – unlike Czechoslovakia – did not have to remain united to assert their independence from outside forces. In this context the republican elections became weapons of liberation for the different peoples living within the federation and played an important role in forcing the pace of communism's demise and the negotiated revolution. The federal structure enabled divisions between core and periphery, between ethnic areas that had supported the rise of communism and those where communism had been imposed, to resurface through the elections. The federal structure also provided a governmental structure through the elections. It proved relatively easy for the previously powerless parliaments of the republics to come alive and begin to assert the interests of their constituents. Elections thus created alternative power centres to communist rule (republican elites), an area of conflict (the struggle to rule independently of the central state) and a structure (federalism) in which to conduct this struggle. Negotiating the end of communism thus became a possibility as nationalist and democratic forces in the republics gained large amounts of legal, institutional and economic resources for the first time. The difference between Yugoslavia, where elections led quickly to ethnic strife, and the USSR, where there was over a year of conflict between the republics and the central Soviet state before the balance of power shifted in favour of the republics after the August 1991 coup attempt, is explained by the attitude of the political elite that was dominant in the core republics of the two states, Serbia and Russia. The Russian elite under Boris Yeltsin was fighting to liberate itself from the Soviet state and therefore had no interest in maintaining the multi-ethnic federation. The Serbian elite under Slobodan Milošević identified Yugoslavia with 'greater Serbia' (a territorial union of all the Serb peoples). They therefore opposed the demise of the federation and went militarily to the aid of the Serbian diaspora in other republics.

Elections in the rest of Eastern Europe had a somewhat different function from the elections in the Soviet Union and Yugoslavia. In most of Eastern Europe, the beginning of 1990 saw some form of power-sharing between the more progressive members of the old communist elite and an anti-communist opposition, both through round tables and the hasty introduction of opposition members into parliaments and governments to replace some of the communist-sponsored deputies and ministers. However, neither communists nor oppositionists had any kind of electoral mandate, and the number of groups that might potentially be consulted about the shape of the post-communist polity rose exponentially as freedom of the press and freedom to form organisations followed the end of the communists' monopoly on power. The voters needed to decide between these groups. A major task of the power-sharing bodies was, therefore, to agree on the rules for free elections which would create democratically legitimated parliaments. These parliaments would be able, among other things, to carry out thorough revisions of the constitution, rather than the urgent and piecemeal amendments which had been made in the immediate aftermath of the revolutions to enable such things as pluralism of political parties.

The need to move from power-sharing to elected government made the elections 'referendums on democracy'. Two countries can clearly be characterised in this way: Poland (1989) and Czechoslovakia (1990). In both these countries, the communists were defeated by a strong vote for large citizens' movements that had previously mobilised popular protest to the regimes. In the GDR, the citizens' movement performed very badly. The political agenda had already shifted, and reunification was seen as the best method of securing democracy. As a result, communism was laid to rest by voting for the parties most unequivocally in favour of a quick union with the Federal Republic of

Germany. The election can none the less be viewed as delivering a vote on democracy. In Romania, a major victory was won by the National Salvation Front, which also enjoyed 'revolutionary legitimacy'. Yet here the similarity with Poland and Czechoslovakia is more doubtful, since it was unclear whether voting for the NSF was the best way to bolster democracy. In many respects, the Romanian vote was more like that in Bulgaria, where a reformed Communist Party won. This pattern was followed later in Albania. A final exception was Hungary, where communism was considered sufficiently un-threatening for a number of democratic parties to compete with each other.

The elections in Eastern Europe (except Yugoslavia) did not only decide the question: 'communism or democracy?' They also fostered interest articu-lation and political debate between independent parties. A large number of very different parties stood in the elections even where there was always going to be a clear victor. We can group the parties that competed in the elections into four general categories.

First, there were communist successor parties. In many countries, these came in two varieties: a small party comprising hardliners who rejected change and clung to their original dogma; and a somewhat larger party that was attempting to transform itself into a western-type social democratic party, attracting the mainstream left-of-centre vote. The latter parties changed their names, policies and leaders, but attempted wherever possible to retain the communists' material assets. Their success, in the medium, if not the short term, was greater than might have been expected. In some countries (Bulgaria and Albania), they won the first elections. In others (Czechoslovakia and eastern Germany), they could not win an election, but obtained between 10 and 20 per cent of the vote in the first two or three post-communist elections, which was surprising given the repressive nature of communism in these countries. A final pattern was Hungary and Poland, where the communists did badly in the first elections, but regained power four years later. The hardliners, however, predictably met with electoral defeat and were unable to improve their situation, since inability to adapt was their most salient characteristic.

Secondly, there were 'historic' or 'traditional' parties. These parties had not existed for forty years, but suddenly sprung up as communism crumbled, and claimed the legacy of a pre-1948 party or pre-World War II party. In some cases, elderly leaders returned from exile and joined forces with younger politicians. The link with the past was often used to back up claims not just to political legitimacy, but also to material assets, since the property of most of the traditional parties had been confiscated when they were banned by the communists. At first sight, these parties should have done well. Forty years of communist rule had left a vacuum in terms of moral and political values, and looking to the past was for many people the most obvious way to fill the void. In practice, however, they had two disadvantages. One was that many of the parties concerned had been involved in the failure of interwar democracy in

Eastern Europe. Memories of the past thus worked against them as well as for them because they were not seen as safe guides to democracy. The other disadvantage they faced was that the changes in the social structure of their countries effected under communism had removed their obvious constituency.[4] In the 1990 elections, only two parties managed to re-enter government after an absence of more than forty years. The Smallholders became a junior coalition partner in Hungary, as did the East German Social Democrats, who were helped by the swift establishment of strong links with their West German counterparts. In Romania, where two revived parties, rather than new parties, provided the main opposition in the election campaign, the majority of the victorious National Salvation Front was the most notable in the region. In the medium term only the Czech Social Democrats had managed by the mid-1990s to regain a solid enough political base to become one of the major parties in their country. The Czech Social Democrats were helped by the failure of the communist successor party to break with orthodox communist ideology. This meant that they were able to articulate a distinct ideological position, an advantage not always afforded other historic parties in the region.

Thirdly, in the GDR, Czechoslovakia, Bulgaria and Poland there were the 'satellite' or 'puppet' parties, which had been allowed to exist throughout the communist period. Their leaderships had endorsed communist policies and been allowed to nominate carefully selected members as candidates on the communists' election lists. The function of the parties had been to provide an illusion of pluralism in monolithic societies and to allow some public participation supportive of communist goals among social groups such as Christians and peasants who could not or would not join the ruling Communist Party. As communism collapsed, these parties quickly exploited their representation in parliament to become an independent political force. Their position had something in common with that of the communist successor parties because, while they had always had much smaller memberships than Communist Parties, they already possessed an organisational base. This gave them a head start over new and revived parties. They also had something in common with the historical parties because some of them were interwar parties which had been emasculated during the communist takeovers of the late 1940s. In East Germany, former puppet parties were unnaturally catapulted to power by the electorate because the Christian Democrats and Liberal Democrats received the backing of the governing parties in West Germany. This led people to consider them the most reliable guarantors of unification. In Poland, Bulgaria and Czechoslovakia, puppet parties representing the rural population had enough of a natural constituency to gain some degree of electoral representation, although they were reformed by mergers with other groups.

Fourthly, there were new parties which became the main actors in post-communist politics. In confused and rapidly changing societies these parties had the problem both of establishing their legitimacy and of finding issues that could be used to present a clear profile to the electorate. Several main categories of new parties can, however, be distinguished.

Revolutionary legitimacy was the most successful means of winning support in the initial elections. Polish Solidarity, the Czech Civic Forum and Slovak Public Against Violence, and the Romanian National Salvation Front won elections because they were perceived as having ousted the communists. They were therefore deemed the most appropriate people to safeguard the achievements of the revolution and lead their countries to democracy. In the GDR, revolutionary legitimacy was not sufficient to win electoral victory for the leaders of the street protests against the communists, since the agenda for safeguarding democracy had already shifted to achieving German unification. One qualifying remark must be made here. What people throughout Eastern Europe wanted was not just democracy but also the material well-being it was thought to bring. Unification was considered to guarantee the fulfilment of both goals. West German parties (on offer to the GDR via their eastern 'sister' parties) were the only actors in first post-communist elections who had a proven track record of economic success.

Nationalist parties, while nowhere receiving sufficiently widespread support to form a government, also gained substantial percentages of the vote (up to 10 per cent) in countries such as Czechoslovakia, Romania and Bulgaria, which were not ethnically homogeneous. Their advantage was that ethnicity was one aspect of social identity that had not been confused by the enormous changes that had taken place under communism. In Yugoslavia, where the nature of 1990 elections was different, nationalist parties representing the ethnic majority also managed to muster sufficient support in all the federal republics to take over the reins of government.

Ecology was a major issue of concern in most post-communist states, but this did not lead to substantial support for Green parties. In the late communist period, expressing concern about the environment had been a good way of implicitly criticising regime performance without using arguments considered ideologically unacceptable, since the communist governments also purported to be worried about ecological problems. After 1989, however, environmental issues became depoliticised, since there was broad agreement among all parties that communism had left an appalling legacy of pollution and something needed to be done about it. (Doing something in practice was a different matter.) Voting Green tended, therefore, often to be a sign of distrust in all other parties.

Economic interests were not a major source of division in the 1990 elections. Most political parties agreed that some moves towards a market economy were necessary, but the electorate was far from sure, after forty years of communism, what their actual personal economic position was compared to other groups in society, and what the implications of economic reform would be for them. In 1990, revived Social Democratic Parties were the main competitors to target economic issues, but they received limited support because much of the electorate associated anything to do with socialism with the communists; socialist voters not totally disillusioned by the entire communist period often voted for communist successor parties. Economic cleavages in the electorate only became significant as the 1990s progressed, and voters had some experience of economic reform on which to base their choices, or wished to protest government competence in economic manage-ment. (When the broad citizens' movements disintegrated during the first democratically elected parliaments, it was usually owing to the emergence of economic disagreements between their different wings.) In the meantime all manner of parties could be, and were, established to represent social groups uncertain about their interests. The choice of parties was often bewildering. For example, peasants and people in rural areas often had a choice between several parties claiming to represent agricultural interests.

In 1990–91, the Soviet Union mixed the various forms of representation that we can see in the rest of Eastern Europe. The nationalist and democratic movements (Democratic Russia, Sajudis, etc.) that were successful in 1990 were akin to the citizens' movements of Solidarity and Civic Forum/Public Against Violence in that they unified people from across the political spectrum against communism. There was also a mass of environmental parties, revived historic parties and new parties. The organisations that appeared in Moldova and the Baltics to represent ethnic Russians against the indigenous peoples of these areas could, if we were generous, be called minority parties. However, none of the parties, associations or movements that emerged during this period were strong as organisations, ideological blocs or representatives of any socio-economic constituency. Political parties in Russia (as, indeed, in Poland) were frequently labelled 'taxi' or 'sofa' parties because it was claimed that their membership could all sit on one sofa or fit in one cab. The success of the nationalist and democratic movements in the 1990 elections camouflaged the ideological divisions within them. They were all to split once the CPSU, the common enemy, was defeated. The weakness of parties and the fragility of the large nationalist and democratic movements meant that there was little development beyond what M. Steven Fish labels 'movement society'. Communism had destroyed the connections that give people common socio-economic and political interests and that lead them to create the institutions of civil society – parties, trade unions and interest associations, etc. As a result, the groups that emerged during *perestroika* could put down few social roots and had to search for constituencies to represent. Their chief activity was to campaign continuously, and particularly against the CPSU, in a sequence of 'complex, interacting, apocalyptic political [i.e. not social or economic] campaigns'. Political society thus resembled a social movement, a 'series of demands and challenges to power holders in the name of a social category that lacks an established political position', rather than the socially structured politics of civil society.[5]

Progress towards creating legitimate democratic government and prospects for consolidation across the area were thus mixed in 1990 (1990–91 for the USSR). The different rates of development reflects the variation in exit points from communism in Eastern Europe (compare, for example, the Polish experience of negotiation through the round table with Romania's experience of civil unrest and the National Salvation Front and the democratic possibilities in each), the fact that the republics of the USSR and Yugoslavia were trying to break free of communist federations and still trying to reach their exit point from communism, and the resources (human, ideological, economic and organisational) that political leaders could call upon to help develop parties and stable governmental institutions.

Yet the elections were the beginning and not the end of democratic progress in the post-communist world. They differed from the first and 'founding' elections in other transitions of the 'third wave' (Latin America, Southern Europe), where the results were pivotal in defining the political actors who would guide the transition to democracy.[6] In Eastern Europe, their importance as referendums on democracy, and in the Soviet Union and Yugoslavia, the dominance of questions of statehood, left other issues of party formation to be decided in second and third elections. For this reason, we shall look at the constitutional choices which were important in determining the influence of political actors in Part III, and only in Part IV do we begin to discuss the development of more stable party systems in each country. It was not only the structure and external environment of post-communist societies which shaped their political destinies, but also the institutional frameworks which governed the distribution of power within their states. Electoral systems will be mentioned frequently in the next two chapters, and yet, in 1990, neither parties nor voters had the practical experience to calculate their effects accurately, either in debating electoral laws (in the case of parties) or in casting their ballots (in the case of voters). A plethora of states changed their electoral laws after the first elections, and voters gradually became able to make informed decisions. Greater experience of parliamentary democracy also highlighted the importance of legal divisions of power between Prime Ministers and Presidents, and this became a focus of many of the battles still to come.

Notes

1. Linz and Stepan (1992). The term 'stateness' used above is taken from this article.
2. *Ibid.*, p. 126.
3. *Ibid.*, p. 131.

4. For an examination of the influence of pre-communist cleavage structures on contemporary party systems in Eastern Europe, see Rivera (1996).
5. Charles Tilly, quoted in Fish (1995a, p. 61). Fish's description of 'movement society' can be found on pp. 61–4.
6. Jasiewicz (1993, pp. 133–4).

CHAPTER 5

The rise of the republics and the demise of the USSR, 1990–91

Introduction

The revolutions in Eastern Europe at the end of 1989 forced a rethinking of political priorities in the USSR. Gorbachev's reforms were relaunched with the revision of Article 6 of the Constitution (on the 'leading role of the party'), and the establishment of the post of President of the USSR. The national-democratic movements that had emerged in 1988–89 gained strength and confidence as the Soviet state's weaknesses and lack of ability to control the demise of its client regimes in Eastern Europe became apparent. Together, the increased confidence and activity of the national oppositions and the new political reforms initiated by Gorbachev began to shape the three interrelated processes that made up the endgame of Soviet power: the CPSU became more and more marginalised as a political force; republican legislatures fell under the sway of national democratic opposition forces, who pressed first for state sovereignty and then for independence; and power at the centre became vested increasingly in state institutions (rather than the CPSU) as Gorbachev tried to preserve something of the Soviet system.

The marginalisation of the party and Gorbachev's increased reliance on the state made the endgame of Soviet power almost impossible for Gorbachev to win. The range of forces opposed to him made it difficult to develop a strategy that could guarantee him a large political constituency, and he was constantly shifting his political position to try to create a support base for himself. This confused friends and foes alike, as Gorbachev seemed to have no clear and consistent political stance.[1] Radicals were alienated by his continued attachment to the CPSU. Party conservatives were angered by his continued efforts at reform. Yet Gorbachev's increased reliance on the institutions of the Soviet state made him an ally of conservative officials, and this was seen as a challenge by republican legislatures which tried to increase their own powers as a response, and alienated some of Gorbachev's more liberal supporters like his Foreign Minister, Eduard Shevardnadze, who resigned in December 1990. His attempts at compromise with nationalist governments in the spring of 1991 divided him from his own government, many of whom were involved in the August 1991 coup against him. In the wake of the failed coup, Gorbachev was left almost totally isolated. His attempts to regain the political initiative and preserve something of the central state and federal system were confounded by national elites working to their own agendas. On 31 December 1991, what remained of the Soviet state was formally consigned to the dustbin of history. In its place a new organisation, the Commonwealth of Independent States (CIS), was established to regulate relations between Russia, Ukraine, Belarus, Moldova, Armenia, Azerbaijan and the five Central Asian states (Kazakhstan, Turkmenistan, Kyrgyzstan, Uzbekistan and Tajikistan). This new body was in no way comparable to the old Soviet state. It was a loose arrangement of consultative meetings between leaders and ministers, with no strong central institutions and no coercive powers.

Politics at the centre, 1990–August 1991

Gorbachev's decision to establish the USSR presidency and press for the revision of Article 6 in February/March 1990 was an acknowledgement that the reforms he had announced in 1988 and carried out in 1989 had, for the most part, failed. Gorbachev was still uncertain of multi-party politics at the start of 1990. In January 1990, he stated that he did not 'see anything tragic about a multi-party system', but that a 'multi-party system [was] not a cure all' and often masked individual ambitions. But such doubts had to be set aside. Events in Eastern Europe showed the fragile nature of Communist Party power and the need to maintain a reformist momentum. A *de facto* pluralist system was beginning to take shape anyway, thanks to the growth of the *neformaly* and the popular fronts, and because the CPSU was beginning to fragment.[2] Conservatives in the party were increasingly vocal in their demands for a Russian Communist Party organisation (Russia was unique amongst the Soviet republics in not having a republican Communist Party). At the end of January 1990, democrats in the party met to form the Democratic Platform, which called for the abandonment of the party's vanguard claims, the abolition of the party's bureaucratic machinery and the reorganisation of local party organisations into constituency parties whose sole purpose would be electoral activity.[3] If the party was to continue to reform and to maintain some vestige of organisational integrity, these developments needed to be controlled. Finally, the prospect of elections in the republics and local elections made it necessary once more to indicate to the party that it had to reform and adapt itself to winning power.

Textbox 5.1 Main events in the USSR, 1990

January	Over 100 killed during military intervention to block nationalist forces in Azerbaijan. CPSU begins to break up as radicals inside the CPSU set up the 'Democratic Platform'.
February	CPSU Central Committee agrees to abolish Article 6 of the Soviet constitution and supports moves towards a presidential system. Supreme Soviet passes bill on presidency at the end of the month.
March	Local and republican elections. Nationalists win in most of the republics. The USSR CPD elects Gorbachev President and changes the constitution to remove Article 6. Lithuania declares independence. Estonia suspends the Soviet constitution.
May	Latvia declares independence. Yeltsin elected head of Russian parliament by 'Democratic Russia' deputies. 'War of laws' begins between the republics and the central government.
July	28th CPSU Congress. Yeltsin and other radicals quit the CPSU.
August–October	Gorbachev attempts to find economic reform strategy. Makes a brief alliance with Yeltsin to support the radical '500 Days' plan for economic reform, but caves in under conservative pressure and begins his 'drift to the right'.
September	Gorbachev granted additional presidential powers by USSR CPD.
December	Shevardnadze resigns as Minister of Foreign Affairs. Gorbachev forces the election of Gennady Yanayev as Vice-President. Gorbachev proposes referendum on the future of the Union.

Revising Article 6 was the natural response to these problems. It continued the policy of pressuring the party to change by making party cadres realise that power was not automatically theirs – it had to be won. It also addressed one of the main complaints of democrats like the Inter-Regional Deputies Group, namely that power in the USSR could not be constitutional and politics could not be democratic while the CPSU retained a constitutional guarantee of political power. Article 6 and the formation of a presidential post were discussed by a CPSU Central Committee plenum in February 1990 and the changes approved by the Supreme Soviet. The new version of Article 6 removed the description of the CPSU as 'the leading and guiding force of Soviet society and the nucleus of its political system, of all state organisations and public organisations'. Instead, the party was charged to 'take part in the elaboration of the policy of the Soviet state and in the running of state and public affairs through . . . representatives elected to the Soviets of People's deputies and in other ways'. The party was to do this alongside 'other political parties, as well as trade union, youth and other public organisations and mass movements'.

On its own, and despite the undefined 'other ways', this new version of Article 6 met radical demands for the transfer of power from the CPSU to elected representative institutions. Gorbachev, however, was not giving power away. The change in Article 6 did not *de facto* alter the ability of party leaders at local level to rule. Changes in the party's organisational structure were made at the 28th CPSU Congress in June 1990, but only affected central party bodies: the Politburo, Central Committee and Central Committee Secretariat were all downgraded. The CPSU thus continued to exercise power locally despite Gorbachev's weakening its influence over policy at the centre. Gorbachev's personal power was secured through the presidential post established at the same time as Article 6 was revised. The new presidency gave Gorbachev constitutional powers far greater than any previous Soviet leader. In particular, the powers of the President lessened the independence of the USSR Supreme Soviet and Congress of People's Deputies (CPD) since the President could dissolve the Supreme Soviet and had extensive prerogatives to veto legislation. The power of the President was backed by the creation of new institutions like the Presidential Council (made up of presidential nominees and key figures from the state like Chair of the Supreme Soviet Anatoly Lukyanov, Prime Minister Nikolai Ryzhkov, the head of the KGB, and the Ministers of Foreign Affairs, Defence, and Internal Affairs) and the Federation Council (which consisted of representatives of the republics).[4] The President's powers were further extended in September 1990 when Gorbachev was granted the right to issue decrees that had the force of law, to form institutions for economic reform and to ensure cooperation between units of the federation.

The powers of the presidency gave Gorbachev the formal instruments necessary to control central policy-making. However, they did nothing to ease the political divisions in the country or the CPSU.

Conservatives within the party saw the revision of Article 6 as yet another attack on the party's privileges and became more convinced of the need for an alternative organisational structure in the CPSU through which they could attempt to 'stop the rot'. They achieved their wish in June 1990 when the Russian Communist Party (CP RSFSR) was formed at a congress of Russian delegates to the 28th CPSU Congress. Ivan Polozkov, the Krasnodar regional Party Secretary and a long-term critic of Gorbachev's policies, was elected First Secretary.[5]

Radicals from across the country objected to the centralisation of powers in the new presidential position. They also criticised Gorbachev for not standing for open election to the new post; he was instead elected to it by the pliant USSR CPD. Gorbachev's failure to stand for election was a tactical error since it meant that the new post lacked the authority that would have been given by a mandate secured through elections – something that the opposition was soon to gain through republican and local elections. Radicals were further alienated by the persecution of Democratic Platform members and the publication of an 'Open Letter' to the group in *Pravda* (the party paper) that called on them to disband.[6] The letter, and the formation of the CP RSFSR just prior to the 28th CPSU Congress, undid any potential good will that the revision of Article 6 might have had. The majority of opposition leaders, including Yeltsin, quit the party publicly and dramatically at the 28th Congress in July.[7]

The revision of Article 6 thus did little to reverse the party's fortunes or preserve its organisational integrity. As 1990 progressed party membership and revenue declined at an increasing rate.[8] The conservative CP RSFSR was a sounding-board for conservative criticism of Gorbachev, but failed to develop into an effective political organisation. Regional party apparatuses became more interested in securing the economic position of the *nomenklatura* by engaging in commercial activity, than in the political leadership that Gorbachev demanded.[9] The focus of political life did change, however, as the creation of the presidency and the republican elections of March 1990 (see below) led to a struggle between the central state and republican legislatures with popular mandates for legislative and political dominance.

Gorbachev's first move after the establishment of the presidency and the republican elections was an attempted show of force.[10] Lithuania declared independence (rather than sovereignty) following the election of Sajudis to power in March 1990 (see below). Gorbachev responded by condemning the action as illegal and imposing sanctions – including an energy blockade – on the republic. This attempt at demonstrating the power of the central state had little effect as the other republics soon declared sovereignty. The 'war of laws', as the struggle between the centre and the republics over whose decisions had binding force became known, began to paralyse government as republics sought to sever ties with central ministries, which in turn tried to preserve their powers. Russia's declaration of state sovereignty was particularly damaging since its size and importance meant that the centre 'lost the reservoir of wealth that had kept it in power'.[11] Republics refused to meet their payments to the central state budget, encouraged their citizens to avoid military service and did not raise retail and food prices as demanded by the centre.

The opposition to the centre from the republics, and the confusion that ensued, made it imperative for Gorbachev to try to define the respective powers of central and republican government. The Federation Council began the attempt to draw up a new union treaty (to replace the 1922 treaty, which was still formally in place) in June 1990. Gorbachev's efforts were doomed from the start. The Baltic republics, Moldova, Georgia and Armenia did not participate in discussions on the new treaty and made it plain that it would not apply to them. Moreover, there were major differences between the republics that did engage in negotiations and Gorbachev as to the principles upon which the new treaty would be based. Most republican leaders wanted the treaty to recognise and codify their declarations of state sovereignty. Gorbachev tried to use the treaty to claw back powers that the republics had arrogated to themselves. The result was an impasse, as Yeltsin was to explain in 1991: 'New draft agreements began to appear one after another. In essence into each of them was dragged the very same model of a union with a strong centre. The principle of sovereignty was recognised only as a decorative frill; in fact it was ruthlessly suppressed.'[12]

With no agreement forthcoming, or imminent, Gorbachev found himself, in 1990, stuck in a Catch-22 situation. It was impossible to secure a future union without the agreement of the new national-republican elites. At the same time, the fact that he could not produce a compromise with them made him more reliant for support on conservatives within the central state. This in turn made it less likely that he could produce a compromise solution to the question of union. It also had a knock-on effect to other policy areas, the most crucial of which was the economy.

The political chaos of *perestroika* had compounded the structural faults of the Soviet economy so that by mid-1990 the USSR was falling rapidly into economic crisis, with growing inflation, rising external debt, declining industrial production and a burgeoning budget deficit (see Table 5.1). Any attempt at averting economic collapse required agreement with the republics. Gorbachev was caught, however, between the need to compromise with the republics and his need to retain conservative political support; as a result he was unable to produce an effective economic reform plan. Negotiations with the new Russian government over the '500 Days' reform plan (so-called because it promised to move the USSR to a market economy within 500 days), drawn up by Stanislav Shatalin and accepted by the Russian government in September 1990, broke down in the face of conservative opposition. Nikolai Ryzhkov, the USSR Prime Minister, insisted on following the reform policies he had launched in late 1989. An attempt was made to unify the two plans and a mixture of the reform packages was accepted by the USSR Supreme Soviet in October 1990.[13] However, in practice no achievable economic policy emerged: the Russian and central governments blocked each other.

Gorbachev's prevarication over economic policy was the first major sign that he was 'drifting to the right' under pressure from conservatives within the Soviet state and because of criticism and threats from groups like Soyuz, the large conservative bloc in the USSR CPD. Gorbachev's reliance on conservative state bureaucrats deepened at the December USSR CPD meeting when Shevardnadze resigned as Minister of Foreign Affairs, warning against the prospect of dictatorship. The liberal orientation of the government was further eroded when Gorbachev forced the election of Gennady Yanayev to

Table 5.1 Selected Soviet economic statistics, 1987–91

	1987	1988	1989	1990	1991
Gross domestic product (per cent change)	—	—	3.0	−2.0	−17.0[a]
Industrial growth rate over previous 12 months (per cent change)	3.5	3.8	1.4	−0.1	−14.7
Budget deficit (per cent share of GDP)	6.4	9.2	8.7	6.2	12–14.0
External debt (billions of US dollars)	39.2	43.0	54.0	52.2[b]	—
Retail price increases (per cent change)	1.3	0.6	2.0	5.6	86.0[a]
Rates of growth in average wages of workers and employees (per cent change)	3.2	3.6	8.2	13.1	10.9

a. CIS republics.
b. Projected figure for June 1990.
Sources: Millar (1993, pp. 45, 47); Russian Economic Trends, 1 (3), p.74; IMF *et al.* (1990, p. 50); IMF (1992, p. 58); Aven (1991, p. 192).

the new post of Vice-President, and appointed two other hardliners – Valentin Pavlov and Boris Pugo – Prime Minister and Minister for Internal Affairs respectively. Gorbachev also tried to wrest back initiative from the republics, to prove that he had a popular mandate and pressure republican leaders to sign a new union treaty by calling a referendum for March 1991 on preserving the union.

However, in January 1991, before the referendum was held, conservatives tried to apply direct force to the problem of the disintegrating union by launching military action in Lithuania and Latvia. Gorbachev might not personally have been to blame for the deaths that ensued in Latvia and Lithuania (he claimed to have been asleep at the time of the Lithuanian killings), but his appointment and support for conservatives, plus the fact that he did not remove them from office after the January events, made him morally culpable. Support for Baltic independence was only fortified by the massacres and made it even less likely that they could be drawn back into the Soviet federal fold.

The Baltic republics, Moldova and Armenia did not take part in the referendum on the Union when it was held in March 1991. Gorbachev still argued that the results of the referendum gave him a mandate for his position on maintaining the Union. In total 76.4 per cent of the electorate that turned out voted 'yes' in favour of Union (see Table 5.2). But Gorbachev's 'victory' was hollow. The Baltic republics held separate referendums on independence

	Textbox 5.2 Main events in the USSR, 1991
January	Military intervention in Lithuania and Latvia. Yeltsin pledges solidarity with the Baltics and the people rally round to defend national parliaments.
February	Majority vote for Union in referendum. Russians vote for the establishment of a Russian presidency.
April	'9+1' agreement signed by Gorbachev and the leaders of nine of the republics. Agree a new union treaty to be signed in August which will substantially revise the balance of power in favour of republics.
June	Pavlov and the conservatives attempt a constitutional coup by asking for more powers for the Prime Minister.
August	Hardliners launch coup attempt on the eve of the signing of the new union treaty (see Textbox 5.3).
September–November	Yeltsin accumulates as much power as is possible in order to begin economic reform. Is granted additional powers for a year by the Russian parliament and appoints his own government, making himself Prime Minister and Yegor Gaidar Minister of Finance. Negotiations for the new union treaty fail.
December	Ukraine votes for independence in referendum. All hope of new union treaty dies. Belarus and Russia persuade Ukraine to join in Commonwealth of Independent States. Central Asian states, Azerbaijan and Armenia join a week later. Gorbachev resigns as President on 25 December. USSR officially ceases to exist on 31 December.

Table 5.2   Results of the referendums on the Union and independence, 1991

Referendum on the Union	*% turnout*	*% voting yes*	*% voting no*
USSR total[a]	80.0	76.4	21.7
RSFSR	75.4	71.3	26.4
Ukraine	83.5	70.2	28.0
Belarus	83.3	82.7	16.1
Referendum on independence			
Lithuania	84.43	90.47	6.56
Latvia	87.56	73.68	24.69
Estonia	82.96	77.73	21.40

a. Includes returns for the Central Asian republics and Azerbaijan. The Baltic republics, Armenia, Georgia and Moldova did not participate.

Source: Adapted from White *et al.* (1993, p. 89).

and a majority voted for full secession from the Union (see Table 5.2) The question[14] voters were asked to respond to in Gorbachev's referendum was ambiguous and could reflect the position of a large part of the opposition as well as of Gorbachev.[15] A 'yes' vote was not, therefore, necessarily a vote in support of Gorbachev. The 'yes' vote for the Union as a whole was inflated by the large number of 'yes' votes in the Central Asian republics and the Russian countryside, the most traditional political areas of the country. Urban Russian voters and those in western Ukraine – the areas where much of the pressure for change originated – were less enthusiastic.[16] Finally, Gorbachev's victory was tainted by the fact that 70 per cent of voters in Russia voted for the creation of a Russian presidency. They thereby supported the development of Russian political institutions and state sovereignty at the same time that they approved of a 'renewed union'.

The failure of the hardliners' show of force in Latvia and Lithuania and the equivocal vote for the Union in the referendum forced Gorbachev to rethink his strategy once more. In April 1991, he met the leaders of nine republics (Russia, Ukraine, Belarus, Azerbaijan and the five Central Asian republics) at Novo-Ogarevo. Together they signed the '9 + 1' agreement in which Gorbachev recognised the sovereignty of the republics, made concessions to Russia over federal taxes and in which all committed themselves to signing a new union treaty (drafts of which were published in June and July).

The '9 + 1' agreement marked the beginning of the end of the USSR, although its signatories were not to know how rapid its demise was to be. The concessions that Gorbachev made at Novo-Ogarevo angered the conservatives who had previously been in alliance with him. In July, Prime Minister Pavlov requested additional powers from the USSR CPD; these would have enabled the conservatives in the government to act independently of Gorbachev. Pavlov's attempt to usurp some of Gorbachev's powers failed after Gorbachev intervened angrily in the legislature's debate. Gorbachev's rebuttal of the conservatives was a short-lived success. The attempt to re-organise the powers of the government was a prelude to the coup attempt on 18 August, two days before the new union treaty was due to be signed. The coup destroyed the balance of power that produced the '9 + 1' agreement and the need for a union treaty, and prompted the short, terminal stage of Soviet power.

The August coup and the collapse of the Soviet Union

The attempted reimposition of central control by the State Committee for the State of Emergency (SCSE) in August 1991 rapidly turned into a farce. The coup was poorly planned and even more poorly executed. It later emerged

---

Textbox 5.3 The August coup, 1991

18 August	State Committee for the State of Emergency (SCSE) convened. Representatives of the SCSE meet Gorbachev at his holiday home at Foros. He refuses to endorse plans for the coup.
19 August	Tanks and troops occupy central Moscow. State of emergency declared. Yeltsin declares the coup illegal and calls for strikes. White House (Russian parliament building) put under siege.
20 August	Demonstrations in Moscow and Leningrad against the SCSE. White House defended by thousands of ordinary citizens. Three die during the night in a clash with tanks.
21 August	SCSE collapses. Boris Pugo commits suicide, other members of the Committee are arrested.
22 August	Gorbachev returns to Moscow. Emergency session of the Russian Supreme Soviet opens.
23 August	Gorbachev addresses Russian Supreme Soviet. Yeltsin suspends the CPSU.
24 August	Gorbachev resigns as General Secretary of the CPSU. Russia recognises Baltic states' independence. Ukraine declares independence.
25 August	Belarus declares independence.
27 August	Moldova declares independence.
29 August	USSR Supreme Soviet suspends CPSU and votes itself out of existence.

---

that two members of the SCSE (its head, Vice-President Yanayev, and Prime Minister Pavlov) were drunk for most of the time.[17] The plotters were unsure of their support amongst the armed forces and the security services and were unable to command the loyalty of key units and officers. They failed to arrest Yeltsin or the leadership of the Russian government, and were divided amongst themselves on the use of force against the opposition. Their attempt to control the media failed as journalists in Moscow joined forces to produce an anti-coup paper, and radio broadcasts from the West went unjammed. They failed to mobilise any popular support for their actions or make alliances with conservatives like the Soyuz group. The plotters' strategy also prevented them from using those coercive instruments that were available to them. The SCSE tried to give their seizure of power a veneer of legality by claiming that they were taking over on the basis of the Soviet constitution, which allowed the Vice-President to take over if the President was, as the SCSE claimed, unable to fulfil his duties. This piece of constitu-tional trickery limited the options of the SCSE to a degree since their claim to be the legal government of the reformed USSR required a modicum of civilised behaviour from them.[18]

The rapid disintegration of the coup attempt was not just a matter of incompetence and poor planning, however. Russia had changed dramatically between 1985 and 1991. A relatively small, but still significant, number of people were prepared to defend their new freedoms by demonstrating in the major cities and defending the White House, the Russian parliament building. Perhaps more important than this open resistance was the way that few people felt the need to obey the SCSE's orders. Previously, fear had induced an apathetic compliance with party and state power. Now there was a feeling that the orders of the SCSE were an irrelevance that could simply be ignored. For the most part army commanders, factory directors and local political authorities neither supported nor rejected the SCSE, so that its 'constituency', the *nomenklatura* appointed by and formerly dependent upon the party, was not activated. This provided Yeltsin and the Russian parliament with the opportunity to resist publicly and demonstrate that the authority of the SCSE did not extend beyond the Kremlin's walls, an impression reinforced by the wait-and-see attitude adopted by most of the other republican leaderships. The result was that the coup collapsed, not so much because it was resisted, but because the junta could do nothing to overcome that resistance: the powers of the Soviet state evaporated before the eyes of the SCSE.

The weaknesses of the central state were also made apparent to Gorbachev when he arrived back in Moscow from his holiday home, and temporary prison, in the Crimea on 22 August. The CPSU was suspended in Russia (it was later banned). Parts of the Soviet state were taken over by Russia and the USSR Supreme Soviet suspended its activities as Lukyanov, its Chair, had been arrested for being a supporter of the SCSE. Gorbachev's hopes for the union treaty that should have been signed on 20 August rapidly began to diminish. His authority had been damaged by the coup since he had appointed most of the members of the SCSE to their posts. In the political vacuum left by the collapse of the coup the republics could decide for themselves what relationship they would have with the remains of the central state. A new version of the union treaty was published in November and Gorbachev strove to have it signed,[19] but it was too late. Yeltsin had begun to accumulate the powers necessary to begin reforming the Russian economy independently of any central authority and the other republics; those republics that had an interest (primarily economic) in being a part of a 'Union of Sovereign States' (mostly the Central Asian republics) did not have the political influence to support Gorbachev. The final death-knell of the Union was sounded by the Ukrainian referendum on independence on 1 December. Over 90 per cent voted for independence (which had been declared back in August) and Leonid Kravchuk was elected president on a pro-independence ticket (see below).

Although the actions of Ukraine and Russia showed that a new union was not going to be formed, some means of communication between the republics was still necessary. The leaders of the newly independent states had to deal with questions of borders and the rights of their citizens living in other states, to divide up the common property of the USSR, and to trade with one another because of their highly integrated economies. The need to deal with these issues led the three Slav states of Belarus, Russia and Ukraine to agree on the formation of a new organisation, the Commonwealth of Independent States (CIS), at Belovezhshkaya pushcha on 8 December. Moldova, the five Central Asian states, Azerbaijan and Armenia agreed to join within a few days and the CIS was formally created with the Alma Ata (capital of Kazakhstan) declaration on 21 December. The CIS was deliberately created as a weak organisation since none of the new states wanted to create, or give the impression that they were creating, a new central political organisation.[20] The CIS was to be a consultative body, made up of Councils of Heads of State and Government and meetings of ministers. Decisions were to be adopted on the basis of consensus, with each state having the right to opt out of any agreement.[21] The establishment of the CIS made the USSR a completely redundant political entity. Gorbachev resigned as President on 25 December. On 31 December the USSR ceased to exist.

The new republican governments: different paths to independence

The moves towards independence made by the republican governments elected in 1990 reflected the different stages of development reached in 1989 by democratic and nationalist movements.[22] The Baltic republics led the way by electing nationalist governments and declaring their independence in 1990. Matters were more complex in Russia and Ukraine, where radical demands were held back by the continuing influence of local communist leaders, ethnic divisions and weaker nationalist and democratic political organisation. Progress in Belarus was slower, but the ice did begin gradually to break. Moldova, on the other hand, embraced the independence cause with fervour, although this exacerbated ethnic tensions within the republic.

However, no matter what the speed of change in the republics, none of them was 'free' until the August coup destroyed the last vestiges of the Soviet state's ability and will to intervene in their affairs. Complete independence was thus slow in coming and this had an affect on the post-communist politics of the future. During the struggle for independence, politicians adopted positions and took part in alliances and movements that were the product of generalised opposition to the USSR, the CPSU and Gorbachev. These alliances, movements and positions had no solid socio-economic constituency or platform, and were not organised into effective political parties: the elections in 1990 were fought by broad-based front organisations, which were unified only in their opposition to Soviet power. This produced leaders like Yeltsin in Russia and Landsbergis in Lithuania, who helped force the demise of the USSR, but who did not have strong parliamentary or party support for policies that would rebuild the nations they had come to lead. Other leaders, like Kravchuk in Ukraine, emerged as compromises were reached between nationalists and communists (either reform-minded or opportunistic). Again, this helped the rise of new nations since it helped break down party opposition to sovereignty and independence. But it too left leaders in office who headed shaky parliamentary coalitions or who commanded legislatures that were replete with members of the old communist elite.

Russia

The parliaments elected in Russia in March 1990 were of the same design as the USSR parliaments elected in March 1989. The Russian people directly elected a Congress of People's Deputies (CPD), which in turn elected a smaller, full-time parliament, the Supreme Soviet. However, Russia's democratic forces were far better prepared for the March 1990 elections than they had been for the 1989 USSR CPD elections. But they still faced formidable problems. Organisationally, they were divided into two allied blocs (which merged after the elections), Elections-90 (based in Leningrad) and Democratic Russia (based in Moscow and some other major industrial towns), and did not have much of a presence in the countryside.[23] Moreover, many local elites still had a firm grasp on their territories and used their power to corrupt the elections. They had slightly less opportunity to do so in 1990 because changes in the electoral law made nominating candidates for deputy easier and reduced the powers of local electoral commissions, and because officials were under pressure in local council elections as well as the Russian CPD elections. But the elections were still subject to bureaucratic interference, dirty tricks and fraud (like ballot stuffing and changing the location of polling stations without prior announcement).

Democratic Russia endorsed 116 candidates for deputy at its founding Congress in January 1990. This was less than 10 per cent of the total number of seats available (1068). But because the nomination process was more open (there were 7018 candidates for the 1068 seats fought) Democratic Russia actually had a much larger number of supporters standing for election as either independents or in affiliated groups than were actually endorsed, and they managed their campaign successfully.[24] As in 1989, the vast majority of candidates were CPSU members, but again the party leadership did not stand for election and regional party First Secretaries avoided the challenge of standing in the more politically advanced urban constituencies.[25] In addition to CPSU-supported candidates and the Elections-90/Democratic Russia supporters, a third group, the Patriotic Bloc, provided a common platform for candidates standing on a Russian nationalist ticket, but it failed to make a substantial impact on voters as it was seen – with some justification – as a front organisation for CPSU conservatives.[26]

The large number of independents standing for office and the fact that the 'Patriotic Bloc' and democratic oppositions were umbrella organisations, rather than parties, meant that it was difficult to see who had won the elections until the Russian CPD met and voting began. The democrats knew, however, that they had done well from the Moscow and Leningrad (which reverted to the name St Petersburg in 1991) returns: they took 25 out of 34 seats in Leningrad and 63 out of 65 seats in Moscow. The voting for local councils also gave some encouragement: Democratic Russia and associate groups gained control over the city councils of Moscow and Leningrad, and had majorities in a number of other industrial centres.[27]

When the Russian CPD did meet, the democrats (who formed into a Democratic Russia parliamentary faction) and the communists (who formed a Communists of Russia faction) were fairly evenly matched. These political divisions were accurately reflected in the loyalties of the deputies elected by the CPD to the Supreme Soviet. Deputies were largely drawn from the bureaucracy, but only a small majority voted for the proposals of the Communists of Russia faction at the first session of the CPD, with 46 per cent of deputies voting for Democratic Russia proposals (see Table 5.3). The vote for neither faction was stable however, so that the democrats could hope to win some votes. Most importantly, Democratic Russia secured the election of Yeltsin as Chair of the Russian Supreme Soviet on 29 May. They also managed to secure a compromise over the election of Russian Supreme Soviet deputies so that it reflected the political divisions within the Russian CPD.[28] As the conflict between Russia and the central government increased in intensity throughout the year the Communists of Russia vote began to unravel. By the time of the Russian CPD's third convocation in March 1991, 492 deputies were consistently voting for radical proposals, 477 for conservative proposals, with 94 deputies holding the balance and swinging between the two groups. At the same time, 108 deputies voted consistently for radical proposals in the Russian Supreme Soviet, 99 for conservative proposals, with 22 floating voters.[29] This turnround was helped, in part, by the defection at the third convocation of the Congress of 170 deputies from the 'Communists of Russia' faction to form a new 'Communists for Democracy' group under the leadership of Alexander Rutskoi (whose reward was to become Yeltsin's Vice-President later in the year).

The shifting allegiances in the Russian CPD and the election of Yeltsin as Chair of the Supreme Soviet meant that the democratic opposition managed to control the agenda of Russian politics, even though they had not been totally victorious in the March 1990 elections. In June 1990 Russia declared state sovereignty, thereby asserting its right to manage its own finances and

Table 5.3 The socio-political composition of the Russian CPD and voting behaviour at the first CPD convocation

	No. of deputies	%	DR^a	CR^b
Top political leaders	69	6	4	96
Upper and middle rank officials (Regional party secretaries from Central Committee officials, Ministers and Deputy Ministers, Military and KGB leaders)	162	15	8	90
Lower rank officials (State and collective farm officials, low rank party and state bureaucrats)	602	57	60	40
Workers and peasants	51	5	74	24
Creative and scientific intelligentsia	179	17	87	11
Total	1063	100	46	52

a. Per cent of deputies who *mostly* voted for Democratic Russia proposals at the first RSFSR Congress of People's Deputies.
b. Per cent of deputies who *mostly* voted for Communists of Russia proposals at the first RSFSR Congress of People's Deputies.

Source: Adapted from Efimova *et al.* (1990, pp. 1–3), and Sobyanin and Yur'ev (1991, pp. 61–4).

conduct relations with other republics and foreign governments as an equal with the central Soviet state. Large public demonstrations in Moscow through-out 1990 and early 1991 kept up public pressure for change. Miners went on strike again in July 1990 and in March and April 1991. In May 1991 the mines were transferred to the jurisdiction of the Russian republic. Most important of all, Yeltsin's election as Chair of the Supreme Soviet meant that Gorbachev had to negotiate with him on the economy and the union treaty. This prevented any compromise over the question of sovereignty, deprived Gorbachev of the ability to place the might of Russia behind his vision of the Union, and stopped Gorbachev from taking measures that might have prevented further economic decline. Yeltsin was forthright in his support for the nationalist movements in the Baltics and in his condemnation of the use of force against them. This position, which he shared with other republican leaders, and his appeals to the armed forces, helped to divide the military and made it more difficult for the hardliners in the central government to launch successful repressive actions.

Russia's move towards independence thus rested heavily on the control that Yeltsin had over the Russian political agenda and the way that this allowed him to deal with Gorbachev. Yeltsin's control over the Russian political scene was secured finally and fully with his direct election as Russian President in June 1991. Unlike Gorbachev, he was elected by the people to the post of President, managing to obtain the 50+ per cent of votes necessary for victory in the first round and in competition with five candidates (see Table 5.4).

Table 5.4 The 1991 Russian presidential elections

	% vote
Boris Yeltsin	57.3
Nikolai Ryzhkov	16.9
Vladimir Zhirinovsky	7.8
Aman-Geľdy Tuleev	6.8
Vadim Bakatin	3.4
Albert Makashov	3.7

Source: Pravda, 20 June 1991, p. 1.

Yeltsin's election was the penultimate action in his personal struggle with Gorbachev and showed the complete reversal of their fortunes. Gorbachev was isolated from his own government, and the CPSU had all but ceased to be a potent political force at national level. Yeltsin, on the other hand, had personal authority to run Russia and popularity. The coup of August 1991 was to provide him with the opportunity to rule without any interference, and boosted his personal popularity even more. But despite Yeltsin's personal political gains during and immediately after the coup, he was faced with a major problem: how to support the power he had won through his leadership of the struggle against the centre.

Yeltsin's basic problem was his lack of a firm political base both inside and outside parliament. The CPSU and the CP RSFSR were suspended and banned after August and the Communists of Russia faction in the Russian CPD disintegrated. But the parliaments still contained a large number of deputies who had always been opposed to Yeltsin. Moreover, although the deputies associated with the Democratic Russia faction had been unified in their opposition to the Soviet state, they had little else in common and had no incentive to continue operating as a cohesive faction after the demise of the central state. Outside parliament, Yeltsin had relied on the Democratic Russia movement to organise support for him. However, it too lost its rationale after the demise of the CPSU. It suffered a series of debilitating splits as it searched for a new purpose and organisational identity.[30] Finally, Yeltsin was now obliged to rule Russia, satisfy popular aspirations and fulfil some of the promises made to the people during the struggle with Gorbachev. The main issue was the economy. Yeltsin was now clearly in charge of the fate of the Russian economy, which was in a state of near-terminal decline. Radical action would be needed to stop total economic collapse and enable Yeltsin to retain his popularity and authority over time.

It has been argued that Yeltsin should have called elections at this stage since his prestige was high: '"democrats" were heroes, communists were hiding and nationalists had yet to emerge'.[31] But elections might not have shored up Yeltsin's position all that much. He had no political party with which to fight elections so the deputy body that emerged after elections would probably have been just as independent of him as the deputies in the existing legislatures. Additionally, the constitutional relationship between the Russian CPD and the President would still have been unclear and a potential source of conflict, and disagreements over economic policy would still have occurred.[32] Instead of calling elections, Yeltsin sought to use the prestige and political capital he had acquired during the coup to increase his personal powers as President and create a government that would carry out radical economic reform (widely referred to as 'shock therapy'). He could do this because in the short term there was 'no coherent opposition with which to negotiate' and thus few limits on his powers.[33] In early November he demanded, and was granted, emergency powers to appoint ministers and issue economic decrees for one year without parliamentary approval from the Russian CPD.[34] Yeltsin took on the post of Prime Minister and appointed Yegor Gaidar, a young academic economist with radical views, as Minister of Finance. Some emergency measures to shore up the economy were taken, and comprehensive economic reform was scheduled to commence on 1 January 1992.

In many ways Yeltsin's accumulation of more power to his presidency was a logical extension of his fight against the central Soviet state. That struggle had been personalised both by Yeltsin's competition with Gorbachev and by the way in which opposition and popular aspirations had been focused on Yeltsin in the absence of strong and effective political parties. In the new conditions of post-communism in Russia, the personalisation of reform was not to be as conducive to democratic progress as the focused battle between Yeltsin and Gorbachev had been for Russian independence. The institutionalisation of political life rather than the personalisation of political power, a major problem of post-communist politics in general and a long-standing historical problem for Russia, was hampered as a battle between President and parliament divided the polity once more.

Ukraine

In March 1990, voters in Ukraine, like all of the other republics except Russia, elected deputies direct to their new Verkhovna Rada (Supreme Council). The Ukrainian opposition, like their Russian counterparts, faced some considerable problems in the Rada elections.

In November 1989, Rukh (the Ukrainian independence movement) had supported the formation of an umbrella organisation, the Democratic Bloc, with which to fight the Communist Party of Ukraine (CPU) in the March 1990 elections.[35] The Democratic Bloc's activities began to force the CPU to make more concessionary statements about Ukrainian state sovereignty within the framework of a new union, and the CPU's electoral platform promised Ukrainian state sovereignty. However, the CPU still retained a large amount of organisational strength and support, particularly in eastern and southern

Ukraine where Russians and russified Ukrainians were in the majority. Rukh was weak in these areas and unable to field candidates in many eastern and southern constituencies. As a result, the Democratic Bloc fielded candidates in only 205 of the 450 Rada constituencies (see Table 5.5). The Democratic Bloc nevertheless did well, winning 120 seats (mostly in the second round of voting, in Kiev and in western Ukraine) and scoring some considerable successes over CPU leaders. But its parliamentary faction, Narodna Rada (People's Council) could not form a majority in the Rada.

The Democratic Bloc's inability to win a majority did not reverse the process of political development away from Soviet power in Ukraine. The Rada declared state sovereignty just after Russia in July 1990, recognising 'the Ukrainian nation's inalienable right to self-determination' and 'exclusive right to control, use and direct the national wealth of the Ukraine'. Although the majority in the Rada saw this declaration as being a part of the process of drawing up a new union treaty, the declaration laid the basis for a shift towards Rukh's position by the CPU. This was further facilitated by the nature of the Rada. The new parliament was split between three factions, Narodna Rada, a large number of floating voters, and the 'Bloc for a Sovereign Soviet Ukraine' based around CPU deputies.[36] The ability of the opposition to influence the agenda of the Rada was helped by a number of factors: many CPU deputies paid little attention to parliamentary politics because of their bureaucratic and party commitments; Narodna Rada was able to apply pressure to reformist CPU deputies; and the disproportionate influence of Narodna Rada members as chairs of Rada committees and members of the Rada Presidium. Finally, the CPU leadership was weakened by the decision of Ivashko to quit Ukrainian politics just a month after his election as Chair of the Rada. Ivashko, who made the extremely poor career move of becoming Deputy General Secretary of the CPSU, was replaced as Chair of the Rada by Leonid Kravchuk, the CPU Central Committee Secretary for Ideology.

Table 5.5 Candidates and deputies of the Ukrainian Democratic Bloc, by region

Region	No. of districts	Candidates	Elected
Eastern Ukraine	150	40	28
Southern Ukraine	76	16	2
Central Ukraine	128	62	19
Western Ukraine	65	56	54
Kiev	22	22	16
Others	19	9	1
Total	460	205	120

Source: Arel (1991, p. 116). More detailed breakdowns of regional representation can be found in Potichnyj (1992, pp. 198–9).

Kravchuk, a supreme pragmatist, soon began to emerge as the dominant figure in Ukrainian politics: when expedient to do so, he bent with the prevailing nationalist wind. He was helped in this by his experience as the CPU's chief ideologist: years of combating nationalism on the CPU's behalf had made him familiar with nationalist concerns and able to talk their language when it suited him. At the same time that he was able to appropriate nationalism, Kravchuk also appealed more to Russians and russified Ukrainians than the nationalists from western Ukraine. In short, Kravchuk had 'a multidimensional political personality that could appeal to ... and seem familiar to diverse audiences'.[37] This enabled Kravchuk to present himself as the only leader of the whole Ukrainian nation.

Public pressure for change within the Ukraine was maintained by demonstrations in Kiev and western Ukraine, and by miners' strikes in March 1991. Following a hunger strike by students in October 1990, the government, headed by Vitaly Masol, resigned, and Kravchuk rejected the first draft of the union treaty.[38] In the March 1991 referendum on the Union 70.2 per cent of Ukrainian voters agreed with Gorbachev's proposition on preserving a 'renewed federation' (see Table 5.2), and in a question on the Ukraine put on the ballot paper by the government, 80.2 per cent approved of Ukraine being a part of a 'Union of Sovereign States'.[39] Ukraine was a signatory of the '9 + 1' agreement in April, but Kravchuk was already positioning himself as a nationalist. Kravchuk did not sign the agreement personally and placed himself at the head of a centrist coalition as the CPU faction in the Rada began to disintegrate into reformists and hardliners.[40]

Command of this new loose coalition, combined with his pragmatism in moving towards the nationalist position, was to enable Kravchuk to take advantage of the political vacuum that followed the August coup attempt. Kravchuk bided his time during the events of August, but as soon as the coup was defeated he moved firmly to the nationalist position. He abandoned the CPU, which was banned on 30 August (but quickly reformed as the Socialist Party of Ukraine, the SPU).[41] Ukraine declared independence on 24 August. A referendum to confirm this decision and a presidential election were scheduled for 1 December. Kravchuk positioned himself as a moderate nationalist in the campaigns for both. This, and the massive support that he received from the media (still largely in the hands of the *nomenklatura*), secured him a convincing victory in the election over more overt nationalist candidates (he received 61.59 per cent of the vote in a six-horse race). Support for independence in the referendum was even higher at 90.32 per cent. Kravchuk's election and the referendum result removed any possibility of the USSR's continued existence. Kravchuk's position and survival were so firmly wedded to the nationalist position that Ukraine was only drawn into the CIS reluctantly and under pressure from Russia and Belarus.

Ukraine, like Russia, thus moved toward a presidential system very rapidly after the August coup – but for different reasons. Yeltsin took on further presidential powers in order to secure his power from threats by the Russian CPD and to begin economic reform. Kravchuk draped himself in nationalist clothes and sought the presidency to stay one step ahead of the nationalists and democrats from Rukh and other parties, and offered some protection to the old elite. This ensured that Ukraine would reform its economy only slowly, because the old elite came under far less pressure from government.

The Baltic republics: Estonia, Latvia and Lithuania

The elections in the three Baltic republics in 1990 saw the inevitable victory of candidates supported by the popular fronts and the formation of governments committed to securing independence.[42]

Lithuania led the way. The first round of elections to the Supreme Council was held in late February so that the Council could meet before Gorbachev became President of the USSR. Candidates endorsed by the pro-independence Sajudis secured 72 seats in the first round of voting (141 seats were available), and a further 17 seats in the second round (see Table 5.6). The small number of Russians in the republic meant that the pro-Moscow Lithuanian Communist Party (Moscow Platform) won no seats and Yedinstvo (Unity), a conservative front organisation that claimed to represent the interests of the republic's Russian minority, only managed to field one candidate.[43]

Elections were held on 18 March in Latvia and Estonia. The Latvian elections produced a similar result to Lithuania. Candidates supported by the Popular Front of Latvia (PFL) won 116 seats in the first round and 5 in the second round to become the majority group in the Supreme Council. Candidates from the Latvian Interfront did far better than the Lithuanian Yedinstvo, winning 39 seats in the first round of voting, because of the large number of Russians in Latvia (see Table 2.2). The Latvian Communist Party,

Table 5.6 Results of the first two rounds of the March 1990 elections in Lithuania

Affiliation	No. of deputies	Sajudis endorsed
No party	64	58
Independent Communist Party	31	17
Lithuanian Communist Party (Moscow Platform)	7	0
Social Democratic Party	9	9
Green Party	2	2
Christian Democratic Party	2	2
Democratic Party	1	1
Total	116	89

Source: CSCE (1990, p. 25).

however, made virtually no impact on the elections as a force independent of the PFL or the Interfront.[44]

The elections in Estonia were much more complex than in Latvia and Lithuania.[45] The latter two republics (along with Russia, Belarus, Ukraine and Moldova) used the Soviet version of a majoritarian system: to be elected a candidate had to secure 50 per cent of votes cast; in the event of no candidate securing 50 per cent of votes a run-off election was held between the two candidates with the most votes in the first round. Estonia used a mixed system of voting: four of the Supreme Council's 109 seats were set aside for members of the Soviet army so as to prevent soldiers' votes from being used to boost support artificially for conservative candidates. The remaining 105 were elected by a form of proportional representation (the single transferable vote system), in which voters rank candidates in a constituency and votes are transferred according to preference from candidates who are eliminated at each round of counting until a clear winner emerges. The complexity of the voting system meant that the balance of parliamentary forces was not clear until the Supreme Council met. The Popular Front of Estonia (PFE) emerged as the largest faction with between 41 and 45 deputies. The 'Free Estonia' faction, made up of reform-minded communists, had between 25 and 29 deputies, and the anti-nationalist Joint Council of Work Collectives and military deputies made up a faction of 27. The PFE's share of seats, together with support from some reform communists, enabled it to continue to press ahead with reform; anti-independence forces did not have one-third of votes in the Supreme Council and therefore could not veto major decisions.

The new nationalist-dominated legislatures faced two decisions when they first met: how far to push along the road to independence and how far to compromise with reform communists. Lithuania broke totally with Moscow on 11 March 1990. It reverted to its old name of the 'Republic of Lithuania' and pushed the reform communists aside by electing Vytautas Landsbergis Chair of the Supreme Council and Head of State. Latvia and Estonia were more cautious. In Estonia, Edgar Savisaar, a former Deputy Head of the State Planning Commission, was elected Prime Minister in April, but no dramatic steps towards independence were taken. Latvia declared *de jure* independence in May and elected Ivars Godmanis as Prime Minister.[46]

The unambiguous stance of the Lithuanian government under Landsbergis caused the full weight of Gorbachev's displeasure to fall on the republic. The USSR CPD declared Lithuanian independence illegal on 15 March and an economic blockade began in April. The blockade was partially successful in that the Lithuanians compromised with Moscow and agreed to talks and a moratorium on the declaration of independence. However, no progress was made in these, or any other negotiations. The three Baltic states were set on independence and unwilling to compromise with Moscow. As negotiations and pressure from the centre began to fail, the campaign against the nationalist governments shifted to conservative movements within the republics. These were encouraged by the hardliners appointed by Gorbachev at the end of 1990 and supported by the Soviet army and renegade OMON (special forces police) units, which broke away from republican interior ministries. The formation of pro-Soviet 'National Salvation Committees' was announced in all three of the republics in December 1990.[47] The Committees claimed to be governments-in-waiting, and their membership included local pro-Moscow communists and military leaders. The establishment of the Committees was a prelude to the events of January 1991, when Soviet troops seized the press centre and the television centre in Vilnius, killing fifteen people, and OMON troops seized the Ministry of the Interior building and killed six people in Riga.[48] The January events only strengthened the Baltic commitment to independence. Barricades were set up to protect the parliaments and mass demonstrations were held against the military. Referendums on independence were held in February and March 1991 in all three republics, with substantial numbers of Russians voting alongside native Balts for independence from Moscow (see Table 5.2).[49]

The failure of coercion and the broad popularity of the independence cause did not secure secession from the USSR. The central, Soviet government could not force the republics to abandon their wish for independence, but the republics in turn were unable to move forward because they relied on the USSR for resources and because their independence was not recognised by the international community.[50] The inability of the three republics to take the final step towards independence meant that they were prevented from developing their political systems, delayed dealing with questions of citizenship and could not begin the complex economic process of dismantling the command economy. Although there was some development of political parties in all three republics, as there was throughout the region, the popular fronts, the reform communists with whom they worked and the anti-independence movements like the Interfronts remained the main focus of political activity. As a result, the Baltic republics – despite the advanced nature of their struggle against Soviet power and their high levels of socio-economic development – continued to possess only very simple forms of interest representation. The main cleavage in Baltic politics was between pro- and anti-independence forces and was frequently represented as an ethnic division, despite the support of a substantial number of Russians for the independence cause.

The independence of all three Baltic states was affirmed rapidly by the international community after the August coup. However, the achievement of complete and internationally recognised independence did not attenuate the basic, ethnic cleavage that dominated Baltic politics. If anything it worsened it. In November 1991, Estonia reintroduced its 1938 citizenship law and removed citizenship from Russians who had emigrated to the new state during the Soviet period. A Constitutional Assembly was also convened to create a new parliament. In the same month, the Latvian Popular Front adopted more radical nationalist positions based on the slogan 'Deoccupation [the withdrawal of Russian troops], Desovietisation [the purge of the bureaucracy], Decolonisation [pressure on Russian immigrants to leave]'. The Latvian Supreme Council restored citizenship to all those who had held it prior to 1940 while deferring a decision on the naturalisation of non-Latvian residents. In Lithuania, which had a far smaller Russian minority, the drift towards a harder nationalist politics was expressed in the first moves towards creating a presidency made by Landsbergis.

In each case the intent was to try to solve some of the problems that becoming a nation-state imposed on the popular front governments. The moves towards restrictive citizenship in Latvia and Estonia sought to create a defined political community that would serve as the constituency of the new state governments; the call for the establishment of a presidency in Lithuania sought to cement the hold of a particular brand of nationalism on the new state's political system. But the moves made in each of the states at the year end were to prove ineffective, largely because they meant that pressing economic problems were not prominent on politicians' agenda. Estonia suffered a governmental crisis in January 1992, which was to lead to fresh elections and a new constitution. The proposed presidency in Lithuania divided Sajudis and the Supreme Council and led to Landsbergis's fall. Latvia continued to press for restrictive citizenship, but could not avoid government crisis and elections. The changes in government that were to take place in 1992 and 1993 show politics in the Baltic states immediately after August 1991 – in so far as they were a continuation of the nationalist struggle – to have been little more than an act of denial, an attempt to perpetuate a form of politics that was not suited to the tasks of national reconstruction.

Belarus

Of all the Soviet republics, Belarus stuck closest to the electoral model used to select deputies for the USSR CPD in March 1989 (see Chapter 2). The Supreme Council consisted of 360 deputies, 50 of whom were delegated by 'public organisations' under the control of the Communist Party of Belarus (CPB). The nomination of deputies was also much more tightly controlled by party organs than in other republics. The result was that only 25 deputies to the new Supreme Council were members of the Popular Front of Belarus (PFB).[51] The Front's poor performance in the elections, and the fact that the majority of deputies were party members, did not mean that there was no change in political life. The party's prestige was damaged by the elections and the Supreme Council was not totally compliant to the old leadership's will. The Chair of the old Supreme Council, Mikalia Dzemyantsei, had to stand in two rounds before he was re-elected by the new deputies. A PFB candidate, Stanislau Shushkevich, was elected as First Deputy Chair. The Chair of the Council of Ministers, Vyacheslau Kebich, retained his post, but his nominees for some ministerial positions were rejected.[52]

The party's hold on power in Belarus thus remained strong after the elections in comparison to the other republics, but it could not use this relative strength to avoid change completely. A compromise between Dzemyantsei and Shushkevich in late July 1990 allowed Belarus to follow the general trend and declare itself sovereign. As in Ukraine, the communist deputies who supported the declaration of sovereignty (145 abstained rather than support it) did not intend it to be a step towards independence. But the intentions of Belarusian communist deputies did not matter. Events in the Baltic republics and opposition to the new union treaty from the Russian government meant that Belarusian support for the Union did not alter the balance of power between the central Soviet state and the republics. The Supreme Council's conservatives could not slow the growth of popular resentment at the pace of change in the republic itself either. The CPB, which reaffirmed its hostility to any kind of change at a Congress in December 1990, became increasingly isolated from the population.

Popular resentment at the slow pace of change finally erupted in April 1991, when strikes broke out in Minsk and spread to other major cities.[53] The strikers demanded that the July 1990 declaration of sovereignty be acted upon, and called for multi-party elections, the removal of party organisations from workplaces and a new constitution. The strikes showed that the support (higher in Belarus than anywhere else in European USSR) for a renewed federation in the March 1991 referendum did not mean satisfaction with the existing order. The Belarusian leadership paid some lip-service to popular demands, but attempted to avoid change by buying off workers with wage rises. The political demands of the strikers were discussed and rejected by the Supreme Council's communist majority. Popular pressure for change was thus stifled by the republican leadership. But they were only delaying the inevitable. Their continued close association with Moscow meant that they depended on the survival of the central state for their continued tenure. When the centre collapsed after the August coup, the leadership had no authority left, particularly since they supported the declaration of a state of emergency. Dzemyantsei was forced to step down as Chair of the Supreme Council and was replaced by Shushkevich. The CPB was suspended temporarily. Fresh elections for the Supreme Council were not called, however, so that Belarus started its post-communist phase with the most conservative legislature in the region.

Moldova

The replacement of Semyon Grossu by Petr Lucinschi as first secretary of the Communist Party of Moldova (CPM) meant that the 1990 elections to the Moldovan Supreme Council were much more open and democratic than could have otherwise been expected. However, the ethnic cleavage in Moldovan politics between Moldovans, Russians and the Gagauz was not healed.

The main features of the election campaign were the opposition to the Popular Front of Moldova (PFM) by the Yedinstvo (Unity) movement, which claimed to represent the rights of the Russian minority, and the way in which the CPM – which experienced a brief rise in popularity with Lucinschi's appointment – tried to regain some political ground by donning some nationalist clothes. Just before the March election, Lucinschi called for state sovereignty for Moldova at a CPSU Central Committee meeting. But the CPM was too far behind the PFM to catch up. The PFM mobilised ethnic Moldovans in rural areas to vote, and in alliance with the Agrarian Party, independents and ecologists won over two-thirds of the seats in the Supreme Council.[54] This victory led to the creation of a new government under the leadership of Mircea Druc and the election of the PFM candidate, Mircea Snegur (who had been a prime mover behind the legislation restoring Moldovan language rights the previous year), to the Chair of the Supreme Council. Snegur and the new leadership then set about breaking the links between the republic and Moscow and weakening the CPM. State sovereignty was proclaimed in June 1990, the CPM was banned from organising in factories and other places of work, and its control over the media was broken.

The actions of the new government began to move Moldova to the forefront of the independence struggle. Like the Baltic republics, the PFM-dominated government refused to take part in negotiations over the Union treaty and opted out of the referendum on the Union in March 1990. The pressure put on the republic's leadership to take part in the referendum, and their dissatisfaction with Gorbachev's 'drift to the right' further radicalised the PFM's leaders (but not Snegur), so that by early 1991 they were pressing for full independence and talking of reunification with Romania.

The radicalisation of the PFM and the refusal to participate in the referendum stimulated a backlash from the Russian minority in Transdnestr and the Gagauz, which was supported by hardliners in Moscow and by local Russian communists. Tiraspol, the main city of Transdnestr, voted itself independent in January 1990, and in April 1990, together with several other city councils in the region, it refused to recognise the PFM-dominated Supreme Council. In September 1990, Transdnestr declared itself an independent republic. Separate elections were held in both Gagauz and Transdnestr in October and November 1990 and anti-Moldovan deputies were elected.[55] The elections provoked inter-ethnic violence between Moldovans and the

Russian and Gagauz minorities which the Soviet state could not contain, and in some instances actively supported. By early 1991 the Moldovan government and Transdnestr were on separate paths of development. The referendum on the union was held in both Transdnestr and Gagauz districts and they voted for the union. In August Transdnestr was unique in its unqualified support for the SCSE. The army threatened to restore Soviet power throughout Moldova but was prevented by the rapid collapse of the coup and resistance on the streets of Chişinău, the republican capital.[56]

The Moldovan declaration of independence after the August coup worsened the ethnic conflict. Paramilitary units were established in Transdnestr to protect Russian rights and began to seize control of the eastern regions of the new Moldovan state with the support of the 14th Army (now nominally under the control of Russia). The split between Moldova and Transdnestr was cemented by the unopposed election of Snegur to the presidency of Moldova in December 1991. Transdnestr and Gagauz took no part in the elections. The PFM also boycotted the election because Snegur had removed Druc from his post as Prime Minister, opposed integration with Romania, and because the PFM did not agree with the establishment of the presidency. The split between the PFM and President Snegur was to divide the Moldovan polity for another two years.

Conclusion

All the governments that emerged in 1990–91 in the republics of European USSR were weak once the CPSU and the Soviet state finally collapsed. The Popular Fronts and mass movements that had been effective in mobilising support for democrats and nationalists at key moments in the struggle with the central state contained too many political currents and could not be transformed into mass political parties to support projects of national reconstruction. By late 1991 they had nearly all either been marginalised and/ or had begun to fragment into a mass of competing, small political parties. This was inevitable to a large extent since they had not been mandated to construct new societies and polities, and the fragmentation was not necessarily problematic. Social interest representation had been condensed in the struggle with the central state, and the dissolution of the fronts was necessary if parties and organisations that could represent the wider social plurality were to emerge. However, the demise of the fronts also meant that there was no unified parliamentary support upon which the leaders of the new states could rely to support the policies necessary for economic and institutional reform. This was to cause crises of government in all of the newly independent states over the following years and to make the already complex problems of post-communist economic and political transformation harder to deal with.

Notes

1. Surovell (1994).
2. Hill (1991).
3. Gill (1994, pp. 122–4).
4. Sakwa (1990, pp. 162–3).
5. Gill (1994, pp. 126–30).
6. Robinson (1995, pp. 177–8).
7. For details of the Congress, see Chiesa (1990); Frank (1990); Rees (1992); Gill (1994, pp. 137–43).
8. Harasymiw (1991).
9. McAuley (1992a).
10. Physical force had already been used in Georgia in April 1989 when Soviet troops had attacked and killed twenty demonstrators. It had been used again in January 1990 in Baku, the capital of Azerbaijan, to stop the Azerbaijani Popular Front from taking power. Over 200 people were killed on this occasion. There was also intervention by the military and Ministry of Internal Affairs troops in inter-ethnic conflict in Uzbekistan, Kyrgyzstan and Tajikistan, and covert (at least) involvement in other conflicts.
11. Walker (1993, p. 173).
12. Cited in White *et al.* (1993, p. 87).
13. Goldman (1991, pp. 216–20).
14. The referendum question was: 'Do you consider it necessary to preserve the Union of Soviet Socialist Republics as a renewed federation of equal, sovereign republics in which the rights and freedoms of people of any nationality will be guaranteed in full measure?'
15. Dunlop (1993, p. 33).
16. White *et al.* (1993, p. 88).
17. The other members of the SCSE were Minister of Defence Dmitry Yazov, Minister of Internal Affairs Boris Pugo, KGB Chairman Vladimir Kryuchkov, Chairman of the USSR Farmers' Union Vasily Starodubtsev, President of the Association of State Enterprises Alexander Tizyakov and Deputy Chair of the Security Council Oleg Baklanov.
18. For descriptions of the events of August 1991, see Gorbachev (1991); Sixsmith (1991); Steele (1994, pp. 59–79); Dunlop (1993, pp. 186–255); Yeltsin (1994, pp. 41–103). Analysis of the coup's causes and significance can be found in Odom (1991); Sakwa (1993a); Gooding (1993).
19. For descriptions of the attempts made by Gorbachev to keep the union alive and the counter actions of Russia, see Gorbachev (1991, pp. 59–76); Dunlop (1993, pp. 260–76).
20. For the Agreement on creating the CIS and its founding Charter see the appendices in Tolz and Elliot (1995).
21. Sheehy (1992a and 1992b); White *et al.* (1993, pp. 92–4).
22. For an overview of elections throughout the USSR in 1990, see Slider (1990).
23. Kiernan (1993, pp. 165–7).
24. Brudny (1993, pp. 144–5).
25. Embree (1991, p. 1066).
26. Kiernan (1993, pp. 164–5).
27. Hosking *et al.* (1992, p. 88); Brudny (1993, p. 145).
28. Kiernan (1993, pp. 192–200).

29. Sobyanin and Yur'ev (1991, pp. 48–9).
30. Brudny (1993, pp. 155–6).
31. McFaul (1993a, p. 89).
32. Robinson (1994, pp. 298–9).
33. Shevtsova (1995, p. 8).
34. Sakwa (1993a, pp. 47–8).
35. Kuzio and Wilson (1994, p. 123).
36. Arel (1991, p. 109).
37. Motyl (1995, p. 111).
38. Krawchenko (1993, p. 78).
39. Solchanyk (1991).
40. Solchanyk (1995, pp. 121–3); Kuzio and Wilson (1994, pp. 159–62).
41. Another successor party named the Communist Party of Ukraine (CPU) was formed later.
42. For an overview of the Baltic elections in 1990, see Taagepera (1990b).
43. CSCE (1990, pp. 11–25).
44. *Ibid.*, pp. 51–66.
45. There were also elections to the Estonian Congress, a rival body to the Supreme Council, in early 1990. The Supreme Council, like those of Lithuania and Latvia, was the official republican legislature and the successor to the old republican Supreme Soviet. The Estonian Congress, which was elected by ethnic Estonians only, was set up by radical nationalists as a parliament untainted by Soviet connections. The Congress had 499 seats (35 for representatives of Estonian organisations from overseas). PFE candidates won 107 seats and were the largest bloc. The Congress did not, however, emerge as a significant political actor since the PFE had no interest in promoting its power. See Taagepera (1993, pp. 174–5).
46. Muiznieks (1993, p. 199).
47. Karklins (1994, pp. 104–6).
48. Foye (1991); Gerner and Hedlund (1993, pp. 150–1); Lieven (1994, pp. 198–9).
49. Girnius (1991); Bungs (1991a and 1991b); Kionka (1991); Taagepera (1993, pp. 192–5); Karklins (1994, pp. 101–4).
50. Bradshaw *et al.* (1994, p. 170).
51. Zaprudnik (1993, p. 149).
52. Urban and Zaprudnik (1993, p. 113).
53. Mihalisko (1995, pp. 134–5).
54. CSCE (1990, pp. 73–88).
55. Fane (1993, pp. 139–40).
56. Socor (1995a, pp. 202–5).

CHAPTER 6

Elections in Eastern Europe, 1990

Introduction

The main question confronting the countries of Eastern Europe in 1990 was what was to replace the Communist Party's monopoly of power which had collapsed at the end of 1989. In 1989 and 1990, certain basic steps were taken nearly everywhere in order to solve this problem, although Albania trailed behind by a year, and in Yugoslavia there was significantly different timing in the various republics. Typically, the Communist Party leader was replaced, the party was renamed and the 'leading role of the party' was removed by a hasty amendment to the constitution. The opposition was either admitted to the government, or, more usually, invited to participate in some form of round-table negotiations, after which elections were held. A new government was formed in the light of the election results, and a President was chosen, often by the new parliament, but sometimes directly by the voters. The parliament was then to use its democratic mandate to legitimate the passing of a completely new constitution, but at this point the complexity of democratic politics intervened. Only one state – Croatia – actually passed a new constitution in 1990 (some, and by no means at all the least democratic, had not reached consensus on the issue by 1996), but numerous constitutional amendments were made.

One difference between the transformations in Eastern Europe and classic revolutions, as mentioned briefly in Chapter 1, was the respect paid to existing institutions and the need to transfer power by legal means. The old system was not simply overthrown, with its structures derided and destroyed. Rather, they were transformed and crafted to the needs of a democracy. Certain features of communist systems facilitated this process. They had paid lip-service to democracy, even if they had their own collectivist definitions of the term. Consequently, they also had, at a very basic level, the infrastructure for democratic decision-making. It had been uniformly abused, and removing the leading role of the Communist Party from the old constitutions was crucial precisely because this had been what had usurped the democratic prerogatives nominally allotted to 'the people' in the old systems. However, the prior existence of constitutions, parliaments, governments and elections made it easier to negotiate a legal transfer of power. Sometimes, new rules had to be made, sometimes old ones merely had to be implemented. But in chaotic times, it helped a little to have at least some structures around which debates could be focused.

Considerable attention is paid in this chapter to the emergent multi-party systems because the political parties were a major new feature in all the countries concerned. (Even Albania had more than one party by the end of the year.) Election systems are also looked at in some detail because the introduction of choices which would influence the distribution of power was novel, and the process for managing this was the subject of much negotiation. Both the formation of political parties and the election systems finally agreed illustrate the diversity between individual states which was to become a hallmark of the region. However, neither attained their final state in 1990, and both subjects will be dealt with in more detail in Chapters 7 and 10.

Albania

For Albania, 1990 was not a year of elections. Yet while Albania lagged well behind the rest of Eastern Europe, 1990 was none the less a year that saw at least the start of serious reforms.[1] This was prompted both by pressure from below in the form of continuing public unrest in the country's cities, most notably Shkodër, and by the leadership's recognition of the need for reform, which had been hastened by the alarming example of the overthrow and execution of Ceauşescu, the ruler of Europe's second most repressive communist state.

In January, limited reforms were announced which involved both a change in the procedures of the Party of Labour of Albania (PLA), and some decentralisation of the economy. The spring and summer saw efforts on Albania's part to join the CSCE and to establish diplomatic relations with the United States, USSR and United Kingdom; in the case of the USSR, these had brought success by July. These moves were accompanied by further tentative steps to relax the state's total control of citizens' lives, including the lifting of the absolute ban on religion and a provision that Albanians were to be allowed to hold passports. Alia's own position was strengthened by changes in the composition of the Politburo in July, and in November, a new electoral law was passed which was to allow contested elections in early 1991. This legislation was more reminiscent of Gorbachev's early attempts at demo-cratising the Soviet Union than Eastern Europe's free elections of 1990: the leading role

Textbox 6.1 Main events in Eastern Europe, 1990

January *Albania* The Central Committee of the Party of Labour of Albania (communists) takes small steps towards economic and political reform.
Bulgaria Leading role of the party removed from the constitution.
Czechoslovakia Prime Minister Čalfa leaves the Communist Party.
Poland The Polish United Workers' Party (communists) dissolves itself; some deputies become Social Democrats, others independents.
Romania The National Salvation Front (NSF) announces that it will contest elections, leading to protest demonstrations by students.

February *Bulgaria* Lilov becomes Communist Party leader; Atanasov government resigns; Lukanov becomes Prime Minister.
Czechoslovakia Former dissident Pithart of Civic Forum (CF) becomes Czech Prime Minister.
GDR The communist Socialist Unity Party (SED) changes its name to the Party of Democratic Socialism (PDS); a Government of National Responsibility is formed, representing thirteen parties and groups.
Romania The NSF and opposition agree to form a Council for National Unity.

March *Bulgaria* The round-table agrees free elections; Mladenov is to be President.
Czechoslovakia Slovak Prime Minister Čič leaves the Communist Party.
GDR Democratic elections (brought forward from May) are won by the Christian Democrats and allies (supported by West German government).
Romania Ethnic disturbances between Romanians and ethnic Hungarians in Tîrgu Mureş leave several dead.

April *Bulgaria* The Communist Party becomes the Bulgarian Socialist Party (BSP).
Czechoslovakia The Czechoslovak Socialist Republic (CSSR) becomes the Czech and Slovak Federal Republic (CSFR).
GDR Coalition government formed of all parties with West German 'sisters' – i.e. Christian Democrats, Social Democrats and Free Democrats – under Prime Minister de Maizière.
Hungary The Hungarian Democratic Forum (HDF) wins elections after the second round of voting.

May *Albania* Laws on travel, human rights and religion are relaxed.
Hungary Antall (HDF) forms coalition government with Smallholders, Christian Democrats and independents.

	Romania Parliamentary and presidential elections are won by the NSF and Iliescu.
June	*Bulgaria* BSP wins elections; Lukanov remains Prime Minister.
	Czechoslovakia Free elections won by CF and Public Against Violence (PAV); Čalfa (PAV) remains federal Prime Minister and Pithart (CF) Czech Prime Minister; Mečiar (PAV) become Slovak Prime Minister.
	Romania Anti-communist demonstrators in University Square, Bucharest are attacked by miners supporting NSF.
July	*Albania* Travel restrictions are eased after demonstrators take shelter in Western embassies. Diplomatic relations with USSR are resumed after a break of nearly thirty years.
	Bulgaria Mladenov resigns the presidency.
	Czechoslovakia The new parliament re-elects Havel President.
	Hungary A further referendum on how to elect President fails as turnout is under 14 per cent.
August	*Bulgaria* The Bulgarian parliament elects Zhelev President; Zhelev leaves the Union of Democratic Forces.
	GDR Social Democrats leave government.
	Hungary Parliament elects Göncz of the Alliance of Free Democrats (AFD) President.
	Romania Nicu Ceaușescu, the late President's son, is sentenced to twenty years' imprisonment (but released two years later on health grounds).
October	*Albania* The most famous Albanian writer, Ismail Kadare, is granted political asylum in France.
	GDR Unification with the Federal Republic of Germany; Eastern Germany reformed into five Länder, and in elections four are won by the Christian Democrats.
November	*Albania* A new election law is passed, allowing for multi-candidate elections in February 1991.
	Bulgaria Lukanov resigns as Prime Minister when economic reform programme defeated in parliament.
	Poland First round of presidential elections; Mazowiecki comes third after Wałęsa and émigré Tymiński.
December	*Albania* After student demonstrations in Tirana, the formation of a multi-party state is announced; riots in other cities; Stalin's name is removed from state institutions. There is a refugee exodus to Greece.
	Bulgaria The non-party Popov replaces Lukanov as Prime Minister.
	Germany First all-German elections are won by the Christian Democrats and their coalition partners.
	Poland Mazowiecki resigns as Prime Minister; Wałęsa wins the presidential election in run-off with Tymiński.

of the party had not yet been abandoned, and pluralism was restricted to a choice among candidates presented by the PLA and its approved mass organisations. However, the initial plans for elections with very limited competition were overtaken by events, and when elections did finally take place in March and April 1991, they were, if not entirely fair, at least democratic and multi-party.[2]

What happened was that the changes from above implemented during the course of 1990 proved insufficient to quell protests from below. The anti-government demonstrations which had started in Shkodër reached the capital, Tirana, in July 1990, and in this case their suppression was accompanied by some demonstrators fleeing into foreign embassies. Within a few days, an initial trickle had turned into a flood, and rapid evacuation abroad was organised for nearly 5000 Albanians who had sought refuge in Western embassies. A further shock to the regime was delivered in October, when the only internationally known Albanian, the novelist Ismail Kadare, defected in Paris and criticised the limited nature of Alia's reforms. Finally, the ruler's hand was forced by the rebelliousness of Albania's youth: in December 1990, student demonstrations in Tirana led the PLA to permit a multi-party system, and within a day, the Democratic Party had been formed.[3]

The intense and unique problems which Albania was to face in the next few years were determined largely by two facts. One was that it had entered both the interwar and the communist period as the most underdeveloped country in Europe. The second was that, in 1990, it telescoped within one year processes of change to the communist system which elsewhere in Eastern Europe had taken place over more than three decades. This was illustrated most graphically by the fact that, just a few days *after* the formation of competing parties had been permitted, the government finally decided to remove Stalin's name from all institutions which it controlled.[4]

Bulgaria

Bulgaria began 1990 in a somewhat different situation from the other Warsaw Pact countries because – despite the substantial changes in the last two months of 1989 – it was still the Communist Party which was setting the political agenda. The ability of the communists to retain power was based in part on their ability to lay all the blame for past problems on Zhivkov, who had been in power for an inordinately long time (as, indeed, had many of them). However, many of those who had opposed Zhivkov most strongly in the independent groupings were themselves products of the communist regime.

In the early months of 1990, democratisation proceeded on a number of fronts. The communist-dominated National Assembly formally removed the leading role of the party from the constitution in January, and a Bulgarian

Communist Party congress at the end of the month – which revealed serious splits within the party – also accepted the resignation of the new President, Mladenov, from the party leadership, so that the beginning of a separation of powers was implemented. Mladenov was replaced as party Chair by Aleksandar Lilov, and Andrey Lukanov, also a communist, became Prime Minister in early February. In April, party members voted by referendum to adopt the name 'Bulgarian Socialist Party' (BSP). At the same time, the round-table talks gradually agreed a number of constitutional amendments, and adopted a law on political parties and a new electoral law to be used for elections in June.

The most notable stipulation of the party law was the ban on parties organising on a religious basis. The consequence of this was that the Movement for Rights and Freedoms (MRF), which was in practice the Turkish Party, was unable to indicate this clearly either in its name or its programme. The electoral law, while not the most complex in the post-communist world, was a compromise embodying elements of several systems. Half the seats (200) were allocated in single-member constituencies, where the winning candidate required 50 per cent of the votes in order to be elected on the first ballot. Where no candidate obtained sufficient votes, a second ballot was held two weeks later. Unlike in Hungary, however, where few candidates won in the first round, in Bulgaria a run-off was required in only 81 of 200 seats (see Table 6.1). The remaining 200 seats were distributed by proportional representation to party lists in 28 constituencies, with the stipulation that a party had to obtain 4 per cent of the list vote nationally in order to gain representation.

When the elections took place, only four parties cleared the 4 per cent hurdle and obtained PR seats. The choice was largely between the Bulgarian Socialist Party and the opposition Union of Democratic Forces (UDF), although 16 seats went to the Bulgarian Agrarian National Union – a puppet party which had been allowed a restricted existence under communism – and 23 went to the Turkish MRF. The UDF had attempted to fight the elections along the lines of a 'referendum on democracy' of the sort which brought success to Solidarity in Poland and the citizens' movements in Czechoslovakia. This attempt failed, however. Despite the unpopularity of Zhivkov, the communist period had not been such a manifest disaster in Bulgaria as elsewhere, given the extremely low level of modernisation at the outset; and the revitalised BSP could advance a credible case that it was able and willing to bring about any changes necessary in Bulgarian society. Additionally, the UDF suffered from a number of disadvantages. Despite the demonstrations of late 1989, it could not realistically claim to be a heroic organisation which had united the people to bring down communism; it also was weakened by the fact that it was the umbrella organisation of a large number of parties and organisations, which hampered both effective leadership and the coherent presentation of policy; and it lacked substantial support in the countryside

Table 6.1 Bulgarian election, 10/17 June 1990

	% vote	PR seats	Round 1 seats Constituency	Round 2 seats Constituency	Total
Bulgarian Socialist Party	47	97	75	39	211
Union of Democratic Forces	36	75	32	37	144
Movement for Rights & Freedoms	6	12	9	2	23
Bulgarian Agrarian National Union	8	16	0	0	16
Others	3	0	3	3	6
Total		200	119	81	400

Source: Ashley (1990, p. 317).

because of its origins among urban intellectual elites, its inability to match the BSP's existing party infrastructure in the provinces, and the fact that its proposed economic policy of 'shock therapy' was not reassuring to much of the electorate. Steady change under the BSP appeared to many the more attractive option. Some of the UDF's disadvantages would have been diminished if, as it had advocated, elections had been held later in the year, when it would have had more time to organise. Its increasing popularity and the waning support of the communists towards the end of the year suggest that this would have helped them. But it would not have solved any of its principal structural problems.[5]

The polarisation of Bulgarian politics into two opposing camps became most significant after the elections. The new parliament, the Grand National Assembly, was to have a duration of only 18 months since, as in many other post-communist countries, it had the functions of a constituent assembly – a body with electoral legitimacy which was to decide the rules by which ordinary, everyday politics would thereafter be conducted. However, changing the constitution required a two-thirds majority, and it was arithmetically impossible for the BSP to attain one without at least some support from the UDF. The first stalemate the National Assembly confronted was in choosing a new President after Mladenov was discredited and resigned in July 1990. Eventually, a compromise was reached whereby the BSP supported the UDF leader, Zhelyu Zhelev, who then resigned his party affiliation.

The BSP faced two other problems, however. One was the reality of trying to effect economic reform, and the party lost popularity as a population expecting improvements found that things were actually still getting worse. The other was fracturing within the BSP itself: the party in a one-party state has completely different goals and functions to a party in a democracy, and as the BSP was confronted by genuine policy dilemmas, it was almost inevitable that widely different views would emerge. These crystallised into a battle between Party Leader Lilov and Prime Minister Lukanov. When there were widespread popular protests over the economy in November 1990, Lukanov resigned.[6]

The first post-communist Bulgarian government had therefore survived for less than six months. It was replaced by a broad coalition government under the non-party Dimitar Popov, a lawyer who was known for his work on the Central Election Commission. The government contained five further independents, as well as representatives of every party or coalition in the National Assembly except the Turkish MRF.

Czechoslovakia

Although communist Czechoslovakia had been one of the most authoritarian of the East European regimes, the weak legitimacy and self-confidence of its rulers after 1968 meant that it 'imploded' to a greater extent than the others. The transfer of power at the end of 1989 was relatively quick and smooth, so that by the beginning of 1990, it had a highly respected former dissident as President and a Government of National Understanding.

In January, the Communist Party recalled more than 100 of its deputies, who were replaced by nominees of the opposition citizens' movements, so that the Communist Party no longer had even a paper majority in the Federal Assembly. Similar developments took place in the Czech and Slovak National Councils. Additionally, some of the communist ministers in the government, including the Federal Prime Minister Marián Čalfa, and later the Slovak Prime Minister Milan Čič, resigned their party membership; a former dissident, Petr Pithart, became Czech Prime Minister. Communists in a large number of other high state offices were also replaced. Legislation was agreed on the registration of political parties, the electoral law was changed and free elections were arranged for June. In the meantime, economic reforms to move the country towards a market economy were already beginning, albeit slowly.

In spite of the seemingly smooth progress of Czechoslovakia towards full democracy, one incident early in the year presaged problems which were later to dominate the country's politics. President Havel suggested to the Federal Assembly that the country's name should be changed from the Czechoslovak Socialist Republic (CSSR) to the Czechoslovak Republic (CSR) – the latter having been its formal title during the interwar years. This seemingly inoffensive proposal became contentious when Slovak deputies suggested that the name 'Czecho-Slovak Republic' would more accurately reflect in the outside world that the country actually comprised two separate nations. This led to a parliamentary 'hyphen war', which most Czechs found ridiculous, while simultaneously considering the issue sufficiently important to continue opposing the hyphen. Eventually, the title 'Czech and Slovak Federal Republic' was accepted as a compromise solution. In the meantime, however, demonstrations had taken place in Bratislava during which demands for an independent Slovak state began to emerge, albeit only from a small minority.

Elections took place on 8–9 June (Czechs and Slovaks hold elections on a Friday afternoon and the following Saturday morning).[7] The new electoral system was one of qualified PR, where seats are allotted to parties in proportion to their vote, provided that they have obtained 5 per cent of the total vote.[8] However, ballot papers were distributed to the voters in advance because of the complexity of the choices which had to be made. First, because of the federal nature of the country, each voter had to vote three times: for the two chambers of the Federal Assembly, and for the Czech or Slovak National Council, depending on which part of the country they lived in. For each of these three elections, they had to select the list of candidates for the party of their choice, but they also had the chance to rearrange the order of the candidates on each list by marking up to four with a 'preferential vote'. The most popular candidates for each party were therefore, in theory, more likely to get elected, although in practice any politician with a sufficiently high profile to gain the large number of preferential votes required to be moved was likely to be near the top of the list already.

Several observations must be made about the elections. The first is that they corresponded to a large extent to the 'referendum on democracy' pattern: as shown in Table 6.2, by far the most popular candidates were the citizens' movements Civic Forum in the Czech Republic and Public Against Violence in Slovakia. One of their most potent electoral slogans had been 'return to Europe' – emphasising the fact that the communist period had been an aberration from the country's democratic interwar history. The second is that support for the citizens' movements was stronger amongst the Czechs (about half) than among the Slovaks (about a third). This was largely because, while both had an equally strong communist vote (just over 13 per cent), Christian Democracy was twice as strong in Slovakia, where Catholicism played a larger role. A third feature of the elections, however, was the substantial minority of the vote in each republic which went to nationalist parties: in the Czech Republic, about 9 per cent of the vote went to a party supporting regional (mainly Moravian) interests, and in Slovakia, the Slovak National Party won about 12 per cent of the vote, and a coalition of Hungarian parties just over 8 per cent. In sum, few people had voted according to economic interests, because few people were sure what these were in a non-communist regime; so they had either voted for or against the former government, by choosing the citizens' movements or the communists, or they had voted according to their religion or nationality, which were the only identities which remained after forty years of system transformation. Parties which had links with the pre-communist period, such as the Social Democrats, did not emerge as a major force.

The governments which emerged from the elections were broad coalitions, based on consensus, and they displayed a degree of continuity with the non-communist governments which had immediately preceded them. The Slovak

Table 6.2 Czechoslovak elections, 8–9 June 1990

	Federal Assembly[a]				National Council	
	Ch. of People		Ch. of Nations			
Czech parties	% vote	Seats	% vote	Seats	% vote	Seats
Civic Forum	53	68	50	50	49	127
Communist Party of CS	13	15	14	12	13	32
Movement for Selfgoverning Democracy/Association for Moravia & Silesia	8	9	9	7	10	22
Christian & Democratic Union	9	9	9	6	8	19
Others	17	0	18	0	19	0
Total		101		75		200

Slovak parties	% vote	Seats	% vote	Seats	% vote[b]	Seats
Public Against Violence	33	19	37	33	29	48
Christian Democratic Movement	19	11	17	14	19	31
Communist Party of CS	14	8	13	12	13	22
Slovak National Party	11	6	11	9	14	22
Coexistence/Hungarian Christian Democratic Movement	9	5	8	7	9	14
Democratic Party	4	0	4	0	4	7
Green Party	3	0	3	0	3	6
Others	8	0	6	0	8	0
Total		49		75		150

a. All percentages relate to total votes cast in either the Czech Republic or the Slovak Republic: official statistics *never* gave percentages for the Federation as a whole.
b. A 5 per cent clause operated for the Federal Assembly and Czech National Council, but only a 3 per cent clause for the Slovak National Council.
Source: Federální statistický úřad (1991, pp. 629–30).

Čalfa from Public Against Violence remained Federal Prime Minister, to balance the Czech Václav Havel as President; Pithart of Civic Forum remained Czech Prime Minister, and Vladimír Mečiar, of Public Against Violence, became Slovak Prime Minister. Apart from the citizens' movements, both Czech and Slovak Christian Democrats provided government ministers, as well as the smaller Democratic Party in Slovakia. Some independent ministers were appointed, too. The only main parties excluded were the communists, the Slovak Nationalists and the Hungarian coalition, although there was some Hungarian participation via Public Against Violence.

The problem of such consensus politics was that it was easier to maintain while the main enemy was perceived to be the old regime; as the governments began to tackle the real problems of a post-communist society, the splits within and between the ruling parties began to show. However, in general terms, 1990 was a year of considerable achievements for Czechoslovakia. The country's institutional framework had been radically altered, and local government reform was followed by local elections in December; freedom and pluralism of the media was established; and, while the issue of Czech-Slovak relations and forming an 'authentic federation' from the rather flawed communist federal structures was the focus of much controversy, by December the Federal Assembly had passed a constitutional amendment on power-sharing between the republics and the federation.

The foundations were also laid for economic reform: the laws permitting citizens to set up private businesses passed in the spring were followed by the first law on the restitution of property confiscated during the communist period in the autumn. Small-scale privatisation began through which small state-owned businesses were auctioned off to private citizens. To many people, the progress of economic reform appeared slow, yet Czechoslovakia, in spite of – or perhaps because of [9] – its strong entrepreneurial traditions in the pre-communist period, had had virtually no legal private enterprise at all in the previous forty years. This initially hampered its economic progress, particularly in the area of foreign investment, but it was a handicap which was rapidly to diminish in the following years, most particularly for the Czechs. Unlike in Poland, where there was an urgent foreign debt problem, the government could afford to take slightly more time to plan its economic changes.

GDR

The German Democratic Republic was the first communist state physically to disappear from the map of Europe. It was also a unique case of post-communist transformation, since the area adopted a ready-made set of democratic institutions and a complete bureaucratic, legal and economic system, as well as receiving more dedicated western help in terms of financial resources and expertise than any of its neighbours. By acceding to the Federal Republic of Germany at midnight 2/3 October 1990, it had become a member of the European Community in less than eleven months from the fall of the Berlin Wall, so it is also the only existing model for the integration of the formerly communist world into European structures.

At the beginning of 1990, however, it had been far from clear which path the GDR would follow. German unification was already on the agenda, both in the slogans of demonstrators and in the plans of politicians, but the timespan envisaged was long. It was thought that the GDR and the Federal Republic of Germany would gradually move towards a confederation, from which one state might eventually emerge. A number of factors accelerated developments.

First, the planned elections were brought forward from May to March, making them the first fully free elections in the former Warsaw Pact area. In part, this was necessitated by the declining legitimacy of the round table of old and new organisations that was negotiating the changes; as the number of new parties multiplied in the early months of 1990, it became more questionable upon whose behalf the opposition groups represented at the round-table actually spoke. Secondly, the importance of the Federal Republic of Germany as a political actor in GDR politics was increasing, although, constitutionally, it had none. A decision by the round table that West German parties should not campaign in the March elections was widely ignored, and the overriding importance of West German political structures was underlined by the results, in which the reformed Communist Party, the Party of Democratic Socialism, was the only major competitor to gain more than a few per cent of the vote which did not have a western 'sister' party (see Table 6.3). The predominance of parties with West German supporters occurred in spite of an electoral system of unrestricted proportional representation which provided new and smaller East German parties with maximum scope to translate any support they had into seats. Thirdly, the result itself was a very clear 'referendum on unification' in two senses. One was that New Forum, the citizens' movement which had done so much to bring down the communists, gained only 3 per cent of the vote; this contrasted markedly with the fate of counterparts abroad such as the Czech Civic Forum and Polish Solidarity. The East German election may be considered to fit the 'referendum on democracy' pattern, but clearly the electorate considered the best way to anchor democracy to be unification with the Federal Republic rather than returning former dissidents to power. The other way in which the electorate opted for rapid unification was by voting predominantly for parties supported by the West German Christian Democrats of Chancellor Helmut Kohl. These wanted the territory of the German Democratic Republic to join the Federal Republic under Article 23 of the constitution, which allowed for the accession of new Länder (regions or states). A lower percentage of votes went to the Social Democrats, who preferred a slower route to unification under Article 146 of the constitution, which envisaged the passing of a new constitution when both parts of the divided Germany were able to vote on one freely.[10]

The election result was, however, something of a curiosity because of the amount of the vote which went to what were, technically, former 'puppet' parties of the communists. While the Social Democratic Party had been revived in autumn 1989 after disappearing on its forced merger with the communists in the late 1940s, the East German Christian Democratic Union (which obtained 41 per cent of the vote) had existed throughout the communist period. The difficulty faced by the West German Christian Democratic Union was that they were loathe to endorse the east German puppet party of the same name, but were aware of the latter's potential in terms of organisational infrastructure, and anxious not to split the centre-right vote. They therefore encouraged both new right-of-centre parties and former puppet parties of the same alleged persuasion to enter an alliance together, although the parties were all entered separately on the ballot paper. Much of the East German electorate, however, was already operating entirely on a forward-

Table 6.3 GDR election, 18 March 1990

	% vote	seats
Christian Democratic Union	41	163
German Social Union	6	25
Democratic Awakening	1	4
[Alliance for Germany total	*48*	*192]*
Social Democratic Party of Germany	22	88
Party of Democratic Socialism	16	66
League of Free Democrats	5	21
Alliance 90	3	12
Democratic Farmers' Party of Germany	2	9
Greens/Independent Women's Association	2	8
National Democratic Party of Germany	0	2
Democratic Women's League of Germany	0	1
United Left/the Carnations	0	1
Total		400

Source: Keesing's Record of World Events (1990), 36 (3), p. 37301.

looking agenda which anticipated unification, rather than staring back into the GDR past, and simply cast their vote for the party with the same name as Chancellor Helmut Kohl's, regardless of the fact that it had formerly co-operated with the communists. By the end of the year, the same mechanism was also working for the Free Democratic Party, which had taken over the apparatus and membership of the old 'puppet' Liberal Democratic Party. It achieved considerable, though fleeting, popularity in the December 1990 elections because the Free Democrat Foreign Minister, Hans-Dietrich Genscher, who was credited with a substantial role in gaining international agreement to unification, happened to be an East German by origin.

There was also a final and major factor which accelerated the formal unification process and was related not to politics but to economics. In the early months of 1990, West German largesse to the GDR was less than had been expected by the East German population, given the Federal Republic's willingness to loan money before the communists had been toppled. Voting for Chancellor Kohl's party was seen in part as a way of reassuring the West German government, thereby encouraging them to invest money; and Kohl's promise to convert the East German mark to the West German mark at the rate of 1:1, which he made shortly before the GDR election, was a further incentive. After the March elections, it became clear that not even the now guaranteed political freedoms would curb the high emigration rate from East to West, still running at several thousand a day. Only by earning Deutschmarks would East Germans happily remain working at home, and currency union was therefore introduced at the beginning of July. The Ostmark was replaced by the Deutschmark. At this point, it was envisaged that Germany would be formally united in December, to coincide with the

Table 6.4 German election, 2 December 1990

	% vote east	% vote total	Total seats
Christian Democratic Union[a]	42	44	319
Social Democratic Party of Germany	24	33	239
Free Democratic Party	13	11	79
Party of Democratic Socialism	11	2	16
Alliance 90/Greens	6	5	8
Others	4	4	0
Total			661

a. In Bavaria, the Christian Social Union
Source: Calculated from Golz (1994, pp. 1129–30).

national elections due in the old Federal Republic. However, as the truly dire
state of the East German economy emerged, coupled with the almost total
lack of native East Germans qualified to tackle the problems, the impatience
of the West German government to take control of the entire problem grew.
The broad East German government coalition, encompassing Christian
Democrats, Social Democrats and Liberals, fell apart in August when the
Social Democratic economic ministers were dismissed, and it became more
and more urgent to regularise a situation where much real power was actually
being exercised in Bonn, technically the capital of a foreign country.

The willingness of the majority of East Germans to place their fate in the
hands of the West German government was confirmed at the ballot box twice
more in 1990. In October, shortly after unification, the five new East German
Länder elected their own parliaments and governments in accordance with
the German federal system, and the Christian Democrats won in four of them.
Finally, in December Chancellor Kohl won an impressive election victory,
as shown in Table 6.4, and his support in the new Länder was higher than in
the old.[11]

In the course of the year, everyday life had changed radically for most East
Germans. However, they were not only in a different situation materially, but
also politically. Whereas, at the beginning of the year, the citizens were
pushing for very rapid changes which the politicians were finding it very hard
to keep up with, by the end of the year the situation had reversed:[12] citizens
found that the entire constitutional, political, legal and economic framework
of their lives had been changed around them, and they were left to undergo a
painful adaptation process.

Hungary

One consequence of the smooth, negotiated transition in Hungary was
that the country approached free elections in March 1990 with a somewhat
more developed party constellation than its neighbours. The elections could

scarcely be considered a 'plebiscite on democracy', since there was no force that could credibly threaten to turn Hungary away from the democratic path and back to a restrictive communist system: leading communists had, after all, been instrumental in bringing about the introduction of a multi-party system and democratic elections. This meant that the opposition saw no need to maintain a united front in the face of external danger because the sort of communists which Hungary had seen in the late 1980s were simply not that dangerous a kind. The elections were therefore mainly about which party should rule the country, rather than about what sort of regime there should be.

Nevertheless, the party spectrum which entered the election was not easily recognisable in terms of Western systems. The parties can be divided into three main groups: those emerging from the communist Hungarian Socialist Workers' Party; those with their roots in anticommunist dissent; and reincarnations of parties which had existed in the precommunist period. As can be seen in Table 6.5, it was the new parties – the Hungarian Democratic Forum (HDF), the Alliance of Free Democrats (AFD) and FIDESZ (the Alliance of Young Democrats) – which were most successful in the elections, obtaining 278 of 386 seats. The revived historical parties obtained 65 seats, and the Hungarian Socialists (reform communists) gained 32.[13]

The results of the elections, which led to the representation of only six parties in parliament, were partly a result of a highly complex electoral system which militated in favour of stronger parties.[14] This system showed all the signs of having been designed by a committee, and incorporated elements taken from almost every European election system except the single transferable vote. First of all, 176 of the parliament's 386 seats were contested in single-member constituencies in a modified first-past-the-post system: a candidate was required to gain 50 per cent of votes cast in order to win in the first round, held on 25 March. Only five candidates managed to do this, so that second ballots took place two weeks later in 171 constituencies. Here, only the most successful candidates ran (usually three), and the seat was allotted to the candidate with the most votes. As an additional complication, a turnout of 50 per cent of a constituency's voters was required for the first ballot to be valid. A further 152 seats were available for allocation by proportional representation to party lists in 20 regions. Only parties with a requisite number of candidates standing for election in single-member constituencies were allowed to present a list, and a party had to obtain 4 per cent of regional votes nationwide in order to be allocated any seats by PR. Finally, residual votes (i.e. votes that had not been given to a winning candidate) from both the single-member constituency and the regional list ballots were distributed to national party lists presented by parties with regional lists in at least seven regions. Ninety seats were allocated in this manner – 58 which had been reserved for the national lists, plus 32 seats 'left over' from those originally earmarked for

Table 6.5 Hungarian election, 25 March/8 April 1990

| | % vote | | Seats | | |
	Regional lists	Individual	Regional lists	National lists	Total
Hungarian Democratic Forum	25	115	40	10	165
Alliance of Free Democrats	21	34	34	23	91
Independent Smallholders Party	12	11	16	17	44
Hungarian Socialist Party	11	1	14	18	33
Alliance of Young Democrats (FIDESZ)	9	1	8	12	21
Christian Democratic People's Party	6	3	8	10	21
Agrarian Alliance	3	1	0	0	1
Independent	–	6	0	0	6
Joint candidates	–	4	0	0	4
Other	13	0	0	0	0
Total		176	120	90	386

Source: Hungarian Central Statistical Office (1991, pp. 202–4).

the regional list election because no party had gained a sufficient quota of votes to win them.

It might be tempting to attribute the fact that Hungary produced almost the lowest voter turnout in the post-communist world for an initial democratic election – 65 per cent in the first round and 46 per cent in the second round – to the extraordinary complexity of the electoral system. In fact, however, the Hungarians had not produced the most complicated ballot paper (a distinction won by the Czechs and Slovaks), and voters had only been required to select one candidate for their constituency and one party list for their region. Reasons for voter apathy can therefore be more realistically sought in the nature of Hungarian politics. The democratic system had been hammered out in negotiations between the elites of the old and new parties, and was not the product of widespread popular protest, as had been the case elsewhere. Consequently, voters did not perceive that they were personally involved in the final struggle of the new versus the old regime.[15]

The election result produced a parliament divided along reasonably clear ideological lines, and hence one that facilitated the formation of the government. The HDF, the winner of the election, represented the populist strand of Hungarian dissent, and it therefore entered a coalition with two traditional parties with a nationalist/Christian orientation, the Independent Smallholders and the Christian Democrats. Their main support was in the countryside and in provincial towns. The opposition was split between the more urban liberal dissidents in the AFD and FIDESZ, and the reform communists in the HSP.[16] Since the new government was going to need to amend the constitution, which required a two-thirds majority in parliament, some accord with the second strongest party, the Alliance of Free Democrats, was essential, and this was achieved by finally solving the problem of how to elect a president. It was agreed that the constitution should be changed to allow parliament to choose the President, after which the AFD member Árpád Göncz was elected.

However, once a government under the premiership of the HDF's József Antall had been installed, the successful formation of democratic institutions needed to be matched by policies to solve the country's economic problems. Conditions for this were at first sight favourable: the government had a reasonably stable majority and the prospect of remaining in power for four years. Additionally, Hungary's lead over its Warsaw Pact allies in the transition to democracy was matched in many respects by its lead in the economic field. Although the country had one of the highest foreign debt burdens in the area, it also had the most developed private sector and the most advanced economic links with the Western world. It had been a member of the International Monetary Fund and the World Bank since 1982, and foreign partners in joint ventures were allowed to repatriate their profits, which made it initially the favoured destination for western investors. It was partly as a consequence of this that Antall's government felt able to avoid the path of economic 'shock therapy'. However, very little was done during its first 100 days in office, and the local government elections in the autumn gave the first indication of the leading party's decline in popularity. This presaged developments over the next few years.

Poland

By mid-1990, Poland – the pioneer of change in Eastern Europe – was in the anomalous position of having the least democratically elected parliament in the region. In some respects, it had commenced 1990 well ahead of its communist neighbours as its non-communist Prime Minister, Mazowiecki, had been appointed in August 1989. Moreover, the parliament had implemented such basic constitutional changes as removing the leading role of the Communist Party and deleting the word 'People's' to make the country's formal name the 'Polish Republic'; and the Finance Minister, Leszek Balcerowicz, had prepared his programme of macroeconomic stabilisation – designed to combat Poland's excessive inflation rate – which led to freeing of prices and imports, as well as strict wage controls, at the beginning of 1990. However, in terms of creating a democratic institutional framework, the country's transition was complicated by the fact that it had erected interim, semi-democratic structures prior to the collapse of communism internationally. Poland still lacked an agreed electoral system for free elections, and the future role of the President – an office occupied by the communist Jaruzelski – was yet to be determined.

By January 1990, the wider environment in which Mazowiecki's government functioned had changed substantially and become less restrictive. This was in part because the dramatic events in neighbouring countries at the end of the previous year had demonstrated definitively that there was now no Soviet threat to limit Poland's room for manoeuvre. But it was also because the Polish United Workers' Party (PUWP), which had been demoralised and shedding its remaining members with enormous speed since its election defeat, finally dissolved itself, yielding a successor called Social Democracy of the Polish Republic under Aleksander Kwaśniewski.

The removal of the internal threat to democracy in the form of a Communist Party provided greater scope for articulating disputes *within* Solidarity. Divisions began to emerge between Mazowiecki's government, the club of parliamentary deputies who had been elected with Solidarity support, and Solidarity's trade union organisation. The latter was still led from Gdańsk by the national hero Wałęsa, who had refrained from putting himself forward for either the parliament or the government.[17] It emerged in the course of 1990, however, that his sights were set on the presidency, and he prepared his campaign by increasing criticism of Mazowiecki and the government that he had originally supported. Wałęsa was known to dislike the fact that Mazowiecki – whom he himself had chosen as premier in the summer – had shown an unexpected degree of independence, and Wałęsa was also critical of the slow pace of change, both in removing old communists and introducing economic reform. The two factors were partly linked, since the failure to carry out widespread privatisation of state enterprises was being accompanied by 'spontaneous privatisation' in which sections of the old communist *nomenklatura* converted its political power into economic power by gaining control of industry and commerce.

By the summer, all vestiges of communist power were so clearly an anachronism that the communist Internal Affairs and Defence Ministers were replaced, and Jaruzelski finally resigned the presidency. It was decided that the next President should be directly elected, and in November 1990 Poland finally had a free election. This accelerated the break-up of Solidarity as a broad and united citizens' movement, but a number of factors complicated the formation of parties in the period prior to the presidential elections.[18] The fact that the forthcoming election was for the presidency rather than the parliament exacerbated the tendency towards personalised rather than programmatic parties. Wałęsa also confused the situation by refusing unambiguously to identify himself with any particular party, although the Centre Alliance, established in May 1990 from one part of Solidarity, clearly saw campaigning for Wałęsa's presidency as one of its main functions. Wałęsa may have calculated that a multiplicity of small parties, rather than the formation of two or three strong ones, would help him maintain his own personal power. However, his aversion to parties was also reminiscent of the views of the interwar Polish leader Piłsudski (greatly revered by Wałęsa), who saw parties as vehicles of politicians' self-interest rather than defenders of a unified national interest. Additionally, Solidarity's own status confused the situation: since it accepted dual membership and had sponsored candidates belonging to a variety of small parties in the 1989 elections, Solidarity's club of parliamentary deputies also contained members of political parties other than those emerging from Solidarity.

By the time of the election, when Wałęsa faced the Prime Minister Mazowiecki in the contest for President, both were backed by part of Solidarity. Wałęsa, however, had a far wider range of other support than Mazowiecki. The surprise of the election was not, therefore, that Wałęsa won, but rather that the Prime Minister failed to come second (see Table 6.6). The distinction of fighting Wałęsa in the second round of the election was achieved not by the candidate of one of the three smaller parties standing in the election, but by the maverick independent Stan Tymiński. While Wałęsa received less than 40 per cent of the vote in the first round (50 per cent was required to win without a second ballot), he gained nearly 75 per cent in the second round, as most of the eliminated contestants and their supporters considered Wałęsa, whatever his faults, an infinitely lesser evil than Tymiński. Nevertheless, the fact that a quarter of the voters had chosen an unknown outsider whose émigré background seemed as dubious as his contacts within Poland, as well as the fact that only 61 per cent of the electorate had turned out for the first round of a highly publicised election, suggested an alarming level of public scepticism about democratic politics.

In the face of his ignominious defeat in the presidential contest, Mazowiecki resigned as Prime Minister, so that Wałęsa took office with the possibility that new parliamentary elections would take place. What remained unclear – to be determined by a new constitution – were the actual powers of the President. This confusion was to underlie many of the battles in Polish politics for more than half a decade.

Table 6.6 Polish presidential election, 25 November/9 December 1990

	% vote	
	1st round	2nd round
Lech Wałęsa (Centre Alliance *et al.*)	40	74
Stanisław Tymiński (Independent)	23	26
Tadeusz Mazowiecki (Democratic Union)	18	
Włodzimierz Cimoszewicz (Left)	9	
Roman Bartoszcze (Polish Peasant Party)	7	
Leszek Moczulski (Confederation for Independent Poland)	3	

Source: Adapted from Główny Urząd Statystyczny (1992, p. 65).

Romania

Throughout 1990, Romania was the country whose progress towards democracy caused most anxiety internationally. This related both to the origin, the composition and the behaviour of the National Salvation Front (NSF), which had emerged in the middle of the protests the previous December. While the NSF portrayed itself as the spontaneous product of revolution, others believed that it derived from an anti-Ceauşescu conspiracy within the Romanian Communist Party, which had been hurriedly implemented as a response to public protest. Although some of the few dissidents who had been active during the revolution found themselves put on to the NSF Council, it comprised in the main influential figures from the Romanian Communist Party: the Chair, Ion Iliescu, had been a top-ranking communist before slipping into obscurity in the course of the 1970s and 1980s owing to distaste for Ceauşescu's policies. The NSF had rapidly assumed the exercise of all state power, appointing Petre Roman as Prime Minister the day after Ceauşescu's execution, and it presented itself as Romania's caretaker prior to free elections, which were initially planned for April 1990, though actually held a month later.[19]

The NSF already began encountering criticism in January 1990. On 12 January, thousands demonstrated in front of its headquarters, demanding, *inter alia*, the banning of the Communist Party – a measure that was immediately conceded by the NSF, although its implementation was clouded by the customary unclarity. The opposition's disquiet increased on 23 January, when the NSF announced that it would itself be competing in the forthcoming elections. The amount of power concentrated in the NSF's hand now took on a far more sinister complexion, since it was effectively abandoning the pretence of being a neutral arbiter of Romania's affairs and becoming a major actor in the political game: the NSF had oversight of elections in which it was itself competing. The elections were moved back to May, to allow the opposition more time to organise, though an extra month was scarcely likely to dent the NSF's overwhelming organisational advantage. More demonstrations took place at the end of the month, which were met by an apparent concession from the NSF, when opposition parties – which had previously been excluded from any interim power-sharing arrangement on the pretext that the NSF was itself a government of national unity – were admitted to a Provisional Council for National Unity. This participation was restricted, however, to preparing the electoral law, and the Council was easily packed by NSF supporters, many masquerading as representatives of newly formed parties. A more ominous development accompanying the late January demonstrations was the mobilisation of a pro-NSF counter-demonstration, most notably miners transported in from outside Bucharest who attacked the crowd.

When the elections finally took place in May, they differed from those elsewhere in the region in two major respects.[20] One was that a President was directly elected at the same time as the parliament. While direct election of the President was an arrangement gradually adopted by a number of other post-communist countries, such elections did not take place simultaneously with general elections. In the Romanian case, the direct election of the President appeared to be a method of confirming the personalised power of Iliescu. The second difference was the very clear victory of both Iliescu and the NSF. Iliescu's victory was a rare example of an election where, although there was provision for a second ballot in the electoral law, none was necessary because one candidate obtained more than 50 per cent of the vote in the first round. As can be seen from Table 6.7, the NSF majority in the parliamentary elections – where it gained two-thirds of the vote – was also higher than that of Civic Forum in the Czech Republic (an example of a broad movement associated with carrying out the revolution) and the Bulgarian Socialist Party (an example of a reformed communist hierarchy retaining power).

Three reasons can be suggested for the victory of the NSF. One was that it combined, in a schizophrenic merger, both the prestige of revolutionary heroism of the sort enjoyed by the Czechoslovak citizens' movements and Solidarity with the organisational strength of a communist successor party. This was possible in part because Ceauşescu had been such a strong focus for popular hatred that the role of other leading communists had been to an extent submerged. The contention that the NSF was not a reincarnation of the Communist Party, and the inexperience of the electorate, added to this confusion. A second reason is simply the lack of opposition. The two most serious rivals of the NSF were the National Liberal Party and the National Peasant Party, which were both revivals of traditional, precommunist parties, and which won a total of only about 10 per cent of the vote. This was not inconsistent with the electoral support of historic parties elsewhere in the region. The Romanian situation differed, however, because none of the myriad of new parties which had formed was any more successful. The use of an election system based on proportional representation without a minimum threshold should have helped smaller parties, but the almost total lack of organised dissent under Ceauşescu had deprived the country of any basis on which such parties could build. It is notable, for example, that both the presidential candidates from the historic parties were émigrés who had not lived in Romania for decades, and who were therefore suspect to voters who had suffered so much over this period. The opposition also had a disadvantage compared to its Bulgarian counterpart in that it failed to unite in any kind of umbrella organisation which could harness all anti-NSF sentiment. Old political rivalries, preserved during emigration, bore some of the blame here. The disunity of the Romanian opposition contrasted, however, with the high degree of organisation among the country's Hungarian minority, who not only voted together in the parliamentary election, but were also successful in

Table 6.7 Romanian elections, 20 May 1990

Lower House (Chamber of Deputies)	% vote	Seats
National Salvation Front	66	263
Hungarian Democratic Federation of Romania	7	29
National Liberal Party	6	29
Romanian Ecological Movement	3	12
National Peasants Party – Christian Democratic Party	3	12
Alliance for the Unity of Romanians	2	9
Agrarian Democratic Party	2	9
Romanian Ecological Party	2	8
Romanian Socialist Democratic Party	1	5
Romanian Social Democratic Party	1	2
Others	7	9
Ethnic minorities	1	9
Total		396

N.B. The 119-seat Upper House (Senate) was elected simultaneously using a similar electoral system.

Presidency	% vote
Ion Iliescu (National Salvation Front)	85
Radu Câmpeanu (National Liberal)	11
Ion Raţiu (National Peasants)	4

Source: Deletant (1990); Nelson (1990).

delivering their vote to the National Liberal candidate opposing Iliescu as President.

A final reason contributing to the NSF's success was the less legitimate advantages it had gained from its prominence in taking over the country since Christmas, and its large degree of control over the rules of the election, such as party finance and media coverage, and the supervision of the voting process. However, while some irregularities in the conduct of the election were reported, the NSF victory was so massive that it cannot be held to have distorted the will of the voters as a whole.

Despite the overwhelming election victories, however, the government was still confronted by many problems, two of which were particularly grave. One was public violence. Riots involving ethnic Hungarians and Romanians in Tîrgu Mureş in March left three dead,[21] and an even more negative impression abroad was created in June, when miners were again transported into Bucharest to clear away students who had been protesting in University Square for two months. This time, there were six deaths, while the police stood by and did nothing.[22] The second problem was the economy. Like so many 1990 election victors, the NSF was to find that fulfilling its promises was more difficult than making them, and relatively little help could be expected from the west as Romania remained almost the least attractive country in Eastern Europe.

Yugoslavia

1990 was the year which marked the end of Yugoslav communism, and highlighted the divergent constellations of forces in each republic which were to lead their people into the unknown. It began with the 14th Congress of the League of Communists of Yugoslavia in January, which represented the demise of Yugoslavia as a communist and a multinational state: nationalism prevailed over communism. Although the Congress voted to introduce political pluralism by ending the communists' leading role, attempts by the League of Communists to reform itself were overtaken by the differences between the republics. Slovene proposals to restructure the federal party into eight independent parties, and, indeed, all other proposals presented by the Slovene delegation, were rejected outright.[23] The Slovene communists left the Congress and were joined by the Croats. From here onwards, although the Federal government and the Federal presidency continued to some extent to function, the party as a federal force did not.

Yugoslavia approached its first multi-party elections for more than half a century in a very different position from other East European states. First, since Yugoslavia had not been in the Soviet orbit, the disintegration of its communist system did not constitute a victory over an alien force, and this intensified the bitterness of the country's internal struggles. There was no unifying sense of national liberation. On the contrary: the ending of the Soviet threat and the example of the newly emerging democracies elsewhere in the region merely removed any motivation the elites of the very different republics could have had to combine forces. Secondly, when free elections took place at intervals later in the year, they were all at republic level, so that this crucial stage in democratic development did not take place at a federal, Yugoslav level. It must be noted particularly that virtually all the parties in the elections were, in essence, national parties: even where they did not designate their nationality in their formal title, or have a specifically nationalist programme, they none the less operated in one republic only.[24] (The major exception, Federal Prime Minister Marković's Alliance of Reform Forces, was an electoral failure.) In this regard, the Yugoslav situation resembled that in Czechoslovakia, where successful parties in the first elections were – with the exception of the Communists – either Czech or Slovak. Yet in two respects, the disintegration of the Yugoslav federation was pre-programmed to a far greater extent than in Czechoslovakia. In Yugoslavia, not even the communist successor parties entered the first elections as federal structures; and no elections took place at federal level. This was not only a historical nationalist legacy, but also a communist one. By impeding the development of a civil society with autonomous horizontal links between independent citizens within different republics, the communist system had largely precluded the possibility of any multinational articulation of common interests. Where

Textbox 6.2 Main events in Yugoslavia, 1990

January	*Yugoslavia* The League of Communists of Yugoslavia begins to collapse at its 14th Congress as the Slovenes leave, and the constitutional guarantee of the leading role of the League of Communists is abandoned.
	Serbia Serious disturbances in Kosovo, with numerous deaths.
February	*Slovenia* The Communists change their party name to Party of Democratic Reform.
March	*Slovenia* The constitution is amended to remove the word 'socialist' from the republic's name.
April	*Croatia* Elections, with a second round in May, are won by the Croatian Democratic Community, whose candidate Tudjman becomes President.
	Slovenia Multi-party elections to the Republican Assembly are held. Kučan, of the post-communist Party of Democratic Reform, is elected President, but the coalition DEMOS government is formed from six anti-communist parties.
May	*Croatia* Croats vote overwhelmingly for autonomy within Yugoslavia in a referendum, but attempts to negotiate this fail.
	Yugoslavia Jović of Serbia takes over the rotating Yugoslav presidency.
July	*Croatia* Croatia makes amendments to its constitution, including the removal of the word 'socialist' from the republic's name.
	Serbia The League of Communists of Serbia becomes Socialist Party of Serbia, with Milošević still leader. A referendum on changing the republic's constitution is won with a massive majority, but is boycotted by Albanians.
	Slovenia The republic's full sovereignty is declared by parliament.
August	*Croatia* The republic's communist member of the federal state presidency is replaced by its Prime Minister, Mesić.
September	*Serbia* The constitution is revised to legalise control over the autonomous provinces of Vojvodina and Kosovo.
October	*Croatia* The Serbs of the Krajina declare their autonomy from Croatia following an unofficial referendum in August.
November	*Bosnia-Herzegovina* In elections to the collective state presidency, all seven seats go to nationalist parties.
December	*Bosnia-Herzegovina* Second-round elections result in coalition government, as the vote is split along religious lines.
	Croatia A new constitution is passed, proclaiming sovereignty and the right to secede.
	Macedonia Gligorov, of the post-communist Party of Democratic Change, becomes President, while a minority 'government of experts' is formed.
	Montenegro The communists win elections.
	Serbia Milošević's post-communist Socialist Party of Serbia wins elections.
	Slovenia A referendum overwhelmingly opts for secession.

independent groups had managed to form, they were locally based, i.e. within a single republic or part thereof.

Since all the republics held elections in 1990, the developments in each will be briefly reviewed in the chronological order of the elections.[25]

Slovenia

Slovenia was the most economically developed, prosperous and culturally western part of the freest and most open communist country in Eastern Europe. It is therefore not surprising that it was eventually able to overcome the disadvantages of its origins in the largely war-torn Yugoslavia and become, by the second half of the 1990s, a leading candidate for integration into European structures. Such an outcome was even easier to predict, however, a decade earlier, before the setbacks of the bloody disintegration of Yugoslavia. In the second half of the 1980s, Slovenia was visibly developing a civil society more vibrant than any other in the entire communist world.[26] When it finally held elections in April 1990, it was marked by two features almost never found in combination elsewhere in Eastern Europe. One was a reformist Communist Party which had voluntarily pursued both economic reform, links with Western Europe, and internal democratisation. In this, it most closely resembled Hungary. The second feature was the development of independent political parties which was consequent to the revitalisation of a civil society. Unlike the Hungarian case, however, where politics to an extent remained an elite concern greeted by public apathy, in Slovenia the immediacy of the struggle against Belgrade-centred Serbian communist domination had mobilised the population into a direct involvement in, and identification with, the country's democratic process.

Both these features were reflected in the results of the election in April 1990. The parliamentary elections were won by the Democratic Opposition of Slovenia (DEMOS in Slovene), which was a broad anti-communist coalition containing six separate parties (see Table 6.8). However, the direct election of the president, which was held simultaneously, was won by the communist leader Milan Kučan, who defeated the DEMOS candidate in the second round. Kučan's victory reflected the duality of the political agenda in Slovenia. Despite the population's desire to move away from communism reflected in the parliamentary election, Kučan as an individual was trusted, on the basis of his track record, to protect Slovenian interests against the remnants of federal power in Belgrade.

Under the new DEMOS government, disputes with the federal authorities over budgetary matters and control of the military continued, and Slovene proposals formally to reshape Yugoslavia into a confederation of sovereign states were rejected. This led, in December 1990, to the holding of a

Table 6.8 Slovenian elections, 8 April 1990

Socio-Political Chamber[a]	% vote	Seats
Slovenian Christian Democrats	13	11
Slovenian Farmers' Alliance	13	11
Slovenian Democratic Alliance	10	8
Greens of Slovenia	9	8
Social Democratic Alliance of Slovenia	7	6
Slovene Craftsmen's Party	4	3
[DEMOS (Democratic Opposition of Slovenia)	*55*	*47]*
League of Communists of Slovenia-Party of Democratic Reform	17	14
League of Socialist Youth of Slovenia-Liberal Party	14	12
Socialist Alliance of Slovenia	6	5
Italian/Hungarian minority (reserved seats)		2
Total		80

a. There were two other chambers in the Assembly, which derived from its origins within the communist system – the Chamber of Associated Labour, which was not elected on a party basis, and a Chamber of Municipalities.

Source: Statistični urad Republike Slovenije (1995, p. 105); Cohen (1995, p. 92–3).

Presidency	% vote	
	Round 1 (8.4)	Round 2 (22.4)
Milan Kučan (LCS-PDR)	44	58
Jože Pučnik (DEMOS)	26	42
Josip Kramberger (Independent)	19	
Marko Demsar (LSYS-LP)	10	

Source: Allcock (1991, p. 359).

referendum which demonstrated overwhelming support for independence, with 88.5 per cent in favour on a 93.5 per cent turnout.[27]

Croatia

In Croatia, both the development of the party system and the 1990 elections results were very different from in Slovenia. Whereas the pluralisation of Slovene politics was a gradual process, in Croatia political parties sprung up within a very short period in 1989 and 1990, and many opposition leaders were former communists who had lost their positions when the nationalist upsurge in Croatia in 1971 had been suppressed.[28] This, together with the problems Croatia faced because of the republic's multinational population, meant that national issues were far more dominant politically in Croatia than in Slovenia. The fact that the country then became embroiled in war for the first few years of its independent existence further impeded the development of pluralist party politics.

The elections held in late April and early May 1990 were won comfortably

Table 6.9 Croatian elections, 22 April/6–7 May 1990

Socio-Political Chamber[a]	% vote (1st round)	Seats
Croatian Democratic Alliance	42	54
League of Communists-Party of Democratic Change	35	19
Serbian Democratic Party	2	1
Others	22	6
Total		80

a. As in Slovenia, this was the most important of the three chambers inherited from the communist system.

Source: Cohen (1995, p. 100).

by the Croatian Democratic Community, a coalition of six parties.[29] The victors were helped by the electoral system, which – unlike the proportional representation used in Slovenia – comprised single-member constituencies and a second round of balloting if no candidate received more than 50 per cent of the vote in the first. This gave them two-thirds of the seats in the republic's most important parliamentary chamber although they had received only 42 per cent of the vote (see Table 6.9).[30] Although the Croatian communists had done much better in terms of the percentage parliamentary vote than their Slovenian counterparts, they were left with far less representation, particularly since the leader of the largest party in the winning coalition, the Croatian Democratic Community's Franjo Tudjman, was elected president by the new parliament. The Croatian communists were also doomed to a further fall in popularity by the fact that they were the chosen party of most of the republic's Serbian voters, who comprised about twelve per cent of the republic's inhabitants.

Tensions increased after the elections because President Tudjman was known as a Croatian nationalist, and the Serbian minority was unenthusiastic about the dismantling of the federation, which would end, and probably reverse, their previously rather privileged position.[31] Resistance to Tudjman was particularly strong in the regions referred to by the Serbs as the Krajina or borderlands, where the majority of the population was Serbian.[32] The second half of 1990 was therefore marked by disputes over policing, an unofficial referendum among Serbs on autonomy, and an eventual declaration of Serb autonomy.

Bosnia-Herzegovina

In many respects, Bosnia-Herzegovina was one of the Yugoslav republics least prepared for democratic elections. Unlike Slovenia and Croatia, and even Serbia, the area had no historical experience of representative institutions,[33] and had had one of the most conservative, hardline communist leaderships in the country in the late communist period. What did appear to be

Table 6.10 Bosnia-Herzegovina elections, 18 November/2 December 1990

Chamber of Citizens and Chamber of Municipalities	Seats
Party of Democratic Action (Muslim)	86
Serbian Democratic Party	72
Croatian Democratic Community	44
League of Communists-Party of Democratic Change	19
Alliance of Reform Forces	12
Other	7
Total	240

Source: Allcock (1994a, p. 82).

in its favour was the fact that it was one of the most genuinely multi-ethnic parts of the country, with a population of Muslims, Serbs and Croats (see Table 3.2). However, the population was most intermixed in the towns, where the more urban Muslim majority tended to live, and the multicultural atmosphere of the cosmopolitan capital Sarajevo was very different from that in the villages.

When elections were held in November 1990, the vote split very strongly along ethnic lines.[34] As can be seen from Table 6.10, the three most successful parties represented the Muslim, Serbian and Croatian communities respectively; these were followed by the reformed Communist Party – which received a lower percentage of the vote than its counterparts elsewhere in Yugoslavia – and the Marković's Alliance of Reform Forces. The leader of the Muslim Party for Democratic Action, Alija Izetbegović, was appointed President by the collective state presidency which had been elected at the same time as the parliament. A Croat was appointed Prime Minister, and a Serb as Chair of the parliament. Such a complex power-sharing arrangement was inherently likely to lead to immobilism in Bosnian politics. However, this was largely an academic problem as Bosnia's instability was soon to be caused, fatally, by events elsewhere in Yugoslavia.[35]

Macedonia

Macedonia was the poorest of Yugoslavia's six republics, and shared Bosnia's problems of lacking any democratic experience. The Macedonians were a relatively new nation, granted their own territory and recognition of their language by the Yugoslav communists after 1945.[36] The most successful party in the November 1990 elections in fact claimed the legacy of the Internal Macedonian Revolutionary Organisation (IMRO), which had been notorious in interwar Europe for its use of terrorism to pursue its nationalist aims. The reformed Communist Party, called the Party of Democratic Change, came second, followed by the Party for Democratic Prosperity, which represented the republic's substantial Albanian minority. As can be seen from Table 6.11,

Table 6.11 Macedonian election, 9 November/29November/9December 1990

	% vote first round	Seats
Internal Macedonian Revolutionary Organisation-Democratic Party for Macedonian National Unity	12	38
League of Communists of Macedonia-Party of Democratic Change	18	31
Party for Democratic Prosperity	12	22
Alliance of Reform Forces	11	19
Party for Democratic Prosperity/National Democratic Party	1	5
Socialist Party of Macedonia	6	4
Party of Yugoslavs in Macedonia	1	2
National Democratic Party	0	1
Independents	1	3
Total		120

N.B. Some parties stood with different coalition partners in different constituencies.

Source: EIU Country Profile Macedonia, Serbia-Montenegro 1994–95 (1995, p. 7); Allcock (1991, p. 332); *Eastern Europe and the Commonwealth of Independent States 1994* (1994, p. 443); Chiclet (1994, pp. 146–7).

this produced a parliament in which the formation of a majority government was almost impossible. This eventually led, in the first quarter of 1991, to the formation of a government largely comprising non-party experts – a pattern later to become familiar in its Balkan neighbours, Bulgaria and Romania. The leading figure in Macedonian politics, the communist Kiro Gligorov, was to become the President, elected by parliament in early 1991.

Serbia

The Serbian elections of December 1990 appeared to confirm Serbia's identity as a Balkan rather than a Central European country: Milošević's Socialist Party of Serbia – a nationalist communist successor party – was a clear victor in the elections. The result therefore resembled the electoral outcomes in Romania and Bulgaria, while Slovenia, for example, could more easily be compared to Czechoslovakia or Hungary. It is true that the Serbian socialists were aided by a majoritarian electoral system, and actually obtained less than half of the votes cast, yet Milošević himself was elected President with 65 per cent support in direct elections.[37] It therefore appeared to be Milošević's nationalism that was preserving support for the former communists.

However, a look at the election results (Table 6.12) and the weak support for all the opposition parties indicates a further characteristic of Serbian politics, namely, that the elections were held before other, non-communist political forces had had a chance to organise. The socialists' opponents lacked any organisational infrastructure or easy access to the media.

Table 6.12 Serbian elections, 9/23 December 1990

Serbian Assembly	Seats
Socialist Party of Serbia	194
Serbian Movement for Renewal	19
Democratic Community of Vojvodina Hungarians	8
Democratic Party	7
Party of Democratic Action	3
Alliance of Peasants of Serbia	2
Alliance of Reform Forces of Vojvodina	2
Others	7
Independents	8
Total	250

Source: Allcock (1994, p. 638).

Presidency	% vote
Slobodan Milošević, Socialist Party of Serbia	65
Vuk Drašković, Serbian Movement for Renewal	16
Ivan Djurić, Alliance of Reform Forces	6
Sulejman Ugljanin, Party of Democratic Action	2
Others (28)	11

Source: Andrejevich (1990b, p. 38).

Nationalism was the dominant ideology of most political parties in Serbia, present not only in the Socialist Party of Serbia, but also among Milošević's anti-communist rivals.[38] Furthermore, two parties representing the Hungarian minority in Vojvodina entered parliament, the Party of Democratic Action was Muslim, and an Albanian party was lacking merely because of the decision of the Albanians of Kosovo to boycott the elections. Nationalism was a particularly potent force in Serbia – and one which Milošević skilfully exploited – not only because the republic contained ethnic minorities to whom the Serbs were denying autonomy, but also because there was a substantial number of Serbs living outside the republic.[39] As the disintegration of Yugoslavia became imminent, the latter were threatened with the prospect of becoming ethnic minorities if the republics in which they lived broke away from Serbia. There was therefore a strong incentive for Serbia to oppose the end of the federation or its conversion into a weak confederation, and to demand that, should the federation end, the internal republican borders had to be renegotiated – effectively allowing for the creation of a Greater Serbia. The strong Serb influence in the Yugoslav People's Army – which became even stronger in the course of 1990 and 1991, as non-Serbs increasingly refused to be conscripted into it, and non-Serb officers joined their own republics' defence forces – gave Serbia the potential to pursue these demands by force. By the time of the 1990 elections, there had already been tension between the Army and the Croatian

Republic in the Serb-populated Krajina area. The Serbian position on minorities was, however, and remained, fundamentally contradictory, since Serbia was unwilling to grant the Albanians of Kosovo the autonomy it demanded for Serbian minorities elsewhere in Yugoslavia.

Montenegro

Montenegro was traditionally Serbia's closest ally, and Montenegrins had – in comparison to their small number in the population as a whole – been very strongly represented in the League of Communists of Yugoslavia. It was therefore not surprising that Montenegro was the only republic apart from Serbia to produce a post-communist election victory. It should be noted, however, that in January 1989, the old guard of Montenegrin communists had been dislodged from power and replaced by a younger and more reformist leadership under Momir Bulatović, who was to win the presidential election in December 1990.

As can be seen from Table 6.13, the party constellation produced by the Montenegrin elections was very similar to that in Serbia. The republic's strong pro-federal orientation is reflected, however, in the fact that the second largest party in parliament (albeit it way behind the communists) was Marković's Alliance of Reform Forces. The People's Party supported a union of Serbia and Montenegro in the case of the Yugoslav federation ending.[40] Finally, the Democratic Coalition comprised parties of the Muslim and Albanian minorities in the country. The election results were a fair indication of future developments, where Montenegro was to end up as Serbia's only partner in the new Federal Republic of Yugoslavia created in April 1992.

Table 6.13 Montenegrin elections, 9/23 December 1990

National Assembly	Seats
League of Communists of Montenegro/Democratic Party of Socialists	83
Alliance of Reform Forces	17
Democratic Coalition	13
People's Party	12
Total	125

Source: Cohen (1995, p. 158).

Presidency	% vote	
	1st round	2nd round
Momir Bulatović, League of Communists of Montenegro	42	76
Ljubiša Stanković, Alliance of Reform Forces	17	24

Source: Allcock (1991, p. 339); Andrejevich (1990b, p. 38).

Conclusion

By the end of 1990, most of Eastern Europe was politically unrecognisable when compared to its situation a year before. The electoral process, despite isolated irregularities, was generally well managed. It achieved its main purpose, which was to select governments that – unlike their communist predecessors – could claim democratic legitimacy when confronting their countries' deep-seated problems. This did not necessarily mean that they knew what to do when they were sworn into office and finally had the chance to untangle the economic mess which the communist system had become. With the exception of Eastern Germany, their compatriots remained the same, and there was relatively little expertise available. Almost everyone was learning on the job. In this respect, the successes were more remarkable than the failures.

Albania and Yugoslavia differed, however, from the former Warsaw Pact states because the year 1990 was largely a prelude to even greater changes which took place in 1991. As discussed in Chapter 4, for Yugoslavia the electoral sequence (that is, holding republican elections but no federal ones) was crucial: they had helped select the major actors in the tragedy which was to follow.

Notes

1. For summarised accounts of the events of 1990, see Milivojević (1991); Staar (1991, pp. 252–9); Vickers (1994).
2. See Loloci (1994).
3. Staar (1991); Zanga (1991a and 1991b).
4. Szajkowski (1994, p. 3).
5. Details of the 1990 elections can be found in Ashley (1990); Bell (1993); Glenny (1993, pp. 164–92); Szajkowski (1994, pp. 93–7).
6. See Perry (1990).
7. See Wightman (1991).
8. Three per cent in the case of the Slovak National Council.
9. The Stalinist purges in Czechoslovakia in the early 1950s had been particularly bad because the communists felt a need to gain firm control on a society with strong democratic traditions; similarly, entrepreneurship of any kind was particularly threatening to communists because it had been so central to interwar society.
10. On the elections, see von Beyme (1991); Osmond (1992).
11. Irving and Paterson (1991); Kitschelt (1991).
12. See Henderson (1993).
13. See Batt (1990); Körösényi (1991); Pittaway and Swain (1994).
14. For an analysis of the effects of the electoral system, see Gabel (1995).
15. See Simon (1993).
16. See Glenny (1993, pp. 72–94), and for more comprehensive coverage, Bozóki *et al.* (1992).

17. For Wałęsa's role, see Batt (1991, pp. 83–8); Glenny (1993, pp. 50–71); Kurski (1993).
18. See Zubek (1992).
19. See Almond (1990); Calinescu and Tismaneanu (1991); Nelson (1991); Rady (1992).
20. On the elections, see Deletant (1990); Mihut (1994); Gallagher (1991); Nelson (1990).
21. Gallagher (1995, pp. 86–96).
22. See Tismaneanu and Tudoran (1993).
23. Silber and Little (1995, pp. 84–6).
24. Seroka (1993, p. 106); Allcock (1994c, pp. 628–9).
25. For basic details on all six elections, see Allcock (1991).
26. See Bibič (1993); Mastnak (1994).
27. Carmichael (1994, p. 629).
28. Cohen (1995, p. 96); Pusić (1994).
29. Andrejevich (1990a); Bennett (1995, pp. 123–31).
30. The Yugoslav republics had complex tricameral republican parliaments, which caused considerable difficulties when they were democratically elected. See Zakosek (1994, pp. 88–91).
31. See Almond (1994, pp. 24–5).
32. There is no technical definition of what is meant by the Krajina. In the 1990s, the term has usually been used to denote the Serb-populated Croatian territory adjacent to the border of Bosnia-Herzegovina which resisted Croatian government control prior to August 1995, although it is also used for Serbian-populated territory within Bosnia-Herzegovina. See Bennett (1995, p. 125); Cohen (1995, pp. 128–30); Klemencić (1996, p. 111).
33. Allcock (1994c, pp. 627–8).
34. Allcock (1994a, pp. 79–84).
35. For further background on Bosnia, see Malcolm (1994).
36. For background on the Macedonian nation, see Allcock (1994d); Poulton (1995).
37. Samardžić (1994).
38. Millar (1994).
39. The 1981 census showed nearly one quarter of citizens who identified themselves as Serbs – about two million people – living outside Serbia. See Table 3.2.
40. Cohen (1995, p. 158).

PART III

REFORM AGENDAS

CHAPTER 7

The nature of
post-communist transitions

Some of the questions about how to build post-communist systems were solved in the course of the overthrow of communism and the elections that followed. However, there was still much to be decided after 1990 in Eastern Europe, and in the former USSR the process of post-communist reconstruction only really began in 1992.

The point has often been made that the transition to democracy is particularly problematic in the post-communist world because the establishment of democratic institutions coincides with economic transi-tion. Additionally, the monolithic nature of post-Stalinist society had removed all autonomous social institutions except the Church. However, there were also many respects in which the transition was simpler. There was a high level of agreement on the desirability of democracy: post-communist societies generally agreed on where their transition was going, even if they did not understand the full implications of living in an open, democratic society. Further, there was an element of 'decolonisation' in the demise of many communist regimes, and the sense of rejecting an alien model helped unify the populace in its search for an alternative. Communist societies also lacked strong vested economic interests: although elites enjoyed privileges and economic advantages which they were loathe to lose, these were generally considered illegitimate and not legally anchored in property rights. The distribution of wealth was far more even than in most Western societies, the Ceauşescu family palaces notwithstanding. The military, too, did not pose a major internal threat in most countries.[1] Finally, one advantageous legacy of communism was the good level of basic education of the population at large.[2]

Nevertheless, in the early 1990s formerly communist states were left with a formidable list of problems all urgently in need of solution. They are presented below in the sort of random order in which they became evident in the early stages of transition:

163

- the creation of democratic institutions – parties, elections, constitutions;
- the introduction of a market economy – privatisation, the removal of state subsidies and price controls, and the establishment of the economic institutions of a free market;
- social problems – unemployment, inequality, crime;
- ethnic problems;
- coming to terms with the past – dealing with the crimes of the former communist regimes.

It is possible to categorise these problems, and thereby explain their significance for post-communist states. Writing in 1990, Ralf Dahrendorf pointed out that different reform tasks take different timespans to deal with: constitutional reform, i.e. the creation of a democratic institutional framework, takes months, economic reform is likely to take years, and changing the social foundations of society may take decades.[3] Claus Offe, in 1991, discussed the problem of the 'triple transition' facing East Central Europe, which may be applied to the post-communist world as a whole. He defined what he describes as 'three hierarchical levels of decision-making'.[4] The first and most fundamental level concerns decisions 'about who "we" are, i.e. a decision on identity, citizenship, and the territorial as well as social and cultural boundaries of the nation-state'. This involves the longest time-span, since nations tend to last for centuries, and decisions are most affected by emotive factors – 'passions, virtue, honour, and patriotism'. The second level relates to the constitution or the institutional framework of the 'regime', which is established using reason, and involves decisions that would normally stretch over decades. The third level comprises the everyday politics of deciding on 'who get what, when and how – in terms of both political power and economic resources'. Decisions here relate to interest, rather than reason or emotion, but governments and the laws they pass often only last for a few years. The challenge facing the former 'Soviet empire' was particularly great because of the simultaneity of transformations taking place on all three levels – the 'triple transition' – which places enormous burdens on a state's decision-making apparatus.[5]

Offe's framework is useful in categorising the problems which were to confront post-communist societies, and will be used to structure the analysis that follows.

Nationhood

It was the first level of decision-making, about questions of nationhood, which was to cause the most spectacular crises. Communist leaderships had always faced difficulties in harnessing the force of nationalism for their own ends because their legitimating ideology of Marxism-Leninism regarded nationalist sentiment as retrograde. In Eastern Europe, the situation was exacerbated by the fact that there were often Russophobic elements to local nationalism, the most notable case being Poland. Engendering strong feelings of patriotism was therefore least dangerous in the states where the communists had come to power by their own efforts: the Soviet Union, Yugoslavia and Albania (although, in the long term, it did not prove effective). However, many of the Warsaw Pact states in Eastern Europe began to veer in a more nationalist direction in the 1980s, as all other efforts to maintain their legitimacy or authority were conspicuously failing. Some minority nationalism also began to emerge –among, for example, Hungarians in Romania and Turks in Bulgaria – although this may be regarded largely as a response to the threats posed by the majority nationalism being promoted by the communist rulers.[6]

There were a number of reasons why nationalism became a dominant issue in post-communist politics. Democratisation brought obvious advantages for national minorities, since the general freedom to air grievances allowed them to raise problems which they had not previously been able to present for public discussion. Citizens also gained the autonomy to organise themselves politically according to sectional interests, and many national minorities chose to form their own political parties. Attempts to ban such parties – for example, in Bulgaria and Albania – ignored the vital issue of why sections of the population considered them desirable. The redistribution processes of post-communism forced minorities not only to promote their own interests, but also to safeguard them. As the foci of both political and economic power shifted, it was possible for ethnic groups to become collective losers in the process.

The post-communist transformation gave an impetus to majority nationalism as well. The removal of communist symbols left a vacuum which was filled by national symbols as the striving for some form of continuity looked back to emblems from the past. This was frequently an issue of political contention, as different parties interpreted the pre-communist past in incompatible ways, and national symbols were often perceived by minorities as exclusive. General tendencies towards xenophobia – which literally means fear rather than hatred of the alien – increased as more open societies exposed wide sectors of the population to foreign influences for the first time. Under communism, international relations had been purely an elite concern, and personnel who dealt with Westerners were particularly strictly vetted. In the 1990s, however, anyone could trade with the West, ordinary people could travel westward and at home they were confronted by the economic power of foreign companies. Their unfamiliarity with the complexity of free societies frequently left them with a feeling of vulnerability and of being exploited and cheated, and such anxieties were not hard to exploit politically. Finally, since nationalist issues were relatively easy to explain to the electorate, they were a tempting tool in the hands of politicians. Nationalism was used not merely by new political forces struggling for national independence, but also by communists struggling to retain a grasp on power. The prime example of this phenomenon was the Serbian communist leader Slobodan Milošević, who in 1997 had been in power longer than any other leader in the post-communist world.

There were also more general explanations of the power of nationalism. The simplest idea is that of the 'freezer' effect: communism had merely put the traditional national enmities of Eastern Europe on ice for forty years, and they emerged perfectly preserved when the system changed. Nationalist myths fell on particularly fertile ground in societies where communism had robbed citizens of objective information about their own histories, leaving them ill-equipped to differentiate between true and false and half-truths. Furthermore, communist states had singularly failed to construct political nations, i.e. citizens who were bound to their political community regardless of ethnicity. All politics was inauthentic in communist society, and belief in the communist state entity in which people had lived sometimes collapsed as quickly as the regimes themselves. The collapse of weak communist institutions often led to their replacement by nationalism as an integrating force, because there was no other available. Democratic or political integration – a belief in the legitimacy of legal institutions – develops slowly, over decades, and was therefore not an available option to the newly elected governments. Economic integration – a belief in the material efficacy of the new system – also failed everywhere, with the possible exception of the Czech Republic and Eastern Germany.[7]

Finally, an important aspect of 'triple transition' was that during post-communist transformation everything was negotiable: the distribution of power and material benefits; constitutional rules; and territorial boundaries and definitions of citizenship. The definition of citizenship was most crucially at issue in Estonia and Latvia, where there were major problems surrounding the status and voting rights of people living on the territory of the new states; but there was also controversy, for example, in Slovakia and Macedonia, where new constitutions were perceived to place Hungarian and Albanian minorities respectively in the symbolic position of being second-class citizens, who did not belong to the mainstream of the political community.[8] But territorial boundaries were also placed in question. For example, the Serbs of the Krajina questioned (with force of arms) whether they were obliged to remain in Croatia if Yugoslavia ceased to exist; and it was even at one point suggested that, since the southern Slovak border with Hungary had been established as the border with Czechoslovakia by the post-World War I Treaty of Trianon, it might possibly be free for renegotiation when an independent Slovak state was formed. This leads on to an important point defining the fate of minority groups under post-communism.

Communist states differentiated 'nations' and 'nationalities' or national minorities. Nations were self-contained units who lived on the territory of a state containing another nation or nations. Under communist federalism, they were normally assigned their own republic. The Slovaks, Estonians and

Croats, to name but a few examples, fell into this category. Nationalities, however, were part of an ethnic group which had a state elsewhere, and were entitled, at best, to autonomy. Hungarian and Albanian minorities fell into this category. They were minorities in two senses: minorities in the states in which they lived, and minorities of their nation as a whole. This differentiation was crucial as the communist federations broke up, as they all came apart at the boundaries of their republics. Groups recognised as nations – for example, the Macedonians, Moldovans and Belarusians – gained independence. Albanian, Serbian and Hungarian minorities did not. Nor did many smaller groups in the former Soviet Union, such as the Tartars and the Chechens. This was where major points of nationalist tension existed.

Constitutions

The second level of politics involves establishing the ground rules of the democratic game. We shall concentrate here on the two main constitutional choices that had to be made when constructing the institutional framework for a democratic polity.[9] The first is the distribution of executive power. It may be concentrated in the hands of a Prime Minister and government which reflect the composition of parliament, while the President is a figurehead with limited constitutional power. This is normally referred to as parliamentarism. Or it may, in a presidential system, be vested in the figure of a directly elected President who chooses their own Prime Minister, albeit constrained by the need to have legislation passed by the parliament. Both the legislature and execu-tive has an electoral mandate, and hence its own source of legitimacy. Semi-presidential systems comprise an (often unclear and contested) combi-nation of both. The second major choice relates to the electoral system, which is in fact normally determined by election laws rather than constitutional provisions. The rules of elections directly affect the party composition of parliament, and, in the longer term, the development of a party system. A majoritarian system, in which the single candidate who wins the most votes in a constituency gains a seat in parliament, tends to promote the development of a two-party system.[10] Proportional representation (PR), where a party is awarded a number of seats commensurate to the votes cast for its list of candidates, normally leads to a higher number of parties in parliament.

In Chapter 1, we argued that the coincidence of having to rebuild society, economy and polity simultaneously is a reason for naming the processes of change underway in Eastern Europe and the former Soviet Union revolu-tionary. However, revolutionary change in post-communism is negotiated, and this was most apparent when dealing with questions such as the role of the President, and the means by which the first democratic parliament – the one most likely to effect lasting constitutional changes – was to be elected. In many cases, particularly in Eastern Europe, the negotiating parties imperfectly understood the consequences which their decisions would have. In the early stages of negotiation, some Communist Parties evaluated their chances of retaining the presidency highly, and were therefore in favour of strong presidential powers. Yet the presidency was often to end up in the hands of their opponents. Similar miscalculations took place over the effects of majoritarian electoral systems.[11] Elsewhere, in much of Yugoslavia and the post-Soviet newly independent states (NIS), former communists made more accurate calculations, or were in a stronger negotiating position, and retained a grip on power.

Parliamentarism versus presidentialism

It is tempting to argue that parliamentary systems are more democratic than presidential ones. Arend Lijphart, in a survey of 22 countries which had been continuously democratic since World War II,[12] found that 18 of them were parliamentary. Only the United States had a clear presidential system, and in Finland, France and Switzerland, the system was mixed. When reviewing the non-communist states in the 'Third Wave' of democratisation, it can also be noted that whereas presidentialism prevails in Latin America, the countries of Southern Europe incline towards parliamentarism. If we look at post-communist states, the tendency towards presidentialism increases as one moves eastward. The Czech Republic, Hungary, Slovakia and Slovenia (the latter in spite of having a directly elected President) are basically parliamentary systems. Bulgaria, Poland and Romania all have a stronger, and directly elected,[13] Presidents, although Poland, the country most noted for its semi-presidentialism, was thought to be moving away from this model after Wałęsa's defeat at the end of 1995. In the rest of former Yugoslavia and most of the NIS, the tendency was towards presidentialism.[14]

There are numerous arguments against presidentialism.[15] They have been put most effectively by Juan Linz,[16] who has identified a number of disadvantages, some of which are particularly grave. First, presidential systems beget 'divided sovereignty', whereby conflict exists between a popularly elected President who has the right to initiate government programmes, and a popularly elected legislature. In the single most famous and durable presidential system of the democratic world, the United States, the executive has a conspicuous failure rate in getting its legislation passed. In the most commonly discussed Western semi-presidential system, the French Fifth Republic, democratic consolidation was assisted by the fact that the presidency and parliament were initially held by politicians of similar complexion for nearly a quarter of a century. Second, presidential systems make politics a 'zero-sum game'. The powers of a presidency are large, even when balanced by those of an elected legislature. Capturing the presidency is therefore very important and creates a 'winner takes all' atmosphere – it is the ultimate majoritarian electoral system. Furthermore, the risks of presidentialism are greatest in new and weak democracies. In a well-developed civil society, political parties, interest associations, strong legal checks and well-defined institutional roles can check some of the dangers of a presidential system. Unfortunately, these have been rare in post-communist states and without them there is the possibility of authoritarianism re-emerging, or democracy becoming 'delegative democracy'.[17] Delegative democracy is a term coined to describe imperfect transitions to democracy. The aim of moving towards democracy is to produce a political system that is representative of the people because of elections, and to have the people's representatives accountable *during* their period in office to their electorate. Delegative democracy only satisfies the first half of this formula. Leaders are elected, but 'whoever wins election to the presidency is thereby entitled to govern as he or she sees fit, constrained only by the hard facts of existing power relations and by a constitutionally limited term of office'.[18] In other words, democracy is secured as the regular, periodic transfer of power by elections, but the only constraints on the use of power are what a leader is allowed to get away with by other elite members.

In the periods covered in Chapters 8 and 9 presidential systems did not fully develop into delegative democracy in most of the countries we are looking at. (The exception might be some of the former Yugoslav states. However, the wars between and in these states conditioned political development heavily so that executive power developed under peculiar circumstances.)[19] More common in 1991–93 was 'insecure presidentialism' – debate and negotiation over what powers the President and parliament should have.[20] The results of debate, where there were results, were mixed. Russia, at the end of 1993, created a presidential system by constitutional referendum. Subsequently, Russia, Belarus and Moldova all began to manifest signs of delegative democracy (see Chapter 11). Elsewhere, and excluding former Yugoslavia, the picture was more mixed. The issue of sovereignty was blurred in Lithuania by the reformed Communist Party's capturing both parliamentary power and the presidency. Ukraine has only recently (June 1996) produced a constitution with provision for a strong presidency; the recent Polish draft constitution contains more restricted presidential powers. Both Ukraine and Poland have suffered long debate over the merits of a presidential system and frequent squabbles over the respective powers of parliament and President.

Presidentialism, does, however, have some advantages in providing strong leadership. Views on the desirability of this vary throughout the post-communist world. The *New Democracies Barometer*, a multinational public opinion survey covering ten post-communist states, asked respondents in 1995 if they agreed with the statement that it was 'best to get rid of parliament and elections and have a strong leader who can quickly decide everything'. Support for this option was highest in the two most eastern countries surveyed, the Ukraine (where 67 per cent agreed strongly or somewhat), and Belarus (where the figure was 56 per cent).[21] Such views obviously offer fertile ground for the establishment and maintenance of a presidential system. Interestingly, support for a 'strong leader' was by far the lowest – 5 per cent, as against a ten-country average of 29 per cent – in Croatia, which had by far the strongest president of all the remaining countries.

It is the exceptional demands of the 'triple transition' that can make it advantageous to have a strong executive to oversee the process of reform. A presidential system may be more likely to produce this than the fragmented parliaments elected in countries with no strong party system.[22] Where Presidents are reformers, the power of their post allows them to push through reforms that do not necessarily have either mass, or significant elite, support. Presidentialism can thus be a factor boosting revolution and conflict at the cost of negotiation and compromise. The clearest example of a reforming President with a divided and more conservative parliament is Boris Yeltsin in Russia. A second President approaching this category is Albania's Sali Berisha, who was not in fact popularly elected, but obtained a two-thirds parliamentary majority, in May/June 1996, by elections condemned as unfair at home and abroad. Both Yeltsin and Berisha have obtained the support of many Western countries in spite of reservations about their democratic credentials simply because their countries have no obvious viable alternative likely to continue what are perceived to be urgently necessary reforms leading to the foundation of a functioning market economy. However, a President who is linked to old elites (like Ukraine's President Kravchuk) can use the power of the post to slow reform and dull one or more aspects of revolutionary change. Old power structures are thereby preserved. These processes can also occur in parliamentary systems, but are less likely to take extreme forms. Parliamentary systems share power out more than presidential systems and allow for a broader range of inputs into the policy process. In other words, they create negotiation of some sort or other. Pressure to moderate or accelerate change can be fed directly into the policy-making process in an orderly, institutionalised fashion through parliament and its committees by representatives of different political, social and economic interests; parliamentary alliances and bargaining can stimulate pacts that may stop or stimulate policy in the short term and act to stabilise politics in the medium to long term.

Electoral systems

The post-communist world is characterised by a large variety of electoral systems, and the diversity has been increased by the tendency in some countries (for example, Poland and Albania) to try out amended systems in successive elections. It is this tendency which led to many choices over electoral systems being made in the period after the first elections of 1990. Nevertheless, there are some general trends which can be identified.[23]

First, where majoritarian systems with single-member constituencies are to be found, it is the post-communist norm to follow the French model whereby the successful candidate is required to obtain 50 per cent of the vote. If no candidate succeeds in the first round, a second ballot is held, normally two weeks later, in which only the leading candidates are permitted to stand. While this system does favour larger parties, it also encourages some degree of coalition-building to take place between the first and second round, and obviates the citizens' need to indulge in complex tactical voting in the first round.

Secondly, where a PR system is used, it is normal for there to be a minimum threshold parties have to reach in order to be awarded any seats at all. This practice has been copied from the Federal Republic of Germany, which in 1949 adopted a 5 per cent threshold to avoid the severe party fragmentation which helped bring down the interwar Weimar Republic. In some post-communist states (e.g. the Czech Republic and Slovakia), the threshold is 5 per cent, while in others it is 4 per cent, or sometimes 3 per cent. It is also common for higher thresholds to be set for multi-party coalitions. This discourages a multitude of parties from forming tactical coalitions in order to enter parliament which subsequently break up and produce a fragmented parliament.

Thirdly, there is an unusually high number of mixed electoral systems, where some deputies are elected on the majoritarian system from single-member constituencies, and others are selected by PR from national or regional party lists. Russia, Poland, Hungary and Albania are examples of mixed systems. Mixed systems are again based on the German model, where every voter has to cast a first vote for a constituency candidate, who will win if they gain the highest number of votes in their constituency, and a second vote for a party list, which will be allotted seats if the party gains more than 5 per cent of the national vote or three directly elected deputies. However, a crucial fact about the German system which is frequently overlooked is that the number of directly elected deputies each party has gained from first votes is subtracted from the number of seats to which it is entitled under PR *before* these are allocated. Hence the overall parliamentary balance is one of PR. In many of the mixed systems of the post-communist world (e.g. Russia) this adjustment between first and second votes does not take place, so that a party that does well in the single-member constituencies takes this advantage with them to parliament. Mixed systems are in part a consequence of negotiated revolution: they represent a compromise between differences of opinion based on the perceived interests of negotiating partners.

When examining the outcomes of post-communist election systems, volatility is a factor that must be taken into account. Comparisons of Western democracies have been undertaken which examine the degree of disproportionality (i.e. the difference between percentage of votes and percentage of seats obtained by parties).[24] It is extremely hard to add data from the 'new democracies' to these existing tables, because a high degree of disproportionality is a characteristic of new electoral systems. The evidence suggests that minimum thresholds in PR systems fail to work effectively the first time round, when the electorate have not had the time to adapt to their implications. Instead of promoting the consolidation of the party system, they merely increase the proportion of citizens whose votes have not been translated into parliamentary representation. The 'wasted vote' given to parties gaining less than the required 5 per cent decreased from 19 per cent in the 1992 Czech National Council elections to 11 per cent in the 1996 Czech elections, and from 20 per cent in the 1992 Slovak National Council elections to 14 per cent in the 1994 Slovak elections. In Bulgaria, with a 4 per cent clause, 25 per cent of the vote was wasted in 1991, when only three parties entered parliament, but only 16 per cent in 1994, when five parties crossed the threshold. Minimum thresholds also fail to work properly first time round because particularly difficult decisions face new political parties who need to merge in order to obtain the crucial percentage of votes necessary to have a share of the parliamentary seats. It would be unfair to suggest that their main handicap is the personal or ideological squabbling between their leaders. Their dilemma is also that they may not have a firm base of dedicated supporters who will follow their lead into a larger coalition. Two parties with 3 or 4 per cent of the vote in the opinion polls are not guaranteed 7 per cent of the vote if they stand together, whether as a newly merged party or a coalition. Their potential supporters' mild distaste for the new partner may well prevail over a weak allegiance to the original party and drive them elsewhere. However, PR systems are more likely to stabilise over time and produce a lower level of disproportionality than majoritarian systems.

Russia has thus far proved an exception to this rule. The 1995 Duma elections created a higher level of disproportionality than the 1993 elections. Eight parties managed to get over the 5 per cent threshold in 1993 with 87 per cent of the PR vote between them. In 1995 only four parties made it over the threshold, collecting a mere 50.5 per cent of votes between them. The growth in 'wasted' votes can be explained by the far larger number of parties and electoral movements in the 1995 elections compared to 1993. Several parties were barred from the PR vote in 1993 since they failed to collect the number of signatures necessary to register on the ballot; this helped push 8 out of the 13 parties in the election over 5 per cent and ensured that more votes were transformed into seats. As a result Russian political elites and voters did not learn from the PR vote in 1993 as party leaders and voters learnt in other post-communist states. Much of the vote in 1995 was cast for small parties with no hope of securing 5 per cent of the vote, and party leaders did not construct electoral coalitions to increase their vote share.

There have been lengthy debates over the advantages and weaknesses of majoritarian and PR electoral systems.[25] The main argument in favour of majoritarianism is that it produces a clear two-party system in which the winning party will have a legislative majority with which to carry out its government's programme, whereas PR will lead to fragmented parties, coalition governments and the danger of immobilism. Furthermore, under PR, the major decisions about government formation are made not by the voters, but by party leaders behind closed doors in coalition negotiations. However, counter-arguments can be made. Two-party systems may be desirable in states where a two-way split of the electorate is possible, either because there is one main political cleavage, or because multiple cleavages tend to coincide (see Chapter 10). However, for a two-party system to be effective there has to be the possibility of an alternation of power between them. This frequently does not apply in profoundly divided communities, where the electorate, for example, may vote on ethnic lines. The danger of majoritarian systems is that they may produce either one-party rule, or a system in which minorities are permanently excluded from power.[26] Alternatively, where there is a high level of fragmentation among both electorate and political parties, majoritarian electoral systems can lead to the election of local 'personalities' rather than party candidates, and highly divided parliaments. Demanding requirements for the validity of elections (such as requiring a high turnout) can exacerbate this even further as we shall see in the case of Ukraine and Belarus (see Chapter 11).

Another major argument against PR systems is that, even where a 5 per cent clause is operating, they make it easier for extremist parties to enter parliament than a majoritarian system. With single-member constituencies, it is likely that only large parties and geographically concentrated ethnic minority parties will gain representation. The counter-argument here is that democracies are not endangered primarily by extremists who gain 5 or 8 or 10 per cent of the vote, but by those who gain over 30 per cent of the vote. An extremist party with 10 per cent of the vote and the parliamentary representation gained thereby under a PR system will be an irritant. The publicity of its electoral success may – if the political situation is already in crisis – enhance its vote further in subsequent elections, but even 30 per cent of the vote will not enable it to overturn democracy. However, a majoritarian system is far more vulnerable in unstable circumstances, because a sudden upsurge of support for extremism to 30 per cent of the vote can unexpectedly produce a parliamentary majority sufficient to change the constitution. There are also questions of what comprises extremism. An illustration of the potential problems is presented by the former Czechoslovakia. The Czech Republic is developing a two-party system with a left–right divide, but in the 1996 elections, neither faction obtained a parliamentary majority because two 'anti-system' parties – the extreme right Republicans and the Communist

Party – both obtained over 5 per cent of the vote (see Table 12.9). As a consequence, the centre-right minority government has to make compromises with its largest, Social Democratic rival, while the electorate is subjected to the distasteful spectacle of the Republicans making openly racist speeches in parliament. Meanwhile, the advantages of a majoritarian system which would be likely to eradicate both the communists and the republicans are discussed. In Slovakia, which has an almost identical electoral system, Mečiar's Movement for a Democratic Slovakia (MFDS) has a firm electoral base comprising over 30 per cent of the electorate, while six other parties gained, in 1994, between 5 and 10 per cent of the vote (see Table 12.4). Mečiar lacked a parliamentary majority, and therefore eventually formed a nationally oriented coalition with two parties often labelled extremist (though less extreme than the Czech Republicans): the Slovak National Party on the right and the Workers' Association of Slovakia on the left. The opposition was divided between three parties on a right–left divide and the Hungarian Coalition. In March 1996, Mečiar began to discuss Slovakia's need for a strong two-party system, and the consequent desirability of altering the qualified PR electoral system to a mixed or majoritarian one. A majoritarian system (calculating on the basis of the 1994 election results) would be likely to eliminate his two extremist coalition partners and give his party a parliamentary majority. But equally, it could potentially eliminate almost all opposition parties apart from the geographically concentrated Hungarian Coalition. More crucially, even a mixed PR–majoritarian system could give the MFDS the three-fifths parliamentary majority necessary to amend the constitution at will. The PR–majoritarian choice is thereby reduced to choosing the lesser evil: the irritant of extremists disrupting the developing left–right divide in the Czech Republic, or the prospect of the MFDS gaining unlimited power in Slovakia. For the post-communist world, this dilemma is central. The prerequisites for alternation of power between two parties are rare.

Bicameralism versus unicameralism

A final decision to be made by post-communist constitution framers was whether to have one or two chambers in their parliament. Here, the region shows no marked divergence from the pattern of Western democracies, where bicameral parliaments are generally to be found in more populous and in federal states.[27] The two remaining federations of the post-communist world – Russia and rump Yugoslavia – both have bicameral parliaments. Elsewhere, a rough 'ten million' dividing line exists. The Czech Republic (10.3m) and Belarus (10.4m) are numerically on the borderline. Belarus has a unicameral parliament, and although a second chamber is stipulated in the Czech constitution, elections to it were only held in November 1996. Ukraine (51.7m) is exceptional in having a unicameral legislature, although proposals for a bicameral parliament were made during recent debates on the Constitution (see Chapter 11). Bulgaria (8.5m), Estonia (1.5m), Hungary (10.3m), Latvia (2.7m), Lithuania (3.7m), Moldova (4.3m) and Slovakia (5.3m) have unicameral parliaments; in Poland (38.6m) and Romania (22.8m) they are bicameral. What is more in question, however, is the actual role of second chambers. Systems of checks and balances are nowhere in the region well established, and the outcomes of decisions to form a second chamber are as yet far from clear.

Constitutional choices and political conflict

The discussion of the constitutional choices facing post-communist states has so far been technical, in that it has mainly described the various systems adopted, their effects, strengths and weaknesses. When discussing the 'triple transition', however, two other factors are of enormous importance. The first is the extent to which the 'second level' of constitutional politics is central to the political contest in individual countries. In a consolidated democracy, the rules of politics have been fixed, and debate over constitutional change mostly relates to fine-tuning and takes place over a long timespan. In many post-communist states, however, this stage has yet to be reached. For example, while the framework of Hungarian democracy is now largely accepted, neighbouring Serbia has been prone to very frequent changes of constitutions and electoral laws, largely to suit the political interests of Slobodan Milošević. In the Czech Republic, most political argument revolves around economic choices, while in Slovakia a bitterly polarised political battle is symbolised by the enmity of President and Prime Minister.

The second factor of importance is the extent to which constitutions and rules guide the political process. However acerbic the Slovak contestation of the second level of politics may be, it is conducted within the framework of constitutionality, and the Prime Minister's power is constrained, for example, by the referral of laws passed by parliament to the Constitutional Court, and by the President's exercise of his constitutional power not to appoint ambassadors he considers unsuitable. In Albania, however, the content of the country's electoral laws is of only secondary importance to the fact that the results of the 1996 election were widely considered to be fraudulent. As long as laws are flouted, the prerequisites for a consolidated democracy are not present.

Economics and everyday politics

We must finish by discussing the remaining items on the checklist of problems presented at the beginning of this chapter. These divide roughly into two categories: problems of economic transformation and some of its attendant social consequences, and problems of 'coming to terms with the past', most particularly prosecuting former communist leaders for their crimes, and excluding those most culpable of collaboration with the regime from public office. It may be argued that both sets of problems were so severe for post-communist governments that they can scarcely be classified as 'everyday politics', and yet in a sense they were, for they were normally dealt with by ordinary laws passed by parliaments. This chapter will not deal in detail with 'lustration laws' (checking officials and candidates for high office for their communist past) or the various attempts to bring former communist leaders to trial. The controversies involved are dealt with in discussion of individual countries where they were a major issue in domestic politics. Economic dilemmas, however, were central to countries throughout the region, and they shared common legacies from their communist pasts.

Economic reform was of immense importance across Eastern Europe and the NIS. Communism had fallen in part because of its shortcomings as an economic system. The area's new rulers knew they would be judged by the success of economic reform, the pain that it caused and the rewards it brought. Economic reform was also judged desirable because it completed the anti-communist revolution. Constructing capitalism would, it was hoped, sweep out those communists who had survived the political demise of Communist Party rule. Furthermore, moving to a market economy would alter social relations by recreating property ownership and economic differentials. This would give democracy and parties more solid social constituencies.

The elites that came to power in the immediate aftermath of communism's fall were not completely free to choose their own economic path. International financial institutions (IFIs), like the International Monetary Fund (IMF), the World Bank and the European Bank for Reconstruction and Development (EBRD), required the adoption of certain policies before they would release much needed financial aid and technical support. Making aid dependent on following certain policies was called 'conditionality'. The economic policy and style IFIs favour is 'shock therapy'. On the other hand, post-communist elites had to contend with *nomenklatura* members (mostly factory directors) who wanted to preserve their power, and citizens who were worried about the effect of reform on their welfare rights (pensions, health care, schooling, etc.). The remnants of the *nomenklatura* and ordinary people worried about welfare prefer that the move towards the market is through a more 'gradualist' passage to capitalism.

The differences between shock therapy and gradualism cover two areas: policy prescription and policy style.[28] Shock therapy is a set of policies designed to effect a rapid and total break with communist economic organisation without regard to existing economic and social organisation. The aim is to get to the market as quickly as possible by creating market mechanisms as quickly as possible. The recommended 'sequencing' (the order in which reforms should take place) of shock therapy is first, price liberalisation and budget stabilisation through the reduction of state spending, and second, mass privatisation. There are some good reasons to launch economic reform this way. Liberalising prices and cutting state spending are ways of fighting inflation, a problem experienced throughout post-communist countries at the onset of reform. However, the first stage of shock therapy aims to do more than cut inflation. Raising prices and cutting state spending are supposed to 'commercialise' economic activity: in theory, state subsidies are reduced and enterprises begin to respond to the chance to make a profit; acting on a commercial criteria leads enterprises to shed excess labour, be technically innovative and use materials economically because they face the 'hard' budget constraints of the market rather than the 'soft' budget constraints of planning (see Introduction). Commercialisation (if it occurs) is nothing short of an economic revolution which sweeps away existing economic and social organisation and practice. Those enterprises unable to reform go under or are snapped up at low prices during privatisation, the second stage of reform. By the time that privatisation begins industry should be more efficient, goods should be flowing to the market and inflation should be controlled.

Gradualism, as its name suggests, does not go in for such dramatic change. There are no firm ideas about policy in gradualist thinking as there are in shock therapy. Gradualism is more about policy style than policy prescription. The difference between policy style in shock therapy and gradualism is summarised in Table 7.1. Shock therapy is confrontational because it aims for rapid change to market economy and recommends specific changes to achieve this. The desire for rapid change and the sequencing of reform confront existing interests and seek to exclude them from policy-making in favour of expert knowledge and to transform/destroy them. In contrast gradualism works through existing institutions. As a result policy is not imposed and does not follow a pattern: policy emerges and is shaped by existing institutions and interests. As policy evolves it can take numerous different forms and sequences. Price liberalisation might be delayed. There will be less cutting back of state subsidies and spending since interest groups can lobby for their share of the state budget. Privatisation will be slower. Proponents of shock therapy argue that gradualism prolongs the pain of moving to the market and runs the risk of making the move harder. Supporters of gradualism argue that it is more realistic, promotes greater social involvement in reform and lessens conflict between pro- and anti-reform elites by incorporating them both into policy-making.

The differences in policy style – leaving aside the differences in policy prescription – between shock therapy and gradualism show much of their relationship to the two parts of negotiated revolution. Shock therapy is revolutionary. Gradualism advances negotiation. However, neither shock

Table 7.1 Economic options in post-communist transitions

Shock therapy	Gradualism
1. **End-point driven.** Choice of policy determined by the goal for the final outcome of the process.	**Focus on immediate problems.** Identifies worst problems, tries to solve them. Ignores the effects of decisions on long-term equilibrium.
2. **Clean the slate.** Emphasises the need to break completely with the past through comprehensive change and institutional destruction in the first stages of reform because of the interconnectedness of problems.	**Use existing institutions.** Recognises that new structures can only be created slowly and accepts that existing institutions are better than no or hastily constructed institutions.
3. **Large leaps.** Bold package to break with constraints of the past, involves the building of many new institutions.	**Small steps.** Emphasises the risk of going too far, too fast and the impossibility of quickly creating a new interrelated network of institutions.
4. **Faith in the new.** Willing to trust in theoretical reasoning as the primary input for the design of society and economy.	**Scepticism.** Searches existing models and methods for help in formulating changes.
5. **Irreversibility.** Weak form – willingness to accept large irreversible changes. Strong form – emphasises the need for them.	**Reversibility.** Advocates policies that produce feedback on their effects and that can be stopped or reversed.
6. **Design and theory.** Sees most important intellectual resource for policy-makers as being the knowledge held by theorists and technocrats.	**Judgement and practice.** Sees most important intellectual resource for policy-makers as practical, accumulated experience that resides in existing economic institutions and social arrangements.

Source: Adapted from Murrell (1992a, p. 13).

therapy nor gradualism has really existed in pure form in post-communism. The demands of IFIs have forced all East European and former Soviet states (with the exception of those former Yugoslav states most embroiled in the war) to make some semblance of dealing with inflation. In those states where there has been more enthusiasm for shock therapy, economic elites and parliaments have frequently reined radical reformers in. The result, more often than not, has been that economic policy has been a mixture of movement, resistance and compromise. This has been particularly apparent in states like Russia where conflict over economic policy overlapped with conflict over constitutional order. Compromise also occurred in Poland where shock therapy was eventually moderated by the succession to power of the Pawlak government after the 1993 elections. Elsewhere, for example in Hungary, the pace of economic reform was slower from the onset because the new government tried to protect the population from some of reform's harsher consequences.

Economic transformation is also of enormous consequence in political terms because it gradually began to affect social stratification. Under communism, the state controlled how most people earned their money, and also how they had spent it. Most people worked for the state, and salary differentials were low. In return, the state or party-controlled organisations massively subsidised 'collective consumption' – e.g. rents, utilities, healthcare, childcare, transport and holiday facilities. All these mechanisms broke down with the end of the communist regimes, though in some countries much more slowly than in others. Many people with skills and initiative, particularly educated professionals, went to work in the private sector for several times their previous state salaries. At the other end of the scale, those who were badly off were hit by severe deprivation as rents, food and transport rose in cost. State benefits became a crippling cost for the national budget, as the poverty line was not far removed from many people's ordinary salaries.

The underlying issue was one of the redistribution of power and economic advantages: 'who gets what and why'. The previous defining criterion of social location, which might bring extra benefits, or promotion at work, was party membership, and this ceased to exist. Other criteria took its place: what people knew, what they owned, and – often crucially – who they knew. The new criteria frequently enabled former elites to retain their privileges. But the uncertainty over the criteria of allocation engendered uncertainty, and also electoral volatility. The level of everyday politics was thus emotionally charged in post-communist societies to an extent far greater than in established democracies.

The impact of the 'triple transition'

Distinguishing between the different levels of politics is important because, just as in discussing the varying modes of transition from communism, it helps to explain why communist federations disintegrated. Frequently, dialogue between republics became impossible because they were preoccupied with different levels of politics. While Slovenia appeared concerned with the issue of its national independence between 1989 and 1991, and the pluralisation and democratisation of its society enabled this striving to be articulated, the underlying drive which propelled it was the desire to consolidate its (by Yugoslav standards substantial) economic prosperity and to develop unhindered still closer contacts with the West. After independence was achieved in 1991, questions of national identity subsided as a political issue, and the new state was not riven by disputes over the constitutional distribution of power. Its political controversies were on a more normal 'everyday' level. In Croatia, on the other hand, the concerns with statehood which were prevalent at the time independence was declared continued. Definitions of citizenship were in dispute, and related both to the (gradually much reduced) Serbian minority, and to the status of Croats abroad. Nationalism rather than an economic cleavage appeared most important in the political system, and there were disputes over the constitutional distribution of power and the functioning of political institutions. In all other former Yugoslav republics, issues of state-hood and constitutional distribution of power likewise prevailed.

In Czechoslovakia, political debate was likewise clouded by divergent agendas. While there were economic differences of opinion between Czechs and Slovaks, these were no greater than those successfully accommodated within different regions of other states. The underlying problem of Czecho-slovakia was not so much arguments or enmity between Czechs and Slovaks, but the fact that the Slovaks were preoccupied with internal battles over their own national identity, while the Czechs were not. After the separation of the state, the Czechs slipped into their new, Czech identity with relative ease, and were able to concentrate solely on the issues of economic distribution which interested the electorate. In Slovakia, however, arguments over the compo-nents of Slovak national identity continued, and these were reflected also in bitter institutional disputes between the prime minister and the president. In Slovakia, politics were contested on all three levels, while the Czechs were concerned with everyday politics.

The case of the former Soviet Union is slightly different. The fragmentation of the federation was concurrent with the fall of the communist establishment and questions of national identity existed in all the successor states. The NIS also had to establish relations between themselves. Questions of economics, the division of Soviet military equipment and the treatment of minorities divided the NIS and made the consolidation of the Commonwealth of Independent States an erratic affair.

A final indication of the divergence between the different parts of former federations is the fact that chances of EU membership (see Chapter 10) vary. Estonia and Slovenia, which are viable candidates, were formerly joined in federations with states whose chances of EU membership are almost non-existent in the immediate future (for example, Ukraine and Serbia). Slovakia's situation is not as favourable as the Czech Republic'. EU accession requirements require the resolution of questions of nationhood and consti-tutional order, and substantial success in economic transformation. Progress on these fronts differs markedly between states which were previously mem-bers of a single federation.

Notes

1. Most of the 'Guidelines for democratizers' relating to the military which are suggested in Huntington (1991) are largely irrelevant to post-communist societies.
2. See Vanhanen and Kimber (1994).

3. Dahrendorf (1990, pp. 2–3).
4. Offe (1991, pp. 869–70).
5. *Ibid.*, p. 871.
6. For discussion of majority and minority nationalism, see J. F. Brown (1988, Ch. 14). See also J. F. Brown (1994, pp. 172–228).
7. For explanation of this argument, see Offe (1994, pp. 231–2).
8. Further examples of how 'the people' is defined in post-communist constitutions can be found in Dimitrijević (1993).
9. For a useful discussion of these choices, see Lijphart (1991a and 1992b); McGregor (1996); Stepan and Skach (1993).
10. This idea is sometimes called 'Duverger's Law', as it was most famously put by the French political scientist Maurice Duverger in the early 1950s. See Duverger (1954, pp. 206–55). For a discussion of the topic, see Sartori (1986).
11. Bulgaria, Croatia, Hungary and Poland are examples of this. See Elster (1993/94); Bennett (1995, pp. 127–8).
12. Lijphart (1984, pp. 68–77).
13. From 1992 in the case of Bulgaria.
14. See Lucky (1993/94) and McGregor (1994) for an overview of presidential powers in Eastern Europe.
15. The merits of presidentialism and parliamentarism have been extensively debated. See the contributions in Linz and Valenzuela (1994); Lijphart (1992a); Sartori (1994); and Shugart and Carey (1992) for a representative sample of opinions.
16. See Linz (1993 and 1994).
17. O'Donnell (1994, p. 59).
18. *Ibid.*
19. For details of presidencies in Yugoslavia, see Varady and Dimitrijevic (1993/94).
20. Some of the disputes between Presidents and Prime Ministers are discussed in Baylis (1996).
21. Rose and Haerpfer (1995, Table 25c). The countries surveyed were Bulgaria, Czech Republic, Slovakia, Hungary, Poland, Romania, Slovenia, Croatia, Belarus and Ukraine. See also Rose and Mishler (1996).
22. Holmes (1993/94).
23. For details of electoral systems in East Europe, see Lucky (1994); McGregor (1993).
24. See Lijphart (1994).
25. See, for example, the debate in *Journal of Democracy*: Lardeyret (1991); Lijphart (1991a and 1991b); Quade (1991).
26. See Horowitz (1993, pp. 29–30).
27. Lijphart (1984, pp. 91–4).
28. The most accessible introduction to the debate over economic reform is in Adams and Brock (1993). More advanced discussions can be found in Murrell (1992a and 1992b). Pro-shock therapy writings include: Åslund (1995); IMF (1992); IMF *et al.* (1990); Lipton and Sachs (1990); Sachs (1993); and the papers in Åslund (1994), Åslund and Layard (1993). More sceptical views of shock therapy can be found in: Murrell (1992a), Murrel (1992b and 1992c); Przeworski (1991 and 1993); Stark (1992 and 1995).

CHAPTER 8

Politics as crisis: Russia and the Newly Independent States, 1992–93

Introduction

Throughout 1992–93 the governments in the successor states to the Soviet Union faced many of the same problems that had confronted the East Europeans on achieving their independence from the Soviet bloc at the end of 1989. The difference was that the governments of the Newly Independent States (NIS) started from a different point politically from other post-communist states.

The post-communist states of Eastern Europe had generally elected governments *after* the collapse of the communist system, or when it was apparent that communist power had reached its terminal stage. They had thus elected governments for the post-communist era. In contrast, the March 1990 republican elections in the USSR had been about getting to post-communism. Presidential elections in Russia and Ukraine in June and December 1991 respectively had given Yeltsin and Kravchuk some grounds to claim that they had a mandate for the post-communist period. But overall few political leaders had a mandate for change. And even if they believed that they did have such a mandate, they still had to secure support for their programmes from legislatures elected under Soviet power. These legislatures were often fractious, if not openly opposed to reform, and conflict between executives and parliaments was to become the norm throughout the area. Lithuania and Estonia tried to resolve some of these problems with elections in 1992. Latvia and Russia followed them in June and December 1993 respectively. (Elections were held in Ukraine, Belarus and Moldova in 1994.) The time that it took to overcome these problems had an effect on politics. Political elites spent most of their time dealing with constitutional reform questions and trying to preserve their own power. As a result they frequently neglected to cultivate political parties (the development of which was further hindered by the delays in elections) and much needed economic reform became a hostage to political struggles.

The picture was further complicated by the fact that all the NIS had to deal with the economic and political problems caused by the collapse of the USSR. Political problems were harder to solve. Questions of citizenship and the rights of Russians living in the NIS, the removal of Russian troops from bases, the division of the USSR's military arsenal, territorial and border disputes, and control over nuclear forces and nuclear disarmament were bound up with attempts to create nation-states in the NIS and relations with Russia. The CIS had little influence on them. It could not develop fully into a forum for the resolution of common problems for the whole area of the former Soviet Union because the Baltic states remained outside of it. Other states resisted its use in these areas because they saw the CIS as a tool of the Russians. Much of the attempt to resolve common problems therefore took the form of bilateral negotiations between the NIS and Russia. These negotiations were to be the cause of great tension in some of the NIS states, adding to the conflict between executives and legislatures. Some moves were made towards solving economic problems through the development of the CIS in 1992 and 1993. This reflected Russian dominance and control over gas and oil supplies to the NIS.[1] A Coordinating-Consultative Committee to prepare agreements was established, as were an Economic Court and various lower-level bodies to discuss policy areas like the environment. Finally, there was an agreement in 1993 on the formation of an Economic Union to create a free market in goods, services, labour and capital throughout the CIS.[2] Although these developments were a sign that cooperation could take place, they had little practical effect in the short term. There was a long gap between an agreement to do something and any action being taken. States opted out of agreements or tried to modify them, and their ratification by national parliaments was slow and uncertain.

The Russian Federation

Russian politics in 1992 and 1993 was dominated by the struggle for power between President Yeltsin and the parliaments, headed by Ruslan Khasbulatov and supported by Vice-President Alexander Rutskoi.[3] This bitter conflict was possible because the constitutional relationship between President and the parliaments was unclear. Yeltsin, as we saw in Chapter 5, had been granted emergency powers by the parliaments after the failed August 1991 coup. The parliaments, however, were able to contest his right to rule. Yeltsin's power to resist was weakened by the fact that he had no solid parliamentary support. The Democratic Russia deputy bloc broke up into several parliamentary factions. Some communist deputies reformed their bloc and new opposition factions appeared. The conflict between President and parliaments was complicated by two other factors.

First, the issue of economic reform was bound up with the struggle for power. This was inevitable because the strategy of 'shock therapy' adopted by Yeltsin and Yegor Gaidar, his Minister of Finance, centred power in the executive branch of government. This alienated the parliaments and gave them an issue (the hardships caused by economic reform) with which to attack Yeltsin. It also cut industrial leaders off from access to the politicians and state funds. Access to politicians and state funds was vital to industrialists because they wanted to protect the control over industry that they had seized as the party-state had declined in the last years of *perestroika* and also because they needed state subsidies to keep their inefficient factories working. Industrialists therefore built up links with the parliamentary opposition to regain their access to state resources and political protection.

Secondly, the central government under Yeltsin had difficulty in getting the regions and republics (areas where there is a large, titular, non-Russian ethnic group) of the Russian Federation to obey its commands. This was because many regional governments were under the control of old elites (an estimated 80–90 per cent of local officials retained their posts after the fall of communism),[4] and republican elites pressed for greater independence from Moscow. These groups often had links with industrialists opposed to government policy and sought to maintain their own power by isolating themselves and their peoples from the effects of economic reform.

The activities of industrialists and regional and republican elites complicated the power struggle at the centre. The political allegiance of both groups was changeable and they allied with the contenders for power at the centre according to expediency. This made it very difficult to construct stable political alliances either for or against Yeltsin. As a result, Russian politics between the start of economic reform in January 1992 and the violent dissolution of the parliaments in October 1993 were highly unstable. The uncertainty of political life and the constant shifting of political forces was detrimental to democratisation in several ways. Politicians were blinkered by the struggle between President and parliament. They concentrated on preserving their power and status and gave little thought to representing the people. Popular apathy towards politics and distrust of politicians grew. There was no consolidation of political parties into effective organisations or vehicles of interest representation (the exception would be the CPRF, the Communist Party of the Russian Federation, which rapidly became the largest party in Russia once the post-August 1991 ban was lifted). Appeals to democracy were replaced by nationalist sloganising as politicians from across the political spectrum attempted to gain support. Political extremism, typified by Vladimir Zhirinovsky, the leader of the Liberal Democratic Party of

Russia (LDPR), grew.[5] The rule of law was flouted by both sides in the attempt to gain advantage in the struggle. This was mirrored by a general growth in lawlessness. Criminal groups expanded to take advantage of political instability and the under-regulated market that was being created.[6] Corruption spread and became endemic. By 1993, it was estimated that over 3000 criminal groups controlled 40 per cent of the turnover in Russia and the CIS.

The politics of economic reform in Russia

Russia embarked on its course of radical economic reform, 'shock therapy', on 2 January 1992. The reforms, introduced in a speech by Yeltsin in October 1991, were based on advice from Western academic economists and international financial institutions (IFIs) like the International Monetary Fund and the World Bank. Their initial design was classic 'shock therapy' (see Chapter 7).[7] Reform was to take place in two stages and would amount to more than a much-needed economic nostrum. The first stage was set to begin in January 1992 and would involve the liberalisation of most prices and the cutting of state subsidies to industry. This was supposed to lead to the stabilisation of the rouble. The reformers argued that it was necessary to embark on reform in this way to get rid of the huge amount of money held by private citizens, to 'commercialise' economic enterprises by removing subsidies and making them work for profits, to create conditions for both internally and externally funded investment, and to secure aid from IFIs. Prices and inflation would rise initially, but would fall as the population's money holdings were depleted, industry responded to free prices by producing more goods and the flow of state money into the economy slowed. There would be some privatisation in this first stage of reform, but it would only involve some retail firms and small companies. Large-scale privatisation of Russian industry and the liberalisation of all remaining prices were to take place in the second stage of reform, which was scheduled to begin in late 1992.

The two-stage reform policy was a radical solution to Russia's vast economic problems and had political implications. As was argued in Chapter 7, 'shock therapy' aims at destroying existing economic institutions and replacing them with new market institutions in one great leap. It ignores the interests that exist in the economy and is based on the ideas of neo-liberal theorists (like Gaidar, the first Minister of Finance, and his successor, Boris Fedorov) and the desire to create a free market as quickly as possible. In Russia, this urge to destroy inherited economic interests and replace them with new market structures was revolutionary in that it aimed to re-engineer society socially – a highly political task – and complete the anti-communist revolution. As in any revolution (see Chapter 1), power had to be centralised – in this case on the Yeltsin presidency – for the successful pursuit of a

---

Textbox 8.1 Main events in Russia, 1992

January	Prices liberalised in Russia in attempt to control inflation, create basis of market economy and break up the power of industrial managers.
April	Russian parliament backs government economic policy but with reservations. Yeltsin forced to compromise on the composition of the government.
June	Privatisation legislation passed. Yeltsin appoints Gaidar acting Prime Minister.
December	Russian parliaments oppose government. Gaidar replaced as Prime Minister by Viktor Chernomyrdin. Yeltsin does deal with the parliaments and gets the promise of a referendum on the constitution.

---

revolutionary goal. Following 'shock therapy' policies thus provided Yeltsin with an argument against parliamentarism and for presidential power. The social re-engineering of society would take place through the displacement of the *nomenklatura*. The *nomenklatura* had taken advantage of the loosen-ing of political controls under Gorbachev to transfer control over enterprises from the Soviet state into their own hands. This made managers *de facto*, if not *de jure*, owners of enterprises.[8] 'Commercialisation' and the ending of state subsidies threatened this *nomenklatura* control because it would create an imperative to reform industrial production. Some factories would close when denied government subsidies, others would reform. This would split the *nomenklatura*. Successful reformers would become a constituency for the government. Unsuccessful enterprise directors would lose control of their enterprises to entrepreneurs or foreign capital, or be forced out by their own workforce.[9]

The gamble on 'shock therapy' was immense: political as well as economic fortunes rode upon its success. However, since 'shock therapy' constituted a broad attack on what remained of the old power structures of the Soviet system, it could not but create its own opposition. This opposition came from both politicians and industrialists. The parliaments, as can be seen from Table 8.1, were a fertile ground for opposition. The only group that supported Yeltsin on a relatively consistent basis was the coalition of reform groups with 267 deputies. The opposition bloc, 'Russian Unity', had the most deputies, while the centre ground of independents and the 'Bloc of construc-tive forces' were as likely to vote against Yeltsin and the government as for them. Taken together, the large number of factions and their very fluid membership would have made the parliament difficult to work with. 'Shock therapy', the appointment of Gaidar and the attempt to centre power on the presidency and the government made it almost impossible for Yeltsin to work with the

Table 8.1 Factions in the Russian Congress of People's Deputies at the end of 1992

	No. of deputies
Coalition of reforms	267
Radical Democrats	51
Democratic Russia	50
Left Centre/Cooperation	59
Free Russia	54
Consensus for Progress	53
Bloc of constructive forces	155
Workers' Union (Reform without Shock)	50
Smena (Change)	54
Industrial Union	51
Independents	259
Deputies with no factional affiliation	208
Sovereignty and Equality	51
Oppositional bloc 'Russian Unity'	359
Rodina (Homeland)	55
Rossiya (Russia)	55
Otchizina (Motherland)	51
Agrarian Union	130
Communists of Russia	68

Source: Sakwa (1993b, p. 67).

CPD and Supreme Soviet. Ruslan Khasbulatov, the Chairman of the Presidium of the Supreme Soviet, was alienated from the government and pushed into opposition. Khasbulatov controlled the agendas of the parliaments and used the powers of his office to subvert Yeltsin and the government's programme of reform. The Vice-President, Alexander Rutskoi, took the side of the parliaments because he saw economic reform as a betrayal of Russia to foreign economic interests.

The instability of the parliaments and the threat to industrialists from 'shock therapy' meant that economic reform and Yeltsin came under attack very rapidly. The first major skirmish was in April 1992 at the sixth meeting of the CPD. The opposition sought to remove the emergency powers that Yeltsin had been granted in late 1991 and called for a halt to 'shock therapy'. They could not, however, gather the support necessary to reverse reforms: the end result was a compromise. Yeltsin retained his emergency powers until the end of 1992 and received a grudging endorsement of economic reform, but had to give up the post of Prime Minister by July. The compromise outcome of the sixth session of the CPD set the tone for the next seventeen months, until the parliaments were disbanded in September 1993. Neither side was able to defeat the other in parliament. As a consequence, compromises were reached which satisfied neither side and led to further politicking and attempts to secure advantage. After the sixth session of the CPD Yeltsin replaced several reformist ministers with moderates (including Viktor Chernomyrdin, the future Prime Minister) to appease industrialists. He balanced this by appointing Gaidar as acting Prime Minister in June 1992 to ensure that the executive remained under his control. The parliaments, in return, used the resignation of the Chairman of the Central Bank of Russia in June to strike back at reform by appointing Viktor Gerashchenko, an opponent of 'shock therapy', to the post.

Gerashchenko's appointment aided industrialist opposition to radical economic reform. Industrialist opposition took two forms. At local level industrialists used their positions to oppose the government by either ignoring the government's instructions and the demands of the inchoate market and carrying on as usual, or by using their structural economic power to subvert reform. The chief effect of the 'carrying on as usual' strategy was a huge build-up of inter-enterprise debt as industry continued to trade by circulating goods on credit.[10] After Gerashchenko's appointment, the Central Bank paid off this debt by issuing credits. This added to inflationary pressures in the economy by increasing the state budget deficit, and allowed enterprises to ignore government attempts at commercialising their activities.

Industrialists used their structural economic power to subvert reform in two ways. First, monopoly producers (who accounted for as much as 40 per cent of industrial production) used their control over markets to take advantage of price deregulation and profiteer: prices were raised, but output remained the same. Again, this added to inflationary pressures. Secondly, managers used their positions to subvert attempts to diversify ownership through privatisation by buying worker support and blocking the flow of information necessary to the privatisation process. This stopped the diversification of ownership from reaching the levels proposed by the government and acted as a barrier to the fuller emergence of a new economic class that could act as a constituency for the government.

Industrialists also became major political players, with several industrialist organisations vying for influence. The most prominent of these organisations was the Union of Industrialists and Entrepreneurs (UIE), headed by Arkady Volsky. In the summer of 1992, the UIE made alliances with two of Russia's better established parties (Rutskoi's People's Party for Free Russia and the Democratic Party of Russia) and the Smena (Change) parliamentary faction to form a new organisation: Civic Union. Civic Union then made an agreement with the Federation of Independent Trade Unions of Russia (the successor to the old communist trade union movement).[11] Civic Union did not argue against the market economy, but pushed for a gradualist solution to the country's economic problems, warning against the destruction of Russia's industrial infrastructure and demanding state help and protection. This position made the organisation appear to occupy the 'centre' ground of Russian politics in the autumn of 1992.[12] Moreover, its backing from industrialists and some political parties and its agreement with the successor to the communist trade union organisation gave it the appearance of being the most representative force in Russian politics.

The rise of Civic Union and the opposition from industrialists at the grassroots to government economic policy put Yeltsin in a difficult position as 1992 drew to a close. Civic Union's emergence appeared to have created a political force that could challenge Yeltsin. Opposition from industrialists, and support for them from the Central Bank under Gerashchenko, had damaged the government's economic policies. Inflation had slowed month by month after the initial shock of price liberalisation in January 1992. By August the rate of increase had fallen to just 9 per cent per month. The emission of credits to pay off inter-enterprise debt and higher wage payments over the summer brought this back up to 23 per cent in October, with food and consumer goods prices rising dramatically. Moreover, Russia's steep decline in industrial production showed no sign of slowing down as industry either could not or would not respond to the possibilities of market production.

The worsening economic situation in the autumn of 1992 strengthened the opposition's hand and forced Yeltsin to rethink his political strategy. In the run-up to the December meeting of the CPD, Yeltsin began to make overtures to industrialists in order to capture support from the political centre. The strategy paid off. Yeltsin won enough support to be able to force another compromise (brokered by Valery Zorkin, the head of the Constitutional Court) at the seventh CPD meeting in December 1992. The composition of the government was changed once again. Gaidar was removed as acting Prime Minister, and Viktor Chernomyrdin, who had the support of industrialists, was approved as his replacement by the CPD. Chernomyrdin immediately made a series of statements which questioned the 'rush to the market' approach of 'shock therapy'. Nevertheless, his appointment did not completely blunt the reformist edge of the government since the post of Minister of Finance was taken over by Boris Fedorov, a committed 'shock therapist'.

The most important part of the December compromise was not the changes to the government, but the agreement that the dispute between parliaments and President should be settled by means of a referendum on the constitution. The referendum was scheduled for 11 April 1993. Under the terms of the deal the CPD was to propose the new constitution and Yeltsin was to be given the opportunity to make amendments to it before the vote. If the two sides could not agree on the terms of the constitution, two separate documents would be put to the people for their decision.

1993: From compromise to conflict

Russia seemed to have resolved its conflict between President and parliament democratically with the agreement on a referendum at the CPD in December 1992. However, the promise of political peace was illusory and shortlived. Compromise was not something that either side really wanted. Rather it was a default solution to the political impasse, necessary because neither side was able to defeat the other, but temporary and not liked by either party. The result, eventually, was that the conflict between parliaments and the President flared up again, and the course was set for the violent resolution of the power struggle that was to come in October 1993. The basis of the new power struggle was, however, different from that of 1992.

The first reason that the power struggle was different was the fragmentation of Civic Union. Civic Union was a victim of its own success. The replacement of Gaidar by Chernomyrdin brought to power a man who was sympathetic to industrialist causes and amenable to being influenced by them. As a result certain industrial groups (particularly the energy sector where Chernomyrdin had made his career) no longer needed political alliances to influence policy. Other industrialists lost interest in opposing the government because they were now in a position to gain from reform. Pressure from

---

Textbox 8.2 Main events in Russia, 1993

March	CPD reneges on deal on referendum and attempts to strip Yeltsin of his powers. Yeltsin decrees emergency rule and referendum. CPD responds by trying to impeach him, but fails. Eventually a deal is done on the referendum.
April	Referendum on economic reform, prospect of new elections for the presidency and the parliaments and confidence in Yeltsin. Yeltsin wins on all questions.
June	Yeltsin calls Constitutional Conference to try to get an agreement on a presidential system from major political actors.
September	Yeltsin brings Gaidar back into the government and then suspends the parliaments and decrees emergency rule. Parliaments meet in emergency session.
October	Pro-parliament demonstrators clash with riot police. Yeltsin calls in the army to restore order. At least 100 people killed. Parliamentary elections and a constitutional referendum are called for December.
December	Victory for Yeltsin on new constitution gives him extra powers as President. Russia's Choice does poorly at the polls. Surprise success for Zhirinovsky's LDP.

parliament and from Civic Union had successfully forced changes in privatisation legislation. Ostensibly the aim of the parliaments and Civic Union was to give workers a stake in the process by allowing them to become owners. In reality worker-led buyouts were a means by which directors gained control over enterprises by controlling which workers represented the shopfloor and by controlling the sale of shares not owned by workers. These shares were sold to dummy companies controlled by directors or were brought directly by management.[13] The privatisation (*privatizatsiya*) of state property quickly became labelled the *prikhvatizatsiya* (taking) of state property, or *nomenklatura* privatisation.

The possibility of gaining from privatisation bought off a significant part of the industrial opposition to the government. In the December 1993 elections (see below) support for Volsky and Civic Union had declined to such an extent that they received just 1.93 per cent of the vote. Those industrialists who could not gain from privatisation continued to support oppositional politics through other industrialist organisations. These did not have the political weight that Civic Union had exerted in late 1992 because of its alliances. Struggle over economic policy became internalised within the government. Economic liberals like Boris Fedorov and Anatoly Chubais – respectively the Minister of Finance and the head of GKI (the State Property Management Committee, which dealt with privatisation) – struggled to continue with economic reform while other ministers distributed resources to clients and friends.

The dying down of conflict over economic policy changed the character of political conflict. The political parties and leaders which had been in alliance with the industrialists in Civic Union, or who had benefited from the danger the group posed to the government, had to seek new allies. The only obvious allies for Rutskoi and Khasbulatov were the nationalists. The nationalists opposed the Yeltsin government for a variety of reasons. For the far left, Yeltsin was a criminal because he had destroyed the USSR. For the far right, Yeltsin was a traitor because he had abandoned the millions of Russians living in the 'near abroad' (as the other former republics are now known colloquially). Both sides hated him for what they perceived to be his policy of kowtowing to Western interests, for selling Russia's economy to Western capitalists and for not defending its culture against Western materialism. Together, the left and the right made up a broad nationalist camp sometimes called the 'Red-Brown Alliance'.[14] Rutskoi made the first move towards the 'Red-Brown' camp. He had already toyed with some of it positions in 1992, echoing its criticisms of 'shock therapy' as a betrayal of the Russian people to Western capitalists, and by declaring that the Russian Army had the right to defend ethnic Russians throughout the 'near abroad'. In the spring of 1993 he moved completely from the centrist positions of Civic Union and tried to claim leadership of the Red-Browns. At the same time he supported Khasbulatov and demanded that the referendum planned for April 1993 be abandoned. This brought Khasbulatov closer to the nationalist opposition as the final confrontation between President and parliaments neared in October.

The reconfiguration of political forces caused by the decline of Civic Union and Rutskoi's move towards the nationalists formed the backdrop to the struggles that developed over the referendum on the constitution, forcing the two sides into ever more irreconcilable positions. In January 1993, Khasbulatov argued that the agreement to hold a referendum was unconstitutional since it had been forced on the parliaments by Yeltsin. Yeltsin responded by suggesting that parliamentary elections be brought forward. Khasbulatov then tried to gain the upper hand by attempting to split Yeltsin from the government. The eighth meeting of the CPD (10–13 March 1993) could not agree on the referendum but removed Yeltsin's special powers (granted in November 1991), stripped him of the right to issue decrees that were equivalent to parliamentary laws and of the right to appoint ministers and regional heads of administration. Chernomyrdin and the government were granted the right to bring legislation direct to parliament so that they could make law independently of the President.

Yeltsin responded on 20 March by decreeing 'special rule' in Russia and stating that the referendum would go ahead on 25 April. At first 'special rule' appeared to mean that the parliaments were dissolved. Zorkin discredited himself as head of the Constitutional Court by condemning this because the decree (published on 24 March) made no mention of the parliaments' dissolution. The CPD met again on 26 March to discuss the latest developments. Zorkin was now unable to mediate as he had in December 1992. Yeltsin and Khasbulatov tried to reach a compromise by agreeing to early elections for both the presidency and the parliaments. This only further destabilised the situation however, as the CPD voted on impeaching Yeltsin and removing Khasbulatov as Chair of the Supreme Soviet. Both votes were unsuccessful, but forced Khasbulatov and Yeltsin to collude. The result was another compromise: it was agreed to hold the referendum on 25 April.

Once again the compromise was not wanted by either side. Since Yeltsin had got his wish – the referendum – Khasbulatov tried to make sure that nothing would come of it and that it would damage Yeltsin. The conditions imposed by the CPD for holding the referendum made it impossible for Yeltsin to win and questions were added to make it a plebiscite on his popularity and policies. Four questions on confidence in Yeltsin, his socio-economic policies, and on calling early elections for both the post of President and the parliaments were asked (see Table 8.2). Fifty per cent of all eligible voters had to support a proposal for it to be legally binding and for fresh elections to be called. As a result, the referendum was legally a draw. A clear majority of voters expressed confidence in Yeltsin and his policies, and supported the call for early parliamentary elections, with only a smaller

Table 8.2 Results of the April 1993 referendum in Russia

	Yes vote		*No vote*		
	% vote	*% electorate*	*% vote*	*% electorate*	*Spoiled ballots*
Do you have confidence in the President of the Russian Federation, Boris Yeltsin?	58.7	37.3	39.2	25.2	2.1
Do you approve of the socio-economic policies carried out by the President and government of the Russian Federation since 1992?	53.0	34.0	44.6	28.6	2.4
Do you consider it necessary to hold early elections to the Presidency of the Russian Federation?	49.5	31.7	47.1	30.2	3.4
Do you consider it necessary to hold early elections of the people's deputies of the Russian Federation?	67.2	43.1	30.1	19.3	2.7

Source: Slater (1993, p. 12).

majority in favour of early elections to the presidency. However, none of the proposals was approved by over 50 per cent of the eligible electorate, only 64 per cent of whom voted anyway. With no legal mandate, Yeltsin could only claim a moral victory over the parliaments and Khasbulatov. He was, however, in no position to effect change to the political system without further struggle. Moreover, to win in this struggle he needed allies. Using his moral victory, Yeltsin tried to build up support for presidential power – and a new constitution guaranteeing that power – by calling a Constitutional Conference.

The Conference (convened at the start of June 1993) was an attempt at forming an alternative representative structure to the parliaments on the grounds that the referendum vote in favour of early parliamentary elections had destroyed the legitimacy of the CPD and Supreme Soviet. Yeltsin's decree establishing the Conference gave it the right to discuss and draft the final text of a new constitution. The Conference was made up of 750 representatives from the regions of Russia, political parties and social organisations, the parliaments, the presidential administration and the government.[15] The Conference started badly when Yeltsin's opening speech angered the majority of delegates, but in mid-July a draft constitution was voted on and accepted. The draft was, however, a hollow victory for Yeltsin because there was no certainty that it would be accepted as the final text of the constitution. The parliaments were less than enthusiastic because they would have been replaced by new legislatures. Moreover, the Conference had highlighted the differences between Yeltsin and the regions of Russia.

The problem of the relationship of the eighty-nine regions and republics that make up the Russian Federation to the centre was not a new one. The relationship between the President, the government and the republics and regions had never been adequately codified after the fall of the USSR and the destruction of the old system of managing regional politics. A Federal Treaty had been signed in March 1992 by most of the republics and all of the regions (Chechnya, which had declared itself independent in September 1991, and Tatarstan, which wanted greater autonomy, refused to sign). The Treaty recognised all as having equal rights and obligations, but allowed the republics the trappings of statehood: constitutions, parliaments, presidents, etc. The regions meanwhile were governed by a combination of presidential represen-tatives (created in August 1991 and supposed to watch over the execution of presidential decrees and orders), 'heads of administration' or governors (at first appointed by Yeltsin but later elected), and the local Soviets (councils) that had been elected in March 1990.[16]

The Treaty was too vague to regulate the relationship between centre and periphery properly for long. Republics and regions tried to negotiate conces-sions for themselves; the regions complained that the rights enjoyed by the republics were unjust and threatened to proclaim themselves republics; the republics threatened to secede from the Federation unless they were granted greater concessions and economic autonomy. The power struggle in Moscow made this administrative chaos worse. Local elites took advantage of the weakness of central government to do what they pleased. The presidency and the parliaments were played off against one another, and the power of local elites and industrialists over the regions and republics was strengthened at the expense of central government. The most visible outward sign of this was the compromise, and then loss of control, over the appointment of governors. Yeltsin was forced to concede that governors should be appointed only with the agreement of local Soviets and relented on some of the appointments he had already made. As a result, the majority of governors were members of the old *nomenklatura*.[17] These governors had little sympathy with the reformers in Moscow, but had many connections to local industrialists. Taxes and contri-butions to the federal budget went unpaid and government economic policy was flaunted as elites cushioned their population from the effects of market reform by subverting the market and by aiding local industrialists' takeover of their enterprises.[18]

The powers of regional leaders were therefore quite extensive by mid-1993 and the establishment of the Constitutional Conference. They were a power-ful constituency to be courted and their support could have swung the consti-tutional struggle. Yeltsin tried to solicit their support by making concessions to them in the draft constitution and by calling for the establishment of a Federation Council with representatives from local Soviets and executives of all eighty-nine regions and republics. The creation of the Federation Council and its acceptance of the draft constitution were vital for Yeltsin's plans to succeed. But regional support for his ideas was lukewarm at best. Local Soviets disliked the draft constitution and the powers that it gave to the executive at the expense of representative institutions, and were angered by Yeltsin's criticisms of Soviets as undemocratic. Many of them commented negatively on the draft constitution and proposed changes to it. Governors and republican leaders were not prepared to back Yeltsin unanimously in the uncertain political climate of autumn 1993.

Khasbulatov was more successful in finding support for his plans after the referendum. He drew closer to Rutskoi and his nationalist allies. Where Yeltsin criticised the Soviets as undemocratic, Khasbulatov defended them as traditional Russian institutions protecting the country from colonialisation by the West. The CPD passed a budget which threatened to double government spending and fuel inflation, attacked the GKI and privatisation, and proposed amendments to the constitution that would have weakened Yeltsin's foreign policy role and control over the armed forces.[19]

Khasbulatov's alliance with Rutskoi and Yeltsin's failure to secure the agreement of regional leaders for the Federation Council made the peaceful resolution of the constitutional crisis impossible: Yeltsin had run out of ways of circumventing the parliaments to secure his vision of a presidential constitution; Khasbulatov and Rutskoi's alliance with the 'Red-Brown alliance' made compromise impossible, since their rhetoric portrayed Yeltsin as a traitor and was implacable in its support for the parliaments against the presidency. Yeltsin made the first moves to break the deadlock. He reappointed Gaidar to the government, dissolved the parliaments on 21 September 1993 in contravention of the constitution and called for elections to a new parliament which would approve the draft constitution.

The events that followed Yeltsin's decree on the dissolution of the parliaments were a combination of tragedy and farce.[20] Some deputies deserted the parliamentary cause when offered new jobs and retirement packages by the government. The parliament building – the same White House that Yeltsin had defended two years earlier – was surrounded and blockaded, the electricity and water cut off. Inside Rutskoi was declared acting President and extremists (most of whom were not deputies) organised for the armed defence of the building. The impasse lasted until Sunday, 3 October, when a demonstration organised by Working Russia (an anti-Yeltsin, neo-Stalinist organisation) broke through the blockade, marched to the White House and joined the armed groups inside the building. Rutskoi tried to organise this enlarged force to seize power. Armed detachments were dispatched to seize the television centre at Ostankino, some 7 kilometres away. Here they met their first real resistance from Interior Ministry troops. (The lax policing and failure to contain the Working Russia demonstration earlier in the day has led some commentators to speculate that the authorities in some way stimulated the revolt so as to crush the parliaments once and for all.)[21] A brief but bloody gun battle broke out around the television centre and the rebel forces were driven back to the White House.

The battle at the Ostankino television station provided Yeltsin with justification for bringing in the Army to crush the parliaments. The Army was initially reluctant: Defence Minister General Pavel Grachev did not want to deploy his forces in a political dispute against ethnic Russians, and there was some doubt as to whether the Army would be willing to fight. Finally, and after several hours of cajoling and a personal appeal by Yeltsin, it was agreed to use Army units for an assault on the White House the next day. On Monday, 4 October, the White House was surrounded by tanks and troops, and bombarded with shells. Rutskoi's appeals for soldiers to change sides were disregarded and no one came to the parliaments' aid. By evening a very one-sided battle was over. The parliament surrendered; Khasbulatov, Rutskoi and some of the other leaders were arrested; martial law and a curfew were temporarily declared in Moscow. In the days that followed, Yeltsin further asserted the powers of the central government by dissolving local Soviets, sacking governors who had opposed him too vehemently, and ordering elections for new regional legislatures in 1994.

Yeltsin's victory over the parliaments and their supporters removed the obstacles to adopting a new constitution guaranteeing presidential power. But there was no mechanism for this constitution to be adopted now that the parliaments had been destroyed. Yeltsin's way around this was to declare that there would be elections to a new legislature and a plebiscite on the new constitution setting up the legislature and establishing its relationship (which was to be a subordinate one) to the presidency at the same time.[22] As a consequence, on election day (12 December), Russia's voters were asked to vote for a constitution establishing a new parliament and to elect this parliament. The new parliament was titled the Federal Assembly and was to consist of two chambers: the upper house, the Council of the Federation (178 deputies, two from each of Russia's republics and regions), and the more important lower house, the State Duma (450 deputies, 225 directly elected from single-member constituencies under majoritarian rules and 225 elected by PR).[23]

This strategy of simultaneous elections and constitutional plebiscite held out the bonus of recreating legitimacy for Yeltsin after the destruction of the old parliaments. By voting for a government party and the constitution, people would signify their support *post hoc* for Yeltsin's destruction of the old parliaments and show that they preferred a presidential system to a parliamentary one. The result would be that Yeltsin's authority would be affirmed at the same time that his actual powers as President were extended and legalised.

Matters were not to turn out quite as Yeltsin hoped they would. Yeltsin secured a narrow (and questionable) victory on the question of the constitution: 54.8 per cent of registered voters turned out, with 58.4 per cent voting in favour of the constitution (for details of the constitution, see Chapter 11).[24] The real test for Yeltsin, however, was not the referendum on the constitution or the selection of deputies to Council of the Federation, but the PR vote for 225 of the seats in the State Duma. The seats in the Federal Council and the vast majority of the 225 constituency seats in the State Duma were filled by governors and other regional leaders (for seats on the Council of the Federation) or won by 'independents' (for the Duma, frequently members of regional political and economic elites) (see Table 8.3). The success of the 'independents' reflected the weakness of party organisation throughout Russia. Voters cast their ballot for well-known local figures rather than people put forward by political parties, which were weak in the provinces and unable to mount effective door-to-door campaigns. The constituency elections were thus not so much about national politics as local power, and they did not pose a threat to Yeltsin.[25] However, in the PR vote the electorate directly signalled their support or disapproval for Yeltsin's policies because they had the chance to vote for or against Russia's Choice, the electoral bloc representing the presidency and led by Yegor Gaidar. Russia's Choice came second with just over 15 per cent of the vote. (The other government party, the Party of Russian Unity and Accord (PRES), got 6.76 per cent.) The overall vote against the

Table 8.3 Results of the elections to the Russian Duma, December 1993

	PR vote		Constituency seats	Total[a]
	% vote	Seats		
LDPR	22.92	59	5	64
Russia's Choice	15.51	40	30	70
CPRF	12.40	32	16	48
Women of Russia	8.13	21	2	23
Agrarian Party	7.99	21	12	33
Yabloko	7.86	20	3	23
PRES	6.76	18	1	19
Democratic Party of Russia	5.52	14	1	15
Other parties	8.72[b]		8	8
Independents			141	141

a. Does not add up to 450 because the election was declared illegal in five constituencies and was not held in Chechnya.
b. No other party got over the 5 per cent threshold of votes to secure representation through the party list system.

For a more detailed breakdown of the election results, the results of all of the constituency elections and maps showing the geographical spread of party support, see Lester (1995, pp. 256–73).

government was much higher. Vladimir Zhirinovsky's LDPR was a surprise leader with 22.92 per cent of the vote; the CPRF and its ally the Agrarian Party got just over 20 per cent of the vote; the liberal reformist, but anti-Yeltsin, Yabloko (Apple, the acronym of the 'Yavlinsky–Boldyrev–Lukin bloc') got 7.86 per cent of the vote. The centrist Women of Russia electoral bloc got 8.13 per cent.

The results of the elections were thus mixed for Yeltsin. Why did the majority vote for the constitution (something Yeltsin wanted), but against Russia's Choice? First, it is a matter of doubt that the constitution was actually passed. There have been persistent rumours of ballot-rigging and no evidence produced to deny them. Secondly, campaigning against the constitution, though possible, was not as extensive as it might have been. Many of the parties opposed to the constitution were denied registration for the PR ballot and did not get television and radio airtime to petition for a 'no' vote. Debate was further inhibited by threats made during the campaign to bar those blocs that opposed the constitution from the election. Thirdly, a protest vote was not necessarily incompatible with a vote for the constitution. Zhirinovsky, who had his eye on the powers of the presidency, campaigned for the constitution. Other voters rejected Russia's Choice because of dislike for the government or Gaidar, or because they were revolted by the destruction of the old parliaments. However, they voted for the constitution simply to solve the question of where power lay: they were tired of the political struggles that had led to the October events and with the endless debate about the constitution.[26]

Ukraine

Ukrainian politics in 1992–93 were dominated by President Leonid Kravchuk's efforts to secure his power and control over both the make-up and the policies of the government. As in Russia there was a connection between economics and politics, but in Ukraine this was complicated by the question of how to build the Ukrainian state.

Kravchuk mixed caution in economic affairs with Ukrainian territorial nationalism (defence of Ukraine's sovereignty and statehood). Both policies were products of the way he had risen to power and his support base. By balancing nationalism and economic caution Kravchuk was able to continue occupying the middle ground of Ukrainian politics: he appealed both to some nationalists and to the old communist elite who controlled industry and were afraid of the effects of economic reform. For a time this balancing act made Kravchuk appear invulnerable to the chaos of Ukrainian politics. Kravchuk, as a Ukrainian joke had it, was so quick on his feet that he did not need an umbrella when it was raining – he could dodge between the drops. This was an impossible act to keep up for any great length of time. Reluctance to reform

---

Textbox 8.3 Main events in Ukraine, 1992–93

1992

January	Kravchuk calls for a round table to discuss formation of government of national accord.
June	Demonstrations in Kiev call for Fokin's resignation.
August	Yeltsin and Kravchuk agree to place Black Sea fleet under joint command for three years and then to divide it.
September	Fokin resigns and Rada forces the government to step down.
October	Kuchma becomes Prime Minister.
November	Kuchma granted emergency powers for six months to deal with the economy.
December	Sharp price rises. Chornovil takes control of Rukh.

1993

January	Deputies from east and south demand reconsideration of government economic policy. Defeated by Kuchma with support from Chornovil and the Rukh faction.
February	Kravchuk calls for a new constitution and early presidential and parliamentary elections.
April	163 Rada deputies sign an open letter to Kravchuk calling for Ukraine to be a nuclear state.
May	Kuchma offers resignation after Rada refuses to extend his emergency powers. Kravchuk tries and fails to abolish the post of Prime Minister and take over as head of government.
June	Kuchma twice attempts to resign. Strikes spread from Donbass and demand a vote of no confidence in Kravchuk, Kuchma and the Rada. Rada agrees to referendum. Kravchuk tries and fails to take control of the government and places Kuchma in charge of a special commission on the economy.
September	Kuchma's resignation is finally accepted. Rada schedules elections to a new 450-seat parliament for March 1994 and to the presidency for June 1994. Kravchuk and Yeltsin agree equal division of Black Sea fleet.
November	Rada ratifies START I with substantial list of conditions.

---

the economy led Ukraine to the brink of bankruptcy. Relations between Kravchuk, the government and the Verkhovna Rada (parliament) soured.[27]

After independence, Kravchuk's nationalism changed from anti-Sovietism to anti-Russianism.[28] The principal policy areas that this affected were Ukraine's relations with the CIS, the question of nuclear disarmament and the issue of the Black Sea Fleet.[29]

Ukraine was the least enthusiastic member of the Commonwealth and resisted attempts to expand its influence. Kravchuk insisted that the CIS was nothing more than a mechanism through which the NIS would disentangle themselves, and that any serious problem between Ukraine and the NIS would be dealt with on a bilateral, state-to-state basis, so that Ukraine's independence and sovereignty would be recognised. As a result, Ukraine did not participate in many of the initiatives put forward in 1992 to develop the CIS. This position softened because of Ukraine's deteriorating economic position and economic pressure from Russia in 1993. In May 1993 Ukraine signed the declaration supporting Economic Union. The qualification of Ukrainian intransigence towards the CIS was, however, tempered by objections to parts of the agreement, and Ukraine would sign on only as an associate member of the agreement.

A similar pattern of events unfolded with regard to nuclear disarmament. Under CIS agreements Ukraine, Belarus and Kazakhstan were supposed to remove tactical nuclear weapons to Russia for dismantling by July 1992 and strategic nuclear weapons by the end of 1994. In May 1992 these states, Russia and the United States signed the Lisbon Protocol, which committed them to signing the Nuclear Non-Proliferation Treaty (NPT) and honouring the Strategic Arms Reduction Treaty (START I), which Gorbachev and George Bush had signed in 1991. Ukraine fulfilled only one of these agreements – the removal of tactical nuclear weapons. (Belarus and Kazakhstan met them all.) Keeping the strategic weapons served several purposes. They kept Ukraine in the international eye and were a possible bargaining chip for more foreign aid. Russian leaders had also made some ill-judged statements about Ukraine's borders with Russia, and keeping the weapons satisfied nationalists' demands that Ukraine be adequately defended from Russia (for example, 163 Rada deputies wrote to Kravchuk in April 1993 calling for Ukraine to be a nuclear state). Debate on ratifying START I dragged into 1993. When the Rada finally voted on START I in November 1993, it heavily modified the original agreements, stating that it would not be bound by the NPT and agreeing to hand over only a portion of the warheads and launchers on its territory for destruction.

Confrontation with Russia was even more direct over the question of the Black Sea Fleet. The Fleet was stationed in the Crimea, an area that had become a part of Ukraine only in 1954 and which is populated mostly by Russians. Russia claimed most of the Fleet for itself on the grounds that it was a strategic force and belonged to Russia under CIS agreements.[30] The Russian parliaments fuelled controversy by insisting that the legality of Ukraine's ownership of Crimea be considered.[31] Kravchuk demanded half the Fleet for Ukraine, partly as a response to this and partly because it helped to maintain his nationalist credentials. This caused a crisis in the Fleet where the majority of officers and sailors were ethnic Russians and wanted the Fleet to remain under Russian control. Kravchuk and Yeltsin agreed in August 1993 to co-manage the Fleet for three years and then divide it. But the matter was destined to remain unresolved. Kravchuk's position on the Fleet softened in 1993 as it had with the CIS. In June 1993, Kravchuk and Yeltsin agreed to divide the Fleet equally between the two countries by the year end. At their next summit in September Kravchuk agreed to swap the Ukraine's share in exchange for cancelling debt to Russia. This proposed deal, which made very good economic sense for Ukraine, was met with cries of horror from nationalists, who threatened to bring impeachment proceedings against Kravchuk. The widespread opposition to the proposal left the future of the Fleet uncertain.

Overall, Kravchuk's nationalism brought mixed results: he demonstrated Ukraine's independence from Russia, and stopped Western governments from forgetting about Ukraine or treating it as an appendage of Russia. His nationalism also won Kravchuk the support of a section of the leadership of Rukh. However, there were few tangible benefits for Ukraine. Ukrainian statehood was assured, but going it alone was not an option that it could afford – as is shown by the slow moves towards accepting that the CIS had some role to play beyond that of a divorce court for the NIS, and the proposal to swap at least part of the Black Sea Fleet for debt. The reason for this was the decline in the Ukrainian economy throughout 1992 and 1993. The worse the economic situation became, the more financially dependent Ukraine was on Russia: Ukraine owed Russia more than any other NIS state and was dependent upon it for energy.[32] However, and perhaps ironically, economic decline meant that Kravchuk relied on his nationalist credentials for authority and support, despite the fact that there had to be some reconciliation with the CIS and Russia. He got credit from nationalists for his overall efforts at strengthening Ukrainian statehood, even as that statehood was compromised and as he lost support because of Ukraine's economic crisis.

The policies that led to economic crisis were, like nationalism, a result of Kravchuk's rise to power. Indeed, there was some relationship between nationalism and caution over economic reform because economic gradualism meant resisting pressure to reform from Russia. The economic reformers in Russia wanted to cut subsidies to other NIS states and ensure that they did not pursue policies which would spur inflation in Russia. Kravchuk had signalled Ukraine's desire to determine its own economic policy in 1991 by announcing that it would introduce a temporary currency, the karbovanets, in January 1992. This was supposed to be the first step towards complete monetary independence and a new currency, the hryvnia, in late 1992. (In the event, the introduction of the hryvnia was delayed until mid-1996.)

Although there was a link between nationalism and economics, a more important influence on economic reform was the former communist, eco-nomic *nomenklatura*. This group had supported Kravchuk in the Rada during his rise to power, and the old elite, although not organised into a political faction, remained the largest bloc in the Rada.[33] The power of the former *nomenklatura* was strongest in the industrial, russified, east and south Ukraine. These areas were dependent on state subsidies and they would not countenance radical economic reform.

The result of Kravchuk's economic caution was economic disaster for Ukraine. The deterioration of the Ukrainian economy led to the downfall of Prime Minister Vitold Fokin in September 1992. His successor, Leonid Kuchma, was the manager of the Southern Machine Construction Plant at Dnepropetrovsk (in eastern Ukraine), the largest rocket and missile plant in the world, and a classic member of the economic *nomenklatura*. Kuchma tried to appoint a team that would create a measure of consensus over reform and move Ukraine forward at a measured pace. His appointments to the economics ministries were from the economic *nomenklatura* and, like Kuchma himself, were all gradualists rather than 'shock therapists'. The need to take action on the economy secured Rada support for Kuchma. In November, the Rada gave him emergency powers for six months so that he could bring in policies to control inflation through a tighter budget and controls on wage increases. The first steps were also taken towards privatising trade and commerce. Kuchma also announced his support for the privatisation of small and medium factories. Large-scale industrial concerns were to be denationalised very slowly and subsidies were to be kept for those who needed them.

Kuchma's policies could not halt the decline of the Ukrainian economy. If anything, the situation worsened in 1993. In 1992, gross domestic product fell by 20 per cent. Inflation was 30–70 per cent a month, and consumer goods in February 1993 were 1305 per cent higher in price than in February 1992.[34] In 1993, inflation reached nearly 10,000 per cent and gross domestic product fell by a further 18 per cent.[35]

Kuchma's failure to control the economy's decline fed straight back into politics. The first challenge came in January 1993, when deputies from the south and east protested against price rises. Support from Rukh helped Kuchma overcome their protests, but the Rada as a whole was critical of his policies. Rukh, which had split in December 1993 and was now led by Vyacheslav Chornovil, an implacable opponent of Kravchuk and the *nomenklatura*[36], appealed for a referendum on new parliamentary elections. Kravchuk tried to turn the anti-government sentiment to his own advantage by taking up Rukh's appeal in February and calling for both new parliamentary and presidential elections. Thereafter, the situation began to develop into a farce.

In May, the Rada refused to extend Kuchma's emergency powers and he offered his resignation in protest. Kravchuk tried to take advantage of the situation and requested that the Prime Minister's powers be transferred to the presidency so that he could run the government directly. The Rada rejected his proposal and refused to accept Kuchma's resignation. The result was a stalemate. Popular dissatisfaction with the government, the Rada and the state of the economy soared. There were more calls for a referendum on elections to the Rada and the presidency, and in June strikes broke out amongst miners in the Donbass and threatened to become nationwide. Again, Kuchma tried to resign and was turned down. Faced with this pressure, the Rada accepted the call for a referendum on public confidence in the Rada and presidency, rather than one on the need for early elections. Kravchuk opposed this move and decreed himself head of government and Kuchma head of a special commission on economic reform. Kuchma tried to resign for a third time and Kravchuk was forced to withdraw his decree. In September, Kuchma tried to resign for a fourth time when the Rada did not meet another plea for special powers. Finally, he got his wish. The Rada requested that Kravchuk take over the government, and voted for elections to a new 450-seat parliament in March 1994 and to the presidency in June 1994. Kravchuk appointed another member of the *nomenklatura* acting Prime Minister and took over direct leadership of the cabinet himself.

The promise of elections to both a new parliament and for the presidency solved the crisis and as 1993 drew to a close most political activity became dedicated to election campaigning. Ukraine thus ended the first period of post-communist politics much as it had started it. The economy was in ruins and dominated by the old elite, and Kravchuk held power thanks to his use of nationalism. Politics had not taken the violent turn that had marred Russian politics but little progress had been made. No new constitution had been adopted and there had been no real institutional development. Perhaps the most significant development, and one that was to influence the outcome of the elections in 1994, was the re-emergence of the left in Ukraine over the course of 1993. Two successor parties to the Communist Party of Ukraine had emerged: the Socialist Party of Ukraine (SPU) and, later, the Communist Party of Ukraine (CPU). The SPU and CPU made progress as parties because they gave pro-Russian and anti-economic reform constituencies an outlet. This helped them in the 1994 elections and coloured much of Ukrainian politics thereafter.

The Baltic states: Estonia, Latvia and Lithuania

Politics became highly differentiated in the Baltic states in 1992–93. Estonia and Lithuania developed quickly: each had elections and new constitutions in 1992. Latvia moved more slowly, with elections to a new parliament in 1993. The differences between the three states are largely a reflection of their ethnic composition, although policies and circumstance also had a part to play. The question of citizenship for minorities was a major issue in Estonia and Latvia,

---

Textbox 8.4 Main events in the Baltic states, 1992–93

1992

January	*Estonia* Crisis over emergency powers for Prime Minister Savisaar leads to resignation of the government. Vähi becomes Prime Minister.
February	*Estonia* Supreme Council passes the enabling legislation for the restored 1938 citizenship law.
May	*Lithuania* Referendum on presidency goes against Landsbergis on technical grounds and he calls for new elections.
June	*Estonia* New constitution confirmed by referendum. New currency (kroon) introduced.
	Lithuania Referendum calling for speedy withdrawal of Russian troops.
July	*Latvia* Latvian ruble becomes the only legal currency.
	Lithuania Vagnorius forced to resign as Prime Minister. Abisala elected to replace him. Parliament decides to hold new elections in September.
September	*Estonia* Elections to presidency and Riigikogu. Meri becomes President.
	Lithuania Agreement with Russia that all troops should be withdrawn by 30 August 1993.
October	*Estonia, Latvia, Lithuania.* Yeltsin issues a decree halting the withdrawal of Russian troops from all three states.
	Estonia Laar elected as Prime Minister.

---

both of which had large Russian minorities (see Table 2.2).[37] The right were able to use this issue – differently in the two countries – and convert it into power. Citizenship questions played no part in Lithuanian politics, and this helps account for the collapse of the right and nationalism.

Economic issues had a less devastating effect on political life in the Baltic states than in Russia. All three states had major economic problems and suffered from economic decline.[38] Production fell as Russian markets were lost and it proved difficult to find new export markets. Prices rose as price liberalisation in Russia had a knock-on affect. But overall the Balts were more successful than most of the other NIS in controlling their economies. Estonia and Latvia introduced new currencies (the kroon and the lats) in 1992 and brought inflation down through tight monetary policies and control of wages. Lithuania was slower to respond, but it too introduced a new currency (the litas) in 1993, and had some success in slowing its economic decline.[39] The three states continued to trade with Russia and remained dependent on Russian energy. However, they also began to expand trade links with the outside world (particularly to Scandinavia) and attracted foreign capital.

	Latvia Guidelines on citizenship passed by Supreme Council.
	Lithuania First round of voting for Seimas and referendum on new constitution, which is accepted.
November	*Lithuania* Second round of voting for Seimas confirms victory for LDLP. Brazauskas elected acting President.
December	*Lithuania* Lubys becomes Prime Minister.
1993	
January	*Lithuania* Landsbergis decides not to run for President.
February	*Lithuania* Brazauskas elected President. Prime Minister Lubys resigns.
March	*Lithuania* Slezevicius becomes Prime Minister.
May	*Estonia, Lithuania* Admitted to Council of Europe.
	Lithuania Homeland Union founded from the Sajudis movement. Landsbergis elected chairman.
June	*Latvia* Elections to Saeima.
	Lithuania New currency, the litas, introduced.
July	*Estonia* Law on Aliens passed.
	Latvia Latvian Way/Farmers' Union coalition government formed under Prime Minister Birkavs. 1922 Constitution reinstated.
October	*Estonia* Local elections show fall in popularity of Laar's Isamaa Party.
November	*Estonia, Latvia* Russians agree to withdraw remaining troops by 31 August 1994.

Despite their success, economic problems endured for all three states. By the end of 1993, all three states' governments, even the Latvian government which had been in power for the shortest time, had suffered a decrease in popularity.

Estonia[40]

Estonian politics was plunged into crisis in January 1992, after a vote on emergency economic powers for Prime Minister Savisaar. Savisaar won the vote because of support from non-Estonian deputies. As a result, his support from the Popular Front of Estonia (PFE), which had a slim majority overall, disappeared and he resigned. Tiit Vähi took over as caretaker Prime Minister until a new constitution and elections were held. On 28 June, a referendum on a new constitution was held and was approved by an overwhelming majority (92.2 per cent) of the 66.3 per cent of voters who turned out. The new constitution established a new parliament, the Riigikogu, which was to have 101 deputies and would serve normally for four years (the first Riigikogu had a special term of two years). The Riigikogu was to be elected by proportional representation and would – normally – elect a president for five years. It was decided to have a direct vote for the first presidential election, with the Riigikogu deciding between the two leading candidates if no one received over 50 per cent of the popular vote.

Outwardly, the acceptance of a new constitution and the elections that it allowed for solved the problem of moving from a government of national liberation to a government of post-communism in Estonia. However, there was one major problem. The 1938 citizenship law, which had been reintroduced in November 1991 and given legal substance by the Supreme Council in February 1992, stripped Russians, and other ethnic groups who had immigrated to the new state during the Soviet period, of their citizenship. Applying for citizenship would take three years (dated from March 1990) and non-citizens were not allowed to vote in elections.

This law meant that nearly 40 per cent of Estonia's inhabitants were disenfranchised in the September 1992 elections. The Riigikogu had only one non-Estonian deputy (a Finn) and no party that directly represented ethnic minorities. Most of the seats (see Table 8.4) were won by electoral alliances, with the Isamaa (Fatherland) alliance gaining the most votes. Isamaa's leader, Mart Laar, formed a coalition government with another alliance, the Moderates, and the Estonian National Independence Party (ENIP). Arnold Rüütel, the ex-communist leader, won 41.8 per cent of the popular vote for President, but was defeated in the Riigikogu vote by Lennart Meri, a former Foreign Minister. Not surprisingly, the election of the Riigikogu as a mono-ethnic parliament and the formation of the Isamaa government did not reverse attitudes towards the Russian minority (one of the coalition members, ENIP, had been a leader in promoting citizenship only for those residents in Estonia since before 1940). The exclusion of the Russian minority from the Riigikogu elections led to protests from Russia. In October, Yeltsin, who had already linked troop withdrawals with citizenship in Estonia, issued a decree halting the withdrawal of all Russian troops from all the Baltic states. In Russian eyes matters did not improve in 1993. Estonia adopted a 'Law on the Language Standard' for citizenship in February 1993. In May 1993, non-citizens were barred from standing in local elections, an act that was anti-constitutional and broke earlier promises made to both the Council of Europe (Estonia had been admitted that month) and to the Russians. The worst moment in relations was reached after the Riigikogu passed a 'Law on Aliens' in July. This required any Russians who had not become citizens to apply for residence permits or be deported; Russia appealed to the UN and threatened Estonian sovereignty. At the same time, communist-dominated local authorities in the Russian towns of Narva and Sillamae organised referendums on autonomy for their districts. Turnout was low, but over 98 per cent of voters supported the call for autonomy.

Some partial integration of the Russian population was achieved towards

Table 8.4 The 1992 Estonian Riigikogu elections

	% vote	Seats
Isamaa	22.0	29
Secure Home	13.6	17
Popular Front	12.2	15
Moderates	9.7	12
National Independence Party	8.7	10
Independent Royalists	7.1	8
Estonian Citizens	6.8	8
Greens	2.6	1
Entrepreneurs' Party	2.3	1
Other	14.3	—

Source: Arter (1995, p. 254).

the end of the year. This was partly due to President Meri taking a fuller role and partly due to the weakening of Laar's Isamaa coalition. Meri refused to sign the Law on Aliens and helped moderate Russian politicans stand in the October 1993 local elections. Representative Assembly and another Russian group did well in the elections, winning a majority on Tallinn (the capital) council between them. Isamaa did badly, winning only five seats (out of 64) in Tallinn, and came behind Vähi's Coalition Party nationally. The Riigikogu modified the Law on Aliens in November to allow retired Russian military officers the right of residency. These acts, and the fact that no international agency (such as the OSCE, the Organisation on Security and Cooperation in Europe) found against Estonia's citizenship laws, helped secure an agreement in November between Estonia, Latvia and Russia which promised the withdrawal of all Russian troops by August 1994.

Latvia[41]

Latvia did not suffer the immediate same shock to its political system as Estonia. The decline of the Latvian Supreme Council was determined by the slow fragmentation of the Popular Front of Latvia (PFL). The fragmentation of the PFL began soon after independence when several factions were formed from within it. However, the biggest PFL loss was not to organised factional activity. Many PFL deputies became independents and did not bother turning up to sessions of the Council or its committees as they were too involved in work outside of parliament. When they did, they voted to suit themselves and their own interests. The PFL's loss of organisational identity caused numerous defeats for the government of Ivars Godmanis. Economic reform at the end of 1992 was forced into place by the IMF. However, it was too late to save the reputation of either the Supreme Council (which accepted economic reform under duress) or Godmanis.

The fragmentation of the PFL and the loss of ministers also created a turbulent political environment outside of the Supreme Council. Party development was chaotic and became more so after elections to a new 100-seat parliament – the Saeima – were announced. Some parties, such as the Latvian Farmers' Union, Ravnopravie (Equal Rights, a Russian organisation), the Democratic Labour Party (the reformed, pro-independence Communist Party) and the right-wing Latvian National Independence Movement (LNIM) had their roots in the pre-independence period. The announcement that the Saeima would be elected by proportional representation (with a 4 per cent barrier to stop some of the smaller parties from securing seats) led to a round of politicking as new groups were formed from the rump of the PFL. Two main groups emerged. Janis Jurkans, a former Foreign Minister, formed Harmony for Latvia-Economic Rebirth, a moderate group that claimed to stand for the original PFL platform and was for the assimilation of Russians. The other group, Latvia's Way, was created with the help of Latvian exiles as a moderate right-wing group to counter a perceived threat from the Democratic Labour Party (this never materialised). Its links with the exiled community gave Latvia's Way an appearance of being above the dirty politics of the Supreme Council, as did the fact that its figurehead leader was the popular head of state, Anatolijs Gorbunovs.

The Saeima election in June 1993 was, like the Estonian Riigikogu election, marred by the exclusion of Russians. The long decline of the Supreme Council had left Latvia unable to develop a policy to deal with its minorities. It thus remained stuck at the position attained immediately after independence, when the Supreme Council had given citizenship only to those who had held it prior to 1940 and had deferred a decision on the naturalisation of non-Latvian residents. This move angered Russia in the same way that Estonia's laws did. More Russians qualified for citizenship in Latvia however, since the country (especially Riga, the capital) had long had a Russian population. Even so, 34 per cent of the country's population were denied citizenship and could not vote in the elections. This helped the moderate right to victory, with the right in general gaining about 70 per cent of the vote overall (see Table 8.5). Latvia's Way formed a government in coalition with the Farmers' Union, support from other parties being sought issue-by-issue to give the government an overall majority. At its first session the Saeima voted to reinstate the 1922 constitution and elected Guntis Ulmanis, from the Farmers' Union, President. Ulmanis then nominated Valdis Birkavs as Prime Minister and he formed a cabinet composed of ten members of Latvia's Way and three members of the Farmers' Union.

The new moderate right government kept the economic policies that had been introduced by Godmanis and the IMF. The moderate nationalist majority also began to introduce more restrictive legislation on minorities. In November, the Saeima voted for a law on naturalisation that set quotas for the

Table 8.5 The 1993 Latvian Saeima elections

	% vote	Seats
Latvia's Way	32.4	36
LNIM	12.4	15
Harmony for Latvia-Economic Rebirth	12.0	13
Farmers' Union	10.7	12
Ravnopravie	5.8	7
Fatherland and Freedom	5.4	6
Christian Democratic Union	5.0	6
Democratic Centre Party	4.8	5
Others	12.5	

number of non-ethnic Latvians who could be naturalised each year. This, like the Estonian Law on Aliens, caused protests from Russia, and Ulmanis refused to sign the law. A law on naturalisation was eventually passed in mid-1994, but this was too late to prevent Russians from being excluded from the 1994 local elections.

Lithuania[42]

In its 1990 declaration of independence, Lithuania proclaimed the re-creation of the 1940 Republic of Lithuania. Although Lithuania looked back to the pre-war independence period for a sense of national identity, its citizenship laws were liberal: anyone who had been resident in the republic in 1989 was granted the right to become a citizen. This made Lithuania's entry into the Council of Europe easier than that of Estonia (they both joined in May 1993) and enabled it to come to an early agreement on complete troop withdrawals with Russia.

Lithuania's ability to deal quickly with its citizenship issue was not just a result of its not possessing the ethnic divisions – or fear of such – that affected politics in Estonia, Latvia, Moldova and Ukraine. Lithuania also managed to escape ethno-politics because it had something approximating a party system at the time of its independence. The early (December 1989) break with Moscow of the Lithuanian Democratic Labour Party (LDLP, the pro-independence communists) under Algirdas Brazauskas and Brazauskas's support for independence meant that the party had solid social support. The LDLP had supported Sajudis, which led the struggle for independence under President Landsbergis, whilst there was still a Soviet Union. But with independence achieved, the LDLP began to act as an independent party. This gave Lithuania something that was missing from all of the other European NIS: a strong left (the LDLP) *and* a strong right-wing party (Sajudis). There were other parties, including ethnic parties like the Polish Union and extremist parties, but the LDLP and Sajudis dominated the political landscape.

This balance between left and right was not, however, immediately apparent after independence and this led Lithuania into crisis. Sajudis, as a mass movement, had drifted to the right in the course of the final struggle with the USSR and supported Landsbergis's calls for the strengthening of the presidency. The move to the right was not popular with many of the Sajudis deputies in the Supreme Council and most of them, regardless of their political position, did not support Landsbergis's desire to build up the presidency. By 1992 neither Landsbergis nor Prime Minister Gediminas Vagnorius could count on a parliamentary majority, but the opposition was not strong enough to overthrow either of them. Landsbergis, supported by Sajudis activists outside the Supreme Council, gathered signatures for a referendum on the presidency and on the immediate withdrawal of Russian troops from Lithuania. The two issues were coupled because Landsbergis was aware that voters would be more likely to turn out for a strong presidency if it was presented as a continuation of the struggle to be free of Russia. The Supreme Council, because of its opposition to the extension of presidential power, separated the votes. The result, as Landsbergis had feared, was defeat for the idea of a strong presidency. In the referendum on the presidency on 25 May 1992, 69.4 per cent of voters supported Landsbergis's proposal. Only 57.5 per cent of the electorate turned out to vote however, and Landsbergis failed on the technical grounds that the 60 per cent of the total registered electorate had not voted as required by law. The referendum on Russian troop withdrawals three weeks later passed effortlessly with a 91 per cent vote for immediate withdrawal.

Landsbergis reacted to the failure of the presidency referendum by calling for new elections, which he thought he could win at the head of Sajudis. He did not get his chance to force an election until July, when dissatisfaction with the state of the economy and with the autocratic style of Prime Minister Vagnorius led deputies to vote for new elections in October. Landsbergis took advantage of this to remove Vagnorius and replace him with Aleksandras Abisala. This, however, was to be his last real use of power.

The first round of elections to the new parliament, the Seimas, were held on 25 October with run-offs for undecided seats in November. The Seimas had 141 seats, 70 of which were elected by proportional representation and 71 from single-member constituencies. It was thought that this mixed electoral system would balance the left (expected to do well in the proportional representation vote) and the right (expected to do well in the single-member constituencies). In the event the LDLP – to universal surprise – did well in both sets of elections because of popular discontent with high inflation and economic decline. The LDLP took 37 single-member seats and gained 44 per cent of the vote and 36 seats through proportional representation (see Table 8.6). This gave it enough seats to form a government on its own. Shocked by coming second, Sajudis and Landsbergis withdrew from the presidential elections scheduled for 14 February 1993. In May 1993, a new party, the Homeland Union (Conservatives of

Table 8.6 The 1992 Lithuanian Seimas elections

	% vote	Seats
LDLP	44.4	73
Sajudis	20.9	30
Christian Democrats	12.4	18
Social Democrats	6.0	8
Union of Nationalists		4
Polish Union		4
Centre Movement		2
Independents		2

Source: Lieven (1994, p. 269).

Lithuania) (HU(CL)), was formed out of Landsbergis's remaining support in Sajudis. The new party retained the loyalty of Landsbergis's support but could not dent the dominance of the LDLP. This dominance was confirmed by the presidential election. Brazauskas, who had been elected acting President by the Seimas in December 1993, defeated Stasys Lozoraitis by 60 per cent of the vote to 30 per cent. Once elected Brazauskas (who as President had to resign from the LDLP) nominated Adolfas Slezevicius as Prime Minister, replacing Bronislavas Lubys who had been put in place as a compromise candidate in December 1992.

The installation of an LDLP government did not lead to a restoration of Soviet power as Landsbergis had prophesied. Instead, the LDLP government wavered between populism and serious economic reform. Pressure from the IMF forced it to take some measures to control inflation after the introduction of a new currency, the litas, in June. This slowed economic decline in 1993 relative to 1992. The LDLP government was further accused of treachery for building closer relations with Moscow and Poland. However, Lithuanian sovereignty was not hurt by these measures, and Brazauskas pressed for and supported the closer integration of the Baltic states with the EU and NATO.

Belarus[43]

In many ways it is difficult to say that Belarus actually reached post-communism even after the collapse of the Soviet state. The Communist Party of Belarus was banned after the failure of the August coup (it was legalised again in February 1993) and the communist Chair of the Supreme Soviet, Mikalia Dzemyantsei, had been replaced by a Popular Front of Belarus (PFB) candidate, Stanislau Shushkevich. But little else changed.

Shushkevich could not implement radical economic reform because the Supreme Council and the government under Prime Minister Vyacheslau Kebich were dominated by members of the *nomenklatura*. The economy was

Textbox 8.5 Main events in Belarus, 1992–93

1992

January	PFB call for a referendum on abolishing Supreme Council and calling new elections.
May	PFB referendum petition considered by Central Electoral Commission.
June	New interim currency to replace the rouble introduced.
October	Supreme Council refuses to call a referendum. Declares elections to be held in March 1994 (one year earlier than scheduled).

1993

February	Communist Party of Belarus relegalised. Sets up the People's Movement of Belarus with two other Communist Parties.
March	Draft of new constitution completed. Contains provision for a strong presidency.
April	Supreme Council approves membership of CIS collective security pact. Shushkevich calls for a referendum on Belarusian neutrality.
September	Agreement on economic union signed with Russia.
November	Trade unions present petition calling for early elections.

more or less totally dependent on trade with other NIS states and received all of its gas supply and 91 per cent of its crude oil from Russia. Russia cut supplies in August 1993 and again in September because of defaulting on debt repayment. In September 1993 Belarus signed agreements with Russia on economic and monetary union but this did not help Belarusian monetary stability. In 1993 the state and collective farms inherited from the USSR was preserved in law when they received the legal right to own land and limit land redistribution for private farming. Privatisation for industry was planned for 1993, but the vouchers with which Belarusian citizens could buy stakes in enterprises were only due to be distributed in 1994. Industrial production fell, as in other states, over both 1992 and 1993, and inflation was rampant. On top of all these problems Belarus continued to pay high clean-up costs because of the nuclear disaster at Chernobyl in 1986.

The hold of the *nomenklatura* over economy, government and parliament meant that the PFB's struggle to decommunise the new country continued. At the same time Shushkevich tried to prise power away from Kebich. Neither the PFB or Shushkevich were successful.

In the spring of 1992 the PFB gathered over 400,000 signatures on a petition calling for early elections. The Central Electoral Commission had no choice but to confirm that this was a legal petition meeting the requirements for calling a referendum. The Supreme Council should have met and set a referendum date within a month of the petition's approval by the Electoral Commission. However, the Supreme Council did not meet until October, and it simply refused to recognise the referendum petition as legal and did not schedule a vote. A small concession was made: elections to parliament were brought forward by a year to March 1994.

At the same time that the Supreme Council was rejecting the referendum on elections, Shushkevich was losing power to Kebich. Kebich's support in the Supreme Council was stronger than Shushkevich's, despite the fact that Shushkevich was Chair of the Supreme Council. Over the summer of 1992, Kebich began to act autonomously of the Supreme Council and arrogated some of its powers (such as signing international agreements) to himself and his government. Shushkevich's control over the Supreme Council suffered further because of his disagreements with it over the draft constitution and links with Russia. The draft constitution (first published in August 1992) proposed the establishment of a presidency. This was rejected by Shushkevich and the PFB who feared that it would lead to authoritarianism. The debate over the constitution dragged over into 1993. In May, the Supreme Council accepted just over half of the proposed constitution's clauses. Debate continued for the rest of the year and was only settled in 1994.

The issue of relations with Russia was far more divisive. Most Belarusian politicians accepted that there had to be close relations with Russia because of the country's economic dependency. What distinguished between them was the question of how far they should go towards partnership – and possibly reintegration – with Russia. Shushkevich and large portions of the PFB leadership supported the CIS but wanted to defend Belarusian sovereignty. The Supreme Council, the government and the *nomenklatura* in general were more predisposed towards moves to reintegration. Matters came to a head in April 1993 over the CIS collective security pact. The Supreme Council, against Shushkevich's wishes, ratified the pact. Shushkevich claimed that the agreement violated Belarusian neutrality and called for a referendum on the neutrality question. In June, the Supreme Council responded by calling for a vote of no confidence in Shushkevich. The vote was overwhelmingly against him, but was rendered invalid by the PFB faction, which walked out and made the session inquorate. Shushkevich survived, but only for a short while (see Chapter 11).

The PFB and Shushkevich thus made little headway against the power of the *nomenklatura* in 1992 and 1993. The only sign that change might come about was popular dissatisfaction with the Supreme Council and the government. The most visible sign of this was the petition submitted to the Council by the trade unions in November 1993. This petition echoed the PFB's call for early elections and contained nearly 750,000 signatures. Despite this show of disapproval in the parliament, there were no guarantees that popular support could be harnessed to finally break the control of the *nomenklatura* in the scheduled elections. Party development was weak and the roots of parties shallow in comparison to the power of former party officials. The PFB had established itself as a party in May 1993 and the relegalised communists had united to form the People's Movement of Belarus. There were no other significant parties and people's loyalties were to the *nomenklatura* that employed them. The prospects of Belarus making progress on its own towards democracy or solving its economic problems looked slight.

Moldova[44]

Moldovan politics underwent a fundamental realignment in 1992–93. The Popular Front of Moldova (PFM) declined in importance as a consequence of its failure to see that reunification with Romania was not a viable political option. President Mircea Snegur moved closer to the CIS to curry favour with Russia over the question of Transdnestr and because of Moldovan economic dependency on Russia. This led Snegur into further conflict with PFM deputies in the Supreme Council (his relations with the PFM were already strained because of their opposition to the establishment of the presidency).

The violence that had flared in Transdnestr after the failure of the August 1991 coup continued in the first few months of 1992 and Moldova lost control of virtually all of the area. This prompted Snegur and the government of Prime Minister Valeriu Muravschi to attempt a military solution. Moldova formed an army in the spring of 1992 and engaged the rebels in Transdnestr in the early summer. The Moldovan forces fared badly against the rebel forces, which were trained, supplied and supported by General Alexander Lebed's 14th Army. The 14th Army was nominally under Russian control, but was in practice obedient to Lebed. Lebed worked his 'defence' of the Russian minority in Transdnestr up into political popularity in Russia. (In 1995 he quit the Army and became a full-time politician – see Chapter 11). The defeat of the Moldovan forces led President Snegur to negotiate with Yeltsin and a ceasefire was signed and monitored by Russian troops brought into the area. The influx of even more Russian troops consolidated the hold of the rebel forces over the area.

The founding of an army and the conflict with Transdnestr placed the weak Moldovan economy under enormous strain and meant that there was no real effort at economic reform. Snegur blamed Muravschi and the government for this and in June they were forced to resign. They were replaced in July by a 'government of national consensus' under Andrei Sangheli. The core support of this new government was the Democratic Agrarian Party of Moldova

---

Textbox 8.6 Main events in Moldova, 1992–93

1992

January	Snegur granted power to appoint government without legislative approval.
March	Moldovan Army formed and attempts to hold territory in Transdnestr.
June	Prime Minister Muravschi forced to resign due to popular discontent over living standards. Fighting between Moldovan forces, 14th Army and Transdnestr rebels.
July	Sangheli becomes Prime Minister and sets up a government of national consensus. Snegur signs agreements with Yeltsin which lead to a ceasefire in Transdnestr.
December	Snegur proposes a referendum on Moldova's future status.

1993

January	Alexandru Mosanu resigns as Chairman of parliament over the referendum.
February	Petr Lucinschi becomes Chairman of parliament.
March	Parliament completes debate on new constitution which declares Moldova an independent state.
July	Snegur asks parliament to ratify Moldovan economic membership of the CIS. Narrowly fails.
August	Parliament becomes inquorate and ceases to function. Russia applies trade sanctions to force Moldova to join the CIS Economic Union.
September	Snegur signs CIS Treaty on Economic Union.
October	New electoral law adopted.

(DAPM, effectively the leadership of state and collective farms and the Moldovan equivalent of the economic *nomenklatura* in other NIS) allied with deputies from Transdnestr, the Gagauz districts, and factions that had broken with the PFM. The advent of the Sangheli government and the ceasefire with Russia showed the direction of politics to be firmly away from the PFM and reunification with Romania.

In December 1992, Snegur came down firmly against the PFM by calling for Moldova to develop independently and announcing a referendum to decide whether the country should unite with Romania, join CIS (the Supreme Council had not ratified the original agreement to join the CIS), or remain independent. This prompted a series of crises in the Supreme Council. The Chairman of the Council, Alexandru Mosanu (a PFM deputy) quit in protest in January. Petr Lucinschi (the former First Secretary of the Moldovan

Communist Party) was elected to replace him. The Supreme Council then proceeded to ratify the constitution which declared Moldova an independent state in March. Snegur described the country as a member of the CIS. In July, he requested the Council to ratify the CIS agreement on Economic Union. Russia added to the pressure to join by applying trade sanctions on the grounds that Moldova was not a CIS member. The vote in the Council failed to ratify the agreement on Economic Union because PFM deputies, taking advantage of the absence of pro-Russian deputies, voted against it and denied it the absolute majority required to make it law. Snegur signed anyway and the majority of pro-government deputies walked out of parliament in protest at the bill's failure. This rendered the Supreme Council inoperative. A majority was finally convened in October, and a new electoral law was passed which set elections for February 1994. This effectively signalled the end of the PFM and any prospect of unification with Romania. Russia acknowledged Moldova's new attitude towards the CIS by removing trade sanctions in December.

Conclusion

The NIS made very little overall progress towards democracy and a market economy in 1992–93. The Russian elections of December 1993 had followed the bloody suppression of the parliaments. An extremist party, the Liberal Democrats under Zhirinovsky, had won the most votes and most of the other parties that had stood in the election were created by the political elite at the last minute (the exceptions were the LDPR and CPRF). They did not look as though they could form the basis of a strong party system. Party development was similarly weak in Ukraine and Belarus. In Moldova, the DAPM was shaping up to be a significant force. But its democratic credentials were thin since it was a creation of the new state's agricultural *nomenklatura*. The Baltic states looked to have made more progress with their elections of new, post-communist parliaments. But this progress was marred by the exclusion of ethnic minorities in Estonia and Latvia. Lithuania's success in achieving an ideological, rather than an ethnic, change of government was also no guarantee of democratic consolidation over the longer term. The victory of the LDLP did not lead to the restoration of communism but it threw the right into confusion and weakened the left–right balance in Lithuania. On top of these political problems the NIS had made little headway in transforming their economies. The Baltic states had achieved some stability, but elsewhere the power of the *nomenklatura* had not been broken. Indeed the first steps towards private property had often strengthened the *nomenklatura*'s grip on the economy. The failure to achieve a clean break with the economic power of the *nomenklatura*, or to build strong new, democratic governments and popular institutions, made it difficult for the NIS to consolidate the democratic practices that they did have. Much of political life was focused on individual politicians. Individual politicians were the source of patronage and resources. Political parties were vehicles for politicians, rather than representatives of social or ideological trends. The high personalisation of politics also fostered corruption, which was widespread in all of the NIS. The law and law enforcement were weak, and deals were done through informal channels rather than through legislatures or proper administrative hierarchies.

Notes

1. Russia supplied all the natural gas used in Belarus, Estonia, Moldova, Lithuania and Latvia and 56 per cent of that used by Ukraine. It supplied 91 per cent of crude oil used in Belarus, 94 per cent in Lithuania and 89 per cent in Ukraine. The others imported virtually all of their refined oil from Russia. See Dawisha and Parrot (1994, p. 175).
2. On the early development of the CIS see Sheehy (1995, pp. 221–5).
3. On the conflict between Yeltsin and Khasbulatov/Rutskoi, see Brudny (1995).
4. White and McAllister (1996, p. 107).
5. For Zhirinovsky's views see Frazer and Lancelle (1994); Klepikova and Solovyov (1995).
6. See Handelman (1994).
7. Lipton and Sachs (1992, pp. 229–30); Åslund and Layard (1993); Åslund (1994).
8. Johnson and Kroll (1991, p. 283).
9. Robinson (1994, pp. 300–1).
10. Ickes and Ryterman (1992 and 1993).
11. Lohr (1993).
12. Ellman (1993); McFaul (1993b). For a critical evaluation of the idea of centrism in Russian politics at this time, see Lester (1995, ch. 5).
13. For details of privatisation, see S. Clarke (1994); Rutland (1994); Boycko *et al.* (1995).
14. On the development of the radical opposition see Hahn (1994); B. Clark (1995, pp. 139–93).
15. Tolz (1993); Sakwa (1993b, p. 83); Löwenhardt (1995, pp. 136–7).
16. Slider (1994, pp. 251–9).
17. *Ibid.*, pp. 256–7.
18. Hanson (1993); Smith (1995, pp. 29–31).
19. Brudny (1995, pp. 93–4); Steele (1994, p. 374).
20. For a more complete description of the events of October, see Brown (1993); Steele (1994, pp. 371–87); B. Clark (1995, pp. 241–64). Opposing Russian views can be found in Buzgalin and Kolganov (1994); Yeltsin (1994, pp. 241–83).
21. See for example Steele (1994).
22. The vote on the constitution was a plebiscite rather than a referendum since the law on referendums required that over half of all registered voters (not just voters who cast a vote) support a constitutional change. See Wyman *et al.* (1994, p. 255).
23. For a more complete analysis of the 1993 election see Urban (1994); Lentini (1995); Sakwa (1995).
24. For doubts on the validity of the referendum and election results, see Tolz and Wishnevsky (1994).

25. See Omel'chenko and Pilkington (1995) for a description of this in the Ul'yanovsk region.
26. For extensive analyses of voters' motives see Hough (1994); Whitefield and Evans (1994); Wyman *et al.* (1995); Baglione and Clark (1995).
27. For a more extended version of this argument, see Motyl (1995).
28. For a historical survey of Russian–Ukrainian relations, see Holman (1994).
29. For another discussion of these issues, see Duncan (1996, pp. 200–1, 203–5).
30. For a survey of the initial dispute over the Fleet, see D. Clarke (1992) and Foye (1992).
31. Many Russians do not regard Ukraine as an independent country because its history is bound up with Russia's. See Lester (1994) for an overview of Russian opinions.
32. See note 1 to this chapter and Whitlock (1993); Dawisha and Parrott (1994, pp. 180–1).
33. Ryabchuk (1992, pp. 53–4); Duncan (1996, p. 202).
34. Dawisha and Parrot (1994, p. 178).
35. Karatnycky (1995, p. 117).
36. Ryabchuk (1992); Solchanyk (1993, pp. 58–60).
37. Minority rights in Latvia and Estonia will be dealt with below. For an overview of the issue in all three Baltic states, see Raun (1994b).
38. For details of the Baltic economies at the start of independence, see Bradshaw *et al.* (1994, pp. 169–79).
39. See W. S. Brown (1993); Dreifelds (1996, pp. 113–41); Girnius (1994, pp. 101–2).
40. For other descriptions of Estonian politics in 1992–93, see Kand (1994); Kask (1994); Kionka (1995); Lieven (1994, pp. 282–89); Melvin (1995, pp. 44–50); Raun (1994a); Stepan (1994).
41. On Latvian politics during 1992–93, see Dreifelds (1996); Lieven (1994, p. 294–302); Melvin (1995, pp. 38–44); Plakans (1994); Smith (1996, pp. 162–6).
42. For other descriptions of Lithuanian politics in this period, see T. D. Clark (1995a); Girnius (1994); Lieven (1994, pp. 259–74); Senn (1994 and 1996).
43. Surveys of politics in Belarus during 1992–93 can be found in Clem (1996); Dawisha and Parrot (1994, pp. 140–3); Lukashuk (1995a and 1995b); Markus (1994a); Marples (1993); Zaprudnik and Fedor (1995).
44. For further discussion of politics in Moldova in 1992–93, see Crowther (1994); Crowther and Fedor (1995); Eyal and Smith (1996); Melvin (1995, pp. 64–77); Miller (1994); Socor (1994a and 1995b).

CHAPTER 9

East European roads to democracy, 1991–93

Introduction

The countries under review were placed under an extremely heavy burden of decision-making between 1991 and 1993. In Albania, this comprised the full range of tasks involved in the transition from communism. In Yugoslavia, the fact that all the republics had long been going their own separate ways was finally confronted in a clash which turned into the first war in Europe since 1945. Elsewhere, the range of problems were more broadly similar. One was the need to pass new constitutions, or, failing this, to make yet more amendments to existing ones. In practice, new constitutions were only imperative for new states. The Yugoslav successor states and the Czech and Slovak Republics had to have them, and while Bulgaria and Romania also passed new constitutions (in 1991), Poland and Hungary did not.

A second problem where approaches between states differed notably was dealing with the communist past, either by lustration laws, which banned certain categories of former communists or communist collaborators from public office, or through the prosecution of former communist leaders.[1] Lustration was most thorough in the former GDR, where citizens were also given access to their own secret police files (an organisational task which would have been hard to cope with without west German resources), and in the Czech Republic. Both had been fairly modern, industrial societies at the advent of communism, and had been subjected to authoritarian forms of communism. Poland and Hungary trailed behind in passing legislation. In Bulgaria and Slovakia, the application of lustration laws was rather temporary; changes of government (from anti-communist to neutral) in 1992 largely ended this phase of politics. Lustration was a contentious and fraught process, opposed not merely by post-communist parties, but also by liberals who found it both legally dubious and unhelpful to national conciliation and building the future. It also left untouched former communist power-bases

219

which related to the control of economic enterprise rather than public service. Criminal prosecution of previous communist rulers was a less rigorous and more symbolic form of coming to terms with the past. For former communist elites who had managed to retain their grip on power – for example, in Romania and Bulgaria – it had the distinct advantage that it was less likely to affect them personally. Only in Albania, where the new anti-communist government installed in 1992 began to prosecute communist/socialist leaders for actions taken after the introduction of democratic structures, did lustration issues clearly appear to be abused for political ends.

The third, and in many respects crucial, problem of the period was economic reform. While the new constitutions and lustration laws produced much controversy and heated political debate in parliament, it was the economy which produced the greatest dilemmas for governments, for it was economics which most directly affected the lives of all their citizens. Whatever the international pressure to reform the economy as quickly as possible, in a democracy it is ultimately the verdict of the voters which decides whether governments will be permitted to continue their chosen economic path. Where ruling parties were ousted at the ballot box, it was most often because of dissatisfaction with the effects of economic reform.

Economic discontent therefore had political outcomes. The most notable in this period – and that which followed – were when the electorate expressed its economic discontent by returning post-communist parties to power. The most spectacular case was presented by the famously anti-communist Poles, who in the autumn of 1993 returned an essentially post-communist alliance to power, but this was not an isolated example. It was occasionally suggested (not least by opposition parties) that this represented a reversion to the communist past. Yet the idea that the electorate were putting communism back in power through the election victories of communist successor parties was fundamentally to misunderstand or misrepresent the essence of Soviet-style communism. Communist Parties in a one-party world did not represent left-wing political views. This is not to deny that some communists were left-wing, or that some (mainly older) Communist Party members were idealists fired by memories of the 'constructive', heroic phase of communism after the Russian Revolution or World War II. None the less, Communist Parties had essentially been power structures. Their power was underwritten in Eastern Europe by the Soviet military threat. Once this was removed, the *invincibility* of their power was removed, but the resources – in the most general sense of the word – at their disposal were not entirely demolished.

In many countries which had been underdeveloped prior to the advent of communism – such as the Balkan countries and Soviet successor states – communists had managed to create a personal power-base unrelated to Soviet power. This derived not from their ideas, but from their everyday contact networks, and their clientelistic power-bases remained sufficiently intact for them to remain in power under their new name. In a second group of countries – Poland, Hungary, eastern Germany and Slovakia – the communists had been ejected from power in initial elections, but had then reformed themselves on a programmatic basis as left-wing social democratic parties. Yet even these parties were not purely social democratic, whatever their aspirations. They were burdened with a hard core of older members who had remained with them less through left-wing conviction than a lack of the imagination and flexibility necessary to move themselves elsewhere. The label 'communist' or 'post-communist', therefore, concealed a wide and confusing range of ideological and economic orientations.

Finally, in this chapter we shall look at the area of post-communist decision-making which had been least predicted in advance – that related to questions of national identity. In some countries, such as Romania and Bulgaria, this led to a steady stream of political controversies relating to the position of minorities. However, in the two multinational federations, where the different nations had been accorded equal rights under the communist system, dissolution of the common state occurred. The means used to achieve this – political negotiation in Czechoslovakia and armed conflict in Yugoslavia – had almost nothing in common. Former communist states had different histories and possessed different structural resources for problem-solving, and there could therefore be varying outcomes of the transition from communism.

Albania

Albania held its first moderately free post-communist election in March 1991 – the last of the East European countries to do so. Since opposition parties had only been legalised the previous December, there had been pressure on the ruling communist Party of Labour of Albania (PLA) to delay the elections so that the communists' organisational advantage would be minimised.[2] This they refused to do, and in view of the increasing chaos enveloping the country, there was something to be said for early elections. Albania's economic situation was deteriorating rapidly, accompanied by continuing public demonstrations (often violently suppressed by the regime), the first strikes, and the onset set of mass emigration. Both the Greek government, which was affected in January 1991 by thousands of Albania's ethnic Greek inhabitants as well as many Albanians crossing the border, and the Italian government, which was hit in March by the arrival of ships commandeered by disaffected young Albanians arriving in the Italian port of Brindisi, were markedly in favour of the Albanians solving their problems at home.

Five opposition parties contested the elections, as well as the PLA and its affiliated organisations. As can be seen from Table 9.1, the elections were clearly won by the PLA, who gained over half the vote and two-thirds of the

---

Textbox 9.1 Main events in Albania, 1991–93

1991

March　　　First elections are won by communist Party of Labour of
Albania (PLA), as other parties have difficulties campaigning
outside cities.

April　　　A law about basic constitutional provisions is passed and
　　　　　　PLA leader Alia elected President.

June　　　Government resigns after massive strike-wave. Bufi (PLA)
　　　　　　becomes Prime Minister of a government comprising
　　　　　　parliamentary parties and experts. The PLA becomes
　　　　　　Socialist Party of Albania.

December　　The Democratic Party (DP) leaves the coalition government.
　　　　　　Bufi resigns and is replaced by Vilson Ahmeti.

1992

March　　　Second elections are won by Democratic Party.

April　　　Alia resigns as President as parliament elects Berisha (DP) as
　　　　　　his replacement. Meksi (DP) forms coalition government
　　　　　　largely comprising DP.

July　　　DP vote decreases sharply (to 43 per cent) in local elections.

September　Former President Alia is placed under house arrest.
　　　　　　After DP split, breakaway leader Gramoz Pashko sets up
　　　　　　Democratic Alliance.

1993

January　　Enver Hoxha's widow is sentenced to nine years'
　　　　　　imprisonment.

June　　　The opposition and the Social Democratic Party boycott
　　　　　　parliament to protest at the failure to adopt a new
　　　　　　constitution. They returned in August.

July　　　Former Prime Minister Fatos Nano arrested on charges of
　　　　　　corruption.

August　　Former President Alia is arrested for abuse of power.

---

seats in parliament; most of the remainder of the seats went to the Democratic Party, with five obtained by the Democratic Union of the Greek Minority (OMONIA). The most unpleasant surprise for the PLA was the failure of its leader, Ramiz Alia, to gain a seat.[3] This was due to two factors. First, the country had a majoritarian election system in which each of 250 constituencies returned one deputy (with a second round of voting being held if no candidate obtained more than 50 per cent of the vote in the first round). A candidate's

Table 9.1 Albanian elections 31 March/7 April/14 April 1991

	% vote	Seats
Party of Labour of Albania	56	169
Democratic Party of Albania	39	75
OMONIA (Greek party)	1	5
Committee of Veterans	0	1
Total		250

Source: Statistical Yearbook of Albania 1991 (1991, p. 30);
Szajkowski (1994, p. 6).

fate, therefore, depended on the votes of the citizens in one constituency only. Secondly, the Albanian electorate was divided by a quite exceptionally strong urban/rural cleavage, with the Democratic Party winning almost all seats in the cities, while the PLA was predominant in the rural areas where most of the population lived: because of the country's very weak infrastructure (and the ban on private cars during the communist period), it was particularly hard for the recently formed Democratic Party to establish a presence outside the major towns. Alia, however, had chosen to stand in a Tirana constituency, where, in accordance with the general voting patterns, the Democratic Party candidate won an outright majority in the first round.

The elections did little to calm the situation in the country. As the PLA's victory was announced, more demonstrations took place in Shkodër, where opposition supporters made allegations of electoral fraud against the PLA (although these were not, in the main, supported by international observers of the election). Four demonstrators were shot dead by the police. The opposition refused the PLA's appeals to cooperate in government, and also objected to the draft of a new constitution presented to the parliament in April, arguing that such changes were premature. In its place, interim constitutional amendments were adopted, which included the provision for an executive president, to be elected by a two-thirds parliamentary majority. Since the PLA possessed such a majority, Alia was confirmed as President and resigned all his party offices.

However, the country's problems did not end here. The first Prime Minister selected, the PLA reformer Fatos Nano, presided over a government comprising solely PLA members, but resigned in June 1991 in the face of massive strikes and continuing protests over the deaths of the Shkodër demonstrators.[4] He was replaced by Ylli Bufi, who was also a PLA member, but who led a government half composed of opposition members. The decades-long PLA monopoly of power was thereby broken. Yet even this government only lasted until December, when it was abandoned by the Democratic Party, and a temporary government under Vilson Ahmeti was formed which largely comprised non-party 'experts'. Albania had been hit by renewed emigration waves and economic chaos occasioned in part by spontaneous decollectivisation of agriculture, and it survived the winter largely thanks to food aid from Italy.

In March 1992, new elections were held, following changes to the electoral law a month earlier.[5] The new electoral law reduced the size of the parliament to 140 members, of whom 100 were chosen from single-member constituencies, while 40 seats were distributed on the basis of proportional representation to parties whose candidates had together obtained more than 4 per cent of the national vote. Since the allocation of these 40 seats took account of how many of each party's deputies had been directly elected, the overall party balance was roughly proportional to the votes they had received.[6]

As can be seen in Table 9.2, the results were a clear defeat for the communists, despite the fact that the PLA had started attempting to deal with its past, and had changed its name to the Socialist Party of Albania (SPA) in June 1991. The victors were the Democratic Party, who, with 62 per cent of the vote, nearly obtained a two-thirds majority. Of the three smaller parties to enter parliament, the Human Rights Union Party was a largely Greek ethnic minority party, and the party's name reflected the fact that parties formed on 'ethnic principles' had by now been banned.

The Democratic Party leader, Sali Berisha, was elected President by the parliament, but only after the constitution had been amended slightly to increase the President's powers.[7] Berisha appointed a government under the premiership of Aleksander Meksi which was largely composed of Democratic Party members (there was one minister each from the Republican and Social Democratic Parties). The Meksi government succeeded in calming the situation in Albania somewhat, and in 1993 the country actually showed positive economic growth rates – albeit from a level below which it was almost impossible to sink. However, in spite of the Democratic Party's numerically strong position in parliament, it did not possess alone the two-thirds majority necessary for passing a new constitution, and it was weakened by splits both within the party leadership itself, and, in summer 1993, with its Social Democratic coalition partner.[8]

Table 9.2 Albanian election, 29 March/5 April 1992

	% vote (1st round)	Seats
Democratic Party of Albania	62	92
Socialist Party of Albania	26	38
Social Democratic Party	4	7
Human Rights Union Party (Greek party)	3	2
Republican Party	3	1
Total		140

Source: Szajkowski, (1994 p. 11).

In some respects, developments in Albania in the early 1990s conformed to a Balkan pattern familiar from Bulgaria or Romania. For example, the first elections were won by the communists, and at one point, the country had to resort to a non-party government of technocrats. The banning of parties based on ethnic principles was reminiscent of Bulgaria, and its tendency to put former communists on trial was reminiscent of both Bulgaria and Romania.

Yet in many ways Albania was also unique. Its economic situation was worse than elsewhere in the post-communist world: rampant unemployment made even the most extreme estimates for eastern Germany look low; the weakness of the country's infrastructure had led state structures virtually to collapse for a period in 1991/92, with the result that there was little orderly control of the decollectivisation process; and whereas crime rates rose alarmingly everywhere in the region, nowhere was the situation as frightening as in Albania. The hopelessness of the country's situation led to more frantic mass attempts at emigration than anywhere else in the post-communist world, and, whereas foreign aid was important to all states emerging from communist rule, the need was nowhere quite as desperate as Albania. Being by tradition a largely Moslem country, Albania was able to extend its international links by becoming a member of the Islamic Conference.[9] Such contacts were also important because of Albania's highly vulnerable geopolitical situation: the danger of the Yugoslav war spreading southwards was considerable, not least because Albanian minorities in Serbia and Macedonia were nearly as numerous as the population of Albania itself.

In terms of political developments, Albania had some unusual characteristics. One of the most alarming was the extent of reprisals against former communists. Ramiz Alia, despite having been an initiator of reform, was arrested in September 1992, within six months of ceasing to be President; and in July 1993, parliamentary immunity was removed from the SPA leader Fatos Nano so that he could be arrested on corruption charges.[10] Therefore, although Albania appeared to be making some progress in 1992 and 1993, its path to democracy was far from assured.

Bulgaria

Bulgaria commenced 1991 with a newly formed multi-party government led by an independent, Dimitar Popov. The previous Bulgarian Socialist Party (BSP) Prime Minister, Lukanov, had been ousted due to internal party dissent, strikes and street violence. Since failure to solve Bulgaria's economic problems had been a major cause of the previous government's fall, the new government set about rectifying the situation. Although it still contained many ministers associated with the BSP, it also included members of the Union of Democratic Forces (UDF) – previously the main opposition grouping – and

---

Textbox 9.2 Main events in Bulgaria, 1991–93

1991

January	Agreement Guaranteeing a Peaceful Transition to Democratic Society signed by leading government parties.
March	BSP apologises for socialism.
July	New constitution is ratified.
October	In the second elections, the UDF becomes the largest party.
November	Dimitrov, the UDF Chair, becomes Prime Minister of a minority government relying on support from deputies of the Turkish party Movement for Rights and Freedoms (MRF).

1992

January	Zhelev re-elected President in direct election; narrow victory over BSP candidate in second ballot.
October	Dimitrov government falls, after itself asking for a vote of confidence, when MRF withdraws support in parliament.
December	Berov (non-party) becomes Prime Minister in government of 'national responsibility' with BSP and MRF support.

1993

January	Twenty-three UDF deputies are excluded from the movement for supporting the Berov government. Other deputies leave soon after.
May	The UDF begins demonstrations against President Zhelev.
June	Vice-President Dimitrova resigns after disagreements with President Zhelev.

UDF ministers held two major economic posts, so that the government marked a notable change in the direction of economic reform. However, it was essentially a typical compromise government without the strength to pursue real reform. Nevertheless, the reforms it carried out met with approval in the West, but price liberalisation led to the costs of many staple items such as food and transport increasing by several hundred per cent in the first quarter of the year. At the same time, there was a sharp decline in industrial output, and Bulgaria was particularly badly affected by the loss of the Soviet market, upon which its exports had been heavily dependent.

Apart from trying to solve the country's economic problems, the major task on the political agenda in the first half of 1991 was the passing of a new constitution. The issue caused sharp controversy, both between the two main groups of parliamentary deputies, the BSP and the UDF, and within the UDF itself. Since the BSP still had a majority in the Grand National Assembly, it was in a good position to influence which draft of the constitution would be adopted, and there were fears that the constitution passed would be too favourable to the interests of the socialists. Since no referendum was to be held on the constitution, no change in the popular mood since the elections of the previous year could be reflected in the decision-making procedure. However a two-thirds majority of votes – which the BSP did not command on its own – was required to pass the constitution, so some opposition support had to be forthcoming. The fact that the constitution was finally passed on 9 July 1991 with the necessary two-thirds majority, and was signed by 309 of the Assembly's 400 deputies, was due to a split within the UDF. Two of the largest parties of which UDF was composed, the Bulgarian Social Democratic Party and one of the country's Agrarian parties, the Bulgarian Agrarian National Union-Nikola Petkov, decided to support the constitution. Other UDF deputies, however, staged a walkout from parliament in May, and by early July, some of them, including the leaders of several parties, were holding a fruitless hunger strike near the parliament building.[11]

Like many new constitutions in the post-communist world, the Bulgarian constitution was not perfect and was unclear on some issues, yet it was none the less an improvement on the country's existing legal framework, establishing, for example, a Constitutional Court. There were also reasonable provisions for future amendment by a two-thirds parliamentary majority. The constitution protected basic human and civil rights, such as freedom of the press and religion, and stated in Article 19 that: 'The economy of the Republic of Bulgaria shall be based on free economic initiative.'[12] On the other hand, as a socialist legacy, Article 48 also affirmed the right to work, and that 'the state shall take care to provide conditions for the exercising of this right',[13] a provision which had elsewhere – for example in eastern Germany – been advocated by some, but deemed impractical as a constitutional provision. The mainly Turkish Movement for Rights and Freedoms (MRF) objected to the constitution on the grounds that there was no reference to minorities, and it included a ban on political parties based on ethnic, racial or religious lines. Yet the preamble at least referred to 'the people of Bulgaria', thus avoiding the phrase 'Bulgarian nation', whose counterpart in the equivalent section of the Slovak constitution was to cause lasting controversy.

A curiosity of the constitution, however, was the position of the President. In a change of the procedure used the previous year, the President was to be directly elected for a term of five years. However, the Bulgarian President, unlike many popularly elected counterparts, has a role broadly similar to that of Presidents elsewhere who are chosen by parliaments. The President can return legislation to parliament for further discussion, but it can be then passed again by a simple majority and the President is thereafter obliged to promulgate it within seven days. He is, however, nominal head of the armed forces, and he also has an (undefined) voice in foreign policy.[14]

With the constitution passed, the Grand National Assembly reverted to being a National Assembly charged with normal legislative functions pending new elections, which took place on 13 October 1991. Bulgaria thus became the first of the former Warsaw Pact countries (excluding the special case of eastern Germany) to hold a second democratic election. This is perhaps symptomatic of one of the interesting features of Bulgarian politics in the early post-communist period, which was that there were rather numerous changes of government, but against the background of what was, at least superficially, a relatively stable party system.

The elections took place according to a new election law which reduced the number of deputies to 240, all of whom were to be elected on the basis of pro-portional representation from parties obtaining more than 4 per cent of the vote nationally.[15] The first controversy in the run-up to the elections con-cerned the admissibility of the MRF, which was generally perceived as the Turkish Party, in the light of the election law's constitutionally based ban on parties formed on ethnic, racial or religious lines. Local attempts to ban the movement's participation in the election were finally overturned by a Supreme Court decision on 20 September. It was clear, however, that the BSP had favoured the movement's banning, and considerable nationalist animosity was generated not only against the country's Turkish minority, but also against the interference of Western countries which had criticised both the attempt to exclude the MRF, and the general principle of banning parties with an ethnic or religious platform.

The final election result (see Table 9.3) was something of a surprise in that only three lists of parties – the UDF, the MRF and an alliance led by the BSP – gained the 4 per cent of the vote necessary to enter parliament. Nevertheless, only one of these three, the Turkish MRF, had actually increased its vote; the UDF lost nearly 2 per cent of its vote, and the BSP 14 per cent. What had happened was that nearly a quarter of the vote in the 1991 elections went to parties which failed to cross the 4 per cent threshold. The UDF had, however, done well given that it had lost two of its largest component parties in the dispute over the passing of the constitution. One of these, the Bulgarian Social Democratic Party, joined a coalition called the UDF (Centre), and a UDF (Liberal) also stood in the elections. The other main UDF breakaway party, the agrarian BANU-Nikola Petkov, not only ran separately in the elections, but also itself split, with its smaller part running under a BANU-United ticket with the BANU which had been represented in the previous parliament. These four party lists won a total of more than 13 per cent of the vote, although none crossed the 4 per cent threshold. Of 31 further coalitions and parties, none obtained more than 2 per cent of the vote.[16]

The fracturing of the UDF was not surprising given the fate of other broad

Table 9.3 Bulgarian election, 13 October 1991

	% vote	Seats
Union of Democratic Forces	34	110
Bulgarian Socialist Party	33	106
Movement for Rights and Freedoms	8	24
Others	25	0
Total	100	240

Source: Szajkowski (1994, pp. 101–4).

anti-communist movements in Eastern Europe, and the loss of some of its components had the advantage of increasing the coherence of its programme. The clearest difference between the UDF and the BSP was in their economic programme, though it must be noted that, although the UDF came out in favour of more radical reform, even the BSP was, by the time of the 1991 elections, distinctly more reform-oriented than it had been in the previous elections. There were, however, other underlying themes in the election campaign, such as the exploitation of nationalism by the BSP, and, perhaps most importantly, the fact that the electorate was still playing out the battle for and against the previous Communist Party which had elsewhere been a feature of the first elections after 1989.

The election left Bulgaria with a fundamental problem, however. Although it had been hoped that it would release the parliament from the partial paralysis experienced in the first part of the year, it produced no clear majority – though with less splits within UDF, it might have done, since less of the opposition vote would have been lost to parties gaining below the 4 per cent threshold necessary for representation. The almost equal division of the ethnic Bulgarian vote between the UDF and BSP meant that the Turkish MRF held the balance of power. Eventually, the UDF formed a minority government under its chair, Filip Dimitrov, but this was reliant on support from the MRF in order to pass its legislative programme. A formal coalition with the MRF would have been politically problematic in the extreme in view of the strength of nationalism among Bulgarians: the UDF had performed particularly badly compared to the BSP in areas with a strong Turkish minority.

1992 commenced with the direct election of the serving President, Zhelyu Zhelev, together with his chosen Vice-President, Blaga Dimitrova. It was not an overwhelming victory, since they failed to gain the 50 per cent of the vote necessary for election in the first round, and they had to enter a run-off with the socialist-backed candidates a week later (see Table 9.4). Yet Zhelev's re-election did present an element of stability in the Bulgarian system. Although his relations with the new UDF government were tense, since he was not as 'dark blue' (hardline anti-communist), he was broadly supportive of the new

Table 9.4 Bulgarian presidential election, 12/19 January 1992

	% vote	
	Round 1	*Round 2*
Zhelyu Zhelev/Blaga Dimitrova (UDF-backed)	45	53
Velko Valkanov/Rumen Vodenicharov (BSP-backed)	30	47
Georges Ganchev/Petar Beron	17	–
Others	8	–

Sources: Eastern Europe and the Commonwealth of Independent States 1994 (1994) p. 217;
Nikolaev (1992, pp. 11–16).

government's programme, and was the least nationalist of the presidential candidates standing.

By the end of the year, however, Bulgaria's first entirely non-communist government had fallen. Its programme had included elements commonly pursued elsewhere by the victors of the first post-communist elections. De-communisation measures were adopted, such as the confiscation of some of the extensive property owned by the Communist Party and its allied organisations. There was also 'lustration' of whole sectors of public employees, such as scientists and university teachers, and attempts at criminal prosecution of former communist leaders were intensified. While the former leader Zhivkov had been arrested as early as January 1990, this was followed in 1992 by charges against a number of other former Politburo members and prime ministers. Zhivkov was finally convicted and sentenced to seven years' imprisonment in September 1992, but his prosecution was complex, and he remained, after conviction, under house arrest rather than in prison. The results of the government's economic reform attempts were also inconclusive. Restitution laws were finally enacted, but proved hard to implement, and despite some denationalisation of small businesses, little progress was made in large-scale privatisation. The contentious issues of land restitution, however, remained a key item still on the agenda.[17]

One of the UDF government's problems was that neither privatisation nor decommunisation have generally proved particularly successful in maintaining popular support in the post-communist world. The UDF also had two particular difficulties of its own. One was that it was still a coalition between a large number of separate parties, and therefore had to expend considerable effort on internal negotiations as well as on running the country.[18] The other was that its minority government depended on MRF support. Although the latter was very concerned about issues such as Turkish-language instruction in schools – a cause to which the UDF was more sympathetic than the BSP – its Turkish electorate, being largely rural and not particularly highly educated, was not a constituency likely to benefit from economic reform. This was the issue which finally led to the MRF siding with the BSP in a vote of no-confidence against the government at the end of October 1992.

Given the party balance in the National Assembly and the improbability of the MRF forming a coalition with the BSP, there were only two realistic options open after the fall of the UDF government: fresh elections, or the installing of another non-party government. For a time, it seemed that President Zhelev would have to call a new election, but the third candidate he nominated to form a government, the non-party economist Lyuben Berov who had been proposed by MRF, finally managed to gain parliamentary approval for a cabinet comprised largely of technocrats. His support came not only from the BSP and MRF, but also from twenty-three UDF rebels in the parliament.

Berov's government relied for its continuation largely on the disinclination of deputies to face new elections for the second time since June 1990; it was hence inherently unlikely to be stable, and it had to survive numerous votes of no confidence before it finally fell in the autumn of 1994. Support from the BSP and MRF, as well as from a breakaway faction of the UDF, was always contingent. While the BSP had voted Berov into power, they refused to support measures introduced by his government if they were likely to harm the BSP's electorate. However, the opposition UDF did not concentrate solely on battling against Berov's government: it was mainly preoccupied with its own internal conflicts, and the struggle against President Zhelev. Although Zhelev had originally come from their own ranks, the UDF blamed him for the fall of the Dimitrov government.

The frequent changes of government in Bulgaria may have staved off major upheavals, but they also held back the rate of change. Under the Berov government, the process of decommunisation slowed during 1993, and despite a commitment to large-scale privatisation, very little actually happened.[19] International factors continued to be unfavourable to Bulgarian industry and exports, and the extreme disadvantage it suffered from the collapse of the Soviet market was compounded by the embargo of trade with its neighbour Serbia, which also disrupted the cheapest trade route to the EU. Bulgaria therefore both began and ended the period 1991–93 in a state of partial parliamentary paralysis, and no definitive progress was made on determining its final political complexion, or in coping with everyday issues such as transforming the economy and dealing with the communist past.

Czechoslovakia

Czechoslovakia must be considered one of the most successful countries in the 1991–93 period. While it clearly had considerable problems with national identity, to the extent that the common state of Czechs and Slovaks only survived until the end of 1992, what is most remarkable is that its difficulties were solved so quickly and efficiently.[20] Arguments between Czechs and

Textbox 9.3 Main events in Czechoslovakia, 1991–93

1991

January	Constitution amended.
March	CF divides into Civic Democratic Party (CDP) under Klaus and Civic Movement; PAV splits as Slovak Prime Minister Mečiar forms breakaway Movement for a Democratic Slovakia (MFDS).
April	Mečiar replaced as Slovak Prime Minister by Christian Democrat Čarnogurský.

1992

June	Klaus and Mečiar win elections in Czech and Slovak republics respectively, where they become Prime Ministers and agree to split the country.
July	Stráský (CDP) becomes Prime Minister of the Federal government, which is a CDP/MFDS coalition with programme to split the country; Havel resigns as President after the new parliament fails to re-elect him.
September	The Slovak parliament adopts Slovak constitution.
November	The Federal Assembly adopts law on the end of CSFR.
December	The Czech Republic adopts constitution; Czechoslovakia ceases to exist at the end of the year.

1993

January	*Czech Republic* Parliament elects Havel Czech President.
February	*Czech and Slovak Republics* Separate Czech and Slovak currencies adopted.
	Slovakia Kováč elected Slovak President by parliament.
April	*Slovakia* MFDS splits, as MFDS deputies form the Alliance of Democrats. The only Slovak National Party (SNP) minister in the government leaves.
October	*Slovakia* MFDS enters formal government coalition with SNP.
December	*Slovakia* A new faction forms in the SNP, which is later to become the National Democratic Party.

Slovaks remained firmly in the political realm, whereas nationality problems in the other two federations formed in the communist period – the Soviet Union and Yugoslavia – also involved the military. There were a number of reasons for this. One related to the country's political culture and the fact that force of arms had not been a traditional way of solving problems and injustices, particularly among the Czechs. Another was that there was no historical enmity between Czechs and Slovaks, since – unlike most neighbouring peoples – neither had ever conquered or massacred the other. Their union in 1918, after the fall of the Austro-Hungarian empire, had been an entirely voluntary decision, based on the fact that they spoke very similar languages (to the extent that in the interwar period, they were often described, normally by Czechs, as two branches of a single nation), and that they felt better able to fend off hostile neighbours by forming a state together.[21] A final reason why it was relatively easy to divide Czechoslovakia was that the Czech and Slovak population of the country was scarcely intermingled at all, as can be seen from Table 9.5. Since only about 0.5 per cent of all Czechs lived in Slovakia, the loss of this territory did not really matter to the Czech nation; and whereas about 5 per cent of Slovaks lived in the Czech Republic, they comprised individuals who had moved there, rather than communities historically settled in the area. Hence they did not form a cohesive pressure group, and their fate was hard to politicise, particularly since most were quite content to remain in the independent Czech Republic.

The relative success of political institution-building in Czechoslovakia is demonstrated by the fact that – although the state itself proved unstable – institutional procedures were used to dismantle it. Furthermore, a considerable volume of fairly complex and controversial legislation was passed in the period prior to the second elections in June 1992, in spite of the fact that the country's governments and parliaments were weighed down by lengthy discussions of the state's constitutional future.

When 1991 commenced, there were a number of problems on the political agenda: the continuation of economic reform; 'coming to terms with the past' (how to deal with former communists); and the rearrangement of the federation and the relative powers of the central parliament and the Czech and

Table 9.5 National composition of Czechoslovakia, 1991

	Czech Republic Total	%	Slovak Republic Total	%	Czechoslovakia Total	%
Czech	9,871,518	96	56,487	1	9,928,005	64
Slovak	239,355	2	4,445,303	84	4,684,658	30
Hungarian	20,260	0	608,221	12	628,481	4
Romany	24,294	0	77,269	1	101,563	1
Polish	52,362	1	3,420	0	55,782	0
Ruthenian	2,307	0	49,099	1	51,406	0
German	40,907	0	7,738	0	48,645	0
Other/not known	51,212	0	26,798	1	78,010	1
Total	10,302,215		5,274,335		15,576,550	

Data for population by mother tongue from census of 3 March 1991. Statistics of both mother tongue and declared nationality tend to underestimate the Romany population, which may be over 10 per cent in Slovakia, and at least 2 per cent in the Czech Republic. See J. F. Brown (1996, p. 7).

Source: Český statistický úřad (1993 p. 413).

lovak National Councils. In the first two areas, considerable successes were achieved. The Czechoslovak economy started off with the advantage of what was, by East European standards, a relatively low foreign debt, but it was disadvantaged by the fact that the economy had remained almost totally unreformed in the 1970s and 1980s, and there was less private enterprise, even on the lowest level of small shops and services, than almost anywhere else in Eastern Europe. A major economic reform programme was launched at the beginning of 1991, and price liberalisation, higher interest rates and the devaluation of the crown led to an increase in retail prices approaching 50 per cent in the first half of the year, although the inflation rate fell sharply thereafter. 'Small privatisation' affecting, for example, shops and services began, as did the restitution of private property confiscated by the communists after 1948. The most ambitious scheme – 'large privatisation' including the use of vouchers – took place in 1992. Citizens were able to buy, for 1000 crowns (about a week's wages), vouchers to exchange for shares in state-owned companies, and the scheme became highly popular after investment funds sprung up which guaranteed high returns to anyone who entrusted them with their vouchers. Economic success was marred, however, by the fact that the effect of the reforms was far harsher in Slovakia than in the Czech Republic. The Slovak economy was much more vulnerable than that in the Czech Republic, since it was not only further from Western Europe and less attractive for foreign investment, but was also far less diverse, and many towns were very dependent on single enterprises in branches of heavy industry, such as military production, which had been favoured by the communists but became largely redundant as the economy was reformed. A consequence of this was that, by the time the next elections were held in June 1992, the low Czechoslovak employment rate of 5.5 per cent concealed over 11 per cent unemployment in Slovakia compared to less than 3 per cent in the Czech Republic.

The process of decommunisation proceeded amid controversy surrounding individuals who claimed they were being falsely accused of secret police collaboration and acting as informers on the basis of inaccurate reports from the very institution being condemned.[22] Initial screening of elected deputies was followed in October 1991 by a law to eliminate high-ranking communist officials and secret police informers from government and state employment for a period of five years. The process was known as 'lustration', and became generally accepted in spite of accusations that it involved notions of collective guilt and the need to prove innocence rather than guilt.

Despite the success of the Federal Assembly in passing contentious legislation in areas such as economic reform and lustration, the major institutional failure of Czechoslovakia lay in the third of the areas mentioned above: redefining the relationship between Czechs and Slovaks. This was most markedly demonstrated by the inability of the parliament to pass a new constitution. The first electoral period had been set at two rather than four years, on the assumption that this would be long enough not only to pass a new constitution for Czechoslovakia, but also to agree constitutions for the Czech and Slovak Republics. This assumption proved false.

Constitutional reform was hard to agree in Czechoslovakia because, being a federation, the government structure was relatively complex, with separate Czechoslovak, Czech and Slovak parliaments and governments.[23] Even the central Federal Assembly itself was bicameral, and in the upper chamber the votes of Czech and Slovak deputies on important legislation were counted separately, with a three-fifths majority of each being required for constitutional amendments to be passed. This meant that a high degree of political consensus was required, but this was hard to reach on issues where Czechs and Slovaks perceived their interests differently. In discussing a new constitution, many Slovak politicians were anxious to emphasise their nation's equality with the Czechs, and wished the passing of a new federal constitution to be preceded by a State Treaty between the Czech and Slovak Republics.[24] The Czechs initially opposed this, but even when the principle had been conceded, no agreement could be reached on the precise provisions of such a treaty, nor could the country's future be decided by a popular referendum since the Federal Assembly was unable to agree on its wording.

Part of the failure to agree was caused by the differing developments within the Czech and Slovak political systems. On the surface, there was, by post-communist standards, a large degree of continuity of governmental personnel in the first few years after the revolution, and the Czechoslovak Federation and the Czech Republic retained the same Prime Minister from the immediate aftermath of the revolution until the second free elections in June 1992. Even though the two citizens' movements, the Czech Civic Forum and the Slovak Public Against Violence (PAV), followed a pattern common to most broad-based anti-communist movements and divided after their success in initial elections, the disintegration of Civic Forum into three separate parties in early 1991 had little effect on the Czechoslovak and Czech governments. In Slovakia, however, progress was less smooth. Arguments within the Slovak PAV were tinged with greater personal bitterness than in Civic Forum, and its division into two factions led to the ousting of the Prime Minister Vladimír Mečiar in April 1991. Mečiar and his followers then split away from PAV to form the Movement for a Democratic Slovakia (MFDS), which left the government. Although the majority of PAV deputies in the Slovak National Council remained with the movement, its coalition partner, the Christian Democratic Movement, had now become the largest party in the government. Therefore the Christian Democrat leader Ján Čarnogurský became the new Slovak Prime Minister. The greatest problem confronting Slovak politics was, however, that Mečiar took with him the majority of the government's electoral support among the population at large. While many leading figures in Public Against Violence considered the dismissal of Mečiar to be essential in view of his unaccountable and unpredictable behaviour, the wisdom of such a move in a nascent democracy was questionable: Mečiar was the most popular politician in Slovakia. And once in opposition, he and the MFDS were free to increase their popular support by mobilising Slovak discontent with both the effects of economic reform and the Slovak Republic's relationship with the Czechs.

By the time the second elections had been held in June 1992, it was clear that party politics in the Czech and Slovak Republics were developing differently, as can be seen from Table 9.6.[25] The largest Czech party in the new Federal Assembly was the Civic Democratic Party, the largest of the three parties to emerge from Civic Forum. It was led by the former Federal Finance Minister, Václav Klaus, who was heavily identified with the successful voucher privatisation. His party stood in the elections with the small Christian Democratic Party, and was easily able to form a centre-right coalition in the Czech National Council together with two smaller parties, the Christian Democratic Union/Czech People's Party and the Civic Democratic Alliance.[26] In Slovakia, the victor was Mečiar's Movement for a Democratic Slovakia, which was only two seats short of an absolute majority in the Slovak National Council. Mečiar's party not only had a considerably more left-wing stance on economic issues, but also had differing views from the parties of the Czech Government on the future of the federation. Since economic reform was very close to the heart of the new Czech leader Klaus, he was prepared to uncouple the Czech Republic from Slovakia rather than countenance the permanent obstruction of his economic policies.

Klaus favoured continuing the federation, but preferred independent states to having a looser confederation; Mečiar favoured a form of confederation, but preferred independent states to a continuation of the federal *status quo*. Shortly after the election, therefore, they agreed to end the common Czechoslovak state. Klaus became Czech Prime Minister, and Mečiar the Slovak Prime Minister. Czechoslovakia remained without a President when Václav Havel resigned after the Federal Assembly failed to re-elect him owing to opposition from many Slovak deputies. The new Federal government was 'self-liquidating' in that its main task was to arrange the dissolution of the country, which took place at the end of 1992. Neither Klaus nor Mečiar's parties had a clear electoral mandate to divide the country, and no referendum was held on the issue. Furthermore, public opinion polls before the elections suggested that neither Czechs nor Slovaks at that point supported the division of the country.[27] It is therefore of some interest to examine reasons for the formation of independent states.

One explanation is nationalism. It has been suggested, on the one hand, that the Czechs regarded Czechoslovakia as a Czech state, and were not prepared to accept the Slovaks as equal partners, and even that Czechs were anxious to rid themselves of the weaker Slovak economy in order to strengthen their chances of entering the European Union. On the other hand, the ending of

Table 9.6 Czechoslovak elections, 5–6 June 1992

| | Federal Assembly* | | | | National Council* | |
| | Chamber of People | | Chamber of Nations | | | |
Czech parties	% vote	Seats	% vote	Seats	% vote	Seats
Civic Democratic Party /						
Christian Democratic Party	34	48	33	37	30	76
Left Bloc	14	19	14	15	14	35
Czechoslovak Social Democracy	8	10	7	6	7	16
Association for the Republic–						
Republican Party of CS	6	8	6	6	6	14
Christian Democratic Union–						
Czechoslovak People's Party	6	7	6	6	6	15
Liberal Social Union	6	7	6	5	7	16
Civic Democratic Alliance	5	0	4	0	6	14
Movement for Self-governing						
Democracy/Association for						
Moravia & Silesia	4	0	5	0	6	14
Others	17	0	18	0	19	0
Total		99		75		200

Slovak parties	% vote	Seats	% vote	Seats	% vote	Seats
Movement for a Democratic						
Slovakia	34	24	34	33	37	74
Party of the Democratic Left	14	10	14	13	15	29
Slovak National Party	9	6	9	9	8	15
Christian Democratic Movement	9	6	9	8	9	18
Hungarian Christian Democratic						
Movement/Coexistence	7	5	7	7	7	14
Social Democratic Party in						
Slovakia	5	0	6	5	4	0
Others	21	0	20	0	20	0
Total		51		75		150

*A 5 per cent clause operated for all elections. The percentage vote is calculated separately for each republic. Since percentages have been rounded up or down, a party may appear to have 5 per cent of the vote yet no seats.

Source: Český statistický úřad (1993, pp. 439–41).

Czechoslovakia has also been blamed on militant Slovak nationalism and long-standing Slovak aspirations for independence. Yet these factors fail to account for the apparent lack of public support for dividing the state.

A second explanation points to the fact that Czech and Slovak societies were structurally very different.[28] The Czech Republic had already been a prosperous, modern, industrial society when Czechoslovakia was formed in 1918, and the communist period had been extremely detrimental to Czech economic development. Slovakia, however, had largely become a modern, industrial society in the communist period. This meant that Slovaks did not view the communist period quite as negatively as the Czechs, since it had been linked with progress of a sort. Yet at the same time, modern Slovakia bore the imprint of communist modernisation, for example its overemphasis on heavy industry, in a way which made its transformation to a market economy more painful than was the case in the Czech Republic. It is notable, however, that by the end of forty years of communism, with its tireless efforts to create excessively uniform conditions and lifestyles for all citizens, the standard of living and education of Czechs and Slovaks had nearly converged, and were much more similar than at any previous point in Czechoslovak history.

A final explanation for the break-up can be sought in the fact that the political elites of the Czech and Slovak Republics had become increasingly separated after the country had become a federation at the beginning of 1969.[29] Many leading Slovak politicians were based in the Slovak National Council in Bratislava, and were separated from the Prague-based federal, Czechoslovak politics in a way that their Czech colleagues were not. Czechs and Slovaks largely voted for separate political parties when democracy was reintroduced after 1989, and the institutional structures did little to encourage them to cooperate: for example, to get into parliament, a party needed to get only 5 per cent of the votes in one of the republics, and not in the country as a whole. There were, therefore, no electoral considerations to stop politicians pursuing political agendas which exacerbated rather than lessened the differences between the federation's republics.[30] Moreover, once Klaus and Mečiar had been elected, a public inexperienced in democratic procedures and unused to being able to influence leaders' decisions was perhaps more compliant in accepting the division of the state than it might have been in a more established democracy.

Czech Republic

Most Czechs had been opposed to the division of Czechoslovakia, which they felt had been forced on them by the Slovaks, and were initially even confused about what their new country's name was: while the Slovak Republic was clearly Slovakia, the Czech Republic had no such obvious short form, and all attempts to create one led to nothing. Hence it remained the Czech Republic. However, despite the fact that the Czechs might have appeared psychologically unprepared for independence, they adjusted to it with an almost unseemly ease. This tended to confirm the allegations of some Slovaks that their former compatriots had always regarded Czechoslovakia as being primarily a Czech state. The continuity of the two states was emphasised in the first month of independence by the fact that the parliament elected the former Czechoslovak President Václav Havel as the new Czech President. Any Czech willingness to create a new identity for their new state also petered out when they were faced with having to choose a new flag: they adopted the old

Czechoslovak one, in complete violation of the agreements on the division of the state, and in the face of Slovak protests.[31]

An important factor in the Czechs' ability to reconcile themselves with the loss of Slovakia was that it removed one of the major sources of conflict from political life. The Czech government was now free to concentrate on everyday problems of post-communist transition. There was some controversy over a law declaring the former communist regime illegitimate, and the government coalition argued over the restitution of Church property, but in the economic field, successes were considerable. Unemployment remained at what was, by international standards, an exceptionally low level of around 3 per cent, a second wave of the popular voucher privatisation commenced in the autumn, and the country's investment rating abroad steadily improved. Prime Minister Václav Klaus and the Czech government were rewarded for this by over 60 per cent approval ratings in public opinion polls, which was exceptionally high by post-communist standards, or, indeed, in comparison with most established Western democracies.

On the level of political institution-building, there were some unresolved problems, such as the organisation of local government and the establishment of an upper chamber of parliament, or Senate. (In the event, the government was to proceed through the entire electoral period, lasting until June 1996, without actually creating the second chamber of parliament stipulated in the new Czech constitution.) Generally, however, the Czech Republic already appeared in the first year of its existence to be a model of post-communist transition. Since the Czechs had been the most modern and prosperous nation ever to be subjected to communism, this was perhaps not altogether surprising.

Slovakia

When Slovakia became an independent country at the beginning of 1993, prognoses for its future progress were not optimistic. Its chances of economic success had not been considered good, yet, although privatisation scarcely proceeded at all in the course of 1993, the economic catastrophe frequently predicted by those outside the country did not take place. The Czech and Slovak currencies had been separated much earlier than originally intended, in February 1993, but an initial devaluation against the Czech crown of about 10 per cent in the following summer proved sufficient to stabilise the Slovak currency.

The political shifts caused by independence were much more evident. The country had a new constitution, passed at the beginning of September 1992, and the most immediate task it laid before the parliament, renamed the National Council of the Slovak Republic, was the election of a Slovak President. Since a three-fifths majority of deputies was required, the choice of a President involved some compromise on the part of the ruling Movement for a Democratic Slovakia. (Slovakia's one unifying political figure, the Prague Spring leader Dubček, would have been an obvious choice, but he had unfortunately died after a car accident the previous autumn.) Prime Minister Mečiar's favoured candidate, Roman Kováč, failed to attain the required support, but in February 1993, a second candidate, Michal Kováč (no relation of the unsuccessful contender), was elected President with the help of some support from the Party of the Democratic Left. President Kováč, who had been a member of the MFDS, had agreed to serve as an independent President, and as the year progressed, his independence exceeded Mečiar's expectations. In the years that followed, the enmity between the two men was to become a focal point of conflict in Slovak politics.

A further problem facing Mečiar was the need to secure a firm parliamentary majority, as his party had only 74 deputies in a 150-member parliament. This process was complicated both by dissension within his own party, marked most notably by the defection of eight deputies in March 1993, and by uneasy relations with the MFDS's most likely coalition partner, the Slovak National Party (SNP). A formal coalition was finally agreed with the SNP in October 1993, but by this time both parties were heading for further splits. In Czechoslovakia, they had been held together by their members' opposition to the Prague-based government; in the independent Slovakia, fundamental disagreements on issues such as economic reform, foreign policy orientation and perceptions of the meaning of democracy became increasingly evident.

Eastern Germany

Many of the problems faced by eastern Germany in the period after German unification belonged to the same categories as those confronting their former Warsaw Pact allies. However, the problems were often quantitatively and qualitatively different because the area was part of a European Community member country. Equally important was the fact that politicians in eastern Germany did not have to carry such a large burden of decision-making as their counterparts elsewhere. By taking over a 'ready-made' system, complete with predetermined institutions, laws and bureaucratic procedures, they avoided the enormous choices available elsewhere.

1990 had been a decisive year everywhere for constructing democratic institutions, but outside the former GDR politicians and parliaments still had the chance to alter their original creations, for example by amending electoral systems or changing the procedure for electing their President, and the first democratically elected parliaments elsewhere were often heavily involved in rewriting their communist constitutions. On top of this, in other post-communist countries there was an enormous amount of legislation to be passed on subjects such as privatisation, tax laws, social security and local government. For the east Germans, these decisions were no longer in their hands. A definitive decision on identity and citizenship and the boundaries of the nation-state had been reached by rejecting the GDR; it no longer existed as an entity, but had been dissolved into five new Länder of the Federal Republic of Germany. By doing this, east Germans had also abandoned decision-making about their constitutional and institutional framework: the west Germans had grown very attached to their Basic Law during forty years of peace and prosperity, and were highly resistant to the idea that it might be amended to incorporate any stray aspirations of their formerly communist-dominated fellow citizens. Two major tasks remained, however: on a practical level, a set of everyday political and administrative procedures had to implemented which had been externally established in the very different conditions of western Germany; and on a psychological level, citizens had to adapt to their new system.[32]

If one looks at the political complexion of eastern Germany, it diverged from that in the rest of the post-communist world in a number of respects. A first difference was the status of former Communist Party members, who were left in a far more unfavourable position than elsewhere. This was mostly a consequence of unification, although the GDR's communist leadership had also been more authoritarian and more despised than many, and had more visibly been keeping its citizens prisoners in their own country. When judging lower-ranking party members, however, east Germans, like many people in other post-communist societies, instinctively understood the everyday compromises that had had to be made to survive in 'the system'. Nobody except a few dissidents had completely clean hands, and it was accepted that Communist Party membership was frequently a sign not of moral turpitude, but of a desire to achieve one's professional potential, for which a party card was a prerequisite. Consequently, being a secret police (Stasi) informer, and betraying one's friends, neighbours and colleagues, rather than mere party membership, tended to be used as the yardstick for identifying new social and political pariahs. West Germans, however, did not need to understand all this, and there was nothing to stop them taking the moral high ground, and condemning everyone and everything connected with the SED regime in exactly the same way as many of them had done before unification. Crucially, however, there were not only moral reasons for discriminating against former communists, but also practical considerations which made it possible. Pragmatism in the continued employment of former party members – many of whom had considerable professional and administrative skill and experience – was far less necessary in eastern Germany than elsewhere, since the most senior positions could, if necessary, be filled by west Germans, who out-numbered east Germans by three to one. Additionally, the rapid assumption of west German administrative, economic and legal structures often made experience of the previous, communist structures a liability rather than an asset, and even those with specialist, technical expertise found it hard to compete with more junior counterparts in the same profession who had had the benefit of training in western conditions. Mass redundancy among white-collar and professional staff in general was also a far more common phenomenon in eastern Germany than elsewhere, since west German taxpayers, already becoming resentful of the cost of unification, were unlikely to tolerate – and pay for – what to a westerner was gross overmanning;[33] in other post-communist countries, there was a greater chance that this would go unnoticed.

The situation which faced former communists was, therefore, that they were considered completely unacceptable partners in the political life which they had previously dominated, and they also found that their 'capital assets' in terms of specialist knowledge and contacts were less easily transferable to the radically different structures of the Federal Republic of Germany than they would have been in any other post-communist area.

The second difference between politics in east Germany and elsewhere in the post-communist world was an almost accidental absurdity whereby, although former Communist Party members were widely considered to be unacceptable by other political parties, members of the former 'bloc parties', that is, puppet parties who had meekly provided second-rank support to the regime throughout the GDR period, were thrust to power in the early 1990s.[34] This was largely because of the electoral decisions made by the east Germans in March 1990, when a party's links to the West German government were considered more important than its past. By 1991, however, the low calibre of politicians from the former bloc parties was beginning to become an enormous problem. This was most noticeable at the level of the five new east German Länder, each of which had a regional parliament, with its own Minister President (Prime Minister) and government. The most successful of these governments was that in Saxony, where a west German Christian Democrat, Kurt Biedenkopf, was Minister President. However, three of the other parliaments were also controlled by the Christian Democrats, alone or in coalition with the Free Democrats, so that a large number of prominent regional politicians had been recruited from the old bloc parties. By 1993, all three Minister Presidents from the former bloc parties had had to be replaced, as well as a number of their ministers, for reasons ranging from incompetence to corruption. Many of their replacements were west Germans. The single Social Democrat-led Land, Brandenburg, had problems of its own. Its Minister President, Manfred Stolpe, was a prominent Protestant churchman, and he was therefore an East German rarity: he had had considerable administrative experience without being contaminated by belonging to the Communist Party hierarchy. However, as he withstood a seemingly never-ending onslaught of allegations of cooperation with the

Stasi, it increasingly appeared that almost no one had been completely innocent in the GDR.[35]

A third distinguishing mark of politics in eastern Germany was the fact that the country was federal in structure. In German politics, the office of Minister President in one of the Länder is prestigious, and is as good a stepping stone to the highest office of Federal Chancellor as becoming a minister of the federal government. This was helpful for the integration of east German politicians into the new Federal Republic. Although a number of west Germans had to be introduced into the east German Land governments in the early days after unification, the Land level none the less acted as an influential political field in which east Germans, despite their inexperience, had a natural political advantage. The east German Länder also had some influence in the Bundesrat, the upper chamber of the German parliament, which had to pass all legislation affecting the work of the Länder. It comprised delegates sent by the Länder governments, and although populous Länder were allowed somewhat more representatives than small ones, the relatively small east German Länder were nevertheless over represented compared to the size of their electorates. Since Land delegations frequently voted according to local interests rather than political party, the Bundesrat often witnessed an east–west split in votes. The issue at stake was normally money: since the new Länder had lower local incomes and a greater need for expenditure, their poverty upset the careful financial balance the west Germans had worked out between federal and Land budgets.

The social and economic problems of integrating east Germans into what became essentially an extension of west Germany were more notable, however, than problems of political integration. East Germany experienced mass unemployment on a level almost unknown in the rest of the post-communist world. Much of it was disguised by short-time working or retraining schemes, and during 1992, the official statistics showing nearly 15 per cent unemployment in the new Länder disguised a rate of over 30 per cent if short-time working, job-creation schemes and early retirement were taken into account.[36] The high level of unemployment was caused by a number of factors: the relatively rapid privatisation of larger state enterprises which had been producing goods of dubious quality in a resource-intensive fashion; the loss of eastern markets as the goods began to be sold for hard currency in 1990; the relatively high (by east European standards) wages of east Germans once they were paid in Deutschmarks; and the east Germans' own tendency, when given a choice, to buy west German rather than east German goods. At the same time, traditional state subsidies were discontinued much more rapidly than in other post-communist countries, and people watched, for example, as their rents went up tenfold. Women were particularly badly affected, as the dramatic increase in unemployment was accompanied by a reduction in state-subsidised childcare.

Yet while much was made of the danger of serious unrest in eastern Germany, particularly when young people on the housing estates indulged in racist violence, the worst racist violence of the period took place in western Germany.[37] West Germans also felt insecure: in the run-up to the December 1990 elections, Chancellor Kohl had made somewhat unrealistic promises that unification would not involve tax rises, but these proved to be untenable. After a brief economic boom brought about by the opening of the east German market to west German goods in 1990, the Federal Republic was hit by an international economic recession. Rents also rose in the west, as the influx of east Germans was matched by the arrival of similar numbers of ethnic Germans taking the chance to emigrate from other previously communist countries, as well as a wave of asylum-seekers from elsewhere. Bitterness between east and west Germans rose, and by June 1991, the west Germans nearly went as far as breaking their forty-year constitutional promise that Berlin was to be the German capital in a narrow parliamentary vote. On an everyday level, over 80 per cent of east Germans complained that they felt like second-class citizens, while many west Germans stereotyped them as lazy and ungrateful.

One reason why east Germany did not explode is simply that the east Germans were *not* second-class citizens. Their complaints were articulated with reference to the concept of citizenship precisely because the fundamental notion that all Germans were equal was virtually uncontested. Although, in the eastern Länder, east Germans were initially paid less than west Germans for doing the same job, everyone acknowledged that this was not a tolerable situation in the long term. It was not just a question that the east Germans had a right to move to any other part of Germany if they wanted to, and that the cream of the workforce would tend to do this if wage differentials continued; the German constitution itself was also unusual in containing a commitment to ensuring 'uniformity of living standards in the federal territory'.[38] Additionally, in spite of the psychological shock of unemployment, east Germany illustrated a point that had been made for many years by disgruntled east Europeans: west European unemployment benefit (in some countries, at least) was higher than normal wages under communism. Therefore, while more people suffered a loss of social status than elsewhere in the post-communist world, on a material level the advantages of the post-1989 changes – for example, the ubiquitous introduction of high-quality western goods into the everyday life of all citizens – were far more widespread.

A final reason why tension between east and west Germans did not escalate relates to the political channels available to east Germans to articulate their discontent. In one sense, these were deficient and there was a potential for discontent to be expressed through non-political channels. All the dominant political parties in the Federal Republic were established west German parties, and these could not be particularly forceful advocates of east German interests, since on issues such as transfer of resources from west to east, the views of the majority west German electorate were very different. Additionally, the two parts of the electorate did not rank political issues in the same order of importance; their political agendas were structured differently, and the western agenda predominated. Only the post-communist Party of Democratic Socialism, whose discredited past limited its scope for gaining political support, had an overwhelmingly east German electorate, and was thus free to mobilise east German discontent with the unification process. However, the fact the German party system operated in the country as a whole also had a positive aspect: unlike in Czechoslovakia, where Czechs and Slovaks had separate parties and the country eventually came apart, in Germany parties acted as an integrating force. Although the east Germans only formed a quarter of the country's population, this is far too large a minority to ignore in an established party system where a few per cent of the vote is known to be crucial in determining whether a party crosses the 5 per cent threshold into parliament, or is able to form an acceptable coalition with a parliamentary majority. It was thus in the vital interest of every party which aspired to govern the Federal Republic to work towards the final goal of bringing new and old citizens together.

Hungary

On the surface, Hungary demonstrated considerable stability in the 1991–93 period. On the political front, it was one of the few former Warsaw Pact countries where no new national elections took place, and the only change of Prime Minister was occasioned by the death in office of József Antall. The party system, which had been somewhat more developed than elsewhere at the time of the first democratic elections, also proved remarkably durable: although many political parties were, as elsewhere in the region, subject to internal conflict and splits, it was to be the same six parties who had entered parliament in 1990 which were returned there by the elections in 1994. Economically, Hungary also appeared to be successful, and for much of the early 1990s it was attracting half of all Western investment in Eastern Europe. Finally, it had, by post-communist standards, one of the most enlightened attitudes towards ethnic minorities. However, on closer inspection there were also some worrying features of developments in Hungary. The political apathy of most citizens, and the early onset of discontent with the country's democratic government, were notable. Additionally, while its international standing remained good, much of the country's initial economic head start over the rest of the post-communist world was allowed to be gradually whittled away.

The alienation of Hungarian citizens from politics was not a new development. In 1990, the country had already produced one of the lowest election

---

Textbox 9.4 Main events in Hungary, 1991–93

1991

September   A Constitutional Court ruling limits the powers of the President.

November   The Independent Smallholders Party (ISP) splits, with a second parliamentary caucas formed.

1992

February   Torgyán, leader of the ISP, attempts to remove his party from government, but most ISP deputies do not follow.

August   The ruling Hungarian Democratic Forum is shaken by controversy when one of its Vice-Presidents, Csurka, publishes an anti-Semitic tract.

1993

January   The heads of state radio and television resign.

June   Csurka, expelled from the HDF, sets up the Hungarian Justice and Life Party.

December   Prime Minister Antall dies after a protracted illness, and is replaced by Interior Minister Boross.

---

turnouts in the area, and referendums on the presidency had been invalidated by the failure of half of all citizens to vote. This pattern was to continue with the turnout for parliamentary by-elections falling to as low as 10 per cent. The largest party in the government coalition, the Hungarian Democratic Forum (HDF), lost most of its popular support shortly after it took office, and for the entire period 1991–93 it ran neck-to-neck with the opposition Alliance of Free Democrats (AFD), while the Alliance of Young Democrats (FIDESZ), and later also the post-communist Hungarian Socialist Party (HSP), were well ahead.[39]

There were several reasons for these developments, which derived essentially from the form of negotiated transition which had taken place in Hungary at the end of the communist period. First, the changes had resulted from agreement between elites and had not been accompanied by mass popular protest, and this fact was reflected in the party system, which corresponded more closely to divisions in elite opinion, rather than the interests of groups in society at large.[40] While the three parties in the government coalition, the HDF, the Independent Smallholders Party (ISP) and the Christian Democratic People's Party (CDPP) were right-wing in so far as they were generally of a nationalist and traditional/Christian orientation, the two liberal opposition parties with dissident roots, the AFD and FIDESZ, tended to be more strongly in favour of movement towards a market economy. Only the post-communist HSP, which had initially been shunned by both the voters and the other parties, had a clear left-wing economic orientation. It was therefore hard for voters disillusioned by the decline in their economic situation to find a political party through which they could articulate their discontent. Secondly, the Antall government enjoyed only the briefest of 'honeymoons' because it suffered from having its performance measured against that of the most tolerant, reformist and competent of Europe's communist regimes. It was not, therefore, bolstered in adversity by widespread popular relief at having been released from a greater evil. Thirdly, the opinion poll popularity of FIDESZ – a somewhat unusual party which only accepted members under 35 years of age – was largely a reaction against party politics *per se*, since FIDESZ initially represented a form of anti-party. Its support was therefore largely emotive, rather than being factually based on the contents of its party programme.

Most of the parliamentary political parties were subject to internal reshaping between 1991 and 1993. The AFD was affected both by disputes between its former dissident members and more conventional politicians, and by disputes over whether its economic policy should have a more liberal or a more social democratic slant; it changed its Chair twice in the period, and hovered between willingness to support 1994 election candidates agreed with FIDESZ, and support for some cooperation with the HSP. FIDESZ itself moved, in April 1993, towards becoming a more standard political party by abandoning its age limit and transforming itself into a more centralised and less grassroots organisation, and also by shifting to the centre-right on economic policy.[41] It was two of the governing parties, however, which were affected by major splits. The ISP leader, József Torgyán, was disaffected by the coalition's failure to honour the party's main election promise of fully restoring agricultural land to its former owners or their heirs, and he attempted to withdraw his party from the government. However, barely a quarter of the ISP parliamentary deputies, and none of its ministers, followed him, so the government's position was not jeopardised by this move.[42] In August 1992, the main ruling party, Antall's HDF, was also shaken by a crisis when one of its Vice-Presidents, István Csurka, published a lengthy tract which was both personally critical of Antall, and extremely anti-Semitic in tone.[43] Although Antall was slow in outright condemnation of Csurka's views, Csurka and his supporters were finally expelled from the HDF in July 1993, and went on to form their own Hungarian Justice and Life Party. Although the government now no longer had a firm majority in parliament, the split in the HDF was not a major one, particularly considering the fact that the party had always contained within it a number of distinct streams of opinion.[44]

Apart from disputes within parties, Hungarian politics was hit by a number of other controversies, which were mainly adjudicated by the Constitutional Court. In September 1991, the Court ruled against President Göncz's attempts to extend his powers beyond largely ceremonial functions: it clarified his role as commander in chief of the armed forces by restricting it to giving guidelines, and also stated that his right not to approve government nominees for state positions was limited to cases where appointments would have endangered an institution's democratic functioning. This was a particularly important issue in Hungary since the President's political origins had been within the AFD rather the government parties, so that the likelihood of his disapproving of government decisions was high.[45] Further protracted disputes broke out (as, indeed, in most other post-communist countries) over the independence of the media: the government accused state radio and television of anti-government bias, while the opposition accused the government of attempting to control the media. In 1992, the matter was referred to the Constitutional Court with reference to both the President's powers to intervene in the appointment and dismissal of the heads of Hungarian radio and television, and the constitutionality of the media law. However, no new media law was passed in 1993, and the impartiality of state-owned broadcasting was to remain a contentious issue at the time of the 1994 elections. A final major constitutional controversy related to dealing with the communist past, which was a particularly sensitive matter in Hungary because there had been a large number of civilian deaths at the time of the Hungarian Revolution in 1956. Since the culprits had never been punished, bringing them to justice was a more prominent concern than the 'lustration' of later secret police collaborators, which was a problem common to all post-communist states. Initial attempts to lift the statute of limitations, which prevented the prosecution of crimes committed more than twenty years ago, were declared unconstitutional in 1992, but in late 1993, the Constitutional Court finally agreed to the prosecution of war crimes and crimes against humanity perpetrated during the 1956 Revolution. On balance, therefore, the Court proved itself a reasonably successful democratic institution, both in terms of impartiality towards government and opposition, and in producing rulings which checked executive power without creating political stalemates.

The economic problems in Hungary fall into two major categories: one was the relatively slow progress of privatisation, and the other public discontent at falling living standards. Since economic reform had begun under the last communist governments in the second half of the 1980s, the country entered the 1990s with a far more developed financial infrastructure for dealing with a market economy than its post-communist neighbours, and it became, for example, the first East European country to open a stock exchange in 1990. It was also far better integrated into international markets, which assisted it in redirecting trade when the CMEA collapsed in 1991. However, the early start with economic reform also had two disadvantages. One was the assumption that Hungary was in a position to continue with a slow, steady pace of privatisation rather than risking any kind of 'shock therapy' of the Polish sort. The second was that the 'spontaneous privatisation' carried out by the managers of state enterprises between 1988 and 1990 was not unproblematic. Even when the process was taken over by a State Privatisation Agency, the tendency was to continue with direct sales to foreign investors or management buyouts, with the consequence that the most profitable enterprises were sold – often at low prices to multinational companies – while less desirable ones remained in state hands. No attempts at 'voucher privatisation' of the Czechoslovak kind were made, and former owners were compensated for property confiscated in the communist period, rather than having their original possessions returned to them under restitution laws.

Popular attitudes to the everyday financial hardships which affected citizens in all countries undergoing transition to a market economy were also particularly negative in Hungary because the previous regime was not perceived to have been so deficient as elsewhere in the region. This emerges clearly in cross-national surveys in which respondents in a number of post-communist countries are asked to evaluate both the past and present economic system, and the one they expect in five years' time.[46] While it was not unusual for many citizens everywhere (except the Czech Republic) to rate the current system far more negatively than both the past and, more particularly, the future system, Hungary stands out among East European countries for its pessimism. Some people did not expect, even in the medium term of five years, that the economic system would be as good as in the past. This indicated a sense of disillusionment about the changes taking place.

Nationalism is a final issue of contention in Hungary. The country is ethnically reasonably homogeneous, although minorities may make up as much as 10 per cent of the population of just over ten million. (Statistics are unreliable because, alongside some Germans, Slovaks and Croats, by far the largest minority community comprises Romanies. These are frequently counted inaccurately in censuses, but are thought to number at least 500,000 in Hungary.) From the 1970s onwards, the Hungarian government had attempted to introduce policies supportive of minorities, although they came in many cases too late, since their efforts followed a long history of coercive assimilation. The crucial issue, however, was not minorities within Hungary, who were dispersed and constituted no threat to the state, but the position of the far larger Hungarian minorities in neighbouring countries. Apart from the longstanding controversy surrounding some two million Hungarians in Romania, the Yugoslav war endangered the Hungarians living in Vojvodina, once an autonomous province of Serbia, and the division of Czechoslovakia placed a question mark over the rights of more than 500,000 Hungarians in the now independent Slovakia, whose government was not averse to exploiting fear of the minority community for nationalist ends. The Antall government's willingness to speak on behalf of Hungarians abroad had a dangerous tendency to provoke paranoia among the 'host' governments, since both Slovakia and Romania had historical memories of Hungary as an imperial nation whose irredentism had led to the annexing of part of its neighbours' territory during World War II. However, 1994 was to show that neither nationalism within Hungary nor the fate of minorities abroad were issues easily amenable to exploitation in elections: the Hungarian Justice and Life Party of the nationalist Csurka failed to enter parliament, and neither of the two most successful parties had shown a strong interest in Hungarians in neighbouring countries. Most people in Hungary perceived the Hungarian nation as more of a political than a cultural entity. For Hungarians in Hungary, the overwhelming political concern was the domestic economy.

Poland

Political developments in Poland in the period 1991–93 presented some interesting contrasts in comparison to other post-communist states. On the one hand, Poland remained in the forefront of the transition process. It had been the country where communist power started to crumble the earliest, terminally in 1980, although the process had been set in train in 1956; and it was the first Soviet bloc country, in 1989, to have a non-communist Prime Minister. It became not only the leader in the transition to a market economy, but also the first East European state to produce a backlash which democratically elected a government comprised of successor parties to those that had existed in the communist period. Yet at the same time, Poland also demonstrated some almost chaotic features in its institutional political structures. The party system was characterised by a fragmentation and instability even higher than the regional norm; the electoral system was changed substantially for the national elections in both 1991 and 1993; and the constitutional distribution of power between the President and the parliamentary government remained an open question for the entire period. In one respect, however, politics in Poland was simpler than in many of its neighbours: it was ethnically one of the most homogeneous of the post-communist states. There were hence no conflicts over issues of citizenship, and while there were differences in emphasis over the importance of Polish nationalism, there was little scope for questions about what the Polish nation actually was. The country was presented with a rather startling array of new neighbours – the Federal Republic of Germany, the Czech Republic, Slovakia, Ukraine, Belarus, Lithuania and Russia – but Poland itself remained constant.

Poland began 1991 with a new Prime Minister. The presidential elections in late 1990 had demonstrated a lack of public confidence in Prime Minister Mazowiecki, who had therefore resigned. The new government, under Jan

---

Textbox 9.5 Main events in Poland, 1991–93

1991

January	Bielecki appointed Prime Minister.
October	43 per cent of electorate vote in first free elections, and 29 parties win seats.
December	Olszewski (Centre Alliance) becomes Prime Minister of minority government.

1992

June	Olszewski replaced as Prime Minister by Pawlak (Polish Peasant Party), who is unable to form a government.
July	Pawlak replaced by Suchocka (Democratic Union), who forms a seven-party coalition.

1993

May	Suchocka government falls in vote of no confidence.
September	Pawlak becomes Prime Minister again, after the Democratic Left Alliance and Polish Peasant Party (both successors of communist era parties) win elections.

Krzysztof Bielecki, did not mark a radical shift in policy, since it retained some ministers from Mazowiecki's government, including the Finance Minister Balcerowicz. It was a form of caretaker government, as there was a clear need for fresh parliamentary elections in view of the fact that the existing parliament had been elected in 1989 on a system which was only partially democratic. The major obstacle to the holding of new elections was the need to pass an electoral law appropriate to a democracy, and this proved to be the first major conflict between President Wałęsa and parliament. The system finally adopted in June 1991 was one of almost pure proportional representation for the lower chamber, the Sejm. In the Sejm 391 seats were distributed proportionally by voters choosing a party list in one of the 37 electoral districts, which had between 7 and 37 seats; 69 seats were then distributed to the 'national lists' of parties gaining at least 5 per cent of the national vote or seats in at least five districts. However, the upper chamber, or Senate, was elected on a majority system.

When the elections finally took place in October 1991, over 100 election committees fielded candidate lists for the Sejm elections in at least one constituency, and 28 parties or coalitions had registered lists in at least five constituencies, and were therefore entitled to present a national list. As can be seen from Table 9.7, the result was a highly fragmented parliament, with 29

Table 9.7 Polish elections, 27 October 1991

Sejm (Lower House)	% vote	Seats
Democratic Union	12	62
Democratic Left Alliance	12	60
Catholic Election Action	9	49
Centre Alliance	9	44
Polish Peasant Party	9	48
Confederation for Independent Poland	8	46
Liberal Democratic Congress	7	37
Peasant Accord	5	28
Solidarity	5	27
Polish Party of the Friends of Beer	3	16
Christian Democracy	2	5
Union of Political Realism	2	3
Labour Solidarity	2	4
Democratic Party	1	1
German Minority	1	7
Party of Christian Democrats	1	4
Party X	0	3
Democratic-Social Movement	0	1
Piast Peasant Election Alliance	0	1
Silesian Autonomy	0	2
Krakow Coalition of Solidarity with the President	0	1
Union of Podhale	0	1
Polish Western Union	0	4
Wielkopolska for Poland	0	1
Peasant Unity	0	1
Orthodox Believers	0	1
Solidarity 80	0	1
Union of Great Poles	0	1
Alliance of Women against Life's Hardships	0	1
Total		460

N.B. Parties are listed in the order of percentage national vote received; this does not always correspond to the number of seats won, since these were distributed on a PR basis in each of 37 constituencies.

Senate (Upper House)	Seats
Democratic Union	21
Solidarity	11
Centre Alliance	9
Catholic Action	9
Polish Peasant Party	7
Liberal Democratic Congress	6
Peasant Accord	5
Confederation for Independent Poland	4
Democratic Left Alliance	4
Party of Christian Democrats	3
Christian Democracy	1
Piast Peasant Election Alliance	1
Nationalist Election Committee	1
Others	18
Total	100

Source: Główny Urząd Statystyczny (1992, p. 66); Millard (1994d, pp. 319–20).

political groupings represented, although some with only one deputy.[47] A symbol of this chaos was the fact that in Poland a beer-lovers party – a phenomenon which had appeared but not succeeded in elections elsewhere in the region – not only won 16 seats, but also later split on internal policy disagreements. This was all worryingly reminiscent of the country's unstable parliamentary democracy after World War I, which was marked by a rapid succession of governments and then followed by authoritarian rule after 1926. While the electoral system was usually blamed for the diversity of parties returned to parliament in 1991, the real problem which made forming a government so difficult was that support had been fairly evenly spread among the major parties, with no single one of them gaining more than an eighth of the vote. A minimum threshold for gaining seats would have made little difference to this, since only 24 per cent of the vote and 13 per cent of the seats went to organisations gaining less than 5 per cent of the national vote; nor, indeed, would a majoritarian 'first-past-the-post' system have helped, as witnessed by the composition of the upper chamber which had been elected by this method.

The fragmentation of the parliament was, therefore, to a considerable extent merely a reflection of the fragmentation of Polish politics. Parties could be split into three groups according to their provenance.[48] The post-communist parties, Social Democracy of the Polish Republic (which formed the core of the Democratic Left Alliance) and the Polish Peasant Party, were reformed successors of parties which had existed under communism. Most of the other major parties, such as the Democratic Union and the Liberal Democratic Congress, had their origins within the Solidarity movement, which had obtained massive electoral support in 1989. The remaining parties were mostly new creations, although the largest, the Confederation for an Independent Poland, had been formed clandestinely during the communist period. The three groups, however, lacked any form of internal coherence, being divided by a myriad of factors such as attitude to economic reform, the protection of agriculture, decommunisation, religion, and – last but not least – personalities. Broad anti-communist fronts had, throughout the region, been prone to split after the first democratic elections, but few had split into so many groups as in Poland.

It took six weeks to form a government after the 1991 elections, and the product of this laborious process was a coalition of five centre-right parties with mainly Solidarity origins. Yet even this did not possess a majority in the Sejm without garnering additional support. The new Prime Minister, Jan Olszewski, began losing his coalition partners almost as soon as he took office, and he was also opposed from the outset by President Wałęsa. The government lasted just six months, and, despite heavy criticism of its economic policy, it was finally brought down in an argument over 'lustration' – dealing with the communist past – during the course of which the Internal Affairs

Minister circulated lists accusing a number of prominent politicians of collaboration with the communist secret police. Such lists were problematic everywhere in the post-communist world, since they inevitably relied for evidence on the files of the very secret police who were being reviled. The Polish lists, however, were also particularly problematic politically, since they included both the President and the leaders of two of the coalition parties.[49]

Following Olszewski's ousting, President Wałęsa initially asked the leader of the Polish Peasant Party, Waldemar Pawlak, to form a government, but he was unable to do so. Finally, a new government, under Hanna Suchocka of the post-Solidarity Democratic Union, was approved in July 1992. It comprised a coalition of seven parties, including several which had belonged to Olszewski's government. Like its predecessor, this government lacked a parliamentary majority and was reliant on the votes of further parties in order to remain in office. However, few politicians had anything obvious to gain by attempting to bring about a change of government in such a divided parliament, so, despite notable differences in the policy orientation of its members, the Suchocka government survived until September 1993. Suchocka had lost a vote of no confidence in May 1993, but Wałęsa dissolved parliament rather than accepting her resignation, and her government remained in office until new elections were held in September.[50]

The elections took place under a new electoral law which aimed to counteract the fragmentation of the previous Sejm. While retaining the same basic voting system as in 1991, parties (except ethnic minority parties) required a minimum 5 per cent of the national vote and coalitions 8 per cent in order to obtain seats on a PR basis in the constituencies, of which there were now 52. Seven per cent of the vote was required for parties to be assigned any of the 69 seats reserved for national lists. However, the effect of this law was in many respects as unsatisfactory as that of the previous one. As can be seen from Table 9.8, it produced a much neater parliament, with only six parties represented in the Sejm, but it also distorted the will of the voters. The two post-communist groups, the Democratic Left Alliance and the Polish Peasant Party, ended up with two-thirds of the seats on the basis of little more than a third of the votes, and over a third of the vote was 'wasted' on parties or coalitions which did not cross the threshold. The scale of the post-communist victory was therefore in part a consequence of the new electoral system, and the fact that politicians and voters had had no time to adapt to its effects. It was, however, also a result of the weakness and division of the post-Solidarity parties, and particularly the failure of the right-of-centre to unite and gain Sejm representation.

The victory of a communist successor party in Poland, with its tradition of staunch popular resistance to communism, was at first sight surprising. However, two factors go some way to explaining it.[51] First, Poland under the Balcerowicz Plan had been the one East European country to implement

Table 9.8 Polish elections, 19 September 1993

Sejm (Lower House)	% vote	Seats
Democratic Left Alliance	20	171
Polish Peasant Party	15	132
Democratic Union	11	74
Union of Labour	7	41
Confederation for Independent Poland	6	22
Non-Party Reform Bloc	5	16
German Minority	1	4
Total		460

Senate (Upper House)	Seats
Democratic Left Alliance	37
Polish Peasant Party	36
Solidarity	10
Democratic Union	4
Non-Party Reform Bloc	2
Union of Labour	2
Liberal Democratic Congress	1
German Minority	1
Others	7
Total	100

Source: Główny Urząd Statystyczny (1994, p. 77); Millard (1994d, pp. 323–4).

genuine economic 'shock therapy'. By 1993, this was beginning to show positive results. The country had recovered from the collapse of the Soviet markets which took place in 1991, and had gone on to produce almost the first positive growth rates in the post-communist world; inflation had been, if not completely conquered, at least reduced from the runaway levels of 1989. However, while private enterprise now accounted for more than half of economic activity, this was largely due to the growth of small businesses and the service sector, and where larger state enterprises were in private hands, they had often been sold to their former communist managers. The sense of injustice this caused was heightened by the fact that there was substantial unemployment, and for many ordinary people on fixed wages, pensions or benefits, living standards had declined markedly. Additionally, Poland had been the one Soviet bloc country where agriculture was largely in the hands of small farmers, and these formed another major social group disaffected by the introduction of free market principles and the removal of state subsidies to agriculture. Such people formed the mainstay of the support of the Polish Peasant Party, which had emerged from the puppet United Peasant Party of the communist period, and which was the other post-communist party to do well in the elections. The second factor which favoured the post-communist parties was the tendency of Solidarity's successors to argue between themselves while, at the same time, the four governments which they had led since 1989 did not appear adequately to have addressed the everyday material problems of many citizens. This assisted the post-communist parties in presenting themselves as calm professionals who were concerned with ordinary people rather than ideological or religious battles.[52]

The 1993 elections left Poland in the strange position of having executive powers shared between a post-communist government and the presidency of the anti-communist hero, Wałęsa. While the country had yet to pass an entirely new constitution, the so-called 'Little Constitution' of October 1992 clarified relations between parliament and President, giving the Sejm and Senate legislative power while executive power was divided between the President and the Council of Ministers (government). The President's powers included 'general supervision in the field of international relations' and 'with respect to the external and internal security of the State', as well as the right to nominate the Prime Minister, although the latter's chosen government was subject to a vote of confidence in the Sejm.[53] Such a semi-presidential system left scope for conflict between President and Prime Minister, and the decisiveness of the election result gave Wałęsa only limited opportunity to choose a Prime Minister of his choice. The task eventually fell to the leader of the Polish Peasant Party, Waldemar Pawlak.

In general terms, however, Poland was showing some signs of stabilisation by the end of 1993. Despite popular dissatisfaction, economic indicators were improving; some progress had been made in defining the role of the President; and the country had a government with a clear parliamentary majority.

Romania

By 1991, the National Salvation Front (NSF) in Romania was suffering from some of the basic problems which afflicted the broad political movements who had been elected to government elsewhere in the post-communist world. These included a tendency to split as ruling politicians had to cope with the real problems of everyday politics, such as economic reform. However, in many respects the problems facing Romania were more severe than elsewhere, and solutions more elusive.

In the course of 1991, the government of the NSF's Petre Roman made attempts at economic reform, with a first land reform act in February, a second stage of price liberalisation in April, and a privatisation law in August. While these measures were helpful in improving Romania's standing with the West, which had been much damaged during 1990, they were not fully supported by the whole of the NSF, nor did they bring about any immediate amelioration in the population's living conditions. During the course of the summer, industrial production was still declining sharply as inflation soared, and strikes were commonplace. One of the NSF's responses to such discontent was that,

---

Textbox 9.6 Main events in Romania, 1991–93

1991

September	Miners demonstrating against the NSF force Prime Minister Roman to resign.
October	Stolojan (independent) becomes Prime Minister of government largely comprised of NSF, with some National Liberals.
November	New constitution passed.
December	77 per cent 'yes' vote in referendum on constitution.

1992

April	NSF splits; Roman faction remains NSF, Iliescu faction becomes Democratic NSF.
September	Second parliamentary and presidential elections; Iliescu remains President after a second round of voting in October, but parliament is deadlocked.
November	Vacaroiu (independent) becomes Prime Minister of government of technocrats and DNSF members, with tacit nationalist support.

1993

May	NSF becomes Democratic Party (DP-NSF).
July	DNSF becomes PSDR (Party of Social Democracy of Romania).
October	Romania is finally admitted to the Council of Europe, after earlier doubts over its democratic credentials in the field of civil rights.

---

although it had won a safe majority in the 1990 elections, by early 1991 it was already seeking coalition partners in order to share the burden of coping with the country's continuing economic crisis. These attempts were largely unsuccessful, despite the signing in July of a charter with three small parties with links to the NSF.

Matters came to a head in September 1991 when thousands of angry miners from the Jiu Valley arrived in Bucharest on hijacked trains, leading to unrest in which three died and hundreds were injured. Whereas, in the previous summer, they had come in support of the government, on this occasion they were protesting against their own living conditions and demanding the resignation of both Prime Minister Roman and President Iliescu. In the event, Roman was ousted while Iliescu survived, and suspicions were voiced either that the President had sacrificed the Prime Minister to save himself, or that Iliescu had created or exploited the chance to rid himself of the leading representative of a faction in the NSF with whose policies he disagreed.

Roman was replaced as Prime Minister by the non-party Theodor Stolojan. The government he formed retained a few NSF members from the previous government, as well as some new ministers who were affiliated to the NSF, but was also half composed of independents and some members of smaller parties, including the National Liberal Party which had previously been in opposition. The NSF had thus succeeded in retaining overall control of the government while broadening its scope. The precise political orientation of the government was not altogether clear, and in some senses it was always regarded as an interim government which aimed to stabilise the economic situation pending new elections. While Roman's forced resignation could be seen as a response to protests about the social effects of his government's policies, Stolojan pledged to accelerate reforms and could not be regarded as an opponent of economic reform: he had resigned from his post of Finance Minister in Roman's government the previous spring because he considered progress towards a market economy was too slow. In practice, however, Stolojan was to achieve little in his year in office, other than the avoidance of further violent manifestations of social discontent; industrial production continued to decline markedly.

By the beginning of 1992, Romanian politics should have had a clearer framework, since the country had the distinction of possessing a new constitution which had been approved in a popular referendum. The draft constitution had been approved by both chambers of the Romanian parliament, which together comprised the Constituent Assembly, by a majority of over 80 per cent in November 1991, the month after the new government had been installed.[54] Criticisms of the new constitution were varied, and included the position of ethnic minorities, the fact that Romania was to be a republic (as opposed to a monarchy) and the powers of the President. However, when the referendum took place in early December, it demonstrated a reasonable, if not overwhelming, level of approval, with over half the total eligible electorate voting in favour: despite some calls for a boycott of the referendum, there was a turnout of nearly 70 per cent, of whom over three-quarters were in favour.

It was, in fact, the situation of the President which was to cause continuing tensions in the political life of Romania, yet this derived in a sense less from the constitutional provisions for presidential powers, which were not particularly extensive compared to Western democracies with directly elected Presidents, but rather from the actual position of power and authority held by President Iliescu in the Romanian political context. Although Iliescu had technically left the NSF in June 1990 since the constitution did not permit the President to be a member of any political party, he remained a prominent actor in the internal disputes of the NSF which erupted in 1992.

The NSF split at its convention in March 1992. The reason lay partly in the ever more open enmity between Roman and Iliescu, which had been apparent since the former's forced resignation the previous September. On a political level, this manifested itself both in arguments over economic policy and over the NSF's links with the communist past: Iliescu accused Roman of attempting to force the pace of economic reform beyond that envisaged by the NSF's original programme, while Roman doubted Iliescu's will to lead Romania to a democratic future. The NSF's poor performance in local elections in February, which was in part a response to the evident divisions within the movement, further exacerbated tensions between its various factions. When Roman's supporters were successful in opposing Iliescu's being chosen as the NSF candidate for the next presidential elections, the conservative faction supporting Iliescu broke away and formed a new party called the Democratic National Salvation Front (DNSF).[55] The NSF thus appeared to have shared the fate of most of the broad political movements spawned at the time of the 1989 revolutions and to have divided along political lines when confronted with the real issues of post-communist politics.

The opposition in Romania also underwent structural changes. At the time of the 1990 elections, it had been largely composed of two very weak 'historic' parties – which had both performed badly – as well as the Hungarian Democratic Federation of Romania (HDFR). In November 1991, opposition parties united in the Democratic Convention, and this was relatively successful in the local elections the next February, although its performance did not match that of the NSF. However, one of the two historic parties, the National Liberal Party (NLP) led by Radu Câmpeanu, left the Democratic Convention in April 1992. This decision was determined by the probability that Câmpeanu would not be selected as the Democratic Convention's presidential candidate and by the consideration that Romanian nationalism could not be effectively exploited within an umbrella organisation which also embraced representatives of the Hungarian minority.

New elections were finally held in Romania in late September 1992. Slight changes had been made in the electoral law since 1990: the number of seats in the lower chamber had been reduced to 328, and the number in the upper chamber increased to 143.[56] The electoral system remained one of proportional representation, where citizens cast their vote for party lists within whichever of the large constituencies they lived. However, seats could now be claimed only by parties which won more than 3 per cent of the vote, and in the case of electoral coalitions, this was increased by 1 per cent for each extra party, up to a total threshold of 8 per cent. The representatives of national minorities were exempt from this provision, since each minority had a right to one seat in the lower chamber, as a consequence of which the total number of deputies actually exceeded 328. For the presidential election, the rules remained very similar to 1990: if no candidate received the support of more than 50 per cent of the total electorate in the first round, the two candidates obtaining the most votes entered a second ballot two weeks later, when the candidate with the most votes would win.

Although these electoral procedures were not exceptional, the Romanian political system remained unusual in two respects. The first was that the two chambers of the Romanian parliament were extremely similar, other than in size: they were elected at the same time, for the same electoral period, used almost identical electoral systems, and had similar legislative powers. The second was that the President was elected at the same time as the parliament. Generally, where Presidents are directly elected by the people, this process does not coincide with parliamentary elections. One effect of the elections being held at the same time was that the presidential election, which obviously focused heavily on the individual candidates, somewhat overshadowed the party political competition which took place in the parliamentary elections.

As can be seen from Table 9.9, it was the presidential election which produced the clearest result, with Iliescu gaining nearly half of the first round vote. This was a consequence both of Iliescu's personal prominence, and of a legal requirements that candidates should be endorsed by 100,000 citizens in order to appear on the ballot paper. This rule had reduced the field to six, which was substantially less than the number of parties presenting lists of candidates in the parliamentary election. Iliescu, for example, was supported by the DNSF and by the nationalist Greater Romania Party (GRP), while the Hungarian HDFR supported the presidential candidate of the opposition Democratic Convention of Romania (DCR), but stood separately in the parliamentary elections.

The result of the parliamentary elections was less clear, with seven parties crossing the 3 per cent threshold. Some observations can be made, however. First, the pro-Iliescu DNSF, which had technically broken away from the NSF, gained 28 per cent, compared to a mere 10 per cent for the NSF of former Prime Minister Roman. (In the presidential elections, where the DNSF supported the incumbent Iliescu, the disparity in the performance of the two parties' candidates was even greater.) One disadvantage faced by the NSF was that they differed from the DNSF in that they were more favourable towards economic reform and more anti-communist, yet both these views were represented more forcefully by the opposition DCR. Secondly, the performance of the opposition, while much improved from the 1990 elections, was nevertheless much weaker than in Bulgaria and Albania, where the opposition had managed to oust communist successor parties in the second democratic elections. The DCR's failure can be explained in part by the internal problems of an organisation which at the time of the elections encompassed eighteen different parties, and had already lost the National Liberal Party (which stood alone in the elections and failed to cross the 3 per cent threshold). The DCR spent much energy debating the restoration of the

Table 9.9 Romanian elections, 27 September 1992

Lower House (Chamber of Deputies)	% vote	Seats
Democratic National Salvation Front	28	117
Democratic Convention of Romania	20	82
National Salvation Front	10	43
Party of Romanian National Unity	8	30
Hungarian Democratic Federation of Romania	7	27
Greater Romania Party	4	16
Socialist Labour Party	3	13
Democratic Agrarian Party	3	0
National Liberal Party	2	0
Others	15	13
Total	100	341

Upper House (Senate)	% vote	Seats
Democratic National Salvation Front	28	49
Democratic Convention	20	34
National Salvation Front	10	18
Party of Romanian National Unity	8	14
Hungarian Democratic Federation of Romania	8	12
Greater Romania Party	4	6
Socialist Labour Party	3	5
Democratic Agrarian Party	3	5
National Liberal Party	3	0
Others	12	0
Total	100	143

N.B. Although a 3 per cent threshold was in operation, in the Chamber of Deputies, seats were reserved for parties of the national minorities, which accounts for the seats allocated to 'others'.

Presidency	% vote	
	Round 1 (27.9)	Round 2 (11.10)
Ion Iliescu (DNSF)	47	61
Emil Constantinescu (DCR)	31	39
Gheorghe Funar (PRNU)	11	–
Caius Dragomir (NSF)	5	–
Ioan Manzatu (Republican Party)	3	–
Mircea Druc (ind.)	3	–

Source: Bing and Szajkowski (1994, p. 349); Shafir (1992, pp. 1–8).

monarchy, an issue on which it was itself divided while the electorate was largely opposed, and partly as a consequence of stances on this issue, it ended up fielding a largely unknown presidential candidate, Emil Constantinescu. Thirdly, nearly 20 per cent of the vote went to the three parties with a predominantly national focus, two of which were Romanian nationalist, and one a representative of the Hungarian minority.

The composition of the parliament did not facilitate government formation, and once again a Prime Minister without party affiliation, Nicolae

Vacaroiu, was chosen. His government was viewed predominantly as representing the DNSF, which was now the largest parliamentary party, although the majority of ministers were independents. The government was potentially extremely vulnerable, since for support it had to rely on the votes not merely of the DNSF, but also of the two nationalist parties, the Greater Romania Party and the Party of Romanian National Unity, and of the small Socialist Labour Party, which was a far left party. This informal alliance embraced parties which on some indicators ranged from far right to far left, although all to some extent shared populist tendencies such as left-wing hostility to economic reform and a right-wing inclination to nationalism. An advantage of this fragile arrangement, however, was that the DNSF did avoid, in the short term, the stigma internationally of being in coalition with extremist parties.

Although the Vacaroiu government survived throughout 1993 without a clear parliamentary majority, little progress was made in solving Romania's many problems. Ethnic tension remained considerable, with the Hungarian minority of some 7 per cent feeling threatened by the demands of Romanian nationalists. Politically, all the main political groups suffered internal problems. The DNSF changed its name in July to the Party of Social Democracy of Romania, and in May the NSF had merged with the small extra-parliamentary Democratic Party and was renamed the Democratic Party-National Salvation Front. The DCR, being a broad umbrella organisation, was affected by divisions within its component parties as well as questions about its own future. The HDFR was also divided between more moderate representatives of the Hungarian minority and those that favoured demands for autonomy. Finally, economic problems were still severe. The year began with shortages of energy and food, a further wave of price liberalisation at the beginning of May 1993 contributed to an inflation rate of nearly 300 per cent, the country was affected by several waves of strikes, and the currency was weak. Little progress was made on privatisation as government supporters remained divided between the need for economic reform and the desirability of preserving a social safety net.

Only in the foreign policy arena were there any notable successes.[57] On 1 February 1993, an association agreement was signed with the European Community, which was only the fourth such agreement with a post-communist state, following those with Poland, Hungary and Czechoslovakia. In October 1993, Romania was accepted as a member by the Council of Europe, despite doubts about the progress of democratisation in the country, and Romania's Most Favoured Nation status was restored by the United States. The country's international standing was of considerable importance to the government and President alike, in view of Romania's rather vulnerable geopolitical situation. Whatever the internal problems, Romania was none the less relatively stable when compared to its eastern neighbour, the Republic of Moldova, and its south-eastern neighbour Serbia, which were, or recently had been, embroiled in warfare.

Former Yugoslavia

Disintegration and war

Yugoslavia in the period under review was dominated by disintegration and war, and it is not the aim of this section to chart the course of the all too numerous military conflicts which arose, and the futile attempts of the UN and the European Community to broker ceasefires and agreements which were almost inevitably violated by some of the parties involved.[58] However, no discussion of the domestic politics and post-communist transition in the Yugoslav successor states is meaningful without reference to their broader context. Two of the six Yugoslav republics – Croatia and Bosnia-Herzegovina – declared independence while not in control of all the territory within their nominal, communist Yugoslav, republican borders; and in a further two – Serbia and Montenegro, which were to form the 'rump Yugoslavia' – domestic politics were radically affected by the international economic sanctions imposed because of their military involvement in the disputed territories of their neighbours. Of the remaining two republics, Macedonia was closely watched by the West because of its historical reputation as an unstable Balkan flashpoint, which could lead to an internationalisation of the Yugoslav war. However, this ever-present danger was in some respects a stabilising factor in the republic's internal politics, as external threats are the most effective motivation compelling divided domestic elites to cooperation and compromise. It was only in the last, and most Western, republic of Slovenia that politics were to any extent dominated by normal day-to-day issues. This is not unconnected to the fact that, as shown by Table 3.4, it was the most ethnically homogeneous of the republics, with over 90 per cent of the population belonging to the titular nationality.

Yugoslavia entered 1991 in a situation where a renegotiation of the relationship between the Federation's republics was urgently necessary. Serbian intransigence was detrimental to achieving such a goal, since both its dominant position in the Yugoslav federation and its fears for the future of Serbian minorities in Croatia and Bosnia-Herzegovina in the case of increased independence of the republics made it a defender of the *status quo*. Serbia's reluctance fundamentally to restructure the territorial distribution of power within Yugoslavia was, however, also supported by the western powers, who – in a period prior to the disintegration of the Soviet and Czechoslovak federations – were unwilling to countenance the notion of border changes of any kind for fear that it would lead to uncontrollable instability. The fact that

Textbox 9.7 Main events in former Yugoslavia, 1991–93

1991

January   *Croatia and Slovenia* The two republics declare a mutual defence pact.
            Macedonia The parliament declares the republic's sovereignty and
            right to secede from the federation.
April   *Yugoslavia* The Socialist Federal Republic of Yugoslavia is renamed
            the Federal Republic of Yugoslavia.
May   *Croatia* A referendum shows 94 per cent of those voting to be in favour
            of independence.
            Yugoslavia The Croat Mesić is prevented from taking his turn to be
            Federal President by Serbia and its allies in the state presidency.
June   *Yugoslavia* Slovenia declares independence, and Croatia the intention
            to secede. A ten-day war follows, after which the Yugoslav National
            Army withdraws from Slovenia and a ceasefire is negotiated in Croatia.
            Agreement is reached on Mesić becoming Yugoslav President.
            The Serbs of the Krajina areas of Croatia and Bosnia-Herzegovina
            announce that they are uniting.
September   *Macedonia* A referendum (boycotted by the Albanian minority) shows
            95 per cent support for independence.
            Serbia (Kosovo) The Albanian population votes in an unauthorised
            referendum for independence, and an independence declaration
            (never internationally recognised) is made the next month.
October   *Bosnia-Herzegovina* The parliament declares the republic's sovereignty,
            but also the willingness to negotiate a form of Yugoslav association.
            Croatia After a three-month EC negotiated moratorium on
            independence, the parliament declares all Federal laws invalid.
            Slovenia The republic cuts all links with federal institutions and
            introduces its own currency.
November   *Macedonia* A new constitution is passed, declaring the country
            independent.
December   *Yugoslavia* The Croats Mesić and Marković resign as President and
            Prime Minister of the Federation.
            Slovenia A new constitution is passed.
            Croatia The 'Republic of Serbian Krajina' is declared in Serbian
            areas of Croatia.
            Bosnia-Herzegovina Bosnian Serbs proclaim their own republic after a
            November referendum against independence from Yugoslavia.

1992

January   *Croatia* UN 'Protected Areas' established, largely in territory outside
            the control of the Croatian government. Croatian (and Slovenian)
            independence is recognised by the EC.
March   *Bosnia-Herzegovina* Independence declared after overwhelming
            support in a referendum held in February (boycotted by Serbs); a
            'Serbian Republic' of Bosnia-Herzegovina is formed, led by Karadžić.
            Croatia UN peacekeeping forces deployed.

	Serbia and Montenegro A referendum supports Montenegro joining Serbia in a new Federal Republic of Yugoslavia.
April	*Bosnia-Herzegovina* The state is officially recognised by the EC and United States.
	Macedonia Admitted to the United Nations as 'Former Yugoslav Republic of Macedonia' (FYROM), amid continuing protests from Greece about any use of the name 'Macedonia'.
	Slovenia Government falls in a vote of no confidence.
	Serbia and Montenegro The Federal Republic of Yugoslavia, comprising Serbia and Montenegro, is created by the promulgation of a new constitution.
May	*Serbia and Montenegro* The first direct Federal elections take place, after which the expatriate Panić is appointed Prime Minister, and Ćosić President. Separate, unofficial elections are held in Kosovo. The United Nations imposes economic sanctions.
	Bosnia-Herzegovina/Croatia/Slovenia All states admitted to the United Nations.
July	*Bosnia-Herzegovina* A 'Croatian Union of Herceg-Bosna', never internationally recognised, is established in areas containing the Croatian minority.
	Macedonia The government is defeated in a vote of no confidence, to be replaced by a new coalition government.
August	*Croatia* New elections again won by the Croatian Democratic Community, with Tudjman directly elected as President.
October	*Serbia and Montenegro* Montenegro adopts a new constitution, incorporating its status as part of the Federal Republic of Yugoslavia.
December	*Serbia and Montenegro* New elections at Federal and republican level are won by socialists, with the victory of Milošević over Federal Prime Minister Panić as Serbian President, and the latter's dismissal as Prime Minister. Ćosić is re-elected as Federal President.
	Slovenia In fresh elections, Kučan is re-elected President, though a new coalition government is formed under a Liberal Democrat Prime Minister, Drnovšek.

1993

January	*Bosnia-Herzegovina* The Vance–Owen Plan for the division of Bosnia-Herzegovina is presented in Geneva.
	Serbia and Montenegro Bulatović is re-elected Montenegrin President.
April	*Bosnia-Herzegovina* The Vance–Owen Plan rejected by Bosnian Serbs after acceptance by the Muslims and Croats.
	Macedonia The republic is admitted to United Nations under the name of 'Former Yugoslav Republic of Macedonia'.
	Serbia and Montenegro UN sanctions strengthened.
June	*Serbia and Montenegro* Federal President Ćosić ousted for allegedly conspiring against Milošević.
December	*Serbia and Montenegro* New parliamentary elections in Serbia.

the era of the communist stabilisation of Yugoslavia had clearly ended was apparently overlooked. Explicit statements by leading Western politicians that an independent Slovenia or Croatia would not be recognised – most notably that of US Secretary of State James Baker made in Belgrade just five days before the scheduled Slovenian declaration of independence – merely removed any incentive the Serbian leadership might have had to compromise in discussions on the future of the federation.[59]

The task of restructuring the way Yugoslavia was governed was complicated by two factors other than the extreme national mix of the country. The first was post-communist transition. The approaches of the different republics to this great historic challenge, and the speed with which they were proceeding, were incompatible. The radically divergent progress of the independent Slovenia by the mid-1990s compared to its more Eastern neighbours is an eloquent testimony to this. The vast scale of the problems caused by post-communist development in Yugoslavia was given scant attention internationally at the beginning of the 1990s because the West had traditionally been preoccupied with communism as a Soviet threat, of which Yugoslavia formed no part. The second factor complicating negotiations in Yugoslavia in 1990 and 1991 was that any new structures acceptable to the Slovenes and Croats would have to be based on a confederation of sovereign states. While successful federalism entails creating complex and sensitive mechanisms for consensus-building and the mediation of disputes, a functioning confederation is arguably even more difficult to construct. It is therefore not entirely surprising that Yugoslavia, with its very weak interwar tradition of democracy followed by over forty years of communism, lacked the political sophistication to achieve this aim. The Slovenes had at least been prepared to discuss a confederation, whereas the Czechs, negotiating with the Slovaks in somewhat different circumstances in 1992, had immediately written off all confederal arrangements as impractical and both opted for and implemented independence in just over six months. The Slovene case was, however, like the Czech/Slovak situation, relatively simple to solve by independence because the country was, by East European standards, ethnically homogeneous to a high degree. Elsewhere in Yugoslavia, complex and time-consuming federal or confederal arrangements had more to recommend themselves because of the problems of multi-ethnicity. However, the successful implementation of such arrangements presupposes a willingness on the part of all the political elites involved to achieve such an outcome.

Slovenia finally declared independence in late June 1991, and was joined by Croatia. While not as well prepared – militarily or administratively – for independence as Slovenia, Croatia was reluctant to remain in the Federation without the support of the Slovene counterweight against Serbian dominance. Yugoslavia at this point lacked a Federal President, as the Serbs had blocked the normal rotation procedure for this office to prevent its assumption by the

Croat Stipe Mesić – an indication of the extent to which the Yugoslav Federation was non-functional. After brief attempts by the Federal authorities to retain control of Yugoslavia's international border in Slovenia, a three-month moratorium on independence was brokered by the European Community, which entailed Serbian agreement to Mesić's accession to the Federal presidency. While there was still a desire on the part of a number of Western governments to see the preservation of Yugoslavia, the fact that the Yugoslav People's Army had used force and caused deaths in the dispute with Slovenia had swung international opinion against Serbia and the Federal authorities. In October, Slovenia reaffirmed its independence, and both Slovenia and Croatia were recognised as independent states by the European Community (under heavy German pressure) in January 1992.

Warfare in Croatia was far more protracted than in Slovenia, and ceasefires agreed from June 1991 onwards were continually violated. The Serbian leadership was by this point less concerned with the continuation of Yugoslavia *per se*, and more with the Serbian minorities whom it wished to see joined in some form of Greater Serbia; the Croatian government was motivated by the fact that Serbs now controlled about a quarter of Croatian territory. An arms embargo on Yugoslavia agreed by the EC and the United States in July, and unanimously approved by the United Nations in September, served mainly to perpetuate the existing Serbian superiority in military supplies and arms production. UN troops were first deployed in Yugoslavia to monitor the border between the Serb and Croatian communities in Croatia; this effectively preserved a situation in which the Croatian government was not in control of all its state's territory.

Macedonia and Bosnia-Herzegovina declared their independence in November 1991 and March 1992 respectively, their hands forced by unwillingness to remain in a Yugoslavia without Croatia and Slovenia. Compared to Slovenia and Croatia, the independence of Bosnia-Herzegovina was rapidly accepted by the international community – despite the fact that its government clearly did not control all the territory of the new state. Diplomatic recognition was granted by the EC and the United States in April, and Bosnia-Herzegovina was accepted into the United Nations in May. However, this led to a new phase in the war, as the Serbs of Bosnia-Herzegovina refused to be separated from Serbia. May saw the start of the protracted siege of the Bosnian capital, Sarajevo. The fact that the old Yugoslavia now no longer existed was confirmed by the forming in April of a new Federal Republic of Yugoslavia comprising merely Serbia and Montenegro. Milošević technically withdrew the Yugoslav People's Army from Bosnia in May, but the Bosnian Serb leader, Radovan Karadžić, and the military commander, General Mladič, had received, and continued to receive, much support from Serbian military strength.

The Bosnian war was greatly complicated by the fact that it was a three-way struggle. The minority Serbian community allied with the rebel Serbs of the Croatian Krajina and set its hopes on the formation of some kind of Greater Serbia uniting all the Serbs of the former Yugoslavia. This was territorially problematic, and created a military imperative to secure land-links between the dispersed areas with majority Serbian populations. The smaller Croatian minority at times cooperated with the Bosnian government, which mainly represented the Muslim community. The Muslims, while the largest of the three communities, comprised 40 per cent, compared to about 32 per cent Serbs and 18 per cent Croats (see Table 3.2). However, Croatia was not entirely averse to the idea of cooperating with Serbia in a partition of Bosnia which would unite many of its Croats and Serbs with the neighbouring republics of Croatia and Serbia, while leaving a much truncated rump Bosnia. Such designs were vastly complicated by the enormous intermingling of the national groups within Bosnia, and the vicious war which took place was marked by a growing international familiarity with the term 'ethnic cleansing'. This entailed the creation of hundreds of thousands of refugees as the armies of all three communities (but most notably by far of the Serbs) terrorised all others in their path so that they fled their homes. The response of the international community was largely restricted to humanitarian aid, economic sanctions against rump Yugoslavia and the repeated brokering of agreements, which were either not accepted by one of the parties or accepted and then violated.

Internal politics

When one turns to look at the domestic political systems in the former Yugoslavia, what one finds, amid the chaos of everyday life, including economic collapse, rampant inflation and the largest shifts of population seen in Europe since the aftermath of World War II, is a high degree of stability of power. Prime Ministers came and went, but no former Yugoslav republic changed its President after independence. (The fact that there was a change of President in the rump Yugoslav Federation serves merely to indicate the lower status of this office.) At first sight this is a pattern not unfamiliar in the rest of Eastern Europe, but there are two crucial differences. First, the changes in Prime Minister in former Yugoslavia did not (with the exception of Slovenia and Macedonia) coincide with a significant change in the party composition of the government. While there was a plurality of parties in each of the new states, most of them had a clearly identifiable ruling party.[60] The exceptions were Slovenia, where shifting party coalitions governed, and Bosnia-Herzegovina, which was not, as an entity, governed at all. Secondly, the Presidents were crucial to the location of effective power in former Yugoslavia.[61] This is reflected in the fact that all the republics eventually opted for the direct election of the President. Only the President of the rump Federal Republic of

Yugoslavia was chosen by parliament, and again, this is indicative of the fact that the office was not a locus of power: President Milošević ruled Serbia, and President Bulatović controlled Montenegro in his shadow. The one exception to dominant presidential power is Slovenia, where President Kučan, although directly elected and respected, had a far more ceremonial role of the sort common in Central Europe. Elsewhere in the new states of the former Yugoslavia, the pattern of party and presidential rule was most reminiscent of that in Romania.

Several reasons can be suggested for the prevalence of presidential and dominant party rule. Conditions of war rendered the option of a strong leader more attractive. Strong presidencies were also more common in the former Soviet Union, and coincided to some degree with societies that had had little independent or dissident activity in the communist period. In the former Yugoslavia, the two factors reinforced each other, as it was particularly easy for leaders holding power in abnormal conditions of warfare to manipulate the system around them and retain power. For example, control of the media – a contentious issue throughout the post-communist world – was particularly strong (though, by communist standards, very far from complete) in the former Yugoslavia, and there were numerous incidents of political opponents being suppressed, most notably in the Albanian Kosovo region of Serbia. Additionally, preservation of single-party dominance by more democratic means was aided in former Yugoslavia by the fact that almost all the republics had initially opted for majoritarian electoral systems, and ruling parties were in an excellent position to prevent any alteration of this *status quo*. Even though second ballots were generally held where no candidate gained more than 50 per cent of the vote, such a system was still highly disadvantageous to the small, struggling and often disorganised oppositions. The electoral systems exacerbated the problems of democracies emerging without anchors in a strong civil society rather than moderating them. It is notable that Slovenia is in this respect once again the Yugoslav exception, as it operated a proportional representation system in parliamentary elections.[62]

Whereas all the republics had held elections in 1990, only four returned to the ballot box in the period 1991–93. The first was Croatia, which held elections (in those parts of the republic which it controlled) in August 1992. The elections were for the lower house of parliament (the far less powerful upper house was elected in February 1993) and for the presidency. As can be seen from Table 9.10, these confirmed the predominance of the Croatian Democratic Community and gave its leader, Franjo Tudjman, the advantage of being directly elected as the state's President.

The elections in Slovenia were perhaps more significant. The republic had mirrored developments elsewhere in East-Central Europe, whereby a broad anti-communist coalition won the first post-communist elections and then came apart. In the Slovene case, the DEMOS coalition oversaw the successful

Table 9.10 Croatian elections, 2 August 1992

Lower House	% vote	Seats
Croatian Democratic Community	44	85
Croatian Social Liberal Party	17	14
Social Democratic Party of Croatia	5	11
Croatian People's Party	7	6
Croatian Party of Rights	7	5
Croatian Peasants' Party	4	3
Serbian People's Party	1	3
Others	15	11
Total		138

N.B. An Upper Chamber was also elected in February 1993.
Source: EIU Country Report Bosnia-Hercegovina, Croatia and Slovenia
(4th quarter 1995, p. 14).

Presidency	% vote
Franjo Tudjman (CDC)	58
Dražen Budiša (CSLP)	22
Davka Dabčević-Kučar (SPP)	6
Dobroslav Paraga (CPR)	6
Others (4)	8

Source: Eastern Europe and the Commonwealth of Independent States
1994 (1994, p. 244).

Table 9.11 Slovenian elections, 6 December 1992

National Assembly	% vote	Seats
Liberal Democratic Party	23	22
Slovene Christian Democrats	15	15
United List	14	14
Slovene National Party	10	12
Slovene People's Party	9	10
Democratic Party	5	6
Greens of Slovenia	4	5
Social Democratic Party of Slovenia	3	4
Others	18	0
Italian and Magyar national minorities (reserved seats)		2
Total		90

Source: Statistični urad Republike Slovenije (1995, p. 106); Bibič (1993, p. 382).

Presidency	% vote
Milan Kučan	64
Ivan Bizjak	21
Jelko Kacin	7
Others (5)	8

Source: Statistični urad Republike Slovenije (1995, p. 109).

attainment of Slovene independence, and the passing of a new constitution in December 1991, and was then dissolved. This was followed by a change of government after a vote of no confidence in May 1992. The new Prime Minister, Janez Drnovšek of the Liberal Democratic Party, remained in office after the elections, as did President Kučan, who, as shown in Table 9.11, managed to be re-elected as President with more than 50 per cent of the vote in the first round.[63]

Finally, the citizens of the rump Yugoslavia, comprising Serbia and Montenegro, also voted – with extraordinary frequency, in the case of the Serbs. A Federal parliament was elected in May 1992, after the creation of the new

Table 9.12 Serbian elections, 20 December 1992

	% vote	Seats
Socialist Party of Serbia	29	101
Serbian Radical Party	23	73
Democratic Movement for Serbia (DEPOS)	17	49
Democratic Community of Vojvodina Hungarians	3	9
Democratic Party	4	7
Group of Citizens from Kosovo and Metohija – Arkan	0	5
Serbian Peasants' Party	3	3
Reform Democratic Forces of Vojvodina	2	2
Democratic Reform Party of Muslims	0	1
Total		250

Presidential elections	% vote
Slobodan Milošević	56
Milan Panić	34
Others (5)	10

Source: Andrejevich (1993, pp. 15–16).

Table 9.13 Montenegrin elections, 20 December 1992/10 January 1993

Parliament	Seats
Democratic Socialist Party of Montenegro	46
People's Party	14
Liberal Alliance	13
Serbian Radical Party	8
Social Democratic Party of Reformists	4
Total	85

Source: EIU Country Profile Macedonia, Serbia-Montenegro 1993–94, p. 24.

Presidency	% vote	
	Round 1	Round 2
Momir Bulatović	43	63
Branko Kostić	24	37
Others (7)	33	

Source: EIU Country Profile Macedonia, Serbia-Montenegro 1992–93, p. 8.

Federal Republic of Yugoslavia. Milan Panić, an émigré businessman, became Prime Minister, and although his attempts at moderation met with some approval in the West, he soon disagreed with the Serbian President Milošević, and stood against him in the new elections for the Serbian President in December 1992.

Panić lost (see Table 9.12), and was shortly afterwards ousted as federal Prime Minister. At the same time, a new Serbian parliament was elected, as well as a new Federal parliament, and parliamentary and presidential elections took place in Montenegro. As can be seen from Table 9.13, the post-communist Montenegrin leader, Bulatović, remained as President, and his Democratic Socialist Party of Montenegro fared better than their Serbian counterparts had done in the parliamentary elections and gained a parliamentary majority.

Table 9.14 Serbian election, 19 December 1993

	% vote	Seats
Socialist Party of Serbia	37	123
Democratic Movement of Serbia	17	45
Serbian Radical Party	14	39
Democratic Party	12	29
Democratic Party of Serbia	5	7
Democratic Community of Vojvodina Hungarians	3	5
Albanian parties (coalition)	1	2
Total		250

Source: Allcock (1994b, p. 638); Cohen (1995, p. 351).

Despite the power wielded by Milošević in Serbia, his Socialist Party of Serbia did not enjoy a majority in parliament after the December 1992 elections, and in an attempt to rid his party of dependence on parties more extreme than his own, Serbia held new parliamentary elections just one year later. As can be seen from Table 9.14, the socialists' performance improved somewhat, but was still just short of an overall parliamentary majority.[64] Under the pressure of a protracted and inconclusive war and with international sanctions crippling the Serbian economy, Milošević's hold on power was not as complete as he could have wished.

Conclusion

In the course of the period under review, many of the electorates made their first judgements on democratically elected governments. The results were varied. The East Germans had already made a definitive and immutable decision about their future in 1990, but had to adapt to its consequences. In Czechoslovakia, the differences in views between Czechs and Slovaks expressed in the 1992 elections led to the demise of the common state. In Albania, a new, reformist government was elected in 1992 as the country stood on the brink of the economic abyss. In Bulgaria and Romania, elections in 1991 and 1992 were indecisive. Perhaps most surprisingly of all, the two countries which had led the transition from communism, Poland and Hungary, returned their successor parties to power – Poland in 1993, and Hungary a little later in early 1994. Finally, where first post-independence elections took place in the former Yugoslavia, they were influenced by the traumatic circumstances of the break-up of the federation.

However, amid this diversity of fortune, what all the states had in common was that the process of transition was far from complete, and many questions remained unanswered relating to both political, economic and national questions. It was only in the period that followed that any measured judgement of successes and failures became possible.

Notes

1. For an overview of the issue, see Welsh (1996).
2. Zanga (1991c).
3. For details of the elections, see Szajkowski (1992 and 1994, pp. 2–7).
4. See Vickers (1994); Zanga (1992a).
5. Zanga (1992b); Vickers (1994); Szajkowski (1994, pp. 8–12); Austin (1993).
6. For details of the electoral law, see Loloci (1994).
7. For tabulated details of presidential powers, see Lucky (1993/94, pp. 66–8).
8. Zanga and Austin (1993).
9. Zanga (1993).
10. For details of these and later trials of former communist leaders, see Imholz (1995).
11. Engelbrekt (1991).
12. International Institute of Democracy (1995, p. 16).
13. *Ibid.*, p. 25.
14. For further details of presidential powers in Bulgaria, see *East European Constitutional Review*, 3 (4)/4 (1).
15. Details of the electoral law are given in Kolarova and Dimitrov (1994).
16. See Szajkowski (1994, pp. 98–104); Kitschelt *et al.* (1995); Bell (1993); Tzvetkov (1992).
17. Engelbrekt (1993); for an account of decollectivisation, see Creed (1995).
18. For the development of the party system, see Karasimeonov (1993).
19. Engelbrekt (1994).
20. The most thorough discussion of the causes of the Czech/Slovak break-up is in Musil (1995). For a good summary, see Elster (1995).
21. For the history of Czech/Slovak relations, see Leff (1988); Kirschbaum (1993).
22. See Siklova (1996).
23. See Olson (1994); Henderson (1994a).
24. See Mathernova (1993).
25. For discussion of the 1992 elections, see Olson (1993); Wightman (1992).
26. The Civic Democratic Alliance had also emerged from Civic Forum; the Civic Movement, its third offshoot, failed to enter parliament in 1992.

27. For opinion poll figures, see Wolchik (1994).
28. See Musil (1993); Bútora *et al.* (1991).
29. The federalisation of Czechoslovakia was the only democratisation project of the Prague Spring to come to fruition after the Soviet invasion, although communist normalisation greatly distorted the way federalism operated. See Leff (1988).
30. For discussion of the importance of elite behaviour, see Henderson (1995).
31. For a discussion of Czech national identity, see Holy (1994).
32. See further Dalton (1994); Fulbrook (1994); Offe (1992).
33. On public service employees in East Germany, see Goetz (1993); Kvistad (1994).
34. On the CDU, see Segert (1995); Clemens (1993).
35. On problems of 'lustration' in East Germany, see Torpey (1993).
36. See Statistisches Bundesamt für die Bundesrepublik Deutschland (1993, pp. 130–1).
37. On nationalism and racism in east and west Germany after unification, see *German Politics*, 3 (2).
38. Art. 106 (3) 2.
39. For public opinion poll figures, see Pittaway and Swain (1994, p. 194).
40. See J. F. Brown (1994, p. 86); Körösényi (1991 and 1994).
41. See Pataki (1993).
42. See Pataki (1992a).
43. See Pataki (1992b). On Hungarian nationalism, see Csepeli and Örkény (1996).
44. On parties and power groups in general, see Szalai (1994).
45. See Mink (1993/94).
46. Rose and Haerpfer (1993, p. 43; 1994, p. 31).
47. On the 1991 elections, see Millard (1992).
48. On Polish parties, see Lewis (1994b); Lewis and Gortat (1995).
49. See Millard (1994b, pp. 483–4); Karpinski (1993).
50. See Vinton (1993).
51. On the 1993 elections, see Chan (1995); Gibson and Cielecka (1995); Marody (1995); Millard (1994c); Wade *et al.* (1995); Zagórski (1994); Zubek (1994 and 1995).
52. For a general evaluation of Polish politics in the early 1990s, see Millard (1994a).
53. See Articles 32, 34, 57. International Institute of Democracy (1995, pp. 393–4, 401–2; also Rzeplinski (1993/94).
54. On the constitution, see Crowther and Roper (1996).
55. See Gallagher (1995, pp. 114–24). For wide-ranging coverage of all aspects of Romanian domestic politics in the 1991–93 period, the most comprehensive source is articles by Shafir and Ionescu in *RFE/RL Research Report*.
56. See Stefoi (1994).
57. See Shafir and Ionescu (1994).
58. On the Yugoslav war, see Almond (1994); Bennett (1995); Crnobrnja (1994); Glenny (1993); Silber and Little (1995).
59. Almond (1994, pp. 39–40); Bennett (1995, p. 154); Cohen (1995, pp. 220–1); Silber and Little (1995, pp. 164–6). The most scathing critique of Western policy in former Yugoslavia is contained in Almond's work.
60. Allcock (1994c, p. 631).
61. See Varady and Dimitrijevic (1993/94).
62. For details of the mixed Croatian system, see Kaspović (1996).
63. See Bibić (1993); Milanovich (1996); Ramet (1993); Zajc (1994).
64. Allcock (1994b); Cohen (1995, pp. 348–56).

PART IV

THE NEW POLITICAL SYSTEMS OF EUROPE, 1994–96

CHAPTER 10

Patterns of post-communist politics

By the mid-1990s, the countries which had once been viewed by many in the West as a homogeneous communist bloc were beginning to separate into definable groups following divergent paths of development. There are many indicators that can be used to measure their progress: economic success, the ability to consolidate democratic institutions and prospects for what is generically termed 'integration into European structures'. Since the last criterion is largely an amalgam of the first two, it is here that we shall start evaluating the general state of post-communist politics in the mid-1990s.

Integration into European structures

If there was one single aim uniting the communist states of Europe when they embarked upon their transformation processes, it was a desire to become more like the countries of Western Europe. It was unclear whether the attraction was democracy or economic prosperity, or even if the distinction was evident. The strength of the motivation also varied radically: opposing views were most prevalent in Russia, where there were grave doubts about the appropriateness of any Western model, while among Czechs the desire to 'return to Europe' was almost frantic. The importance of acceptability by European organisations was therefore based not only on practical considerations, but also on emotive factors.

The most important institution in the 1990s, which dominated aspirations for European integration, was the European Union (European Community prior to 1993). Ten states managed to achieve association agreements: the Soviet Union's six former Warsaw Pact allies, the three Baltic Republics and Slovenia.[1] In the run-up to the Intergovernmental Conference (IGC) which commenced in 1996, the majority of them submitted formal applications for membership, and discussions over their membership were to start six months after the ending of the IGC, which it was assumed would mean early 1998. It was generally accepted that the chance of any East-Central European state joining the EU depended less on the former's ability to harmonise its legislation and democratic practices with that of the EU, and more on the EU's own ability to reform itself. Without a major revision of the Common Agricultural Policy, the expense of accepting any former communist country – and most particularly Poland, which was both relatively large and relatively agrarian – would be prohibitive. Nevertheless, there were five clear 'front-runners' for EU membership: the 'Visegrad Four' (Czech Republic, Hungary, Poland and Slovakia) and Slovenia. Slovenia had been a late starter, both because of its history as a former Yugoslav republic and because of disputes with Italy, and Slovakia's chances of membership were jeopardised because of EU concerns about its internal democratic development (see Chapter 12).

The post-communist constellation of applicants for NATO membership was slightly different. Again, the organisation had a 'half-way' house, the Partnership for Peace (PfP) programme, which includes Albania, Macedonia, Russia and Ukraine. In practice, PfP is open to any post-communist country not actually fighting a war. It currently excludes Bosnia-Herzegovina, Croatia and rump Yugoslavia; Belarus and Moldova have expressed an interest in joining. However, chances for full membership of NATO are limited. When, in July 1996, the US Congress voted $60 million of military aid for preparing the Czech Republic, Hungary and Poland (but not Slovakia) to join NATO it seemed clear that these were the three states most likely to gain speedy membership.

Other membership criteria exist for the Council of Europe, which has more of a symbolic than a practical importance for post-communist states. Russia was accepted, as, eventually, were Albania and Macedonia, and Croatian membership was achieved in October 1996. A more telling test of economic international acceptability was posed by the OECD, which accepted first the Czech Republic in late 1995, followed by Hungary and then Poland in 1996.

When analysing the patterns of membership of international organisations, it is hard to avoid a form of historic determinism. The East-Central European countries which had been part of the Austro-Hungarian empire (though only partially so in the case of Poland) generally stood the best chance of EU membership. The two countries which were structurally the best prepared were the Czech Republic and Slovenia, both of which had been ruled by the Austrians. Hungary and Poland stood somewhere in between, while the two countries with the greatest problems were those who had been subjected to Hungarian rule, and whose young democracies were still struggling with their newly acquired nationhood and attendant conflicts over national identity. Slovakia was in danger of being ejected from the leading group of contenders for EU membership, while Croatia had never belonged to it in the first place because it had been embroiled in warfare almost solidly since independence.

Three groups of states lag somewhat behind the leaders. First, there are the three Baltic states, which fall into a category of their own. They suffer from being former Soviet republics, and two of them – Latvia and Estonia – have inherited considerable problems over questions of citizenship owing to the presence of very large Russian minorities. They have in common the fact that they are predominantly Protestant or Catholic in religion, which reflects their earlier histories, and none of them was a Soviet republic in the interwar period. However, they are viable candidates for EU entry in many respects. Secondly, there are the states of South-East Europe, which are mainly Orthodox or Muslim in religion and were all once subject to Ottoman rule. They subdivide into the former Warsaw Pact states, Bulgaria and Romania, whose chances of integration into European structures are greater, and the former Yugoslav republics, Macedonia and the current Federal Republic of Yugoslavia comprising Serbia and Montenegro. All have certain aspects of their mode of transition from communism and the ability of parts of the former communist elites to remain in power by pre-emptive reform in common. Catholic Croatia might be assigned to this group, though purely because of its inability to fit anywhere else in the mid-1990s.

A final group of states comprises Russia and the two states geographically and culturally closest to it, Belarus and Ukraine. Moldova, an uneasy creation of former Romanian territory and the Russian lands of the Transdnestr added by Stalin, also falls into this group. All four are substantially different in many respects, but share the worst chances of integration into European structures.

Finally, Bosnia-Herzegovina defies any attempt at classification. This is perhaps not surprising, since it is the one post-communist state whose future existence is severely in doubt.

Economics

The economic progress of the post-communist states is hard to measure in statistics. Three of the most important indicators are presented below: changes in Gross Domestic Product (GDP), in consumer price inflation and in unemployment rates. It must be emphasised, however, that no single authoritative source of comparable data exists. Many international organisations publish varying figures, having used different bases of computation, and all are reliant on the raw data compiled within the countries themselves. Communist accounting practices were notoriously unreliable, and such a situation cannot be corrected overnight.

Caveats must also be made about the meaning of statistics. For example, the decline in GDP experienced everywhere in the early post-communist years does not necessarily indicate a matching drop in the wealth of a country. Some of the fall in industrial output occurred because factories ceased producing

Table 10.1 Growth of real GDP (per cent)

	1990	1991	1992	1993	1994	1995
Visegrad Four and Slovenia						
Czech Republic	1.2	−14.2	−6.4	−0.9	2.6	4.8
Hungary	−3.5	−11.9	−3.0	−0.9	2.0	1.5
Poland	−11.6	−7.6	2.6	3.8	5.0	7.0
Slovakia	−2.5	−14.5	−7.0	−4.1	4.8	7.4
Slovenia	−4.7	−8.1	−5.4	1.3	5.5	4.8
Baltic Republics						
Estonia	−8.1	−11.0	−14.2	−6.7	6.0	3.0
Latvia	2.9	−8.3	−35.0	−15.0	−2.0	−1.0
Lithuania	−5.0	−13.1	−37.7	−24.2	1.7	5.0
South-East Europe						
Albania	−10.0	−27.7	−9.7	11.0	7.4	—
Bulgaria	−9.1	−11.7	−7.3	−2.4	1.4	2.5
Croatia	−8.6	−14.4	−9.0	−3.2	0.8	—
Macedonia[b]	−9.9	−12.1	−14.0	−14.1	−7.2	—
Romania	−5.6	−12.9	−10.0	1.3	3.4	6.9
Former Soviet Union, excluding Baltic Republics						
Belarus	−3.0	−1.2	−9.6	−11.6	−21.5	0.0
Moldova	−1.5	−11.9	−29.0	−9.0	−22.0	−3.0
Russia	—	−13.0	−19.0	−12.0	−15.0	−4.0
Ukraine	−3.0	−12.0	−17.0	−17.0	−23.0	−12.0

a. Estimate.
b. A slightly different calculation base is used in Macedonia.

Sources: EBRD (1995); 1995 data and Czech and Slovak Republics 1990: *Eurasia Economic Outlook* (May 1996).

low-quality goods which no one had wanted, and which were quite impossible to sell after the collapse of the large and undiscriminating Soviet market. Also, although there had been a thriving and unmeasured black market of goods and services everywhere in the communist world, the production of state-run industry was still far easier to measure than the output of the large number of small private entrepreneurs – many in the areas of services and trade – which sprung up in the early 1990s. Many of the statistics do not, therefore, properly capture the fruits of private enterprise.

Similarly, inflation rates often tell us little about how people were actually living, as this depended on the structure of their income – something which was in a great state of flux in the early years. It is fair to say, however, that the sense of insecurity among citizens was greater where there was rampant inflation, which wiped out the savings of decades. Official unemployment rates, too, can hide much. Sometimes, they encompass many people who are not actively seeking employment because they are content to work in the 'black economy'. In other cases, such as that of Albania, official statistics (although high) are lower than general estimates of the number of people without employment. It

Table 10.2 Consumer price inflation rates (per cent)

	1990	1991	1992	1993	1994	1995
Visegrad Four and Slovenia						
Czech Republic	10.0	56.7	11.1	20.0	10.0	7.9
Hungary	28.9	35.0	23.0	22.5	18.8	28.3
Poland	585.8	70.3	43.0	35.3	32.2	21.6
Slovakia	10.4	61.2	10.1	23.1	13.4	7.2
Slovenia	550.0	117.7	201.3	32.3	19.8	8.6
Baltic Republics						
Estonia	23.1	210.5	1076.0	89.8	48.0	28.9
Latvia	10.5	124.4	951.2	109.1	35.7	24.2
Lithuania	8.4	224.7	1020.5	409.2	72.0	28.8
South-East Europe						
Albania	0	36.0	226.0	85.0	22.6[a]	—
Bulgaria	26.3	333.5	82.0	73.0	96.3	32.9
Croatia	136.0	149.0	937.0	1,150.0	–3.0	—
Macedonia	—	—	1,691.0	350.0	122.0	—
Romania	5.1	174.5	210.9	256.1	131.0	27.8
Former Soviet Union, excluding Baltic Republics						
Belarus	—	93.0	1558.0	1994.0	1875.0	80.0
Moldova	4.2	98.0	1276.0	789.0	327.0	23.8
Russia	5.6	92.7	1354.0	896.0	302.0	130.0
Ukraine	4.2	91.0	1,210.0	4,735.0	891.0	180.0

a. Estimate.

Sources: EBRD (1995); 1995 data and Czech and Slovak Republics 1990: *Eurasia Economic Outlook* (May 1996).

is also hard to say what employment figures tell us about the state of the economy. Communist societies employed many people who were doing no useful work. Low unemployment figures, therefore, tend to indicate a failure to restructure state-run industry, rather than a buoyant, flourishing economy. It is commonly suggested that they indicate both in the case of the Czech Republic. Nevertheless, high unemployment rates, where owing to mass redundancies, were politically significant in inducing a sense of anxiety and discontent in the public at large.

In spite of all these caveats, some patterns do emerge when looking at the statistics, and they tend to reinforce the groupings of countries which emerge when looking at chances of integration into European structures. Table 10.1 illustrates that 1994 was an important turning point for the countries of East-Central Europe as they finally entered a period of economic growth. The same was generally true of the Baltic republics and South-East Europe, although here progress was more halting.

When examining inflation rates (see Table 10.2) it is clear that only three countries have the problem under real control: the Czech Republic, Slovakia

Table 10.3 Unemployment rates (per cent – end of year figure)

	1990	1991	1992	1993	1994	1995
Visegrad Four and Slovenia						
Czech Republic	0.8	4.1	2.6	3.5	3.2	2.9
Hungary	2.5	8.0	12.3	12.1	10.4	10.4
Poland	6.1	11.8	13.6	15.7	16.0	14.9
Slovakia	1.5	7.9	11.0	14.4	14.8	13.1
Slovenia[b]	4.7	8.2	11.1	14.5	14.6	14.5
Baltic Republics						
Estonia	—	0.1	1.9	2.6	2.0	2.5
Latvia	0.0	0.1	2.1	5.3	6.5	6.5
Lithuania	—	0.3	1.0	2.5	4.2	7.3
South-East Europe						
Albania	7.6	8.6	26.9	29.0	19.5[a]	—
Bulgaria	1.5	11.5	15.6	16.4	12.8	11.1
Croatia	—	—	12.9	12.8	12.6	—
Macedonia[b]	—	18.0	19.0	19.0	19.0	—
Romania	—	3.0	8.4	10.2	10.9	8.9
Former Soviet Union, excluding Baltic Republics						
Belarus	—	—	0.5	1.5	2.5	—
Moldova	—	0.004	0.7	0.8	1.2	1.4
Russia	0.0	0.1	0.8	1.1	2.1	8.0
Ukraine	0.0	0.0	0.3	0.4	0.4	0.6

a. Estimate.
b. Annual average.

Sources: EBRD (1996); 1995 data, all data for Moldova, and Czech and Slovak Republics 1990: *Eurasia Economic Outlook* (May 1996).

and Slovenia. Elsewhere, it is the trends which are important. In Poland and the Baltic states, inflation was a long-standing problem which was finally being brought under control; but in Hungary, the rise in inflation in 1995, after the post-communist government had taken office, was acutely felt by the population and translated into political disillusionment. In south-east Europe, the situation was unstable: in Bulgaria, for example, the government lost control of the economy in 1996 and the inflation rate was set to rise again markedly. In the states of the former Soviet Union, the situation remained grave. Inflation has slowed in Russia, Moldova, Ukraine and Belarus, but control over government spending, the revenue-gathering powers of central authori-ties and the consolidation of capitalist economics are weak in all four countries.

When looking at the employment rates (Table 10.3), several pictures emerge. First there is the very low unemployment rate in the Czech Republic, which – together with the country's low inflation rate and the general economic health that had led to its acceptance into the OECD – was not unrelated to the success of Klaus's government in becoming the first market reformers to be endorsed (though only just) by their electorate for a second term in office. Secondly, there is a band of former East European states with high but stable rates between about 10 and 15 per cent. Finally, in the former Soviet Union, unemployment rates are low. The overall picture (with the Czech exception) is that any measure of economic transformation brings with it high unemployment rates. These were often instrumental in bringing election defeat to incumbent governments, thereby leaving them with a fundamental dilemma: failing to reform brings economic disaster, and reforming electoral disaster.

Democracy and party politics

In Part III, we discussed the significance of constitutional choices and institutional structures in establishing democracy in the post-communist states. A further important aspect in consolidating democracy is the development of political party systems. Chapter 4 examined its post-communist starting point at the first elections in 1990. By the mid-1990s the party landscape had changed markedly. It was becoming possible to analyse the party constellations according to categories familiar to Western political science, although these highlighted many features peculiar to the post-communist world.

The origins of political parties

A first point which needs to be emphasised is the importance of the origin of political parties. In many West European countries, the formation of political parties was linked to an extension of suffrage and the attendant need for mass organisations. Parties grew from below, because they articulated the interests of groups in society who strove for parliamentary representation.[2] In the post-communist world, the genesis of political parties was different. The first elections at the beginning of the 1990s were usually organised within the space of a few months. The new political actors who managed to get elected were thereafter engaged in a process of party formation which to a major degree took place within parliaments. The differentiation of political views on specific issues was most marked at elite level where the first elections had returned broad anti-communist movements to power. The ruling party in a one-party state and the mass opposition movements that rose against them in the late 1980s were fundamentally different from political parties in a democracy. They were not formed to articulate the interests of a specific group or groups in society, but claimed to represent the united goals of all people. They therefore embraced a broad range of opinions, even if these are not openly articulated. Differences of opinions and factions among both members of a communist elite party and mass oppositions emerged into daylight for the first time when vital decisions on the economic and constitutional future had to be made.

Another problem for parties which form at elite level in parliament is that they do not always reflect the sentiments of the electorate: there is no organic link between the party and a mass base in the population. In Czechoslovakia, for example, two of the largest groups, in terms of parliamentary and government strength, which emerged from the broad citizens' movements – the Civic Movement from Civic Forum and the Civic Democratic Union from Public Against Violence – failed to poll even the 5 per cent of the vote necessary to enter parliament in the 1992 elections. Democratic Russia, the mass citizens' movement that provided much of the initial support for Boris Yeltsin, faded to complete insignificance after 1991. Further, the relations between, and coalition potential of, political parties often reflect their elite origins. Where a ruling party splits – such as the Movement for a Democratic Slovakia or the National Salvation Front in Romania – the bitter fighting between the two factions often precludes their future cooperation as independent parties. At the same time, relations between the breakaway group and the rest of the opposition can be clouded by the new party's previous involvement in government. Personality conflicts between leading politicians also often lead to a plethora of small opposition parties arguing between themselves rather than uniting to produce an attractive programme addressing the concerns of the electorate. This was characteristic of Bulgaria, Romania and Russia. Indeed, the fate of Yegor Gaidar's Russia's Choice – the party set up to represent the then Russian government in the December 1993 Duma elections – is exemplary. The party split after its poor showing in the 1993 elections and a splinter party (Forwards Russia!) has not cooperated with Russia's Choice subsequently. Moreover, Russia's Choice has not been able to form electoral alliances with other liberal reformist parties such as Yabloko, because of its past record in government and personality clashes between rival party leaders.

By the mid-1990s, party leaderships in some countries were learning to move in the available 'issue space' – that is, to develop programmes that appeal to specific sectors of the electorate. Three factors interfered with this effort.

First, marketing was an alien idea in the communist world and was a skill that political parties had to learn from scratch. Ironically, former communists were sometimes better at addressing the masses. In the former regime, the Communist Party had unrealistically claimed to represent the entire population, yet for politicians this could provide a better training in dealing with broad sectors of society than the preoccupation with the moral superiority of their cause found among some members of the opposition.

Secondly, there were initially very marked similarities between the programmes of many parties. Populist promises to improve citizens' economic situation, or to reduce crime, were widespread. This notwithstanding, by the mid-1990s enough parties – in East-Central Europe at least – had a track record in government for voters to make some informed judgement on the likelihood of promises being fulfilled.

Thirdly, parties in the post-communist world lacked 'core voters', that is social groups who formed a firm base of support, and had, in Western Europe, often inherited their voting behaviour through generations.[3] While party allegiances did gradually begin to form, they could not be as firmly rooted, since the economic interests of the electorate were not as clearly defined and were in a greater state of flux. Electoral volatility was least among citizens who voted according to 'ascriptive' (or immutable) characteristics such as nationality or region. Sometimes such characteristics can overlap and reinforce one another, but volatility is still possible because many parties may seek to represent voters with these characteristics. Ukraine, where voting is strongly influenced by the confluence of region and ethnicity, is a good example of this phenomenon, with a large number of parties seeking the electoral favour of voters in both eastern and western Ukraine.

Communist successor parties, too, often have firm 'core electorates'. Although they have shed many of their members since 1989, they have often retained a firmer base of support than many new parties possess. The Communist Party of the Russian Federation (CPRF) is one of the main beneficiaries of a 'core electorate', as we shall see in Chapter 11. However, it should also be borne in mind that having a 'core electorate' is not always beneficial since it can lead to parties being pigeonholed and rejected by other voters. Again, the CPRF is a good example of this: it is seen by many Russian voters and commentators as the 'party of pensioners' or the 'party of economic losers' (the two are not mutually exclusive categories).

Political cleavages

Although parties had problems establishing themselves as representatives of major sections of society, it is none the less possible to talk about nascent cleavage systems in post-communist politics. A political cleavage is a fault-line through a political community which affects how citizens vote. Where there is one major cleavage – for example, economic differences – a two-party system is likely. Where there are several, which frequently occurs in states which are mixed ethnically or in religion, a multi-party system is more likely. Sometimes, cleavages are mutually reinforcing, that is, a number of characteristics which help determine voting behaviour are normally found together. For example, rural communities are often traditionalist and religious. Where cleavages are cross-cutting, they divide societies in several different directions.

A number of lists have been compiled of the cleavages relevant to politics in democratic countries. Arend Lijphart, looking at the twenty-two states which were democracies between 1945 and 1980, identified the following: socio-economic, religious, cultural–ethnic, urban–rural, regime support, foreign policy and post-materialism.[4] All of these are present in some parts of the post-communist world with the exception of the last, and most recently added member of the list: post-materialism.[5] The existence of such a cleavage is dependent on a level of material prosperity not yet achieved there. The distribution of the remaining cleavages in individual post-communist states depends on a number of factors.[6] The reasons why they will be different from cleavages in the established democracies becomes clear if we look back at one of the most famous accounts of the developments of cleavages in Western Europe. Lipset and Rokkan identified four critical lines of cleavage as follows:

> Two of these cleavages are direct products of what we might call the *National* Revolution: the conflict between *the central nation-building culture* and the increasing resistance of the ethnically, linguistically, or religiously distinct *subject populations* in the provinces and the peripheries; the conflict between the centralizing, standardizing and mobilizing *Nation-State* and the historically established corporate privileges of the *Church*.
>
> Two of them are products of the *Industrial* Revolution: the conflict between the *landed interests* and the rising class of *industrial entrepreneurs*; the conflict between *owners and employers* on one side and *tenants, labourers and workers* on the other.[7]

Such distinctions originating from the history of Western Europe are hard to apply to the post-communist East, but are useful in highlighting some of the ways in which it differed. First, communism had destroyed the established privileges of the Church. While religious belief still affected some voters' value orientations, secularism had become widespread, and Churches are now not generally regarded as legitimate actors on the political scene. Christian Democratic parties in Eastern Europe were lucky to obtain 10 per cent of the vote in an election, excluding the exceptional case of eastern Germany where the party's strength had not originated within a post-communist society, but was imported from West Germany. Secondly, the 'industrial revolution' had been structurally very different in most of the countries we are looking at. Modernisation, marked by the shift of the labour force from the primary sector (agriculture) to the secondary sector (industry), and the urbanisation attendant on this, had generally been completed in the early communist years. The most notable exceptions to this are the Czech Republic and eastern Germany, which were economically far ahead of their neighbours at the onset of communism. For much of the postwar period, communism was clearly holding them up from progressing to a more complex society where the tertiary (service) sector takes over from industry as the main employer.[8] The collectivisation of agriculture (in most countries) had also changed the structure of rural communities.

It was therefore inherently likely that party systems, as they developed, would have certain post-communist specifics. In determining their cleavage structures, an initial problem is posed by terminology. Use of 'left' and 'right', which often dominates discussion of western parties, may not mean the same in the east. For while in East-Central Europe 'the right' was understood to mean free market reformers, in Russia it could mean anti-market nationalists – a group that can include many communists. Further, both 'left' and 'right' are usually used in the former communist world to refer to the socio-economic positions of voters and parties rather than to their value orientations. There is no organic link between support for the free market on the one hand and social conservatism, traditionalism or authoritarianism on the other (although racist and extreme nationalist parties are, interestingly, instinctively identified as being right-wing). In some respects, revolutionary change in the post-communist world is 'back to front', since it is moving in the direction of less, rather than more equality in society.[9]

It is partly in consequence of this that parties are sometimes grouped differently in Eastern Europe compared to Western Europe. Herbert Kitschelt predicted in 1991 that 'all East European party systems will be centred around a pro-market/libertarian versus anti-market authoritarian axis. In contrast, West European party systems in the late twentieth century tend to be oriented towards an anti-market/libertarian versus pro-market/authoritarian axis.'[10] What this means is that in the West, those with right-wing, pro-market economic views tend to be socially conservative, traditionalist and authoritarian; those who are left-wing economically and support greater equality and redistribution by the state tend to be socially liberal. In the post-communist world, however, advocates of the free market and rapid economic reform tend to be less authoritarian, while supporters of state intervention in the economy (which, of course, is the *status quo*) will tend to be conservative and authoritarian.

The fact that economic free market ideas and zeal for reform exist without many of the value orientations normally understood as right-wing is one factor which makes it hard for 'right-wing' economic reformers to gain widespread and stable electoral support. Their lack of social conservatism limits their ability to build bridges to the electorate in rural communities, who are often poorer and in a worse position to benefit from marketisation, but would be likely to vote for right-of-centre parties in a western democracy. The urban–rural split is extremely strong in many post-communist states, and it is generally former communists who retain control of the countryside. The Democratic Agrarian Party of Moldova is a very good example of former communists who have used their control over the rural vote to ensure political power.

Surveys aimed at determining the structure of party cleavages in post-communist states have mainly been conducted in East-Central Europe.[11] They indicate that there is already a degree of programmatic structuring in the party systems of the area – that is, that parties can be differentiated on the basis of their programmes, and that there is some consistency between voters' views, their voting behaviour and the proclaimed programmes of the parties they choose. Differences in cleavage structures can be noted, which suggest that it is not merely institutional factors such as electoral systems which determine the shape of a country's party system. As we shall see in Chapter 12, in the Czech Republic a very clear socio-economic cleavage dominates the party system, whereas in Poland – known for its large numbers of parties – there are multiple cross-cutting cleavages. These include socio-economic factors, religion, authoritarianism and attitudes towards the former communist regime.

The complexity of cleavage structures in post-communist Europe is also relevant to the discussion in Chapter 7 on the disadvantages of majoritarian electoral systems which are alleged to create two-party systems. The history of party politics in at least three countries – Bulgaria, Romania and Slovakia – was one of a number of small opposition parties trying to unite to defeat one strong rival of a broadly nationalist orientation. Their failure to do so was related in part to the cleavage structures of their countries. First, in all three, during all or most of the period 1994–96, the opposition to the government included parties representing ethnic minorities. These were hard to integrate into a united opposition bloc, particularly for electoral purposes. To do so would be likely to drive all wavering and nationally inclined opposition voters among the majority community firmly into the government camp. Secondly, uniting all the parties opposed to a nationalist or authoritarian government entails ignoring left–right cleavages based on socio-economic interests. This weakens programmatic differentiation between the main electoral alternatives. More practically, it risks driving economically left-wing voters behind the government. An example of this problem is provided by the fate of the Party of the Democratic Left in Slovakia, which entered a multi-party coalition including economically right-wing Christian Democrats after the fall of the second Mečiar government in spring 1994, but then lost many of its voters in the autumn 1994 elections. In systems with multiple cleavages, the effect of constitutional engineering aimed at forcing the development of a two-party system may thus threaten to create a state dominated by a single party. A variant on this is the way in which majoritarian systems have favoured not a party, but a specific group – 'the party of power', particularly powerful local elites – in some countries. In Belarus, Ukraine and Russia majoritarian electoral systems have led to the election of large numbers of independent candidates or candidates from parties with strong roots in local political and economic administration, such as the communist successor parties of Ukraine which are strong in eastern Ukraine, or the Agrarian Party and CPRF in Russia.[12] This has not led to one party dominating political life, but has ensured a large measure of elite continuity between communism and post-communism.

Different types of party

Party systems are not merely determined by institutional frameworks and the political cleavages in the societies whose interests they represent. In some post-communist states, parties attempted to adapt their programmes to appeal to the broadest section of the community likely to vote for them. But there are other ways of gaining votes.

Although much attention is paid throughout this book to political parties because of the centrality of their role in the political process, it cannot be assumed that this reflects the views of citizens in post-communist states. Although many derogatory comments are made about political parties in western countries, they are none the less normally considered as vital components of a democratic society. In formerly communist states, they may merely be regarded as groups of self-seeking individuals who wish to gain personal advantage at the expense of an undefined 'national interest'. Memories of the 'leading role of the party' can create negative feelings towards parties as a whole. In much of Eastern Europe, where multi-party (though not, in the main, democratic) systems existed for most of the interwar period, parties are historically linked to political failure. Trust in parties is extremely low; the multinational *New Democracies Barometer* found in late 1995 that they were generally the least trusted organisations in political life.[13] Both governments and parliaments received somewhat higher ratings.

Against this background, and given the short time which parties have had to form, it is not surprising that their organisations and structures rarely resemble those in Western Europe. Herbert Kitschelt notes that three pure types exist: apart from programmatic parties, there are also charismatic parties, who rely on voters rallying around their leader, and clientelistic parties, which are usually a form of 'patronage organisation', which provides benefits to their followers:

> Clientelistic and charisma-based party systems have a chance to survive as long as (1) they deal with unsophisticated, uneducated voters for whom the discrepancy between democratic rules and party performance is not noticeable or problematic and (2) they do not operate in an environment of economic growth and sectoral change that upsets the balance of political coalitions rafted by such party systems.[14]

Such conditions exist in much of the post-communist world, as the election of local elite members in Belarus, Russia and Ukraine indicates. Kitschelt further rejects the *tabula rasa* approach, which suggests that the party systems of post-communism started from scratch at the beginning of the 1990s.[15] He suggests that the form which party systems take relates to a number of factors: the institutional framework (whereby parliamentarism and electoral systems without personalised voting favour programmatic parties); the form of communist rule which existed and the mode of democratic transition (see Chapter 1); the duration of previous periods of democratic rule; and the levels of economic backwardness, which are linked to the timing of industrial-isation.[16] When these factors are combined, it emerges that the worst chances of achieving a programme-based party system are those of Serbia and the former Soviet Union (with the exception of the Baltic Republics), followed by Romania and Bulgaria. Croatia under this basis of calculation is in the same group as the Baltic States and Slovakia.[17]

The precision of such calculations is not of vital importance. But when looking at the parties which fought for office throughout the communist world, it is important to bear in mind that their social and historical environments differed substantially. Political structures were merely a complex reflection of everything else which affected the development of individual countries.

Notes

1. For background on these ten countries and their chances of accession, see Weidenfeld (1995).
2. See LaPalombara and Weiner (1966) abridged in Mair (1990, pp. 25–30).
3. It should be noted, however, that by the 1990s a process of 'partisan dealignment' was taking place in much of the western world. Voting behaviour was becoming more volatile as the electorate no longer identified with traditional allegiances.
4. Lijphart (1984, pp. 127–41). For further suggestions of major cleavages, see also Daalder (1966) and Sartori (1976).
5. The seminal work on post-materialism is Ingelhart (1977).
6. For a discussion of this point focusing on pre-communist cleavage structures and modes of transition, see Rivera (1996).
7. Lipset and Rokkan (1967) abridged in Mair (1990, pp. 91–138).
8. For the Czech case, see Musil (1993).
9. Markowski (1995, pp. 4–5).
10. Kitschelt (1992, p. 20).
11. See Kitschelt (1995a); Evans and Whitefield (1995a); Whitefield and Evans (1996); Markowski (1995).
12. The best analysis of this is for the Ukrainian case and can be found in Birch (forthcoming).
13. Rose and Haerpfer (1995). On a 10-country average, 14 per cent trusted parties, 23 per cent were neutral, and 62 per cent distrusted them. Only in the Czech Republic did respondents trusting or neutral to parties outnumber those that distrusted them. See also Rose (1995).
14. Kitschelt (1995b, pp. 449–50).
15. Kitschelt (1995a, p. 3); Kitschelt (1995b, p. 451).
16. Kitschelt (1995b, pp. 451–5).
17. *Ibid.*, p. 457.

CHAPTER 11

The difficulties of democratic consolidation: Russia and the NIS, 1994–96

Introduction

The main question facing the successor states to the USSR at the start of 1994 was whether they could break out of their low levels of democratic institutionalisation, and take decisive steps towards political stability and democratic government. Few of the Newly Independent States (NIS) had managed to create effective party systems or break the power of entrenched elite groups in 1992–93. Most have not made much progress in the years that have followed. As a result, the personalisation of politics deepened: politics was privatised and became a closed game played by elite groups (the 'party of power') to satisfy their private interests. Chains of administrative responsibility – never strong – eroded as branches of government, ministries of state and sub-national executives (regional governors and republican presidents), developed policy to suit themselves. Cabals formed within government or presidential administrations to petition for some interest or other. National interests were unclear and largely forgotten as corruption and clientelism grow.

The privatisation of politics was a particular problem in Russia, Ukraine, Belarus and Moldova, where the distinction between public and private spheres is weak. Officials treat state property and their offices as their personal possessions. Law and democratic ideas about accountability have little effect on the behaviour of officials. Powerful oligarchs in ministries, sub-national government and major economic concerns threaten one another and the integrity of the state. Clientelism and patronage create protection networks, what Russians call *krysha. Krysha* is the Russian word for 'roof'. In contemporary Russian political and economic life it signifies the personal connections and chains of mutual obligation that make up protection networks and provide 'cover' for economic and political activity. These connections can be to state bodies (like the security services), to powerful politicians or regional political leaders, to major economic companies, to organised crime or, ideally, to some combination of the above.[1]

There are two means of breaking the personalisation of politics. First, economic reform can create market economics and generate wealth. Markets can provide opportunities and incentives other than those offered, or controlled, by political elites and the state; the more wealth created by capitalist economy the more attractive these alternative opportunities and incentives will be. Opportunities and incentives created by markets are, of course, never available equally to all and are to a great extent under the control of elites. However, the variety of choices and incentives in most developed market economies does limit the amount of power held by political elites.

The progress towards market economies in the NIS has, however, continued to be slow. Most of the governments in the region are formally committed to economic reform. However, internal political squabbles, weak coalitions and lack of political will have meant that reform has not been pursued diligently. Most of the area's economies drifted in 1994–96 (see Chapter 10). Estonia was the only economy to achieve real stabilisation. The two other Baltic states lagged behind it and suffered from banking crises in 1995 and 1996. Ukraine started to reform more seriously in this period, but the influence of lobby groups was strong because of the election of an industrialist, Leonid Kuchma, to the presidency, and because the left-dominated Rada was anti-reform. Economic reform barely started in Belarus, although some reform legislation was introduced and a few prices were freed. Moldova's economy stabilised, but again there was little serious commitment to reform.

The second means of escaping from personalised politics (on which we shall concentrate in this chapter) is to construct polities that are governed by law and balanced by strong civil society. Developing the rule of law in the NIS has been slow because some states have only recently adopted constitutions, and also because there is a large degree of political control over judiciaries and because judicial rulings against presidents and governments have been ignored or circumvented. Strong civil societies have yet to emerge. The development of political parties has at once been both extensive and shallow: there are vast numbers of parties in all of the NIS countries, but few of them have deep roots. Electoral systems and low voter loyalty to existing parties have encouraged elites to fragment and set up new parties instead of working within existing ones, or to stand as independent candidates. Party politics have thus had only a limited impact on the power of executives throughout the region.

The Russian Federation

Russia started 1994 in a state of great uncertainty. The defeat of the old parliaments and the introduction of the new constitution made it beyond doubt that Russia was entering a new phase of post-communist political life. However, the contours of this new phase were unclear. The powers of the President were now strong, but there were doubts about Yeltsin's ability to use them. In the end Yeltsin emerged as the central figure in Russian politics because of the powers allocated to the President in the new constitution. But he has not used his powers to any positive end except his re-election. Moreover, no interest group or party has been able to muster support, either to take power or to force Yeltsin to adopt their agenda.

Russian politics under the new constitution

The President of the Russian Federation is granted extensive power under the constitution adopted in December 1993.[2] The President can appoint and dismiss ministers with the Prime Minister and nominate candidates for Prime Minister. The Duma cannot reject the President's candidates for Prime Minister more than three times; if it does he can dissolve it and call fresh elections. The President has extensive powers of appointment in the military and the judiciary, and over regional officials. The President has the right to initiate legislation (a right also shared by the government) and referendums, and his decrees have equal status to law. The President can block decisions taken by regional governors and republican presidents. The President can veto legislation from the Duma and the Council of the Federation; the Duma and the Council of the Federation can reinstate vetoed legislation but have to muster two-thirds support for a vetoed bill in both chambers of parliament – a very difficult thing to do. Further, Duma laws on taxation and the federal budget only come into effect if approved by the government.

Checks on presidential and government power from the Federal Assembly are weak. The Council of the Federation ratifies presidential decrees on states of emergency and the deployment of troops outside of the Russian Federation. The Duma can hold a vote of no confidence in the government, but the President can reject its finding. If a second vote is held within three months and this goes against the government, the President has a choice: he can disband the government or dissolve the Duma. There are some limits to the President's powers to dissolve the Duma: the President cannot dissolve the Duma for any reason until a year after a Duma election, during the last six months of the presidential term of office, during a state of emergency or if the Duma is trying to impeach him. Impeachment is far from easy. The President has to be accused of treason or some other major crime and this has to be supported by one-third of Duma deputies. Next, a Duma committee has to be established to verify the charges. Its findings for impeachment have to be supported by a two-thirds vote of all deputies in the Duma, and by the Supreme and Constitutional Courts. If the Duma, the Supreme Court and the Constitutional Court all find against the President, a resolution to impeach the President is put to the Council of the Federation, where it has to be passed by a two-thirds vote of all deputies. All these procedures have to be brought to a conclusion within three months.

With such powers at his disposal why did Yeltsin not stamp his authority on Russia and transform it once and for all? First, it is doubtful whether Yeltsin actually knew what he wanted to do in 1994. The ideas on radical economic reform pursued in 1992 had come from academic economists brought into government. Yeltsin had little emotional commitment to them. His political activity in 1993 had been almost entirely directed to securing his power. No agenda for broader change had been developed during this struggle. In his address to the Duma in February 1994, Yeltsin pledged more help for those who had lost from economic reform, and a more assertive foreign policy to strengthen the Russian state and protect Russians living in the other NIS. These promises were a sop to the parliamentary opposition and an attempt by Yeltsin to regain some of the ground he had lost since the October events. They did not amount to a philosophy of change that could underpin policy.

More importantly, political power granted by law does not automatically equate to authority and the certainty that one's orders will obeyed. Yeltsin possessed political power from the consitution, but his authority was low. He was, therefore, dependent upon others to support him and had to be cautious about policy. This caution governed his relations with the Federal Assembly, the government, regional elites and powerful economic groups.

Of the two chambers of the Federal Assembly, the Council of the Federation was the most amenable to Yeltsin. Deputies to the Council of the Federation are regional leaders. Hardline opposition deputies from the left and nationalists are in a minority. In January 1994, most deputies considered themselves affiliated to Russia's Choice (see Table 11.1). Support for Russia's Choice did not reflect Council deputies' political beliefs: they were interested in power and wished to identify themselves with what had been the presidential party in the 1993 elections. Their desire to court power continued after Democratic Russia lost its influence in government. The Council signalled its support for Yeltsin by electing Vladimir Shumeiko, a former Deputy Prime Minister and Yeltsin supporter, as its Chairman. The pro-Yeltsin/pro-government faction was only just short of an absolute majority in the Council, and could count on the support of centrist deputies to carry most votes.[3]

The Duma, the lower chamber of the Federal Assembly, was not as malleable as the Council of the Federation. The political affiliations of deputies in the Duma were far more concrete than those of Council of the Federation deputies. The firmer political support for parties in the Duma was

Table 11.1 Political affiliations in the Federal Assembly (number of seats)

	State Duma			Council of the Federation
	Jan. 1994	*Jan. 1995*	*Oct. 1995*	*Jan. 1994*
Pro-reform (Total)	106	97	62	46
Russia's Choice	76	67	49	40
PRES	30	30	13	4
Russian Movement for Democratic Reforms				2
Moderate reformers (Total)	25	28	27	26
Yabloko	25	28	27	3
Independents				23
Centrists (Total)	103	94	141	36
New Regional Policy	65	60	37	
Women of Russia	23	22	20	
Democratic Party of Russia	15	12	11	
Stability (founded 1995)			37	
Russia (founded 1995)			36	
Independents				36
Opposition (Total)	163	159	153	20
LDPR	63	60	55	
CPRF	45	45	47	15
Agrarian Party	55	54	51	3
Other				2
Others	52	69	57	48

Source: Adapted from Lester (1995, pp. 274–5), Remington (1994, p. 83), Halligan and Mozdoukhov (1995, p. 12).

due to the election of half the Duma deputies by proportional representation, and because access to power and resources was controlled by party factions. The officially registered factions (those with a minimum of 35 deputies) had better facilities, access to state officials, controlled the Duma committees, and could be used to lobby government and strike deals. Membership of factions were not totally stable as a comparison of their composition in January 1994 and January and October 1995 shows. However, the factions functioned relatively well despite shifts in membership and the appearance of new groups. The influence of factions made debate in the Duma far more structured than in the old parliaments, and the Chairman of the Duma could not control its agenda as Ruslan Khasbulatov had controlled the old parliaments.[4] This was a point in Yeltsin's favour: there was far more room for the government to manoeuvre and strike deals with factions and individual parliamentarians. On the negative side, however, the basic, intractable anti-Yeltsin vote from the Communist Party of the Russian Federation (CPRF) and the Agrarian Party was much larger than in the Council of the Federation. Moreover, Yeltsin could not count on the total support of all the deputies listed in the pro-reform or centrist categories either. Deputies from Yabloko, for example, were as likely to vote against the government as for it. As 1994 progressed pro-reform deputies from Russia's Choice (soon renamed Russia's Democratic Choice) became more disillusioned with the government and its economic policies, and often voted against it. It remained to be seen how factions like Zhirinovsky's LDPR, or new groups like New Regional Policy (a centrist group formed by independents) would vote on specific issues in January 1994, but Yeltsin could not count on their automatic support. The Duma made it clear that it was going to be independent fairly quickly. Ivan Rybkin, an Agrarian Party deputy and a former organiser of the CPRF faction in the disbanded CPD, was elected Chairman, and in February 1994 the Duma voted to free the coup leaders from August 1991 and the prisoners awaiting trial for their part in the October 1993 events.

Uncertainty about the Duma's relationship to the presidency was matched by uncertainty about where power lay in the government, the relationship between the centre and the regions, and the growing power of private economic interests. Prime Minister Viktor Chernomyrdin appeared to be far more secure in his post than Yeltsin after the December 1993 elections. Chernomyrdin had not associated himself with any party or electoral movement in December 1993. As a result, the protest vote in the elections was perceived as either directly against Yeltsin, or against the radical economic reformers whose electoral vehicles stalled.[5] Yegor Gaidar (the leader of Russia's Choice) resigned as First Deputy Prime Minister and Boris Fedorov quit as Finance Minister. Only two liberal reformers remained in the government: Anatoly Chubais, the Deputy Prime Minister with responsibility for privatisation, and Andrei Kozyrev, the Foreign Minister. The bulk of the government were of a similar background and inclination to Chernomyrdin: former state and enterprise officials with links to industrialist organisations and powerful corporations.[6]

Finally, Yeltsin's ability to use the powers that he held under the new constitution were limited by the need to deal with the regions and powerful economic interests. The power of regional leaders grew dramatically after the dissolution of the central parliaments in October 1993.[7] New regional representative institutions (to be called dumas or assemblies) were set up, but with fewer powers than the old Soviets. Governors were empowered to decide how regional dumas and assemblies were to be elected and the number of deputies that were to serve in them. Regional governors had the right to veto duma and assembly decisions. Electoral malpractice in the elections to the dumas and assemblies in 1994 and 1995 was rife. Gerrymandering and the distribution of a disproportionate number of seats to rural areas were particularly common. As a result, many regional dumas and assemblies are packed with local officials or their clients, the so-called 'party of power'.

The power of major industrial concerns (like Gazprom, the major oil producers like LUKOil, or firms like KamAZ) and financial operations (such as Most Bank) was even more invidious. Politicians and major economic concerns service each others' interests by acting as *krysha* for one another: politicians fix competition, secure tax breaks, etc., so that their favoured firms can thrive; in return companies provide resources to politicians that can be used for campaigning and the extension of patronage networks. Cherno-myrdin had the best links (and *krysha*) of all – to Gazprom, the most powerful company in Russia. Gazprom is a giant gas company that controls 95 per cent of Russian natural gas production, and hence a large proportion of Russia and the NIS's energy supply.[8] Many of the ties between enterprises and politicians are longstanding and date back to the links between bureaucrats, enterprise directors and the first entrepreneurs during the *perestroika* period. The con-solidation of enterprise directors' ownership through privatisation in 1992–93 (see Chapter 8) enabled these connections to flourish and gain in political significance. The size of some banks and industrial concerns, and the diversity of their interests, is immense. Most Bank, for example, is one of the largest banks in Russia and has powerful media interests, owning a major daily newspaper and a national television station.

The power of business interests and regional governors, Chernomyrdin's strength relative to Yeltsin's low personal authority and opposition in the Duma balanced Yeltsin's power as President. Outwardly, political peace was guaranteed by an agreement on 'Civic Accord' signed in April 1994 by 245 representatives of parties, regional governors, and major interest groups (only the CPRF, Agrarian Party and Yabloko refused to sign).[9] The document bound signatories to keep the political peace for two years. They were to refrain from trying to secure 'destabilising constitutional amendments'. The Federal Assembly was supposed to adopt new laws on elections, parties and Federal rights as quickly as possible. The government promised to fight inflation and promote economic growth after the falls in production in 1992–93. Regional leaders agreed to defend the unity of the Federation. The 'Civic Accord' was window dressing: there was no conflict because no one could muster the support, the will or the resources to try to make things happen. Real politics – the decision-making about who gets what, when and how – became hidden from public view with conflict internalised in the government and presidential administration. Decisions were taken by lobby-ing ministries, deals were struck between the government and factions in the Duma, and cliques in the presidential administration sought Yeltsin's ear. The influence of hidden politicking and the lack of positive direction in policy can be seen in the most important domestic policy issue of 1994–96: the inter-vention in Chechnya.

The decision to intervene in Chechnya in December 1994 was largely a result of politicking within the government and presidential administration. In 1991 the Chechens, who have a long history of opposition to the Russian state,

Textbox 11.1 Main events in Russia, 1994 to July 1996
(see also Textbox 11.2 on the Chechen conflict)

1994

January	Economic reformers quit the government in response to the December 1993 Duma elections.
February	Treaty signed between Federal government and Tatarstan.
April	Civic Accord adopted.
December	Russian troops invade Chechnya.

1995

May	Our Home is Russia Party set up by Chernomyrdin.
June	General Alexander Lebed resigns as commander of 14th Army in Moldova to go into Russian politics.
July	Yeltsin hospitalised with heart complaint.
October	Yeltsin hospitalised for second time.
November	Registration of parties for Duma elections.
December	Duma elections. CPRF head the poll.

1996

January	Removal of last reformers from government. Russia admitted to Council of Europe.
March	Duma vote condemns the agreements that founded the CIS.
April	Treaty with Belarus establishing Community of Sovereign States. Zyuganov issues electoral platform.
May	Korzhakov calls for the election to be postponed. Bulk of democratic forces declare their support for Yeltsin.
June	First round of voting in the presidential elections. Yeltsin makes Alexander Lebed (third in the voting) Secretary of the Defence Council. Defence Minister Grachev is removed from office. Three senior hardliners in the government are removed for plotting to upset the second round of voting.
July	Yeltsin disappears from public view on eve of second round of the presidential elections. Rumours circulate about his ill-health. However, he beats Zyuganov convincingly in the second round of voting. Fighting breaks out again in Chechnya. Chubais appointed head of the presidential administration.

declared independence from the Russian Federation under the leadership of Dzhokar Dudayev, a former Soviet airforce general. Russia tried to intervene militarily and failed. Thereafter, Chechnya refused to take part in any treaty or agreement with Russia. Dudayev built up the powers of the presidency and the area was destabilised by violent clashes between pro- and anti-Dudayev forces. Chechnya earned the reputation of being one of the former Soviet Union's biggest arms bazaars and home base of extensive organised crime networks. This reputation was not entirely undeserved, although all major ethnic groups in post-communist Russia are involved in organised crime, and the weapons sold in Chechnya's capital, Grozny, were often of Russian provenance.

By mid-1994, Chechnya was highly unstable and some action had to be taken to settle the question of its status within the Russian Federation. There were options other than war: the February 1994 Treaty with Tatarstan proved that there could be an accommodation of federal and republican interests.[10] The Russians could have just waited the Dudayev regime out; the rise of opposition, although sponsored by Russia, proved Dudayev was unpopular; Chechnya was impossible to rule and on the verge of collapse because of incompetence, conflict and Russian blockades. However, events spiralled out of control because they were driven by private interests and a struggle to control regional policy and represent the regions in their negotiations with the central, federal authorities.[11] Being able to claim leadership of the regions in their relations with the centre meant immense political power and control over vast resources and patronage in the form of federal subsidies to the regions. The struggle to control regional policy involved Vladimir Shumeiko, the Chairman of the Council of the Federation, and Sergei Filatov, head of the presidential administration, on one side, and Sergei Shakrai, a Deputy Prime Minister and Minister for Nationalities and Regions on the other. Shakrai had support from Chernomyrdin. Shumeiko and Filatov had Yeltsin's ear and the support of what came to be known as the 'party of war' – which included Yeltsin's friend and head of the presidential guard, General Alexander Korzhakov, the heads of the 'power' ministries (the Defence Minister, the head of the FSB,[12] the Federal Security Service and the Minister of Internal Affairs) and important state officials like the Chairman of the Security Council. Shumeiko and Filatov argued for a policy of no compromise over the status of Chechnya. Shakhrai argued for a treaty with Chechnya similar to that signed with Tatarstan. Shakrai won the support of the Duma, but was removed from his ministerial post (he stayed on as a Deputy Prime Minister) in May 1994 following machinations within the presidential circle. He was replaced by Nikolai Yegorov, an ally of Shumeiko's.

Shakrai's removal left Russia without an overt Chechen policy. Contacts between the Chechens and the Russians deteriorated, with Filatov rejecting Chechen requests for talks on the area's status in August 1994. Russian policy was reduced to covert support for anti-Dudayev forces. The conflict between pro-Dudayev forces and the Russian-backed opposition escalated in the autumn of 1994.[13] The opposition fared badly and the FSB provided tank and air support for their November 1994 attack on Grozny. When this assault failed several Russians were captured and FSB involvement was exposed. The compromising of the FSB forced Yeltsin to make a decision about Chechnya. Private interest outweighed other considerations: Russia went to war because of Yeltsin's wish to appear strong and protective of Russia's borders. The 'party of war' promised a quick and convincing victory. Yeltsin's nationalist critics would be outflanked and the restoration of national prestige by force of arms would be a vote-winner in the December 1995 Duma and 1996 presidential elections. War also suited the private ends of the 'party of war'. They were keen to increase their influence over Yeltsin, and hence over policy. The 'party of war' were authoritarian and nationalist in their political outlook and wanted a voice in economic policy-making to strengthen state control and protect the military industrial complex, their constituency. The 'party of war' were also tainted with accusations of corruption and abuse of power. If Yeltsin's prestige rose after a military victory they would not have to fear a new President coming to power and holding them accountable for their individual and collective abuses of office.

The lack of any alternative policy options and the arguments of the 'party of war' pushed Russia towards military intervention. At the end of November Yeltsin issued a presidential decree 'On Measures for the Restoration of the Constitutional Order and Enforcement of Laws in the Chechen Republic' and the Security Council (headed by Yeltsin) told Defence Minister Grachev to prepare for a full-scale military intervention. On 11 December three columns of Russian troops invaded Chechnya.

The decision to invade pitched Russian troops against an implacable enemy. Many Chechens put aside their dislike of Dudayev to fight the greater, Russian enemy. Russian tactics were inadequate and Russia's conscript troops were poorly prepared for combat. Indiscriminate shelling and bombing by the Russian forces led to high civilian casualties. Grozny was eventually brought under Russian control, but its capture did not bring an end to the conflict. The fighting moved to the mountains where Chechen forces waged a guerrilla war. Attempts at pacifying the countryside led to human rights abuses by the Russians: villages were bombed regardless of whether they contained Chechen forces; thousands of Chechens were illegally detained and tortured in the 'filtration' camps set up to separate combatants and non-combatants; Russian troops killed civilians, most notoriously at the village of Samashki where at least 120 civilians were massacred.[14]

Struggling to hold on to power: from Chechnya to the 1996 presidential elections

The Russian army's inability to bring the war to a quick conclusion made the invasion of Chechnya more than a military disaster. Chechnya became a political embarrassment to Yeltsin, a vote-loser rather than the hoped for vote-winner. There was widespread condemnation of the invasion from foreign leaders.[15] Domestic political reaction was equally hostile. The war was a gift for anti-Yeltsin forces, who argued that the invasion showed Yeltsin's authoritarianism. The only parliamentary faction to support the invasion unambiguously was Zhirinovsky's Liberal Democratic Party (LDPR). The fate of Russian troops in Chechnya was brought direct into Russian homes by independent television, which did not censor its reports and attacked the invasion. General Alexander Lebed, the commander of Russia's 14th Army stationed in Moldova, attacked the military high command for incompetence and contrasted the Chechen invasion to his own actions in protecting Russians in Transdnestr.

Despite its effect on Yeltsin's popularity, the Chechnya débâcle did not weaken his links to the 'party of war'. Yeltsin trusted its members, particularly Korzhakov, and knew that they depended upon him: he was their patron and their power was based on their association with his presidency. Even after the crisis at Budennovsk in June 1995 (see Textbox 11.2), there was only a limited purge of the 'party of war'. Yeltsin thus did little in 1995 to reverse the damage done to his prestige by Chechnya. His political reputation was further compromised by his health problems in 1995. In July, he went into hospital for a month following a heart attack. Further coronary complications in October put him in hospital for another month. Opinion polls throughout 1995 regularly put Yeltsin well down the list of favoured candidates for the presidency, with only 2–3 per cent of respondents saying they would vote for him.

The problems caused by Chechnya were worsened by the government's lack of support from any political group outside of the 'party of war' and the 'party of power'. Reformist parties like Russia's Democratic Choice and Yabloko had broken with Yeltsin over the invasion. Chechnya increased support for the CPRF, the best organised and most numerous party in Russia because of its inheritance of the CPSU's membership and organisational framework. New political threats were also emerging. Chief among these was Alexander Lebed. Lebed resigned from the army in June 1995 citing his disgust at the Chechnya operation and attempts to transfer him from Transdnestr to a Siberian military district. Lebed joined the Congress of Russian Communities (KRO), a nationalist group with links to the military industrial complex. Opinion polls soon listed him as a strong contender for the presidency with about 8 per cent support (the other strong contender at the time was Yabloko's Grigory Yavlinsky who had about the same level of support).

In any other year the split between parties and the executive would not have been too important: politics would have carried on in the corridors of the Kremlin away from public view. However, elections to the Duma were scheduled for December 1995 and the presidential elections had to be held in 1996. Without a political party in the elections Yeltsin and the government

---

Textbox 11.2 The war in Chechnya

1991

September   Coup in Chechnya, Dzhokar Dudayev becomes leader.

October   Dudayev elected President of Chechnya and Chechen declaration of independence.

November   Yeltsin declares state of emergency in the area. Failure of attempted Russian intervention. State of emergency is revoked and troops withdraw.

1993

May–June   Demonstrations against Dudayev. Opposition forced to flee from Grozny, the Chechen capital, after forces loyal to Dudayev fire on them.

1994

June   Armed clashes in Grozny between forces loyal to President Dudayev and the opposition.

August   Armed clashes in north of the republic between forces loyal to President Dudayev and the opposition.

October   Chechen opposition tries to seize Grozny.

November   Chechen opposition tries to seize Grozny for second time. Russian tanks support the opposition. Attack fails and Russians are captured.

December   Russian troops invade Chechnya.

1995

January   Grozny is brought under Russian control. Many Russian troops and civilians killed in the fighting.

February   Russians begin to take control of the countryside as Chechens withdraw to the mountains.

---

faced the threat of a total schism between the government and the Duma after December 1995. Moreover, the Duma elections were widely seen as a trial run for the presidential elections. Party leaders would decide whether to run or not according to how their party fared in the Duma election.

To counter their isolation Yeltsin and the government began to organise two political parties in the spring of 1995. Chernomyrdin set up Our Home is Russia (or NDR from the Russian Nash Dom – Rossiya) as a centre-right party. The founding members of the party included the Stability faction (one of two factions the government helped found at the start of 1995), eight cabinet ministers, sixty regional leaders or their deputies, Shakrai's PRES party (and

April	Chernomyrdin announces Russian ceasefire in Chechnya to last to early May. Breaks down after Chechens infiltrate Grozny. Russians massacre Chechen civilians in Samashki.
May	Yeltsin vetoes law passed by both the Duma and the Council of Federation calling for unconditional talks with the Chechens.
June	Chechens under Shamil Basaev take hundreds of Russian hostages in the Russian town of Budennovsk. Chernomyrdin negotiates the Chechens' withdrawal and the release of the hostages after military action fails. Peace talks demanded by Basaev begin in Grozny.
July	Agreement with Chechens on a ceasefire, partial withdrawal of Russian Army, exchange of prisoners and the disarming of Chechens. No political agreement is reached and clashes between security forces and Chechens continue.
August	Russians pull troops out of parts of southern Chechnya. No significant disarmament of Chechen forces. Russians lose their military advantage.
December	Heavy fighting as anti-Russian forces try to prevent voting in the Duma election. Russians begin to take back some of the territory they withdrew from earlier in the year.
1996	
January	Chechen forces under Salman Raduev (Dudayev's son-in-law) seize hostages in the Dagestani town of Kyzlar and are then besieged at the village of Pervomaiskoe.
March	Yeltsin unveils peace plans as a part of his electoral campaign.
April	Dudayev killed by Russian air strike. Succeeded by Zelimkhan Yanderbiev.
May	Peace deal signed in Moscow. Yeltsin visits Chechnya.
July	Chechens protest that the terms of the peace deal are being broken by Russia. Fighting restarts.

its Duma faction), and the New Regional Policy faction. The party was backed by Gazprom and many leading banks. The support of regional leaders enabled the party to create a national organisation very quickly.[16]

The second pro-government party was formed by Ivan Rybkin, the Chairman of the Duma. Rybkin's party (which eventually had the less than inspiring title of the Electoral Bloc of Ivan Rybkin) was supposed to be a centre-left party. Rybkin failed to persuade the Agrarian Party (of which he was a member) or any other significant leftist or centre party to join his movement.

Chernomyrdin, Rybkin and the presidential administration were quite cynical in forming two parties. They hoped that two parties would enable them to monopolise the centre ground of politics, take enough seats in the Duma to prevent any other group from controlling the political agenda in the run-up to the presidential election, and discourage anyone but Yeltsin or a designated successor from running for the presidency. However, this plan was flawed. Rybkin's bloc would never gain momentum because cooperation with the government was anathema to the left. Consequently, few inroads were ever going to be made into the vote of the CPRF in particular, and the left in general. It was also unclear who would vote for either party or what the centre ground of politics was. The fragmentation of political life and of support for political parties had not slowed since 1993. Politicians from across the political spectrum set up parties in the hope of getting across the 5 per cent threshold and into the Duma. We have already mentioned Alexander Lebed and KRO. Boris Fedorov formed a group called Forward Russia! which mixed free market economics with some nationalist themes. Alexander Rutskoi formed Derzhava (Great Power), a nationalist organisation. Alternatives to the CPRF included former Soviet Prime Minister Nikolai Ryzhkov's Power to the People group, and Communists-Working Russia. In total 43 parties and electoral movements were to be registered for the PR vote in the Duma elections.

Russia went to the polls for the Duma elections on 17 December 1995. There was no vote on the Council of the Federation: the two seats allocated to the 89 regions and republics of the Federation are in future to be filled by the regional chief executive (the Governor or President) and the head of the regional duma or assembly. As in 1993 the elections were not without controversy. The biggest scandal concerned the attempt by the Central Electoral Commission to bar Yabloko, Democratic Russia (now a small liberal party) and Derzhava from the PR vote because of irregularities in their lists of candidates. Yabloko and Derzhava were reinstated after widespread protest. Violence flared up in Chechnya as Dudayev loyalists tried to prevent voting in the Duma elections and for a puppet republican government. Again, as in 1993, the opinion polls were not a totally accurate predictor of how Russia would vote.

The final result – the CPRF's taking the largest share of the vote and only a few parties crossing the 5 per cent threshold – was not unexpected. The CPRF emerged as the biggest party for three reasons.[17]

First, the CPRF had the best party organisation of all the competing parties, the largest membership and the clearest party identity. This enabled it to campaign more effectively at grassroots level and meant that it retained a core of supporters. Table 11.3 shows the results of a survey on the consistency of party vote between the December 1993 and the December 1995 Duma elections. The percentage of people who voted for the same party in both 1993 and 1995 is shown in bold type. The CPRF held 68 per cent of its vote between the two elections, 21 per cent more than any other party.

Table 11.2 The 1995 State Duma election results and comparison to the 1993 elections

	% PR vote	PR seats	Single-mandate seats	Total	1993 PR %
Left (Total)	32.22				
CPRF	22.30	99	58	157	12.40
Communists-Working Russia	4.53		1	1	
Agrarian Party	3.78		20	20	7.99
Power to the People	1.61		9	9	
Nationalist (Total)	19.94				
LDPR	11.18	50	1	51	22.92
KRO	4.31		5	5	
Derzhava	2.57				
Pro-Reform (Total)	19.06				
Yabloko	6.89	31	14	45	7.86
Workers' Self-Government	3.98		1	1	
Russia's Democratic Choice	3.86		9	9	15.51
Forward Russia!	1.94		3	3	
Pro-Government (Total)	11.24				
Our Home is Russia	10.13	45	10	55	
Rybkin Bloc	1.11		3	3	
Others (30 parties)	17.51		14	14	
Independents			77	77	141 (seats)

Secondly, the CPRF had the best anti-Yeltsin and anti-government credentials. The CPRF faction in the Duma had been the most consistent in opposing the government and the war in Chechnya. Its record helped the CPRF take some of the protest vote that had gone to the LDPR in December 1993. Table 11.3 shows that around 15 per cent of LDPR voters in 1993 defected to the CPRF in 1995. The CPRF also picked up the votes of disgruntled Agrarian party voters and a sizeable tranche of the vote given to parties that had run in 1993 but failed to compete effectively or at all in 1995 (the 'others' category in Table 11.3).

Thirdly, the CPRF was more than a single-issue party. Most of the other opposition and anti-reform electoral movements appealed to nationalists only. The CPRF blended rhetoric about Russia as a great power and the need to re-create the Soviet Union with criticisms of the government's economic policy. It could thus appeal to nationalist voters and to those dispossessed by reform. This lifted the CPRF above the nationalist parties who were all scrambling for the votes of one narrowly defined section of the electorate. The CPRF's 'record' also spoke for it. As the successor to the CPSU, the CPRF benefited from nostalgia for the time when Russia had been at the centre of a superpower, and there had been order, low crime and economic stability.

The results of the other parties also contained some surprises. The LDPR

Table 11.3 The consistency of party vote in Duma elections, 1993–95 (per cent)

Party voted for in 1993	Party voted for in 1995								
	CPRF	Women of Russia	Yabloko	Russia's Democratic Choice	Our Home is Russia	KRO	LDPR	Other	Did not vote
CPRF	**68**	2	3	1	2	1	1	10	13
Agrarians	29	9	0	4	7	5	5	22	20
Women of Russia	5	**34**	11	4	11	5	5	21	7
Yabloko	5	3	**43**	5	11	8	0	14	10
Russia's Choice	11	4	8	**19**	12	3	6	26	15
LDPR	15	5	5	0	6	1	**47**	16	9
Other	21	2	7	5	15	7	4	**22**	17
Did not vote	8	4	6	2	6	3	6	15	**49**

Source: Wyman (1996, p. 18)

did much better than expected. Most polls forecast that the LDPR's share of the vote would fall to about 5 per cent. The LDPR actually came third with just over 11 per cent of the vote. This was a huge drop on 1993, but was accounted a victory because it secured 50 of the 225 seats allocated through the PR vote and was won against a larger nationalist field (KRO, Derzhava and four other groups) than had stood in 1993. NDR did better than the opinion polls predicted (polls predicted a NDR vote of about 5–7 per cent). However, NDR still had a vote share that was less than Russia's Choice achieved as the 1993 presidential party and it won fewer of the single-mandate seats than Russia's Choice had in 1993. However, NDR did manage to beat Yabloko and take third place in the PR vote.

Only the CPRF, the LDPR, NDR and Yabloko managed to secure enough votes to carry them across the 5 per cent threshold to a share of the 225 seats allocated by the PR results. Did the electoral failure of most of the 43 parties and electoral movements signify that support for the main parties or political trends had solidified? The answer can only be a qualified yes.[18] In Table 11.2 we can see the vote for broad political trends (left, nationalist, pro-reform, etc.). The combined anti-government vote from the left and nationalists is 52.16 per cent of the vote in 1995 compared to about 43 per cent in 1993. Party allegiance inside these large categories was not stable, however. The CPRF, as has been noted, kept 68 per cent of its vote from 1993. No other party managed to retain even 50 per cent of its vote, and Russia's Democratic Choice did particularly badly (see Table 11.3). On average, 57 per cent of the electorate in 1995 voted for a different party from the one they had supported in 1993. This measure of electoral volatility is six times higher than the figure for Western European elections in the 1980s, and higher than for recent elections in Poland, Hungary, the Czech Republic and Slovakia.[19]

There were some signs that the vote was influenced by social cleavage. Voting for the CPRF and the LDPR was highest in rural areas and small towns and cities, and among older (age 40+) citizens and the less well educated. The LDPR vote was stronger among workers than the CPRF vote, but the CPRF took a larger number of votes from pensioners, and had a higher share of the vote in large cities than the LDPR. NDR and Yabloko took more votes among residents of Moscow, St Petersburg and other large cities, professional people and the under forties. The anti-government vote was, as in 1993, highest in the 'red belt': the southern agricultural districts of the country, and the run-down industrial areas of the Urals, Siberia and the Pacific seaboard. However, although the identifiable electoral cleavages are largely the same in 1993 and 1995, the high rate of electoral volatility makes it difficult to see cleavages as definite determinants of party vote; at best they indicate broad rejection or acceptance of the government.

The results of the single-mandate constituency votes look slightly more encouraging because parties were more successful in 1995. In 1993, 141 of the

225 single-mandate constituencies went to independents; in 1995 their share of single-mandate seats fell to 77. However, this was not as dramatic a change as the raw data seem to indicate. The independents who won in 1993 were often local dignitaries, or people who had their support. The same type of person won in 1995 under a party flag. Party 'victories' were not, therefore, necessarily a sign of voter partisanship for parties: many people voted for one party in the PR vote and for a local candidate – no matter what their party affiliation – in the single-mandate vote. This split-ticket voting helps explain the success in single-mandate constituencies of parties that did not cross the 5 per cent threshold in the PR vote (the Agrarian Party, for example, took twenty single-mandate seats, the Rybkin bloc took three seats). Similar arguments have been made concerning many of the single-mandate constituencies won by the CPRF.[20] The stronger showing of parties cannot be taken as an unqualified sign of increased party identification among elites either: Russian elites show a marked propensity to trade party allegiances for advantage.

The CPRF's electoral success made its leader, Gennady Zyuganov, the favourite for the presidential race. The CPRF also became the largest faction in the new Duma (see Table 11.4). The CPRF 'lent' some of its faction to the Agrarian Party so that it had the thirty-five deputies necessary for registration as an official faction. Their choice of Duma Chairman, a CPRF deputy, won easily. CPRF deputies also became Chairs of nine of the Duma's committees, including the committees on economic policy, legislation and security.[21]

The dominance of the left in the new Duma provoked an immediate reaction from Yeltsin, who shuffled the government in an attempt to recapture the popular mood. Chubais was fired by Yeltsin as Deputy Prime Minister. Kozyrev resigned as Minister for Foreign Affairs because he had been elected to the Duma. He was replaced by Yevgeny Primakov, the head of the Federal Intelligence Service, the KGB's successor in external espionage. Primakov was a member of the last CPSU Politburo and is seen as unsympathetic by the West. The CPRF welcomed his appointment. Filatov, a liberal despite his role in pushing Russia towards war in Chechnya, was replaced as head of the presidential administration by Nikolai Yegorov.

Table 11.4 Factions in the State Duma in January 1996

	Seats
CPRF	149
NDR	55
LDPR	51
Yabloko	46
Russian Regions	42
Popular Power	37
Agrarian Party	35

Source: Transition, vol. 2 (4), p. 10.

The removal of the last liberals from the government marked the peak of Yeltsin's flirtation with the 'party of war'. The government reshuffle did not bring any immediate change in Yeltsin's poll ratings. Table 11.5 shows how his rating changed over the course of the presidential election campaign. In January 1996, only 8 per cent of poll respondents said they would vote for Yeltsin if the presidential election were held on the following Sunday. Worse, more people believed Zyuganov would win the election than believed Yeltsin would be victorious, and more people did not want Yeltsin to win in any circumstances than Zyuganov. Yeltsin's fortunes were not helped by another Chechen incursion into the Federation in January, which led to another round of hostage-taking and Russian demonstration of martial incompetence.

However, if we follow the development of the polls in Table 11.5 we can see that Yeltsin steadily began to draw level with Zyuganov. By March more people were convinced that Yeltsin would win the elections than Zyuganov, and he was in second place according to voting intentions. This was the turning point in Yeltsin's fortunes. To win the presidency a candidate has to secure over 50 per cent of the votes cast. If no candidate receives over 50 per cent in the first round of voting a run-off election is held between the top two candidates. When Yeltsin came second in the polls the election started to turn into a two-horse race. No candidate was ever going to win 50 per cent of the vote in the first round (16 June); the battle was to get to the second round and run against Zyuganov and the CPRF. When Yeltsin gained enough support to put him in the second round the other non-communist candidates began to fall away. In April, 17 per cent more people believed Yeltsin was going to win than Zyuganov. In May, more respondents said they would vote for him rather than Zyuganov, and over half of respondents thought he was going to win.

How did Yeltsin achieve this reversal of fortune? The turnaround was due as much to the failure of the other anti-Zyuganov candidates (see Textbox 11.3) as it was to Yeltsin. None of the other candidates was able to attract any more support than they had at the start of the race; all they could do was to lose supporters to Yeltsin or Zyuganov. Early frontrunners like Zhirinovsky, Lebed or Yavlinsky appealed to a narrow segment of the electorate only and they could not win over each other's supporters. Yeltsin, however, could appeal to other candidates' supporters. He uniquely represented something to everyone: he was a nationalist to Zhirinovsky and Lebed supporters, a reformer for Yavlinsky voters, an anti-communist to everyone. The closer Yeltsin got to getting into a run-off with Zyuganov the more this effect worked for him. Democrats in particular began to defect to him as an anti-communist, and he got endorsements from Russia's Democratic Choice and other groups. Even the recently sacked Filatov and Chubais came to work for his re-election campaign.

Yeltsin also had the benefit of running as the incumbent. Being the incumbent has some electoral advantage in many parts of the world. It was

Table 11.5 Opinion polls and the Russian presidential election, January to June 1996

Which candidate would you vote for if the presidential election is held next Sunday (per cent)?

	Jan.	Feb.	March	April	May	June
Boris Yeltsin	8	11	15	18	28	36
Gennady Zyuganov	20	24	25	26	27	24
Alexander Lebed	10	8	10	10	6	10
Grigory Yavlinsky	13	9	11	10	9	8
Vladimir Zhirinovsky	10	12	9	8	7	6
Other	22	29	16	15	11	5
Against all/difficult to say	17	17	14	11	11	11

Who will win the presidential election in your opinion (per cent)?

	Jan.	Feb.	March	April	May	June
Boris Yeltsin	14	21	29	40	52	57
Gennady Zyuganov	18	22	24	23	21	19
Difficult to say	40	39	35	28	21	12

Which candidate would you not like to be elected President under any conditions (per cent)?

	Jan.	Feb.	March	April	May	June
Boris Yeltsin	43	40	37	37	36	29
Gennady Zyuganov	14	21	26	27	29	31

Source: Adapted from All-Russian Centre for the Study of Public Opinion polls in *Segodnya*, 13 June 1996

crucial for Yeltsin and provided the means to get his campaign off the ground. The presidency gave Yeltsin resources and access to powerful economic and regional lobbies. All were put to work. Yeltsin's campaign tours to the provinces were punctuated by his signing decrees on building new schools, hospitals, libraries, giving out machinery to farmers, and tax breaks to firms and regions. This was buying votes with state revenues, but there was little that the oppo-sition could do to stop it. The media – with the exception of communist and nationalist newspapers – covered Yeltsin's campaign to the virtual exclusion of everyone else. There was very little effort to be neutral and report the campaign objectively on state or independent television and radio. Regional leaders swung behind the Yeltsin campaign, fearing that the CPRF would rein in their powers.

Zyuganov's campaign lacked the same impetus as Yeltsin's. He had a core of supporters, but found it difficult to make inroads into other camps. Zyuganov was not helped on the campaign trail by his lack of charisma relative to Yeltsin, and his difficulty in getting access to the media. The communist label counted against him too. Zyuganov tried to present himself as a moderate whose aim was to restore Russian national pride and develop

---

Textbox 11.3 Candidates in the Russian presidential election,
June 1996 (first round)

Vladimir Bryntsalov	Age 49. Duma deputy, millionaire businessman. Member of the Russian Socialist Party. Registered after appeal to Supreme Court.
Svyatoslav Fedorov	Age 68. Famous eye surgeon, leader of the Party of Workers' Self-Government, Duma deputy.
Mikhail Gorbachev	Age 65. Former President of the USSR and General Secretary of the CPSU. Currently has no party affiliation and chairs a think tank in Moscow.
Aleksandr Lebed	Age 46. Ex-Lieutenant General and Commander of 14th Army in Moldova, former co-leader of the Congress of Russian Communities (KRO), Duma deputy, no current party affiliation.
Martin Shakkum	Age 44. Think tank director, no party affiliation. Registered after appeal to Supreme Court.
Yury Vlasov	Age 60. Former world champion weightlifter, former democrat turned extreme nationalist. Member of the Popular Patriotic Party.
Grigory Yavlinsky	Age 42. Economist, leader of the Yabloko Party, Duma deputy.
Boris Yeltsin	Age 65. President, no party affiliation.
Vladimir Zhirinovsky	Age 50. Leader of the Liberal Democratic Party of Russia (LDPR), Duma deputy, candidate in 1991 Russian presidential election.
Gennady Zyuganov	Age 52. Leader of the Communist Party of the Russian Federation (CPRF), Duma deputy.

---

economic justice. Many voters feared that this was an act. Others believed Zyuganov, but were scared off by more orthodox members of the CPRF and some of the hardliners that gathered in its electoral alliance. Some voters thought twice about voting for Zyuganov because of the electoral success of the CPRF in the Duma elections of December: a CPRF president and CPRF-dominated Duma would concentrate too much power in one party's hands.[22]

Finally, Yeltsin proved to be effective in countering the CPRF political agenda. In March, the CPRF faction sponsored a successful resolution in the Duma on the legality of the December 1991 Belovezhskaya pushcha agreement that had set up the CIS and brought a final end to the USSR. Yeltsin accused them of wanting to take the country back to the Soviet system, and outflanked them by signing an agreement with Belarus, which established a 'Community of Sovereign States'. He signed populist decrees ending military conscription and moved to end the war in Chechnya, his biggest vote-loser. He called a ceasefire and negotiations at the end of March. Dudayev was killed by a Russian air strike in April, and the new Chechen leader, Zemlikhan Yanderbiev, was quickly brought to Moscow where a deal was signed which ensured a cessation of hostilities until the elections were over.

Yeltsin's use of his position, the failure of the other candidates and the obstacles that Zyuganov faced helped make Yeltsin the first round winner on 16 June (see Table 11.6). The only surprise in the first round was the success of Alexander Lebed, who came third with a higher than expected 14 per cent. Lebed's success was due in part to help from the Yeltsin camp, which did not criticise him and helped him get access to television a few days before the vote. This probably helped Lebed gain some extra votes, and denied them to Zyuganov: Lebed and Zyuganov were campaigning on some common issues like anti-corruption, nationalism, criticism of the war in Chechnya and a more assertive foreign policy.

Yeltsin's first-round victory did not mean he was assured of winning the second round. Turnout was lower than expected in the first round. If it fell again in the second round, Zyuganov's share of the vote was expected to rise. The CPRF organisation was believed to be effective at getting the vote out and his core support was electorally disciplined: his voters would turn out no matter what; Yeltsin's voters would not. To solve this problem the date of the second round of the election was brought forward by the Central Electoral Commission and the day was changed. Previous elections and votes had been held on Sundays. For the second round, the vote was changed to Wednesday, 3 July. It was believed that this would increase turnout among urban voters and boost Yeltsin's chances.

Yeltsin also had to make sure that voters who had supported other candidates in the first round supported him in the second. Yeltsin looked set to pick up votes from minor candidates like Vladimir Bryntsalov, and votes from democrats like Grigory Yavlinsky. Capturing the vote of Lebed and Zhirinovsky, who had come third and fifth, was vital however, because their voters were split evenly between Yeltsin and Zyuganov, with a large number of their voters not committed to either side. Yeltsin used his incumbency advantage and brought Lebed into the presidential administration, appointing him Secretary of the Security Council and presidential aide on national security issues. Defence Minister Grachev, whom Lebed had criticised frequently for his handling of the Chechnya campaign and reported corruption, was fired as part of the deal.

Lebed's appointment was supposed to win over his voters and a section of Zhirinovsky's. But before the second round vote a very bizarre event occurred. On 19 June, two of Yeltsin's re-election team were detained in the Kremlin by guards under the command of Korzhakov. The two aides were questioned for eleven hours in an attempt to get incriminating evidence against Prime Minister Chernomyrdin. While they were being questioned

Table 11.6 Results of the Russian presidential election, June and July 1996

	First Round % vote	Second Round % vote
Boris Yeltsin	35.28	53.82
Gennady Zyuganov	32.03	40.31
Alexander Lebed	14.52	
Grigory Yavlinsky	7.34	
Vladimir Zhirinovsky	5.70	
Svyatoslav Fedorov	0.92	
Mikhail Gorbachev	0.51	
Others	0.73	
Against All	1.54	4.83
Turnout	69.65	68.89

Source: Rossiiskaya Gazeta, 22 June 1996, *OMRI Russian Presidential Electoral Survey* (e-mail version), no. 15.

journalists from independent television got hold of the story. They broadcast it and informed Chubais, who was also working for the Yeltsin campaign. Chubais rang Lebed, who announced that this was an attempt by hardliners in the presidential administration to subvert the election. The story was plausible: Korzhakov had called for the elections to be cancelled before the first-round vote, and most commentators suspected that he, and other hardliners, feared they would be held responsible for the war in Chechnya and tried for corruption if Yeltsin lost. Yeltsin had censured Korzhakov for his remarks, but it now looked as though the hardliners were preparing a coup. If Chernomyrdin was compromised and forced to step down, a hardliner could be made Prime Minister; Yeltsin could then be removed as President, and the new Prime Minister would take over as President under the constitution. Korzhakov, the head of the FSB, and a hardline Deputy Prime Minister were all rapidly removed from their posts.

The strange events in the Kremlin did not influence the second round of voting. The turnout of voters fell slightly, but was high enough to balance out the communist vote. Enough Lebed voters and others changed to Yeltsin for him to defeat Zyuganov by a handsome margin (see Table 11.6).

Did Yeltsin's victory, accompanied as it was by the removal from power of key hardliners and a return to government of Anatoly Chubais (as head of the presidential administration in place of Yegorov), signal that Russia is on the way to democracy at last? The prospects do not look promising. The peace deal signed with Chechnya unravelled after the election, with the Russians accused of breaking the terms of the agreement. Lebed brokered a new peace deal, but this exposed differences over the future direction of Russia within the executive. Lebed soon found himself in dispute with other members of the government and was sacked by Yeltsin on 17 October 1996 after Lebed's rivals had accused him of trying to overthrow the government. Finally, Yeltsin's heart problems returned to the news shortly after his re-election. Yeltsin managed to struggle through his presidential inauguration, but was soon hospitalised. In November 1996 he had a quintuple heart by-pass operation. He survived this operation and soon announced that he would be returning to work. However, it was uncertain how much authority Yeltsin still had as President. In case of the President's sudden death in office or complete incapacitation, the constitution provides for the Prime Minister to take over and for fresh elections to be held within three months. Most of Russia's main politicians were positioning themselves for this eventuality and it thus appeared that the second Yeltsin administration might be much shorter than the first.

Apart from the immediate problems before the new administration, Russia still needed to deal with deep structural problems before its weak democracy was secured. Yeltsin's victory and the fall of some of the conservatives in his circle does not break the power of economic lobby groups, regional elites or corrupt politicians. These may well continue to conduct policy between themselves and in private, away from public scrutiny. The main democratic means of public influence on policy-making, party and interest group politics were still at a low level of development. Moreover, there were few signs that they will develop at any speed. Finally, the Russian economy looked set for another bout of inflation if the election promises made by Yeltsin were cashed in. There are no signs of any dramatic economic recovery or the political will to implement policies that might achieve such a reversal of fortune.

Ukraine

Campaigning for the Verkhovna Rada and the presidency were the main foci of Ukrainian political life in early 1994. After the elections, political life was occupied by attempts to establish the relationship between the two institutions.

The Ukrainian party system was shaped by concerns about economic change and nation-building, with parties 'best organised at opposite ends of the political spectrum among the nationalist right and the anti-nationalist left'.[23] The main left parties were the Communist Party of Ukraine (CPU), the Socialist Party of Ukraine (SPU) and the Agrarian Party (APU). All campaigned on an anti-economic reform ticket, and argued that Ukraine should not develop a strong presidential system. The three parties differed on relations with Russia: the CPU campaigned for union with Russia and other NIS in a new federation; the SPU and APU argued for an independent Ukraine with strong links to Russia, particularly strong economic relations. Similar policy positions to the SPU and APU were held by two small left-centre parties, the Labour Party (LPU) and Civic Congress (CCU). The far

Textbox 11.4 Main events in Ukraine, 1994 to June 1996

1994

January	Presidents Kravchuk, Clinton and Yeltsin sign an agreement in Moscow on nuclear disarmament.
March	Elections to the Rada. Left-wing parties win the largest number of seats.
June	First round of presidential election fought by seven candidates. Vitaly Masol appointed Prime Minister.
July	Second round of presidential election. Leonid Kuchma beats the incumbent, Leonid Kravchuk.
August	Kuchma issues decrees increasing his power over central and regional government.
October	Rada votes for economic reform package and ratifies Nuclear Non-Proliferation Treaty. IMF approves credit package to Ukraine. World Bank issues a loan of $500 million.
November	Kuchma visits United States and receives additional aid grants. Ukraine becomes fourth largest recipient of US aid.

1995

March	Prime Minister Masol resigns and is replaced by Yevheny Marchuk.
April	Rada passes vote of no confidence in Marchuk government. Kuchma orders a new government be chosen.
June	Constitutional compromise agreed giving power to presidency and heading off dispute over the competencies of the presidency and Rada. Agreement signed with Russia over the division of the Black Sea fleet.
September	Ukraine signs Partnership for Peace agreement with NATO.

1996

March	Rada Constitutional Commission approves draft constitution. Kuchma issues decree ordering privatisation of all remaining state-owned companies.
May	Withdrawal of all nuclear warheads from Ukraine completed. President Kuchma sacks the Prime Minister.
June	Rada approves the draft constitution submitted by the Constitutional Commission, but gets bogged down in revisions. Kuchma decrees a referendum on the constitution. This forces Rada to reconsider and pass the constitution.

right was marked out by its nationalism and anti-democratic rhetoric more than anything else. Mostly this took the form of anti-CIS rhetoric, although some far right parties called for the creation of a new Ukrainian state which was to include parts of Moldova and Belarus. The far right also called for the extension of presidential power. However, they were divided over economic policy, with some favouring the extension of private property and some arguing for state control.

The centre ground of Ukrainian party politics was dominated by the creation of electoral alliances. Centre-left parties joined with industrialists associations to form the Inter-Regional Bloc of Reforms (I-RBR) under the former Prime Minister, Leonid Kuchma. I-RBR had support among the economic elite in the south and east of Ukraine, favoured closer cooperation with Russia and the CIS and was for modest market reform. The centre-right/national democratic bloc was based around Rukh, which, with several smaller parties and political and cultural groups, formed the Democratic Coalition Ukraine. The parties clustered in the Democratic Coalition Ukraine all favoured market reform and were in particular opposed to continued *nomenklatura* power in the economy. Their chief areas of disagreement with the I-RBR group of parties was over attitudes to Russia. Rukh and its partners looked west to Europe. Some also favoured keeping an independent Ukrainian nuclear deterrent. (Ukraine had signed another agreement on nuclear disarmament with Russia and the United States in January 1995.)

The results of the March elections and the April run-offs can be seen in Table 11.7. There were two chief influences on the results: regionalism and the electoral laws that established a majoritarian system.[24] The electoral laws help account for two aspects of the result: the high number of independent deputies elected (168 in total, although some were associated with I-RBR as Table 11.7 shows) and the high number of unfilled seats (112 after both the March and April elections). The electoral laws favoured independent candidates because they made it easy to nominate local candidates, and because parties had difficulty getting their message across. The laws guaranteeing equal access to the media meant that parties' messages were lost in the sheer volume of party programmes and information about independent candidates. The large number of unfilled seats was caused by the need to secure an absolute majority (over 50 per cent of the vote) from over 50 per cent of the registered electorate in order to be elected. These stringent electoral rules made it very difficult to secure positive results; either turnout was too low, or no candidate got an absolute majority. After the second round of voting 338 deputies were elected and the Rada was just quorate. Repeat elections had to be held in July, August, November and December 1994, and December 1995. Even after the December 1995 elections 31 seats were still unfilled.[25]

The regional influence on the vote shows in the geography of parties' electoral success (independents did well everywhere).[26] The left took their

Table 11.7 Elections to Ukrainian Rada, March–April 1994

	% vote	Seats
Left (Sub-total)	18.55	147
Communist Party of Ukraine	12.72	86
Socialist Party of Ukraine	3.09	26
Agrarian Party of Ukraine	2.74	35
Centre (Sub-total)	1.84	33
Inter-Regional Bloc of Reforms		20[a]
National Democrats (Sub-total)	9.10	48
Rukh	5.15	27
Far Right (Sub-total)	2.10	20
Other Parties	1.93	
Total of Parties	33.52	

a. Elected as independents

Source: Adapted from Wilson (1995, p. 365) and Birch (forthcoming).

seats in the east and south; the I-RBR did surprisingly poorly in these areas. The left's success rested on their greater organisation, their support from rural areas and the high vote for the CPU in the Donbass mining area.[27] The national democrats and the far right did best in west Ukraine, and won the majority of their seats there. Central Ukraine was split between the national democrats and the left, with Rukh taking seats in Kiev and the APU taking some seats in rural areas.

The left were to attract further support once the Verkhovna Rada met and factions began to form. The CPU, SPU, APU and Rukh all set up factions, and the I-RBR created a bloc from independent deputies. Deputies from the far right parties sat as independents in the Verkhovna Rada.[28] The left's dominance led to the election of SPU leader Oleksandr Moroz as Chairman of the Rada, and Kravchuk's nominee for Prime Minister, Vitaly Masol (previously Prime Minister from 1987 to 1990), was ratified. However, attention switched to the presidential election before any real legislative work got under way.

The presidential election was dominated by the same two issues as the parliamentary election: economic change and Ukrainian statehood. However, the influence of these issues on the vote in the presidential election was different to the parliamentary elections. Elections to the Ukrainian presidency take the same form as for the Russian presidency. Seven candidates stood in the election: the incumbent, Leonid Kravchuk, former Prime Minister and I-RBR leader, Leonid Kuchma, and Oleksandr Moroz, SPU leader and new Rada Chairman were the main contenders (see Table 11.8 for the other candidates). Kravchuk campaigned on the issue of Ukrainian statehood and indepen-dence.[29] This reflected his move to the right during 1992 and 1993, and gave him strong support in western Ukraine. Moroz and Kuchma both tried to appeal to the centre, east and south of Ukraine. Both advocated reconciliation and better links with Russia. Moroz and Kuchma differed on economics and the presidency: Moroz favoured a parliamentary system and gradual economic reform with strong state involvement in the economy; Kuchma argued for the creation of a strong executive and economic reform based on monetary reform.

The attitudes of the presidential candidates influenced the distribution of their support in the first round of voting. Kravchuk's nationalism helped him to top the polls in the west and he picked up enough support in central Ukraine to give him the overall lead (see Table 11.8). Kuchma and Moroz split most of the eastern and southern vote between them. Kuchma did best in the areas bordering Russia and in the Crimea; Moroz attracted votes in the Donbass, the socialist heartland.

Kravchuk was not able to transform his first round lead into overall victory. Rukh endorsed Kravchuk for the second round and he picked up some of the minor candidates' votes. However, the number of votes that swung to Kuchma in the second round was greater than those available to Kravchuk. Kuchma picked up Moroz's votes in the east and south because of his more moderate position on Ukrainian statehood and relations with Russia. In parts of central Ukraine he gained both Moroz's votes, thanks to his position on Russia, and some of Lanovyi's votes, thanks to his position on economic reform. This enabled Kuchma to take the lead in parts of central Ukraine. Increased turnout in the south also helped increase Kuchma's overall share of the vote. Kuchma beat Kravchuk easily with 52.1 per cent of the vote to Kravchuk's 45.1 per cent.

The geographical spread of voting meant that Kuchma and the left deputies in the Rada had a common electorate. However, they had different political agendas and these dominated Ukrainian political life over the next two years.[30] Kravchuk was able to secure part of the economic reforms he had campaigned for, and this helped to slow the state's economic decline. However, Kuchma could not obtain a two-thirds vote in the Rada for the presidentialist constitution that he desired. The left wanted the new constitution to adapt the 1978 Soviet Ukrainian constitution. There was no provision for a presidency in this constitution. The left had a large enough proportion of the Rada's deputies to ensure that its preferences on constitutional order could not be ignored.

Kuchma increased his power in August 1994 by subordinating central and local government to the office of the President. This let him control the cabinet's agenda and meant that the Masol government could not take any decision on economic reform without Kuchma in attendance. Kuchma also appropriated the right of patronage to his office by decreeing his control over all appointments to state organisations. However, Kuchma could not control the Rada and did not have the means of sanctioning it available to the Russian

Table 11.8 Ukrainian presidential election, 1994

	First round % vote	Second round % vote
Leonid Kravchuk	37.7	45.1
Leonid Kuchma	31.3	52.1
Oleksandr Moroz	13.0	
Volodymyr Lanovyi	9.3	
Valery Babich	2.4	
Ivan Pliushch	1.3	
Petro Talanchuk	0.5	

Source: Wilson (1995, pp. 368–9).

President after December 1993. Kuchma tried to gain such powers in December 1994 when he presented a draft law on state power to the Rada. Although he had majority support in the Rada for the law, Kuchma could not get the two-thirds vote needed to change the constitution. An interim 'Constitutional Agreement' (sometimes called the 'small constitution') was introduced in June 1995 while a Constitutional Committee made up of representatives from all parliamentary factions was established to produce a fresh draft constitution.

The Constitutional Commission finally reported in March 1995. However, there was no agreement on the content of the new constitution within the Committee, let alone within the Rada as a whole. Matters were complicated by Kuchma's suggestion that the Rada be replaced by a bicameral assembly. Many Rada deputies feared this would allow Kuchma to play one chamber of parliament off against another. Left deputies further objected to the draft's lack of welfare guarantees, excision of Soviet era state symbols (such as the flag) and to the dropping of Russian as a state language. Various votes were held in June, but no agreement was forthcoming. Kuchma finally broke the deadlock by decreeing that a referendum on a constitution providing for a bicameral parliament be held. This was a threat against all factions of the Rada since it proposed the Rada's replacement with a bicameral parliament. The threat focused deputies' attention, and on 28 June they voted to accept a version of the document that strengthened the presidency, but preserved the Rada as a unicameral parliament with 450 deputies.

The late passage of the constitution – coupled as it is with regional-based party opposition to the presidential order, low levels of party development and no reform of the electoral system – make it difficult to assess the degree to which Ukraine has moved to consolidate democracy. The checks on the President's use of his power are untested and Kuchma has yet to establish stable president/government relations. The electoral system will continue to produce high levels of support for the CPU and the SPU in the east and the south, while the presidency will go to a candidate who can win the centre and control either the east and the west. Ukraine's politics look set, therefore, to be regionally based and party politics to be deformed by the electoral system.

The Baltic states: Estonia, Latvia and Lithuania

The Baltic states were in a very different position to Russia and Ukraine at the start of 1994. They had all adopted new constitutions in 1992–93 and elected new legislatures and governments. They had also made far more progress towards economic reform and integration with Western Europe than the other NIS (see Textbox 11.5). However, these successes did not mean that democracy was fully consolidated in the Baltic states. Estonia, Latvia and Lithuania had the outward form of democratic politics, but it remained to be seen whether they could fill that form with content. Baltic politics remained fluid and unstable in 1994–96. In Estonia and Latvia the low popularity of ruling coalitions encouraged some parties to break with them. This caused high turnover in government and tense relations between coalition partners. Dissatisfaction also led to the proliferation of political parties in Estonia and Latvia. Like other post-communist states, Estonia and Latvia were already prone to high levels of party fragmentation and formation because of the weakness of electoral cleavages and their PR election systems. Coalition instability helped increase the rate of party formation as members of the political elite established parties in the hope of entering government. Government crisis in Lithuania came from financial scandal, but the Lithuanian Democratic Labour Party (LDLP) and President Brazauskas retained control of power. Party politics remained relatively stable too as Landsbergis's Homeland Union (Conservatives of Lithuania) HU(CL) sought to build up support so as to challenge the LDLP in 1996.

Estonia and Latvia also continued to experience poor relations with Russia over citizenship, and the rights of Russians were the major issue dividing the two countries. Estonia's relations with Russia were further complicated by arguments over territory and accusations of spying. Estonian–Russian relations briefly improved in 1994 when a deal was signed on the final removal of Russian troops from Estonia. Since then relations have worsened. In January 1995, the Riigikogu passed legislation extending the minimum period of residence needed to qualify for Estonian citizenship from two to five years.[31] The agreement on troop withdrawals was not ratified by the Riigikogu until December 1995. The delay was caused by Estonian fears that ratifying the deal meant rejecting the 1920 Tartu treaty between Russia and Estonia. For Estonians acceptance of the 1920 treaty means recognition of the continuity between present-day Estonia and the independent Estonia of the interwar years. The treaty also had territorial implications since the border it defined between Russia and Estonia includes territory that is now within the Russian

Federation. Latvia's relations with Russia were marred by the passage of a citizenship law in 1994. The first version of the law set quotas on the number of people who could be naturalised each year and President Ulmanis returned the law to the Saeima after Russian and international pressure. A modified version was passed in July 1994, with the quotas technically removed. The right to apply for citizenship is now controlled by age: non-Latvians under 20 could apply for citizenship from 1 January 1995, those between 20 and 25 could apply from 1 January 1996, etc. This amounts to much the same thing as quotas even though there is no fixed number given for the number of people who can apply year on year: non-Latvians over 40 will have to wait until the year 2000 to apply and 300,000 non-Latvians will not be eligible until 2001–2003.[32]

Estonia

The Isamaa-led coalition government under Mart Laar was deeply unpopular by the end of 1993. Elections to the Riigikogu were not due until March 1995, but there were doubts about Laar's government staying in office until then. Isamaa had performed badly in the October 1993 local elections (see Chapter 8). Laar's position was further weakened in January 1994 when he clashed with President Meri over the composition of the government. Over the course of the year, Laar's style of government alienated several cabinet ministers and by September 1994 he could no longer command a parliamentary majority. A vote of no confidence in the Laar government was called and passed; a new coalition government was formed under Andres Tarand from the Moderates electoral alliance.

The collapse of support for Laar was not just due to his style of rule; it was also part of a major reorganisation of the parties that had fought the 1992 election, and the emergence of new parties and alliances (necessary because of the 5 per cent threshold used in the Estonian PR system) created to fight the 1995 election. On the centre-right of the political spectrum, Isamaa lost members to two new right-wing parties, the Right-Wingers Party and the Reformist Party, but was joined by Estonian National Independence Party (ENIP, one of its coalition partners) in an electoral alliance. Tarand's Moderates also lost members to the Reformist Party. The remnants of the Popular Front of Estonia turned into the Centre Party under Edgar Savisaar. The centre-left Secure Home electoral alliance from the 1992 Riigikogu elections changed its name into the Coalition and Rural People's Association when joined by the Rural People's Party, set up by former President Arnold Rüütel for the election.[33] There were few policy differences between the centre-right and the centre-left. The centre-left (the Centre Party and the Coalition and Rural People's Association) favoured support for groups hurt by the move to a market economy, and appealed in particular to pensioners and farmers. The centre-right (Isamaa, the Reform Party, ENIP and the Right-Wingers Party)

Textbox 11.5 Main events in the Baltic states, 1994 to June 1996

1994

March   German Foreign Minister Klaus Kinkel states all three Baltic states should be admitted to the EU.

April   *Latvia* Agreement with Russia on troop withdrawals.
               Lithuania Campaign for referendum on compensation for savings lost as a result of inflation and illegal privatisation.

May   *Latvia* Local elections. Latvia's Way performs badly.

June   *Estonia* Two parties quit the ruling Isamaa coalition. Yeltsin decrees that Estonian claims on Russian territory are invalid.
               Latvia Legislation passed setting a quota on the number of Russians who can take Estonian citizenship a year. Quota removed after Russian pressure, but language tests remain.
               Lithuania Changes made to government after pressure from Seimas.

July   *Estonia, Latvia and Lithuania* All sign free trade agreements with EU.
               Estonia Agreement with Russia on troop withdrawals and the rights of retired Soviet military personnel in Estonia.
               Latvia Prime Minister Birkavs and the government resign after the Farmers' Union withdraws from coalition. Gailis becomes Prime Minister.

August   *Estonia and Latvia* Withdrawal of Russian troops completed.
               Lithuania Referendum on compensation for savings lost as a result of inflation and illegal privatisation held. Vote is invalid due to low turnout.

September *Estonia* Vote of no confidence in the Laar government passed in the Riigikogu.

October   *Estonia* Tarand becomes Prime Minister.

November   *Estonia* New government approved by Riigikogu.

1995

January   *Estonia* Law passed lengthening the minimum period of residency required for citizenship.
               Lithuania Law on restitution of Catholic Church property seized during the communist period is passed.

February   *Estonia* President Meri calls for territorial claims against Russia to be dropped.

	Latvia Admitted to Council of Europe.
March	*Estonia* Elections to the Riigikogu. Coalition Party and Rural People's Association win most seats. Vähi becomes Prime Minister.
	Lithuania Law on restitution accepted with President Brazauskas's revisions. LDLP performs badly in local elections.
April	*Latvia and Lithuania* Become associate members of the EU.
September	*Latvia* Elections to Saeima. Samnieks wins most seats.
November	*Estonia* Agreement with Russia on borders.
	Lithuania Prime Minister Slezevicius survives vote of no confidence in Seimas.
December	*Estonia* Applies for EU membership. Riigikogu ratifies July 1994 agreements with Russia on troop withdrawals and the rights of retired Soviet military personnel.
	Latvia Skele coalition government approved by Saeima.
	Lithuania Applies for EU membership. Banking crisis begins.

1996

January	*Estonia* Estonian delegates to the Council of Europe's Parliamentary Assembly vote against Russia's admittance to the Council of Europe.
	Lithuania Government crisis over banking crisis.
February	*Lithuania* President Brazauskas persuades the Seimas to remove Slezevicius from the post of Prime Minister and names Laurynas Stankevicius his successor.
March	*Estonia* 64 Riigikogu deputies send letter of condolence to Dudayev after his son-in-law is killed. Russian Duma calls for economic sanctions.
	Lithuania Stankevicius presents economic programme to Seimas to deal with financial crisis. Seimas approves new government.
April	*Estonia* Riigikogu passes law making it almost impossible for Russians to stand in local elections. President Meri sends the law back for reconsideration.
	Lithuania President Brazauskas calls Seimas elections for October. Formation of Stankevicius government is completed.
May	*Latvia* Coalition threatened after Prime Minister Skele sacks the Minister of Agriculture. Coalition partners are further divided over the prospect of re-electing President Ulmanis.
June	*Latvia* Saeima re-elects Ulmanis as President.

were against increasing state spending to compensate the victims of change.[34] Aside from these differences on social protection, there was no fundamental disagreement over the need for economic reform through financial stability. This meant that there were countless ways that the parties could combine in coalitions after the elections.

The 1995 Riigikogu elections were different from the 1992 elections in several respects. The Riigikogu elected in 1995 was not an ethnically homogeneous legislature. Some 50,000 non-ethnic Estonians had been naturalised by the time of the elections and were entitled to vote and this helped the Russian 'Our Home is Estonia' alliance get across the 5 per cent threshold and take six seats in the Riigikogu.[35] The right vote split in 1995 thanks to the setting up of the Right-Wingers and Reform Parties. The success of these two parties, the Centre Party and the Coalition and Rural People's Association reduced the share of the vote taken by Isamaa/ENIP from just over 30 per cent to 7.9 per cent. Minority parties and parties at the ends of the political continuum also fared less well than in 1992. The 'Fourth Power' electoral alliance of Greens and Royalists, failed to secure re-election; the communist-led Justice electoral alliance and the right-wing Estonian Citizens/Better Estonia both failed to get across the threshold.

The 1995 election and the lack of ideological differentiation between parties showed the shallowness of electoral cleavages, and the ease with which parties could be set up in the centre ground of politics and take seats. The Rural People's Party, the Right-Wingers and the Reform Party had all been set up with the election in view and polled well. Only the Coalition and Centre parties did well *and* had a significant political and electoral history. Estonia thus had a party system, but parties were a creation of the electoral system as much as they were representative of defined ideological or social constituencies. Many parties were vehicles for politicians seeking power: the electoral system demanded that politicians be members of parties if they wished to have access to power; the weakness of electoral cleavages meant that new parties could be formed and stand a chance of electoral success. The fluidity of the Estonian party system did not end after the elections and the rise and fall of coalition governments was also not affected.

The Coalition and Rural People's Association and the Centre Party formed a coalition government in April 1995. The leader of the Coalition Party, Tiit Vähi, became Prime Minister and Edgar Savisaar of the Centre Party took the post of Interior Minister. The Vähi government pledged to carry on the policies of the Laar/Tarand governments. The new government maintained the impetus for economic reform by producing a plan for a balanced budget in September 1995. However, changes in the government were forced in October after Vähi sacked Savisaar over allegations of illegal phonetapping. The continued support for Savisaar from his Centre Party forced Vähi's whole government to quit. However, President Meri asked Vähi to form another

Table 11.9 Estonian election, March 1995

Party	Electoral Alliance	% vote	Seats
Coalition Rural Union Pensioners and Family Party Rural People's Party	Coalition and Rural People's Association	32.2	41
Reform Party		16.2	19
Centre		14.2	16
Isamaa ENIP	Isamaa/ENIP	7.9	8
Rural Centre Social Democrats Central Trade Union Organisation	Moderates	6.0	6
Estonian United People's Party Russian Party	Our Home is Estonia	5.9	6
Right-wingers		5.0	5
Others		15.2	0

Source: Adapted from Arter (1995, p. 260) and Norgaard *et al.* (1996, p. 88).

government, and he allied the Coalition and Rural People's Association with a party from the centre-right, the Reform Party. The Centre Party meanwhile replaced Savisaar as leader with Andra Veidemann. In March 1996 the party and its parliamentary bloc split when Veidemann quit to form a new group. ENIP and Isamaa formally merged to create the Isamaa Alliance in December 1995 and in April 1996 the Moderate Party was formed by two of its electoral allies. The Estonian party system was thus still evolving after 1995 and as it does so the interchangeability of government coalition parties will evolve with it. There was some continuity in government in 1996 thanks to President Meri's re-election in September. However, there were further changes in government at the end of 1996 after coalition disputes. Prime Minister Vähi constructed yet another coalition government in December, but this government looked weak since Vähi could not strike a deal with the Reform Party and could thus rely on the support of only 41 of the 101 Riigikogu deputies.

Latvia

Latvia's political development was very similar to that of Estonia. The moderate-right government of Valdis Birkavs collapsed in the summer of 1994 after the withdrawal of a coalition partner and local elections in which coalition parties performed poorly. A new government with the same major coalition partner was formed and elections were held in 1995. The elections did not see the ruling coalition suffer a defeat of the same magnitude as the

Isamaa coalition parties in Estonia. None the less the ruling coalition could not form a new, stable government and a new coalition grouping came to power.

Latvia's failure to introduce a law on citizenship by the time of the May 1994 local elections meant that only people who had been resident in the country before 1940 or who were descended from a 1940 resident were entitled to vote. Consequently, many Russians and other minorities, who made up over one-third of the population of voting age, were excluded. There were further language requirements that had to be satisfied in order to register as a candidate for local office. The exclusion of the Russians and other minorities meant that nationalist parties won the majority of seats in the local elections just as they had taken most seats in the Saeima elections in late 1993. However, Latvia's Way, the leading party in the ruling coalition, did not do well. It took seats, but other right parties like the Latvian National Independence Movement (LNIM) did much better.[36]

The poor performance of Latvia's Way in the local elections was a sign that it had not managed to grow from being a party based around a few political personalities and set up to fight a national election to a political party with grassroots organisations. This was further evinced a month after the local elections when the coalition collapsed after Latvia's Way quarrelled with its coalition partner, the Farmers' Union, over tariff levels for imported agricultural goods and subsidies paid to farmers.[37] The opposition was not able to muster enough support to form a new coalition, although LNIM tried. After a month another coalition based around Latvia's Way took shape. A new government was finally approved by the Saeima in September 1994: Birkavs became Foreign Minister and Maris Gailis, Prime Minister.

The crisis and the formation of the new coalition government realigned Latvian parliamentary politics and created a left–right spectrum within the Saeima. The right built on the experience of trying to construct a coalition to form a parliamentary caucus, the National Bloc. The National Bloc gathered together thirty-three deputies from LNIM, the Farmers' Union and two other right parties to form an opposition to the new government.[38] The government moved to the left. The most ardent supporters of economic reform were removed from the cabinet and the government, ironically, adopted the sort of economic policy on tariffs and subsidies that the Farmers' Union had asked for.[39] Economic reform was not pursued with vigour and recovery slowed. Inflation did not fall noticeably between 1994 and 1995, and the closure of one of the countries biggest banks raised the budget deficit. Industrial and agricultural production fell in 1994 and mass privatisation (started in May 1995) progressed slowly.[40]

Unfortunately, the left–right divide within the Saeima did not translate neatly into party formation for the September 1995 Saeima elections. The alliances made during 1994 on both the left and the right fragmented as parties sought electoral advantage for themselves. New parties were formed by splinter groups from the main parties. Other parties simply did not develop strong organisations. Latvia's Way only became a political party in the autumn of 1994; only invited individuals were allowed to join and by the end of 1994 it only had 400 members.[41] In total nineteen parties were on the PR list for the elections (only a minority of Russians in Latvia could vote because of the difficulties they faced in obtaining naturalisation). Only nine parties got above the new 5 per cent threshold (the threshold had been 4 per cent in 1993) to gain seats in the Saeima (see Table 11.10). Latvia's Way and its coalition partners did poorly. On the left, the Concord Party lost votes to the Latvian Socialist Party and the Unity Party. Latvia's Way's share of the vote dropped by 15 per cent from 1993 as it took responsibility for public dissatisfaction with slow economic recovery. It lost seats in the political centre to Samnieks (In Charge), which had been established in April 1994 and campaigned for tighter economic management and trade links with Russia. The right vote fragmented: Zigerist's Party/Movement for Latvia (headed by Joahims Zigerist, who has convictions for inciting racial hatred in his native Germany, speaks poor Latvian and claims Latvian nationality through his father) and the National Conservative Party were both formed from factions of LNIM and took its 1993 vote; Fatherland and Freedom doubled its number of seats from 1993; the Farmers' Union fought the election in alliance with the Christian Democratic Union and they lost ten seats between them.[42]

The fragmented support for parties in the election made it difficult to form a new coalition. Two compromise blocs were formed. Samnieks, the Unity and Concord parties formed a broad-based coalition with the Zigerist's Party under the title National Reconciliation Bloc. Fatherland and Freedom, the Farmers' Union and the National Conservative Party re-formed the National Bloc. President Ulmanis asked the Fatherland and Freedom leader Maris Grinblats to form a government. Grinblats failed to win the Saeima's support in November. In December, a National Reconciliation Bloc coalition headed by Samnieks leader, Ziedonis Cevers, was also rejected. After further political realignment a coalition was formed from the majority of parties in the Saeima under the leadership of Andris Skele. The coalition included: Samnieks (with Skele as Prime Minister and Cevers as one of three Deputy Prime Ministers); Latvia's Way (Birkavs took the post of Foreign Minister, Gailis became a Deputy Prime Minister and Environment Minister); Fatherland and Freedom (Grinblats became a Deputy Prime Minister and Minister for Education); the Unity Party, the National Conservative Party, the Farmers' Union and Christian Democrats, and Green Party took other ministerial positions. The coalition had a commanding majority in the Saeima thanks to the involvement of so many parties (only the Zigerists, the Socialist Party and the Concord Party were not included). Managing so many different groups, personalities and party leaders has not been easy. Ministers from the different parties have frequently criticised one another. In May 1996, Skele dismissed the Minister

Table 11.10 Latvian election, September 1995

	% vote	Seats
Samnieks	15.3	18
Latvia's Way	15.1	17
Zigerist's Party/Movement for Latvia	14.7	16
Fatherland and Freedom	11.6	14
Unity Party	7.2	8
National Conservative Party	6.2	8
Farmers' Union/Christian Democratic Union	6.1	8
Latvian Socialist Party	5.7	6
Concord Party	5.6	6
Others	12.5	0

of Agriculture, whose Unity Party promptly quit the coalition. Once again the argument between coalition partners was over agricultural subsidies: the Unity Party wanted them to be preserved; other coalition partners wanted them removed so that Latvia could conform to EU and World Bank criteria. The coalition came under further pressure in June 1996 when Ulmanis came up for re-election. Samnieks nominated Ilga Kreituse, the chairwoman of the Saeima, and the Farmers' Union and other parties continued to support Ulmanis. Ulmanis won on the first ballot with 53 votes. After the election, and to try to prevent further conflict, five of the coalition parties drew up a coalition agreement for one year and this has held thus far.[43]

Lithuania

Politics in Lithuania were not crisis-free between 1994 and 1996, but there was no fundamental challenge to the government and ruling party as there was in Estonia and Latvia. Neither did its ruling party, the LDLP, nor President Brazauskas have to stand for re-election: elections for the Seimas were scheduled for October 1996, with presidential elections to follow in 1997. There was no real struggle for power between the Seimas and the President either. The LDLP had a majority in the Seimas thanks to its convincing victory in the 1992 elections. Brazauskas resigned his membership of the LDLP on becoming President in 1993, but there were no policy differences between him, the government and the LDLP parliamentary caucus, and he controlled the political agenda for the most part.[44] With the LDLP's hold on power so firm, the main questions in Lithuanian politics were whether the opposition could develop sufficiently to challenge it in October 1996, and how far LDLP policies would alienate voters and increase opposition support.

Opposition to the LDLP could achieve little by directly attacking the government through the Seimas because of the LDLP's majority. Landsbergis and HU(CL) tried to discredit the LDLP from outside of the Seimas by taking advantage of popular discontent with economic reform and the government.

In 1993 HU(CL) organised petitions calling for discussion of a law to compensate for savings lost as a result of economic change. The LDLP-controlled Seimas ignored the petitions and the law. In April 1994, HU(CL) began gathering signatures again, this time for a referendum to approve a law against illegal privatisation and compensation for lost savings. This law would have index-linked savings and compensated for losses caused by inflation since 1991. Some privatised enterprises would also have been returned to the state. HU(CL)'s promotion of the referendum was economic populism and enabled HU(CL) spokespeople to accuse the government – which opposed the law – of seeking to protect *nomenklatura* privatisation. HU(CL) managed to gather over 500,000 signatures to secure the holding of the referendum; however, when the referendum was held, only 37 per cent of registered voters turned out so that the result was not legally binding.

The low turnout in the referendum was not a sign of the LDLP or the government's popularity. The government found itself embroiled in political controversy at the start of 1995 when the Seimas passed a law limiting the restitution of property seized under communism from the Catholic Church.[45] President Brazauskas refused to sign the law, realising that it played into the opposition's hands: the Church was more trusted according to opinion polls than the government; Slezevicius and the LDLP, as the main successor party to the Lithuanian Communist Party, looked to be justifying the communist party's actions, and taking revenge for some priests' support for the HU(CL) referendum. The LDLP confirmed this impression by accusing the Church of seeking undue influence in politics and of being a threat to democracy.

A revised version of the law on restitution was passed at the end of March 1995. Before then, however, the LDLP faced public censure in local elections. It is difficult to draw a direct line from the controversy over the restitution law to the local election results. But the LDLP did badly and the restitution law controversy may have brought conservative voters to the polls despite a generally low turnout. Continued economic problems did not help government fortunes either. The vote share of the HU(CL) and the Christian Democrats improved to 29.1 and 16.9 per cent (Sajudis and the Christian Democrats had got 20 and 12 per cent in the 1993 elections). The LDLP's share of the vote plummeted from 44 per cent in 1993 to 19.9 per cent in the local elections. The newly formed Peasants Party took 6.9 per cent of the vote.[46]

The LDLP's prestige was hit further in 1996 by government scandal. In December 1996, the Lithuanian Joint-Stock Innovation Bank and Litimpeks Bank (the two largest banks in the country) were closed amid accusations of fraud and insolvency. In January 1996, it was revealed that Prime Minister Slezevicius had withdrawn a large amount of money from the Lithuanian Joint-Stock Innovation Bank just before accounts were frozen and that he had done this knowing that the bank's operations were about to be suspended. The Seimas opposition immediately called for Slezevicius's resignation. Initially,

Brazauskas supported Slezevicius; but he withdrew this support after two ministers tried to resign from the government and criminal charges were brought against Slezevicius for abusing his position. The LDLP ruling council continued to support Slezevicius and he stayed in office. At the end of January, Brazauskas signed a decree calling for the Seimas to vote to remove Slezevicius. The government was collapsing (the Interior Minister resigned for the same crime Slezevicius was accused of, and the Seimas supported Brazauskas's decree on 8 February 1996). Brazauskas appointed Laurynas Stankevicius Prime Minister, and a new cabinet and government programme were presented to the Seimas and accepted in March and April respectively.

The bank scandal has reinforced popular perceptions of the LDLP, namely that it has difficulty managing the economy, that its ministers are arrogant in the use of their power and that it supports corrupt economic activity. These popular beliefs helped HU(CL) and the Christian Democrats repeat their local election success in the October 1996 elections. Twenty-three parties were registered for the PR vote in the elections. However, only five managed to get over the 5 per cent threshold to secure a share of the 70 Seimas seats distributed by PR: HU(CL) received 29.7 per cent of the vote and 33 seats; the Christian Democrats overtook the LDLP, gaining 9.9 per cent of the vote and 11 seats to the LDLP s 9.7 per cent and 10 seats; the Centre Union and the Social Democratic Party took 8.2 and 6.6 per cent of the vote and gained 9 and 7 seats respectively. HU(CL)'s lead in the PR vote was bolstered in the 71 single-mandate constituency voting. In the first round voting in October it secured the only two outright victories in the single mandate constituencies, with Landsbergis and former Prime Minister Gediminas Vagnorius winning their seats. In the second round voting on 10 November, HU(CL) won 35 seats, the Christian Democrats and Social Democrats took 5 seats each, and the LDLP 2 seats. The mixed PR and majoritarian electoral system thus helped to keep the number of parties that can effectively compete in elections low since small fringe parties were not able to take many of the non-PR seats. HU(CL)'s success made Landsbergis the firm favourite for the 1997 presidential race. In the meantime Lithuania began a period of cohabitation. The HU(CL) domination of the Seimas was secured by a formal coalition agreement with the Christian Democrats, which gave the Christian Democrats three ministerial posts (including Foreign Affairs and Defence) in the new government under Vagnorius. At the first meeting of the new Seimas Landsbergis was elected Seimas Chairman by 107 votes to 28.

Belarus

Belarus adopted a new constitution and elected a President in 1994. But it did not make any significant progress towards democracy or breaking the political or economic power of the *nomenklatura*. By mid-1996 the political and human rights situation in the country had deteriorated to such an extent that the European Parliament's Commission on Foreign Policy and Security demanded that a draft trade treaty between the EU and Belarus be suspended until Belarus improves its observance of human rights.

1994 started badly for democrats: Supreme Council Chairman Stanislau Shushkevich finally lost his long struggle with the old guard majority in the Supreme Council and the government under Prime Minister Vyacheslau Kebich. The conservative majority in the Supreme Council called a vote of no confidence in both Shushkevich and Kebich after they had been accused of corruption by Alexander Lukashenko, the Chairman of a Supreme Council commission on corruption. Kebich survived the vote of no confidence easily. Shushkevich lost the vote of confidence by 209 votes to 36.[47]

Shushkevich's removal increased Kebich's hold over the Belarusian political system. The new Chair of the Supreme Council, Mechyslau Hryb, was an ally of Kebich's. Kebich pushed his political agenda through the Supreme Council. In March, a constitution providing for a strong presidency was passed by the Supreme Council (Shushkevich had opposed this). In April, Lukashenko's anti-corruption commission was closed down by order of the Supreme Council. In the same month, Kebich signed a Treaty on Monetary Union with Russia. Shushkevich and the Popular Front of Belarus (PFB) had opposed any deal with Russia that eroded the sovereignty of Belarus. The Treaty on Monetary Union threatened to compromise Belarusian sovereignty heavily. Russia gained the right to use military installations in Belarus free of charge, and the Russian Central Bank was to control monetary policy and the issue of currency. In the event, the Treaty was not fully implemented. Russia made use of Belarusian military bases, but did not take control of Belarus's money supply. The Belarusian government continued to subsidise industry, agriculture and prices, and Russia feared that full monetary union would increase its own inflation rate.[48]

The adoption of a new constitution and establishment of a presidency made it necessary to hold elections. Kebich was expected to win the presidency given his control over Belarusian politics: support from the *nomenklatura* would deliver the vote for him. The electoral law is similar to that of Russia and Ukraine: the winning candidate has to secure an absolute majority of votes (over 50 per cent) to win; if no candidate is victorious in the first round of voting a second round run-off between the top two candidates is held; over 50 per cent of the registered electorate have to vote for the election to be valid. Six candidates stood in the first round of voting in June 1994: Kebich, Lukashenko, Shushkevich, PFB leader Zyanon Paznyak, communist leader Vasil Novikau, and collective farm union leader Alexander Dubko. Kebich, Lukashenko, Novikau and Dubko all campaigned on conservative platforms, arguing for close links with Russia and against radical economic change.

Textbox 11.6 Main events in Belarus, 1994 to June 1996

1994

January	Supreme Council votes to remove Shushkevich from his post as Chair. He is replaced by Hryb, an ally of Prime Minister Kebich.
March	Supreme Council adopts new constitution. Office of President is created.
April	Agreement on monetary union signed with Russia. Supreme Council anti-corruption commission is dissolved.
June	First round of presidential elections fought by six candidates.
July	Lukashenko elected President in a run-off election with Kebich. Mikhas Chyhir appointed Prime Minister. Privatisation halted.
September	Russians announce that there is no prospect of monetary union with Belarus.
November	Lukashenko increases the powers of the presidency over local government.

1995

February	Supreme Council passes a law enabling it to impeach the President by a two-thirds vote of its deputies. Friendship treaty with Russia.
April	Lukashenko threatens to suspend Supreme Council after it rejects his proposals for referendum questions on relations with Russia. PFB deputies go on hunger strike.
May	Parliamentary elections and referendum.
September	Constitutional Court begins investigation of presidential powers at the request of Supreme Council Chair Hryb.
October	Conflict grows between Lukashenko and Supreme Council. Three newspapers closed by presidential order and the main publishing house is forbidden to print them.

Lukashenko argued for reunification with Russia and against any privatisation of industry. Shushkevich and Paznyak stood for market reform and Belarusian national sovereignty.

The results were a surprise: Lukashenko won the first round with 44 per cent of the vote. Kebich came second with 17 per cent, Paznyak and Shushkevich followed with 12 and 9 per cent, Dubko got 6 per cent and Novikau 4 per cent. Lukashenko's first-round victory was then converted into a huge second-round victory when he got 81.1 per cent of the vote.[49] Lukashenko achieved his surprise victory because he promised more than Kebich, was not associated with the country's economic decline and because he wore the mantle of an anti-corruption campaigner. However, there was little practical,

December	Final round of voting in the Supreme Council elections. Supreme Council finally becomes quorate.

1996

January	Sharetsky elected Chair of the Supreme Council. Lukashenko orders state officials to ignore Constitutional Court rulings that suspend presidential decrees. The Court appeals to the Supreme Council.
February	Lukashenko appoints key state officials by decree and without the Supreme Council's assent as required by the constitution.
March	Agreement with Russia on a new union treaty. Supreme Council votes for the agreement. Mass protests in Minsk (the capital of Belarus) are suppressed with violence by riot police.
April	New Union treaty signed in Moscow to create the Community of Sovereign Republics. Demonstrations in Minsk on the day of the signing are followed three weeks later by demonstrations to commemorate the tenth anniversary of the Chernobyl nuclear disaster. Both demonstrations are suppressed by riot police. Over 200 people arrested.
May	Further demonstrations against Lukashenko on 1 and 30 May to protest detention and trial of earlier arrestees.
June	European Parliament Commission for Foreign Policy and Security demands that a provisional trade agreement with Belarus be suspended pending improvements in human rights and democracy in Belarus. Supreme Council Chair Sharetsky criticises Lukashenko.

substantive difference between Lukashenko and Kebich on policy. Lukashenko talked of reunification with Russia, but the best that could be hoped for was Russian indulgence and support. Russia's failure to implement fully the Treaty on Monetary Union showed that it was not going to burden its economy to too great an extent with Belarusian problems. A friendship treaty was signed between the two countries in February 1995. Russia was the chief beneficiary, gaining the right to station troops on Belarusian territory. The treaty provided for a customs union (set up in May 1995), but no real economic integration was planned. Lukashenko's accusations of corruption in government were just rhetoric. The new government blended young reformers and ministers from the Kebich government.[50] Lukashenko had accused some of the latter of corruption. Similar accusations were soon levelled against his own administration. However, press reports of the accusations were censored, and nothing was done to purge government of corrupt officials.

With reunification with Russia impossible, Lukashenko and the new government struggled to develop an agenda for economic reform, and Belarus's economy continued its decline. Lukashenko's uncertainty over economic policy contrasts sharply with his certainty over political power. The office of President has considerable powers in the constitution. Lukashenko added to them in November 1994 when he persuaded the Supreme Council to amend the law on local government. Elected local councils were suspended under the new law, and their responsibilities passed to regional executive agencies. The heads of regional executives were appointed by the President, who also had the right to approve any appointments that they made. This gave Lukashenko immense power over all branches of executive government.

A partial check on the powers of the President was introduced in January 1995 when the Supreme Council adopted rules for the impeachment of the President: if the President is charged with violating the constitution or a serious crime the Supreme Council can impeach him by a two-thirds vote. However, Lukashenko's power continued to grow and become more authoritarian, and the Supreme Council found itself in a strange position in relation to Lukashenko. The Supreme Council's term of office ended in 1995. The 1994 constitution established a smaller, 260-seat Supreme Council (down from 360 seats). Elections were scheduled for May 1995. Lukashenko wanted a referendum held at the same time as the elections. He proposed four questions for the referendum: on the President's right to suspend the Supreme Council, on relations with Russia, on the re-introduction of Russian as the state language, and on the re-introduction of Soviet era state symbols. The Supreme Council rejected all but the first question on relations with Russia. Eighteen PFB deputies led by Paznyak went on hunger strike. Lukashenko threatened to suspend the Council unless it conceded to his demand for a referendum, and the PFB deputies were forcibly removed from the Supreme Council building by riot police. This show of strength cowed the Supreme Council; it accepted modified referendum questions with the proviso that the question on the President's right to dissolve the Supreme Council was not legally binding.

The referendum and elections to the new Supreme Council were held in May. All Lukashenko's referendum questions were accepted: 83.1 per cent voted for Russian to have equal status with Belarusian as a state language; 75 per cent voted for the introduction of new state symbols; 82.4 per cent expressed agreement with Lukashenko's attempts to further economic integration with Russia (the friendship treaty and customs union of February 1995); 77.6 per cent agreed that the President should have the right to suspend the Supreme Council if it violated the constitution. At the same time that Lukashenko received this endorsement of his policies, the legislature was weakened. Belarus's majoritarian electoral laws are the same as Ukraine's, although their effect is more severe in Belarus. Only eighteen deputies were elected in the first round of voting on 14 May. Turnout fell for the second round of run-off elections at the end of the month and only 102 more deputies were elected. The low number of deputies elected was not just because of the electoral system. Party development was very weak. The PFB failed to gain any seats in the first round of voting. The rural *nomenklatura* of collective farm managers were most successful: most of the deputies elected were from rural areas, and were independents or members of the CPB and the Agrarian Party. Little information on parties reached voters because of the paltry sums of money allocated to candidates by the state for campaign expenses, KGB censorship of electoral materials and government control over the press (four newspapers had been brought under government control in April).

With only 120 deputies elected after the first two rounds of voting the Supreme Council was inquorate. The legislative arm of government was left in limbo: the old Supreme Council continued to meet and operate while further elections were planned for November and December. Lukashenko argued that the old Supreme Council had no legitimacy. Lukashenko's dictatorial style of government flourished in the vacuum. In July, he altered the budget by decree. A strike by unpaid metro workers in August was ended by force, and fifteen trade union leaders were arrested. Supreme Council deputies' immunity from arrest was removed by presidential decree, and an opposition deputy was arrested for helping organise the metro strike. In October, Lukashenko extended his control over the government by appointing two officials from his administration as Deputy Prime Ministers.

The new Supreme Council finally became quorate after two more rounds of elections in November and December 1995. Lukashenko encouraged voters to stay at home in the hope that low turnout would render the elections invalid. The political make-up of the new Supreme Council can be seen in Table 11.11. The largest group of deputies are independents and will probably support Lukashenko. The CPB and the Agrarian Party are the only parties with a significant presence in the Supreme Council. The PFB failed to secure any seats. The largest pro-reform group is the United Civic Party, which has become the base for the opposition Citizens' Action faction in the Supreme Council.[51] The Supreme Council elected Semyon Sharetsky from the Agrarian Party Chair of the Supreme Council.

The period since the formation of the new Supreme Council has been one of intense political conflict. Hryb and the old Supreme Council had attempted to constrain Lukashenko's power by asking the Constitutional Court to rule on the constitutionality of his decrees. The Court found against Lukashenko in several cases over the last few months of 1995. In January 1996, Lukashenko ordered state officials to ignore the rulings of the Court. In turn, the Court appealed to the Supreme Council to uphold its rulings. Lukashenko showed his contempt for the Supreme Council by appointing several officials without

Table 11.11 Belarusian Supreme Council after third round of elections, December 1995

	Seats
CPB	42
Agrarian Party	33
Civic Unity Party	9
Party of People's Accord	8
Party of All-Belarusian Unity and Accord	2
Belarusian Social Democratic Grammada	2
Other parties	7
Independents	95
Unfilled seats	62

Supreme Council assent. Violent demonstrations marked the announcement and signing of the agreement between Yeltsin and Lukashenko creating a Community of Sovereign Republics. More demonstrations followed as the arrest and detention of earlier demonstrators was protested. In June 1996, Sharetsky criticised Lukashenko for not dealing with Belarus's economic collapse and warned that the Supreme Council would take action if Lukashenko did not.

Lukashenko's reaction to the new Supreme Council's election was typical: he tried to increase his powers and create a new parliament over which he would have more control. In late July 1996 Lukashenko announced that he would call a referendum to change the constitution. These changes would lengthen his term of office, create a new two-tier parliament, which would include many presidential nominees, and allow for more presidential control over the appointment of the judiciary. The months that followed Lukashenko's announcement of the referendum were marked by political turmoil. Deputies tried to gather signatures to begin impeachment proceedings. The Supreme Council wrangled with Lukashenko over the questions on the referendum. Prime Minister Mikhail Chyhir resigned on the eve of the referendum in November in protest at the questions. The international community was scathing of the questions on the referendum and the voting procedures. Russia tried unsuccessfully to mediate between Lukashenko and the Supreme Council so as to head off a total breakdown in relations. Voters finally chose between two draft constitutions: the Supreme Council's and Lukashenko's. The Supreme Council also had questions on the ballot proposing that there be elections to local authorities and on the budget. Lukashenko added questions on changing the national holiday to a date commemorating Belarus's Soviet past, on stopping the sale of private property and on the death penalty. Lukashenko's constitution and proposals won the day, although the vote is of dubious validity. The 'passage' of the new constitution gives Lukashenko the power to shape Belarusian politics as he wills. It remains to be seen if he will be able to use these powers. Whether he does or not, the future of Belarus looks bleak. The Community of Sovereign Republics has disappeared from the Russian political agenda since the presidential elections, and does not look likely to provide Belarus with an economic lifeboat. Belarus has nothing to offer Russia but territory; Russia already has the use of military facilities in Belarus and thus has no need of the area for strategic advantage. Belarus is most likely fated to further economic decline, a weak nation-state with an authoritarian President.

Moldova

Moldova continued to move away from the political positions adopted by the pro-Romanian PFM in the struggle for independence during 1994. Elections to a new legislature, the Parlamentul (parliament), were held in February 1994 and a new Constitution was adopted in July. The rapprochement between the Moldovan majority and the Russian and Gagauz minorities continued slowly and there has been no resumption of armed conflict between Moldova and Transdnestr.

The February 1994 elections completed the removal of the PFM from power. The new Parlamentul was elected by PR with a 4 per cent threshold. Only four parties managed to cross this threshold (see Table 11.12). The high vote and victory for the Democratic Agrarian Party of Moldova (DAPM) makes the 1994 Moldovan elections unique among the NIS countries that we are covering since it unambiguously returned a ruling party to power. The DAPM's electoral success reflected popular disenchantment with the PFM, a desire for continued consensus politics among ethnic elites, and the party's strength among rural leaders, and hence rural voters. The PFM, retitled the Christian Democratic Popular Front (CDPF), slumped, and fell behind the Congress of Peasants and Intellectuals, a more moderate pro-Romanian group founded by PFM dissidents. The Socialist Party and Yedinstvo won backing from those parts of the urban population that had suffered most from economic reform, and from Russian and Gagauz voters.[52] Support for Moldova as an inde-pendent state and the political decline of pro-Romanian political groups were further confirmed by a referendum held on 6 March. Just over 75 per cent of registered voters participated, with 95 per cent of them rejecting reunification with Romania in favour of independence.

The referendum and election results meant that there was no political change. The DAPM majority ensured the return to power of the Sangheli government and Lucinschi was re-elected Chair of the Parlamentul. The Parlamentul went on to ratify agreements and legislation delayed by the PFM's boycott of the legislature in 1993. Moldova's membership of the CIS and the treaty on CIS economic union were ratified in April. A new

---

Textbox 11.7 Main events in Moldova, 1994 to June 1996

1994

February	Elections to the new Parlamentul (parliament). Agrarian Party wins most seats.
March	Referendum shows that majority favour independence and are against unification with Romania.
April	Parlamentul votes to join CIS. President Snegur and Igor Smirnov (leader of Transdnestr) issue a declaration on solving the Transdnestr problem.
July	New constitution introduced after Parlamentul vote.
October	Agreement with Russia on withdrawal of 14th Army from Transdnestr.
December	Law passed giving extensive rights to the Gagauz.

1995

March	Large demonstrations by students, workers and others in Chişinău over language, cultural and educational issues. Parliament approves privatisation plans.
April	Voters in Transdnestr oppose the withdrawal of Russian troops in referendum. Agrarian Party wins nearly half of seats in local elections. Separate elections in Transdnestr are won by the Patriotic Bloc.
June	General Lebed resigns as commander of 14th Army to go into Russian politics. 14th Army is downgraded to an operational group. Moldova joins Council of Europe.
July	Snegur resigns from the Democratic Agrarian Party to form a new, presidential party, the Party of Rebirth and Consolidation. Accuses the Agrarian Party of trying to weaken the presidency. Prime Minister Andrei Sangheli becomes leader of Agrarian Party.
August	Snegur elected chair of the Party of Rebirth and Consolidation.
November	Russian Duma passes a resolution declaring that Transdnestr is of strategic interest to Russia.
December	Voters in Transdnestr ratify a constitution that declares the region independent and vote to join the CIS.

1996

March	Snegur tries to remove Defence Minister by decree.
April	Constitutional Court rules that Snegur's removal of the Defence Minister is unconstitutional.
June	Transdnestr accepts status as a republic within Moldova, but the agreement is not signed into law. Parlamentul sets 17 November as the date for presidential elections.

Table 11.12 Moldovan election, February 1994

	% vote	Seats
DAPM	43.2	54
Yedinstvo/Socialist bloc	22.0	27
Congress of Peasants and Intellectuals	9.2	11
Christian Democratic Popular Front	7.5	9

Source: King (1995, p. 11).

constitution was passed in July with guarantees on the rights of ethnic minorities. The new constitution did not solve the question of Transdnestr's status, although it provides for Transdnestrian autonomy. Various agreements have been reached with Russia over troop withdrawals. The implementation of these agreements has been blocked by Transdnestr's leaders, who have been unwilling to cede authority to Chișinău.[53] Transdnestr held parallel local elections to Moldova's in March and April 1995, and a referendum on troop withdrawals (93 per cent of voters objected to plans to withdraw the 14th Army). The Patriotic Bloc, which favours Transdnestrian independence and the restoration of the USSR, won most seats with 90 per cent of the vote. In December 1995, Transdnestr held another referendum, this time on the area's status and constitution, and elections to a regional parliament. A constitution declaring Transdnestr an independent state was approved by 82 per cent of voters, with 89 per cent voting for Transdnestr to join the CIS. The elections were won again by the Patriotic Bloc. Moldova declared both the referendums and elections unconstitutional. Negotiations eventually led to Transdnestr being recognised as a republic within Moldova in June 1996. This agreement has yet to become law however, and the Russian withdrawal from the area is not complete.

The greater stability brought to Moldovan politics by the elections and new constitution lasted until mid-1995 when President Snegur quit the DAPM. Snegur accused the government of trying to reduce his powers and of not being fully committed to economic reform. In August, Snegur formed and was elected head of a new party, the Rebirth and Consolidation Party. Snegur's action exposed a split within the DAPM leadership between himself, Prime Minister Sangheli and Parlamentul Chairman Lucinschi. All three were manoeuvring for advantage in the presidential elections scheduled for late 1996 and trying to set up parties as electoral vehicles. Lucinschi has connections to the left-wing Party of Social Progress (established in January 1995). Sangheli commands the DAPM's support and became its leader after Snegur's resignation. By forming his own party Snegur was trying to put some ideological distance between himself and the other two contenders. He also created open conflict between his office, the government and the DAPM. The DAPM faction in the Parlamentul voted three pro-Snegur deputies out of their posts as Deputy Chair of the Parlamentul and heads of Parlamentul commissions. The Constitutional Court reinstated them, but the DAPM faction repeated the vote and dismissed them again. In October, Snegur used demonstrations over living standards and the name given to the language in the constitution (it is listed as Moldovan, but student protesters favour Romanian) to pressure the government: demonstrations ended with a promise of a debate in the Parlamentul on the government's performance. Relations between Snegur and the government worsened in March 1996 when Snegur tried to dismiss the Defence Minister by decree. Snegur was forced to reinstate the minister after government protests to the Constitutional Court led to its ruling that Snegur's decree was unconstitutional.

Snegur's attempt to distance himself from the DAPM and support for some opposition demands on the name of the state language paid few dividends. Snegur gained the support of the CDPF for the presidential elections that were held in November and December 1996 and this helped him to take the lead in the first round of voting, with 38 per cent of the vote. The DAPM candidate, Prime Minister Sangheli, was undermined by corruption scandals and came fourth. Sangheli's poor showing helped Parlamentul Chairman Lucinschi secure second place in the first round vote with 27 per cent of the vote (the third place candidate was Communist Party candidate and an ethnic Russian; there were nine candidates in all). By coming second and securing a place in the second-round vote, Lucinschi found himself in an analogous position to that of Kuchma in Ukraine in 1994. His share of the vote grew by a far larger proportion than that of the first round leader, Snegur, as voters who had supported the Communist candidate or who were fearful of the more nationalist Snegur transferred their allegiance to him. In the second round vote Lucinschi beat Snegur with 54 per cent of the vote. But despite the fact that the incumbent lost, Lucinschi's victory means political continuity. The position of the DAPM as the dominant party has not been seriously altered, and Lucinschi will not introduce radical economic reform. Relations with Russia will be close and may threaten Moldovan sovereignty as the opposition claimed in the presidential campaign. However, this threat will probably not amount to much more than has already been suffered since independence because of Russian interference in Transdenstr.

Conclusion

The length of time that it took to put into place new constitutions and elect new parliaments, and the rocky relationship between executives and parliaments throughout the region, makes it difficult to assert with any degree of confidence that democracy is safely and widely installed outside the Baltic republics. In the Baltic republics there is still a considerable amount to be done before democracy is consolidated fully: Estonia and Latvia have weak party systems, fragile coalition governments and are effectively mono-ethnic polities; the Lithuanian party system is unproven, while the country faces the prospect of the Saeima and presidency falling under the control of opposing political forces.

Despite their problems, the political systems of the Baltic states are effective representative democracies in comparison to the rest of the NIS. Politicians in Russia, Ukraine, Belarus and Moldova are to a greater or lesser extent still unaccountable to their electorates, or to any other regulatory mechanism such as the law. They thus resemble the descriptions of presidentialism and 'delegative democracy' given in Chapter 7. The powers of presidents are generally strong, and incumbents have tended to rule as they see 'fit, constrained only by the hard facts of existing power relations and by a constitutionally limited term of office'.[54] Constraints, such as they are, have usually only been negative: rulers have been held in check by the balance of forces among elites. There are few positive constraints, such as constitutional and institutional constraints, on presidents and executives. Where the latter exist, ways around them have often been found. Presidents have used threats – like the calls for referendums by President Kuchma of Ukraine during the debate over the new Ukrainian constitution – and have used the resources of their office – like Russia's Boris Yeltsin during the 1996 election – to maintain or increase their power. The power of executives is a recurring issue throughout the political systems of the NIS, with elites controlling politics and the distribution of resources, like mini-presidents, at local level. With so much power and influence resting in the hands of individuals, it should not be surprising that corruption and abuse of power is rife. President Lukashenko of Belarus is the worst of the bunch, but he is not alone.

Can the situation be saved? Quick and uniform change is probably unlikely. However, there are now more potential sources of change than existed a few years ago. Pressures may develop on some leaders in the region to control elites and corruption. Alternatively, and this would be best, society may find some new organisational vehicles or popular voices to help correct the flawed democratic polities of Russia, Ukraine, Belarus and Moldova.

Notes

1. For a fuller description of *krysha*, see Shlyapentokh (1996).
2. For more on the constitution, see Thorson (1993); Lane and Ross (1995, pp. 18–19).
3. T. D. Clark (1995b, pp. 379–82).
4. Fish (1995b, pp. 345–6).
5. Yeltsin's personal approval rating dropped from 30 to 20 per cent between the autumn of 1993 and the spring of 1994; the number of people who thought that he should resign rose from 29 to 40 per cent; 32 per cent of people thought Yeltsin and his coterie to blame

'for the fact that democracy in Russia is being defeated', only 12 per cent blamed Chernomyrdin and the government. See Aron (1995, pp. 327–9).

6. Åslund (1995, pp. 201–2).
7. The section below draws on Gelman and Senatova (1995).
8. See Kryukov and Moe (1996).
9. More details on the Civic Accord can be found in Tolz (1994).
10. See Teague (1994).
11. See Schneider (1995, pp. 158–60) for a fuller exposition of the argument that follows.
12. The FSB was one of the successor organisations to the KGB and was responsible for internal security. At the time the Chechen war broke out the FSB was called the FSK, the Federal Counter-intelligence Service. We use its current name throughout to avoid confusion.
13. This section draws on Baev (1996, pp. 141–8).
14. Human rights abuses in Chechnya are detailed in Bovay (1995).
15. On international reaction to Chechnya, see Kuzio (1995b and 1996).
16. For a more detailed analysis of the foundation of Our Home is Russia, see Belin (1995).
17. For a fuller discussion of the CPRF, see Sakwa (1996).
18. At the time of writing there are only a few published analyses of the 1995 election, for example Buzgalin and Kolganov (1996); Kagarlitsky (1996); and Oates (1996). This chapter also draws on Wyman (1996).
19. Wyman (1996, p. 3).
20. Orttung (1996, p. 8).
21. *Ibid.*, p. 7.
22. Sakwa (1996, p. 23).
23. Wilson (1995, p. 364). This section draws on the descriptions of parties and their programmes in Wasylyk (1994) and Kuzio (1995a).
24. For fuller analysis of the Rada elections see Arel and Wilson (1994); Birch (1995, 1996b and 1997); Kuzio (1995a); Wilson (1995).
25. Birch (1996a).
26. Holdar (1995, pp. 123–30).
27. Birch (1995, p. 95); Arel and Wilson (1994, p. 14).
28. For details see Wilson (1995, p. 366).
29. The best description of electoral platforms in the presidential race can be found in Birch (forthcoming).
30. The next section draws on Bojcun (1995, pp. 77–82).
31. Norgaard *et al.* (1996, pp. 200–2).
32. *Ibid.*, p. 196
33. Taagepera (1995, p. 329).
34. Arter (1996, p. 258).
35. Melvin (1995, p. 50); Norgaard *et al.* (1996, p. 202).
36. Bungs (1994a).
37. Bungs (1994b).
38. Girnius (1995a, p. 15).
39. Dreifelds (1996, pp. 95–6).
40. For a fuller analysis of Latvian economic trends between 1994 and 1996, see Paeglis (1995).
41. Dreifelds (1996, p. 96).
42. See Davies and Ozolins (1996).
43. Norgaard *et al.* (1996, p. 76).

44. This section draws on Girnius (1995b).
45. Norgaard *et al.* (1996, p. 95).
46. Markus (1995, p. 47).
47. Markus (1994b); Zaprudnik and Fedor (1995, p. 57).
48. Markus (1994c, pp. 5–6).
49. Markus (1995, p. 48).
50. See Markus (1996).
51. See King (1995, pp. 9–11); Socor (1994b).
52. King (1995, p. 23).
53. See Ionescu and Munteanu (1996).
54. O'Donnell (1994, p. 59).

CHAPTER 12

The new democracies of Eastern Europe

Introduction

Two main questions must be highlighted about the progress of the countries under review in the mid-1990s. The first – most relevant for some of the former Yugoslav states, Albania and Romania – is whether democracy had successfully been established at all. Many of the problems relating to the personalisation of politics outlined at the beginning of Chapter 11 apply, albeit to a somewhat lesser degree, to many of the states of South-Eastern Europe. The second question, more appropriate for the countries of East-Central Europe, is whether or not their democracies were being consolidated.

One test for determining whether a democracy has been consolidated is the 'two turnover' test suggested by Samuel P. Huntington. By this criterion a consolidation is achieved 'if the party or group that takes power in the initial election at the time of transition loses a subsequent election and turns over power to those election winners, and if those election winners then peacefully turn over power to the winners of a later election'.[1] No post-communist country has yet had time to progress this far, but Hungary and Poland were half-way there: elections passed power to post-communist parties, and there were reasons to expect that they would hand it back if they lost the subsequent election. The Czech Republic and Slovenia also had good chances of 'passing' the test as the time came at some point in the future, while Slovakia was in a rather curious position. Although power had changed hands at both the 1992 and 1994 elections, in both cases it moved in the same direction. Mečiar's first two governments had been removed from power through losing their support in parliament, only to be returned by the voters at the next elections.

One cannot, therefore, talk about consolidated democracy anywhere in the region, yet there were some signs of stabilisation. An example of this is provided by Table 12.1, which presents electoral turnouts in most of the elections held in the area in the seven years which started with Solidarity's

Table 12.1 Electoral turnout in post-communist Eastern Europe

	1989	1990	1991	1992	1993	1994	1995	1996
Albania			99	90				80
Bulgaria		90	80	P75		74		P63
Croatia		85		75			69	
CSFR		96		85				
Czech Rep.		97		85				76
E. Germany		93 Mar.				73		
		75 Dec.						
Hungary		65				69		
Macedonia		85				76		
Montenegro		75						67
Poland	62	P61	43		52		P65	
Romania		86		73				73
Serbia		72		69	62			
Slovakia		95		84		76		
Slovenia				75				74

Where two-round elections were held, the turnout given is for the first round; second round turnouts were always lower.
'P' indicates that the election concerned was a presidential one, without a simultaneous parliamentary election.

election victory in Poland in June 1989. The pattern is one of convergence towards a respectable average of somewhat over 70 per cent.

A second pattern emerges from Table 12.2, which shows the Presidents and Prime Ministers of each state in the region from the time of negotiated revolution until June 1996. It is notable that the turnover of Prime Ministers is relatively high, with the average period in office only just exceeding 18 months. Presidencies were far more stable, however, and a majority of countries had only seen one President in the 1990s. In many cases, this is a positive feature. Men (again, there were no women) such as the Hungarian president Göncz and the Czech President Havel were respected figures who competently fulfilled the role of providing 'checks and balances' in the consolidating democracies. But the phenomenon becomes questionable when dealing with countries where Presidents held more power. In semi-presidential Poland, one of the few countries to see more than one President, the office was successfully transferred from Wałęsa to Kwaśniewski at the end of 1995. President Iliescu of Romania, however, wielded considerable influence over his country's political system for seven years from December 1989. The problem becomes more severe when examining the former Yugoslav republics. While President Gligorov of Macedonia was a point of stability in a country trying to establish democracy in adverse circumstances, President Tudjman of Croatia and President Milošević of Serbia dominated their states' political systems and controlled the rules of the political contest. It was impossible to predict what would happen when they finally left office.

Table 12.2 Prime Ministers and Presidents in post-communist Eastern Europe

State	Prime Minister		President	
Albania	Fatos Nano	May 91	Ramiz Alia	Apr. 91
	Ylli Bufi	June 91	Sali Berisha	Apr. 92
	Vilson Ahmeti	Dec. 91		
	Aleksander Meksi	Apr. 92		
		July 96		
Bosnia-Herzegovina	Jure Pelivan	Dec. 90	Alija Izetbegović	Dec. 90E
	Mile Akmadžić	Nov. 92		
	Haris Silajdžić	Oct. 93		
	Hasan Muratović	Jan. 96		
Bulgaria	Andrey Lukanov	Feb. 90	Petar Mladenov	Nov. 89
		June 90	Zhelyu Zhelev	Aug. 90
	Dimitar Popov	Dec. 90		Jan. 92E
	Filip Dimitrov	Nov. 91		
	Lyuben Berov	Dec. 92		
	Reneta Indzhova	Oct. 94		
	Zhan Videnov	Jan. 95		
Croatia	Stipe Mesić	May 90	Franjo Tudjman	May 90
	Josip Manolić	Aug 90		Aug. 92E
	Franjo Gregurić	July 91		
	Hrvoje Šarinić	Aug. 92		
	Nikica Valentić	Apr. 93		
	Zlatko Matesa	Nov. 95		
Czechoslovakia	Marián Čalfa	Dec. 89	Václav Havel	Dec. 89–
		June 90		July 92
	Jan Stráský	June 92–Dec. 92		
Czech Republic	Petr Pithart	Jan. 90	Václav Havel	Jan. 93–
		June 90		
	Václav Klaus	June 92		
		June 96		
Hungary	József Antall D	May 90	Árpád Göncz	Aug. 90
	Peter Boross	Dec. 93		June 95
	Gyula Horn	June 94		
Macedonia	Nikola Kljušev	Mar. 91	Kiro Gligorov	Jan. 91
	Branko Crvenkovski	Sept. 92		Oct. 94E
		Dec. 94		
Montenegro	Milo Djukanović	Jan. 91	Momir Bulatović	Dec. 90E
		Jan. 93		
		Nov. 96		Jan 93E
Poland	Tadeusz Mazowiecki	Aug. 89	Wojciech Jaruzelski	Aug. 89
	Krzysztof Bielecki	Jan. 91	Lech Wałęsa	Dec. 90E
	Jan Olszewski	Dec. 91	Aleksander	Dec. 95E
	Hanna Suchocka	Jul. 92	Kwaśniewski	
	Waldemar Pawlak	Oct. 93		
	Józef Oleksy	Mar. 95		
	Włodomierz Cimoszewicz	Feb. 96		

Table 12.2 *Continued*

State	Prime Minister		President	
Romania	Petre Roman	Dec. 89	Ion Iliescu	May 90E
		May 90		Oct. 92E
	Theodor Stolojan	Oct. 91	Emil Constantinescu	Nov. 96E
	Nicolae Vacaroiu	Nov. 92		
	Victor Ciorbea	Nov. 96		
Serbia	Dragotin Zelenović	Jan. 91	Slobodan Milošević	May 89
	Radoman Bozović	Dec. 91		Nov. 90E
	Nikola Sainović	Jan. 93		Dec. 92E
	Mirko Marjanović	Feb. 94		
Slovakia	Milan Čić	Dec. 89	Michal Kováč	Feb. 93
	Vladimír Mečiar	June 90		
	Ján Čarnogurský	Apr. 91		
	Vladimír Mečiar	June 92		
	Jozef Moravčík	Mar. 94		
	Vladimír Mečiar	Dec. 94		
Slovenia	Lojže Peterle	May 90	Milan Kučan	Apr. 90E
	Janez Drnovšek	May 92		Dec. 92E
		Jan. 93		
Yugoslavia	Ante Marković	Jan. 89–	Janez Drnovšek	May 89
		Dec. 91	Borisav Jović	May 90
			Stipe Mesić	July 91–
				Dec. 91
Federal Republic	Milan Panić	July 92	Dobrica Ćosić	June 92
of Yugoslavia	Radoje Kontić	Feb. 93	Zoran Lilić	June 93
		Nov. 96		

'E' indicates that the President was directly elected. 'D' indicates that the postholder died in office. Dates given are those of entering office. Dates of leaving office are also given where there was no successor. Underlining indicates parliamentary elections.

In such cases, continuity in the presidency was a sign that the process of democratic consolidation had yet to begin. Power had not even changed hands once.

Albania

Just as Albania had been an exception in Eastern Europe throughout the communist period, so it remained in the mid-1990s. In some respects, progress under the Democratic Party (DP) of Sali Berisha was as satisfactory as could have been expected, yet in the establishment of basic democratic structures, the country was clearly wanting.

Given that the communist Albania of Enver Hoxha had been the most nationalist and isolationist of all the states in Europe, the country was

---

Textbox 12.1 Main events in Albania, 1994–96

1994

April	Former Prime Minister Nano sentenced to twelve years' imprisonment for misappropriating public funds while in office.
July	Former President Alia sentenced to nine years' imprisonment for corruption and human rights abuses.
August	Five ethnic Greek leaders arrested and jailed for spying.
November	The draft constitution of President Berisha is defeated in a popular referendum.
December	The Social Democrats and Republicans leave the Democratic Party government (although one Social Democrat minister leaves the party and remains in government).

1995

September	'Lustration' laws ban former top communist officials and secret police collaborators from public office for six years.

1996

May	President Berisha's Democratic Party wins a two-thirds parliamentary majority in an election marred by the most blatant fraud in post-communist Eastern Europe.

---

surprisingly untroubled by a preoccupation with national identity – perhaps because it had too many other concerns. The division of Albanians themselves into the northern Geg clans and the southern Tosks never became a major political issue, but the country was not without the more usual minority problems, since there was a Greek minority in the south of the country, whose size ranged from 60,000 to 300,000 according to whether Albanian or Greek figures were used. Although relations with Greece were frequently uneasy as a result of disputes about the Greek minority, compromises proved possible. The latent danger of a conflict over the Albanian minorities in former Yugoslavia was also avoided, largely due to government awareness of the country's extreme international vulnerability. This made Albania enthusiastic about NATO membership (it was the first East European country formally to apply), and it was accepted into the organisation's Partnership for Peace in January 1994. In July 1995, it also finally became a member of the Council of Europe, despite earlier doubts regarding Albania's lack of a new constitution and continuing concern about the independence of the judiciary.[2]

On the economic front, some developments were also achieved, and in 1994 inflation was reduced from three to two figures (see Table 10.2). While the economic plight of ordinary citizens cannot be overestimated, it has to be seen in the context of the desperately low level of development both before and during the communist period, and the catastrophe of total collapse which had threatened during 1991 and 1992. While the European Commission's 1996 *Eurobarometer* report showed that in 1995 Albania had had by far the lowest GDP per head in Europe, the Albanians as people showed by far the most optimistic attitudes in the post-communist world.[3] They gave the most positive responses about the direction the country was going in general, about satisfaction with democracy, about respect for human rights, about the advantages of a market economy and about improvement in their personal financial situation in the last and the next year; and they also had the most positive image of the European Union. Yet the sheer consistency of the positive responses gives, above all, an indication of Albanian awareness of the depths from which they were rising. What they do not reveal are the underlying political problems of the country.

The Albanian optimism in general terms was not transferred into overwhelming approval of the government. The Socialist Party of Albania (SPA) began to regain support after its 1992 election defeat, and the popularity of President Berisha waned as criticism of his authoritarian tendencies increased both from the opposition and from within his own party and coalition partners. What was most alarming, however, was Berisha's inclinations to change the rules of the political game when they did not suit him. This emerged on a number of occasions. While Berisha had originally enjoyed the two-thirds majority support in parliament necessary to be elected President after the 1992 elections, he soon lost it, and proved unable to find a draft constitution able to garner the two-thirds of votes necessary for approval by the legislature. He attempted to resolve this problem not by compromise, but by circumventing parliament and putting the constitution to a popular referendum in late 1994, which he lost. This was thought to reflect not so much objections to the content of the constitution as a protest against Berisha's personal style and the corruption of many of the supporters around him.[4] There were, however, also faults in the constitution in that it did not provide for sufficient division of powers: it gave the President not only the right to name the Prime Minister, but also the continued right to propose High Court and Constitutional Court judges to be approved by parliament.[5] Interference with the judiciary was particularly contentious, as Berisha was involved in a protracted battle with the judge who headed the Supreme Court soon after the referendum defeat.[6]

Furthermore, Berisha also took measures which would increase his chances of winning the next election in spite of his declining popularity. Although trials against leading communists such as Ramiz Alia had already been completed, 'lustration' laws against former leading communists and informers were adopted the autumn before the election, which debarred a rather large number of likely candidates from running for parliament, often on the grounds of dubious evidence.[7] The election laws themselves were also amended so that 115 rather than 100 of the 140 parliamentary seats were to be elected in single-member constituencies, thereby substantially reducing the PR element of seat distribution. This was an attempt to ensure the DP not only a majority in parliament, but also the two-thirds majority necessary to change the constitution. Such a high majority is almost impossible for any single party to achieve in a democracy.

The culmination of all Berisha's dubious measures were the elections themselves. Allegations of intimidation began before the elections, and the opposition made the mistake of protesting against irregularities on election day by abandoning polling stations several hours before balloting finished, so that the count itself took place without any supervision. When the DP announced it had won the election within a few hours of the close of voting – in a country without sophisticated computer equipment or exit polling, and with an electoral system based on individual constituency results and second round run-offs – Albania's democratic credentials collapsed.[8] The official results of the election are given in Table 12.3, not because they are assumed to reflect accurately the way Albanians voted, but because they affected the composition of the new government formed.

Table 12.3 Albanian election, 26 May/2 June/16 June 1996

	No. of seats
Democratic Party of Albania	122
Socialist Party of Albania	10
Republican Party	3
Party for the Defence of Rights and Freedoms (Greek party)	3
Balli Kombëtar	2
Total	140

Source: OMRI Daily Digest, Part II, 24 June 1996.

Whatever Albania's relative successes in controlling national conflict and starting the long, uphill struggle of economic recovery, it had thus far failed in the fundamental task of creating democratic institutions.

Bulgaria

Bulgaria commenced 1994 in a rather ambivalent position, since it had made no great progress in its post-communist transition, but it had at least managed to avoid manifest signs of instability. Politics, while contentious, remained non-violent, in contrast to its neighbours Yugoslavia and Romania and its own pre-communist past.

Textbox 12.2 Main events in Bulgaria, 1994–96

1994

February	Bulgaria joins NATO's Partnership for Peace.
September	Berov's government resigns.
October	An interim government appointed with Indzhova as Prime Minister.
December	The Bulgarian Socialist Party (BSP) and its smaller coalition partners win a parliamentary majority in elections. Dimitrov replaced by Kostov as Chair of Union of Democratic Forces.

1995

January	Videnov, the BSP leader, becomes Prime Minister.
November	The BSP maintain their vote in local elections, but fail to win in Sofia and several other major cities.

1996

June	The opposition hold a primary election to choose their presidential candidate, and the incumbent Zhelev loses to Stoyanov.
November	Stoyanov wins the presidential election in a second-round run-off. Against a background of severe economic problems, the future of the BSP Videnov government is placed in question.

The basic structure of Bulgaria's emergent party system bore some resemblance to that in Romania, although it was less fragmented.[9] The major division was between, on the one hand, a larger, more nationalist and economically left-wing post-communist faction, mainly represented by the Bulgarian Socialist Party (BSP), and on the other hand, a somewhat smaller and rather heterogeneous umbrella organisation of new and historic parties represented by the Union of Democratic Forces (UDF). The dilemma which faced UDF politicians was that uniting in the face of the powerful BSP enemy, while appearing in some respects a sensible tactic, had disadvantages as well, since much effort had to be spent on internal negotiations. The diversity of views held by UDF member organisations, as well as the fact that it was hard to gauge the strength of individual parties, also made it very difficult for them to present the electorate with a programmatically coherent alternative to the BSP. Their platform was therefore based rather generally on rejection of the communist past and opposition to the BSP. Politics in Bulgaria, as in Romania and Slovakia, tended to be a stand-off between two factions who both claimed the mantle of democracy, and who both maintained that they represented the best interests of the people while the other side merely damaged them. More complex articulation of interests, while not absent, was subordinate to the general battle between the two polarised political groups. A final element, which the Bulgarian party system had in common with Romania and Slovakia, was that a substantial ethnic minority from the former ruling imperial masters – in the Bulgarian case Turks rather than Hungarians – voted for its own party. Arithmetically, the existence of this third 'alien' political grouping radically increased the likelihood of parliament being deadlocked in a situation where no one had a legislative majority.

This was precisely what had happened in Bulgaria after the 1991 elections, where first a UDF government ruled with informal support from the Turkish Movement for Rights and Freedoms (MRF), and then the government of the independent Berov took over in what bore more resemblance to a BSP government with informal MRF support. Berov finally resigned in September 1994, and an interim Prime Minister, Reneta Indzhova, took over until elections were held in December.

The elections produced a clear majority for the BSP under the leadership of Zhan Videnov, which gained 44 per cent of the vote and 125 of the parliament's 240 seats (see Table 12.4).[10] The BSP stood in coalition with two small left-wing splinters from other parties, the Political Club Ecoglasnost, which received the Environment Ministry in the new government, and the Bulgarian Agrarian National Union-Aleksandar Stamboliiski, which received the Agricultural Ministry and a deputy premiership. (The latter was but one of many Bulgarian parties carrying the BANU label; Bulgaria spawned agrarian parties claiming the heritage of the interwar BANU in the same way that Romania produced a myriad of supposedly liberal parties.) The UDF did worse in the elections, having lost 10 per cent of the total electorate since 1991. This was due to the increased popularity of the BSP, and to the fact that the UDF had shed some of its members before the election. Since 1992, the UDF had been divided into a hardline 'dark blue' and strongly anti-communist core under the UDF leader Filip Dimitrov (who resigned after the 1994 election defeat), and a moderate 'pale blue' wing which was less nationalist, more liberal politically, and less intransigently anti-communist. It was UDF defectors from the latter wing which formed the mainstay of two new parties which fought the 1994 elections. The left-of-centre Democratic Alternative for the Republic, which aimed at reconciliation between the two main blocs in Bulgarian politics, narrowly failed to enter parliament with 3.79 per cent of the vote. However, the right-of-centre People's Union (PU) was more successful. This had been formed from a merger of the Democratic Party, a major UDF party which had left the organisation just before the elections, and the largest of the many BANUs. It was right-wing economically and strongly supported the privatisation of industry and agriculture, but it lacked the dogmatic anti-communism of the UDF hardliners. Two other parties entered parliament.

Table 12.4 Bulgarian election, 18 December 1994

	% vote	Seats
Bulgarian Socialist Party (with coalition partners)	44	125
Union of Democratic Forces	24	69
People's Union	7	18
Movement for Rights & Freedoms	5	15
Bulgarian Business Bloc	5	13
Others	16	0
Total		240

Source: Darzhaven Vestnik, 31 December 1994, pp. 9–10; Engelbrekt (1995, pp. 19–22).

One, predictably, was the MRF, although its vote had decreased since the previous elections. It had been affected by splits, and the Turkish electorate were disoriented by the support the MRF had given indirectly to the BSP by voting with the Berov government.[11] The other new party to enter parliament was the Bulgarian Business Bloc under the returned émigré, Georges Ganchev. Although its voters were largely young and moderately well educated, the party was right-wing populist and attracted a protest vote from people disillusioned by the performance of the more established political parties.

The 1994 elections indicated that there was some structuring to the Bulgarian party system, with a strong left-wing party pitted against parties representing individual strands of opposition to it.[12] There were also demographic differences between the voters of the various parties. Like most post-communist parties, the BSP was more successful among older people, and there was a notable urban–rural cleavage, with the UDF doing best in the capital Sofia and other large cities.[13]

Videnov's first year in power was not unsuccessful, and the BSP maintained its vote in the November 1995 local elections. Economically, inflation was under control, being measured in two rather than three figures in 1995, and politically, the European Commission's *Eurobarometer* survey showed that public satisfaction with democracy was rising, albeit from a startling low.[14] (In 1994, Bulgaria had produced the lowest rating ever for anywhere in the post-communist world, including the normally more pessimistic former Soviet Union, when 87 per cent more respondents had given negative than positive replies when asked if they were satisfied with the way democracy was developing.) However, by early 1996, it was clear that the economy was deteriorating seriously, as the currency fell, prices rose, shops were hit by bread shortages and there was a wave of strikes.[15] The BSP was caught in what was to become a classic dilemma of post-communist parties who became election victors: it could not deliver on its promises, and the party became divided between conservatives who still wished to try and modernisers who knew that urgent solutions were needed to the country's economic travails.

Politically, the rapid economic collapse was unfortunate for the BSP because 1996 was an election year, with presidential elections due in late

October. Just at a time when the BSP was in disarray, the opposition showed signs of organisation, with the UDF and PU agreeing on the original idea of arranging a primary election open to all voters to choose their joint candidate for presidency. Each group selected one candidate, and the MRF also joined in the procedure, advising its supporters to choose between the two according to their conscience.[16] The primary took place in June, with a 12 per cent turnout, and appeared to have been successful in persuading the incumbent President, Zhelev – who was opposed by the UDF – not to stand, as he was defeated by almost 2 to 1 by the UDF's Petar Stoyanov. It was Stoyanov and his vice-presidential candidate Kavaldzhiev who won the presidency against the BSP contenders in a second round in early November 1996 (see Table 12.5).

The fact that, in 1996, Bulgaria was beset by economic difficulties while the political situation showed some signs of stabilisation was indicative of a deeper, underlying problem. This was that in many respects, relatively little had actually changed in Bulgaria since 1990. A consequence of the communist-led democratisation that had taken place at the turn of the decade was that the BSP, although led by a young man, still contained many leading figures and government ministers with pasts in the higher echelons of the communist *nomenklatura*, and it was not really a modern Social Democratic Party. The UDF's period in office had been very short, and the 'technocratic' governments had, like the BSP governments, mainly comprised members of the previous elites (and, indeed, this was also true of the UDF itself). Since almost all the modernisation processes which had taken place in Bulgaria so far had occurred during the communist regime, there was very little experience available to suggest how transformation might be effected using any other procedures.

Table 12.5 Bulgarian presidential election, 24 October/3 November 1996

	% vote	
	Round 1	*Round 2*
Petar Stoyanov/Todor Kavaldzhiev (UDF)	44	60
Ivan Marazov/Irina Bokova (BSP)	27	40
Georges Ganchev/Arlin Antonov (BBB)	22	
Others	7	

Source: OMRI Daily Digest, Part II, 30 October 1996; *OMRI Daily Digest*, Part II, 4 November 1996.

Czech Republic

By 1996, the Czech Republic had clearly emerged as the most stable and economically successful of the former Soviet bloc countries, which was a considerable achievement for a state that had technically existed for less than

---

Textbox 12.3 Main events in the Czech Republic, 1994–96

1994

March   The Czech Republic joins NATO's Partnership for Peace.
November   Local elections indicate that the Civic Democratic Party (CDP)
               is still clearly the most popular.

1995

October   The Czech crown becomes convertible.
November   The Czech Republic becomes the first post-communist country
               to join the OECD.
               The small Christian Democratic Party merges with the CDP,
               with whom it ran in the 1992 elections.

1996

January   The Czech Republic applies to join the European Union.
June   Elections return Klaus's centre-right government coalition to
               power, but a strong vote for the Social Democrats deprives it of
               its parliamentary majority.
November   In the first elections for the parliament's upper chamber, the
               three government parties obtain a majority, but there is no CDP
               landslide despite the use of a majoritarian voting system.

---

four years. However, it may be argued that what this indicated was not the consummate skill of Czech politicians, so much as the importance of pre-communist traditions in determining the fate of post-communist states. In political, social and economic terms, the Czechs had been the most advanced nation to undergo communist rule, and it had emerged from the communist period with (by communist standards) a high standard of living and a low level of international debt.[17] This enabled them within just a few years to overcome the structural problems derived from having had an exceptionally rigid communist government, and to achieve the distinction of becoming the first post-communist state admitted to the OECD. In all predictions of the post-communist states most likely to be accepted into NATO and the European Union in the first wave, the Czech Republic featured as a firm candidate. However, Czech aspirations frequently appeared to be even more ambitious, with the Czech Prime Minister Václav Klaus aiming for Czech admission to the EU before any of the country's Visegrad partners. The frantic Czech efforts to return to where they had once belonged – which had been embodied in Civic Forum's 1990 election slogan 'Back to Europe' – on occasion led them to underestimate the disadvantages inherited from forty years of communist rule, and the extent to which their market economy was only in its infancy.

From the point of view of political analysis, the 'normality' of the Czech party system according to West European standards was demonstrated by the fact that it was structured around a left–right cleavage based on economic interests.[18] The 1992 elections had produced a governing coalition of centre-right parties with a parliamentary majority, but the existence of a clear left–right cleavage in Czech politics was only really to emerge in the course of the parliament's term as it became increasingly obvious that the opposition to the government was consolidating around the Czech Social Democratic Party. While the Social Democrats had only obtained about 7 per cent of the vote in 1992, their popularity rose steadily thereafter, and by early summer 1995, opinion polls indicated that they were supported by about 20 per cent of the electorate, compared to just over 25 per cent for Klaus's Civic Democratic Party (CDP), the largest of the governing parties.[19] This was a particularly significant development because it was the only example in the post-communist world of a major left-wing party which was social democratic in origin rather than being a communist successor party.[20]

The reasons why this happened in the Czech Republic were twofold. First, because the Czech Lands had been relatively modern and industrial in the pre-communist period, Social Democracy had a firm history in the area. The party had been founded in the nineteenth century, and had been a regular partici-pant in Czechoslovak governments between the wars.[21] Secondly, the Prague Spring and Warsaw Pact invasion in 1968 had led to the Czechoslovak Com-munist Party being purged of most of its more dynamic, reform-minded elements (particularly in the Czech rather than the Slovak Republic). A consequence of this was that the Czech communist successor party had proved exceptionally impervious to 'social-democratisation' of the type that had taken place in Hungary, Slovakia and Poland. Even when reformist elements had broken away from the Communist Party – as many of its parliamentary deputies did after 1992 – they had been unable to carry the electorate with them. This was in some measure because the industrial nature of pre-war Czech society had also meant that communism had indigenous roots there. The Communist Party had been strong in the interwar period, and had performed well in the fairly free 1946 elections, obtaining 40 per cent of the vote in the Czech part of the country. This continuity was most clearly demonstrated by the fact that the Communist Party of Bohemia and Moravia, which regained parliamentary representation in 1996, was the only communist successor party in Eastern Europe which still retained the label 'communist' in its official designation.

The results of the June 1996 Czech elections (shown in Table 12.6) were interesting for a number of reasons. Klaus's centre-right coalition government was returned to power with all three constituent parties maintaining or slightly

Table 12.6 Czech election, 31 May–1 June 1996

	% vote	Seats
Civic Democratic Party	30	68
Czech Social Democratic Party	26	61
Communist Party of Bohemia and Moravia	10	22
Christian Democratic Union-Czech People's Party	8	18
Association for the Republic-Republican Party of Czechoslovakia	8	18
Civic Democratic Alliance	6	13
Others	11	0
Total		200

Source: Czech press, 2 June 1996.

increasing their 1992 percentage of the vote, which was an admirable achievement considering that governments dedicated to market reforms had been ejected by the electorate at the earliest opportunity almost everywhere else in the post-communist world. However, what was a triumph in the international context actually appeared like a defeat within the Czech Republic. First, despite maintaining its percentage of the vote, the government only obtained 99 of the 200 seats, and thereby lost its parliamentary majority. The reason for this was that elections were conducted by proportional representation with a 5 per cent threshold, and in 1996 a smaller number of votes than in 1992 were 'wasted' by being given to parties with less than 5 per cent. Secondly, the personal victory of the elections belonged to the Social Democrat leader Miloš Zeman, whose party had quadrupled its vote in four years and surpassed all expectations by gaining a mere 3 per cent less of the vote than Klaus's CDP.

A weakness in the Czech political landscape, which led to a minority government having to be formed in spite of the fact that the party system was relatively clearly divided between a centre-right government and a left-wing social democratic opposition, was that nearly 20 per cent of the vote had gone to two parties which were not considered as acceptable coalition partners by either of the two main factions. The communists had obtained over 10 per cent of the vote, and the openly racist Republicans over 8 per cent. Until these parties' voters could be integrated into the mainstream of Czech politics, the chances of either a left- or right-wing government obtaining a parliamentary majority were reduced.

There were, however, other reasons why the Czech Republic could not maintain that it had completed the transition – or, in the Czech case, the reversion – to being a standard West European country. It can be argued that the government's electoral success (in comparison to the performance of leaders implementing economic reform elsewhere in the post-communist world) was to a considerable extent due to the fact that it protected much of the population from the hardships of 'shock therapy'. State subsidies for rents and utilities remained; the state paid mothers four years' maternity benefit; and the exceptionally low unemployment rate of around 3 per cent was possible in part because large enterprises were shielded from bankruptcy by indirect state control via investment funds and banks. Klaus's predilection for using Thatcherite rhetoric to lend legitimacy to his economic reforms disguised the fact that the Czech Republic still bore more resemblance to a social welfare state than a *laissez-faire* market economy.[22] It was, therefore, the period after the 1996 elections which would demonstrate how far Czech parties labelling themselves as 'right' were actually prepared to go in this direction. However, since they were now operating with a minority government, any moderation of right-wing principles could be assigned to the need for some compromise with the Social Democrats.

Generally, the reactions to the results of the 1996 elections to the lower chamber showed that the Czech political system had considerable reserves for adapting to the unexpected. Klaus's minority government proved willing to negotiate some issues with the Social Democrat leader Zeman, who was made Chair of the parliament. The elections to the upper chamber, or Senate, which had been delayed until November 1996, also demonstrated some sophistication on the part of the electorate, despite a disappointingly low turnout of 35 per cent. Voters were faced for the first time with a majoritarian election system, where the leading two candidates fought a second round in 78 of 81 constituencies where no one had obtained 50 per cent in the first round. After a substantial CDP lead in the first round, supporters of other parties banded together in the second round to deprive Klaus of an overall majority (see Table 12.7). Despite the fifth of voters who had chosen 'anti-system' parties in June 1996, an overwhelming majority of citizens were firmly committed to democracy to a greater extent than elsewhere in the post-communist world.

Table 12.7 Czech Senate election, 15–16/22–23 November 1996

	Seats
Civic Democratic Party	32
Czech Social Democratic Party	26
Christian Democratic Union	13
Civic Democratic Alliance	7
Communist Party of Bohemia and Moravia	2
Democratic Union	1
Total	81

Source: OMRI Daily Digest, Part II, 25 November 1996.

Eastern Germany

Since the GDR's adoption by an EC member state in 1990, it has become increasingly rare for developments in eastern Germany to be discussed together with those elsewhere in the post-communist world, rather than as an aspect of the domestic politics of the Federal Republic of Germany. The area of the former GDR is almost never included in multinational surveys of attitudes and lifestyles of citizens in post-communist societies. This exclusion is partly a rational reflection of the fact that the conditions of post-communist transition in eastern Germany diverge so greatly from those elsewhere that meaningful comparison is impossible, since it is distorted by there being too many variables. However, the east German case remains of some interest as an 'ideal type' of post-communist transition in which western structures and legislation were directly transferred to a post-communist state, with all the rights and obligations this entailed. Further, the enormous economic cost for the Federal Republic of Germany of modernising the area's infrastructure presaged the expense which the European Union would have to face in the case of the accession of independent East-Central European states.[23]

The eastern German case is also of relevance for examining the 'fit' of a typical western party system when superimposed on a post-communist society.[24] Eastern Germany did not, by East European standards, have a complex cleavage structure and would have been likely, even as an independent state, to develop a right–left divide based on divergent economic interests. It was ethnically highly homogeneous, had relatively low regional and urban/rural disparities in the standard of living, and was Protestant and secular in its religious orientation. When compared to the west German electorate, however, there were several major differences in voting patterns confirmed by the 1994 elections. These are shown by Table 12.8, which shows the vote of the electorate in the east separately, although – unlike in the 1990 Federal elections – this was not a distinction which existed in electoral law. The first is that the vote for the right-of-centre Christian Democrats (CDU) was 4 percentage points lower in east than west. This difference is actually rather small when one considers the lower incomes of most east Germans, the fact that they were more likely to benefit from state intervention in the economy, and the demographic lack in the former GDR of part of the CDU's core electorate – Catholics and practising Protestants. This suggests that the CDU vote is bolstered by issues such as the perceived economic competence of the government, and an emotive desire to push towards a market economy. A higher percentage of workers voted for the CDU in the east than in the west. The Social Democratic Party (SPD) vote was nearly 6 percentage points lower in the east than in the west,[25] but this fact is easily explained, since nearly 18 per cent of the east German vote went to the post-communist Party of Democratic Socialism (PDS).[26] Although the PDS vote was partly a protest vote by east Germans who resented the extent to which their country had been 'taken over' by west Germany, it also reflected the social welfare agenda in the minds of the electorate. It was this that had helped post-communist parties to power in, for example, Poland and Hungary. Finally, it must be noted that both the

Table 12.8 German election, 16 October 1994

	% vote east	% vote total	Total seats
Christian Democratic Union[a]	38	41	294
Social Democratic Party of Germany	31	36	252
Party of Democratic Socialism	20	4	30
Greens	4	7	49
Free Democratic Party	4	7	47
Others	2	4	0
Total			672

a. In Bavaria, the Christian Social Union.
Source: Calculated from Golz (1994, pp. 1129–30).

Free Democrats (FDP) and the Greens polled worse in the east than in the west. The weakness of the Greens reflects the limited appeal of the 'post-materialist agenda' in states grappling with the problems of post-communism, whereas the FDP is a somewhat curious west German phenomenon of a party lacking many core voters which has come to be supported in elections either by voters who wish to see a coalition government, or by those who have misunderstood the voting system.

There are difficulties, however, in trying to derive lessons from the east German experience for elsewhere in the area. These lie less with the unique external environment of the transition, and more in the fact that the case of the GDR was not typical for the communist world as a whole. Eastern Germany had entered the communist period more modern and industrial than its eastern neighbours, and its economic advantage was maintained throughout the forty years of communist rule. In 1989, its mode of transition was nearest to 'implosion', or rapid collapse of communist structures. It was normally compared to Czechoslovakia (although its similarity with the Czech part of the country was greatest), and the Czech Republic by the mid-1990s was proving to be one of the most successful transitions from communism to democracy and a market economy. Successful integration of eastern Germany into western structures does not, therefore, mean that this goal will eventually be achieved elsewhere in the post-communist world. Failure, however, would almost certainly presage failure everywhere else.

Hungary

Hungary commenced 1994 with a new Prime Minister, Peter Boross, not because of any internal political disputes, but because of the death in office of József Antall in December 1993. A far more significant turning point in Hungarian politics came with the second elections in May 1994 (see Table 12.9). These were won decisively by the post-communist Hungarian Socialist

---

Textbox 12.4 Main events in Hungary, 1994–96

1994

February	Hungary joins NATO's Partnership for Peace.
May	Elections give the post-communist Hungarian Socialist Party (HSP) under Horn a parliamentary majority, but it decides to form a coalition with the Alliance of Free Democrats.
December	In local elections, the HSP retains its large lead over other parties.

1995

January	Finance Minister Békesi resigns after disputes with Horn.
June	Parliament re-elects Göncz President by a large majority.

1996

March	Hungary is invited to join the OECD. An IMF loan is agreed.
June	Draft constitution rejected by parliament.

Party (HSP), which polled a third of the votes in the first round, but – because of the limited nature of proportional representation in Hungary (see Chapter 6) – obtained 54 per cent of the seats in parliament. The result was not unexpected in the light of the previous government's longstanding unpopularity, and it scarcely came as a shock to the West since post-communist parties had by this point already been voted to power by the electorates of Poland and Lithuania. Even the fact that the new Prime Minister, Gyula Horn, had been born in 1932 and therefore had a much longer communist past than the younger leaders of social-democratised post-communist parties in, for example, neighbouring Poland and Slovakia was not regarded negatively. Horn had been Foreign Minister in the last, reformist communist government, and was therefore known in the West as the man who had symbolically cut the wire of the Iron Curtain to Austria in June 1989, and had also opened the border in real terms to fleeing East Germans in September 1989.

There were several reasons for the HSP's victory. The former centre-right government was identified with economic failure, and its members' rather backward-looking election campaign, which attempted to invoke the threat of communism, was not likely to have corrected this impression. The protracted 'media war' which it had fought had also made it appear very undemocratic, a disadvantage which outweighed any gains made from positive media coverage. The HSP, however, like their Polish counterparts, attempted to remain aloof from the squabbles of the election campaign while projecting an

Table 12.9 Hungarian election, 8/29 May 1994

	% vote regional lists	individual	Seats regional lists	national lists	total
Hungarian Socialist Party	33	149	53	7	209
Alliance of Free Democrats	20	16	28	25	69
Hungarian Democratic Forum	12	5	18	15	38
Independent Smallholders Party	9	1	14	11	26
Christian Democratic People's Party	7	3	5	14	22
Alliance of Young Democrats (FIDESZ)	7	0	7	13	20
Agrarian Alliance	2	1	0	0	1
Entrepreneurs Party-Liberal Civic Alliance	1	1	0	0	1
Others	10	0	0	0	0
Total		176	125	85	386

Source: Ágh and Kurtán (1995, pp. 23–4).

image of calm professional competence.[27] They made it clear that they were forward-looking and prepared to continue both with economic reform and the pursuit of Hungary's integration into Europe, but they offered in addition a promise of restoring the social security to which the population had been accustomed under the previous regime. This was the greatest single factor in their victory. It may even be suggested that Hungary's first respectable election turnout – 69 per cent in May 1994 – was due less to the voters' having acquired a sudden enthusiasm for democracy, and more to the fact that politicians had finally found an election issue that mobilised them.

Although the HSP had a reasonably safe parliamentary majority, they chose to form a coalition government with the Alliance of Free Democrats (AFD).[28] The AFD were the second largest party in parliament, and obtained three of the fourteen cabinet posts. This was a hopeful sign of political reconciliation, since the coalition contained both former ruling communists and the dissidents whom they had once persecuted. The coalition was advantageous for the AFD, since they would otherwise have been the only parliamentary party apart from FIDESZ which had no experience of government, and it also gave them leverage to promote the more reformist wing of the HSP, most notably by supporting the HSP Finance Minister László Békesi. For the HSP, the coalition improved their image abroad, since they were not a pure post-communist government, and at home, they could share the responsibility for any economic hardships to come. The coalition also gave the government the two-thirds parliamentary majority necessary to change the constitution, but this was not an overriding concern.

The formation of the HSP/AFD coalition was also indicative of the rather ambivalent cleavage structure of Hungarian politics. Although the previous government had been generally considered to be centre-right, the parties which comprised it were right-wing largely in terms of conservative, traditional and slightly authoritarian value orientations, rather than in support for pro-market reforms. On the other hand, the HSP – unlike, for example, post-communist parties in Bulgaria, Romania and Serbia – was distinctly less nationalist than most of its competitors, and defined itself less in outright opposition to pro-market reforms, and more in terms of a particular dedication to maintaining a structure of social welfare.[29] It shared in common with its coalition partner, the AFD, a degree of support for social liberalism. And although the AFD was to argue with its HSP partners on many economic issues, it was far from clear that the AFD was any nearer to the former governing parties on these.

Although the HSP succeeded in retaining its popularity in the local elections of December 1994, the country soon became engulfed in economic problems. During the new government's first year in power, the Forint was devalued several times, there were early substantial rises in energy prices, and although privatisation slowed down, unemployment did not decrease and labour conflicts emerged. Above all, however, there remained an urgent financial need to reform and limit state spending on social security, yet such a move would run directly counter to the HSP's most potent election promise. This dilemma led to a high-profile conflict between Finance Minister Békesi, who appreciated the need to implement a government austerity programme, and the HSP leadership, who were nervous of alienating both the public, whose expectations they themselves had awoken, and their own trade union wing. Békesi eventually resigned in March 1995, but his successor, Lajos Bokros, proceeded to produce an economic stabilisation plan which differed little from the demands of his predecessor and therefore met with the approval of the HSP's more reform-minded coalition partner, the AFD. Domestically, the plan led to a strike-wave in autumn 1995, and the HSP's support in opinion polls sank so far that at one point it was overtaken by the Independent Small-holders Party (ISP).[30] The ISP leader Torgyán, who had left the previous centre-right government (see Chapter 9), was still prepared to promote populist but unrealistic economic promises. Internationally, however, the government's tough economic measures restored some confidence in the Hungarian economy to the point where in spring 1996, Hungary was accepted into the OECD as its second post-communist member after the Czech Republic.[31] This was extremely important for the government, which had set Hungary's integration into West European political and security structures as its main aim.

The fate of economic reform in Hungary was significant, because it confirmed a pattern evident from developments in Bulgaria and Poland, where post-communist parties had also won elections in 1993 and 1994. This was that voters rejected the hardship of economic reform and returned former communist parties to power, but that the newly installed post-communist governments were economically unable to deliver on their election promises.

In terms of political institution-building, however, the Hungarian picture was more hopeful. President Göncz was re-elected to office by parliament in June 1995 and in December 1995, the country managed to pass a new media law,[32] thereby finally addressing an issue which had been the subject of disputes before the Constitutional Court in the first half of the 1990s. However, by the summer of 1996, parliament had yet to pass a new constitution; a draft was voted down by the HSP in June because it did not provide enough 'social rights'.

The continuity in the presidency was matched by the ability of coalition governments and Prime Ministers to remain in power for full electoral periods, and the even more remarkable fact that – notwithstanding the complexities of political cleavages in Hungary – the same six parties were returned to parliament in 1994 as in 1990. They were not, admittedly, entirely stable: the HDF had split in two in spring 1996 and its already much diminished popularity sank still further; and the HSP remained a party of a collective nature which combined different ideological groups and varying degrees of commitment to leftist values and reform.

Nevertheless, in the whole of the post-communist world (excluding eastern Germany, where the territory's adoption into an existing democracy had stabilised political structures), only the Czech Republic came near to Hungary's level of political continuity. The comparative turbulence of Hungarian politics can largely be explained by the fact that the state of the economy, and consequently the level of economic hardship experienced by the population, were objectively far worse in Hungary than in the Czech Republic. These were, however, essentially acerbic battles on the level of everyday politics, where questions of 'who gets what and why' are decided. The other levels of politics – institutional structures and questions of national identity – remained largely untouched by them.

Poland

Although the Polish elections of September 1993 had produced a clear victory and a safe parliamentary majority for the two post-communist groups – the Democratic Left Alliance (DLA) and the Polish Peasant Party (PPP) – Polish politics in 1994 and 1995 produced nothing which resembled one-party rule. Executive power was effectively split three ways: between the two parties of the governing coalition, who had many disagreements, and President Wałęsa, who enjoyed substantial powers for vetoing legislation and determining the appointment of ministers (particularly in the 'power ministries' of Defence, Foreign Affairs and the Interior) under Poland's semi-presidential system.

Disputes between the two governing parties were caused by two factors. First, the leader of the smaller PPP had provided the Prime Minister, Pawlak,

---

Textbox 12.5 Main events in Poland, 1994–96

1994

February   Poland joins NATO's Partnership for Peace.
April   Poland applies to join the European Union.
                   The Democratic Union and the Liberal Democratic
                   Congress merge to form the Freedom Union.

1995

February/March Pawlak of the Polish Peasant Party resigns as Prime Minister
                   and is replaced by Oleksy of the Democratic Left Alliance.
November   Kwasniewski wins a narrow victory over Wałęsa in the
                   second round of the presidential elections.

1996

January   Oleksy resigns as Prime Minister.
February   Cimoszewicz appointed Prime Minister.
June   A draft constitution is completed by the Constitutional
                   Commission.

---

and in return, the DLA controlled the key economic ministries. (This arrangement derived in part from the fact that Aleksander Kwaśniewski, the leader of the DLA's largest component Social Democracy of the Polish Republic, had his sights set on the presidential contest at the end of 1995.) However, Pawlak was not slow to exploit the power of his office, particularly where direct negotiation with Wałęsa over the appointment of ministers was possible. The second reason for the disagreements was that the two post-communist parties had some conflicting basic interests. The PPP had a firm constituency of voters among Poland's small farmers, who wished to see a continuation of state subsidies to agriculture, while the DLA was more concerned in assuring some continuation of economic reform, while also protecting, where possible, the interests of industrial workers and the weaker members of society who had voted for it.

On top of the tensions between the two parties came Wałęsa's predilection for opposing the government by vetoing legislation. In Poland, vetoed laws then required a two-thirds majority in order to be passed when returned to parliament. Further disputes with the President arose from difficulties in agreeing with him successors for the Defence and Foreign Ministries when the postholders resigned. Crisis point was finally reached in February 1995, when the President threatened to dissolve parliament for its failure to pass a budget, although the budget had in fact been passed and was being delayed purely by Wałęsa's refusal to sign it. While the parliament resolutely threatened to impeach him if he took such a move, the governing parties effectively gave in when Pawlak – whom Wałęsa had opposed since his appointment – was replaced by DLA member Józef Oleksy in early March.

For the remainder of 1995, Polish politics was largely dominated by the forthcoming presidential elections. These were finally won by Kwaśniewski in a tense second round against Wałęsa (see Table 12.10). However, the entire campaign was a good illustration of the complex structure of political cleavages underlying the Polish party system. Parties were split on three main issues.[33] The first was a left–right economic split: a market economy versus state intervention. The second was a left–right split where the terms are understood differently and indicate libertarian or authoritarian positions, or – most potently in the Polish context – secular versus religious feelings. The third related to the evaluation of the communist past, and is most simply described as post-communist versus post-Solidarity. The fragmentation of the Polish party system, indicated by the fact that seventeen candidates were officially registered for the 1995 presidential elections although they required 100,000 signatures to do so, reflected in part the fact that all three cleavages were cross-cutting, i.e. almost every conceivable permutation of views on the three major issues, and on some others, actually existed. Of the six parties that had actually entered parliament in 1993, the DLA and PPP were both post-communist, but the PPP was more left economically than the DLA, but, in view of its rural constituency, less secular. The Union of Labour was a post-Solidarity party, but was left of centre economically and secular. The Democratic Union (including ex-premiers Mazowiecki and Suchocka) was a post-Solidarity party which merged in April 1994 with the post-Solidarity Liberal Democratic Congress (including ex-premier Bielecki) to form the Freedom Union. Unlike the Union of Labour, it was strongly pro-market, but also Catholic. The Freedom Union also contained internal divisions, and its 1996 presidential candidate, Jacek Kuroń – formerly of the Democratic Union – was very much on the left of the party. Wałęsa's party, the Non-Party Bloc to Support Reform, was more moderately pro-market, but more strongly Catholic. The Confederation for Independent Poland was left-wing economically, but Catholic and strongly nationalist.[34] To this selection one must also add the Christian National Party, which did not manage to enter parliament, but which was left-wing economically and very strongly Catholic.

The battle finally fought in the second round of the presidential elections was essentially between Wałęsa and the communist past, and in particular about whether Kwaśniewski's party had really distanced itself from the past.[35] The outcome had been very uncertain, since, although Kwaśniewski had been the leading candidate in most opinion polls and did narrowly win, it had been suspected that in a second round the anti-communist vote against the idea of

Table 12.10 Polish presidential election, 5/19 November 1995

	% vote	
	Round 1	*Round 2*
Aleksander Kwasniewski	35	52
Lech Wałęsa	33	48
Jacek Kuroń	9	
Jan Olszewski	7	
Waldamar Pawlak	4	
Tadeusz Zielinski	4	
Hanna Gronkiewicz-Waltz	3	
Others (6)	5	

Source: Summary of World Broadcasts, EE/2455 C/6, EE/2467 C/6.

Poland being represented by a post-communist President might be enough to gain Wałęsa second-round support even from voters who objected to his somewhat authoritarian and erratic style of politics. What is important is that, despite the salience of economic issues in the 1993 parliamentary elections, this was not the main division between the final two presidential candidates. Politics was still heavily influenced by two specifically Polish factors. One was Catholicism. There had been controversial debates both on abortion and religious education in schools, and the preference of the Catholic Church for Wałęsa was explicit. Secondly, and in many respects linked, was the long battle between Solidarity and the communists which had been waged throughout the 1980s.

Even after the presidential elections, when the DLA had obtained both the presidency and the premiership, the cut and thrust of Poland's politics did not end. One of Wałęsa's parting acts was to bring down Prime Minister Oleksy through (never proven) allegations of passing information to the Russians. He was replaced in early 1996 by the DLA's Włodzimierz Cimoszewicz. A draft constitution, finally presented by the Constitutional Commission in June 1996, somewhat reduced the powers of the President, and its chances of being passed were obviously increased by the fact that the presidency and the government were of the same complexion.

Despite the apparent turbulence of Poland's domestic politics, and the fact that the pace of economic reform had declined under the post-communist government, Poland's general standing with the West was not affected. In mid-1996, it was considered to be the leading candidate, together with the Czech Republic, for NATO membership, and to be destined for the first wave of EU membership, whenever that might be. However, the sheer size both of Poland itself and of its underdeveloped and rather unproductive agricultural sector were considered major problems for the integration of East-Central Europe into the EU. None the less, the general balance sheet of Poland's transition to being a stabilised democracy and a market economy was viewed positively by Western institutions.

Romania

From 1994 to 1996, Romanian politics demonstrated what was, at least superficially, a measure of stability. Rather surprisingly, given the lack of a clear parliamentary majority, the government of the non-party Nicolae Vacaroiu survived the entire electoral period from 1992 until the elections in November 1996. However, this should not disguise the fact that the party composition of the government had been subject to significant change, and that it had had to survive successive votes of no confidence, sometimes with slim majorities. The Romanian party system was still uncrystallised, and on many vital issues there was little programmatic differentiation between the parties. In part, this reflected the fact that Romania had been one of the communist countries with the least developed dissident movements: politics in the post-communist era was still largely conducted at an elite level.

The battles of elite politics were visible both within the governing parties and the opposition. Although the government was nominally led by an independent, the main party in government was the Party of Social Democracy of Romania (PSDR), which was the larger successor to Iliescu's National Salvation Front. It found itself in a position which was in some senses similar to the third government of Mečiar's Movement for Democratic Slovakia (see below). It could not rule alone, because it was well short of a parliamentary majority; and for the sake of international respectability would have preferred to avoid a coalition with more extremist parties. However, in the end the compromises involved in negotiating the support of smaller, more extreme parties were less than those required by making agreements with the stronger opposition groupings, who were more fundamentally hostile to the PSDR. In August 1994, the Party of Romanian National Unity (PRNU) under Georghe Funar formally entered the coalition, and it was joined in January 1995 by another nationalist party, the Greater Romania Party (GRP) of Corneliu Vadim Tudor, and by the Socialist Labour Party (SLP), which was an unreformed successor to the Romanian Communist Party.

This government alliance was uneasy, and already began to come apart in November 1995, when the GRP withdrew its support from the government in the wake of official moves against Tudor for attacking President Iliescu in a newspaper article in October. There had also been previous problems with the PRNU, who wished to ban the Hungarian Democratic Federation of Romania (HDFR) (a move that would not have been out of line with the bans on parties with a ethnic basis existing in Bulgaria and Albania), and the PRNU did eventually leave the government in September 1996. The SLP left in March 1996. The fundamental problem for Romania was that what held the government together was essentially nationalist sentiments. These were underpinned by the parties' similar views on economic policy, where they all occupied left-wing positions in favour of substantial state involvement in the

Textbox 12.6 Main events in Romania, 1994–96

1994

January	Romania becomes the first post-communist country to join NATO's Partnership for Peace.
July	The government of Vacaroiu survives a fifth vote of no confidence, and an attempt to impeach President Iliescu fails.
August	The nationalist Party of Romanian National Unity (PRNU) formally joins the government coalition.

1995

January	The nationalist Greater Romania Party (GRP) and left Socialist Labour Party (SLP) join the government coalition.
March	Three member parties leave the opposition Democratic Convention of Romania (DCR).
November	The GRP leaves the government. Death of Corneliu Coposu, leader of the DCR's largest party, the Christian Democrats. The government survives a sixth vote of no confidence.

1996

March	The SLP leaves the governing coalition.
June	The opposition DCR outperforms the Party of Social Democracy of Romania (PSDR) in local elections.
September	The PRNU leaves the government.
November	President Iliescu and the PSDR are defeated in elections, and the DCR's Victor Ciorbea becomes Prime Minister.

economy. In the Romanian context, this combination of left-wing economic policies and nationalism was not surprising, as a feature of the Romanian communist regime had been that – from the late 1950s onwards – the rulers had attempted to legitimate their power by mobilising national sentiment. The PSDR, although it denied that it was neo-communist and claimed to be social democratic, was linked with figures prominent in the former communist regime, and after it was joined in government by the smaller extremist parties, it became unacceptable to international socialist organisations.[36] The three smaller government partners were more open about their admiration for the communist regime, and were therefore labelled parties of 'radical continuity'.[37] The PRNU was based on the regional elites in Transylvania, where Funar had become mayor of Cluj in 1992, and where the majority of the country's Hungarians lived.[38] While it claimed to have liberal economic views, in practice its nationalist aversion to foreign ownership of anything Romanian precluded such a policy. The GRP was slightly more extreme on nationalist issues, had a broader geographical spread of support, and defined itself as left of centre economically. The SLP, while profiling itself on its left-wing policies and communist legacies, was also clearly nationalist.

The opposition which confronted the government was unable effectively to exploit the arguments between partners of the ruling coalition because it was itself internally divided. It comprised three main groups. In the Social Democratic Union (SDU), a major role was played by Roman's Democratic Party-National Salvation Front, had once been part of a governing formation. The Hungarian Democratic Federation of Romania (HDFR) represented the country's largest ethnic minority, and had at times formed part of the Democratic Convention of Romania (DCR), although it was ejected in February 1995 for its espousal of territorial autonomy. Finally, there was the DCR itself, which had started life as an attempt to unite the opposition.[39] It comprised a changing array of organisations and several different strands of politics, ranging from the Christian Democracy of its largest member, the National Peasant Party Christian Democracy, to a social democratic wing, whose main representative left in February 1995 and was later to join the Social Democratic Union. In the middle was a kaleidoscope of supposedly liberal parties, whose adherence to both each other, the DCR and the principles of liberalism fluctuated.[40] What bound all the above groupings together was opposition to the government, yet arguments between politicians at leadership level were inevitably more prominent than efforts to offer a coherent electoral programme to the country's voters. Only the HDFR had a clearly defined constituency of support, and that was based on ethnicity.[41] All these problems notwithstanding, local elections in June 1996 indicated that the opposition was leading over the parties which had at some points been members of Vacaroiu's government. The country as a whole also continued to demonstrate an urban/rural cleavage, with the opposition polling well in larger towns and cities.

The generally uncrystallised state of party politics was matched by controversy over other areas of Romanian democracy, such as freedom of the media, the independence of the judiciary and the role of the secret police.[42] Ethnic relations were tense and confrontational, with the Hungarian minority dissatisfied with provision of mother-tongue education, and both the government and the remainder of the opposition resolute that discussion of territorial autonomy was unacceptable. The country's post-communist transition was slow and halting, but some small progress was made in the economy and international relations. Although repeated attempts at privatisation usually amounted to less than had been hoped, by the end of the period inflation had been brought under control and there were modest but at least positive growth rates. Efforts at integration into European structures also continued, with enthusiasm being shown for both NATO and EU membership. And although Romania appeared to be a country beset by many problems, it has to be remembered that its starting point at the end of 1989 had been infinitely worse, in terms of both economic hardship, deprivation of human rights and suppression of national minorities than that of any other of the Soviet Union's East European satellites.

A watershed in Romanian politics finally came in the November 1996 elections (see Table 12.11), when Iliescu lost the presidency to the DCR's Emil Constantinescu. At the same time, the PSDR lost the parliamentary elections, and the DCR chose Victor Ciorbea, the Mayor of Bucharest, as Prime Minister, charged with the difficult task of shaping a completely new coalition government, while Iliescu abandoned his nominal presidential neutrality and returned to the PSDR as Chair. It at last appeared that democracy had been established in Romania.

Table 12.11 Romanian elections, 3 November 1996

Lower House (Chamber of Deputies)	% vote	Seats
Democratic Convention of Romania	30	122
Party of Social Democracy in Romania	22	91
Social Democratic Union	13	53
Hungarian Democratic Federation of Romania	7	25
Greater Romania Party	4	19
Party of Romanian National Unity	4	18
Others	20	0
Minority organisation		15
Total		343

N.B. The 143-seat Upper House (Senate) was elected simultaneously using a similar electoral system.

Presidency	% vote	
	Round 1 (3.11)	Round 2 (17.11)
Emil Constantinescu (DCR)	28	54
Ion Iliescu (PSDR)	32	46
Petre Roman (SDU)	21	
Others	19	

Source: OMRI Daily Digest, Part II, 8 November 1996, 11 November 1996.

Slovakia

For the Slovak Republic, 1994–96 were years of trying to establish its identity as an independent state in the post-communist world.[43] Of the 'Visegrad Four' countries, who stood the best chance of being accepted into NATO and the European Union, it was the only one which had to grapple with the difficulties of founding the institutions of statehood. Although the Czech

Textbox 12.7 Main events in the Slovak Republic, 1994–96

1994

February	Slovakia joins NATO's Partnership for Peace.
	The two parties in the government coalition – Movement for a Democratic Slovakia (MFDS) and the Slovak National Party (SNP) – both split, depriving the government of a parliamentary majority.
March	After a critical speech to parliament by President Kováč, Mečiar's government is brought down in a vote of no confidence; the opposition forms a broad coalition government under the premiership of Moravčík pending new elections set for September/October.
October	MFDS again wins the elections without a parliamentary majority.
November	The European Union issues first démarche to Slovak government, criticising attempts to concentrate power at the first meeting of the parliament, and threats to remove the Democratic Union representatives from parliament on technical grounds.
December	Mečiar becomes Prime Minister for the third time, after finally forming a government with the SNP and far-left Workers' Association of Slovakia.

1995

May	The parliament passes a vote of no confidence in President Kováč, which has no constitutional effect.
June	The Slovak Republic applies to join the European Union.
August	President Kováč's son, who is suspected of involvement in an international fraud case, is kidnapped and delivered to the Austrian police. The complicity of the Slovak secret service and government in the kidnapping is later alleged.
October	A second EU démarche is issued, criticising in particular the tension between the government and the President.

1996

February	Kováč's son is finally returned to Slovakia by an Austrian court.
June	Disputes over the privatisation of financial institutions lead to major arguments among the coalition parties, but the government survives.

Republic was also technically a new state, in practice the Czechs had had far more experience than the Slovaks of the complexities of running a country, and had effectively been able to take over much of the expertise in operating such Prague-based organisations as the Ministry of Foreign Affairs and the National Bank. The Slovaks, in comparison, had to start almost from scratch.

The difficulties of new statehood were reflected in the political system as well. Whereas in the Czech Republic the major political cleavage was an economic one between right and left, in Slovakia the main cleavage revolved around issues of Slovak nationhood. There were even disputes about which days were appropriate for national holidays, stemming from different evaluations of the independent Slovak state which had existed during World War II. While political parties could often be roughly identified as right and left, it soon emerged that there were two separate left–right spectra, one on the nationalist side and one on the more cosmopolitan side of Slovak politics. These two spectra alternated in government. An additional issue complicating the political scene was the fact that the Hungarian minority, which comprises over 10 per cent of the population, has tended to vote for separate Hungarian parties.

1994 was a year of three governments. At its outset, Prime Minister Mečiar's Movement for Democratic Slovakia (MFDS), which designated itself as centrist (and could be considered as such insofar as it had no clear left or right economic profile), was ruling in coalition with the Slovak National Party (SNP). However, their government was deprived of its majority when both parties lost some of their deputies in splits, and after a critical state of the nation speech by President Kováč in March, the government was brought down in a vote of no confidence. It was replaced by a left–right coalition of opposition parties under the premiership of Jozef Moravčík, who had until recently been the Foreign Minister for MFDS. The new government comprised the post-communist Party of the Democratic Left (PDL), some centre-right parties comprising defectors from the MFDS and SNP who eventually merged in the Democratic Union (DU), and the Christian Democratic Movement of former Prime Minister Čarnogurský.[44] It was a minority government, and relied on tacit support from Hungarian deputies. The advent of the new government was generally welcomed internationally, and relations with the Hungarian minority improved substantially. However, the government was short-lived, since soon after it entered office, it was agreed that early elections – the first to be held in the newly independent Slovakia – would take place on 30 September–1 October 1994.

The new elections returned Mečiar to the premiership for the third time (see Table 12.12). However, since the MFDS had only 61 of the 150 parliamentary seats, it required coalition partners, and Mečiar took until December to find some and form a government. He was eventually forced to take as partners both the SNP and a new far left party, the Workers' Association of Slovakia, which had split from the post-communist PDL.[45] The coalition was somewhat problematic for Slovakia as it comprised three parties with no affiliation to mainstream West European party groupings, and

Table 12.12 Slovak election, 30 September–1 October 1994

	% vote	Seats
Movement for a Democratic Slovakia/Agrarian Party of Slovakia	35	61
Common Choice (Party of the Democratic Left/Green Party in Slovakia/Social Democratic Party of Slovakia/Farmers' Movement)	10	18
Hungarian Coalition (Hungarian Christian Democratic Movement/Coexistence/Hungarian Civic Party)	10	17
Christian Democratic Movement (with Standing Conference of the Civic Institute)	10	17
Democratic Union (with National Democratic Party)	9	15
Workers' Association of Slovakia	7	13
Slovak National Party	5	9
Others	14	0
Total		150

Source: Štatistický úrad Slovenskej republiky (1995, pp. 459–62).

internationally they were all regarded with suspicion and thought to have nationalist and authoritarian tendencies.

The policies of Mečiar's third government contained a number of different strands. On the economic front, it halted the second wave of voucher privatisation commenced by the short-lived Moravčík government, and quickly moved towards direct sales of enterprises. This process displayed strong elements of clientelism, as lucrative deals were made in favour of purchasers with links to the coalition parties. Politically, Mečiar tended towards a concentration of power in government hands, with the ruling coalition largely controlling, for example, parliamentary committees and supervisory boards for television and radio, the Slovak Information Service, and the National Property Fund (which was in charge of privatisation).[46] In judging this, it has to be remembered that Mečiar's experiences as Prime Minister had been almost unique, in so far as he had twice been ousted from office by former supporters in parliament, only to be returned to power by the electorate. It was not, therefore, entirely unnatural that he showed an almost obsessive concern about surrounding himself in all positions of power with people he considered loyal.

Mečiar's preoccupation with the disloyalty of previous allies also displayed itself in a desire for revenge against them. After the 1994 elections, his wrath was directed in particular against the Democratic Union – a political party composed largely of defectors from the parties of the second Mečiar government – and President Kováč, who had been a MFDS member at the time of his election to office. Unsuccessful attempts were made to eject the DU from parliament on the rather tenuous grounds that some of the 10,000 signatures it had had to collect to support its standing for parliament had allegedly been forged. The campaign against Kováč included, in the course of

1995, a vote of no confidence by parliament and a demand for his resignation by the government, neither of which encouraged his departure.[47] Most controversially, however, when Kováč's son, Michal Kovač Jnr., was kidnapped in August 1995 against the background of complex allegations of involvement in a fraud case, government complicity was suspected.[48]

Domestic political disputes impacted on Slovakia's foreign policy. Although the programme of Mečiar's third government prioritised the desire for integration into European structures, much of Slovakia's internal politics appeared counter-productive to this goal. The European Union issued Slovakia with two démarches, the first in November 1994 relating largely to attempts to oust the Democratic Union from parliament, and the second in October 1995 as a reaction to attacks against the President. International concern was also expressed about the language law passed in autumn 1995, which caused alarm amongst the Hungarian minority, and the Criminal Law presented to parliament in spring 1996, which appeared, among other controversial provisions, to make spreading untruths about Slovakia abroad a criminal offence.

Slovakia's balance sheet for the first few years of independent existence was mixed. Its international standing rose markedly in late 1995, when it became clear that the country was obtaining unexpectedly good economic results despite a lack of foreign investment. Yet internally, society was heavily polarised, and the government showed that the Slovak Republic was a young state still battling for its identity both by a great susceptibility to foreign criticism, and a tendency to define people as being 'for' or 'against' Slovakia, and as 'good' or 'bad' Slovaks. However, although the democratic credentials of Mečiar's government were often questioned, the democratic institutions established by the Slovak constitution proved quite robust. Despite the obvious desire of the government to rid itself of President Kováč, it found itself unable to, because there was no constitutional mechanism for doing so, and the country's democratic political culture restricted – though did not totally preclude – any anti-constitutional possibilities for doing so.[49] Similarly, although Mečiar showed signs of wanting to 'change the rules of the game' and raised the possibility of changing the electoral system in spring 1996, it was unclear how he could ever obtain the parliamentary majority to do this. The government's desire to establish the prestige and legitimacy of the independent state also meant that nationalist tendencies were tempered by a desire to be acceptable to an international community which was often reviled for being 'anti-Slovak'.

The country therefore ended up, in 1996, in a position where there were fears that it would, at the decisive moment, be excluded from the first group of post-communist countries to be admitted to NATO and the European Union. Yet in terms of its standard of living and economic progress, it could not reasonably belong in a second group comprising, for example, Bulgaria,

Romania and the Ukraine. Slovakia was the object of substantial criticism from the EU precisely because it was in the 'lead group' of post-communist countries, from which high standards were expected. The flaws in its democracy were also, ironically, well-publicised abroad, largely because it was in the fortunate position of having a strong and vocal opposition to the government. The Slovak Republic can therefore best be characterised as a deviant case among the Visegrad countries, which had particular problems because it was a new state with an insecure and contested national identity. What remained to be seen was how quickly these problems could be overcome.

Former Yugoslavia

In 1996, the Dayton Agreement signed at the end of 1995 produced a cessation of fighting in the former Yugoslavia of a greater durability than all those agreed previously in international negotiations.[50] This notwithstanding, the situation remained tense, and hopes of lasting stability in Bosnia-Herzegovina were tenuous. It was mainly the situation of Croatia and Serbia which had been clarified somewhat.

Several factors had helped bring about the Dayton Agreement. One was the increasing willingness of the Serbian leader Milošević to bow to the economic pressure of sanctions, and the threat they posed to the internal stability of, and hence his grip on power in, Serbia. This led to his distancing himself from the rebel Bosnian Serb leader, Radovan Karadžić, from August 1994 onwards. The withdrawal of Serbian military support from the Serbs of Bosnia and the Krajina was instrumental in bringing about Croatia's greatest military success when, in August 1995, Operation Storm finally asserted Croatian control of the Krajina for the first time. This gave the Croatian government power over almost all the territory of its republic (with the exception of eastern Slavonia, on the border with Vojvodina). It also reduced the size of the Serbian minority in Croatia, since most of the Krajina's Serb population fled in front of the Croatian army. A further factor inducing the Serbs to negotiate was a show of force by NATO in the late summer of 1995, when its planes attacked Bosnian Serb positions near Sarajevo and knocked out their air defence system at Banja Luka.

While Croatia gained the advantage of controlling most of its territory – and the Croatian leader Tudjman capitalised on the military victory by holding, and winning, elections to the parliament in October 1995 – Serbia's position was also to an extent improved by Milošević's abandonment of the rebel Serbs. UN sanctions against the Federal Republic of Yugoslavia were suspended in November 1995, and the state began to gain diplomatic recognition from the countries of the European Union in the spring of 1996. However, although the internal politics of the former Yugoslav republics

---

Textbox 12.8 Main events in former Yugoslavia, 1994–96

1994

March   *Slovenia* Slovenia joins NATO's Partnership for Peace.
Croatia/Bosnia-Herzegovina Washington Agreement on a
Croatian-Bosnian confederation and a Bosnian federation signed
by Croatian and Muslim leaders.

August   *Serbia* Serbia breaks off political and economic relations with the
Serb Republic.

October   *Macedonia* President Gligorov and the post-communist coalition
government remain in power after presidential and
parliamentary elections; the nationalist Internal Macedonian
Revolutionary Organisation gains no seats after boycotting the
second round because of alleged irregularities in the first.

1995

August   *Croatia* The Croatian army recovers most of the Krajina area in
Operation Storm.

October   *Croatia* Tudjman's Croatian Democratic Community wins new
elections with a large majority.
Macedonia President Gligorov is injured in an assassination
attempt by car bomb.

November   *Macedonia* Macedonia joins the Council of Europe, the OSCE
and NATO's Partnership for Peace.
Serbia and Montenegro UN sanctions are suspended.

December   *Bosnia-Herzegovina* Dayton Agreement signed in Paris.

1996

April   *Serbia and Montenegro* Britain announces that it will recognise
the Federal Republic of Yugoslavia, following the lead of France.

September   *Bosnia-Herzegovina* In a flawed election process, voters divide
along ethnic lines.

November   *Serbia and Montenegro* Despite victory for the post-communist
parties in Montenegrin and Federal Yugoslav elections, the
opposition coalition Zajedno takes the largest towns in Serbian
local elections and Milošević's unwillingness to accept the result
leads to the largest demonstrations against his rule yet seen.
Slovenia Inconclusive result to parliamentary election.

---

had stabilised somewhat by the mid-1990s, patterns of party politics bore little
resemblance to those of Western Europe. While many of the new states were
dominated by a single party, their hold on power was often tenuous, and the
desire of the current rulers to remain in government was not conducive to a

deepening of democracy. A fundamental problem was that, except in Slovenia, battles were still being fought on three different levels of politics: nation-building, institution-building and the everyday politics of redistribution.

Outside Slovenia, politics in all the republics was heavily influenced by the process of state-building, and was affected by disputes over the symbols of nationhood and the status of the different nationalities which comprised their populations. Macedonia even lacked an internationally agreed name for its state, owing to Greek protests that the word 'Macedonia' implied a claim to lands in northern Greece, and the new state also had to abandon use of the Star of Vergina as a state symbol under Greek pressure. Internally, its substantial Albanian minority sought constitutional equality with the Macedonians as a state-building nation, although the government did make efforts to appoint ethnic Albanians to positions of powers, such as government ministers, judges and ambassadors. Croatia was still engaged in securing all the territory within its formal boundaries, and the nationalist government laid an emphasis on Croatian nationhood which was threatening to those Serbs who still remained after Operation Storm. Montenegro had an uneasy relationship with the far larger Serbia within the Federal Republic of Yugoslavia, and the opposition was divided between advocates of full independence and those who favoured complete integration with Serbia. Serbia did nothing in the first half of the 1990s to improve its disastrously bad relations with the Albanian majority in the once autonomous region of Kosovo. The Albanians sought independence, and their participation in the Serbian state institutions was virtually non-existent, while Milošević responded by efforts to strengthen the Serb presence in Kosovo demographically through the settlement there of the Serbian refugees from Krajina who had recently arrived in Serbia. Bosnia-Herzegovina, in spite of the Dayton Agreement and the elections held in September 1996, remained a fundamentally unstable state structure, whose long-term viability was questionable.

The institutional foundations of democracy were also fragile (outside Slovenia) marked, for example, by disputes over the fairness of electoral procedures. In Macedonia, the leading opposition party boycotted the second round of elections in 1994 in protest at alleged irregularities in the first round. In Croatia, the new electoral law used in the 1995 elections was highly dubious since it reserved 12 parliamentary seats from 127 for Croatians living abroad, including those in Bosnia-Herzegovina, and all twelve of these were won by President Tudjman's Croatian Democratic Community.[51] The status of the opposition-dominated Zagreb city council was also a source of conflict and international criticism in 1996. In the Federal Republic of Yugoslavia, there was heavy Serbian government interference with the composition of federal bodies. In Bosnia-Herzegovina, functioning institutional structures had yet to be established at all. Freedom of the press and the independence of the judiciary were also at risk.

Finally, the tasks of reconstructing a post-communist market economy were immeasurably complicated by the effects of war. Warfare is not only destructive but expensive, and defence was the largest item in the Croatian state budget. Communications within Croatia were also disrupted for much of the period by the rebel Serb control of part of its territory. Serbia and Montenegro's economies were devastated by international sanctions and runaway inflation. Macedonia was badly affected by itself having to implement sanctions against Serbia, which had been its largest trading partner, and this situation was further exacerbated by its being embargoed for much of the period by Greece owing to the dispute over the country's name. In Bosnia-Herzegovina, economic interests were reduced to acquiring the minimum necessary for physical survival. The refugee problem was a drain on state resources everywhere, and also placed a question mark over issues of ownership. The immense problems faced by other post-communist states when dealing with privatisation and restitution should theoretically have been somewhat less in the former Yugoslavia, where – alone with Poland in the com-munist world – land had not been collectivised, although major industry and most urban dwellings had been in state ownership. However, the tremendous shifts in population which had resulted from 'ethnic cleansing', and the notional right of return for displaced persons embodied in the Dayton Agreement, complicated matters enormously. Only Slovenia, building on its communist period superiority, was able to progress towards EU membership, albeit long hampered by an outstanding disputes with Italy about postwar property confiscations.

However, even if the former Yugoslavia had not been plagued by conditions of warfare, interest articulation by political parties would have been a complex affair since in all republics there was a multiple cleavage structure very far from the left–right model of dominant economic concerns familiar in the West. Even Slovenia, the most advanced of the post-communist countries, was governed by a coalition containing a broad range of opinions, and this was near to disintegration in the run-up to elections at the end of 1996. In Croatia, nationalism had proved the focus of the anti-communist vote in the first 1990 elections, and Tudjman's Croatian Democratic Community (CDC) managed to remain in power not only in the second elections of 1992, but also in further elections held in the wake of military victory in October 1995 (see Table 12.13). However, the continuation of the war may merely have delayed programmatic differentiation among political forces. There were expectations that the CDC, like most broad movements in democracies, was bound to disintegrate. This process had begun in April 1994, when the speakers of both chambers of the parliament, Josip Manolić and Stipe Mesić, left to form the Croatian Independent Democrats, although their new party met with minimal success in the subsequent elections.

In Macedonia, post-communists won an easy election victory in 1994 (see

Table 12.13 Croatian elections, 29 October 1995

Lower House	% vote	Seats			
		PR	Constit.	Other	Total
Croatian Democratic Community	45	42	21	12	75
Croatian Social Liberal Party	12	10	2	0	12
Social Democratic Party of Croatia	9	8	2	0	10
Coalition (led by Croatian Peasants Party)	18	16	2	0	18
Croatian Party of Rights	5	4	0	0	4
Croatian Independent Democrats		0	1	0	1
Minority seats		0	0	7	7
Total		80	28	19	127

N.B. Eighty seats were distributed by PR to parties gaining 5 per cent of the vote; 28 were distributed on a majoritarian system in single-member constituencies; 12 were distributed by PR to Croatians abroad; and 7 were reserved for minorities.

Sources: Toulon (1996, pp. 150–2); *EIU Country Report Bosnia-Hercegovina, Croatia and Slovenia* (4th quarter 1995, p. 14).

Table 12.14), but the major, nationalist opposition party which had led in the 1990 elections had boycotted the second round of the elections. A coalition was formed with the Albanian Party of Democratic Prosperity, but the Albanian political representation was also split on nationalist lines.

In Serbia, it was hard to differentiate parties on any accustomed Western criterion. Even Vuk Drašković's Democratic Movement for Serbia (DEPOS) and several smaller opposition parties were in some respects nationalist, though not in the same way as Milošević's ruling socialists; and Vojislav Šešelj's Serbian Radical Party was more extreme still than the socialists.

A brief look at politics in the former Yugoslavia seems to suggest that national identity was the mainstay of the party system: not only did governing parties represent the nationalism of the majority people in most republics, but many of the smaller parties to enter parliament were representatives of minorities. However, other political cleavages were also important. Most notable of these was the urban/rural split familiar from Bulgaria and Romania, which was particularly conspicuous when the opposition won council elections in prestigious capital cities. Post-communist nationalist populism had a limited appeal to more educated, modern urban populations. Within Croatia, there was a notable difference in the political orientation of the rural Serbs of the Krajina, who were extremely nationalist and had declared autonomy from the Croatian state (which they were mostly to leave after 'Operation Storm'), and the urban Serbs, of whom there had been some 100,000 in Zagreb. Within Serbia itself, support for Milošević was higher among the rural population. In Bosnia-Herzegovina, too, the political views of inhabitants of the cosmopolitan capital Sarajevo differed markedly from those in the villages surrounding it. In addition to the urban/rural divide, a communist/anti-communist cleavage was apparent. When economic values and differences between conservative/

Table 12.14 Macedonian elections, 16/30 October 1994

	Seats
Social Democratic Alliance of Macedonia, Liberal Party, Socialist Party of Macedonia (Alliance for Macedonia)	95
Party for Democratic Prosperity	10
National Democratic Party	4
Social Democratic Party of Macedonia	1
Party for the Full Emancipation of Romanies	1
Democratic Party of Turks/Islamic Road	1
Democratic Party of Macedonia	1
Independents	7
Total	120

Source: Statistical Yearbook of the Republic of Macedonia 1995 (1995, p. 63).

Presidential elections	*% vote*
Kiro Gligorov	78
Ljubiša Georgievski	22

Source: Calculated from *Summary of World Broadcasts* (1994) EE/2144 C/10.

traditionalist and more progressive orientations are superimposed on such divides, it can be seen that the potential for a fragmented party system is present.

Such party fragmentation increases the chances of any party in power fending off the challenges of the opposition because the latter will be weakened by internal divisions. Where governments have strong control of the media, as in the former Yugoslavia, the development of a modern democracy is further constrained. The war also delayed and distorted normal political development.

Yet, as 1996 drew to a close and the former Yugoslavia had enjoyed nearly a year of relative peace, there were some hopeful signs. In Bosnia-Herzegovina, the implementation of the Dayton Agreement was flawed, and the fairness of the elections held in September 1996 was highly questionable. Voters divided on national lines in the fashion first manifest in the 1990 elections, and the collective presidency, comprising a Moslem, a Serb and a Croat, could barely agree on where and how to meet. However, the country at least avoided open descent into warfare again.

In Croatia, the health of 74-year-old President Tudjman appeared, by November 1996, to jeopardise the continuation of his rule, while an attempt to close down the country's last independent radio station led to a demonstration of some 100,000 people on the streets of Zagreb. The largest demonstrations took place, however, on the streets of Belgrade. While November 1996 saw federal elections in the Federal Republic of Yugoslavia (Serbia and Montenegro) and republican elections in Montenegro (see Table 12.15) return the ruling post-communist forces to office, local elections in Serbia

Table 12.15 Montenegrin elections, 3 November 1996

	Seats
Democratic Socialist Party	45
National Unity coalition	19
Party of Democratic Action	3
Democratic League of Montenegro	2
Democratic League of Albanians	2
Total	71

Source: OMRI Daily Digest, Part II, 6 November 1996.

were won by the opposition in most of the country's cities. It was Milošević's attempts to annul the result of the election to Belgrade City Council which brought up to 200,000 people on to the streets in continued demonstrations which called the President's entire political record into question.

Again, Slovenia proved the exception in former Yugoslavia. Here, the November 1996 parliamentary elections, once more conducted on a PR basis, failed to produce a conclusive result (see Table 12.16), although the Liberal Democratic Party of Prime Minister Drnovšek remained the largest party. However, coalition negotiations were able to proceed according to 'normal' criteria of the programmatic similarity of parliamentary parties. The country's favourable credentials as one of the leading contenders for EU membership were not jeopardised.

Table 12.16 Slovenian election, 10 November 1996

	% vote	Seats
Liberal Democratic Party	27	25
Slovene People's Party	19	18
Social Democratic Party of Slovenia	16	16
Slovene Christian Democrats	10	10
United List of Social Democrats	9	10
Democratic Party of Pensioners of Slovenia	4	5
Slovene National Party	3	4
Total		88

Source: Summary of World Broadcasts (1996) EE/2767 A/5, EE/2770 A/10, EE/2774 A/14.

Conclusion

The development of the political systems of Eastern Europe is a process which has yet to be concluded. All the states had entered the post-communist period with differences in their economic, social and political structures, in spite of the homogenising effects of the communist system. By 1996, however, the diversity was far greater. Politically, all had party systems constructed around different cleavage patterns, and the democratic foundations of politics diverged in strength from those approaching a similarity with western systems to those who were only questionably democracies. Economically, there were wide variations in both the progress of economic reforms and in the toler-ability of everyday living conditions for their citizens. The differences between the states of Eastern Europe had always been greater under communism than was generally recognised in the West, where the main dividing line had been between those who were allied to the Soviet Union and the two who were not. Once removed from Soviet influence, the indications were that historical, cultural and economic differences which pre-dated communist rule were prevailing over the homogenising influences which had for forty years been imposed from outside. While post-communist states had initially confronted broadly similar categories of problems, the resources necessary and available for their solution differed widely. Even within former Yugoslavia, where all republics had for forty years been under the same form of non-Soviet com-munism, the difference in progress achieved was as wide as in Eastern Europe as a whole.

Notes

1. Huntington (1991, pp. 266–7).
2. Schmidt (1995b).
3. *Central and Eastern Eurobarometer No. 6* (1996).
4. Zanga (1995).
5. Schmidt (1995a).
6. Abrahams (1996).
7. *Ibid.*; Sullivan (1996). For regular updates on the constituional situation in Albania, see also the 'Constitution Watch' section of *East European Constitutional Review*.
8. Schmidt (1996).
9. The number of parties was none the less still substantial; for details, see Andreev (1996).
10. On the 1994 elections, see Karasimeonov (1995); Dimitrov (1995); Crampton (1995).
11. On the MRF, see Ganev (1995).
12. On left and right in Bulgaria, see Kanev (1996).
13. Krause (1995).
14. *Central and Eastern Eurobarometer No. 6* (1996).
15. Krause (1996a).
16. Krause (1996b).
17. Only the GDR had approached Czechoslovakia in terms of material living standards in the communist period.
18. See Kitschelt (1995a); Whitefield and Evans forthcoming; Markowski (1995).
19. Kettle (1995).
20. For a discussion of Social Democracy in the Czech Republic, see Vermeersch (1994).
21. For an account of interwar Czech politics, see Mamatey and Luža (1973).
22. For discussion of this point, see Henderson (1996).
23. For wide-ranging coverage of politics in the new Germany, see Smith *et al.* (1996).

24. For detailed coverage of the 1994 elections, see the special edition of *German Politics*, 4 (2).
25. On the SPD in Eastern Germany, see Silvia (1993).
26. Since this was less than 5 per cent of the total vote nationally, the PDS would have been excluded from parliament if it had not managed to gain three direct mandates from candidates standing in single-member constituencies. On the PDS, see Oswald (1996).
27. On the HSP, see Ágh (1995), and comparatively on communist successor parties in general, Evans and Whitefield (1995b); Ishiyama (1995); Mahr and Nagle (1995); Waller (1995).
28. On the coalition, see Racz and Kukorelli (1995).
29. Kitschelt (1995a); Evans and Whitefield (1995a); Ágh (1995); Markus (1994).
30. Szilagyi (1996a).
31. Szilagyi (1996b).
32. Szilagyi (1996c).
33. See Markowski (1995); Kitschelt (1995a).
34. On Polish nationalism, see Millard (1994e).
35. On the presidential election, see Millard (1996); Osiatynski (1995).
36. See Shafir (1995a).
37. See Shafir (1994).
38. On the PRNU, see Gallagher (1995).
39. On the DCR, see Shafir (1995b).
40. For an account of the complexities of Liberal politics in Romania, see Shafir (1995c).
41. On the HDFR, see Craiutu (1995).
42. On the deficiencies of Romanian democracy, see Gallagher (1996).
43. Bútora and Bútorová (1993).
44. Henderson (1994b).
45. For the 1994 elections, see Wightman and Szomolányi (1995); Szomolányi and Mesežnikov (1995); Abraham (1995).
46. See Malova (1995).
47. See Zifcak (1995).
48. Fisher (1996).
49. For discussion of the Slovak constitution, see Bealey (1995).
50. Further details can be found in the regular reports on the progress of the Dayton Agreement, as well as on domestic politics in former Yugoslavia, which appear in *Transition*. See also Open Media Research Institute (1996).
51. See Kaspović (1996).

Annotated bibliography

Below is a brief guide to the books readers may find most useful as further reading for each of this book's chapters. Footnotes throughout the text also suggest specific sources, most particularly works that deal with single countries. The number of books available for the earlier periods covered in this book is understandably by far the highest; journal articles, frequently about a single country, are a far richer source for the later chapters. Full details of all the works referred to are given in the References section.

Introduction

A number of books have appeared recently which deal comprehensively with the communist period. For Eastern Europe, the best systematic history is in Joseph Rothschild, *Return to Diversity: A political history of East Central Europe since World War II*, and George Schöpflin, *Politics in Eastern Europe 1945–1992*, as well as Geoffrey Swain and Nigel Swain, *Eastern Europe since 1945*, Ben Fowkes, *The Rise and Fall of Eastern Europe*, and, for a more limited range of countries, Paul G. Lewis, *Central Europe since 1945*. Jacques Rupnik, *The Other Europe*, and Vladimir Tismaneanu, *Reinventing Politics: Eastern Europe from Stalin to Havel*, provide a more discursive background to the region, while J.F. Brown, *Eastern Europe under Communist Rule*, gives excellent coverage of the two decades leading to the crises of the late 1980s. R.J. Crampton, *Eastern Europe in the Twentieth Century*, has the advantage of covering both the interwar and the communist period. There are a large number of histories of the USSR to choose from. Geoffrey Hosking, *A History of the Soviet Union*, and Mary McAuley, *Soviet Politics 1917–1991*, both cover the entire Soviet period. John Keep, *Last of the Empires. A History of the Soviet Union 1945–1991* is a more detailed history of the post-war development of the USSR with good coverage of the Gorbachev period too. For examinations of how communist systems functioned, see Leslie Holmes, *Politics in the Communist World* and Stephen White *et al.*, *Communist and Postcommunist Political Systems*.

Chapter 1 Describing radical change and post-communist politics

Three of the works cited in this chapter are important for examining radical social and political change, and for contemplating democratic transitions in comparative context: Theda Skocpol, *States and Social Revolutions*, is a classic examination of the structural causes and outcomes of social revolution; Guillermo O'Donnell, Philippe Schmitter and

Laurence Whitehead (eds.), *Transitions from Authoritarian Rule* is a four-volume work covering both the theoretical nature of democratisation and providing case studies of transitions in Latin America and Southern Europe; Samuel P. Huntington, *The Third Wave: Democratization in the late twentieth century*, is a synthesis of the ideas generated by earlier researchers and provides a guide to many of the political choices facing politicians during transition. Geoffrey Pridham and Tatu Vanhanen (eds.), *Democratisation in Eastern Europe: Domestic and international perspectives*, is extremely useful, and also covers the 1990 elections, and a much simpler textbook with some analysis of Soviet developments is David S. Mason, *Revolution in East-Central Europe*.

Chapter 2   The USSR: The difficult rebirth of politics

There are many different interpretations of Gorbachev and his reform policies. Rachel Walker, *Six Years that Shook the World. Perestroika – the impossible project*, is an accessible and informative introduction to the period and its immediate aftermath. Stephen White, *After Gorbachev*, provides a very detailed account of all aspects of Gorbachev's reform policies. Gorbachev's thoughts on reform can be found in his *Perestroika. New thinking for our country and the world*. Archie Brown, *The Gorbachev Factor*, concentrates on Gorbachev's personal contribution to reform and gives a very favourable account of his role. Richard Sakwa, *Gorbachev and his Reforms, 1985–1990*, and Jonathan Steele, *Eternal Russia. Yeltsin, Gorbachev and the mirage of democracy*, provide more critical examinations of Gorbachev's reform. Angus Roxburgh, *The Second Russian Revolution. The struggle for power in the Kremlin*, gives an overview of the struggles that went on in the Kremlin during Gorbachev's rule. More detail on the 1989 elections and the establishment of the CPD can be found in Michael Urban, *More Power to the Soviets. The democratic revolution in the USSR*, and Ben Kiernan, *The End of Soviet Politics. Elections, legislatures and the demise of the Communist Party*. The emergence of independent political groups is chronicled in M. Steven Fish, *Democracy from Scratch. Opposition and Regime in the New Russian Revolution*, Geoffrey Hosking et al., *The Road to Post-Communism: New political movements in the USSR, 1985-1991*, and Vera Tolz, *The USSR's Emerging Multiparty System*.

Chapter 3   Eastern Europe: Negotiated revolution and popular revolution

An outstanding analytic account of the revolutions in Eastern Europe is provided by J.F. Brown, *Surge to Freedom: The end of communist rule in Eastern Europe*. Gale Stokes, *The Walls Came Tumbling Down: The collapse of communism in Eastern Europe*, includes much useful historical background to the events of 1989, while Timothy Garton Ash, *We the People: The revolution of 89*, provides an eye-witness account of many of the most important events, and Mark Frankland, *The Patriots' Revolution: How East Europe won its freedom*, presents much colourful description. *The Times Guide to Eastern Europe* is a more factual source, as well as the very systematic Stephen White (ed.), *Handbook of Reconstruction in Eastern Europe and the Soviet Union*. Judy Batt, *East Central Europe: From reform to transformation*, is extremely useful for a more limited number of countries.

Chapter 4   Creating democratic legitimacy

Ralf Dahrendorf *Reflections on the Revolution in Europe*, provides a broad discussion of the problems facing countries embarking on democratisation. Sten Berglund and Jan Åke Dellenbrandt (eds.), *The New Democracies in Eastern Europe*, places the elections in historical context, while Bogdan Szajkowski (ed.), *Political Parties in Eastern Europe and the Soviet Union*, provides a wealth of factual detail for both the Soviet Union and Eastern Europe.

Chapter 5   The rise of the republics and the demise of the USSR, 1990–91

Archie Brown, *The Gorbachev Factor*, Richard Sakwa, *Gorbachev and his Reforms, 1985–1990*, Jonathan Steele, *Eternal Russia. Yeltsin, Gorbachev and the mirage of democracy*, Rachel Walker, *Six Years that Shook the World. Perestroika – the impossible project*, and Stephen White, *After Gorbachev*, all cover the political machinations that accompanied the demise of the USSR. Ian Bremmer and Ray Taras (eds.), *Nations and Politics in the Soviet Successor States*, provides an excellent overview of the rise of nationalism throughout the USSR and in all of the republics covered in this book. Further details of developments in individual republics can be found in Juris Dreifelds, *Latvia in Transition*, John Dunlop, *The Rise of Russia and the Fall of the Soviet Empire*, Taras Kuzio and Andrew Wilson, *Ukraine: Perestroika to Independence*, Anatol Lieven, *The Baltic Revolution. Estonia, Latvia, Lithuania and the Path to Independence*, Alfred Senn, *Lithuania Awakening*, Rein Taagepera, *Estonia: Return to Independence*, and Jan Zaprudnik, *Belarus at a Crossroads in History*.

Chapter 6   Elections in Eastern Europe, 1990

The best sources of information on the 1990 elections are journal articles on individual countries, although they are also covered by the final chapters of many books on the communist period and the events of 1989, such as Joseph Rothschild, *Return to Diversity*. For factual details *Electoral Studies* produced a special issue on 'Elections in Eastern Europe' at the end of 1990. Misha Glenny, *The Rebirth of History*, contains a wealth of background and analysis on the emerging issues of East European politics in 1990, while Stephen Whitefield (ed.), *The New Institutional Architecture of Eastern Europe*, looks at the structural aspects of the emerging democratic systems in the various countries under discussion.

Chapter 7   The nature of post-communist transitions

For a detailed discussion of issues of economic reform see Adam Przeworski, *Democracy and the Market*. The issues surrounding choices of different constitutional structures are explained in Giovanni Sartori, *Comparative Constitutional Engineering: An inquiry into structures, incentives and outcomes*, and Arend Lijphart, *Democracies: patterns of majoritarian and consensus government in twenty-one countries*.

Chapter 8   Politics as crisis: Russia and the newly independent states, 1992–93

Stephen White *et al.* (eds.), *Developments in Russian and Post-Soviet Politics* provides an overview of many of the most pressing problems facing the successor states of the USSR, with particular reference to Russia. Karen Dawisha and Bruce Parrot, *Russia and the New States of Eurasia. The politics of upheaval,* and Graham Smith (ed.), *The Nationalities Question in the Post-Soviet States*, and Vera Tolz and Ian Elliot (eds.), *The Demise of the USSR. From communism to independence,* provide more detailed introductions to events throughout the area. Richard Sakwa, *Russian Politics and Society*, is a very detailed and useful analytic account of Russian politics between 1991 and the middle of 1993. Peter Lentini (ed.), *Elections and Political Order in Russia. The implications of the 1993 election to the Federal Assembly*, complements Sakwa's book by providing an account of the 1993 elections. Jeremy Lester, *Modern Tsars and Princes. The struggle for hegemony in Russia*, and John Löwenhardt, *The Reincarnation of Russia. Struggling with the legacy of communism, 1990–1994*, are very different, but very useful, interpretative accounts of the development of Russian politics in this period. Boris Yeltsin's account of events can be found in his *The View from the Kremlin*. Detailed accounts of developments in individual successor states are not that common. Among the few guides that do exist are Helen Fedor (ed.), *Belarus and Moldova: country studies* and Ole Norgaard *et al.*, *The Baltic States after Independence.*

Chapter 9   Eastern European roads to democracy 1991–93

J.F. Brown, *Hopes and Shadows*, provides a readable, but analytic account of the period covered by this chapter, while Stephen White, Judy Batt and Paul G. Lewis (eds.), *Developments in East European Politics*, provides both thematic and country-by-country coverage. Gordon Wightman (ed.), *Party Formation in East-Central Europe*, concentrates on a single aspect of transition, as does Bogdan Szajkowski (ed.), *Political Parties in Eastern Europe, Russia and the Successor States.*

Chapter 10   Patterns of post-communist politics

For a comparative discussion of Eastern Europe in the context of Europe as a whole, see Richard Rose, *What is Europe?*; for an introduction to the literature on the development of party systems, see Alan Ware, *Political Parties and Party Systems*, and Peter Mair (ed.), *The West European Party System.*

Chapters 11 and 12   The difficulties of democratic consolidation: Russia and the NIS, and The new democracies of Eastern Europe

The best source of information on more recent events is the bi-weekly *Transition* produced by the Open Media Research Institute, which also published *Building Democracy 1995: The OMRI annual survey of Eastern Europe and the former Soviet Union. Communist and Post-Communist Studies*, *East European Constitutional Review*, *East European Politics and*

Societies, *Europe-Asia Studies*, and *The Journal of Communist Studies and Transitional Politics* specialise in covering the area, but articles of interest are frequently to be found in journals with a broader remit such as *British Journal of Political Science*, *Electoral Studies*, *Foreign Affairs*, *Foreign Policy*, *Government and Opposition*, *International Affairs*, *Journal of Area Studies*, *Journal of Democracy*, *Orbis*, *Social Research*, *World Politics*, *The World Today*.

References

Abraham, S. (1995) 'Early elections in Slovakia: a state of deadlock', *Government and Opposition*, 30 (1), pp. 86–100.

Abrahams, F. (1996) 'Tenuous separation of powers', *Transition*, 2 (3), pp. 51–3.

Adams, W. and Brock, J.W. (1993) *Adam Smith Goes to Moscow*, Princeton, NJ: Princeton University Press.

Ágh, A. (1995), 'Partial consolidation of the East-Central European parties: the case of the Hungarian Socialist Party', *Party Politics*, 1 (4), pp. 491–514.

Ágh, A. and Kurtán, S. (eds.) (1995)*Democratization and Europeanization in Hungary: The first parliament (1990–1994)*, Budapest: Hungarian Centre for Democracy Studies.

Akhavan, P. and Howse, R. (eds.) (1995) *Yugoslavia the Former and Future: Reflections by Scholars from the Region*, Geneva: Brookings/UNRISD.

Alexeyeva, L. (1987) *Soviet Dissent: Contemporary movements for national, religious, and human rights*, Middletown: Wesleyan University Press.

Allcock, J. B. (1991) 'Yugoslavia', in Szajkowski, B. (ed.), *The New Political Parties of Eastern Europe and the Soviet Union*, Harlow: Longman, pp. 293–368.

Allcock, J. B. (1994a) 'Bosnia and Hercegovina', in Szajkowski, B. (ed.), *Political Parties of Eastern Europe, Russia and the Successor States*, Harlow: Longman, pp. 79–89.

Allcock, J. B. (1994b) 'Yugoslavia, Federal Republic of Yugoslavia', in Szajkowski, B. (ed.), *Political Parties of Eastern Europe, Russia and the Successor States*, Harlow: Longman, pp. 633–68.

Allcock, J. B. (1994c) 'Yugoslavia, Socialist Federal Republic of Yugoslavia', in Szajkowski, B. (ed.), *Political Parties of Eastern Europe, Russia and the Successor States*, Harlow: Longman, pp. 615–32.

Allcock, J. B. (1994d) 'The contradictions of Macedonian nationality', *Journal of Area Studies*, 4, pp. 139–58.

Almond, M. (1990) 'Romania since the revolution', *Government and Opposition*, 25 (4), pp. 484–96.

Almond, M. (1994) *Europe's Backyard War: The war in the Balkans*, London: Heinemann.

Andreev, A. (1996) 'The political changes and political parties', in Zloch-Christy, I. (ed.), *Bulgaria in a Time of Change: Economic and political dimensions*, Aldershot: Avebury.

Andrejevich, M. (1990a) 'Croatia goes to the polls', *Report on Eastern Europe*, 1 (18), pp. 33–7.

Andrejevich, M. (1990b), 'The election scorecard for Serbia, Montenegro, and Macedonia', *Report on Eastern Europe*, 1 (57), pp. 37–9.

Andrejevich, M. (1993), 'The radicalization of Serbian politics', *RFE/RL Research Report*, 2 (13), pp. 14–24.

Arel, D. (1991) 'The parliamentary blocs in the Ukrainian Supreme Soviet: who and what do they represent?', *Journal of Soviet Nationalities*, 1 (4), pp. 108–43.

Arel, D. and Wilson, A. (1994) 'The Ukrainian parliamentary elections', *RFE/RL Research Report*, 3 (26), pp. 6–17.

Aron, L. (1995) 'Russia between revolution and democracy', *Post-Soviet Affairs*, 11 (4), pp. 305–39.

Arter, D. (1995) 'Estonia after the March 1995 Riigikogu election: still an anti-party system', *Journal of Communist Studies and Transitional Politics*, 11 (3), pp. 249–71.

Ascherson, N. (1981) *The Polish August: The self-limiting revolution*, New York: Viking.

Ash, T. Garton (1983) *The Polish Revolution: Solidarity 1980–82*, London: Jonathan Cape.

Ash, T. Garton (1990), *We the People: The revolution of 89*, Cambridge: Granta.

Ashley, S. (1990) 'Bulgaria', *Electoral Studies*, 9 (4), pp. 312–18.

Åslund, A. (1991) *Gorbachev's Struggle for Economic Reform*, London: Pinter, 2nd edn.

Åslund, A. (ed.) (1994) *Economic Transformation in Russia*, London: Pinter.

Åslund, A. (1995) *How Russia became a Market Economy*, Washington: Brookings Institution.

Åslund, A. and R. Layard (eds.) (1993) *Changing the Economic System in Russia*, London: Pinter.

Austin, R. (1993) 'What Albania adds to the Balkan stew', *Orbis*, 37 (2), pp. 259–79.

Aven, P. (1991) 'Economic policy and the reforms of Mikhail Gorbachev. A short history', in Peck, M. and Richardson, T. (eds.), *What is to be done? Proposals for the Soviet transition to the market*, New Haven, CT: Yale University Press .

Baev, P. (1996) *The Russian Army in a Time of Troubles*, London: Sage.

Baglione, L.A. and Clark, C.L. (1995) 'Participation and the success of economic and political reforms: a lesson from the 1993 Russian parliamentary election', *Journal of Communist Studies*, 11 (3), pp. 215–48.

Batt, J. (1990) 'Political reform in Hungary', *Parliamentary Affairs*, 43 (4), pp. 464–81.

Batt, J. (1991) *East Central Europe from Reform to Transformation*, London: Royal Institute of International Affairs.

Baylis, T.A. (1996) 'Presidents versus prime ministers. Shaping executive authority in Eastern Europe', *World Politics*, 48 (3), pp. 297–323.

Bealey, F. (1995) 'The Slovak constitution', *Democratization*, 2 (2), pp. 179–97.

Bebler, A. (1993) 'Yugoslavia's variety of communist federalism and her demise', *Communist and Post-Communist Studies*, 26 (1), pp. 72–86.

Belin, L. (1995) 'The Chernomyrdin bloc surges forward', *Transition*, 1 (15), pp. 21–6.

Bell, J.D. (1985) *The Bulgarian Communist Party from Blagoev to Zhivkov*, Stanford, CA: Hoover Institution Press.

Bell, J.D. (1993) 'Bulgaria', in White, S., Batt, J. and Lewis, P.G., *Developments in East European Politics*, Basingstoke and London: Macmillan, pp. 83–97.

Bennett, C. (1995) *Yugoslavia's Bloody Collapse: Causes, course and consequences*, London: C. Hurst.

Berend, I. (1990) *The Hungarian Economic Reform*, Cambridge: Cambridge University Press.

Berezkin, A., Kolosov, V., Pavlovskaya, M., Petrov, N. and Sirnyagin, L. (1989) 'The geography of the 1989 elections of people's deputies of the USSR (preliminary results)', *Soviet Geography*, 30 (8), pp. 607–34.

Berglund, S. and Dellenbrant, J.A. (1994) *The New Democracies in Eastern Europe: Party systems and political cleavages,* Aldershot: Edward Elgar, 2nd edn.

Beyme, K. von (1991) 'Electoral unification: The first German elections in December 1990', *Government and Opposition*, 26 (2), pp. 167–84.

Bibič, A. (1993) 'The emergence of pluralism in Slovenia', *Communist and Post-Communist Studies*, 26 (4), pp. 367–86.

Bing, R. and Szajkowski, B. (1994), 'Romania', in Szajkowski, B. (ed.), *Political Parties of Eastern Europe, Russia and the Successor States*, Harlow: Longman, pp. 343–405.

Birch, S. (1995) 'The Ukrainian parliamentary and presidential elections of 1994', *Electoral Studies*, 14 (1), pp. 93–9.

Birch, S. (1996a) 'The Ukrainian repeat elections of December 1995', *Electoral Studies*, 15 (2), pp. 281–2.

Birch, S. (1996b) 'Nomenklatura democratization: electoral clientelism and party formation in post-Soviet Ukraine', mimeo, University of Essex.

Birch, S. (forthcoming) 'Electoral systems, campaign strategies, and vote choice in the Ukrainian parliamentary and presidential elections of 1994', *Political Studies*.

Bojcun, M. (1995) 'Ukraine under Kuchma', *Labour Focus on Eastern Europe*, 52, pp. 70–83.

Bova, R. (1992) 'Political dynamics of the post-communist transition: a comparative perspective', in Bermeo, N. (ed.) *Liberalization and Democratization. Change in the Soviet Union and Eastern Europe*, Baltimore: The Johns Hopkins University Press.

Bovay, N. (1995) 'The Russian armed intervention in Chechnya and its human rights implications', *International Commission of Jurists. The Review*, 54, pp. 29–56.

Boycko, M., Shleifer, A. and Vishny, R. (1995) *Privatizing Russia*, Cambridge, MA: MIT Press.

Bozóki, A., Körösényi, A. and Schöpflin, G. (eds.) (1992) *Post-Communist Transition: Emerging pluralism in Hungary*, London: Pinter.

Bradshaw, M., Hanson, P. and Shaw, D. (1994), 'Economic restructuring' in Smith, G. (ed.), *The Baltic States. The national self-determination of Estonia, Latvia and Lithuania*, Basingstoke: Macmillan.

Braun, A. and Day, R. (1990) 'Gorbachevian contradictions', *Problems of Communism*, 39 (3), pp. 36–50.

Brown, A. (1992) 'New thinking on the Soviet political system', in A. Brown (ed.) *New Thinking in Soviet Politics*, Basingstoke: Macmillan.

Brown, A. (1993) 'The October crisis of 1993: context and implications', *Post-Soviet Affairs*, 9 (3), pp. 183–95.

Brown, A. (1996) *The Gorbachev Factor*, Oxford: Oxford University Press.

Brown, J.F. (1988) *Eastern Europe and Communist Rule*, Durham, NC and London: Duke University Press.

Brown, J.F. (1991) *Surge to Freedom: The end of communist rule in Eastern Europe*, Twickenham: Adamantine Press.

Brown, J.F. (1994) *Hopes and Shadows: Eastern Europe after communism*, Harlow: Longman.

Brown, J.F. (1996) 'A year of reckoning', in Open Media Research Institute, *Building Democracy 1995: The OMRI annual survey of Eastern Europe and the Former Soviet Union*, New York: M.E. Sharpe, pp. 1–14.

Brown, W.S. (1993) 'Economic transition in Estonia', *Journal of Economic Issues*, 27 (2), pp. 493–503.

Brudny, Y. (1993) 'The dynamics of Democratic Russia, 1990–1993', *Post-Soviet Affairs*, 9 (2), pp. 141–70.

Brudny, Y. (1995) 'Ruslan Khasbulatov, Aleksandr Rutskoi, and intraelite conflict in postcommunist Russia, 1991–1994', in Colton, T.J. and Tucker, R.C. (eds.), *Patterns in Post-Soviet Leadership*, Boulder, CO: Westview.

Bugajski, J. (1987) *Czechoslovakia: Charter 77's decade of dissent*, New York: Praeger.

Bungs, D. (1991a) 'Polls show majority in Latvia endorses independence', *Report on the USSR*, 3 (11), pp. 22–5.

Bungs, D. (1991b) 'Voting patterns in the Latvian independence poll', *Report on the USSR*, 3 (12), pp. 21–4.

Bungs, D. (1994a) 'Local elections in Latvia: the opposition wins', *RFE/RL Research Report*, 3 (28), pp. 1–5.

Bungs, D. (1994b) 'Latvian government resigns', *RFE/RL Research Report*, 3 (30), pp. 8–10.

Bútora, M. and Bútorová, Z. (1993) 'Slovakia: The identity challenges of the newly born state', *Social Research*, 60 (4), pp. 705–36.

Bútora, M., Bútorová, Z. and Rosová, T. (1991) 'The hard birth of democracy in Slovakia: The eighteen months following the "Tender" revolution', *The Journal of Communist Studies*, 7 (4), pp. 435–59.

Buzgalin, A. and Kolganov, A. (1994) *Bloody October in Moscow. Political Repression in the Name of Reform*, New York: Monthly Review Press .

Buzgalin, A. and Kolganov, A. (1996) 'Russia: The rout of the neo-liberals', *New Left Review* (215), pp. 129–36.

Calinescu, M. and Tismaneanu, V. (1991) 'The 1989 revolution and Romania's future', *Problems of Communism*, 40 (1), pp. 42–59.

Carmichael, C. (1994) 'Slovenia', in *Eastern Europe and the Commonwealth of Independent States 1994*, London: Europa Publications, pp. 627–30.

Carter, F.W. and Norris, H.T. (eds.) (1996) *The Changing Shape of the Balkans*, London: UCL Press.

Central and East European Eurobarometer No. 6 (1996), Brussels: European Commission.

Český statistický úřad (1993), *Statistická ročenka České republiky '93*, Prague: Český statistický úřad/Český spisovatel.

Chan, K.K. (1995) 'Poland at the crossroads: the 1993 general election', *Europe-Asia Studies*, 47 (1), pp. 123–45.

Chiclet, C. (1994) 'La Macédoine en 1993', in Lhomel, E. and Schreiber, T. (eds.), *L'Europe centrale et orientale*, Paris: La documentation française, pp. 137–48.

Chiclet, C. (1996) 'La Macédoine en 1994–1995', in Lhomel, E. and Schreiber, T. (eds.), *L'Europe centrale et orientale*, Paris: La documentation française, pp. 171–81.

Chiesa, G. (1990) 'The 28th Congress of the CPSU', *Problems of Communism*, 39 (4), pp. 24–38.

Clark, B. (1995) *An Empire's New Clothes. The end of Russian's liberal dream*, London: Vintage.

Clark, T.D. (1995a) 'The Lithuanian political party system: a case study of democratic consolidation', *East European Politics and Society*, 9 (1), pp. 41–62.

Clark, T.D. (1995b) 'Voting patterns in the Russian Council of the Federation', *Journal of Communist and Transitional Politics*, 11 (4), pp. 372–83.

Clarke, D. (1992) 'The saga of the Black Sea Fleet', *RFE/RL Research Report*, 1 (4), pp. 45–49.

Clarke, S. (1994) 'Privatization: The politics of capital and labour', in White, S., Pravda, A. and Gitelman, Z. (eds.), *Developments in Russian and Post-Soviet Politics*, Basingstoke: Macmillan, 3rd edn.

Clarke, S. and Fairbrother P. (1993) 'The origins of the independent workers' movement and the 1989 miners' strike', in Clarke S. *et al.*, *What about the Workers? Workers and the transition to capitalism in Russia*, London: Verso.

Clem, R. (1990) 'Belorussians' in Smith, G. (ed.) *The Nationalities Question in the Soviet Union*, Harlow: Longman.

Clem, R. (1996) 'Belarus and the Belarusians' in Smith, G. (ed.) *The Nationalities Question in the Post-Soviet States*, London: Longman.

Clemens, C. (1993) 'Disquiet on the eastern front: The Christian Democratic Union in Germany's new Länder', *German Politics*, 2 (2), pp. 200–23.

Cohen, L.J. (1995) *Broken Bonds: The disintegration of Yugoslavia*, Oxford: Westview Press, 2nd edn..

Colomer, J.M. and Pascual, M. (1994) 'The Polish games of transition', *Communist and Post-Communist Studies*, 27 (3), pp. 275–94.

Comisso, E.T. (1979) *Workers' Control under Planning and Socialism: Implications of Yugoslav self-management*, New Haven, CT: Yale University Press.

Craiutu, A. (1995) 'A dilemma of dual identity: the democratic alliance of Hungarians in Romania', *East European Constitutional Review*, 4 (2), pp. 43–9.

Crampton, R.J. (1987) *A Short History of Modern Bulgaria*, Cambridge: Cambridge University Press.

Crampton, R.J. (1994) *Eastern Europe in the Twentieth Century*, London: Routledge.

Crampton, R.J. (1995) 'The Bulgarian elections of December 1994', *Electoral Studies*, 14 (2), pp. 236–40.

Creed, G.W. (1995) 'An old song in a new voice: decollectivisation in Bulgaria', in Kideckel, D.A. (ed.), *East European Communities: The struggle for balance in turbulent times*, Oxford: Westview Press, pp. 25–46.

Crnobrnja, M. (1994) *The Yugoslav Drama*, London: I.B. Tauris.

Crowther, W. (1994) 'Moldova after independence', *Current History*, 93 (585), pp. 342–47.

Crowther, W. and Fedor, H. (1995) 'Moldova', in Fedor, H. (ed.), *Belarus and Moldova: Country studies*, Washington: Federal Research Division, Library of Congress.

Crowther, W. and Roper, S.D. (1996) 'A comparative analysis of institutional development in the Romanian and Moldovan legislatures', in Olson, D.M. and Norton, P. (eds.), *The New Parliaments of Central and Eastern Europe*, London: Frank Cass.

CSCE (Commission on Security and Cooperation in Europe) (1990) *Elections in the Baltic States and Soviet Republics*, Washington: US Government Printing Office.

Csepeli, G. and Örkény, A. (1996) 'The changing facets of Hungarian nationalism', *Social Research*, 63 (1), pp. 247–86.

Daalder, H. (1966) 'Parties, elites and political developments in Western Europe', in LaPalombara, J. and Weiner, M. (eds.), *Political Parties and Political Development*, Princeton, NJ: Princeton University Press, pp. 43–77.

Dahrendorf, R. (1990) *Reflections on the Revolution in Europe*, London: Chatto & Windus.

Dalton, R.J. (1994) 'Communists and Democrats: Democratic attitudes in the two Germanies', *British Journal of Political Science*, 24 (4), pp. 469–93.

Davies, P. and Ozolins, A. (1996) 'The Latvian parliamentary elections of 1995', *Electoral Studies*, 15 (1), pp. 124–8.

Davies, R.W. (1989) *Soviet History in the Gorbachev Revolution*, Basingstoke: Macmillan.

Dawisha, K. and Parrot, B. (1994) *Russia and the New States of Eurasia. The politics of upheaval*, Cambridge: Cambridge University Press.

Deletant, D. (1990) 'The Romanian elections May 1990', *Representation*, 29 (108), pp. 23–6.

Deletant, D. (1995) *Ceauşescu and the Securitate: Coercion and disssent in Romania, 1965–1989*, London: Hurst & Co.

Dimitrijević, V. (1993) 'Ethnonationalism and the constitutions: the apotheosis of the nation-state', *Journal of Area Studies*, 3. pp. 50–6.

Dimitrov, R. (1995), 'Bulgaria', in Weidenfeld, W. (ed.), *Central and Eastern Europe on the Way into the European Union*, Gütersloh: Bertelsmann Foundation Publishers, pp. 23–47.

Dreifelds, J. (1989) 'Latvian national rebirth', *Problems of Communism*, 38 (4), pp. 77–94.

Dreifelds, J. (1996) *Latvia in Transition*, Cambridge: Cambridge University Press.

Dubravčić, D. (1993) 'Economic causes and political context of the dissolution of a multinational federal state: the case of Yugoslavia', *Communist Economies & Economic Transformation*, 5 (3), pp. 259–72.

Duncan, P.J.S. (1996) 'Ukraine and the Ukrainians' in Smith, G. (ed.), *The Nationalities Question in the Post-Soviet States*, London: Longman.

Dunlop, J. (1993) *The Rise of Russia and the Fall of the Soviet Empire*, Princeton, NJ: Princeton University Press.

Duverger, M. (1954) *Political Parties: Their organization and activity in the modern state*, London: Methuen.

Eastern Europe and the Commonwealth of Independent States 1994 (1994) London: Europa Publications.

EBRD (European Bank for Reconstruction and Development) (1995) *Transition Report 1995*, London: European Bank of Reconstruction and Development.

Efimova, L., Sobyanin, A. and Yurev, D. (1990) *K voprosu ob antagonizme*, Moscow: ANSSR Voter's Club.

EIU Country Profile Macedonia, Serbia-Montenegro 1992–93 (1993), London: Economist Intelligence Unit.

EIU Country Profile Macedonia, Serbia-Montenegro 1993–94 (1994), London: Economist Intelligence Unit.

EIU Country Profile Macedonia, Serbia-Montenegro 1994–95 (1995), London: Economist Intelligence Unit.

Electoral Studies (1990), 'Special issue on elections in Eastern Europe', 9 (4).

Ellman, M. (1993) 'Russia: The economic program of the Civic Union', *RFE/RL Research Report*, 2 (11), pp. 34–45.

Elster, J. (1993/94) 'Bargaining over the presidency', *East European Constitutional Review*, 2 (4)/3 (1), pp. 95–8.

Elster, J. (1995) 'Consenting adults or the sorcerer's apprentice?', *East European Constitutional Review*, 4 (1), pp. 36–41.

Embree, G.J. (1991) 'RSFSR election results and roll call votes', *Soviet Studies*, 43 (6), pp. 1065–84.

Engelbrekt, K. (1991), 'Constitution adopted, elections set', *Report on Eastern Europe*, 3 (33), pp. 1–5.

Engelbrekt, K. (1993) 'Bulgaria: The weakening of postcommunist illusions', *RFE/RL Report on Eastern Europe*, 2 (1), pp.78–83.

Engelbrekt, K. (1994), 'Bulgaria: Balkan "oasis of stability" facing drought?', *RFE/RL Research Report*, 3 (1), pp. 106–10.

Engelbrekt, K. (1995) 'Political turmoil, economic recovery', *Transition*, 1 (1).

Eurasia Economic Outlook (May 1996) Pennsylvania: WEFA.

Evans, A. (1993) *Soviet Marxism-Leninism. The decline of an ideology*, Westport: Praeger.

Evans, G. and Whitefield, S. (1995a) 'Social and ideological cleavage formation in post-communist Hungary', *Europe–Asia Studies*, 47 (7), pp. 1177–204.

Evans, G. and Whitefield, S. (1995b) 'Economic ideology and political success: communist-successor parties in the Czech Republic, Slovakia and Hungary compared', *Party Politics*, 1 (4), pp. 565–78.

Eyal, J. (1990) 'Moldavians', in Smith, G. (ed.) *The Nationalities Question in the Soviet Union*, Harlow: Longman.

Eyal, J. and Smith, G. (1996) 'Moldova and the Moldovans', in Smith, G. (ed.), *The Nationalities Question in the Post-Soviet States,* London: Longman.

Fane, D. (1993) 'Moldova: breaking loose from Moscow', in Bremmer, I. and Taras, R. (eds.) *Nations and Politics in the Soviet Successor States*, Cambridge: Cambridge University Press.

Federální statistický úřad, Český statistický úřad, Slovenský štatistický úrad (1991), *Statistická ročenka '91 České a Slovenské Federativní Republiky*, Prague: SEVT.

Fish, M. (1995a) *Democracy from Scratch. Opposition and regime in the new Russian revolution*, Princeton, NJ: Princeton University Press.

Fish, M.S. (1995b) 'The advent of multipartism in Russia, 1993–95', *Post-Soviet Affairs*, 11 (4), pp. 340–83.

Fisher, S. (1996) 'Slovakia: backtracking on the road to democratic reform', in Open Media Research Institute *Building Democracy 1995: The OMRI annual survey of Eastern Europe and the Former Soviet Union*, New York: M.E. Sharpe, pp. 25–35.

Fitzpatrick, S. (1994) *The Russian Revolution*, Oxford: Oxford University Press, 2nd edn.

Fowkes, B. (1995) *The Rise and Fall of Communism in Eastern Europe*, Basingstoke: Macmillan, 2nd edn.

Foye, S. (1991) 'Gorbachev denies responsibility for crackdown', *Report on the USSR*, 3 (4), pp. 1–4.

Foye, S. (1992) 'CIS: Kiev and Moscow clash over armed forces', *RFE/RL Research Report*, 1 (3), pp. 1–3.

Frank, P. (1990) 'The Twenty-eighth Congress of the Communist party of the Soviet Union: a personal assessment', *Government and Opposition*, 25 (4), pp. 472–83.

Frankland, M. (1990) *The Patriots' Revolution: How East Europe won its freedom*, London: Sinclair Stevenson.

Frazer, G. and Lancelle, G. (1994) *Zhirinovsky. The little black book: Making sense of the senseless*, Harmondsworth: Penguin Books.

Friedgut, T. and Siegelbaum, L. (1990) 'Perestroika from below: the Soviet miners' strike of 1989', *New Left Review* (181), pp. 5–32.

Friedheim, D.V. (1993) 'Regime collapse in the peaceful East German revolution', *German Politics*, 2 (1), pp. 97–112.

Friedrich, C. and Brzezinski, Z. (1956) *Totalitarian Dictatorship and Autocracy*, Cambridge, MA: Harvard University Press.

Fukuyama, F. (1989) 'The end of history?', *National Interest* (16), pp. 3–18.

Fukuyama, F. (1992) *The End of History and the Last Man*, New York: Free Press.

Fulbrook, M. (1992) *The Two Germanies, 1945–1990*, London: Macmillan.

Fulbrook, M. (1994) 'Aspects of society and identity in the new Germany', *Daedalus*, 123 (1), pp. 211–34.

Fulbrook, M. (1995) *Anatomy of a Dictatorship: Inside the GDR 1949–1989*, Oxford: Oxford University Press.

Gabel, M.J. (1995) 'The political consequences of electoral laws in the 1990 Hungarian elections', *Comparative Politics*, 27 (2), pp. 205–14.

Gallagher, T. (1991) 'Romania: the disputed election of 1990', *Parliamentary Affairs*, 44 (1), pp. 79–93.

Gallagher, T. (1995) *Romania after Ceauşescu: The politics of intolerance*, Edinburgh: Edinburgh University Press.

Gallagher, T. (1996) 'A feeble embrace: Romania's engagement with democracy, 1989–94', *Journal of Communist Studies and Transition Politics*, 12 (2), pp. 145–72.

Ganev, V.I. (1995), 'The mysterious politics of Bulgaria's "Movement for Rights and Freedoms"', *East European Constitutional Review*, 4 (1), pp. 49–53.

Gelman, V. and Senatova, O. (1995) 'Sub-national politics in Russia in the post-communist period: a view from Moscow', *Regional Politics and Policy*, 5 (2), pp. 211–23.

Gerner, K. and Hedlund, S. (1993) *The Baltic States and the End of the Soviet Empire*, London: Routledge.

Gibson, J. and Cielecka, A. (1995) 'Economic influences on the political support for market reform in post-communist transitions: some evidence from the 1993 Polish parliamentary elections', *Europe–Asia Studies*, 47 (5), pp. 765–85.

Gilberg, T. (1990) *Nationalism and Communism in Romania*, Boulder, Col.: Westview Press.

Gill, G. (1994) *The Collapse of a Single-party System. The disintegration of the Communist Party of the Soviet Union*, Cambridge: Cambridge University Press.

Gill, G. (1995) 'Liberalization and democratization in the Soviet Union and Eastern Europe', *Democratization*, 2 (3), pp. 313–36.

Girnius, S. (1991) 'Referendum in Lithuania', *Report on the USSR*, 3, (13) .

Girnius, S. (1994) 'Lithuania: former communists fail to solve problems', in Tolz, V. and Elliot, I. (eds.), *The Demise of the USSR. From communism to independence*, Basingstoke: Macmillan.

Girnius, S. (1995a) 'Reaching west while eyeing Russia', *Transition*, 1 (1), pp. 14–18.

Girnius, S. (1995b) 'State takes the moral high ground', *Transition*, 1 (7), pp. 18–20.

Glenny, M. (1993), *The Fall of Yugoslavia: The third Balkan War*, London: Penguin Books, 2nd edn.

Glenny, M. (1993), *The Rebirth of History*, London: Penguin Books, 2nd edn.

Główny Urząd Statystyczny (1992) *Rocznik statystyczny 1992*, Warsaw: Zakład wydawnictw statystycznych.

Główny Urząd Statystyczny (1994) *Rocznik statystyczny 1994*, Warsaw: Zakład wydawnictw statystycznych.

Goetz, K.E. (1993) 'Rebuilding public administration in the new German Länder: transfer and differentiation', *West European Politics*, 16 (4), pp. 447–69.

Goldman, M. (1991) *What Went Wrong With Perestroika*, New York: W.W. Norton.

Golz, H.-G. (1994) 'Der Wechsel fand nicht statt', *Deutschland Archiv*, 27(11), pp. 1128–34.

Gooding, J. (1993) 'Perestroika and the Russian revolution of 1991', *The Slavonic and East European Review*, 71 (2), pp. 34–56.

Gorbachev, M. (1987a) *Reorganization and the Party's Personnel Policy: The report and concluding speech by the General Secretary of the CPSU Central Committee at the Plenary Meeting of the CPSU Central Committee, January 27–28, 1987*, Moscow: Novosti.

Gorbachev, M. (1987b) *On the Tasks of the Party in the Radical Restructuring of Economic Management: The report and concluding speech by the General Secretary of the CPSU*

Central Committee at the Plenary Meeting of the CPSU Central Committee, June 25–26, 1987, Moscow: Novosti.

Gorbachev, M. (1987c) *Perestroika. New thinking for our country and the world*, London: Collins.

Gorbachev, M. (1991) *The August Coup. The truth and the lessons*, London: HarperCollins.

Gow, J. (1992) *Legitimacy and the Military: the Yugoslav Crisis*, London: Pinter.

Hahn, G. (1994) 'Opposition politics in Russia', *Europe–Asia Studies*, 46 (2), pp. 305–35.

Hahn, J. (1988) 'An experiment in competition: the 1987 elections to local Soviets', *Slavic Review*, 47 (2), pp. 434–47.

Halligan, L. and Mozdoukhov, B. (1995) 'A guide to Russia's parliamentary elections', *CTE Briefing*, 1.

Hammond, T. T. (ed.) (1975) *The Anatomy of Communist Takeovers*, New Haven, CT: Yale University Press.

Handelman, S. (1994) *Comrade Criminal. The theft of the second Russian revolution*, London: Michael Joseph.

Hanson, P. (1993) 'Local power and market reform in Russia', *Communist Economies and Economic Transformation*, 5 (1), pp. 45–60.

Harasymiw, B. (1991) 'Changes in the party's composition: the "destroyka" of the CPSU', *Journal of Communist Studies*, 7 (2), pp. 133–60.

Hazan, B. (1990) *Gorbachev's Gamble. The 19th All-Union Party Conference*, Boulder and Oxford: Westview Press.

Henderson, K. (1992) 'The search for ideological conformity: sociological research on youth in the GDR under Honecker', *German History*, 10 (3), pp. 318–34.

Henderson, K. (1993) 'The East German legacy', in Whitefield, S. (ed.) *The New Institutional Architecture of Eastern Europe*, Basingstoke and London: Macmillan, pp. 56–78.

Henderson, K. (1994a) 'Czechoslovakia: cutting the Gordian knot', *Coexistence*, 31 (4), pp. 309–24.

Henderson, K. (1994b) 'The Slovak Republic', in Szajkowski, B. (ed.), *Political Parties of Eastern Europe, Russia and the Successor States*, Harlow: Longman, pp. 525–44.

Henderson, K. (1995) 'Czechoslovakia: the failure of consensus politics and the break-up of the federation', *Regional and Federal Studies*, 5 (2), pp. 111–33.

Henderson, K. (1996) 'Did the right win the Czech election?', *Contemporary Politics*, 2(3), pp. 127–38.

Hill, R. (1991) 'The CPSU: from monolith to pluralist?', *Soviet Studies*, 43 (2), pp. 217–235.

Hill, R. and Frank, P. (1986) *The Soviet Communist Party*, Boston: Allen and Unwin, 3rd edn.

Holdar, S. (1995) 'Torn between East and West: the regional factor in Ukrainian politics', *Post-Soviet Geography*, 36, no. 2, pp. 112–32.

Holman, G. Paul (1994) 'Russo-Ukrainian relations: the containment legacy' in Duncan, W. Raymond and Holman, G. Paul (eds) *Ethnic Nationalism and Regional Conflict. The former Soviet Union and Yugoslavia*, Boulder and Oxford: Westview Press.

Holmes, L. (1986) *Politics in the Communist World*, Oxford: Clarendon Press.

Holmes, L. (1993) *The End of Communist Power. Anti-corruption campaigns and legitimation crisis*, Oxford: Polity Press.

Holmes, S. (1993/94) 'The postcommunist presidency', *East European Constitutional Review*, 2 (4)3 (1), pp. 36–9.

Holy, L. (1994) 'Metaphors of the natural and the artificial in Czech political discourse', *Man*, 29 (4), pp. 809–29.

Horowitz, D.L. (1993) 'Democracy in divided societies', *Journal of Democracy*, 4 (4), pp. 18–38.

Horvárth, A. and Szakolczai, A. (1992) *The Dissolution of Communist Power: The case of Hungary*, London: Routledge.

Hosking, G. (1990) *A History of the Soviet Union*, London: Fontana, revised edn.

Hosking, G., Aves, J. and Duncan, P. (1992) *The Road to Post-Communism: New political movements in the USSR, 1985–1991*, London: Pinter .

Hough, J. (1977) *The Soviet Union and Social Science Theory*, Cambridge, MA: Harvard University Press.

Hough, J. (1994) 'The Russian election of 1993: public attitudes towards economic reform and democratization', *Post-Soviet Affairs*, 10 (1).

Hungarian Central Statistical Office (1991), *Statistical Pocket Book of Hungary 1990*, Budapest: Statiqum Ltd.

Huntington, S.P. (1991), *The Third Wave: Democratization in the late twentieth century*, Norman and London: University of Oklahoma Press.

Ickes, B.W. and Ryterman, R. (1992) 'The interenterprise arrears crisis in Russia', *Post-Soviet Affairs*, 8 (4), pp. 331–61.

Ickes, B.W. and Ryterman, R. (1993) 'Roadblock to economic reform: inter-enterprise debt and the transition to markets', *Post-Soviet Affairs*, 9 (3), pp. 231–52.

IMF (1992) *The Economy of the Former USSR in 1991*, Washington: International Monetary Fund.

IMF *et al.* (1990) *The Economy of the USSR. Summary and recommendations*, Washington: The World Bank .

Imholz, K. (1995), 'Can Albania break the chain? The 1993–94 trials of former high communist officials', *East European Constitutional Review*, 4 (3), pp. 54–60.

Ingelhart, R. (1977) *The Silent Revolution: Changing values and political styles among Western publics*, Princeton, NJ: Princeton University Press.

International Institute for Democracy (1995) *The Rebirth of Democracy: 12 constitutions of Central and Eastern Europe*, Strasbourg: Council of Europe Press.

Ionescu, D. and Munteanu, I. (1996) 'Likely presidential rivals gear up for elections', *Transition*, 2 (2), pp. 50–2.

Irving, R.E.M. and Paterson, W.E. (1991) 'The 1991 German general election' *Parliamentary Affairs*, 44 (3), 353–72.

Ishiyama, J.T. (1995) 'Communist parties in transition: structures, leaders and processes of democratization in Eastern Europe', *Comparative Politics*, 27 (2), pp. 147–66.

Janjić, D. (1993) 'Socialism, federalism and nationalism in (the former) Yugoslavia: lessons to be learned', *Journal of Area Studies*, 3, pp. 102–19.

Jasiewicz, K. (1993) 'Structures of representation', in White, S., Batt, J. and Lewis, P.G., *Developments in East European Politics*, Basingstoke and London: Macmillan.

Johnson, S. and Kroll, H. (1991) 'Managerial strategies for spontaneous privatization', *Soviet Economy*, 7 (4), pp. 281–316.

Jones, R. (1989) *The Soviet Doctrine of 'Limited Sovereignty' from Lenin to Gorbachev: The Brezhnev doctrine*, Basingstoke: Macmillan.

Joppke, C. (1993) '"Exit" and "voice" in the East German revolution', *German Politics*, 2 (3), pp. 393–414.

Kagarlitsky, B. (1990) *Farewell Perestroika: a Soviet chronicle*, London: Verso.

Kagarlitsky, B. (1996) 'The Russian parliamentary elections: results and prospects', *New Left Review* (215), pp. 117–28.

Kaminski, B. (1991) 'Systematic underpinnings of the transition in Poland: the shadow of the round-table agreement', *Studies in Comparative Communism*, 24 (2), pp. 173–90.

Kand, V. (1994) 'Estonia: year of challenges', *RFE/RL Research Report*, 3 (1), pp. 92–5.

Kanev, D. (1996) 'Bulgaria: "Left" and "right" in the emerging party system', in Matynia, E. (ed.), *Grappling with Democracy: Deliberations on post-communist societies (1990–1995)*, Prague: Slon.

Karasimeonov, G. (1993) 'Sea-changes in the Bulgarian party system', *Journal of Communist Studies*, 9 (3), pp. 272–8.

Karasimeonov, G. (1995), 'Parliamentary elections of 1994 and the development of the Bulgarian party system', *Party Politics*, 1 (4), pp. 579–87.

Karatnycky, A. (1995) 'Ukraine at the crossroads', *Journal of Democracy*, 6 (1), pp. 117–30.

Karklins, R. (1994) *Ethnopolitics and Transition to Democracy. The collapse of the USSR and Latvia*, Baltimore: Johns Hopkins University Press.

Karl, T. Lynn and Schmitter, P.C. (1991) 'Modes of transition in Latin America, Southern and Eastern Europe', *International Social Science Journal* (128), pp. 269–84.

Karpinski, J. (1993) 'Poland: towards a left victory', *Uncaptive Minds*, 24 (3), pp. 119–28.

Kask, P. (1994) 'National radicalization in Estonia: legislation on citizenship and related issues', *Nationalities Papers*, 22 (2), pp. 379–91.

Kaspović, M. (1996) '1995 parliamentary elections in Croatia', *Electoral Studies*, 15 (2), pp. 269–74.

Keane, J. (1988), *Civil Society and the State: New European perspectives*, London: Verso.

Keep, J. (1995) *Last of the Empires. A history of the Soviet Union 1945–1991*, Oxford: Oxford University Press.

Kettle, S. (1995) 'The rise of the Social Democrats', *Transition*, 13 (1), pp. 70–4.

Kiernan, B. (1993) *The End of Soviet Politics. Elections, legislatures and the demise of the Communist Party*, Boulder and Oxford: Westview Press.

King, C. (1995) *Post-Soviet Moldova. A borderland in transition*, London: Royal Institute of International Affairs.

Kionka, R. (1991) 'Estonia says "yes" to independence', *Report on the USSR*, 3 (11).

Kionka, R. (1995) 'Estonia: a difficult transition', in Tolz, V. and Elliot, I. (eds.), *The Demise of the USSR. From communism to independence*, Basingstoke: Macmillan.

Kirschbaum, S.J. (1993) 'Czechoslovakia: the creation, federalisation and dissolution of a nation-state', *Regional Politics and Policy*, 3 (1), pp. 69–95.

Kitschelt, H. (1991) 'The 1990 German federal election and national unification' *West European Politics*, 14 (4), pp. 121–48.

Kitschelt, H. (1992) 'The formation of party systems in East Central Europe', *Politics and Society*, 20 (1), pp. 7–50.

Kitschelt, H. (1995a) 'Party systems in East Central Europe: consolidation or fluidity?, *Studies in Public Policy Number 241*, Glasgow: University of Strathclyde.

Kitschelt, H. (1995b), 'Formation of party cleavages in post-communist democracies: theoretical propositions', *Party Politics*, 1 (4), pp. 447–72.

Kitschelt, H., Dimitrov, D. and Kanev, A. (1995), 'The structuring of the vote in post-communist party systems: the Bulgarian example', *European Journal of Political Research*, 27 (2), pp. 143–60.

Klemencić, M. (1996) 'Croatia rediviva', in Carter, F.W. and Norris, H.T. (eds.), *The Changing Shape of the Balkans*, London: UCL Press.

Klepikova, E. and Solovyov, V. (1995) *Zhirinovsky. The paradoxes of Russian fascism*, London: Viking.

Kolarova, R. and Dimitrov, D. (1994) 'Bulgaria', *East European Constitutional Review*, 3 (2), pp. 50–5.

Kornai, J. (1992) *The Socialist System. The political economy of communism*, Oxford: Clarendon Press.

Körösényi, A. (1991) 'Revival of the past or new beginning? The nature of post-communist politics', *The Political Quarterly*, 62 (1), pp. 52–74.

Körösényi, A. (1994) 'Intellectuals and democracy in Eastern Europe', *The Political Quarterly*, 64 (4), pp. 415–24.

Krause, S. (1995) 'Bulgaria: socialists at the helm', *Transition*, 1 (4), pp. 33–8.

Krause, S. (1996a) 'Bulgarian president defeated in opposition primary', *OMRI Analytical Brief*, 1 (142), electronic version.

Krause, S. (1996b) 'Bulgaria: problems remain unsolved as government stumbles onward', *Transition*, 2 (17), pp. 36–9.

Krawchenko, B. (1993) 'Ukraine: the politics of independence', in Bremmer, I. and Taras, R. (eds.) *Nations and Politics in the Soviet Successor States*, Cambridge: Cambridge University Press.

Kryukov, V. and Moe, A. (1996) *The New Russian Corporatism? A case study of Gazprom*, London: Royal Institute of International Affairs.

Kuran, T. (1991) 'Now out of never: the element of surprise in the East European revolution of 1989', *World Politics*, 44 (1), pp. 7–48.

Kurski, J. (1993) *Lech Walesa: Democrat or Dictator?*, Boulder, CO: Westview Press.

Kusin, V.V. (1972) *Political Groupings in the Czechoslovak Reform Movement*, London: Macmillan.

Kuzio, T. (1995a) 'The 1994 parliamentary elections in Ukraine', *Journal of Communist and Transitional Politics*, 11 (4), pp. 335–61.

Kuzio, T. (1995b) 'The Chechen crisis and the "near abroad"', *Central Asian Survey*, 14 (4), pp. 553–72.

Kuzio, T. (1996) 'International reaction to the Chechen crisis', *Central Asian Survey*, 15 (1), pp. 97–109.

Kuzio, T. and Wilson, A. (1994) *Ukraine: Perestroika to independence*, Basingstoke: Macmillan.

Kvistad, G. O. (1994) 'Accommodation or "cleansing": Germany's state employees from the old regime', *West European Politics*, 17 (4), pp. 52–73.

Lane, D. and Ross, C. (1995) 'From Soviet government to presidential rule', in Lane, D. (ed.) *Russia in Transition. Politics, privatisation and inequality*, London: Longman.

LaPalombara, J. and Weiner, M. (1966) 'The origins of political parties', in LaPalombara, J. and Weiner, M. (eds.), *Political Parties and Political Development*, Princeton, NJ: Princeton University Press, pp. 3–42.

Lardeyret, G. (1991) 'The problem with PR', *Journal of Democracy*, 2 (3), pp. 30–5.

Leff, C. Skalnik (1988) *National Conflict in Czechoslovakia: The making and remaking of a state*, Princeton, NJ: Princeton University Press.

Lentini, P. (1991) 'Reforming the electoral system: the 1989 elections to the USSR Congress of People's Deputies', *Journal of Communist Studies*, 7 (1), pp. 69–94.

Lentini, P. (ed.) (1995) *Elections and Political Order in Russia. The implications of the 1993 election to the Federal Assembly*, Budapest: Central European University Press.

Lester, J. (1994) 'Russian political attitudes to Ukrainian independence', *Journal of Communist Studies and Transitional Politics*, 10 (2), pp. 193–233.

Lester, J. (1995) *Modern Tsars and Princes. The struggle for hegemony in Russia*, London: Verso.

Lewis, P.G. (1990) 'Non-competitive elections and regime change: Poland 1989', *Parliamentary Affairs*, 43 (1), pp. 90–107.

Lewis, P.G. (1994a) *Central Europe since 1945*, Harlow: Longman.

Lewis, P.G. (1994b) 'Political institutionalism and party development in post-communist Poland', *Europe–Asia Studies*, 46 (5), pp. 779–99.

Lewis, P.G. and Gortat, R. (1995) 'Models of party development and questions of state dependence in Poland', *Party Politics*, 1 (4), pp. 599–608.

Lieven, A. (1994) *The Baltic Revolution. Estonia, Latvia, Lithuania and the path to independence*, New Haven, CT: Yale University Press, 2nd edn.

Lijphart, A. (1984) *Democracies: Patterns of majoritarian and consensus government in twenty-one countries*, New Haven, CT and London: Yale University Press.

Lijphart, A. (1991a) 'Constitutional choices for new democracies', *Journal of Democracy*, 2 (1), pp. 72–84.

Lijphart, A. (1991b) 'Double-checking the evidence', *Journal of Democracy*, 2 (3), pp. 42–8.

Lijphart, A. (ed.) (1992a) *Parliamentary versus Presidential Government*, Oxford: Oxford University Press.

Lijphart, A. (1992b) 'Democratization and constitutional choices in Czecho-Slovakia, Hungary and Poland 1989–91', *Journal of Theoretical Politics*, 4 (2), pp. 207–23.

Lijphart, A. (1994) *Electoral Systems and Party Systems. A study of twenty-seven democracies 1945–1990*, Oxford: Oxford University Press.

Linz, J.J. (1993) 'The perils of presidentialism', in Diamond, L. and Plattner, M.F. (eds.) *The Global Resurgence of Democracy*, Baltimore: The Johns Hopkins University Press.

Linz, J.J. (1994), *The Failure of Presidentialism*, Baltimore: The Johns Hopkins University Press.

Linz, J.J. and Stepan, A. (1992) 'Political identities and electoral sequences: Spain, the Soviet Union, and Yugoslavia', *Daedalus*, 121 (2), pp. 123–39.

Linz, J.J and Valenzuela, A. (eds.) (1994) *The Failure of Presidential Democracy*, Baltimore: The Johns Hopkins University Press.

Lipset, S.M. and Rokkan, S. (1967) 'Cleavage structures, party systems, and voter alignments: an introduction', in Lipset, S.M. and Rokkan, S. (eds.) *Party systems and voter alignments*, New York: Free Press, pp. 1–64.

Lipton, D. and Sachs, J. (1990) 'Creating a market economy in Eastern Europe: the case of Poland', *Brookings Papers on Economic Activity* (1), pp. 75–133.

Lipton, D. and Sachs, J. (1992) 'Prospects for Russia's economic reforms', *Brookings Papers on Economic Activity* (2), pp. 213–65.

Lohmann, S. (1994) 'The dynamics of informational cascades: the Monday demonstrations in Leipzig, East Germany, 1989–91', *World Politics*, 47 (1), pp. 42–101.

Lohr, E. (1993) 'Arkadii Volsky's power base', *Europe–Asia Studies*, 45 (5), pp. 811–29.

Loloci, K. (1994) 'Electoral law in Eastern Europe: Albania', *East European Constitutional Review*, 3 (2), pp. 42–50.

Lomax, B. (1976) *Hungary 1956*, London: Allison and Busby.

Löwenhardt, J. (1995) *The Reincarnation of Russia. Struggling with the legacy of communism, 1990–1994*, Durham, NC: Duke University Press.

Lucky, C. (1993/94) 'Table of presidential powers in Eastern Europe', *East European Constitutional Review*, 2 (4)/3 (1), pp. 81–94.

Lucky, C. (1994) 'Table of twelve electoral laws', *East European Constitutional Review*, 3 (2), pp. 65–77.

Lukashuk, A. (1995a) 'Belarus: a year on the treadmill', in Tolz, V. and Elliot, I. (eds.) *The Demise of the USSR. From communism to independence*, Basingstoke: Macmillan.

Lukashuk, A. (1995b) 'Belarus', *East European Constitutional Review*, 4 (2), pp. 84–90.

Lydall, H. (1990) *Yugoslavia in Crisis*, Oxford: Clarendon Press.

Mahr, A. and Nagle, J. (1995) 'Resurrection of the successor parties and democratization in East–Central Europe', *Communist and Post-Communist Studies*, 28 (4), pp. 393–409.

Mair, P. (ed.) (1990) *The West European Party System*, Oxford: Oxford University Press.

Malcolm, N. (1994) *Bosnia: A short history*, London and Basingstoke: Macmillan.

Malova, D. (1995) 'Slovakia: parliamentary rules and legislative dominance', *East European Constitutional Review*, 4 (2), pp. 78–83.

Mamatey, V.S. and Luža, R. (eds.) (1973) *A History of the Czechoslovak Republic 1918–1948*, Princeton, NJ: Princeton University Press.

Markowski, R. (1995) 'Political competition and ideological dimensions in Central Eastern Europe', *Studies in Public Policy Number 257*, Glasgow: University of Strathclyde.

Markus, G.G. (1994) 'Parties, camps and cleavages in Hungary', in Waller, M., Coppieters, B. and Deschouwer, K. (eds.), *Social Democracy in a Post-Communist Europe*, Ilford: Frank Cass, pp. 154–70.

Markus, U. (1994a) 'Belarus: slowly awakening to new realities', *RFE/RL Research Report*, 3 (1), pp. 42–6.

Markus, U. (1994b) 'The Russian–Belarusian monetary union', *RFE/RL Research Report*, 3 (20), pp. 28–32.

Markus, U. (1994c) 'Belarus elects its first president', *RFE/RL Research Report*, 3 (30), pp. 1–7.

Markus, U. (1995) 'Still coming to terms with independence', *Transition*, 1 (2), pp. 47–51.

Markus, U. (1996) 'A new parliament, despite the president', *Transition*, 2 (1), pp. 62–3.

Marody, M. (1995) 'Three stages of party system emergence in Poland', *Communist and Post-Communist Studies*, 28 (2), pp. 263–70.

Marples, D. (1993) 'Belarus: the illusion of stability', *Post-Soviet Affairs*, 9 (3), pp. 253–77.

Mason, D.S. (1992) *Revolution in East-Central Europe: The rise and fall of communism and the Cold War*, Boulder, CO: Westview Press.

Mastnak, T. (1994) 'The Slovene story', *Praxis International*, 13 (4), pp. 373–88.

Mathernova, K. (1993) 'Czecho-Slovakia: constitutional disappointments', in Howard, A.E.D. (ed.) *Constitution Making in Eastern Europe*, Washington: Woodrow Wilson Center Press, pp. 57–92.

McCauley, M. (ed.) (1977) *Communist Power in Europe*, New York: Barnes and Noble.

McAuley, M. (1992a) 'Politics, economics and elite realignment in Russia: a regional perspective', *Soviet Economy*, 8 (1), pp. 46–88.

McAuley, M. (1992b) *Soviet Politics 1917–1991*, Oxford: Oxford University Press.

McFaul, M. (1993a) *Post-Communist Politics. Democratic Politics in Russia and Eastern Europe*, Washington: Center for Strategic and International Studies.

McFaul, M. (1993b) 'Russian centrism and revolutionary transitions', *Post-Soviet Affairs*, 9 (3), pp. 196–222.

McGregor, J.P. (1993) 'How electoral laws shape Eastern Europe's parliaments', *RFE/RL Research Report*, 2 (4) pp. 11–18.

McGregor, J.P. (1994) 'The presidency in East Central Europe', *RFE/RL Research Report*, 3 (2) pp. 23–31.

McGregor, J.P. (1996) 'Constitutional factors in politics in post-communist Central and Eastern Europe', *Communist and Post-Communist Studies*, 29 (2), pp. 147–66.

Melvin, N. (1995) *Russians beyond Russia. The politics of national identity*, London: Pinter.

Mihalisko, K. (1995) 'Belarus', in Tolz, V. and Elliot, I. (eds.), *The Demise of the USSR. From communism to independence*, Basingstoke: Macmillan.

Mihut, L. (1994) 'The emergence of political pluralism in Romania', *Communist and Post-Communist Studies*, 27 (4), pp. 411–22.

Milanovich, M. (1996) 'Slovenia in the new geopolitical context', in Carter, F.W. and Norris, H.T. (eds.), *The Changing Shape of the Balkans*, London: UCL Press, pp. 25–49.

Milivojević, M. (1991) 'Albania', in White, S. (ed.), *Handbook of Reconstruction in Eastern Europe and the Soviet Union*, Harlow: Longman, pp. 2–14.

Millar, J.R. (1993) 'The economies of the CIS: reformation, revolution or restoration?', in Kaufman, R.F and Hardt, J.P, (eds.), *The Former Soviet Union in Transition*, Armonk, NY: M.E. Sharpe .

Millar, N.J. (1994) 'Serbia chooses aggression', *Orbis*, 38 (1), pp. 59–66.

Millard, F. (1992) 'The Polish parliamentary elections of October 1991', *Soviet Studies*, 44 (5), pp. 837–55.

Millard, F. (1994a) *The Anatomy of the New Poland*, Aldershot: Edward Elgar.

Millard, F. (1994b) 'The shaping of the Polish party system, 1989–93', *East European Politics and Societies*, 8 (3), pp. 467–94.

Millard, F. (1994c) 'The Polish parliamentary election of September 1993', *Communist and Post–Communist Politics*, 27 (3), pp. 295–313.

Millard, F. (1994d) 'Poland', in Szajkowski, B. (ed.) *Political Parties of Eastern Europe, Russia and the Successor States*, Harlow: Longman, pp. 313–42.

Millard, F. (1994e) 'Nationalist themes in Polish politics', *Journal of Area Studies*, 4, pp. 43–55.

Millard, F. (1996) 'The 1995 Polish presidential election', *Journal of Communist Studies and Transition Politics*, 12 (1), pp. 101–9.

Miller, M. (1994) 'Moldova: a state-nation. Identity under post-communism', *Slovo*, 7 (1), pp. 56–71.

Mink, A. (1993/94) 'Hungary', *East European Constitutional Review*, 2 (4)/3(1), pp. 68–71.

Misiunas, R. and Taagepera, R. (1993) *The Baltic States. Years of Dependence 1940–1990*, London: Hurst.

Mlynář, Z. (1990) *Night Frost in Prague: The end of humane socialism*, London: C. Hurst.

Morrison, J. (1991) *Boris Yeltsin. From Bolshevik to democrat*, London: Penguin Books.

Motyl, A. (1995) 'The conceptual president: Leonid Kravchuk and the politics of surrealism', in Colton, T. and Tucker, R. (eds.), *Patterns in Post-Soviet Leadership*, Boulder and Oxford: Westview Press.

Muiznieks, N. (1993) 'Latvia: Origins, evolution, triumph', in Bremmer, I. and Taras, R. (eds.), *Nations and Politics in the Soviet Successor States*, Cambridge: Cambridge University Press.

Murrell, P. (1992a) 'Conservative political philosophy and the strategy of economic transition', *East European Politics and Societies*, 6 (1), pp. 3–16.

Murrell, P. (1992b) 'Evolutionary and radical approaches to economic reform', *Economics of Planning*, 25 (1), pp. 79–95.

Murrell, P. (1992c) 'Evolution in economics and in the economic reform of the centrally planned economies', in Clague, C. and Rausser, G. (eds.), *The Emergence of Market Economies in Eastern Europe*, Oxford: Basil Blackwell.

Musil, J. (1993) 'Czech and Slovak society', *Government and Opposition*, 28 (4), pp. 479–95.

Musil, J. (ed.) (1995) *The End of Czechoslovakia*, Budapest: CEU Press.

Nelson, D.N. (1990) 'Romania', *Electoral Studies*, 9 (4), pp. 354–66.

Nelson, D.N. (1991) *Romania after Tyranny*, Boulder, San Francisco and Oxford: Westview Press.

Nikolaev, R. (1992) 'The Bulgarian presidential elections', *Report on Eastern Europe*, 2 (6).

Norgaard, O. *et al.* (1996) *The Baltic States after Independence*, Aldershot: Edward Elgar.

Nove, A. (1986) *The Soviet Economic System*, London: Allen and Unwin, 3rd edn.

Nove, A. (1989) *Glasnost' in Action. Cultural renaissance in Russia*, London: Unwin Hyman.

O'Donnell, G. (1994) 'Delegative democracy', *Journal of Democracy*, 5 (1), pp. 55–69.

O'Donnell, G. and Schmitter, P. (1986) *Transitions from Authoritarian Rule: Tentative conclusions about uncertain democracies*, Baltimore: The Johns Hopkins University Press.

O'Donnell, G., Schmitter, P. and Whitehead, L. (eds.) (1986) *Transitions from Authoritarian Rule* (4 vols), Baltimore: The Johns Hopkins University Press.

O'Neil, P.H. (1996) 'Revolution from within: institutional analysis, transitions from authoritarianism, and the case of Hungary', *World Politics*, 48 (4), pp. 579–603.

Oates, S. (1996) 'Vying for votes on a crowded campaign trail', *Transition*, 2 (4), pp. 26–9.

Odom, W. (1991) 'Alternative perspectives on the August coup', *Problems of Communism*, 40 (6), pp. 13–19.

Offe, C. (1991) 'Capitalism by democratic design? Democratic theory facing the triple transition in East Central Europe', *Social Research*, 58 (4), pp. 876–892.

Offe, C. (1992) 'German reunification as a "natural experiment"', *German Politics*, 1 (1), pp. 1–12.

Offe, C. (1994) *Der Tunnel am Ende des Lichts. Erkundungen der politischen Transformation im Neuen Osten*, Frankfurt: Campus Verlag.

Okey, R. (1994) 'Historical background to the Yugoslav crisis', *Journal of Area Studies*, 4, pp. 124–38.

Olson, D.M. (1993) 'Dissolution of the state: political parties and the 1992 election in Czechoslovakia', *Communist and Post-Communist Studies*, 26 (3), pp. 301–14.

Olson, D.M. (1994) 'The sundered state: federalism and parliament in Czechoslovakia', in Remington, T.F. (ed.), *Parliaments in Transition: The new legislative politics in the former USSR and Eastern Europe*, Oxford: Westview Press, pp. 97–123.

Omel'chenko, E. and Pilkington, H. (1995) 'Stabilization or stagnation? A regional perspective' in Lentini, P. (ed.), *Elections and Political Order in Russia. The implications of the 1993 elections to the Federal Assembly*, Budapest: Central European University Press.

Open Media Research Institute (1996) *Building Democracy 1995: The OMRI annual survey of Eastern Europe and the Former Soviet Union*, New York: M.E. Sharpe.

Orttung, R. (1996) 'Duma elections bolster leftist opposition', *Transition*, 2 (4), pp. 6–11.

Osiatynski, W. (1995) 'After Walesa: the causes and consequences of Walesa's defeat', *East European Constitutional Review*, 4 (4), pp. 35–44.

Osmond, J. (ed.) (1992) *German Reunification: A reference guide and commentary*, Harlow: Longman.

Oswald, F. (1996) 'The Party of Democratic Socialism: ex-communists entrenched as East German regional protest party', *Journal of Communist Studies and Transition Politics*, 12 (2), pp. 173–95.

Paeglis, I. (1995) 'A sluggish pace for economic recovery', *Transition*, 1 (22), pp. 50–3.

Paniotto, V. (1991) 'The Ukrainian Movement for Perestroika – "Rukh": a sociological survey', *Soviet Studies*, 43 (1), pp. 177–81.

Pataki, J. (1992a) 'Role of Smallholders' Party in Hungary's coalition government', *RFE/RL Research Report*, 1 (14), pp. 20–3.

Pataki, J. (1992b) 'Istvan Csurka's tract: summary and reactions', *RFE/RL Research Report*, 1 (40).

Pataki, J. (1993) 'Hungary's youth party comes of age', *RFE/RL Research Report*, 2 (21), pp. 42–5.

Pavković, A. (1994) 'The Serb national idea: a revival 1986–92', *Slavonic and East European Review*, 72 (3), pp. 440–55.

Perry, D.M. (1990), 'Lukanov's government resigns; new prime minister nominated', *Report on Eastern Europe*, 2 (51), 1–5.

Pittaway, M. and Swain, N. (1994) 'Hungary', in Szajkowski, B. (ed.), *Political Parties of Eastern Europe, Russia and the Successor States*, Harlow: Longman, pp. 185–245.

Plakans, A. (1994) 'The tribulations of independence: Latvia, 1991–1993', *Journal of Baltic Studies*, 25 (1), pp. 63–72.

Popovski, V. (1995) 'Yugoslavia: politics, federation, nation', in Smith, G. (ed.), *Federalism: The multiethnic challenge*, London and New York: Longman.

Potichnyj, P. (1992) 'Elections in the Ukraine, 1990', in Gitelman, Z. (ed.), *The Politics of Nationality and the Erosion of the USSR*, Basingstoke: Macmillan.

Poulton, H. (1995), *The Macedonians*, London: C. Hurst.

Pridham, G. (1994) 'Democratic transitions in theory and practice: Southern European lessons for Eastern Europe', in Pridham, G. and Vanhanen, T. (eds.), *Democratization in Eastern Europe. Domestic and international perspectives*, London: Routledge.

Pridham, G. and Vanhanen, T. (eds.) (1994) *Democratization in Eastern Europe: Domestic and international perspectives*, London: Routledge.

Przeworski, A. (1991) *Democracy and the Market. Political and economic reforms in Eastern Europe and Latin America*, Cambridge: Cambridge University Press.

Przeworski, A. (1993) 'Economic reforms, public opinion, and political institutions: Poland in the East European perspective', in Pereira, L.C.B., Maravall, J.M. and Przeworski, A., *Economic Reforms in New Democracies. A social-democratic approach*, Cambridge: Cambridge University Press.

Pusić, V. (1994) 'Constitutional politics in Croatia', *Praxis International*, 13 (4), pp. 389–404.

Quade, Q.L. (1991) 'PR and democratic statecraft', *Journal of Democracy*, 2 (3), pp. 36–41.

Racz, B. and Kukorelli, I. (1995) '"The second-generation" post-communist elections in Hungary in 1994', *Europe–Asia Studies*, 47 (2), pp. 251–79.

Rady, M. (1992) *Romania in Turmoil*, London: I.B. Tauris.

Ramet, S. P. (1993) 'Slovenia's road to democracy', *Europe–Asia Studies*, 45 (5), pp. 869–86.

Ratesh, N. (1991) *Romania: The entangled revolution*, New York: Praeger.

Rau, Z. (ed.) (1991) *The Reemergence of Civil Society in Eastern Europe and the Soviet Union*, Boulder, CO: Westview Press.

Raun, T. (1994a) 'Post-Soviet Estonia, 1991–1993', *Journal of Baltic Studies*, 25 (1), pp. 73–80.

Raun, T. (1994b) 'Ethnic relations and conflict in the Baltic states', in Duncan, W. Raymond and Holman, G. Paul (eds.), *Ethnic Nationalism and Regional Conflict. The Former Soviet Union and Yugoslavia*, Boulder and Oxford: Westview Press.

Rees, E. (ed.) (1992) *The Soviet Communist Party in Disarray. The XXVIII Congress of the Communist Party of the Soviet Union*, Basingstoke: Macmillan.

Remington, T. (1989) 'A socialist pluralism of opinions: Glasnost and policy-making under Gorbachev', *The Russian Review*, 48 (3).

Remington, T. (1994) 'Representative power and the Russian state', in White, S., Pravda, A. and Gitelman, Z. (eds.), *Developments in Russian and Post-Soviet Politics*, Basingstoke, Macmillan.

Rivera, S.W. (1996) 'Historical cleavages or transition mode? Influences on the emerging party systems in Poland, Hungary and Czechoslovakia', *Party Politics*, 2 (2), pp. 177–208.

Robinson, N. (1992) 'Gorbachev and the place of the party in Soviet reform, 1985–1991', *Soviet Studies*, 44 (3), pp. 423–43.

Robinson, N. (1993) 'Parliamentary politics under Gorbachev: opposition and the failure of socialist pluralism' in White, S., di Leo, R. and Cappelli, O. (eds.), *The Soviet Transition: from Gorbachev to Yeltsin*, London: Cass.

Robinson, N. (1994) 'From coup to coup to ... ? The post-communist experience in Russia, 1991–1993', *Coexistence*, 31 (4), pp. 295–308.

Robinson, N. (1995) *Ideology and the Collapse of the Soviet System. A critical history of Soviet ideological discourse*, Aldershot: Edward Elgar.

Roper, S.D. (1994) 'The Romanian revolution from a theoretical perspective', *Communist and Post–Communist Studies*, 27 (4), pp. 401–10.

Rose, R. (1995) 'Mobilizing demobilized voters in post-communist societies', *Party Politics*, 1 (4), pp. 549–63.

Rose, R. (1996) *What is Europe? A dynamic perspective*, New York: HarperCollins.

Rose, R. and Haerpfer, C. (1993) 'Adapting to transformation in Eastern Europe', *Studies in Public Policy No. 212*, Glasgow: University of Strathclyde.

Rose, R. and Haerpfer, C. (1994) 'New Democracies Barometer III: learning from what is happening', *Studies in Public Policy No. 230*, Glasgow: University of Strathclyde.

Rose, R. and Haerpfer, C. (1995) 'New Democracies Barometer IV', *Studies in Public Policy No. 262*, Glasgow: University of Strathclyde.

Rose, R. and Mishler, W. (1996) 'Representation and leadership in post-communist political systems', *Journal of Communist Studies and Transition Politics*, 12 (2), pp. 224–47.

Rothschild, J. (1993) *Return to Diversity. A political history of East Central Europe since World War II*, Oxford: Oxford University Press, 2nd edn.

Roxburgh, A. (1991) *The Second Russian Revolution. The struggle for power in the Kremlin*, London: BBC Books.

Rueschemeyer, D., Stephens, E.H. and Stephens, J.D. (1991) *Capitalist Development and Democracy*, Oxford: Polity Press.

Rupnik, J. (1988), *The Other Europe*, London: Weidenfeld and Nicolson.

Rutland, P. (1985) *The Myth of the Plan*, London: Hutchinson.

Rutland, P. (1991) 'Labor unrest and movements in 1989 and 1990' in Hewett, E. and Wilson, V. (eds.) *Milestones in Glasnost and Perestroika: politics and people*, Washington: Brookings Institute.

Rutland, P. (1994) 'Privatization in Russia: one step forward: two steps back?', *Europe–Asia Studies*, 46 (7), pp. 1109–131.

Rutland, P. (1996) 'Has democracy failed Russia?' in Leftwich, A. (1996), *Democracy and Development. Theory and practice*, Oxford: Polity Press.

Ryabchuk, M. (1992) 'Authoritarianism with a human face?', *East European Reporter*, 5 (6), pp. 52–6.

Rzeplinski, A. (1993/94) 'Poland', *East European Constitutional Review*, 2 (4)/3 (1), pp. 71–5.

Sachs, J. (1993) *Poland's Jump to the Market Economy*, Cambridge, MA: The MIT Press.

Sakwa, R. (1990) *Gorbachev and his Reforms, 1985–1990*, Hemel Hempstead: Philip Allen.

Sakwa, R. (1993a) 'A cleansing storm: the August coup and the triumph of perestroika' in White, S., di Leo, R. and Cappelli, O. (eds.), *The Soviet Transition. From Gorbachev to Yeltsin*, London: Cass.

Sakwa, R. (1993b) *Russian Politics and Society*, London: Routledge.

Sakwa, R. (1995) 'The Russian elections of December 1993', *Europe–Asia Studies*, 47 (2), pp. 195–227.

Sakwa, R. (1996) *The Communist Party of the Russian Federation and the Electoral Process*, Glasgow: University of Strathclyde Studies in Public Policy no. 265.

Samardžić, S. (1994) 'Democracy in postcommunism – a political instrument or the substance of politics: the case of Serbia', *Praxis International*, 13 (4), pp. 405–15.

Sarotte, M.E. (1993) 'Elite intransigence and the end of the Berlin Wall', *German Politics*, 2 (2), pp. 270–87.

Sartori, G. (1976) *Parties and Party Systems: A framework for analysis*, Cambridge: Cambridge University Press.

Sartori, G. (1986) 'The influence of electoral laws. Faulty laws or faulty method?', in Grofman, B. and Lijphart, A. (eds.), *Electoral Laws and their Political Consequences*, New York: Agathon Press.

Sartori, G. (1994) *Comparative Constitutional Engineering: An inquiry into structures, incentives and outcomes*, Basingstoke: Macmillan.

Schmidt, F. (1995a) 'Between political strife and a developing economy', *Transition*, 1 (1), pp. 8–13.

Schmidt, F. (1995b), 'Winning wary recognition for democratic reforms', *Transition*, 1 (15), pp. 3–7.

Schmidt, F. (1996) 'Election fraud sparks protests', *Transition*, 2 (13), pp. 38–9, 63.

Schmitter, P.C. with Karl, T.L. (1994) 'The conceptual travels of transitologists and consolidologists: How far to the East should they attempt to go?', *Slavic Review*, 53 (1), pp. 173–85.

Schneider, E. (1995) 'Moscow's decision for war in Chechnya', *Aussenpolitik*, 46 (2), pp. 157–67.

Schöpflin, G. (1993) *Politics in Eastern Europe 1945–1992*, Oxford: Basil Blackwell.

Segert, D. (1995) 'The East German CDU: An historical or a post-communist party?', *Party Politics*, 1 (4), pp. 589–98.

Senn, A. (1990a) *Lithuania Awakening*, Berkeley: University of California Press.

Senn, A. (1990b) 'Toward Lithuanian independence: Algirdas Brazauskas and the CPL', *Problems of Communism*, 39 (2), pp. 21–8.

Senn, A. (1994) 'Lithuania's first two years of independence', *Journal of Baltic Studies*, 25 (1), pp. 81–8.

Senn, A. (1996) 'Post-Soviet political leadership in Lithuania', in Colton, T. and Tucker, R. (eds.), *Patterns in Post-Soviet Leadership*, Boulder and Oxford: Westview Press.

Seroka, J. (1993) 'Yugoslavia and its successor states' in White, S., Batt, J. and Lewis, P.G., *Developments in East European Politics*, Basingstoke and London: Macmillan, pp. 98–123.

SFRJ Savezni zavod za statistiku (1989), *Statistički godišnjak Jugoslavije 1989*, Belgrade.

Shafir, M. (1985) *Romania: Politics, Economics and Society*, London: Pinter.

Shafir, M. (1992) 'Romania's elections: more change than meets the eye', *RFE/RL Research Report*, 1 (44).

Shafir, M. (1994) 'Romania', *RFE/RL Research Report*, 3 (16), pp. 87–94.

Shafir, M. (1995a) 'Ruling party formalizes relations with extremists', *Transition*, 1 (5), pp. 42–6.

Shafir, M. (1995b), 'Agony and death of an opposition alliance', *Transition*, 1 (8), pp. 23–8.

Shafir, M. (1995c) 'The "centripetfugal" process of unifying the liberals', *Transition*, 1 (15), pp. 49–53.

Shafir, M. and Ionescu, D. (1994) 'Romania: a crucially uneventful year', *RFE/RL Research Report*, 3 (1), pp. 118–21.

Shaikevich, A. (1992) 'Prostranstvo narodnykh deputatov. (Analiz poimennykh golosovanii na II i III s'ezdakh narodnykh deputatov)', *Istoriya SSSR* (1), pp. 1–15.

Shawcross, W. (1990), *Dubcek and Czechoslovakia 1968–1990*, London: The Hogarth Press.

Sheehy, A. (1992a) 'Commonwealth emerges from a disintegrating USSR', *RFE/RL Research Report*, 1 (1), pp. 5–8.

Sheehy, A. (1992b) 'Commonwealth of Independent States: an uneasy compromise', *RFE/RL Research Report*, 1 (2), pp. 1–5.

Sheehy, A. (1995) 'The Commonwealth: an uneasy partnership', in Tolz, V. and Elliot, I. (eds.), *The Demise of the USSR. From communism to independence*, Basingstoke: Macmillan.

Shevtsova, L. (1995) 'Russia's post-communist politics: revolution or continuity?', in Lapidus, G. (ed.), *The New Russia. Troubled transformation*, Boulder and Oxford: Westview Press.

Shlyapentokh, V. (1996) 'Early feudalism – the best parallel for contemporary Russia', *Europe–Asia Studies*, 48 (3), pp. 393–411.

Shtromas, A. (1994) 'The Baltic states as Soviet republics: tensions and contradictions' in Smith, G. (ed.), *The Baltic States. The National Self-Determination of Estonia, Latvia and Lithuania*, Basingstoke: Macmillan.

Shugart, M.S. and Carey, J.M. (1992) *Presidents and Assemblies. Constitutional design and electoral dynamics*, Cambridge: Cambridge University Press.

Siklova, J. (1996), 'Lustration or the Czech way of screening', *East European Constitutional Review*, 5 (1), pp. 57–62.

Silber, L. and Little, A. (1995) *The Death of Yugoslavia*, London: Penguin Books/BBC Books.

Silvia, S.J. (1993) 'Left behind: the Social Democratic Party in Eastern Germany', *West European Politics*, 16 (2), pp. 24–48.

Simecka, M. (1984) *The Restoration of Order*, London: Verso.

Simon, J. (1993) 'Post-paternalist political culture in Hungary: relationship between citizens and politics during and after the "melancholic revolution" (1989–1991)' *Communist and Post-Communist Studies*, 26 (2), pp. 226–38.

Singleton, F. (1985) *A Short History of the Yugoslav Peoples*, Cambridge: Cambridge University Press.

Sixsmith, M. (1991) *Moscow Coup. The death of the Soviet system*, London: Simon and Schuster.

Skilling, H.G. (1976) *Czechoslovakia's Interrrupted Revolution*, Princeton, NJ: Princeton University Press.

Skilling, H.G. (1981) *Charter 77 and Human Rights in Czechoslovakia*, London: Allen & Unwin.

Skilling, H.G. (1989) *Samizdat and an Independent Society in Central and Eastern Europe*, London: Macmillan.

Skocpol, T. (1979) *States and Social Revolutions. A comparative analysis of France, Russia and China*, Cambridge: Cambridge University Press.

Slater, W. (1993) 'No victors in the Russian referendum', *RFE/RL Research Report*, vol. 2 (21), pp. 10–19.

Slider, D. (1990) 'The Soviet Union', *Electoral Studies*, 9 (4), pp. 295–302.

Slider, D. (1994) 'Federalism, discord and accommodation: intergovernmental relations in post-Soviet Russia', in Friedgut, T.H. and Hahn, J.W. (eds.), *Local Power and Post-Soviet Politics*, Armonk, NY: M.E. Sharpe.

Smith, G. (1995) 'The ethno-politics of federation without federation' in Lane, D. (ed.), *Russia in Transition. Politics, privatization and inequality*, Harlow: Longman.

Smith, G. (1996) 'Latvia and the Latvians', in Smith, G. (ed.), *The Nationalities Question in the Post-Soviet States*, London: Longman.

Smith, G., Paterson, W.E., and Padgett, S. (eds.) (1996) *Developments in German Politics 2*, Basingstoke and London: Macmillan.

Sobchak, A. (1992) *For a New Russia*, London: HarperCollins.

Sobyanin, A. and Yur'ev, D. (1991) *S'ezd narodnykh deputatov v zerkale poimennykh golosovanii*, Moscow: mimeo.

Socor, V. (1991b) 'Moldova resists pressure and boycotts union referendum', *Report on the USSR*, 3 (13).

Socor, V. (1994a) 'Moldova: democracy advances, independence at risk', *RFE/RL Research Report*, 3 (1), pp. 47–50.

Socor, V. (1994b) 'Moldova's political landscape: profiles of the parties', *RFE/RL Research Report*, 3 (10), pp. 6–14.

Socor, V. (1995a) 'Moldova', in Tolz, V. and Elliot, I. (eds.), *The Demise of the USSR. From communism to independence*, Basingstoke: Macmillan.

Socor, V. (1995b) 'Moldova: facing Russian pressure', in Tolz, V. and Elliot, I. (eds.), *The Demise of the USSR. From communism to independence*, Basingstoke: Macmillan.

Solchanyk, R. (1991) 'The referendum in Ukraine: preliminary result', *Report on the USSR*, 3 (13).

Solchanyk, R. (1993) 'Ukraine: a year of transition', *RFE/RL Research Report*, 2 (1), pp. 58–63.

Solchanyk, R. (1995) 'Ukraine', in Tolz, V. and Elliot, I. (eds.), *The Demise of the USSR. From communism to independence*, Basingstoke: Macmillan.

Staar, R.F. (ed.) (1991) *Yearbook on International Communist Affairs*, Stanford, CA: Hoover Institution Press.

Staniszkis, J. (1984) *Poland's Self-Limiting Revolution*, Princeton, NJ: Princeton University Press.

Stark, D. (1992) 'Path dependence and privatization strategies in East Central Europe', *East European Politics and Societies*, 6 (1), pp. 17–51.

Stark, D. (1995) 'Not by design: the myth of designer capitalism in Eastern Europe', in Hausner, J., Jessop, B. and Nielsen, J. (eds.), *Strategic Choice and Path-Dependency in Post-Socialism. Institutional Dynamics in the Transition Process*, Aldershot: Edward Elgar.

Statistical Yearbook of Albania 1991 (1991) Tirana: Statistical Directory in the Ministry of Economy.

Statistical Yearbook of the Republic of Macedonia 1995 (1995) Skopje: Statistical Office of the Republic of Macedonia.

Štatistický úrad Slovenskej republiky (1995) *Štatistická ročenka Slovenskej republiky 1994*, Bratislava: VEDA.

Statistični urad Republike Slovenije (1995) *Statistical Yearbook of the Republic of Slovenia 1995*, Ljubljana.

Statistisches Bundesamt für die Bundesrepublik Deutschland (1993) *Statistisches Jahrbuch 1993*, Wiesbaden: Metzler Poeschel.

Steele, J. (1994) *Eternal Russia. Yeltsin, Gorbachev and the mirage of democracy*, London: Faber and Faber.

Steenbergen, B. van (1992) 'Transitions from authoritarian/totalitarian systems: recent developments in Central and Eastern Europe in comparative perspective', *Futures*, 24 (1), pp. 158–72.

Stefoi, E. (1994) 'Romania', *East European Constitutional Review*, 3 (2), pp. 55–8.

Stepan, A. (1994) 'When democracy and the nation-state are competing logics: reflections on Estonia', *Archives Européens de Sociologie*, 35 (1), pp. 127–41.

Stepan, A. and Skach, C. (1993), 'Constitutional frameworks and democratic consolidation: parliamentarianism versus presidentialism', *World Politics*, 46 (1), pp. 1–22.

Stokes, G. (1993) *The Walls Came Tumbling Down: The collapse of communism in Eastern Europe*, Oxford: Oxford University Press.

Sullivan, M. (1996), 'Socialists on the campaign trail', *Transition*, 2 (11), pp. 38–9, 64.

Surovell, J. (1994) 'Gorbachev's last year: leftist or rightist?', *Europe–Asia Studies*, 46 (3), pp. 465–87.

Swain, G. and Swain, N. (1993) *Eastern Europe since 1945*, Basingstoke: Macmillan.

Swain, N. (1992) *Hungary: The rise and fall of feasible socialism*, London and New York: Verso.

Sword, K. E. (ed.) (1990), *Times Guide to Eastern Europe*, London: Times Books.

Szajkowski, B. (ed.) (1991) *Political Parties of Eastern Europe and the Soviet Union*, Harlow: Longman.

Szajkowski, B. (1992) 'The Albanian election of 1991', *Electoral Studies*, 11 (2), p. 157–61.

Szajkowski, B. (ed.) (1994) *Political Parties of Eastern Europe, Russia and the Successor States*, Harlow: Longman.

Szalai, E. (1994) 'The power structure in Hungary', in Bryant, C.G.A. and Mokrzycki, E. (eds.) *The New Great Transformation? Change and continuity in East-Central Europe*, London and New York: Routledge, pp. 120–43.

Szilagyi, Z. (1996a) 'Communication breakdown between the government and the public', *Transition*, 2 (6), pp. 41–3.

Szilagyi, Z. (1996b) 'Hungary's OECD membership is now official', *OMRI Analytical Brief*, 1 (47), electronic version.

Szilagyi, Z. (1996c) 'Hungary has a broadcast media law, at last', *Transition*, 2 (8), pp. 22–5.

Szomolányi, S. and Mesežnikov, G. (eds.) (1995) *Slovakia: Parliamentary Elections 1994*, Bratislava: Slovak Political Science Association.

Taagepera, R. (1989) 'Estonia's road to independence', *Problems of Communism*, 38 (6), pp. 11–26.

Taagepera, R. (1990a) 'A note on the March 1989 elections in Estonia', *Soviet Studies*, 42 (2), pp. 329–39.

Taagepera, R. (1990b) 'The Baltic states', *Electoral Studies*, 9 (2), pp. 300–11.

Taagepera, R. (1993) *Estonia: Return to independence*, Boulder and Oxford: Westview Press.

Taagepera, R. (1995) 'Estonian parliamentary elections, March 1995', *Electoral Studies*, 14 (3), pp. 328–31.

Teague, E. (1994) 'Russia and Tatarstan sign power-sharing treaty', *RFE/RL Research Report*, 3 (14), pp. 19–27.

Terry, S. Meiklejohn (1993) 'Thinking about post-communist transitions: how different are they?', *Slavic Review*, 52 (2), pp. 333–7.

Thorson, C. (1993) 'Russia's draft constitution', *RFE/RL Research Report*, 2 (48), pp. 9–15.

Tishkov, V. (1990) 'An assembly of nations or an all-union parliament? (An ethno–political analysis of the USSR Congress of People's Deputies and Supreme Soviet)', *Journal of Soviet Nationalities*, 1 (1), pp. 101–27.

Tismaneanu, V. (1989) 'Personal power and political crisis in Romania', *Government and Opposition*, 24 (2), pp. 177–98.

Tismaneanu, V. (1992) *Reinventing Politics: Eastern Europe from Stalin to Havel*, New York: The Free Press.

Tismaneanu, V. and Tudoran, D. (1993) 'The Bucharest syndrome', *Journal of Democracy*, 4 (1), pp. 41–52.

Todorova, M.N. (1992) 'Improbable maverick or typical conformist? Seven thoughts on the new Bulgaria', in Ivo Banac (ed.), *Eastern Europe in Revolution*, New York: Cornell University Press, pp. 148–67.

Tökés, R. (ed.) (1979) *Opposition in Eastern Europe*, London: Macmillan.

Tolz, V. (1990) *The USSR's Emerging Multiparty System*, New York: Praeger.

Tolz, V. (1993) 'Drafting the new Russian constitution', *RFE/RL Research Report*, 2 (29), pp. 1–12.

Tolz, V. (1994) 'The civic accord: contributing to Russia's stability?', *RFE/RL Research Report*, 3 (19), pp. 1–5.

Tolz, V. and Elliot, I. (eds.) (1995) *The Demise of the USSR. From communism to independence*, Basingstoke: Macmillan.

Tolz, V. and Wishnevsky, J. (1994) 'Election queries make Russians doubt democratic process', *RFE/RL Research Report*, 3 (13), pp. 1–6.

Tormey, S. (1995) *Making Sense of Tyranny. Interpretations of totalitarianism*, Manchester: Manchester University Press.

Torpey, J. (1993) 'Coming to terms with the communist past: East Germany in comparative perspective', *German Politics*, 2 (3), pp. 415–35.

Toulon, B. (1996), 'La Croatie en 1994–1995', in Lhomel, E. and Schreiber, T. (eds.), *L'Europe centrale et orientale*, Paris: La documentation française, pp. 141–52.

Tzvetkov, P.S. (1992), 'The politics of transition in Bulgaria: back to the future?', *Problems of Communism*, 41 (3), pp. 34–43.

Urban, M. (1989) *An Algebra of Soviet Power: Elite circulation in the Belorussian Republic 1966–1986*, Cambridge: Cambridge University Press.

Urban, M. (1990) *More Power to the Soviets. The democratic revolution in the USSR*, Aldershot: Edward Elgar.

Urban, M. (1994) 'December 1993 as a replication of late-Soviet electoral practices', *Post-Soviet Affairs*, 10 (2), pp. 127–58.

Urban, M. and Zaprudnik, J. (1993) 'Belarus: the long road to nationhood', in Bremmer, I. and Taras, R. (eds.), *Nations and Politics in the Soviet Successor States*, Cambridge: Cambridge University Press.

Vanhanen, T. and Kimber, R. (1994) 'Predicting and explaining democratization in Eastern Europe', in Pridham, G. and Vanhanen, T. (eds.), *Democratization in Eastern Europe. Domestic and international perspectives*, London: Routledge.

Varady, T. and Dimitrijevic, N. (1993/94) 'Ex-Yugoslavia', *East European Constitutional Review*, 2 (4)/3 (1), pp. 75–81.

Vardys, V. Stanley (1978) *The Catholic Church, Dissent and Nationality in Soviet Lithuania*, New York: Columbia University Press.

Vardys, V. Stanley (1989) 'Lithuanian national politics', *Problems of Communism*, 38 (4), pp. 53–76.

Vermeersch, J. (1994) 'Social democracy in the Czech Republic and Slovakia', in Waller, M., Coppieters, B. and Deschouwer, K. (eds.), *Social Democracy in a Post-Communist Europe*, Ilford: Frank Cass, pp. 119–35.

Vickers, M. (1994) 'Albania', in *Eastern Europe and the Commonwealth of Independent States 1994*, London: Europa Publications, pp. 108–15.

Vickers, M. (1995) *The Albanians: A modern history*, London: I.B. Tauris.

Vinton, L. (1993) 'Walesa applies political shock therapy', *RFE/RL Research Report*, 2 (24), pp. 1–11.

Vojnić, D. (1995) 'Disparity and disintegration: the economic dimension of Yugoslavia's demise' in Akhavan, P. and Howse, R. (eds.), *Yugoslavia the Former and Future: Reflections by Scholars from the Region*, Geneva: Brookings/UNRISD, pp. 75–111.

Wade, L.L., Lavelle, P. and Groth, A.J. (1995), 'Searching for voting patterns in post-communist Poland's Sejm elections', *Communist and Post-Communist Studies*, 28 (4), pp. 411–25.

Walker, R. (1993) *Six Years that Shook the World. Perestroika – the impossible project*, Manchester: Manchester University Press.

Waller, M. (1995) 'Adaptation of the former communist parties of East-Central Europe: a case of social-democratisation?', *Party Politics*, 1 (4), pp. 473–90.

Ward, C. (1993) *Stalin's Russia*, London: Edward Arnold.

Ware, A. (1996) *Political Parties and Party Systems*, Oxford: Oxford University Press.

Wasylyk, M. (1994) 'Ukraine on the eve of elections', *RFE/RL Research Report*, 3 (12), pp. 44–50.

Weidenfeld, W. (ed.) (1995) *Central and Eastern Europe on the Way into the European Union*, Gütersloh: Bertelsmann Foundation Publishers.

Welsh, H.A. (1994) 'Political transition processes in Central and Eastern Europe', *Comparative Politics*, 26 (4), pp. 379–94.

Welsh, H.A. (1996) 'Dealing with the communist past: Central and East European experiences after 1990', *Europe–Asia Studies*, 48 (3), pp. 413–28.

Wheaton, B. and Kavan, Z. (1992) *The Velvet Revolution: Czechoslovakia 1988–1991*, Boulder, CO: Westview Press.

White, S. (1989) 'Reforming the electoral system' in Joyce, W., Ticktin, H. and White, S. (eds.), *Gorbachev and Gorbachevism*, London: Cass.

White, S. (1991a) *Gorbachev and After*, Cambridge: Cambridge University Press.

White, S. (ed.) (1991b), *Handbook of Reconstruction in Eastern Europe and the Soviet Union*, Harlow: Longman.

White, S., Batt, J. and Lewis, P.G. (eds.) (1993) *Developments in East European Politics*, Basingstoke and London: Macmillan.

White, S., Gardner, J., Schöpflin, G. and Saich, T. (1990) *Communist and Postcommunist Political Systems: An introduction*, Basingstoke: Macmillan, 3rd edn.

White, S., Gill, G. and Slider, D. (1993) *The Politics of Transition. Shaping a post-Soviet future*, Cambridge: Cambridge University Press.

White, S. and McAllister, I. (1996) 'The CPSU and its members: between communism and postcommunism', *British Journal of Political Science*, 26 (1), pp. 105–22.

White, S., McAllister, I. and Rose, R. (1996) *How Russia Votes*, Chatham NJ: Chatham House Publishers .

Whitefield, S. (ed.) (1993) *The New Institutional Architecture of Eastern Europe*, Basingstoke and London: Macmillan.

Whitefield, S. and Evans, G. (1994) 'The Russian election of 1993: public opinion and the transition experience', *Post-Soviet Affairs*, 10 (1), pp. 38–60.

Whitefield, S. and Evans, G. 'The ideological bases of politics in the Czech Republic and Slovakia', *Political Studies*, forthcoming.

Whitlock, E. (1993) 'Ukrainian–Russian trade: the economics of dependency', *RFE/RL Research Report*, 2 (43), pp. 38–42.

Wightman, G. (1991), 'Czechoslovakia: the 1990 elections', *Parliamentary Affairs*, 44 (1), pp. 94–113.

Wightman, G. (1992) 'The 1992 parliamentary elections in Czechoslovakia', *The Journal of Communist Studies*, 8 (4), pp. 293–301.

Wightman, G. (ed.) (1995) *Party Formation in East-Central Europe*, Aldershot: Edward Elgar.

Wightman, G. and Szomolányi, S. (1995) 'Parties and society in Slovakia', *Party Politics*, 1 (4), pp. 609–18.

Wilson, A. (1995) 'Parties and presidents in Ukraine and Crimea, 1994', *Journal of Communist Studies and Transitional Politics*, 11 (4), pp. 362–71.

Wolchik, S. (1991) *Czechoslovakia in Transition: Politics, economics and society*, London: Pinter.

Wolchik, S. (1994) 'The politics of ethnicity in post-communist Czechoslovakia', *East European Politics and Societies*, 8 (1), pp. 153–88.

Wyman, M. (1996) 'Developments in Russian voting behaviour: 1993 and 1995 compared', paper presented to the BASEES Annual Conference, May 1996.

Wyman, M., Miller, B., White, S. and Heywood, P. (1994) 'The Russian elections of December 1993', *Electoral Studies*, 13 (3), pp. 254–71.

Wyman, M., Miller, B., White, S. and Heywood, P. (1995) 'Parties and voters in the elections', in Lentini, P. (ed.), *Elections and Political Order in Russia. The implications of the 1993 elections to the Federal Assembly*, Budapest: Central European University Press.

Yeltsin, B. (1990) *Against the Grain*, London: Jonathan Cape.

Yeltsin, B. (1994) *The View from the Kremlin*, London: HarperCollins.

Zagórski, K. (1994) 'Hope factor, inequality, and legitimacy of systematic transformations: the case of Poland', *Communist and Post-Communist Studies*, 27 (4), pp. 357–76.

Zajc, D. (1994) 'The formation of parliamentary coalitions in Slovenia and the functioning of the first democratic parliament', in Ágh, A. (ed.), *The Emergence of East Central European Parliaments: The first steps*, Budapest: Hungarian Centre of Democracy Studies, pp. 97–107.

Zakosek, N. (1994) 'The Croatian parliament during the period of democratic transition: constitutional and policy aspects', in Ágh, A. (ed.), *The Emergence of East Central European Parliaments: The first steps*, Budapest: Hungarian Centre of Democracy Studies Foundation, pp. 86–96.

Zanga, L. (1991a) 'Students protest and the party responds', *Report on Eastern Europe*, 3 (2), pp. 1–4.

Zanga, L. (1991b) 'A watershed year', *Report on Eastern Europe*, 3 (6), pp. 1–6.

Zanga, L. (1991c) 'The multiparty elections', *Report on Eastern Europe*, 3 (14), pp. 1–6.

Zanga, L. (1992a) 'Albania: fall of government plunges country into chaos', *RFE/RL Research Report*, 1 (2), pp. 17–19.

Zanga, L. (1992b) 'Daunting tasks for Albania's new government', *RFE/RL Research Report*, 1 (21), pp. 11–17.

Zanga, L. (1993) 'Albania moves closer to the Islamic world', *RFE/RL Research Report*, 2 (7), pp. 28–31.

Zanga, L. (1995) 'Corruption takes its toll on the Berisha government', *Transition*, 1 (7), pp. 12–14.

Zanga, L. and Austin, R. (1993) 'Albania's growing political instability', *RFE/RL Research Report*, 2 (36), pp. 27–32.

Zaprudnik, J. (1989) 'Belorussian reawakening', *Problems of Communism*, 38 (4), pp. 36–52.

Zaprudnik, J. (1993) *Belarus at a Crossroads in History*, Boulder and Oxford: Westview Press.

Zaprudnik, J. and Fedor, H. (1995) 'Belarus', in Fedor, H. (ed.), *Belarus and Moldova: country studies*, Washington: Federal Research Division, Library of Congress.

Zifcak, S. (1995) 'The battle of presidential power in Slovakia', *East European Constitutional Review*, 4 (3), pp. 61–5.

Zubek, V. (1991) 'The threshold of Poland's transition: 1989 electoral campaign as the last act of a united Solidarity', *Studies in Comparative Communism*, 24 (4), pp. 355–76.

Zubek, V. (1992) 'The rise and fall of rule by Poland's best and brightest', *Soviet Studies*, 44 (4), pp. 579–608.

Zubek, V. (1994) 'The reassertion of the left in post-communist Poland', *Europe–Asia Studies*, 46 (5), pp. 801–37.

Zubek, V. (1995) 'The phoenix out of the ashes: the rise to power of Poland's post-communist SdRP', *Communist and Post-Communist Studies*, 28 (3), pp. 275–306.

Index